# Live Your Own Life

*To Mary Frances who*
*with a little time will*
*be a true New Bernian!*
*Enjoy! Mary Moulton Barden*
*March 20, 2004*

## Women's Diaries and Letters of the South

Carol Bleser, Series Editor

# Live Your Own Life

## The Family Papers of
## Mary Bayard Clarke, 1854–1886

Edited by Terrell Armistead Crow
and Mary Moulton Barden

University of South Carolina Press

© 2003 University of South Carolina

Published in Columbia, South Carolina, by the
University of South Carolina Press

Manufactured in the United States of America

07  06  05  04  03    5  4  3  2  1

**Library of Congress Cataloging-in-Publication Data**

Clarke, Mary Bayard, 1827–1886.
  Live your own life : the family papers of Mary Bayard Clarke, 1854–1886 /
edited by Terrell Armistead Crow and Mary Moulton Barden.
    p. cm. — (Women's diaries and letters of the South)
  Includes bibliographical references (p.  ) and index.
  ISBN 1-57003-473-7 (alk. paper)
    1. Clarke, Mary Bayard, 1827–1886. 2. Clarke, Mary Bayard, 1827–1886—
Family. 3. Poets, American—19th century—Biography. 4. Poets,
American—19th century—Family relationships. 5. Women—North
Carolina—Biography. 6. Plantation life—North Carolina. 7. North
Carolina—Biography.   I. Crow, Terrell Armistead, 1951–. II. Barden,
Mary Moulton, 1927–. III. Title. IV. Series.
PS1299.C6Z469 2003
811'.4—dc21
[B]                                                              2002013747

For Bardie and Jeff, with love and thanks

# Contents

# Illustrations

# Series Editor's Preface

*Live Your Own Life: The Family Papers of Mary Bayard Clarke, 1854–1886* is the seventeenth volume in what had been the Women's Diaries and Letters of the Nineteenth-Century South series. This series has been redefined and is now titled Women's Diaries and Letters of the South, a change that enables us to include some remarkably fine works from the twentieth century. This series includes a number of never-before-published diaries, some collections of unpublished correspondence, and a few reprints of published diaries—a potpourri of nineteenth-century and, now, twentieth-century southern women's writings.

The series enables women to speak for themselves, providing readers with a rarely opened window into southern society before, during, and after the American Civil War and into the twentieth century. The significance of these letters and journals lies not only in the personal revelations and the writing talent of these women authors but also in the range and versatility of the documents' contents. Taken together, these publications will tell us much about the heyday and the fall of the Cotton Kingdom, the mature years of the "peculiar institution," the war years, the adjustment of the South to a new social order following the defeat of the Confederacy, and the New South of the twentieth century. Through these writings, the reader also will be presented with firsthand accounts of everyday life and social events, courtships and marriages, family life and travels, religion and education, and the life-and-death matters that made up the ordinary and extraordinary world of the American South.

A number of elements make *Live Your Own Life* a notable addition to the series, and it is worthwhile to name only a few of them. That Mary Bayard Clarke was "Tenella," a famous North Carolina poet, now nearly forgotten, and a professional woman writer, made her distinctive in her time. The sheer amount and variety of her surviving correspondence over thirty years is remarkable. Her newspaper and magazine writings, poetry, and copious personal and professional letters demonstrate that nineteenth-century southern women could—if they possessed sufficient intelligence, perspicacity, and gumption—lead remarkable lives. *Live Your Own Life* is filled with surprising occurrences and astonishing discoveries. For example, living in Texas during that state's secession crisis, Clarke covered the events for the *New York Herald*. Returning to North Carolina during the Civil War, she supported the southern cause with her pen while her husband fought for the Confederacy.

Another remarkable turn of events was her husband's defection to the Republican Party in Reconstruction North Carolina. It was a hard blow to Mary and her family. She had to muzzle her pro-South political journalism for the sake of domestic harmony but kept busy throughout the sixties and seventies as a writer and magazine editor. The editors of this volume have accomplished a remarkable "reconstruction" of their own, making it possible for Mary Bayard Clarke to tell her life story in her own words.

Another element of distinction for *Live Your Own Life* is that it is the result of a remarkable collaboration between Terrell Armistead Crow and Mary Moulton Barden, great-granddaughter of Mary Bayard Clarke. The editors have combined the highest caliber of documentary editing skills with the immediacy of a strong family connection. Their perspicacity comes close to that of "Tenella."

Carol Bleser

# Preface

The bulk of the papers reproduced in this volume are held in private collections or repositories, especially the William John Clarke Papers and the Wootten, Moulton, and Clarke Family Papers housed at the Southern Historical Collection, University of North Carolina at Chapel Hill. The manuscripts available for research are voluminous. The editors selected for inclusion those documents deemed most significant in relating the story of Mary Bayard Clarke's evolution from an elite southern woman of the planter class to an articulate professional journalist who challenged many of the gender roles typically assigned to southern women. As a consequence, numerous interesting documents had to be sacrificed to keep the publication within manageable bounds. Nevertheless, the richness of the papers is revealed by the selections herein.

The editors have made every effort to transcribe the letters and articles exactly as written or printed. Original spelling, punctuation, and capitalization have been retained; however superscript letters have been printed as regular letters. When a writer omitted punctuation, the editors followed the original source. In some instances, when it was unclear whether a letter was capitalized or a mark was anything more than a slip of the pen, editorial judgment was used in deciding what to print.

# Acknowledgments

It has taken a quarter century for this book to become a reality. During all this time, we have worked with the support and encouragement of many wonderful friends and colleagues. Dr. Graham A. Barden Jr., who recognized from the first the historical importance of the letters, helped to track down references, and read and copied book and microfilm articles. Dr. Graham A. Barden III kept the editing of his mother on track by providing computer expertise, while Maryann Barden Berry constantly cheered on her mother. Likewise, the editors offer their warmest thanks to Jennifer and David Crow and to Sue Armistead for their unflagging tolerance, interest, and undoubted amusement while we labored over this book.

Our gratitude for the advice and help of scholars who have used the collection also needs to be recorded. Brenda Koffman, a history student at Yale, came to New Bern twice to help sort the jumble of papers while using them for a senior term paper. Dean Paul Escott of Wake Forest University, Dr. Thomas Parramore of Meredith College, and Dr. Alan Watson of the University of North Carolina at Wilmington all used the collection and recognized its importance. We also extend our deepest appreciation to John David Smith, Graduate Alumni Distinguished Professor of History at North Carolina State University. His interest in the project included well-directed bibliographic suggestions that immeasurably improved the work.

Without the assistance of many fine archivists and librarians, details that strengthen the book would have been difficult to find. Archivists at Duke University, the University of North Carolina at Chapel Hill, the Virginia Historical Society, and the Library of Congress cheerfully answered research queries. In particular, Steve Massengill, head of the Nontextual Materials Unit at the North Carolina State Archives, and Jerry Cotten, photographic archivist for the North Carolina Photographic Collection at the Southern Historical Collection, shared their expertise in the field of historical photography and supplied copies of the images that appear in this book. Chris Graham, an associate curator at the North Carolina

Museum of History, also helped to evaluate an early Civil War photograph. Don Lennon, head of Special Collections for the Joyner Library at East Carolina University, provided research facilities and encouragement over the years. Kevin R. Young, a San Antonio historian and author, and Josephine Myler, librarian for the city of San Antonio, took the time to identify many of the Texans found in the book. Members of the staff of the New Bern–Craven County Public Library, especially Victor T. Jones Jr., Marea Kafer Foster, and John Leys, offered timely information on nineteenth-century New Bern and its inhabitants. Series editor Carol Bleser has welcomed this volume into USC Press's distinguished Women's Diaries and Letters of the South publication series. We are grateful to be included and to share such good company as the other titles in the series.

In the beginning, Mary Lib Miller, Jo Aiken, Terry Stewart, and Meredith Nelson helped to decipher difficult handwriting. Peggy Langston typed the Civil War letters of William J. Clarke, Mary Bayard Wootten Larson typed the Texas letters, and Kathy Davis typed the bulk of the other letters with the assistance of Sinoda and Pamela Brown. Their efforts made the move from typewritten to computerized pages much easier.

Without question, the descendants of Mary Bayard Clarke have expressed a lively interest in the project while letting us use their collections of family documents. Frances Martin Finnerty of Brevard gave unstinting access to her collection of letters. Clare Crawford-Mason and her son Victor Crawford of Washington, D.C., provided helpful information. Victor proved invaluable in tracing long-lost family members and in locating and identifying family pictures. Mary Gibson Speer of Missouri City, Texas, filled an important gap in the story with pictures and letters of her great-great-grandmother, Frances Devereux Miller. William and Devereux Joslin and their sister Nell Joslin Styron of Raleigh provided access to the Devereux and Pollock family Bibles. Robert Cannon Hobson of Nashville, Tennessee, and his niece Laura Hobson of Memphis sent information and photographs of Nora Cannon and her children, as did Fred Deupree of Jackson, Mississippi. John Baker of Richmond, Virginia, provided images of Devereux family members from his family album. Louise Morgan of Morganton, North Carolina, also supplied pictures, letters, and genealogical information of Rufus Morgan.

We also want to extend our sincere thanks to other family members who generously gave permission to use family documents in the book: Warren and Rachel Moulton of Charlotte and Celia Lively Eudy of Kinston, North Carolina, and Robert and Lee Martin of Havre de Grace, Maryland.

Lastly, we would like to thank an individual whose intellect, patience, and sense of humor have proved a mainstay to us personally and professionally. Dr. Jeffrey J. Crow, deputy secretary of the Office of Archives and History in the North Carolina Department of Cultural Resources, has provided encouragement and informed criticism of the manuscript at every stage of its development. Jeff's suggestions on further areas of research and on how best to organize a voluminous collection of documents helped to focus our efforts. His objectivity in evaluating the papers, his thorough grounding in the historical editing process, and his proofreading skills have immeasurably enhanced this publication.

# Abbreviations

| | |
|---|---|
| *DNCB* | *Dictionary of North Carolina Biography* |
| *JSH* | *Journal of Southern History* |
| MBC | Mary Bayard Clarke |
| *NCHR* | *North Carolina Historical Review* |
| NCT | North Carolina Troops |
| NCV | North Carolina Volunteers |
| SHC | Southern Historical Collection, Wilson Library, University of North Carolina |
| *SHQ* | *Southwestern Historical Quarterly* |
| *SLM* | *Southern Literary Messenger* |
| UNC | University of North Carolina |
| VHS | Virginia Historical Society |
| WJC | William J. Clarke |

# Cast of Characters

### Pollock Family

**Thomas Pollock III** married **Eunice Edwards**, a daughter of Jonathan Edwards of Massachusetts. Thomas and Eunice Pollock had four children: Elizabeth, Thomas, **Frances**, and George Pollock. Of these children, Thomas, George, and Elizabeth Pollock died without descendants.

George Pollock was a wealthy North Carolina planter who died without heirs and intestate. The bulk of his property went to his sister, Frances Pollock, who had married Irishman John Devereux.

### Devereux Family

**John Devereux** (1761–July 1844) and **Frances Pollock Devereux** (1771–June 3, 1849).

The Devereux had three children: Frances Ann Devereux, George Pollock Devereux, and **Thomas Pollock Devereux**.

Frances Pollock Devereux married Episcopal bishop and Confederate General Leonidas Polk.

George Pollock Devereux married Sarah Johnson of Connecticut. Their children were Lillie Devereux Blake and Georgina Devereux Townsend.

**Thomas Pollock Devereux** (November 17, 1793–March 7, 1869) married first **Catherine Ann Johnson** (d. 1836) of Connecticut. Their children were Frances, Elizabeth (Betsy), John, Catherine, **Mary**, Honoria (Nora), and Sophia Devereux.

Frances Devereux married Henry Watkins Miller. Offspring: Henry M., Katie, and George Miller.

Elizabeth (Betsy) Devereux married Thomas Jones. Offspring: Thomas, William, Elizabeth (Betty), and Rachel Jones.

John Devereux Jr. married Margaret Mordecai. Offspring: Annie Lane, Thomas Pollock, Catherine Johnson, Ellen, Margaret, John, Laura Margaret, and Mary Livingston.

Catherine Devereux married Patrick Edmondston. No children.

Nora Devereux married Robert Cannon. Offspring: Robert, Katie, Nonie, Sadie, and Mattie Cannon.

**Mary Bayard Devereux** married **William J. Clarke**. Offspring: Frank, William (Willie), Mary (Mai), and Thomas (Tom) Clarke.

Thomas Pollock Devereux married second Ann Mary Maitland of New York. Offspring: Susan H. Devereux.

## Clarke Family

William F. Clark married first Anne Marie Robateau. Offspring: **William J. Clarke**. He married second Catherine B. Hollander (Halander). Their offspring were George H., Virginia Elizabeth, Julia L., Mary, and Charles D. Clark.

# THE PAPERS OF MARY BAYARD CLARKE

Mary Bayard Devereux Clarke wrote voluminously in family letters, published poems, and newspaper articles over five decades in the nineteenth century. Her array of correspondents and omnivorous reading habits reflected a lifelong zest for learning and self-evaluation and an enduring sense of humor. She could not resist a good story or its storyteller, nor could she quench her interest in meeting people or assessing new ideas. The richness of these papers and others written by family members, housed in private collections and repositories in several states, provides the rare opportunity for tracing the development of one southern woman from the time she was ten years old until her death in 1886. Glimpses of a pretty and flirtatious young society woman emerge, as does the picture of an older woman with greater depth and intellectual development who had been seasoned by war, ill health, poverty, and the vicissitudes of life. Her friendships with North Carolina legislators, governors, planters, judges, army officers, and a wide circle of women writers in the late nineteenth century reveal how a traditionally reared southern lady found the strength to take decisive steps outside of "woman's place" in the home and into the public world of writing for a variety of southern and northern publishers.

Southern women of the planter class traditionally followed a prescribed existence centralized in their immediate households and a network of family households similar to their own. The dominant importance of the plantation and slave economy molded the lives of all southern women, white and black. For women of the elite planter class, the sharp distinctions of race and class clearly translated into specific gender roles; they were expected to be dutiful daughters, wives, and mothers living under the protection and guidance of male relatives. Southern plantation culture, rural in nature, emphasized a hierarchical structure that placed men, as the head of households, at the top of the South's social, political, and economic systems. The master controlled the plantation and all its inhabitants, white and black. The women in the planter's family lived from childhood to maturity in a culture that reinforced male dominance and women's subordination as the natural order of gender relationships.

The domestic world of planter women has been described as the "cult of true womanhood" by Barbara Welter and others historians. The ideal model for elite white women was that of the pious and pure lady who confined herself largely to the domestic concerns of her family. This concept of "lady" embodied whiteness, privilege, and gender.[1] Although individual planter women might face unhappiness in their domestic arrangements, personal unhappiness did not translate into a rejection of southern patriarchy or of the gender roles of men and women. Elite white women, placed safely on a pedestal that circumscribed their opportunities as individuals, found that many privileges came with their position, although property rights rested in the hands of their husbands and fathers. Planter women benefited from the labor of the black men and women enslaved on plantations. They received the opportunity to superintend their households in fairly stable economic conditions, attend parties, travel to resorts, and receive protection from the men of their families. These women were willing supporters of an economic system that brought wealth and prestige to themselves and their heirs, in spite of the limitations it placed on their opportunities to enter the public arena occupied by men. They preferred the society of their families and close friends and rarely engaged in clubs or social organizations.[2]

In addition, the emphasis on domesticity affected women's educational and job opportunities within the antebellum South. Schools and academies for the daughters of the planter elite provided basic educational skills and social polish, but they were not designed to prepare women to work. Clear evidence of this can be found within the correspondence of the Devereux family. John Devereux Sr., the patriarch of his family, instructed his daughter Frances Devereux on what was expected of her while she attended a school in Maryland. Writing in 1821, he said, "a modest diffident and soothing style, as well in writing as in conversation when combined with simplicity of character and truth, are amongst the finest ornaments of the female mind, a bold, self-sufficient, and positive manner, is the very reverse, and ought to be avoidd both by men & women—"[3] The goal for young southern ladies was matrimony, not employment. Southern ladies were not encouraged to leave the protection of their private sphere to enter the public world.

Mary Bayard Clarke, although born into a wealthy North Carolina planter family that treasured tradition and revered the South's patriarchal society, maintained an uneasy relationship with the demands and expectations of friends and family throughout her life. Described by one acquaintance as a woman "who makes revolutions,"[4] Mary Bayard Clarke frequently tested the limits of the prescribed roles allotted to southern planter women while simultaneously enjoying the privileges that social rank and wealth brought to her and her family before the Civil War. She detested rural life, she received an excellent private education from a northern tutor hired by her father, her husband did not come from the planter class, and she actively engaged in publishing poetry and newspaper articles as a married woman (albeit under a nom de plume during the antebellum period). Her father and other family members opposed Clarke's ambition to become a published author. The tension between her pride of class and her independence and strength of character set the stage for a bittersweet and sometimes turbulent existence for this articulate woman. Her development during the nineteenth century reflected her upbringing as well as her individuality—tradition versus change—and revealed how experiences before, during, and after the Civil War tested her character and forged a woman who was different from the one that grew up as a privileged member of the elite North Carolina planter class.

## Familial Background, Parents

Born on 13 May 1827, Mary Bayard Clarke was one of seven surviving children of Thomas Pollock Devereux and his first wife, Catherine Ann Johnson Devereux of Connecticut.[5] Her five full sisters—Frances, Elizabeth, Catherine, Nora, and Sophia—and her brother, John, provided support for each other during their early years. Her father owned several large plantations and became one of North Carolina's largest slaveholders. An 1813 graduate of Yale University and a successful lawyer, Thomas P. Devereux prospered during the antebellum period while serving both as reporter for the state's supreme court and as manager of family plantations until 1839. In that year, his mother's inheritance of 1,500 slaves forced him to resign his position on the court to devote his time to running the family estate.[6]

Catherine Ann Bayard Johnson Devereux, who descended from a prominent New England family, died of consumption in White Sulphur Springs, Virginia, on 18 July 1836.[7] Within one year, Thomas P. Devereux married Ann Mary Maitland of New York, the daughter of New York merchant Robert Maitland. They had one daughter, Susan Harrison Devereux. The marriage proved a mixed blessing to his other children, however, who bitterly resented their father's remarriage so soon after their mother's death.[8]

Thomas P. Devereux, in addition to his legal career, became a prominent member in the state's Whig Party. He remained committed to the Union until late in the sectional crisis and condemned the states' rights tendencies of his children.[9] Married to a northern woman and financially dependent on northern and southern merchants,[10] Devereux failed to see anything beneficial in the prospect of destroying the Union and "lived by borrowing" before the Civil War. After the war he found himself saddled with overwhelming debts with no way to repay them. By a deed dated 20 October 1868, Devereux gave his entire estate to court-appointed trustees working for a committee of creditors.[11] He died in 1869, and his son spent the remainder of his life trying to work the estate free from this crushing load of debt.[12]

## DEVEREUX FAMILY LIFE

The prospect of financial ruin and the loss of both necessities and luxuries were far removed from the decades of privilege the Devereux family enjoyed before the war. The daughters of the family received an education similar to their brother's Yale studies from a northern tutor hired for that purpose. The Devereux family enjoyed a pleasant home, the opportunity to stay at White Sulphur Springs and similar resorts, and a wide network of friends and family. Nevertheless, each of the first six daughters seemed anxious to get away from the home of their father and stepmother.

## FRANCES DEVEREUX MILLER

Frances Devereux (1816–81), the eldest daughter, married the prominent Raleigh lawyer and politician Henry Watkins Miller in 1837.[13] Frances, a strong-minded and determined woman who rarely indulged in self-reflection, helped to rear her youngest sisters and brother, but her sense of responsibility sometimes led her into a domineering role over their adult lives. Frances Miller's ingrained support of southern gender roles for women and her efforts to enforce them eventually led to a bitter estrangement with Mary Bayard Clarke.

Frances's marriage, although socially respectable, encountered deep problems that worried her family. Henry Miller, a renowned orator, lawyer, and political strategist, suffered from alcoholism.[14] Perhaps because of the difficulties in her marriage, Frances Miller developed the resilience needed to make the decision to open a boardinghouse in Raleigh after her husband's sudden death in 1862. Her parents and some of her siblings opposed this step, viewing it as being unacceptable for a woman of her class, but it is possible that Mary Bayard Clarke and her husband supported the decision.[15] Frances survived the outcry and successfully operated her boardinghouse for many years, housing legislators, judges, and other socially prominent individuals.

Despite her nontraditional role as a businesswoman and her insistence on self-determination, Frances Miller remained proud of her family's heritage and enjoyed her position within Raleigh society. She took an unconventional step to protect her family, but she never directly challenged or rejected southern society's expectations for elite southern women. Indeed, her adherence to the South's patriarchal society propelled Frances into open conflict with another sister who cherished her independence and individuality. Mary Bayard Clarke, a guest in the Miller home at the end of the war, experienced her first rift with Frances when Clarke opened what appeared to her acquaintances as a friendly line of communication with the invaders. Frances firmly condemned her sister's actions and independence.

The bitter exchanges between the sisters ironically were exacerbated when Mary Bayard Clarke's husband joined the Republican Party in 1868. The political animosities this step caused reverberated throughout the extended Devereux family. Familial anger was further compounded when Mary Bayard Clarke then attempted the novel task of trying to bring prominent women into the public work force. She worked as a clerk for a Republican supreme court justice and unsuccessfully attempted to become the North Carolina Supreme Court's first woman librarian.[16]

The decision to pursue the librarianship proffered by Republicans ended sisterly interaction between Frances and Mary for many years. Shortly before she died in August 1881, Frances made some rapprochement with her sister, but the old years of closeness never returned.[17]

## ELIZABETH (BETSY) DEVEREUX JONES

The firmness exhibited by Frances Miller was less apparent in Elizabeth Devereux (1818–79). Another cultivated belle, she married Thomas Francis Jones (?–1857) in 1836 and moved to Perquimans County. Once again, a seemingly respectable marriage encountered difficulties. The entire Devereux family experienced embarrassment and distress in 1846 when Jones killed Dr. Daniel Johnson of Perquimans County in a duel fought over Elizabeth Devereux Jones. After Thomas Jones's death in 1857, his widow and four children lived very quietly indeed. The later correspondence of Elizabeth Jones reveals a woman who relied on her children and other family members for support and who quietly acquiesced to her fate. She died an impoverished but respectable southern lady who mourned her past life but did little to try to improve her existence.

### John Devereux Jr.

John Devereux Jr. (1819–93) followed in his father's footsteps by attending Yale University, earning a law degree, and managing numerous estates and slaves in North Carolina that he inherited from his grandfather.[18] He married into Raleigh's prominent Mordecai family and seemed destined to follow the same road his father had traveled.

During the Civil War, Devereux became chief quartermaster for the state of North Carolina and served ably in that role. He and his wife lived in Raleigh and helped family and friends as they could. When the war destroyed the base of Devereux's wealth, he struggled to reduce estate debts with limited success. His financial difficulties had an impact on his sisters as well, because the legacies Thomas Pollock Devereux left them were dependent on John Devereux's working the estate free of debt.

### Catherine Devereux Edmondston

Catherine Ann Devereux Edmondston's (1823–75) taste for literature and writing found an outlet in the Civil War journal she kept, which was published by the North Carolina Division of Archives and History in 1979 as the *"Journal of a Secesh Lady": The Diary of Catherine Ann Devereux Edmondston, 1860–1866*. Educated and extremely well read, Kate Edmondston embodied the traditional values that defined a woman of the South's planter class. Within the pages of her diary, Kate revealed a strong personality fully capable of making judgments about the events and people around her, yet she dutifully deferred to her husband's tastes and opinions.[19] Somewhat jealous of the literary reputation of her sister, Mary Bayard Clarke, Edmondston frequently commented on how much she disapproved of women who published.[20] During the Reconstruction period, however, she did choose to publish, anonymously, a pamphlet called *The Morte d'Arthur*. In it she attacked the conduct of northern soldiers while praising the chivalry of the South.[21] It is interesting to note that in her will Catherine Edmondston left small sums to each of her widowed sisters, but there were no bequests to Mary Bayard Clarke.[22]

## HONORIA (NORA) DEVEREUX CANNON

Mary Bayard Clarke's younger sister, Honoria (Nora) Devereux Cannon (1829–88), was closest to her in age and temperament. Both were young when their mother died but old enough to remember her clearly. Perhaps because of their mother's death and the lack of rapport with their step-mother, neither of these Devereux daughters followed quite so traditional a path as did their elder sisters and brother.

In 1846 Nora married Robert Cannon, a North Carolina physician, and they moved to Somerville, Tennessee. The Civil War disrupted their prosperous existence, which Nora described in letters home to her father.[23] Although Nora Cannon deeply regretted the loss of property and denounced the faithlessness of her former slaves, she was not one to wring her hands over circumstances she could not control.

Ironically, the Cannons survived the entire war without physical mishap only to have Robert Cannon accidentally shot and killed at a Halloween party in 1865.[24] His death left Nora without a means of support and with five young children, the youngest born after Robert Cannon's death. Nora left her son with members of her husband's family and with daughters Katie, Nora (Nonie), Sarah (Sadie), and baby Mattie returned to North Carolina to the loving arms of her sisters. Initially, Nora and her daughters lived with various family members, but she continued to evaluate her options to secure schooling for her daughters without being financially dependent on relatives. She eventually became a teacher at St. Mary's, a prominent Episcopal female academy "for young ladies" in Raleigh. Her daughters were able to attend the school with the help of scholarship funds, and she earned a regular income for the first time. Although Nora received from St. Mary's only a small salary, which she augmented by sewing and writing, she felt a deep sense of satisfaction about earning her own way.[25]

Nora never returned to a dependent position. She eventually moved back to Somerville, Tennessee, where she became the first woman in the state to be elected to public office when she took the position of county superintendent of public instruction for Fayette County in 1881. Nora Cannon's ability to expand her vision of women's roles after the Civil War brought her success and satisfaction. Having made the decision from necessity of working outside the home, Nora relished the new world she entered.

## Sophia Devereux Turner

The youngest surviving full sister of Mary Bayard Clarke was Sophia Chester Devereux (1833–80). Sophia was only three when her mother died, and she grew up under the care of her father and stepmother. There are clear indications that Sophia's life as a child and as an adult was extremely unhappy. She escaped the confines of the Roanoke plantations by marrying Josiah Turner Jr. in 1856. Turner, from Hillsborough, North Carolina, was a notorious political brawler. After the war, he became a rabid opponent of Radical Reconstruction and Republicans in North Carolina. In November 1868 he purchased and assumed editorship of the *Daily Sentinel,* a Raleigh newspaper, and wrote vituperative articles denouncing Republicans and their policies.[26]

Turner's attacks on Radical Reconstruction led him into direct opposition with Mary Bayard Clarke's husband William, who joined the Republican Party in 1868. Mary Bayard Clarke, knowing how it would be, frequently traveled north to avoid the bitter political strife during Reconstruction.[27] As late as 1878 Mary Bayard Clarke noted in a letter to a northern friend that, "I hate elections, all the old bitterness rises up in them and Republicans here need expect no mercy socially."[28]

How Sophia Turner reacted to the conflict can be surmised from an undated letter she wrote William Clarke around 1868, in which she begged him to tell her that he was not a scalawag. She wistfully added, "Do not feel angry with me I feel ever grateful for the welcome your fireside gave me in my chilled & unhappy girlhood."[29] Other torments pursued Sophia. At some point in the 1870s, she became addicted to morphine and was institutionalized by her husband in the Dorothea Dix insane asylum in Raleigh, where she died on 25 September 1880.

## Mary Bayard Devereux Clarke

Long before the disruptions and family sorrows of the Reconstruction period occurred, Mary Bayard Clarke faced distinct challenges as she entered the public world of publishing. This deliberate step moved her outside the private sphere that sheltered southern ladies. Although careful to couch her correspondence with editors in a manner that emphasized her position as a lady, Clarke ambitiously sought publication of her poetry and prose. Before the Civil War, she had earned a reputation as a poet and columnist using the pseudonym Tenella and worked to publish the first compilation of poems written by North Carolina poets. It appeared in 1854 as *Wood-Notes; or, Carolina Carols: A Collection of North Carolina Poetry.*[30]

The delight she felt in having a book published spurred her desire to make an impact on southern literature. The name Tenella appeared frequently in southern newspapers and periodicals. She wrote a fascinating series of columns about a trip to Cuba in 1855 for the *Southern Literary Messenger* and contributed to other papers. Her writings, which occasionally earned income, augmented her growing literary reputation as Tenella.[31] Mindful of the need to reassure her family and potential editors that she remained committed to the southern ideal of the lady, Clarke gladly used a pseudonym rather than her own name for her publications. In a letter she wrote to a potential editor she was courting, she astutely underscored her reasons for using Tenella. "I have one request to make which I trust you will comply with, and it is that I may never appear in the Messenger except under my Nom de plume. Say what you like about Tenella but nothing at all about Mrs. Clarke. When Mary Forrest applied to me for a sketch of my life and selections from my writings, I wrote to her that I wished the 'Public' to know nothing about me except my signature; and this feeling is so strong that I will give up writing rather than appear out of my social circle except as Tenella."[32] The following year she elaborated on her reasons for using a nom de plume to the same editor, with the telling comment that she did it to please her father, who disapproved of her publishing articles anonymously or otherwise.[33]

Although willing to ameliorate her father's disapproval by keeping her true identity secret, a common device used by women and male writers in the nineteenth century, Mary Bayard Clarke did not hesitate to publish material under her own name after he died. Clarke's decision to use her own name on her published work marked a significant departure from the South's expectations of a lady. The move into publishing was partly dictated by economic necessity, but using her own name also reflected her ongoing ambition to achieve recognition as an author.

Interestingly, the urgent need to earn money to support her family had led Clarke to seek a wider venue for her work long before the war began. In 1848 Mary Bayard married an old Raleigh friend and Mexican War hero, William J. Clarke.[34] Her father had disapproved of the marriage and made the couple wait a year before he gave his consent. Significantly, the marriage did not occur in Raleigh with the father of the bride giving his daughter away. Instead, they were married in Louisiana by Mary Bayard's uncle, Bishop Leonidas Polk, shortly after Clarke returned from the Mexican War. Some of Mary Bayard Devereux's poetry in the year before her marriage described the estrangement with her father and her later delight in finally receiving his approval for the marriage. In an unpublished poem simply titled "December 25, 1848," written at the Polk plantation, Mary Bayard joyfully recorded that she had received her father's approval of her marriage:

> Now may my soul aloud rejoice
> Its darkest bond is broken,
> An earthly Father's cheerful voice
> The wished-for word has spoken.
> Father above! to Thee I raise,
> Upon this glorious day,
> My heart in thankfulness & praise,
> That *this* dark cloud is rolled away.[35]

In "I've Been Thinking," written in 1857, she reveals more clearly how her wedding day had been tinged with sadness with "No sister's loving finger" to twine lilies in her hair and only friends, but no father, "standing round me."[36]

Thomas P. Devereux's reasons for opposing the marriage are not known. William J. Clarke had earned a law degree from the University of North Carolina, but his father came from Raleigh's merchant class, which may have displeased the aristocratic Devereux. Clarke's entry into the Mexican War may have given Devereux pause, as well, if he worried about the possibility of his daughter becoming a young widow. Another source of friction undoubtedly centered on Clarke's politics. The wealthy Devereux was a Whig of long standing, with friends numbering among that party's elite. William Clarke preferred the Democratic Party, whose members were regarded by many Whigs as being socially undesirable.[37] It is also possible that Devereux questioned Clarke's business acumen, a doubt that blossomed into a certainty by the late 1850s. According to North Carolina's 1850 census, Clarke owned eight slaves,[38] four females and four males. He also inherited a house and mill in Raleigh, but he never became a planter and continually experienced financial difficulties. Thomas P. Devereux presented a substantial wedding gift to Mary Bayard and William, and he also made various loans to Clarke that amounted to nearly $10,000 that were not repaid.[39] Devereux, himself strapped for cash by the late 1850s, was not pleased with his son-in-law's business performance.

William Clarke, whose ambitions lay in the political and business arenas rather than in agriculture, was anxious to receive an appointment from the federal government. He expended considerable effort in pushing his claims to a variety of political offices and served as comptroller for North Carolina. By 1854 Clarke sought to become the United States consul to Cuba.[40] The Clarkes visited Cuba in 1855 to ascertain the cost of living and whether the tropical climate would prove beneficial to Mary Bayard Clarke, who suffered from chronic lung problems and feared she would die from consumption as her mother had done. The letters Mary and William sent from Cuba to friends and family in North Carolina reveal their disappointment in the hope of living there permanently. Expenses were high, the climate did not agree with Mary Bayard, and the salary offered the American consul did not seem tempting enough for them to stay. At least, this was the explanation they sent home to friends and family.[41]

Nevertheless, the Cuba visit provided a delightful interlude for Mary Bayard Clarke, who disliked country life and preferred the amenities found in cosmopolitan settings. Clarke, throwing aside the ladylike concepts of duty and motherhood, left her three children in Raleigh with family and friends and, for the first time in her adult life, found herself completely free from family expectations of a proper southern matron's actions. She wrote a series of detailed letters during her extended stay, portions of which were revised for publication as articles in the *Southern Literary Messenger*. Her colorful descriptions of the natural beauty of the island and of its people provide a lively portrait of a Cuba torn with concerns over American filibusterers, conflicts between the Creoles and Spanish authorities on the island, and the intricacies of Cuban society. An energetic woman, she left society friends in the hotels and walked or rode horseback through the streets of Havana—to the consternation of those who worried about her safety and the propriety of a woman wandering, even with a male escort, through the city streets. She assessed the foods she ate, studied the buildings she visited, and thoroughly enjoyed herself. She was careful, however, to reassure her Raleigh relatives that her life of "dissipation" was inexpensive.[42]

Mary Bayard Clarke continued to develop her poetry during her Cuban visit. She had a talent for composing what she sometimes called her "doggerel"—quick, witty rhymes about people or events. One acquaintance she met there had an impact on raising her awareness of her writing abilities, however. According to one who appreciated Mary Bayard's literary talents, an editor of the *National Intelligencer* admired her work and urged her to pursue serious creative writing. Writing years after the Cuban excursion, the writer identified only as "L. P. H." described his first meeting with Mary Bayard Clarke in Cuba.

Some years ago, during a "health trip to the tropics," it was my good fortune to spend four months in the company of a lady who is now well known in Southern literature, not only as "Tenella," the *nom de plume* she first adopted, but also by her real name of Mrs. Mary Bayard Clarke. . . . The first time I ever saw her was at the Tacon theatre. She was leaning on the arm of Mr. Gales Seyton, of *The National Intelligencer,* and surrounded by three or four British naval officers. . . . Shortly after this I met her at a ball given by the British Consul General, in the Aldamer palace, and was presented to her by Mr. Seyton, and from that time saw her almost daily for four months, during which she reigned the acknowledged queen of the small but select society of English and Americans residing in the city of Havana. . . . But while to casual observers Mrs. Clarke was but the *enfant gatè* of society, to those who looked further she was also the highly cultivated and intellectual woman. . . . Speaking of her quickness, and the felicitous skill with which she threw off little *jeu d'esprits,* in the shape of *vers de societie,* one day to Mr. Seyton, he replied: "She is capable of better things than she has yet done, and if she lives long enough will, I predict, make a name for herself among the poets of our country. I may not live to see the noon-tide of her success, but I can already see its dawn." He did not live to see much more than its dawn, but he instigated and suggested much that has brightened that success.[43]

### The Texas Years

The enjoyment of Cuba's delights ended in 1855, when the Clarkes returned to the United States by way of New Orleans. After careful consideration, they moved to Texas to improve their fortunes. This busy interlude led to an interruption in Mary Bayard Clarke's creative writing, but her letters to family in North Carolina after her arrival in Texas provided ample scope for her descriptive abilities. The family letters to Frances Miller, especially, record the delight Clarke felt in breathing prairie air, the difficulties of the journey, and the pain occasioned by moving away from her family.

The Clarkes enjoyed the company in San Antonio of Oliver Dudley Cooke, a New England relative of William Clarke, who became Clarke's law partner in San Antonio. Their friendship and close association extended through the Civil War (the Yankee Cooke joined North Carolina's Twenty-Fourth Regiment) and Reconstruction, with Cooke's standing as godfather to the Clarkes' youngest child. The Clarkes' first three children had all been born in Raleigh: Frank or Franc (1849–1913), William or Willie (1850–1901), and Mary or Mai (1852–1931). Their fourth child, Thomas

(1858–1913), was born in San Antonio. Mary Bayard Clarke wryly noted that, when she unpacked the baby clothes, the sight of them made her feel sick. There were difficulties enough without the worries of childbirth.

Frontier life in San Antonio kept the Clarkes on their toes. Their furniture was delayed for months at Port Lavaca, and both of the senior Clarkes exercised their ingenuity in fabricating household items. Concerns about local schools; the volatile mixture of Germans, Irish, Spanish, and Americans in the city; and the high price of food affected them. Their main social outlet came from association with army officers and their wives, although there were also several local families they cultivated. The Clarkes met Robert E. Lee, Albert Sydney Johnston, Louis T. Wigfall, and others during the San Antonio years. The Clarke children enjoyed fishing, riding on the prairie, balloon ascensions, viewing army camels in the streets of San Antonio, and the excitement of living at an army post. The relaxed style of western entertaining especially pleased Mary Bayard Clarke, as did the chance to ride on the prairie and join in pecan-gathering expeditions with friends. She wrote Winchester Hall in 1856 that "I can no longer be considered an invalid for I eat, sleep, walk, and ride on horseback, and work like a well person. The weather is so charming it is hard to stay in the house. I often resolve on Monday that I will be very domestic all the week, and get through lots of sewing, but at the first invitation to join a party and go out nutting I start up like a war-horse at the sound of the trumpet, pack the children in a carriage, jump on a horse and am off for the day gathering not only pecans, but health and strength from the fresh breezes of the prairie."[44]

The threat of Indian raids, desperadoes, and problems associated with hiring white and black servants provided new experiences as well. In an article published in 1877 by the *Inland Monthly Magazine,* Clarke wrote under her own name a dramatized account of her stay in Texas but used one of her alternate pseudonyms—Stuart Leigh—as the name for the story's main character. In "Mrs. Leigh's Indian Waiter," Clarke described the domestic warfare waged between her German and Irish servants, a battle with a Texas-sized swarm of grasshoppers, her short-lived employment of a young Native American as a house servant, and some of the San Antonio customs for "impromptu parties" and other entertainment. On a darker note, during her Texas stay Mary Bayard also defended her home against an intruder, surprising herself in the process.[45] Another San Antonio transplant confirmed the lawlessness prevalent in San Antonio in 1857. "Three or four weeks ago, robberies & murders occured every night. A dozen or fifteen men and women were killed for money in a few weeks. A Vigilance Committee was formed—& three weeks ago, a great fight occurred at noonday in the streets, in which five men were killed. Since then ten or a dozen have been hung & a great many bad men driven away."[46] Mary Bayard Clarke's transformation from a pampered belle into a woman of action had begun. The lessons learned in Texas would stand her in good stead during and after the Civil War.

The Texas years provided another critical test for William and Mary Bayard Clarke. Planning to pursue a legal career in his adopted state, Clarke studied Texas law in preparation for certification by the Texas bar. He also continued to search for other ways to economic fortune and prominence. A strong proponent of states' rights, Clarke immersed himself in politics and joined the local chapter of the Knights of the Golden Circle, a secret society that began in Cincinnati, Ohio, before the Civil War. The Knights established quasi-military castles or groups and developed a garbled ideology that covered everything from expansionist hopes for acquiring northern Mexico to plans for promoting secession from the United States.[47] The San Antonio castle monitored Union sympathizers, formed a network of conspirators, and later helped organize armed resistance to the United States Army even before Texas seceded from the Union. William Clarke also formed business connections with Samuel Maverick and a Judge Paschal,[48] which led to a disastrous involvement with the local railroad. Both the Clarkes initially were thrilled by William Clarke's appointment as president of the San Antonio and Mexican Gulf Railway, which had been officially chartered in 1850 by Samuel Maverick and others.[49] As president of the railroad, Clarke assumed responsibility for obtaining investments from northern businessmen to fund the purchase of rails and rolling stock. Mary Bayard Clarke mentioned the appointment with satisfaction in one letter, but disillusionment soon set in. William Clarke, acting from an unswerving sense of personal honor, refused to accept a salary from the cash-strapped company during the months he stayed in New York City negotiating with potential investors. This laudable aim had the unfortunate consequence of leaving his wife and children without funds. A primary responsibility of the white southern patriarch was to protect and provide for his family, and William Clarke failed to meet this obligation. Letters written to his wife in response to those received from her indicate how troubled Mary Bayard Clarke became. Although her letters to William no longer survive from this period, her sense of urgency is evident. She was pregnant with their fourth child, she had no money to hire household help, and she had three children to feed. To make ends meet, she eventually taught in a school run by Oliver Cooke, and she voiced her displeasure to William, including her "mortification" at having to ask for money from his business partners. Her sense of desperation led her to write to her father to request financial assistance and that slave children be sent to her from North Carolina to perform household work. He agreed to supply the funds but stipulated that the money should be used for her needs and not those of William. He added with some acerbity, "If the rail road is to be so miserable an affair as not to pay the current house keeping expenses of the officers it becomes a question whether your husband should be any longer troubled & perplexed with it. God preserve you in his holy keeping & bring you safely out of all troubles."[50] Mary Bayard, facing economic difficulties and stranded in Texas without the benefit of a male member of her family, learned to make decisions and devise solutions without the advice or assistance of her husband. She also began to question some of William's decisions.

William Clarke's business difficulties continued unabated, probably aggravated by the economic recession of 1857. He suffered greatly from the knowledge that the Devereux family and his wife considered him a poor manager, but he asked his wife to have faith in him. Writing to her in August 1858, he noted, "It seems to me that at one period of my life I should have gone raving mad to know that the idol of my soul, for whom I would gladly coin my heart's blood, was enduring such things; but like an egg I have been so long in hot water that I have become hardened. But take courage my own darling, show that fortitude and constancy that my brave wife has never been lacking in!"[51]

His use of the word constancy is interesting, because unidentified members of the Devereux clan apparently believed there was another reason why Clarke had left his wife unattended for so many months in Texas. He noted in a letter to her dated 5 September 1858, that he had received three communications from her family suggesting he had left Mary Bayard Clarke because he was jealous or unhappy with her conduct. The patriarchal Devereux clan was only too willing to believe that Mary Bayard would stray from the path of purity and true womanhood without firmer control from her husband. Only half-jokingly William Clarke said, "They . . . seem to think that my protracted stay is in consequence of diminished affection for you, or it may be they fear that you will elope with Mr. Cooke, Mr. Jones or that bete noir James Taylor—all of which are equally ridiculous. . . . If poor James Taylor is with you, you had better get rid of him as easily as possible. If he will not take any hint you had better inform him that the state of your health is such as to render it very incovenient for him to be in the house during my absence, and if he does not then leave send his trunk to the hotel."[52] Concerns over Mary Bayard Clarke's reputation surfaced occasionally over the years. Her quick wit and intelligence attracted male friends, with whom she thoroughly enjoyed conversing and flirting. Her liveliest correspondence was reserved for select male friends. Although William Clarke rarely objected to these friendships, her family did not hesitate to censure her conduct as unbecoming for a southern lady.

William Clarke returned to Texas by late 1858, but business affairs sagged and he considered moving farther west. Letters from John and Thomas Pollock Devereux written in August 1859 urged Mary's return to North Carolina instead. Thomas P. Devereux also decided to provide yearly financial support to his daughter in Texas, with the stipulation that, "I shall insist upon the property, when bought, being so settled that it shall remain yours & your childrens for your & their use & comfort forever, without any possibility of its being taken for other purposes." He acknowledged this might jeopardize her "domestic happiness" but could think of no better way to ensure his daughter's welfare.[53]

It is difficult to gauge William Clarke's reactions to these arrangements. Scattered letters and unpublished poems indicate a deep love and respect between William and Mary Clarke.[54] Nevertheless, in a letter written 21 February 1860, to Thomas P. Devereux, William Clarke was forced to defend his expenditures and stated that he did not seek assistance from Devereux "except when forced by necessity."[55] There is no indication that Clarke's business affairs improved dramatically in the waning years before the Civil War. Mary Bayard Clarke's efforts, therefore, to publish articles and an entire book of poetry during the Texas years undoubtedly sprang from both a real financial need and personal satisfaction.

## Civil War

When Texas seceded from the Union on 1 February 1861, both William and Mary Clarke saw in the crisis a chance to salvage their personal situation as well as to support the new nation. William Clarke worked closely with secessionist forces in San Antonio and participated in events leading to the surrender of the United States Army garrison in that city. He believed his experience in the Mexican War qualified him for a high army appointment and lost no time in pressing his claims with Confederate and Texas authorities. Mary Bayard Clarke anonymously covered San Antonio events as a reporter and wrote a lengthy article about the enforced surrender of the army garrison for the *New York Herald* that mentioned the work of her husband. Interestingly, the way she wrote the column implied the reporter was male.[56]

Both of the Clarkes favored states' rights and the protection of slavery and looked forward with sanguinity to a quick southern victory. William Clarke hastened to Montgomery, Alabama, to advance his military career with Confederate authorities. He had the strong support of both the Texas delegation and old North Carolina acquaintances. He finally accepted a captaincy in the regular army but made plans for a quick promotion via a state regiment in North Carolina.[57] He had a regular salary to help support his family, and he knew the honor attached to military service would please his wife and in-laws. A letter he wrote to Mary on 23 May 1861, attested to his relief after his military commission.

> At times my heart has been so weighed down by care . . . that I have felt that prayer for myself was a mockery. . . . I look back with a shudder to the long, long days when I was idle, unable to do any thing for you because no man had ["]hired" me. I now feel as if I were ascending a gentle hill with the sun in the east shining on my back and all the shadows pointing forward, and thy cheerful voice crying "excelsior."[58]

Although monetary concerns lessened with Clarke's army appointment, other undercurrents worried Mary Bayard. Left in Texas with no clear idea of when her husband would return, suffering from indifferent health, and having experienced a prolonged and unpleasant separation from her husband only a little more than a year before, Mary Bayard Clarke did not relish the idea of waiting in Texas with no idea of what to expect in the future. Her husband wrote that he would send her whatever salary he could spare, but the distance between North Carolina and Texas and the uncertainties of war likely fanned her fears. Too, he wrote her a somewhat cryptic letter with an enclosure (which no longer survives) from an unidentified family member. William instructed her to burn the letter and never tell her family she had read it. Based on Clarke's comments, it appears that the Devereux family still questioned Mary's unsupervised status in Texas.[59]

## CIVIL WAR NORTH CAROLINA

William Clarke returned to North Carolina by June 1861 as a recruiting officer for the Confederacy. Shortly thereafter he received an appointment as colonel of the Fourteenth Regiment, North Carolina Volunteers (later

the Twenty-fourth Regiment, North Carolina Troops). Before he left
Montgomery, he tried to reassure his wife that she would be safe in Texas
and advised her to abandon her plans to visit North Carolina that summer
because "the circuitous route, which is the only safe one" was untenable.[60]
William Clarke penned this letter on 23 May 1861. By 25 June Mary
Bayard Clarke was in Raleigh with her family and a free black woman she
had employed for several years in Texas to help with the children and
household tasks. Her husband may have felt the journey was too dangerous to attempt, but similar fears did not deter Mary Bayard Clarke.
She and her children traveled in an open barge for a portion of the trip,
experiencing storms, sunburn, and general discomfort.[61] The adventure
added zest to the difficulties, however, and the fact that Mary Bayard
Clarke undertook the journey without her husband underscores how
much she had been strengthened by the Texas years. The Devereux family
doubted her reasoning abilities or discretion, but she became increasingly
self-confident in setting goals and accomplishing them.

The Clarkes' welfare thereafter followed that of the Confederacy.
William Clarke ably led his regiment throughout the war until he suffered
a severe wound at the Battle of Drewry's Bluff in Virginia in 1864. His war
letters to his family provided them with vivid descriptions of battles, camp
life, officer rivalries, and his growing despair as hope for victory evapo-
rated. His letters were carefully preserved by his wife, and many of them
also give insight into the family's welfare. Mary Bayard Clarke's letters to
William apparently did not survive the war, which is not surprising given
the hardships of the campaigns. Much can be gleaned, however, from other
correspondence, references in the *Edmondston Diary,* and Mary Bayard
Clarke's creative writings.

The start of the war found Mary Bayard Clarke throwing herself
wholeheartedly into her husband's military enterprise. She made the regimental flag, wrote and published patriotic poems, and daringly left her
children with relatives to follow her husband to Virginia and North Carolina camps on several occasions. She enjoyed being the colonel's lady, taking horseback jaunts with junior officers, and meeting friends. Not
unexpectedly, her absences did not meet with approval from some Devereux family members. Proper southern mothers were supposed to stay
with their children and supervise their upbringing, not gallivant at the
front. The fear of what others would say about this conduct had Devereux
tongues wagging. Mary Bayard Clarke created an additional furor by leaving her children in Raleigh under the supervision of Jane Espy, the free

black woman she brought from Texas. Neither Mary Bayard Clarke's brother or her sisters liked Jane or her free status. They distrusted Jane's care of the Clarkes' four children and blamed her for any poor conduct detected in Frank, Willie, Mary, or Tom. The ever-blunt Frances Miller threw down the gauntlet in an undated letter written in 1861, in which she threatened Jane and criticized William and Mary.[62]

To remove Jane from harm's way, the Clarkes hired her to work for William's regiment, where she performed ably.[63] Jane, who had worked for army officers garrisoned in San Antonio, approved the idea. The relationship between Jane and the Clarkes can only be caught in brief references in letters and in Mary Bayard's "Mrs. Leigh's Indian Waiter." When William Clarke was in Montgomery, he regularly sent a "howdy" to Jane, his slave Sam Taylor, and other employees in his home. Jane provided good service to Clarke's regiment until she became ill and Clarke removed her to Lewisburg to recover. After the war, Jane's contact with the Clarke family is harder to document, but when Mary Bayard Clarke became ill in 1865, it was Jane who nursed her back to health.[64]

Similarly, the Clarkes had a fairly relaxed relationship with their slave Sam Taylor. Taylor went with them when they moved to Texas from North Carolina, and he helped them make the transition to frontier life. When Mary Bayard Clarke left Texas at the start of the Civil War, she placed family papers and heirlooms with Sam to guard during the Clarkes' absence. Her trust in Sam was not misplaced. He wrote to William Clarke on 6 December 1865, noting that, "I have your trunk Still with me which my Mistress pack before She left here." He took the opportunity to thank William Clarke for never selling him, although he could have, but pointed out the difficulties of his life in Texas.[65] Sam Taylor apparently never returned to North Carolina, nor did the Clarkes see him again although there was at least one other exchange of letters.

Although the Clarkes never owned many slaves, they clearly enjoyed the benefits of having slaves handle the heavy work of cooking, washing, and cleaning house. During Reconstruction, Mary Bayard Clarke frequently bemoaned the lack of a cook or housekeeper. Eventually, as money became tighter, the Clarkes periodically had to forego the assistance of servants. Mary Bayard Clarke adjusted as best she could but saw the absurdity in her situation as well. Writing to a friend in Chicago in 1878, Mary Bayard Clarke admitted, "for the first time in my life I am without a house keeper, and I dont take kindly to it and cant teach a cook when I dont know how to cook anything but oysters and coffee, pickles and preserves,

I am well up in the fine arts of house keeping but Oh the drudgery! that gets me in the *small of my back* and I have *struck* work."[66]

The war years brought hardships to the Clarke family, without a doubt, but they also offered opportunities for development and freedom that were not to be found during their antebellum years in North Carolina. Mary Bayard Clarke, in addition to joining her husband on numerous occasions at his military camps, wrote extensively in support of the southern cause. Many women writers, north and south, produced patriotic songs, poems, and stories in support of the troops. Mary Bayard Clarke's poetry, published in various southern newspapers, enjoyed considerable success, especially her poems "The Battle of Manassas," "The Battle of Hampton Roads," "The Rebel Sock," and "Lines on the Death of Annie Carter Lee." Several of these poems later appeared in compilations of southern poetry produced after the war.[67] Most of her war poetry was published without remuneration, but the thrill of helping the cause offered payment enough. Mary Bayard Clarke also worked tirelessly to secure supplies and stores for her husband's regiment. She wrote one Virginia publisher a lively account of her travels across North Carolina as she scoured the countryside for food and clothing.[68]

Mary Bayard Clarke enjoyed the chance to see and be seen, but other matters continually required her attention. Ill health troubled her throughout the war years and after, and this took a toll. Despite her family's belief that she did not provide adequate care for her children, Mary Bayard Clarke worked hard for their well-being. Her two oldest boys' education was suffering. Teachers, when found, became teachers lost as fees rose during the inflationary years of the war. Mary Bayard Clarke had great hopes for Frank and Willie Clarke and wanted them to receive the type of education Devereux children had enjoyed for generations. Wartime exigencies made this an impossibility. Keeping children in clothing and shoes became difficult, too, and considerable ingenuity was required to manufacture them. A major problem they all faced was where to live. The Clarkes did not own a home in North Carolina. They were, in a unique way, refugees throughout the war. Mary Bayard Clarke wrote in 1861, "I am rich in sisters, and have no less than five homes in the State,"[69] but this seeming blessing led to unwanted family scrutiny. Family members did not hesitate to voice their opinions, and this troubled Mary Bayard Clarke, who had begun to chafe at the restrictive role her family expected women to follow. Her self-reliance was not easily resigned, and her distaste for living accommodations with her family is clear. In 1863 she philosophically wrote to son Willie, "I shall have to go to Conniconara to spend the winter; I had many plans but they have all failed and Grandpa thinks I had better be there, I am very sorry that we cant do as we like, but if I go there I can afford to send you to a better school, and as Mrs Primrose thinks of sending Rob and Willie to Davidson I shall try and get you in there with them."[70]

William J. Clarke could offer little but commiseration during the war years as he led his regiment into battles and carried on a furious argument with his commanding officer, General Robert Ransom. Mary Bayard kept him informed of her tribulations over schools and the lack of a permanent home, and he offered advice when he could.[71] His efforts to comfort or advise his wife may not have had the effect he intended, however. As Mary Bayard Clarke struggled with finding shelter, educating her children, gathering supplies for the regiment, and writing her thoughts in published verse and prose, she became increasingly assertive in stating her opinions and had less patience with her husband's quarrels with his superiors. Worried about William's request to transfer out of Ransom's brigade, she predicted the request would be denied; and she was right.[72] Meanwhile, William continued to fret about a promotion that never materialized.

In the spring of 1864, the Clarkes faced a new crisis when William Clarke was badly wounded at the Battle of Drewry's Bluff around 15 May[73] and returned to Raleigh to be nursed by his wife and family. Mary Bayard Clarke relished the opportunity to care for her husband, and she took pride in his military accomplishments. Observing the number of refugees in Raleigh, many of them able-bodied men, she expressed her "contempt" for their cowardice and asserted they were not "worth the powder and shot it would take to kill" them.[74] She hugely enjoyed the role she played as the devoted wife of a wounded war hero. It must have been a soothing interlude to have some time together, as well as a relief to Mary Bayard to know her husband was safe for a time from the battlefields of Virginia.

While convalescing, William Clarke made inquiries to see if he could afford to send his eldest son to the University of North Carolina.[75] The high cost prevented him from doing so, but he clearly tried to help his wife with some of her burdens. As the family's expenses continued to climb while Confederate money plummeted in value, Mary Bayard Clarke manufactured gloves, shirts, drawers, and other clothing items from a variety of sources. She also turned her thoughts to moneymaking enterprises. William Clarke returned to active duty on 1 January 1865.[76] By 17 January Mary Bayard was writing son Willie about her work as a government clerk, which she hoped to turn into a permanent position.[77] She also resurrected the plans to have a book of her poetry published "for the benefit of the fund to protect the graves of our dead about Winchester,"[78] which had been rejected by a northern publisher just before the start of the war.

These efforts came none too soon, because on 5 February 1865, William Clarke was captured by Union forces near Dinwiddie Courthouse in Virginia and imprisoned for the remainder of the war.[79] By April 1865 the federal army had occupied Raleigh. Hopes of employment with the state's Confederate officials ended at that point, but Mary Bayard Clarke's determination to support her family did not falter. She and her sons in the occupied city sold pies, lemonade, and newspapers to the detested Yankees to obtain a little money. They did it with a fierce loyalty to family pride and the South and with a bitter resentment of the Union army and other northern authorities.

## Reconstruction and the Conservatives

The twilight period between the federal occupation of Raleigh and William's release from prison further defined Mary Bayard Clarke's independence. In 1866 she published a series of articles in the *Old Guard* that recounted with verve and vinegar the verbal combat that she and other Raleigh women experienced with the occupying forces. Interestingly, Mary Bayard Clarke clipped and pasted these articles into a scrapbook and penciled in the identities of some of the unnamed Raleigh residents described in the articles. In the three articles, "General Sherman in Raleigh," "Gen. Sherman's Officers Among the Ladies of Raleigh," and "Gen. Sherman's Officers Among the Ladies of Raleigh. (*Concluded*)," Clarke expressed personal sorrow at the Confederacy's fall and anger over the changes wrought by the occupying forces. Yet, it is also clear that she derived a great deal of enjoyment from verbal repartee with the enemy.[80] It was during this period, in 1865, that Frances Miller attacked Mary Bayard Clarke's interactions with federal officers and threatened to send her home to their father. Reading Clarke's denunciations of the North in these articles, it is difficult to explain the ferocity of Miller's attack unless she believed Clarke enjoyed her interactions with the Yankee foes a little too much. It is possible, too, that Clarke used the 1866 articles to justify or excuse her conduct to a censorious southern community.

In 1866 Mary Bayard Clarke wrote another article, this time at the request of former governor Zebulon B. Vance, titled "The South Expects Every Woman to Do Her Duty." Published in the *Old Guard* and signed

with Clarke's alternate pseudonym, Stuart Leigh, the article clearly outlined Clarke's strategy to annoy the Union army and recommended it to
other southern women.[81] As Reconstruction in North Carolina began to
unfold, Mary and William worked with the state's Conservative Party in
an effort to halt Reconstruction policies. The 1868 convention that convened to consider a new state constitution and other legislation received
stinging ridicule from Mary Bayard Clarke's pen. She became, in fact, an
effective spokesperson for the Conservatives, writing numerous newspaper articles on their behalf.

At the same time, Clarke never lost sight of her creative writing. For
a short time in 1866 she worked as an editor for *Field and Fireside*
(Raleigh), which was published by W. B. Smith & Co., the same company
that published her book of poetry *Mosses From A Rolling Stone; or, Idle
Moments of a Busy Woman* in 1866. Clarke's position as editor did not last
because of differences with the owners.[82] She also published for the *Sentinel, Southern Home Journal* (Baltimore), *Literary Pastimes* (Richmond), *The
Land We Love* (Charlotte), *Old Guard,* and other northern papers. Nevertheless, she wearily admitted in a letter to Winchester Hall in 1866 that,
"Though there is a demand for my correspondence and contributions
when they are furnished gratis, I can not get much money from Southern
editors; they are too poor to pay well."[83]

One of her more curious series began when she wrote in the guise of
Betsey Bittersweet, who was supposed to be a semiliterate white woman.
The Bittersweet series took aim at African Americans, Republicans,
Reconstruction, northern schoolteachers, and any other likely target. The
articles, written to produce laughter and ridicule, were filled with racial
and class stereotypes as well as derogatory language. One article, "The
Union Washing Machine," written for the *Sentinel* around 1868, was a
broad metaphor for Reconstruction that referred to the "UNION WASH-
ING MASHIN," "the AMERIKIN MANGLE," and "SHERMAN'S
WRINGER."[84] It is unclear how much of her original text was altered by
the editor of the *Sentinel,* but the Betsey Bittersweet series only became more
vituperative over time and probably accurately reflected Mary Bayard
Clarke's sentiments.

The tone of the Bittersweet articles is in sharp contrast to another
article she wrote in the same period. In an untitled newspaper clipping
published in 1868 and inscribed by Mary Bayard Clarke as being written
"For the Journal of Commerce," she elegantly applauded the work of the
Conservatives, noting, "a body of delegates, representing the respectable

portion of the people of North Carolina, went into Convention in the city of Raleigh to organize a steady and determined resistance to the radicals, both Northern and Southern, who are attempting to force negro supremacy upon them."[85]

Mary Bayard Clarke's pursuit of publishers may be one reason she selected her topics. To earn money she needed to write articles that sold. Indeed, one of her wildest successes was a two-part series devoted to "Aunt Abby The Irrepressible," published in 1867 in *The Land We Love.* Leaving no stone unturned in her search for paying jobs, Clarke also wrote lyrics for hymns and the libretto for an opera.[86]

Mary Bayard Clarke also worked during these years to raise money and collect goods to help young southern girls orphaned by the war. She allowed some of her war poems to be included in others' compilations, which were sold to raise money for educating these young women.[87] The destruction of the plantation system led many former planter women to work together for the first time to support each other and to help those in need from their class. Mary Bayard Clarke joined with women friends to form a network of support for those impoverished by the late war. Interestingly, *Mosses from a Rolling Stone,* on which she pinned so many hopes for the war dead, did not contain any of her war poetry. It consisted of many of her favorite poems that had been published in a variety of publications during the antebellum period. Clarke helped to market the book by writing to friends, advertising in newspapers from Louisiana to Virginia, and sending copies to select friends who would encourage sales. One of the first copies went to Robert E. and Mary Custis Lee in Lexington, Virginia, under the signature of her young daughter, Mary Devereux Clarke, a gift both Lees graciously acknowledged.

Mary Bayard Clarke also tried to assist her husband in finding employment in North Carolina. While he was still in prison, William Clarke had briefly considered returning to Texas after the war.[88] A letter from Brantz Mayer, a United States Army officer living in Baltimore after the war, alluded to a letter from Mary Bayard Clarke that suggested the Clarkes also considered Mexico as a new home.[89]

Apparently, Mary Bayard Clarke preferred the odds in her home state. By 1866 William Clarke had begun negotiations with New York investors to open a sawmill near Keoco Mills, North Carolina. Mary Bayard Clarke wrote her old tutor in February 1866 that she hoped the sawmill would bring some financial relief. Realistic about their prospects, she admitted, "I hate country life, I have no health for its pursuits and enjoyments and love a little society but in the present state of affairs these are but feathers —and to go where we would not always be worried about the Almighty dollar is my first desire."[90] Although the hope for a better future seemed promising, the sawmill venture failed. By November 1866 Mary Bayard Clarke wrote to Frank that, "Father is very low spirited and seems to think no money is to be made by lumber but he wont turn his attention to any thing else. . . . If you need money write either to me or Mr Cooke not to your father he is in such a state of mind that I have to keep him as free from anxiety as possible and so morbid about money he says he wont wear his watch because he does not wish to be at the expense of paying the tax on it."[91]

The need to keep William J. Clarke "free from anxiety" was real. In addition to financial worries, political unrest, child-rearing responsibilities, and running the household in an isolated area, Mary Bayard Clarke faced a serious decline in her husband's physical and mental health.[92] Later letters indicate that the "irritation" William Clarke experienced was not temporary. Whether the illness was caused by mental stress, his imprisonment, financial burdens, or pain from his war wounds, his instability led to further complications when Clarke developed a drinking problem by the mid- to late-1870s. His drinking, while not excessive at first, gradually increased and affected his marriage and career.[93]

## RECONSTRUCTION AND THE REPUBLICANS

Given the Clarkes' involvement with the Conservative Party, it is easy to imagine the jolt their acquaintances received when William joined the Republican Party by July of 1868. Old friends and family members considered it opportunism on Clarke's part, because he received an appointment from Republican Governor William W. Holden on 24 December 1868, as a superior court judge.[94] Indeed, in Clarke's pocket diary he kept during 1868, he recorded on 27 April how depressed he was by the Conservatives' defeat and noted, "Ardently do I hope for the organization of a new party where a Democrat can have some chance."[95] It is possible that he thought working with the Republicans offered the best way to protect the power of southern whites by mitigating the most onerous Reconstruction policies. Given Clarke's pronounced sense of integrity as an officer, however, it is highly likely that after he took the Oath of Allegiance he meant to abide by its terms. As the Conservatives mounted an increasingly vicious white-supremacy campaign, Clarke weighed his options and apparently decided that the rule of law would not be found in the Conservatives' ranks. In the draft of an election speech he made for the Republicans in Goldsboro in 1868, Clarke stated,

> I honestly believe that we now have to decide the question of peace, or war. If I had not so thought, I had remained in the quiet and seclusion of private life. . . . I assure you it requires a strong sense of duty to induce me to take an antagonistic position to many cherished friends, . . . and to expose myself to the torrent of invective, and vituperation, which is poured forth with a facility and profusion absolutely astonishing. But a man whose patriotic instincts carried him into two wars, and who has participated in twenty battles, will probably have sufficient fortitude to risk the stings of wasps and hornets.[96]

The stings from the Conservative camp were not understated. Family and friends deserted the Clarkes. Still, the new Republican associates brought a different world into focus. William Clarke, once his decision was made, stood firm for Republican policy although he distrusted many of the "unscrupulous and tricky Yankees"[97] who moved into the state and dominated the party. Mary Bayard Clarke's reaction was more nuanced. The Republicans were less judgmental of her and her ambitions, which proved attractive. They did represent, however, all that she had scorned for most of her life. Her planter antecedents must have warred with William's political apostasy. The adjustment required ongoing effort, and she abandoned the field during heated political elections, preferring the quiet afforded by visits to northern states that included New York, Massachusetts, Connecticut, Pennsylvania, and Illinois.

Significantly, Mary Bayard Clarke wrote little in support of Republican politics. She stood by her husband and later worked as co-editor with him in 1880 on the Republican newspaper *Signal,* but she did not submit political articles as she had before. Her work instead focused on women's issues, education, health, and women's work outside the home, and some North Carolina readers considered her ideas fairly controversial. In one early editorial, Mary Bayard Clarke stated her purpose as editor of a literary "Woman's Exchange" in a political paper, explaining she felt "that the time had not come when a family paper could maintain itself, simply on its literary merits, however readable it might be made." She even offered to send female subscribers who objected to the Republican politics in the paper "only the first and fourth pages, leaving the inside a blank— on which they can write their own political creed." She added she had "successfully conducted a woman's paper in Chicago" and hoped to use "the latent talent that lies hid in many of our women, simply because they have not the courage to put pen to paper for publication."[98] When readers began responding to her articles with criticism or questions, especially when her editorials were viewed as "upsetting the established order of our dear old conservative State," she firmly replied that the Civil War had changed the state twenty years previously and progress could not be turned back. Tellingly, she noted that, before the war, "if the daughters of our most prominent men had taken positions as clerks in the capitol, and gone there daily to their duties, just as their brothers might have done," they would have been ostracized, but "their grand-daughters have done it with perfect propriety."[99] Clarke found plenty to write about during the postbellum years, although politics seemingly did not interest her. This decision may have reflected lack of opportunity, but it also indicated that her enthusiasm for politics was considerably diminished by the opprobrium her family had experienced over the years.[100]

Although Mary Bayard Clarke turned away from politics as much as she could, she did not turn away from family responsibilities or from the unexplored vistas brought by her new Republican associations. New friends offered opportunities for personal and sometimes financial advancement. Republican judges on the state supreme court enjoyed her company and respected her abilities. Judge Edwin Reade, in particular, encouraged her and approved of her efforts to find salaried work. He also helped Mary Bayard to purchase a home in New Bern, North Carolina, in 1869.[101] In September 1868 Judge Reade, writing to her as a friend and as his "secretary," asked to meet her in Washington, D.C., and revealed how intrigued he was with the vibrant Mrs. Clarke.[102]

Mary Bayard Clarke was in Washington, D.C., to work on a short biography of Zebulon B. Vance she was writing for *Literary Pastime*. She needed access to his official letterbook as Confederate governor of North Carolina, a document which had been confiscated and removed to the War Office in Washington, D.C. Use of the letterbook required the express written permission of President Andrew Johnson, which she had no trouble in procuring. President Johnson proved no more immune to her manipulation than any other man she had known. In a splendid account of her meeting with the president, written in a letter to son Willie, she described her latest conquest, boasting that the president endorsed her petition "in the strongest manner, telling me he was proud of me as a North Carolinian, giving me an immense bouquet and himself escorting me to the door and handing me out to the amazement of the outsiders. It was funny to see the surprised looks as I passed with my petition in a great official envelope endorsed 'War Office' in one hand and my bouquet in the other."[103]

The publishing opportunities of the 1870s provided income that helped the Clarke children, although funds were always short. All four of the children received educations, and Mary Bayard Clarke closely monitored their work and achievements while sending encouragement or admonitions. This close involvement with her children was something she had missed with her mother's early death, and she carefully ensured that each child received support and the chance to develop as an individual.[104]

Efforts on behalf of her children, however, were hampered by William Clarke's growing depression after his defeat for reelection as judge in 1874. His loss of the judgeship and its steady income forced him back into private law practice, where he found it difficult to collect fees in a cash-poor climate. Later, his son Willie used his political connections to acquire for his father the office of clerk of court for Craven County. The entire family hoped for William Clarke's success, but he struggled for the rest of his life to make ends meet. The lack of income remained an open wound between William and Mary Clarke, because Mary's health was beginning to fail and she worried about the future. Their married daughter, writing to her husband in California in 1879, recognized the strain on her parents. "Mother is about to worry herself to death, & with good reason if not having any money is a reason. I hope we will die before we feel to each other as Fada & Mother seem to do. I think both are to blame, in this matter, at least."[105]

Despite these travails, William Clarke remained optimistic and deeply attached to his family. He wrote a heartfelt "love letter" to his wife in 1882 in which he alluded to his problems, their separation, and his need to be reunited with his wife. He somberly noted he had gone to church to pray for guidance and added, "I do not think that the mercies of God are clean gone from me, but He certainly seems to be slow to hear my prayers."[106]

## A JOURNALISTIC CAREER

During the 1870s, Mary Bayard Clarke increasingly turned to social commentary in her newspaper columns. In the process, she blossomed intellectually. Her writing did not always earn much, but she thrived in a world that encouraged her to reach beyond the home into the business world formerly reserved for men. She wrote countless book reviews; assessed and rejected much of the suffrage movement while admitting to "a strong and unshaken belief in the right of every woman who works for payment, to receive as good treatment in a business point of view, as if she were a man;"[107] and discussed theology, hygiene, science, labor relations, evolution, and America's Centennial celebration. She worked with several Chicago women writers to found a short-lived periodical for women called *Current Thought*. She became an advocate for working women, and she tried to teach her southern sisters that there were many good things to be learned from their northern counterparts. One of her 1877 articles, "Woman North and South," attracted attention in several states, and it provides a measure of her development from the days of her Conservative advocacy in the 1860s. Examining southern culture, she observed that the southern woman "is more conservative . . . than her Northern sister. . . . She regards a woman's club, whether a literary, artistic, or social one, as a monstrosity, and leaves all work and amusement outside of home to her husband, brother or son, except the societies of her church. . . . But all this is changed, and the Southern woman grows yearly better adapted to the great social and domestic change in her circumstances produced by the war. Necessity is forcing her to be more self-reliant and more self-supporting. . . . and it is to be hoped . . . the women of the two sections may approach nearer to each other, for each may learn something by doing so."[108]

Clarke also established a deep friendship with Dr. Nathan W. Abbott of Chicago, Illinois. Abbott enjoyed the company of several women writers he knew in Chicago, which is where he met Mary Bayard Clarke in 1877. After her return to North Carolina, the two exchanged long letters in which they considered religion, science, health, and other topics. Clarke admitted to him things she probably did not discuss with her family, including health problems, her age, and that "point of life, which you can understand, when I need all my strength and vitality to meet the demands made on me."[109] This deeply treasured friendship allowed Clarke to talk freely without resorting to subterfuge to please or mollify family. Perhaps it offered an intellectual companionship she found increasingly elusive with her husband.

## "I Feel Life a Muddle"

Writing, housework, and financial and familial crises, although faced energetically, weakened Mary Bayard Clarke's health as the years progressed. She suffered a devastating stroke in 1883 that left her partially paralyzed and temporarily despondent.[110] With considerable courage, she accepted this challenge as she had so many others. By April 1884 she cheerfully wrote Hall that she was considering buying a tricycle and that she was greatly enjoying the gift of a "caligraph" or typewriter that one loving friend had sent her.[111] Although troubled with some memory loss, Mary Bayard continued to read and explore her world through books and correspondence.

Pressing family events also demanded attention during the last decade of Mary Bayard Clarke's life. She saw three of her children married, and she enjoyed the births of two grandchildren to her daughter, Mary Clarke Morgan. This joy was dimmed in 1880 when Mary Clarke Morgan was widowed after her husband Rufus Morgan died from consuming poisonous mushrooms shortly before she was to join him at his apiary business in California. This calamity troubled the entire family and placed additional strains on limited incomes, because the young widow and her two children, one an infant, lived thereafter with William and Mary Clarke. Some of Mary Bayard Clarke's writings in the 1880s, in which she urged women to receive more than "book learning," probably reflected her distress about her daughter's situation. Her daughter's traditional education, which Mary Bayard Clarke had worked so hard to pay for, did not ready her daughter for earning a living in her young widowhood.

In the last month of 1885, Mary Bayard Clarke, knowing that her own husband's death was imminent and believing that her daughter's long-term security would be assured only if she remarried, encouraged a courtship with a New Hampshire emigrant who arrived in New Bern in December 1885. George Moulton, who later worked as a merchant and salesman in and around New Bern, had traveled south to locate his cousin's grave in New Bern's National Cemetery and to test the business waters. While there he met the young widow Mary C. Morgan and decided to stay. Mary Bayard Clarke, ever a realist, checked on Moulton's credentials in New Hampshire and decided this man would suit her daughter.[112] Mary Morgan and George Moulton seemed to be compatible, but the speed of their courtship reflected Mary Bayard Clarke's orchestration.

William J. Clarke, who became ill in 1885, died on 23 January 1886. Mary Bayard Clarke ensured that the last four months of his life were peaceful and "petted him like a spoiled child,"[113] but the strain weakened her. The following month William E. Clarke married Bessie Howerton. The preparations for this event provided the coup de grace. Mary Bayard Clarke suffered a second paralytic stroke in March and knew she was dying. With the will and sense of purpose she had exhibited for years, she arranged for the marriage of her daughter to George Moulton at her sickbed on 14 March 1886. She died on 31 March 1886.

Although prosperity never materialized for William and Mary Clarke, their efforts on behalf of their children bore fruit. Frank, who married a young woman from Michigan, eventually became a leader in that state's development of teaching facilities for the deaf and dumb. The youngest son, Thomas, followed in his brother's footsteps and pursued a similar career in the state of Washington. Willie, a successful lawyer and Republican politician, became postmaster for New Bern and enjoyed his family life until he was tragically drowned with two of his children and a neighbor's child in a boating accident. Mary Clarke Morgan Moulton bore three more children with George and reared all five in her mother's home in New Bern, the Louisiana House. Her descendants occupy the house to this day, and others live nearby. The wealth of family documents they preserved in New Bern provide a great gift to the history of the state and the region. Mary Bayard Clarke's genuine talent as a writer, the variety of people and experiences she encountered, and her national prominence combine to tell a powerful story. Clarke faced great joy and adversity over the course of six decades, and she learned from all that came her way. Reared as a southern lady who was expected to devote herself to the private sphere of her household, this talented woman refused to remain a passive observer of life. Mary Bayard Clarke traveled a long road from southern belle to accomplished woman of letters, and her journey provides a fascinating look at an "irrepressible" southern woman.

### Notes

1. Barbara Welter, "The Cult of True Womanhood, 1820–1860," *American Quarterly* 18 (summer 1966): 151–74; Drew Gilpin Faust, *Mothers of Invention: Women of the Slaveholding South in the American Civil War* (Chapel Hill: University of North Carolina Press, 1996), 7.

2. Elizabeth Fox-Genovese, *Within the Plantation Household: Black and White Women of the Old South.* (Chapel Hill: University of North Carolina Press, 1988), 38–39, 44–45 (hereafter cited as Fox-Genovese, *Within the Plantation Household*). A seminal analysis of southern women can be found in Anne Firor Scott's *The Southern Lady: From Pedestal to Politics, 1830–1930* (Chicago: University of Chicago Press, 1970).

3. John Devereux to Frances Pollock Devereux, 26 November 1821, Wootten, Moulton, and Clarke Family Papers no. 4805, Southern Historical Collection, Wilson Library, University of North Carolina at Chapel Hill (hereafter cited as Wootten, Moulton, Clarke Papers, SHC).

4. Brantz Mayer to Mary Bayard Clarke, Raleigh, 16 April 1866. Letter in possession of Mrs. Graham A. Barden Jr., New Bern, N.C. (hereafter cited as the Barden Collection).

5. Beth G. Crabtree and James W. Patton, eds., *"Journal of a Secesh Lady": The Diary of Catherine Ann Devereux Edmondston, 1860–1866* (Raleigh: North Carolina Division of Archives and History, 1979), xxii (hereafter cited as the *Edmondston Diary*).

6. *Edmondston Diary*, xxiv–xxv.

7. M. V. Murts or Wurts to Miss Frances Devereux, no date, ca. July 1836, Wootten, Moulton, Clarke Papers, SHC.

8. In a letter from Elizabeth Devereux Jones to Sophia Devereux Turner, 7 September 1878, Jones commented, "Oh! if our Mother had only been spared to us how different would have been the lives of every one of her children! I know we would have had greif, every human being must have, but I am sure they would not have been of the kind we have all been called to bear! & all of our lives would have been so different had we had her to go to to tell our troubles & get from her such loving good advice & counsel! Yes we have all needed her, every one has suffered for the want of her love." Josiah Turner Papers no. 730, Southern Historical Collection, Wilson Library, University of North Carolina at Chapel Hill (hereafter cited as Turner Papers, SHC). Mary Bayard Clarke expressed her feelings in an 1857 poem titled "I've Been Thinking." She described her childhood as a "sad and dreary time" and noted "How rapidly we scattered, From the time our Mother died." Mary Bayard Clarke, Manuscript Letterbook, no pagination, Barden Collection (hereafter cited as MBC Letterbook).

9. *Edmondston Diary*, 34.

10. John Devereux Jr. to Mary Bayard Clarke, 6 August 1859, Barden Collection.

11. *Edmondston Diary*, xxiii–xxiv.

12. Ibid, xxvi–xvii.

13. Ibid, xxx–xxxi.

14. In a sketch of Henry Watkins Miller that appeared in *Grandfather's Tales of North Carolina History*, Richard B. Creecy noted that Miller's brilliance and opportunities "were thrown to the winds, he fell before the tempter and his life is now the best temperance lecture in the whole history of North Carolina." Richard B. Creecy, *Grandfather's Tales of North Carolina History* (Raleigh: Edwards and Broughton, Printers, 1901), 159.

15. *Edmondston Diary*, 272, 283. Catherine Edmondston wondered at her sister's decision. "Attempted but vainly to dissuade sister F from her wild scheme of opening a boarding house. What infatuation it is! And so soon after her husband's death! I can neither comprehend or have any patience with it—this pretence of Independence." The Clarkes may have supported Frances's decision, because Frances refers to their bitterness at her not "upholding" Mary Bayard Clarke as she had upheld Frances. Frances Miller to William J. Clarke, 20 July 1870, Barden Collection.

16. Mary Bayard Clarke to William J. Clarke, 21 July [1868], William John Clarke Papers no. 153, Southern Historical Collection, Wilson Library, University of North Carolina at Chapel Hill (hereafter cited as Clarke Papers, SHC).

17. Frances Devereux Miller to William J. Clarke, 12 October 1880. In this short letter Miller asked William to visit her when he was in Durham, noting that she saw "no reason in your continuing angry when your wife has held out her hand." Clarke Papers, SHC.

18. Margaret Devereux, *Plantation Sketches* (Cambridge, Mass.: privately printed, 1933), 2, 14.

19. *Edmondston Diary,* 345. Kate Edmondston recalled on 21 January 1863, "Do you remember, Madam, how you wept & cried the first year of your marriage when your husband said 'that the first duty of woman was to attend to the cooking'? I do not mean to accuse you of neglecting it—that you had too high a sense of your duty as a wife ever to do. What pained & mortified you was the exaltation in which he placed it. He was not fault finding, simply expressing his sense of woman's mission. 'Was it for *this* that you had been educated' Was 'it for *this* that such tastes had been cultivated in you?' . . . You could not worship at such a shrine! and yet, Madam, have you not long years ago seen and confessed that your husband was right?; that a well ordered table, well cooked, well prepared food was the keynote to health, happiness, and usefulness? Remember how you exulted in a passage in Plutarch's Paulus Emilius that it required more genius to order a feast well than to marshal an Army!"

20. *Edmondston Diary,* 282. On 22 October 1862, Edmondston commented, "O! beware of stepping out of your sphere. . . . Then indeed you would forget a woman's first ornament, modesty. Women have no business to rush into print; so wide an arena does not become them."

21. *Edmondston Diary,* 733. What may be the only surviving copy of *The Morte d'Arthur* is in the Barden Collection.

22. *Edmondston Diary,* xii.

23. *Edmondston Diary,* 10 June 1863, 401–2; 9 September 1863, 463–65.

24. *Fayette County Historical Society Bulletin* 1 (Nov. 1988): 81.

25. Nora Cannon to Willie Clarke, 25 February [1872 or 1873], Barden Collection.

26. Samuel A. Ashe, ed., *Biographical History of North Carolina from Colonial Times to the Present,* vol. 3 (Greensboro, N.C.: Charles L. Van Noppen: 1906), 415–26 (hereafter cited as Ashe, *Biographical History*).

27. William J. Clarke to Mary Bayard Clarke, 21 August 1870, Wootten, Moulton, Clarke Papers, SHC.

28. Mary Bayard Clarke to Dr. Nathan Abbott, 16 May 1868, Barden Collection.

29. Sophia Devereux Turner to William J. Clarke, [ca. July 1868], Barden Collection.

30. William E. Clarke manuscript, "Mary Bayard Clarke," p. 4, Francis Martin Finnerty Papers, Brevard, N.C., reproduced courtesy of owner (hereafter cited as Finnerty Papers). Mary Bayard Clarke's son explained the origin of his mother's nom de plume. "It was the custom amongst the girls of New Orleans to take the name of some flower, as a pet name, amongst themselves. There was a very fragant species of jessamine called 'Tenella'—(the tender sweet little one) This name was given to Mary Bayard Devereux by her girl friends and she afterwards adopted it as her nom de plume—"; Mary B. Clarke to John R. Thompson, 31 October 1854, John Esten Cooke Papers, 1840–96, 2nd 82:G, Special Collections Library, Duke University, Durham, N.C. In this letter she also proposed writing a series of articles on "lady like subjects" about a proposed trip to Cuba. She had already received an offer from a northern editor but confessed that "being entirely Southern in my feelings and opinions I would prefer contributing to some periodical in our part of the Union. I have written occasionally for the New Orleans Pecayune and the Home Journal."

31. Mary Bayard Clarke to Dr. Bagby, 12 March 1861, Bagby Family Papers, Virginia Historical Society (hereafter cited as Bagby Papers, VHS).

32. Mary Bayard Clarke to Dr. Bagby, 16 December 1860, Bagby Papers, VHS.

33. Mary Bayard Clarke to Dr. Bagby, 8 April [1861], Bagby Papers, VHS.

34. William J. Clarke served as a captain in the Twelfth Regiment, United States Army. He was brevetted major for gallantry at the Battle of National Bridge, where he was severely wounded. He was mustered out of regular service on 25 July 1848. Clarke suffered considerable pain for the remainder of his life from these and later wounds he received during the Civil War. Ashe, *Cyclopedia of Eminent and Representative Men of the Carolinas of the Nineteenth Century, with a Brief Historical Introduction of South Carolina by General Edward McCrady, Jr., and on North Carolina by Hon. Samuel A. Ashe,* vol. 2 (Madison, Wis.: Brant and Fuller, 1892), 126–27 (hereafter cited as Ashe, *Cyclopedia of Eminent and Representative Men*); Elizabeth Gregory McPherson, ed., "Unpublished Letters from North Carolinians to Polk," *North Carolina Historical Review* 17 (Apr. 1940): 139–40 (hereafter cited as McPherson, "Unpublished Letters to Polk").

35. MBC Letterbook.

36. MBC Letterbook.

37. Just before leaving for the Mexican War, William J. Clarke wrote a letter to President Polk to relate how unpleasantly he had been treated because of his politics. In it Clarke said, "If the President knew how much I have been persecuted for being a Democrat he would make me a Colonel just to spite the Opposition—They have made my life bitter to me and this my native place disagreeable and I want to get away from it." McPherson, "Unpublished Letters to Polk," 139.

38. 1850 Census, Wake County Slave Schedule, Raleigh, p. 667.

39. Thomas Pollock Devereux to Mary Bayard Clarke, 10 August 1858, Barden Collection.

40. In letters to Governor David S. Reid in 1854 and 1855, Clarke furiously denounced his lack of support in the Pierce administration for the consulate post and asked the governor's assistance in securing the position. On 3 January 1855, Clarke fumed, "If N.C., the only State of any consequence that has santioned Gen'l Pierce's administration, if the true blue Democrats who have stood by him thro' good report and thro' evil report, in sunshine & in storm are to be disregarded, then my pretentious claims I had almost said to the office may be overlooked." Clarke added despairingly, "My friend, I am in need of help; as the death of our friend Dr. Scott has terribly involved me, and if I do not receive this appointment I shall be compelled to sell out and leave N.C. I intended to leave for Cuba next week but I shall wait until I hear from you." William J. Clarke to Governor D. S. Reid, David S. Reid Papers PC 1.8, North Carolina State Archives, Raleigh, N.C.

41. Mary Bayard Clarke to Frances Miller, 24 March [1855], Barden Collection.

42. Mary Bayard Clarke to Frances Miller, 24 March [1855], Barden Collection.

43. "La Tenella," *Home Journal* (New York), undated clipping [ca. 1867], MBC Scrapbook 1, Barden Collection. The identity of the Gales Seyton mentioned is unclear. In 1855 the editors of the *National Intelligencer* were Joseph Gales Jr. and William Winston Seaton. Joseph Gales Jr., who suffered from poor health in the 1850s, died in 1860. William Winston Seaton died in 1866. Robert Neal Elliott Jr., "The Raleigh Register, 1799–1863" (Ph.D. diss., University of North Carolina at Chapel Hill, 1953), 46–47, 68, 85–86, 91, 93, 152, 283, 304–6.

44. Mary Bayard Clarke to Winchester Hall, 1856, quoted in *Poems by Mrs. Mary Bayard Clarke, With a Sketch of Her Life by Winchester Hall* (New York: Broadway Publishing, 1905), xv (hereafter cited as Hall, *MBC Poems*). Years later, Robert E. Lee sent a copy of one of Mary Bayard Clarke's poems to his daughter Agnes with the notation, "Mrs. Clarke who wrote the lines on Genl Polk, is the lady who composed those on dear Annie. I knew her well in Texas, where she went for the benefit of her health." Robert E. Lee to Agnes Lee, in care of Dr. C(ary) C(harles) Cocke, Bremo Bluff, Fluvana Co. Virginia, 12 August 1864. Lee Family Papers, VHS.

45. Mary Bayard Clarke, "Mrs. Leigh's Indian Waiter; and How She Came to Get Him," *Inland Monthly Magazine,* July 1877, 48–63; Mary Bayard Clarke to Winchester Hall, 1856, Hall, *MBC Poems,* xv–xvii. Clarke republished the story as a serial years later in the Raleigh *Signal.*

46. George Denison, San Antonio, to Eliza Denison, Vermont, 21 June 1857. Papers of George Denison, Manuscript Collection, MMC–0249, Library of Congress.

47. For more information, see Frank L. Klement, *Dark Lanterns: Secret Political Societies, Conspiracies, and Treason Trials in the Civil War* (Baton Rouge: Louisiana State

University Press, 1984), 1–15; Mark C. Carnes, *Secret Ritual and Manhood in Victorian America* (New Haven, Conn.: Yale University Press, 1989), 7–8; Kevin R. Young, *To the Tyrants Never Yield: A Texas Civil War Sampler* (Plano, Tex.: Worldware Publishing, 1991), 25–34.

48. Samuel A. Maverick was born in South Carolina but moved to Texas by 1835. He became a prominent rancher, businessman, and politician. Walter Prescott Webb and H. Bailey Carroll, eds., *The Handbook of Texas,* vol. 2 (Austin: Texas State Historical Association, 1952), 161 (hereafter cited as *Handbook of Texas*). The "Judge Paschal" probably referred to Isaiah Addison Paschal, a lawyer, jurist, and legislator originally from Georgia. He served on the bench of a Louisiana circuit court in the 1830s and moved to San Antonio in 1845. Ron Tyler, ed. in chief, *The New Handbook of Texas,* vol. 5 (Austin: Texas State Historical Association, 1996), 80 (hereafter cited as *New Handbook of Texas*).

49. *Handbook of Texas,* 544.

50. Thomas Pollock Devereux to Mary Bayard Clarke, 10 August 1858, Barden Collection.

51. William J. Clarke to Mary Bayard Clarke, 30 September 1858, Wootten, Moulton, Clarke Papers, SHC.

52. William J. Clarke to Mary Bayard Clarke, 5 September 1858, Wootten, Moulton, Clarke Papers, SHC.

53. John Devereux Jr. to Mary Bayard Clarke, 6 August 1859; Thomas Pollock Devereux to Mary Bayard Clarke, 12 August 1859. Both letters, Barden Collection.

54. Undated poem, ca. 1858, MBC Letterbook. Written to her absent husband and titled "To ————," these lines were written by Mary Bayard Clarke about her love for her husband:

> But does not my spirit come to thee at night
> To gladden and cheer thee with dreams of delight,
> Or is it in fancy alone that I hear,
> Thy passionate whisper breathed into my ear?
>
> Does my head never now on thy bosom recline
> Does thy lip never lovingly cling unto mine?
> Oh! surely it is not in mem'ry alone,
> I live o'er those moments of rapture we've known?

55. William J. Clarke to Thomas Pollock Devereux, 21 February 1860, John Devereux Papers, PC 34.2, State Archives, North Carolina Division of Archives and History, Raleigh, N.C.

56. Newspaper clipping, MBC Scrapbook 1, "Interesting from Texas," 17 February 1861, with a handwritten notation by Mary Bayard Clarke's daughter, Mary Clarke Moulton: "Letters to the New York Herald written from San Antonio de Bexar in the Spring of /61' By Mother." Barden Collection. The article

is simply signed "Our San Antonio Correspondence." Mary Bayard Clarke alluded to this article in a letter and said, "one can never be half so spicy as when writing strictly incog." Mary Bayard Clarke to Dr. Bagby, 19 March [1861], Bagby Papers, VHS.

57. A letter dated 1 April 1861, from P. N. Luckett, quartermaster general of Texas to Confederate Secretary of War Leroy P. Walker recommended Clarke's appointment in the southern army with the same rank he held in the United States Army during the Mexican War. Luckett referred to Clarke's efficient work during the surrender of the federal garrison in San Antonio "at a time when the Southern cause needed friends." War Department Collection of Confederate Records, Record Group 109, Clarke, William J., National Archives and Records Administration, Washington, D.C. Clarke pinned his military hopes on North Carolina rather than on Texas because he believed most of the fighting would be in that area of the Confederacy. He wrote Mary that if she wished it, he would return to Texas instead, but he preferred trying North Carolina. William J. Clarke to Mary Bayard Clarke, 22 May 1861, Barden Collection.

58. William J. Clarke to Mary Bayard Clarke, 23 May 1861, Wootten, Moulton, Clarke Papers, SHC.

59. William J. Clarke to Mary Bayard Clarke, 23 May 1861, Wootten, Moulton, Clarke Papers, SHC.

60. William J. Clarke to Mary Bayard Clarke, 23 May 1861, Wootten, Moulton, Clarke Papers, SHC.

61. Mary Bayard Clarke to Winchester Hall, 1861. Hall, *MBC Poems,* xvii.

62. Frances Miller to Mary Bayard Clarke, undated, ca. summer 1861, Barden Collection.

63. A bill dated October 1861 to the Confederate government for the services of Jane Espy for two weeks of work at the Lewisburg Hospital can be found in the Clarke Papers, SHC.

64. Mary Bayard Clarke to Winchester Hall, 1865. Hall, *MBC Poems,* xvii.

65. Samuel Taylor to William Clarke, 6 December 1865, Clarke Papers, SHC.

66. Mary Bayard Clarke to Nathan W. Abbott, 16 May [1878], Barden Collection.

67. Mary Bayard Clarke's friend Emily V. Mason published two editions of *The Southern Poems of the War* (Baltimore: John Murphy, 1868), which included several poems by "Tenella" and by "Mrs. M. B. Clarke."

68. Mary Bayard Clarke to Dr. Bagby, 8 October 1861, Bagby Papers, VHS.

69. Mary Bayard Clarke to Dr. Bagby, 8 October 1861, Bagby Papers, VHS.

70. Mary Bayard Clarke to Frank and Willie Clarke, 27 September [1863], Finnerty Papers.

71. William J. Clarke to Mary Bayard Clarke, 1 December 1862; William J. Clarke to Mary Bayard Clarke, 6 February 1863. Both in Wootten, Moulton, Clarke Papers, SHC.

72. William J. Clarke to Mary Bayard Clarke, 11 February 1863, Barden Collection.

73. Louis H. Manarin and Weymouth T. Jordan Jr., eds., *North Carolina Troops: 1861–1865, A Roster,* vol. 7 (Raleigh, N.C.: Division of Archives and History, 1979), 251 (hereafter cited as Manarin and Jordan, *Roster of NC Troops*). Kate Edmondston noted in her diary that "Colonel Clarke's wound is more serious than we at first heard. His shoulder 'is crushed' and peices of bone are already being discharged from it. Poor man, disabled I fear for life! Mr E has written & urged him to come to our house so soon as he can travel, offering to go for him, but it will be some time ere he can leave the Surgeon's hands I fear. He is at a friend's house in Richmond." 25 May 1864, *Edmondston Diary,* 566.

74. Mary Bayard Clarke to Willie Clarke, 20 July 1864, Finnerty Papers.

75. Charles Phillips to William J. Clarke, 26 July 1864, Clarke Papers, SHC.

76. Manarin and Jordan, *Roster of NC Troops,* 7:251.

77. Mary Bayard Clarke to Willie Clarke, 17 January [1865], Finnerty Papers.

78. Mary Bayard Clarke, Raleigh, to Miss Deane, New Orleans, 23 February 1866, Barden Collection; Hall, *MBC Poems,* xix. On 11 October 1865, the publishing firm of W. B. Smith & Co. of Raleigh, N.C., obtained copyright to the manuscript "Mosses from a Rolling Stone: or Idle Moments of a Busy Woman By Tenella," which they published in 1866.

79. Manarin and Jordan, *Roster of NC Troops,* 7:251.

80. [Mary Bayard Clarke], "General Sherman in Raleigh," *Old Guard,* Apr. 1866, 231; Terrell Armistead Crow and Mary Moulton Barden, "Mary Bayard Clarke and the Yankee Occupation of Raleigh," *North Carolina Literary Review* 8 (1999): 29–38.

81. "The South Expects Every Woman to Do Her Duty. [BY A LADY OF NORTH CAROLINA.]," *Old Guard,* Aug. 1866, 482. This clipping was pasted into one of Mary Bayard Clarke's scrapbooks and annotated by her as being, "Written at the request of Governor Vance." She also inked in her initials as author. MBC Scrapbook 1, Barden Collection.

82. Mary Bayard Clarke agreed to have W. B. Smith & Co. publish in *Field and Fireside* a fictional story she had written titled "Chalmette." The story was "a tale of Creole Life in Louisiana." "North Carolina Authors, Mrs. Mary Bayard Clarke," newspaper clipping, no date, MBC Scrapbook 1, Barden Collection. The publisher's decision to serialize the story angered Clarke, who objected that this decision had exposed her to ridicule or injured her reputation as an author. The dispute led to a legal agreement in January 1866, which permitted the publisher to finish part of the story but kept full copyright to the story in Mary Bayard Clarke's hands. Clarke Papers, SHC.

83. Hall, *MBC Poems,* xix.

84. Undated newspaper clipping, ca. 1868, MBC Scrapbook 2, Barden Collection, titled "The Union Washing Machine." The clipping contains the printed

heading, "For the Sentinel. Newbun, North Carlina." The manuscript version of this article originally had been sent by Mary Bayard Clarke to Daniel H. Hill for publication in *The Land We Love*. He turned it down, saying in a brief note to Mary Bayard that it was "too rebellious my friend." She then sent it to the *Sentinel* for publication.

85. Undated, untitled clipping, MBC Scrapbook 1, Barden Collection. Signed "C."

86. R. E. Lee to Miss Mary Clarke, 14 March 1866, Barden Collection; M. C. Lee to Mary Bayard Clarke, 15 March 1866, Barden Collection; Hall, *MBC Poems,* xix. One of the hymns written by Mary B. Clarke, "The Shadow of the Cross," pasted into MBC Scrapbook 1, Barden Collection, was published by J. C. Garrigues & Co. of Pennsylvania, which copyrighted it in 1869. The music was written by R. M. McIntosh.

87. Emily Mason to Mary Bayard Clarke, 10 July [1866], Barden Collection.

88. William J. Clarke to Mary Bayard Clarke, 29 April 1865, Barden Collection.

89. Brantz Meyer to Mary Bayard Clarke, 5 April 1866, Barden Collection.

90. Mary Bayard Clarke to Miss Deane, 23 February 1866, Barden Collection.

91. Mary Bayard Clarke to Frank Clarke, 7 November 1866, Clarke Papers, SHC.

92. Mary Bayard Clarke to Frank Clarke, 20 November [1866], Clarke Papers, SHC.

93. Mary Bayard Clarke to William J. Clarke, undated, ca. January 1880, Clarke Papers, SHC.

94. Clarke succeeded Charles Randolph Thomas as a Republican judge on the North Carolina Superior Court after Thomas resigned in April 1868. James L. Lancaster, "The Scalawags of North Carolina, 1850–1868" (Ph.D. diss., Princeton University, 1974), 76, 297 (hereafter cited as Lancaster, "Scalawags of North Carolina").

95. William J. Clarke Pocket Diary, no pagination, 27 April, 13 August 1868. On 20 July he noted, "The Republicans seem to be rallying to me. God knows I need help and encouragement." Clarke Papers, SHC.

96. William J. Clarke, manuscript speech, undated [1868], Clarke Papers, SHC.

97. William J. Clarke to Mary Clarke Morgan, 28 June 1874, Barden Collection.

98. Mary Bayard Clarke, "Letter from the Editor, Humphrey House, Goldsboro, Feb. 22." [1880] *Signal* (Raleigh), MBC Scrapbook 2 clipping, Barden Collection.

99. Mary Bayard Clarke, "Woman's Work," *Signal* (Raleigh), MBC Scrapbook 2 clipping, [ca. February 1880], Barden Collection.

100. Ashe, *Cyclopedia of Eminent and Representative Men,* 2:126–27.

101. Handwritten copy of draft of deed from "E G Reade" to Mary Bayard Clarke for "Purchase of E Front house." Finnerty Papers.

102. Judge Edwin J. Reade to Mary Bayard Clarke, 7 September 1868, Barden Collection.

103. Mary Bayard Clarke to Willie Clarke, 11 October 1868, Barden Collection. Willie Clarke responded to his mother's letter on 18 October 1868, and laughingly wished he could have heard his mother cajole the president. Barden Collection.

104. Mary Bayard Clarke to Willie Clarke, 2 February [1873], Wootten, Moulton, Clarke Papers, SHC.

105. Mary Clarke Morgan to Rufus Morgan, 30 March 1879, Barden Collection.

106. William J. Clarke to Mary Bayard Clarke, 15 January 1882, Barden Collection.

107. Unidentified newspaper clipping written by Mary Bayard Clarke, 25 December [1881], MBC Scrapbook 1, Barden Collection.

108. Mary Bayard Clarke, "Woman North and South," *Current Thought, Literature, Fashion, Society and Home Topics* 1, no. 1 (Oct. 1877), MBC Scrapbook 1, Barden Collection.

109. Mary Bayard Clarke to Dr. Nathan Abbott, 16 May 1878, Barden Collection.

110. Mary Bayard Clarke to Winchester Hall, November 1883. Hall, *MBC Poems,* xxiii.

111. Mary Bayard Clarke to Winchester Hall, April 1884. Hall, *MBC Poems,* xxiv. The caligraph currently is on display at the New Bern Academy, part of the Tryon Palace Historic Sites and Gardens, North Carolina Division of Archives and History.

112. Will Bartlett to George Moulton, 5 March 1886, Barden Collection.

113. Mary Bayard Clarke to Winchester Hall, January 1886. Hall, *MBC Poems,* xxv.

Live Your Own Life

*John Esten Cooke Papers, 1840–96, 2nd 82:G,*
*Special Collections Library, Duke University*
*Mary Bayard Clarke to John R. Thompson*

Raleigh October 31st [1854]

J R Thompson Esq[1]

Dear Sir

I take the liberty of sending you by to day's mail a copy of Wood-Notes[2] which after many vexatious delays made its appearance a few days ago. The compilation of these Carolina Carols has been with me such a labor of love that I feel I am unable to judge them impartially; many of them are from the pens of personal friends, and others from those whom I have been taught to consider the brightest ornaments of our State.

As I cannot suppose it likely you will be sufficiently interested in the volumes to read them both, I would most respectfully suggest that the poems of Luola, and "A day upon the Hills" by J M Lovejoy[3] are most worthy of your notice.

I enclose some lines written a few days ago for the Messenger which I hope will please you, tho' there is a diversity of opinion respecting them among those persons who have seen them in Manuscript, some thinking them very good, and others pronouncing them a decided failure. I shall leave home in about a month for New Orleans where I am to remain a few weeks before going for the winter to the island of Cuba. I have received a proposition from a Northern editor to write light letters on "lady like subjects" for his paper during my travels which may extend into Mexico. Before closing with him I would like to know whether it would be agreeable to you to receive such letters for the Messenger[4] and on what terms as I am so ignorant in such affairs that I know not whether the offer is a good one or not; being entirely Southern in my feelings and opinions I would prefer contributing to some periodical in our part of the Union. I have written occasionally for the New Orleans Picayune and the Home Journal

Hoping you will let me hear from you at your earliest convenience I remain

Very respectfully

Yours

Mary B Clarke

1. John Reuben Thompson (1823–73) was a noted southern editor, poet, and journalist. He became owner and editor of the periodical *Southern Literary Messenger* (Richmond) in 1847. Two others closely associated with the *Messenger* were William Macfarlane and John W. Fergusson. They acquired ownership of the publication in January 1853, while Thompson continued to serve as editor until 1860. All three men, as well as future *Messenger* editor George W. Bagby, played a prominent role in publishing Mary Bayard Clarke's poetry until the periodical ceased publication in 1864. John S. Patton, ed., *Poems of John R. Thompson* (New York: Charles Scribner's Sons, 1920), xx–xxiii (hereafter cited as Patton, *Thompson Poems*); *Who Was Who in America, Historical Volume 1607–1896* (Chicago: Marquis–Who's Who, 1963), 528.

2. *Wood-Notes; or, Carolina Carols: A Collection of North Carolina Poetry* (Raleigh, N.C.: Pomeroy, 1854). This two-volume publication, edited by Mary Bayard Clarke, was the first compilation of poems written by North Carolina poets.

3. Jefferson Madison Lovejoy was born in Vermont but moved south in 1838 to teach in North Carolina. In January 1842 he opened the Raleigh Male Academy, known locally as the Lovejoy Academy. Elizabeth Reid Murray, *Prehistory through Centennial,* vol. 1 of *Wake: Capital County of North Carolina* (Raleigh, N.C.: Capital County Publishing, 1983), 308–9 (hereafter cited as Murray, *Wake County*); William S. Powell, *Dictionary of North Carolina Biography,* vol. 4 (Chapel Hill: University of North Carolina Press, 1991), 101 (hereafter cited as Powell, *DNCB*).

4. Clarke wrote four articles for the *Messenger* based on her experiences in Cuba: "Reminiscences of Cuba, Part I," 21, no. 9 (Sept. 1855): 566–75; "Reminiscences of Cuba, Concluded," 21, no. 10 (Oct. 1855): 593–97; "Some Farther Reminiscences of Cuba," 21, no. 11 (Nov. 1855): 700–708; and "Some Farther Reminiscences of Cuba, Part II," 21, no. 12 (Dec. 1855): 745–50. All of the articles, signed with her nom de plume Tenella, are available on the World Wide Web as part of *Making of America,* jointly developed by the University of Michigan and Cornell University, 1996, http://moa.umdl.umich.edu/.

*Barden Collection*
*Mary Bayard Clarke to Mr. Winston*

Matanzas[1] [Cuba] March 7th [1855]

My dear Mr Winston[2]

I have been waiting to see something of the country before I wrote to you. And have had no opportunity of doing so until the last two or three days. Owing to the unsettled state of the island arising from the Capt General's[3] fear of Fillibusters[4] and conspiracy, we concluded by the advice of the American Consul[5] at Havana not to go out of the city until things were a little more quiet; consequently we were obliged to give up our plan of keeping house near here as this place has been reported to be the head quarters of the conspirators. But I believe that we might with safety have come here a month ago and I am very sorry we did not; When Col Robertson (the consul) would look very solemn and tell us we were standing over a volcano; that there was a far spreading conspiracy to revolt against the Spanish government, and he had positive information that there was an expedition all ready to land, I used to think there was at least some foundation for his fears, and as he was holding a responsible office did not like to ask the source of his information, the same feeling activated William, and I was really provoked when I found he professed to be a medium for spiritual communications and got most of his news from the other world. When William wrote Sister[6] last we were in Havana and I was quite sick with a cold and obliged to stay in bed to keep warm, as windows without glass, no fires, no carpets and brick floors are not either comfortable or healthy with the thermometer at 45 and a strong north wind; and until this week we have not had more than two consecutive warm days; consequently I have never felt before that I was really improving for what I gained in the warm weather I lost immediately in the cold. William and I left Havana on Tuesday at day light and reached this place by one o'clock. Sue[7] had heard so much of the dirt and discomfort of the hotels that she would not come, having been here once and found the large hotel even worse than the description; but as I wished to see the country I determined to brave it, and come for at least one day, to see the valley of the Youmori and the Coumbré mountain; I was quite unwell when I made up my mind and had to get up at four o'clock so I considered my self a martyr to sight-seeing, and have received my reward. Instead of going to the large hotel we have put up at a quaint little affair kept by a French woman, it is very small, very rough, and very queer, but as clean as any hotel in this country; our landlady is very obliging and gives us the best fare we have had yet. She cannot speak a word of english, but fortunately has a servant who knows a little and can help me out of a difficulty, for my Spanish and french are *not* inexhaustable, and now that I have to do without Sue's help I travel with my dictionary in my hand but even then it is impossible to understand servants and common persons, for they speak a patois that reminds me of a Spanish story I have heard, in reference to the language spoken in the Basque provinces, which is unintelligible to all but the natives; the story says the devil lived there seven years and only learnt his own name, tho' he studied hard all the time to communicate with the people; finally he

quit them saying he had no use for them, for they would certainly con-
taminate all his subjects if they entered his dominion.

The country between this and Havana is considered the most beautiful in the island, but it is a scenery I should soon tire of; with the exception of palms it is almost entirely destitute of trees; you ride for miles and
miles thro' a dead level of waving sugar cane, varied occasionally by fields
of plantain or patches of pine apples. As you approach Matanzas the country becomes more broken and the sugar estates look more habitable; but
generally speaking they are the hotest looking places imaginable the house
stands near the sugar house (where the Steam engine is going constantly)
entirely destitute of trees, except perhaps a few scattered palms, Sometimes you see avenues of these and the Zapoté tree, but as the planters seldom live on their estates they take little pains to improve them and I have
seen none that can compare with Conniconara as a residence. Near Havana
there are many beautiful quinta's or country seats, but they are small, and
you see that they are either show places or the residences of the wealthy
men who don't care to live either in the city or the country; they seldom
contain more than three or four acres and are not real country places. The
quinta of Count Palitina is a beautiful place and I drive out there very often
for the pleasure of walking thro' the garden; an avenue of Palm trees a
quarter of a mile long leads to the house which is a small one for this country, it stands on a hill and the gardens are back of it and laid out in terraces
Here are statues fountains and vases in profusion with clusters of palms,
groves of Zapote's, Mammees and Almonds, plantations of Bananas and
avenues of Orange and Lime trees. The Zapote resembles our live oak and
bears a fruit about the size of a very small orange, which looks more like
an Irish potato than any thing else, it is the same colour but rough on the
outside and divided inside like the orange, the seed are like the water-
melon only twice the size; I dont like them at all, as they are a sickish sweet
without flavour. The Mammee is the same coulor as the Zapote but the
size and shape of a small cantelope the inside is pumpkin coloured but the
seed is very different from the melon as each apple has but one which fills
a cavity about the size of that in a small nutmeg melon. The pine apples are
just coming into season now, and are as different from those we get as if
they were not the same kind of fruit; they are so sweet that I thought the first
I tasted had been preserved and the flavour is about five times as high as any
I ever saw before. They never cut them, but break them by sticking a fork
into them which alone would show how superior they are, they are soft to
the center and not harder than a ripe cling stone peach. The plantain which

is a principal food of the negroes is planted in rows about six feet apart and on the cafétel, or coffee estates serve to shade the coffee plants which are set out between them; the banana is only a superior kind of plantain and the smaller they are the more delicate is their flavour. I live on them principally as they are considered very healthful and I can eat more of them than the pine apple without fear of being made sick. The entire absence of fences strikes one very much as they ride thro' the country there are many beautiful hedges of cactus and plants that I do not know, and I am often reminded of Robinson Crusoe's stake fence which sprouted after the rainy season and became a thick hedge, for there is a plant here that they stick down in the same way not four inches apart and weave reeds between until it takes root, when the reeds gradually fall, and the hedge remains. Sometimes you see stone walls like that at the rock quarry, they are generally covered with creeping plants of different kinds and look very picturesque.

But I must tell you about a ride I took up the Columbré this afternoon, it was the most beautiful sight I ever saw and tho' I am tired out by the ten miles rough travel I cant send my letter off without giving you my impressions while they are fresh. I did not think I should have an opportunity of riding on horse-back here; and left my habit and hat in Havana; so when I was told by a young gentleman staying here, to whom we had been introduced, that I should lose the best part of the view unless I went on horse back, we determined to set our wits to work and procure horse saddle and dress if they could be had in Mantanzas; he accordingly went out among his friends, and got one to go with him to the livery stables; here their report was bad indeed, for not a horse could be found sufficiently surefooted to climb the mountain; but Mr Hermandez, (the friend of my friend who is named Theriaté) said if I would wait until this evening he would have both horse and saddle brought from his sugar estate. We accordingly deferred our trip, and I manufactured an impromptu skirt of my blanket shawl which being a long one was easily done. Mr. Theriate supplied me with a hat, and I rigged myself out at four o'clock in a black silk basque, a plaid skirt with large checks of orange and blue, and a panama hat. I could not help laughing at the figure I cut when ready to mount and laughed still more when I saw my steed, for about half past four one of my cavaliers rode up in a great pet because he could not get a horse to suit him, as Mr Hernandez had not sent for the one he spoke of, his sister having been taken suddenly very ill, he forgot all about it, and could not join our party. With some difficulty Mr. Theriate had procured a pony who was pronounced tolerably sure footed tho' very stubborn; he was so small that when I was on him he was nearly hid by my impromptu skirt and I could not help compairing my self to Triptolemus Yellowby in Walter Scott's Pirate; who when he mounted his shetland pony had to hold up his knees to keep his feet off the ground, and hid his horse entirely with the ample folds of his Sunday cloak. It took a good deal of pinning up to keep my skirt from interfering with my pony's feet, but at last the guide was satisfied and we set out. When we got to the foot of the mountain or rather ridge, we took it single file and I soon found my pony had not been slandered for a more obstinate animal I never rode; at last I gave up the battle and let him choose his own gait while I gave my attention to the view before me. Just at our feet lay the bay of Matanzas, a beautiful circular basin in which the water looked as blue as a June sky; it is entirely shut in by hills and if it were deeper would rival Havana. The Coumbré which we were climbing is a circular ridge enclosing the valley of the Youmori, it is about ten or fifteen miles round and has only one opening wher the river flows out; here it looks as if a passage had been cut directly thro' so perpendicular are the sides; there is just room enough for the river to flow out and a narrow road to run along one bank of it. It is a very small river and about a mile from its mouth seperates into several little streams that lose themselves in the valley which is entirely shut in except where the river flows out. We went up the outer side of the ridge next the sea shore and stood with the valley on one side and the sea on the other. We were so high that the vessels looked like fishing craft, and the palms on the valley not higher than a man; the sugar cane looked like grass and the large sugar houses like white cottages dotted at short distances a part tho' there were miles between them. All along the ridge were beautiful country places most of them going to decay, and either shut up or inhabited only by negroes. We passed just in front of the house we were to have had, which was like the rest, the beautiful garden entirely overgrown and the house itself fast becoming a ruin for want of a little care; The view of both sea and valley is very fine and I should have enjoyed living there very much We rode along the ridge for some distance before we commenced our descent into the valley, which was rather more dangerous than our ascent but my little horse whom I named for the time Triptolemus carried me safely down tho his gait was anything but easy. This valley was the scene of the slaughter of the Indians that Bellow mentioned in his history of Cuba; he says that the superstition is that their blood enriched the land. whether that is the case or not I leave you to decide. it is certainly very productive but I think the water of the Youmori has more to do with that than the blood of the Indians. We rode straight thro' it and came out by the river which gets its waters in some mysterious way, it being quite respectable at its mouth, tho' very likely the sea flows up, as our guide told us it some times in a storm came up into the valley, which from its formation may have been at one time a bay for aught I know. I thought as we came down into and could see no way of getting out without going back, of Dr. Johnson's Happy Valley and think if he could have caught a glimpse of this he would have made Rasselas a prince of Cuba instead of Abysinia. I can assure you that as well as I remember the descriptions of parts of the Happy valley this would answer very well for it, for in some places the sides of the mountain were so steep and rocky that not even a goat could have climb there, in others they were covered with trees among which the palm reigned supreme lifting its feathery crown far above the rest, While the bottom was dotted over with houses, and covered with fields of sugar cane; every part of it is in high cultivation and thro' the houses dwindle down as you approach into overseers cottages and the palaces melt into large Sugar houses surrounded with heaps of cane and [burgis?] (which is the cane after the juice is expressed) as they are generally well white washed "distance lends enchantment to the view" and you see nothing but the beautiful. Owing to the great heat, the planters seldom or I may say never have residences in the valley, they have beautiful ones as I mentioned, on the ridge but only live in them for a few months in summer.

I have written this at intervals so if there are any repetitions please excuse them; I am obliged to close in haste now so that I can catch the steamer we left Matanzas this morning and I write these closing lines in Havana let Sister have this when you are done with it as I shall write her of something else I enclose a note for her and one for Mrs Martindale[8] William desires to be remembered to you he is very well indeed. With many thanks for your kind attention to the children I remain yours affectionately

Mary

1. A large town on the northwest coast of Cuba noted for its spectacular scenery.

2. Patrick A. Winston was William Clarke's law partner. He also served as reporter to the North Carolina Supreme Court. Unsigned article by Mary Bayard Clarke, "Social Reminiscences of the Hon. George E. Badger," newspaper clipping from *The Land We Love* 1, no. 4 (Aug. 1866): 282–86, MBC Scrapbook 1, Barden Collection. According to a notation inscribed in the scrapbook, this article was republished in the *Observer* (Raleigh).

3. Jose de la Concha was governor of Cuba in 1855. Basil Rauch, *American Interest in Cuba: 1848–1855* (New York: Columbia University Press, 1948; Reprint, New York: Octagon Books, 1974), 277, 289 (hereafter cited as Rauch, *American Interest in Cuba*).

4. Cuba was the target of several filibustering expeditions led by American expansionists interested in acquiring the island as a potential new slave state. George H. Gibson, "Opinion in North Carolina Regarding the Acquisition of Texas and Cuba, 1835–1855, Part II," *North Carolina Historical Review* 37 (Apr. 1960): 185–201 (hereafter cited as *NCHR*); Robert E. May, *John A. Quitman: Old South Crusader* (Baton Rouge: Louisiana State University Press, 1985): 236–52.

5. Colonel William R. Robertson was acting American consul during the Clarke visit to Cuba. Rauch, *American Interest in Cuba,* 277.

6. Frances Devereux Miller.

7. Susan Edwards Johnson was Mary Bayard Clarke's cousin from Stratford, Connecticut. Herbert M. Schiller, ed., *A Captain's War: The Letters and Diaries of William H. S. Burgwyn 1861–1865* (Shippensburg, Pa.: White Mane Publishing, 1994), 166n (hereafter cited as Schiller, *A Captain's War*).

8. The 1860 census listed Earline Martindale as the head of household, age 33, seamstress. Her children were Henry H., age 19, clerk; Florence, age 17; Ella, age 21, teacher; Louisa Privette, age 15; and John Spellman, age 11. 1860 Census, Wake County, Raleigh Township, North Carolina: 170, Household no. 536.

*Barden Collection*
*Mary Bayard Clarke to Frances Miller*

Hotel Cubano [Havana] March 24th [1855]

My dear Sister

It seems to me I do nothing but write, yet I cannot keep up my correspondence as I would like for want of time to tell what I see and do to each one. I wrote you but a short letter by the last Steamer because William wrote, and none the steamer before because I sent such a very long one to Mr Winston which I told him he must consider common property. The weather now is really warm and I am improving rapidly but for a constant tho' slight feverishness I should call my self quite well; my trip to Matanzas was of great service to me and if Sue was only willing I should greatly prefer staying there, she does not like it however and we are very comfortable here, having delightful rooms, a very obliging host and hostess and a perfectly quiet house, at this season of the year a person cant be very gay any where in Cuba and we have no temptation to dissipation. We dont get up until eight o'clock; William not until nine when we breakfast. This is a very substantial meal here as a greater part of the business of the day is got thro' with before it comes on; those who get up have coffee immediately after rising but I found I could not stand the long time before breakfast and as I dont get up, dont care for coffee prefering a nap instead; for breakfast we have all kinds of meat, eggs fried plaintains rice etc, with claret and water, and after we have finished, coffee is handed to us. We seldom have any company in the morning, so we read sew study or amuse ourselves as we can until dinner at three, I dont care much for my dinner but a great deal for desert which always consists of fruit Oranges pine apples, bananas etc.—and after it coffee which is generally drank with a kiss made of white of egg and sugar just as we have them at home, two of these dropped in a cup of coffee render it delightful. At five o'clock the fashionable day begins then all the ladies either go out in their volantes[1] or sit at the windows to receive company, gentlemen very often pay calls by stopping in the street and talking for ten or fifteen minutes to a lady in the window; at eight o'clock every body goes to the Plaza de Armas a large square just in front of the Capt General's palace, those ladies who are not two lazy get out of their volantes and walk around it while the band plays but generally the Creoles sit still in their volantes which are drawn up in a line all around the square the beaux go up and chat or sit on the benches and critisize until nine o'clock, when the band plays the *retraiter* (a Spanish march) and in ten minutes the square is deserted and the company go to some confectioners like Pizzine's only on a much larger scale; we always patronize the Dominique and as we seldom go to the Plaza withou meeting several acquaintances generally have quite a party, Now dont think us very dissipated but listen while I tell you what we drink—Simply *Pinalis* and what is pinalis you say; I am shocked at your ignorance Sister, why it is the most fashionable drink in Havana and not to know it argues yourself unknown–well, I was ignorant *once* so I wont disown you but enlighten your mind. Pinalis is the white of egg beaten very light with a little sugar and baked in rolls until perfectly crisp but not brown it is very different from the kisses, if possible I shall bring some home as a curiosity, two of these rolls are brought to you on a silver waiter with a glass of ice water and half a green lime you mix it to suit yourself and have when it is ready a kind of lemonade of a very peculiar and to me agreeable flavor twenty five cnts gives a party of five as much as they can drink so our dissipation is not very expensive; at ten we are generally at home and find the whole house quiet, not a soul is in the street except the watchmen who make it a point to wake you every half hour by screaming as loud as possible the hour and the state of the weather. Yesterday Sue and I ordered a volante to return some visits and while we were waiting for it a funeral procession passed that was most novel to me, first came a crowd of negroes, then a company of soldiers, then the coffin carried on the shoulders of four men while four more held long purple ribbons attached to it; then came a long procession of soldiers and volunteers all smoking and laughing then the citizens, and lastly the volantes all empty I counted one hundred and twelve of them the whole was an hour and a half passing and before more than two thirds had passed the other end of the procession returned having been to the grave and burried the man so that the narrow street presented the singular spectacle of two processions, on one side a merry crew with gay music returning from the funeral and on the other a line of volantes going to it. We had to give up our ride as it was impossible to get a carriage all having been engaged to follow in the wake. I forgot to mention that the hearse headed the volante's tho' the coffin was carried by men. It is against the law to take a coffin out of the city gates screwed down, generally they are carried thro' the streets open and as they open in half and the lid is as deep as the coffin the corpse is entirely exposed. And is taken out of the coffin at the grave and burried, while the coffin is returned to the undertaker. It is also against the law to ride thro' the streets with the curtain of your volante buttoned down tight unless it is raining, then you must leave a little hole or put your hand out. It is also against the law if a person is hurt to do any thing for him until the Doctor comes, if he is cut you must not even stop the blood. This law Sue and I have willfully infringed for yesterday one of the waiters fell from the second story piazza into the paved court below and as you may suppose was nearly killed. Everybody ran to him and he was picked up and carried into the house for dead yet not one offered to do any thing and when orderd shook their heads and said it was against the law Sue bathed his head while I not knowing exactly what was best ran for mustard as I remembered Dr Haywood[2] used it on William after his fall; In the best Spanish I could command I told one of the waiters who had always been particularly obliging to get me the mustard and a knife while I got the cloth, but he shook his head and said I dare not Senora; and we absolutely had to do every thing ourselves. Even the clerk of the house, an American would do nothing but send for the Dr and put cold water on the man. He told me if a person was stabbed or cut in the street and went into a druggest's the druggest dared not even stop the flowing of the blood until the Dr came and ordered it to be done. The other day we attended a pic nic given by Mrs Crawford the British Consul's wife to the officers of two English men of war; it was at the Bishops garden and I enjoyed it very much for the officers are all pleasant and have been here so long we have got pretty well acquainted with them; my particular friend among them is the surgeon a middle aged man who wears a wig and stands a poor chance among the belles when the young lieutenants and middies are about; He and I took a long stroll thro' the garden and I wished so much for Mr Winston for I found that I had discovered a treasure in the Dr's knowledge of plants he told me more about them than any one else could and I never enjoyed a walk more for at each step I saw some plant I had never even heard of before. Among the party was the Hon Miss Murray a maid of Honour to Queen Victoria, whose passion was botany she had her herbarium and her botanical dictionary along and all the party were sent out to bring her specimens while she sat in Queenly state beneath the shade of the bamboo cane laying down the law to every one. On my return from my stroll I found her thus with her toady at her feet holding her books and not knowing who she was thought her a very vulgar looking middle aged woman of course I should not have been so presumptuous had I known before hand that she was maid of honour to the Queen but the opinion was formed before I discovered who she was and some how it was unchanged. Imagine a very coarse woman not unlike Miss Deane³ and about her age, dressed in a sky blue tissue a pink scarf a black lace cap and a profusion of pea green ribbon talking very loud and showing every tooth in her head when she spoke, her neck which was very much exposed was her only good point and around it was tied a string of blue glass beads!! they were undoubtedly *glass* for they were as large as ◯ that and broken in several places; her breast pin was of tourqueois and diamonds as large as my palm and from it depended a cross of equal magnificence bracelets and earrings to match and gold chain enough to hang her. On the subject of botany she was dictatorial and positive to an alarming degree but otherwise she seemed chatty and good natured enough. She asked me some questions about the palm trees and in all meekness I gave her what I thought was a very correct reply having heard it from Dr Turnbull not five minutes before, but she informed me I was entirely mistaken and when I told her I had just got it from a scientific man she very patronizingly said well you are not then to blame for your ignorance but I make it a point never to believe what I am told, but to see for myself. Our dinner was very merry we all assisted in laying it out and when it was half ready found the sun had moved so we must too; accordingly we moved in procession across the garden a gentleman with a table cloth went first and we all followed with what we could pick up Capt

Dobbin of the Buzzard bore a huge turkey and was joked on leaving the Buzzard for another foul, the Hon Miss Murray had a loaf of bread I the salad bowl while the middies as a general rule prefered taking charge of the champagne with the exception of the tallest who was appointed head nurse to keep the children out of danger which office he fulfilled by perching them in trees where they could not get down. Last week we were invited to a party on board the Princeton one of our ships, we went at five and returned at seven so you see we do not injure ourselves with late hours. We go to service every sunday on board ship and have the pleasure if inclined of Talking with the parson during the week. We miss our English and Russian friends very much they are now in Mexico and we will probably meet in New Orleans; where I hope to go by the middle of April at the latest tho' Sue says she will not, we will visit Nora on our return, I have not had a line from her since I left home tho' I have written more than once. I think I shall go to San Antonio as William has pretty well made up his mind to live there in future if he likes it. He could not make money here as consul since they have reduced the salary to $6000 for it is a most expensive place rent for a house that would accomodate our family and allow William to have his office below which is the custom with business men, would be about a hundred dollars a month, servants hire, the lowest is twelve dollars a month often fifteen or twenty and every thing else in proportion; after all I would rather live in Raleigh than any where I have yet been. We have not heard a word from home for a fortnight or more as we got no letters by the last steamer and Mai's[4] picture is yet to come. I am getting almost wild to see the children and have to determine I wont think of them, tho' I cant say I keep my determination very well. The US Steamer Princeton is here and leaves in a few days for Washington City so I am going to send Kate and Henry[5] a box by one of the officers if I can get him to take charge of it. We intend if possible to send some of our baggage back to Wilmington by sea direct and I shall put all my curiosities in that trunk. I enclose some seed of what is called here Amarilla tho' the hon Miss Murray says it is a species of Bignonia, the flower is certainly like it but not the leaf and it is a shrub and not a vine

I dont know whether it will live in our climate or not give my best love to Mr Winston Brother Henry and Miss Healy and twenty kisses to my little darlings I am always trying to imagine how Mai looks and if I meet a child about her size in the street I am bound to kiss it if it is decently clean. The style of dressing children of her age and a little older is most remarkable a [book?] muslin chemise and a petticoat without any waist simply hooked round the waist is their only encumbrance I constantly meet them with no other garments on; if they are in arms the petticoat is dispensed with and the chemise only comes about half way to the knee. William and Sue send love, they are both well. Do write at once for if we leave the first of April I shall barely have time to get it Tell every body howdye and believe me yours lovingly

Mary

PS William told me he had given Aunt Bettie[6] directions about the garden but I suppose either he was mistaken or she has forgotten, so please do what you think best, I told Aunt Bettie some body must be hired to tend it but leave it to you to decide what is best Mai's picture did not come I expect Gen Concha has it, as it looked suspicious

I had closed my letter when your last reached me and as the steamer is fortunately detained by a Norther I shall have time to say a few more words. I am very sorry to hear Willie has been so sick and feel as if I could not stay away from them another week but to come home now would be madness and William says he can only say he shall be there by the last of May, he will not hear of my coming any earlier and says even that depends on the weather; he did not write as soon as he saw me because he ws taken so sick, but he has written you several letters more than any one else and one or the other of us has written by every steamer. I hope Mr Winston got my long letter from Matanzas in that I told you why I said nothing of my health. it seems to depend entirely on the weather what I gain in the warm I lose if it turns cool in fifteen minutes after it changes I get a sore throat and a headach I should never advise any one to come here for health the changes are very sudden and Sue's rapture over Cuba must have been because she was in love. I have no desire to live here and shall go to New Orleans just as soon as William thinks it prudent for us to do so. I am very sorry there should be any trouble about the children I did not think it right to leave them with Mrs M unless I gave her the entire control of them. I said nothing about their going to see you only once a week but told her I wished them to be with you whenever it was convenient and she thought it best. After your conversation with William on the day Mrs Shober dined with us he was unwilling to trouble you with them as he said you did not like my expressing a decided wish that they should not be under Miss H and felt that I made a convenience of you it was not until the day before I left that he consented to my leaving Mary with you and only at my earnest solicitation as I felt she would really be more of a pleasure than a trouble to you I dare say Mrs Martindale is over particular with the boys just as she is with her sewing which you laugh at her so much about and I believe it would be as useless to ask her to alter in one as in the other. I was rather pleased when Franc told me in his letter that he sometimes called her Mother as I thought it showed they were contented and happy; and I am sure they will not do so when I come back or if they do it is but a trifle and unless it particularly hurts your feelings and makes you think I am really dead I should not mind it if I were you. I was astonished to hear of Julia Taylor's marriage Of course she married Mr Busbee[7] well I only hope she wont repent it I have been interrupted by a man with pine apple dresses and have bought one for you which you are not to know of until William gives it to you as it is his idea he told me to get you something pretty for him and I only tell you that you may count it in getting your summer dresses I have also bought Miss Healy a muslin as I could think of nothing useful and ornamental that I thought would suit her; the linens make beautiful morning dresses but for full dress are not pretty except the linen cambric which are $17 and not dressy Is Mrs Martindale's family in mourning. I went to get her a dress and think a linen would suit her. I shant bring any body a shawl but you unless I am commissioned and then it shant be red for there are none to be had now Mrs Dy requests me to get her a dress and two for Sue, all of muslin. Sophia is to send some commissions but I dare say they will come when I am in New Orleans. Once more good bye

Yours truly M

1. A common form of conveyance in Cuba.

2. This probably was Edmund Burke Haywood of Raleigh, one of the Clarke and Devereux family physicians who later had a distinguished role in North Carolina's Confederate medical corps. In 1879 he served as vice president of the North Carolina Medical Society. Ashe, *Cyclopedia of Eminent and Representative Men*, 2:230–36; Powell, *DNCB*, 3:83–84.

3. According to one source, Deane was the tutor hired by Thomas P. Devereux to instruct his daughters. They "had at home the benefit of a University curriculum; and two of Mrs. Clarke's children, quoting from memory of their mother's statement, say that she had under a governess, Miss Dean, an Englishwoman, the full Yale University curriculum as pursued at college by her brother, some years her senior." "Mary Bayard Clarke, 'The Queen Poetess of Carolina Bards,'" unpublished essay, William John Clarke Papers, Southern Historical Collection, Wilson Library, University of North Carolina at Chapel Hill (hereafter cited as Clarke Papers, SHC).

4. The Clarke family's nickname for daughter Mary Devereux Clarke.

5. Kate and Henry were two of Frances and Henry Miller's children.

6. Clarke family slave.

7. Anne Eliza Gales Taylor married Perrin Busbee of Raleigh. It is unclear whether the Julia Taylor referred to in this letter is actually Anne Eliza Gales Taylor Busbee. Powell, *DNCB,* 1:287–88.

❧

*Barden Collection*
*William J. Clarke to Frances Miller*

Havana March 31st 1855.

Dear Sister

I cannot suffer an opportunity of writing to you and informing you of our welfare to pass unimproved. Indeed it would be a most ungracious return for your kindness in keeping us so well informed as to matters & things at home, were I to fail to write to you or some other person in Raleigh by every opportunity. We were very sorry to hear that you had been sick & heard that our dear boys had also been sick with great pain. I feared that they would not get thro' the winter very well after having had the measles, tho' I had no expectation of so severe a winter. We have been greatly distressed by hearing of the death of so many of our friends & acquaintances. I am very thankful that I brought Mary away for when I see how she is affected by the slightest change in the weather, I almost feel that our trip, inconvenient and expensive as it is, has saved her life.[1] You do not appear to have received my letters which I regret because I have written very few others having determined to enjoy myself and rest all I could. The weather has been worse since we have been here than it ever was known to be before. In addition to this the political troubles have been such that a gloom has been thrown over every thing. I send you a representation of the execution of a man of high standing and superior education the father of nine children.[2] Today they executed an American citizen named Estrampes[3] for landing arms at Barracoa, a port on the north side of the island Estrampes had no trial. He was not present when he was tried, could not examine witnesses, and tho' the Amer. Consul protested against the whole proceedings & demanded a trial as prescribed by the treaty they garroted him this morning. He died like a hero, and bore himself so gallantly that the guard cried and sobbed over him. He attempted to speak three times but they beat the drums to drown his voice. His last words were "Liberty forever, death to tyranny." A few days ago they tore down the arms of the Amer. acting consul at Sagua, a village about 40 miles distant & brought him here a prisoner. In short they seem determined to force our country to war, and I think that we are fast becoming a mock & bye-word to all foreigners who see the indignities offered to our flag & officials. They are making great preparations for war and I really believe that the ignorant and conceited fools think that they could conquer the United States. While I write I hear the constant reports of fire arms. The volunteers are firing at the target. Such is the excitement that if a servant clearing off the supper table drops the crockery, the people in the next house run out into the streets crying out "fillibusteros, los yankees." More than sixty arrests were made in one day this week—

We that is our party are treated however with great kindness & respect. Mary and Cousin Sue are now out with Lieut. Col. Pujol[4] (Poohol) the Capt. Gen'l's chief aid, who is very attentive to us. I have been conducted by him and Col. Arcost thro' the Punta fort, the Morro & Cabañas forts and fort Principe. The Americans are leaving with the expectation that our Gov't. will stand no more kicking but immediately retalliate. We expect to leave tomorrow week (the 8th) for New Orleans where we will stop a few days when I (and possibly Mary) will go to San Antonio in Texas to look at the place as every body says it is the very place for Mary to enjoy health and for me to make money at the practice of the law. A furious norther is now blowing and the waves dashing against the sea walls throw the spray fifty feet high. I wish you could stand with me and see how very beautiful the white crested waves look on the deep blue waters of the gulf.—We expect after my return from Texas to go up the Mississippi river to Memphis where we will stop and go to see Nora.[5] You had better direct your next letter to New Orleans. The daguerreotype of dear little Mary has not come to hand—We tried all over this city to get a set of coral for Kate but could not find any that you would like the least. Indeed with the exception of a very few articles this is a very poor place to shop, and then most articles sell at an exorbitant price. The gong is ringing for supper so I must close. Give my love to the boys, kiss dear little May for me, and present my regards to Mr. Miller & Mr. Winston & believe me as ever

Very truly & affectionately Yours

William J. Clarke

1. Mary Bayard Clarke worried throughout her life that she would succumb to consumption as her mother had done. Although she suffered from severe coughs, consumption never materialized.

2. The drawing Clarke sent back to his family in North Carolina showed the execution of Ramon Pintó on 22 March 1855. Pintó, a respected citizen of

Havana, was accused of plotting the assassination of Governor-General Concha. Amelia M. Murray, *Letters from the United States, Cuba and Canada,* vol. 2 (London: John W. Parker and Son, 1856), 85.

3. Franciso Estrampes, the leader of a Cuban junta working for the over-throw of the Spanish government, was caught smuggling guns and executed. Rauch, *American Interest in Cuba,* 289.

4. Fevruin [?] Pujol was Captain-General Concha's chief aide. He wrote and signed an entry in Spanish in the MBC Letterbook, dated "Habana 25 de Marco de 1855."

5. Nora Devereux Cannon, Mary Bayard Clarke's sister.

❧

*Barden Collection*
*Mary Bayard Clarke to Frances Miller*

Port Lavacca[1] Jan 30th [1856]

My dear Sister

Here we are at last in Texas after a most disagreeable voyage which has left me as usual very unwell but I am glad to say not so much so as I feared I should be; while the children are as bright as buttons. William wrote you a short letter while we were lying off Galveston bar where we lay two days and nights, Monday we landed and were visited by several acquaintances John Manly[2] among the number, as the Steamer staid there all day. we went ashore and dined at the hotel with John Hutchens[3] who took us out driving and showed us the Lions. I would not live there for a fortune; the town you know is built on an island which is little more than a slalt [sic] marsh and tho' it is thirty miles long it is so flat that it looks as if a Storm would some day sink it in the ocean We had a smooth run to Indianola[4] where we left the steamer and taking a sail boat not as long as your front passage came over or rather up here a distance of fourteen miles which we performed in the short space of five hours as there was no wind; we might have come in the stage but that route is twenty miles over a shocking road. I was broken down when we got here and felt like covering up my head and crying I never felt so desolate and miserable scarcely in my life but I did not give up to it as I knew it was more body than mind. This morning I feel better and able to go on if we can get a conveyance which is doubtful. The house we are at is as clean as possible and the people very obliging but there are few comforts and I would rather go on as soon as I can while the weather is good tho' William seems to think I ought to rest Our party has been increased by a little girl of fourteen the daughter of one of my acquaintances in New Orleans. whom we are taking out to her

Grandmother who resides in San Antonio with her son in law Majer Bel-ger.[5] I wrote you from New Orleans that we had a house ready for us but our furniture is still here and it will be a month before we can go to house keeping; that which we sent from Raleigh is at Galveston having arrived just a day before us. We have met with a great deal of kindness and made many pleasant acquaintances. William has already been employed in two cases and if I can only keep well and the children are healthy I am sure we shall be happy here. William improves daily I think the sea voyage did him good tho' he would not admit It he was very unwell in New Orleans and I was real uneasy about him. Mary has had not an hour's sickness except colds and sea sickness since you saw her and is as fat and solid as heart could desire she has out grown her pantalets and her dresses are above her knees Willie too has been perfectly well, but Franc has not he is however picking up again Aunt Bettie is sure she is going to die *some time* but views it very philosophcally thinking she has passed thro' so much that she cant endure much longer but she is looking better than I ever saw her and has had with all her exposure no rheumetism William says will you please have that Peach brandy he left in your care packed in a box after bottling, and send it to Thomas A Adams Esqr New Orleans,[6] by Norfolk care of Aex. McPheeters,[7] He has just come in and reports that he has a conveyance that will take half our baggage and our selves so I must close as I will have to divide clothes, the roads are awful and we will be a week getting to San Antonio Sam[8] is well and sends howdye

Yours in haste<br>Mary

1. Port Lavaca, Texas, once the county seat of Calhoun County, became a center of transportation for southern and western Texas. "San Antonio, Texas," *New Handbook of Texas,* 5:281–82.

2. This possibly was John Waldo Manly, the son of Basil and Sarah Manly of North Carolina. His brothers were Charles Manly (governor of North Carolina from 1849 to 1851) and Matthias Manly, a lawyer and jurist. Powell, *DNCB,* 4:209, 210, 211.

3. John Henry Hutchings, a Galveston merchant and banker, moved to Texas from North Carolina in 1845. During the Civil War, he served as a state judge and commissioner of the Confederate States court. "Hutchings, John Henry," *The Handbook of Texas Online,* accessed 15 June 2000, http://www.tsha.utexas.edu/handbook/online/articles/view/HH/fhu50.html (hereafter cited as *Handbook of Texas Online*).

4. Indianola, Texas, a deep-water harbor, became a prosperous shipping port by the 1850s. In 1852 it was selected as county seat of Calhoun County, replacing Port Lavaca. "San Antonio, Texas," *New Handbook of Texas,* 5:281.

5. James Belger of New York was an assistant quartermaster in San Antonio from 1853 to 1855. He was breveted major during the Mexican War and continued in service until 1879. Francis B. Heitman, *Historical Register and Dictionary of the United States Army, From its Organization, September 29, 1789, to March 2, 1903,* vol. 1 (Washington: Government Printing Office, 1903; reprinted by University of Illinois Press, Urbana, 1965), 207 (hereafter cited as Heitman, *Historical Register*).

6. Thomas Austin Adams, a prominent New Orleans businessman, lived in the Garden District. Adams, born in Boston, moved to New Orleans in 1842 to found the Crescent Mutual Insurance Company, a branch of the New York house. S. Frederick Starr, *Southern Comfort: The Garden District of New Orleans* (New York: Princeton Architectural Press, 1998), 45–46, 52, 77.

7. A letter dated 20 November 1855, from the firm of A. M. McPheeters & Co. to Major William J. Clarke of Raleigh, is located in the Clarke Papers, SHC. The letter indicates that Clarke was seeking to ship his family's furniture to Galveston, Texas.

8. Sam Taylor was one of the Clarke slaves.

∞

*Barden Collection*
*Mary Bayard Clarke to Frances Miller*

San Antonio Feb 7th [1856]

My dear Sister

Here we are at last after a most fatiguing journey that has knocked me up entirely I wrote you from Lavaca and was obliged to close my letter in haste as we set off as soon as we could get a conveyance. The roads were in such a shocking condition that we were obliged to leave part of our baggage behind us and at one o'clock set out in a four horse ambulance to go twelve miles that night, "Ambulance," sounds very Spanish, dont it? and it looks Spanish too for it is nothing but a great coarse carryall with three seats under which our trunks and bags were stowed. Of all roads that I ever crossed I think that was the worst, a mile and a half an hour was our speed and often the wheels sunk to the middle in the soft sticky black mud, which was so tenacious that it would fill up the space between the spokes until the wheel seemed one solid mass.[1] The prairie that William thought so beautiful in the spring was as Aunt Bettie said nothing but a "broom straw old field"; not a house tree or fence was visible, and not a human being did we meet until we reached our stopping place at half past eight. You can guess that we were too tired to be nice, and the little house about the quality of Old Mr Cards was most welcome; it was built of slabs and the partitions were of cloth; but you never sat down to a better supper than the good lady gave us. Her coffee, venison steaks, biscuits bread corn cakes peach preserves and cakes would have done credit to Mary and Lucy[2] in their most amiable and Successful moods; and the beds were far better than any I ever saw in a Carolina country tavern Franc and Mary were both taken sick here with cholera morbus and continued unwell tho' the journey The little girl whom I mentioned in my last as being under my care was attacked the next night so I had a great deal of anxiety, but Willie fortunately escaped and is in better health than ever before while Mary and Franc are getting well again.

The next day with all our speed we could only go eighteen miles, and we were five days going the hundred and thirty, while our expenses were just a dollar a mile as we had to pay $100 for the conveyance. I never passed thro' a more desolate country, the road runs on a ridge and the farms lie back in the valleys; they tell us that it is well settled off the road but there we scarcely saw a habitation except those where we stopped which were stage houses

We got here monday evening and tired out as I was I was glad to lie down as soon as possible. Dr and Mrs McCormick[3] came at once to see us, and the latter welcomed me as warmly as tho' I had been her friend too. It was pleasant to feel that some body was glad to see us. They had a room ready for us the first of Jan but a friend stopping a day or two with them was taken with typhoid fever and is still sick there, so they could not take us to their house which had been their intention. Here we are paying enormous prices for miserable fare, so we have decided to camp out until our furniture arrives. I did not get any kitchen utensils in New Orleans and we have bought such as we shall need and will make out with them. Our stove is just like yours and cost the same, but crockery is awful the commonest, cost as much as the iron stone ware I bought in Philadelphia; and provisions are extravagant sugar from 15 to 25 cts a pound coffee 25 Lard 20 eggs 25 butter not good at 50 wood at present $5 a load owing to the unusually cold weather. Every body congratulates us on our house so I suppose the rent is not unreasonable tho' it seems enormous $350. The house is of stone right on the ground with only a loft above where we cannot even put the servants to sleep as wood is so scarce that the ceilings of all but one room are composed of cloth nailed to the rafters and white washed, there are but four rooms; two about the size of Mrs Martindales front rooms and two shed rooms with nothing but the shingles for ceiling so our loft is confined to *one room* which can only be reached by a ladder set in our neighbors yard There is not a closet or pantry in the house; the kitchen is of stone with a dirt floor and a chimney that half fills it; it has two rooms neither of them as large as your dressing room; there is neither smoke house or store room and not a place I can lock up.

Mrs Lewis (Sarah Collins that was)[4] has just been to see me she says I am just in Texas fashion as they dont have furniture here, and pantries are unknown luxuries The people seem very kind and accomodating one gentleman offered us a table another a bed stead mattress and pillows with sheets and blankets until our own come, and with what Mrs McCormick can spare we shall get along very comfortably if we can only keep well. We have certainly taken hold of the rough end first for the weather is bad being unusually cold and wet and the *dry climate* has lost its reputation but every thing shows that this is unusual, the oleanders and oranges at Galveston were all killed down tho' they were fully grown showing that for some years at least they could not have has such weather.

The mexicans who are the principal waggoners have teams of six or eight oxen each that with a heavily loaded cart or dray-like waggon generally perform the journey from the coast in four days They take no care of their oxen and in consequence they have lost large numbers this year and it will probably be a month at least before we get our furniture which is all at Lavacca. The US Quarter master is offering 2.50 a hundred and yet cannot get up the government stores.

Dr McCormick says he has lent out the furniture of one room to a friend who is simarly situated and has been daily expecting to hear his furniture was on the way for six weeks. Hard ware and dry goods are not dearer than in Raleigh and excellent beef and turkeys are more reasonable, but flour is from 16 to 20 dollars a barrel, house rent very high and servants wages just what they choose to ask Sarah Lewis has no children and says she only keeps one as she cannot hire black and wont have white. she says every body lives from hand to mouth here, and the demand for marriageable women so great that if you have a good servant by the time she is sixteen some soldier marries her and they set up for themselves. But the country is improving rapidly people are not ashamed to live as they can and appearances are not thought of. The society seems very pleasant and I think after we get settled and "learn the ropes" we shall find ourselves better off here than in Raleigh Please read this letter to Mrs Primrose[5] and

Mrs Raboteau[6] and tell them I will write to them when I am settled. I shall also write Mrs Martindale and tell her whether I think she had better risk these high prices after I see what the profits are

The children send love to all they will write next week to Mrs M and you. Tho' the weather has been so cold I have been much better since I left the coast the air does not feel keen and I can breathe it even when very cold without that oppression and pain in the chest that it has given me for some time back but of course I cannot yet tell what the effect of the climate will be on me Mary is a little beauty the picture of health for her sickness only made her pale a day or two people stop her in the street and call her into their houses to look at her her hair curls in ringlets about as tight as Margarets[7] and reaches the edge of her dress I will write a good story about her with love to all believe me yours lovingly

Mary

1. The trip from Indianola to San Antonio was noted for its mud bogs at certain times of the year. George Denison, a San Antonio lawyer, wrote to his mother in Vermont on 26 February 1856, that the streets of San Antonio were covered in mud "about three feet deep." Papers of George Denison, Manuscript Collection, MMC–0249, Library of Congress.

2. Slaves, probably owned by Frances Miller.

3. Dr. Charles McCormick, originally from Washington, D.C., entered the army as an assistant surgeon on 30 August 1836. He became a major surgeon by December 1853 and was breveted lieutenant colonel for faithful and meritorious service during the Civil War. He died on 28 April 1877. Heitman, *Historical Register,* 1:659.

4. Unidentified.

5. Eliza Tarbox, originally from Connecticut, eventually married John Primrose of Raleigh, a good friend of William J. Clarke. According to one family source, Mary Bayard Devereux first met William Clarke at the Tarbox-Primrose wedding. Eliza's husband was dead before 1860, when the Wake County census listed Eliza Primrose as being forty years old with real estate worth $3,000 and personal property worth $15,000. Her children were John, William, and Robert Primrose. Powell, *DNCB,* 5:147; undated typescript document, Finnerty Papers; 1860 Census, Wake County, Raleigh Township, North Carolina: 51, Household no. 417.

6. William J. Clarke's father, William F. Clark of Raleigh, had married Anne Maria Raboteau in 1817. Their only child was William J. Clarke. Anne Maria Raboteau died in 1822. Her two brothers were John S. and Charles C. Raboteau. The Mrs. Raboteau referred to in this letter probably was Charles Raboteau's wife, Sarah A. Wynne, whom he married in 1843. William Clarke served as bondsman

for their wedding. "Raboteau/Rabideou/Robdeau Family," Victor Crawford Papers, 20 November 1997, Private Collection, Washington, D.C. (hereafter cited as Crawford Papers).

7. Margaret Mordecai Devereux, wife of Mary Bayard Clarke's brother, John Devereux Jr.

❧

*Barden Collection*
*Mary Bayard Clarke to Frances Miller*

Feb. 14, 1856
San Antonio Feb 14th [1856]

Dear Sister,

Ho for a valentine! from the "promised land," "the Italy of America," the imortal Texas!! I wrote you before we left the hotel, but now we are keeping house I am sure you want to know how we are getting along. Famously I can assure you, and in real Texan style. I have six wooden chairs, a pine table and a lot of kitchen ware, all my own and a borrowed bedstead mattress and bedding for "self and the children", Sarah[1] for a cook and Aunt Betty for a washer. while I do the house work, Frank sets the table, and William smokes reads law and studies Spanish. He was most terrible deceived in thinking good servants could be got here the truth is there are none to be had under $20 a month often 30, and they are germans[2] who can not as a general rule speak english and are so good for nothing that I find it is quite the fashion here to do without. Such prices I never heard of as everything commands, but fees are as high in proportion as every thing else. William was shown a list of the charges adopted by the lawyers and it is the rule of the bar to abide by them and not do work for less and he told me what he charged $4 for in Carolina was there marked 25 which is about the lowest. I cannot tell you much about the climate, the weather has been charming for the past week and I am now writing without a fire while Mary is playing out without her sack with bare neck and arms. Those persons who like to live here tell me that this is the usual weather from October to Christmass and after the first of Feb. between those dates the cold wet Northers prevail rarely lasting more than three days; they also tell me the summers are not very hot and the nights always cool. On the other hand those who dont like the country say it is very hot in summer very changable all winter and one vast mud puddle between christmas and Feb; all however admit that it is very healthy and I am certainly better here than any place I have yet tried I can do twice as much with half the fatigue I experienced at home and seem to breathe from the bottom instead of the top of my lungs. I used to think there was some exaggeration, or at any rate imagination in the stories that were told of the exhilerating effects of the air here but it is all true, it is a real pleasure to *live,* the mere breathing the air is a luxury.

We have had everything to discourage us and disgust us, for the living is so expensive that we cannot afford to keep any thing like the table we did at home, and when I first came to this house the mud was so deep and sticky that Sam had to stop and scrape my feet every ten steps—and that too in the heart of the city, but with all the disadvantages of mud, dust which penetrates every where and ruins your clothes, and shoes, a small inconvenient house and no servants but Sarah and Aunt Bettie I would not go back to morrow—for the climate compensates for every thing if it will only keep as pleasant as it has for the past week. I like the people too what I have seen of them; the most refined and well educated are the army ladies and the officers but there are some very nice residents my predecessor here was Mrs Wilcox a daughter of Andrew Jackson Donaldson,[3] She is very gay having lived much abroad but she is not after my taste being too Western. I met her yesterday at Mrs Lewis' where we dined and she called this morning and sat an hour with me giving me her experience when she first came her a bride or rather a new housekeeper as she had been travelling for some months. She said her husband gave a dinner party for twelve and told her to send to a public garden and buy her vegetables, she did so ordering what she thought a plenty, but not too much and the bill was eight dollars—!!!

The people seem very plain as a general rule and there is neither style or fashion observed Sarah Lewis says the only trouble she has in associating with them is their inclination to be too intimate, and the danger you run of being thought proud if you dont meet them half way. Some persons say that the prices have risen since the head quarters was moved here, that may effect house rent and butter and eggs and so on but not flour and groceries for the Comissary lays in his supplies in New Orleans and has Government wagons to transport them. So the Officers families are better off than we are as they receive their groceries at what they cost in the place where they were purchased The high prices are all that I mind for I could put up with every thing else but like the Irishman I am afraid we shall find out "we cant afford to live" for our appetites increase alarmingly, and I often think I am the ditto of the overseers wife who when she lived on the river had plenty to eat and no appetite and when she lived in the piney woods she had a "*monstrous*" appetite and nothing to eat. But William is encouraged by all the lawyers they tell him if he only sticks to it he must do well at the bar as the business is increasing steadily and the town growing rapidly. Whatever the country may be in Spring I cant think the city could ever be even decently good looking, the houses are mostly Mexican with either dirt or brick floors barred windows and no fireplaces, the Germans and Americans who have built here until within the last few years seem to have merely put up temporary dwellings; building material of the best kind is cheap, a soft stone that may be cut or sawn and hardens by exposure to the air,[4] but all wood is very dear. Four languages are spoken about equally German french Spanish and english; of course the American society is small independent of the army but the officers and their wives are many of them stationary, there are about two hundred here now and over a thousand troops. I am to drive out to morrow morning to the encampment to see them mount guard at eight o'clock, and take breakfast with Dr McCormick at half past seven, so you see it must be pleasant weather for me to go out so early. I have a fire made when we get up but rarely keep it up, and the children are begging to take off their winter drawers but of course I say no—I got caught very nicely last night in the midst of my work by a spruice young gentleman who had evidently done the impossible in the toilet line. The children were all in bed in a pallet and William was reading the life of Philip by Prescott aloud; we always need fire in the evenings and as we are rather short of clothes owing to being obliged to leave our trunks at Lavacca, I concluded I would iron a few that Aunt Bettie might not be obliged to stop washing next day; I had just got a pair of drawers most conspicuously spread out when there was a knock; I thought it was Dr McCormick—as our next neighbor an officer is sick and he is in the habit of visiting him at that hour I had therefore only time to jerk them up on hearing it was not his voice when William ushered in a total stranger in, a Mr Hanson of Burke Co NC originally, who felt he said that we were "home folks;" I think he might after his homely reception.

I have not heard a word from home since I left New Orleans not even a paper was waiting for us tho William ordered them all here; I am longing to hear something of you. I dont even know whether Sophia[5] is married, please send her this letter for really with all I have to do and all I have to tell, I cant write as I would like, to each one.

I had to stop to write for the children before they went to bed, much to Miss Mary's indignation who insists its her Aunty and Franc and Willie shant write to her. I did not even suggest a word to Franc who dictates very freely but poor Will finds it hard work, he says he wishes he was back for then he could tell you every thing and would not have to write. I shant insist on his doing it again for I dont want him to think he is obliged to write. I think he pines more after Minny than any one else he very often says, "Oh me I want to go to school to Mrs Martindale and see Minny so bad" but he wont hear of going to any body else and I dont intend to send them yet tho' there is a little school on the next square. Mary can talk very plainly now and is very good she says she is Father's little woman Mother's lady bird and Aunties darling. Yesterday a lady asked who made her loops she replied Mother but immediately corrected herself and said no Aunty. Aunt Betty is I believe the most dissatisfied of the whole and her great trouble is that she cant wash clean with this limestone water, she wont hear of going to the creek as others do and was almost ready to cry when a neighbor told her to put [Cey?] in the water, then she is sure that some of these yellow Mexicans will remember Mars William and shoot him or stab him one, and she frets very much that he wont carry a pistol all the time. As for Sam he has a perfect arsenal in his room two pistols and a dirk Sunday I went out and asked Franc if he knew where Sam was. "Well Mother he said he would just ramble about a bit and see if he could not find some pretty girls." So I suppose he intends to console himself

I have been out very little and returned only one or two of my visits, to morrow night we drink tea with Major Belger the comandant of the Alamo Several ladies are waiting for me to get fixed before they call but I dont believe we will get our furniture for six weeks. I went out this morning to get some matting for my parlor but not a yard could be had owing to the state of the roads the merchants have not received their fall goods yet and I suppose we may be six months without some of our boxes but we are living here with ten times the comfort and half the expense were we at at the hotel for Guion's[6] is magnificent to it. I have just begun to garden, we have a good garden spot and can water it whenever it needs it by irrigation. William wants to say a few words, so I will close with love to all

I copy Willie's letter as he was too sleepy to wait for Franc to get thro'

Yours lovingly

Mary

*[Enclosure, Franc Clarke to Aunty, Feb. 14, 1856]*

Dear Aunty

Father and Mother and Brother and I walked yesterday to the San Pedro Springs,[7] and we all thought they were nothing but a river sunk some where else and bursting out there; the several springs all run into one small lake which looks as if you might walk on it, it is so green with water lillies. Father saw some that were open but I only saw the buds. We sat under a summer house thatched with rushes and drank lager beer; all under the trees are benches and tables and people go out there and drink beer and eat ice cream but we only drank beer. I like this climate best & if all my friends were here I should like this better than Raleigh. Father brother and I went fishing in the river and did not catch any fish but to day we went to the creek and had better luck. Brother Will beat all of us he caught four Tell Mr Winston if he has got enough money to come out here for as he is such a fisherman he will like it as he will have a creek and a river both, the creek is just at the foot of our garden and the river about half a mile off—I saw a small white fish in the canal this evening that seemed the father of all the rest, he had got in very shallow water and was fidgeting about and trying to get out, before I could come to catch him he made one spring & sprang into deep water and in an instance was out of sight We spent the day at Mr Lewis' and he let me see how the forcing pump worked I like Mrs Lewis and Mr Lewis and like their place also Mrs Lewis gave me some seed and Mr Lewis gave me two fishing hooks Good night Aunty

Your dear little Franc

*[Enclosure from Willie, written by MBC to FM]*
Dear Aunty

I want to see you please come out here and bring Mrs Martindale I caught 4 fish this evening, no it wasnt this morning for this morning I went to see a little boy named Willie,[8] he lives in a big house and has a pony I am tired now but I love you and wish I could talk to you your little

Willie

*[Enclosure from William J. Clarke to Frances]*

San Antonio February 15th 1856

Dear Sister:

Mary, the scribe, who handles the pen of a ready writer, having kept you so well advised of our movements I have been relieved of the necessity of writing to you as often as I should have done, and as I intend doing hereafter. We have seen sights since we left Tennessee, and I never have had my fortitude more severely tried than since our arrival in this place. Every thing seemed to be discouraging and adverse. The weather was very bad and uncomfortable, the streets were almost impassable for mud mire and water, our furniture had not then, nor has it yet arrived tho' it has been three months in Lavaca, 140 miles distant, the hotel that was very good last year has changed hands and was very poor, and our children were cooped up in a miserable little room, so we determined to go into our house to camp out there, sleeping on the floor and living in quite a primitive style. We have become a little used to our rough mode of living and the weather is now so spring like and delightful that we feel composed and almost happy. It is said that there is something very exhilarating in the air, I believe it or I should have advised Mary to put my razor out of sight, the bouie knife was lost on the journey. I have taken to the dilegent reading of the book of Job. I have a fellow feeling for the worthy old patriarch. Mary is very well and has already improved greatly and my little birdie is the very picture of health, she remembers you perfectly and is as talkative as a magpie and when she meets strangers one of the first things is to tell them about Antie.

I should not have commenced writing if I had not thought that I had another sheet page to write on, and we are out of paper and it is too far to the book store for me to get more tonight. I shall write you sometime next week.

Present my regards to Mr Miller and tell him I am hopeful about getting into practice after awhile. The lawyers seem to have plenty to do, tho many of them are very negligent of their business. I have borrowed the Texas laws and spend my days in reading them and studying Spanish.

I have recd. two Standards[9] which gave me all the news I have rec'd. from home, Mr. Roulhac's death[10] etc. The weather is now like the usul winter weather in this climate, very pleasant and Sam and I are engaged in gardening Good night dear Sister

Affectionately
Wm. J. Clarke

1. According to the 1860 Bexar County census, the Clarkes employed an Irish servant named Sarah. 1860 Census, Bexar County, San Antonio Township, Texas: 385, Household no. 730.

2. After Texas entered the Union, San Antonio became one of the largest cities in Texas. A large portion of its population were German immigrants, who outnumbered Hispanic and English-speaking citizens until after 1877. Frederick Law Olmsted visited San Antonio in 1856 and enjoyed the picturesque city with "Its jumble of races, costumes, languages and buildings; its religious ruins . . . ; its remote, isolated, outposted situation and the vague conviction that it is the first of a new class of conquered cities into whose decaying streets our rattling life is to be infused." *New Handbook of Texas,* 5:796–97, 799; Frederick Law Olmsted, *Journey through Texas: A Saddle-Trip on the Southwestern Frontier* (Austin, Tex.: Von Boeckmann-Jones Press, 1962), 79 (hereafter cited as Olmsted, *Journey through Texas*).

3. Clarke actually meant Andrew Jackson Donelson, a soldier, diplomat, and lawyer who served as charge d'affaires to the Republic of Texas and helped to negotiate the annexation of Texas to the United States in 1844. His daughter, Mary Emily Donelson Wilcox, was married to John M. Wilcox, a lawyer originally from North Carolina. Pauline Wilcox Burke, *Emily Donelson of Tennessee,* vol. 1 (Richmond, Va.: Garrett and Massie, 1941), 17; 1860 Census, Bexar County, San Antonio Township, Texas: 404, Household no. 1021; Mary Bayard Clarke, "Interesting from Texas," 17 February 1861, *New York Herald,* undated newspaper clipping, MBC Scrapbook 1.

4. Adobe.

5. Sophia Chester Devereux married Josiah Turner of Hillsborough, North Carolina, on 24 February 1856.

6. Guion's National Hotel in Raleigh, owned by E. P. Guion, was a favorite of state legislators and other prominent visitors. Murray, *Wake County,* 159.

7. Olmsted admired San Antonio's San Pedro Springs and beer garden. He described the springs as, "a wooded spot of great beauty but a mile or two from the town and [it] boasts a restaurant and beer-garden beyond its natural attractions. The San Antonio Spring may be classed as one of the first water among the gems of the natural world. The whole river gushes up in one sparkling burst from the earth. . . . The effect is overpowering." Olmsted, *Journey through Texas,* 83.

8. Willie H. Maverick, son of San Antonio businessman, lawyer, and railroad developer Samuel A. Maverick. After the Civil War, Willie Maverick and his brother George attended the University of North Carolina and the University of Virginia. Willie Maverick continued to correspond occasionally with Willie Clarke in later years. Rena Maverick Green, ed., *Samuel Maverick, Texan: 1803–1870* (San Antonio, Tex.: Privately printed by Rena Maverick Green, 1952), 328, 364.

9. *North Carolina Standard,* a Raleigh newspaper.

10. Joseph Blount Grégoire Roulhac was a North Carolina merchant and graduate of the University of North Carolina. Powell, *DNCB,* 5:255–56.

*Barden Collection*
*William J. Clarke to Frances Miller*

San Antonio, February 24th, 1856—

Dear Sister:

On this rainy Sunday I seat myself for the purpose of writing to you a long letter, which I assure you is quite an undertaking for me, and I have been so long accustomed to write business letters where there is so much to say and then you are done, that I find it somewhat of a task to write about every thing in general and nothing in particular. Willie's idea is, that writing is a great bore tho' he would talk a great deal to the person he is addressing were they present. I hope that the ingenuity of man will yet devise some contrivance by means of which you can set down before an instrument and talking just as you would to a friend find it all recorded in transmissible form. Wouldn't I give you some long epistles if that were the case?

Well to begin at the beginning I thank you very much for your letters of the 24th. ult. and 5th. inst. We recd. the last yesterday. The servants were very much gratified by the letter to them. They have been a great comfort to us, and have cheerfully and patiently borne every hardship and inconvenience. Sarah and Aunt Betty do all the work with a little help from Mary, who says that she can do without fatigue double as much work as in Raleigh, which she attributes to the bracing and invigorating effect of the climate. She is in better health and spirits than she has been in for years. You would be surprised to see how *ironical* she has become, a day's washing is a mere circumstance to her. The children have been generally well, tho' the have been a little sick from overeating. Little Mary is as fat as a house pig, as rosy as a milkmaid, and as bad as she can be. Her mother told her that Auntie was coming to see her and that she was going to put up a bedstead for Anty to sleep on. A few days after Mrs. McCormick sent us a bed-stead and some other furniture, directly Mary saw it she cried out "my Anny's bed" and persists in calling it so. She is very indignant if her Mother ventures to sit on my lap or kiss me. She says that she is a lady, and when a gentleman wanted to kiss her she said "I tant kiss mans but you may tiss my hand." She is now playing around me and when I asked her what I should tell you she says send her a kiss. She has nearly outgrown all her clothes, and insists every afternoon on being dressed up and going to Santonio. She is considered by every body uncommonly pretty, and aunt Betty says if all the children were as smart as she it would be no use for old folks to try to fool them. If she meets an old gentleman whose looks she likes she calls him grandpa and by this means has made so many friends that the confectioners will find that their business has been considerably increased since she came to town. Her forwardness in talking surprises every one. When she was sea sick she said with an indescribable accent of weariness, "Oh fome, feet fome, no place like fome." Every thing she sees belongs either to her or Anny. But it would take a volume to tell you all that little darling's smartness. Your account of the severity of the winter in N.C. did more than any thing else to ceconcile aunty Betty to Texas. Gentlemen who have been in the country 25 and 30 years tell me that they have never seen anything to compare to the severity of the present winter. Large numbers of cattle have died from exposure as it has not heretofore been necessary to shelter them and no shelters were provided. In three weeks time every thing will be green and flourishing "like the land of Egypt as thou comest unto Zoar," tho' now from the joint ravages of the grasshoppers[1] and the winter it looks like Sahara. We have our garden spaded up and about half of our seed sowed. Sam and I feel ourselves very much at a loss in gardening, but I think I shall enjoy it after things begin to grow. We are living just as we were when Mary last wrote to you Our furniture has not arrived and I fear it will be some time before we get it. I never expected to live in such style as we have since I have been here. Every thing seems to have gone contrary. Our furniture had been long enough on the way when we started to have gone to Europe and since it has been here in Texas to have been sent to the Rocky mountains. As the Yankey says it is a very shiftless country. A move to a distant country is at all times and under all circumstances attended with many inconveniences and annoyances, but this, with the exception that we have enjoyed health and met with no personal injury has been attended with all you can possibly conceive. At times my fortitude and endurance have been put to the severest tests, and I have been greatly discouraged, but I have not suffered myself to succumb to "the difficulties of the way," for despondency in me would have been reflected with ten-fold intesity from my little party who would have been in absolute despair. So you may imagine what a weight has been upon me. Mary has borne up with great fortitude and proved in all our late trials, as she has done in all which have ever come on us, a help-meet indeed to me. But tho' I have undergone so much I never have regretted coming out here. I feel a deep confidence that I and my family will enjoy health and that I shall succeed as well in my profession as I could reasonably expect, and that five years hence I shall be better off in every respect than I would have been had I remained in Raleigh, even supposing Mary could have stood the climate. The immigration to this city exceeds every thing I have ever heard of. Men who have travelled over the whole world are settling here and say that it is the healthiest and most desirable place to live in they have ever seen. The people are very kind & friendly and our reception has been as cordial as we could have expected. The house we are living in is not as comfortable as your old house was, and I don't like the neighbourhood as we are surrounded with Germans, French, and Mexicans. Rents are so enormous, and the conveniences of rented houses so few, that I hope to be able to buy a nice lot during this year and to build next. We have been perfectly amazed at the high prices of every thing and will find living very expensive but things will gradually become cheaper. There can be no doubt but the great number of immigrants is the cause in a great measure of this, but when these immigrants become producers instead of consumers, the supply of produce increasing in a greater ratio than the demand will lower prices. And I cannot think that it will be many years before a railroad will run from this to the coast[2] which should make groceries cheaper here than in Raleigh. It is incomprehensible to me that sugar & molasses should be 25 percent higher here in a sugar growing country than with you. There is a large sugar field just back of our garden. The cane was cut and rolled between two wooden rollers like an apple mill, and giving the juice one boiling the owner sold it readily for molasses. Almost everything seems to grow well here and I have seen thousands of fruit trees carried about to be set out, while vines and ornamental trees and shrubs are in great demand. The Mexicans seem to have caught the spirit and in a few years the valley of the San Antonio will blossom like the rose. Wheat grew finely over the whole plain in the days of the Spaniard but now not a stalk is raised. All the flour is brought from New Orleans and consequently for the last few years sells for from $15 to $22 a barrel. The meal is quite good and we get it at $1.10 a bushel. This reminds me that I should tell you how smart I have become. What do you think of my going to market before sun-rise three times a week? I have also become quite a carpenter likewise, and with the aid of Sam have made cupboards and wardrobes which we on account of the scarcity of plank covered with cotton cloth. Mary's ingenuity is fully taxed to invent contrivances to supply the deficiency of closets and pantries etc. You must tell George[3] that there is a nice little creek as near our house as from your house to the bank and that it is full of perch and catfish, and that Franc & Willie can go a fishing and that they have caught a several fish. They are very good boys and say their lessons every day to their mother.

I have not yet commenced practicing law as my licenses were left in one of our trunks which we had to leave in Lavaca as the roads were so bad that we could not bring them with us and we have not received them yet. I have been diligently engaged in reading law and studying Spanish. I am well pleased with the statute law of this state and think that N.C. would have done well while revising her laws had she consulted the Texas statue book and adopted some of them. I have been kindly received by the members of the bar, and as I generally find them busy when I call at their offices and this is quite a business place I doubt not when I put my hook in I shall get a bite. Fees are a little higher than anything else and a lawyer receives not less than $10 for any service. The simplest contract or plainest deed is $25. There is a regular tariff of fees, a copy of which I shall send to Mr. Miller.

Our mails are very much out of joint at present but as the roads improve we shall get letters and papers sooner and more certainly than at present. Your letters and a few Standards contain all the news we have recd. from R. I hope you will not forget that almost anything will interest us. We have had some very pleasant spring-like weather and after the rain of today shall have dried off the ground which it will do in a day or two the weather will be fine and the walking good and we shall be able to take our walks again & wish that you were here to breathe our invigorating and exhilarating air. Mary wishes to add a postscript, and I will be more generous to her than she was to me when she last wrote to you and give her the rest of this page. Excuse this dull and uninteresting letter. I will try to be less prosy in my next. Remember me to Mr. M. & George & believe me

Very sincerely Yours,<br>William J. Clarke

Dear Sister

William has said so much that there is little left for me to add except that I am very sorry to hear you are so unwell and so lonely, I too have many lonely or rather sad moments, for I am so busy all the time I can hardly feel lonely and William having as yet no office is always at home. Teaching the children and attending to Mary besides the other things I have to do fully occupy me Aunt Betty and Sarah do the cooking and washing between them and I am consequently obliged to look after Mary who is the perfect sprite of mischief her love for her father is the strongest of her feelings she is perfectly devoted to him and so jealous that she flies into a passion if he kisses me and if I sit on his knee I am instantly ordered up, she is very interesting as she can speak very plainly and makes many very pertinent and some rather *im*pertinent remarks. I often ask her what Auntie is doing now? to which she generally replies "brushing her hair" that being her favourite amusement, sometimes she says "making a *cidar*" but yesterday answered "hooping Betsey" her hair curls very prettily and she is a real beauty and as healthy as possible all her affection is lavished on her father and Willie but she runs to me when in trouble or "so beepy" (sleepy); the Indian rubber doll is as great a favourite as ever and rejoices in the name of Lucky Jones or as she calls it Sutty a very appropriate cognomen. Please get from Dr E B Haywood my picture of Grace Greenbrod and Irish Sketches by Mrs Hall if left with him I shall loose them as he will forget that he promised to send them by William. Tell Harriett[4] Aunt Betty has written her a long letter and I directed it as she desired direct to Mrs Fisher's[5] care. Give my love to all not forgetting Mrs Martindale I will write her next week Yours lovingly

Mary

1. Clarke wrote an autobiographical account of the grasshopper wars in her two-chapter story, "Mrs. Leigh's Indian Waiter," originally published in 1877. She republished it in the *Signal* (Raleigh) 1, nos. 15–21 (28 Apr.–7 July 1880).

2. William Clarke became involved in local plans to build a railroad connecting San Antonio to Port Lavaca. On 11 October 1856, William Clarke was elected president of the San Antonio and Mexican Gulf Railroad Company. Among the other San Antonio entrepreneurs concerned with the project were Samuel Maverick, Volney E. Howard, and John C. French. The San Antonio and Mexican Gulf Railroad Company, chartered on 5 September 1850, had only five miles of track in operation by 1858. *New Handbook of Texas,* 5:807–8.

3. A son of Henry and Frances Miller.

4. Possibly a Fisher family slave.

5. This probably was Julia Clarke Fisher, William J. Clarke's half-sister. She was married to Jefferson Fisher of Raleigh, North Carolina.

*Barden Collection*
*Mary Bayard Clarke to Frances Miller*

San Antonio May 5th [1856]

Dear Sister,

I sent you a short note in a letter I wrote Mrs Primrose and a day or two since we received a whole mail from you, as Franc & Willie's letters, Mary's containing the cap, and Sam's all arrived the same day. Thank you for the cap and for the poetry it was only the other day I was trying to say it to Mary, and I do wish you could hear her repeating like a little brid "To whit to whit to wee" But oh how insulted she was about the cap, she declared I had no right to it, it was her *ridolet*[1] her Aunty sent her, and that bad old Mother should not have it, I had to whip her and lock it up out of sight before there was any peace—for such a torrent of abuse and invective as I received you cant imagine; the other letter she would not allow to be opened it was her letter from her Auntie and I should not read it, she would lock it up in her *bots* (box) and nobody should touch it, and it was not for an hour after the storm subsided that she would let her father read it to her. I am happy to tell you that all our books and the chests containing the linen and the box of books arrived the other day with one of the boxes that had half a table in it. They got wet a day or two before getting here and the linen was slightly mildewed and two books injured, dont you remember telling William you found the box in which the books were was not strong enough? it was not, and must have been staged either at Norfolk or Lavaca for fourteen penny nails were driven into some of the books and one or two are missing but perhaps they may be in other boxes, lamp oil had been spilt on the box and injured three books but fortunately neither handsome or valuable ones With these exceptions every thing was safe; the decanters pitchers tumblers, glass bowl etc that were with the linen and books all came safely not a crack or break, even my little clock that belonged to Dr Scott was so well put up that on unwinding it it commenced working and when I set it on the table went on just where it stopped at home. You can guess dear Sister how much we all thought of you when we were unpacking and Mary believes you sent all the boxes for her use she had a great tantrum over the chess box for I commenced at once with the rule that they were only to be used to play chess with and she very indignantly exclaimed, when Willie said "We promised Auntie we would not play with them when she gave them to us" ["]Oh what a story my Auntie sent them purpose for her baby to play with" I have fixed up my passage as a parlor for the little furniture would have been lost in a room. Truly tis as Goldsmith says "sending the ruffles when wanting a shirt" for we need bedsteads mattresses cups & saucers dishes and above all summer clothes and we have in their places books pictures looking glasses cut glass, parian ware and a full supply of—*Baby Clothes!*[2] which latter articles being all wet had to be washed immediately and I really felt sick at my stomach when I saw them all on the line besides this we have the half of a table the half of a carpet and the half of a lamp!!! But I am happy to say the childrens summer things are here and my work stand containing Mary's dresses so I am going to work for her to morrow the little dress Kate made her just fits her and as it was hopeless to wait for her to grow to the length I altered the skirt and she wore it yesterday and looked very sweetly in it, she went to Mrs McCormick's and staid to tea and you would have laughed at the grown up airs she put on; she sat up at the table and behaved beautifully, coquetting most admirably with Mr Igleheart. William calls her a pocket edition of Sue Johnson. When I get all my furniture I am going to draw the house and mark where each thing stands. Sam has made me very nice book shelves out of the boxes and put up some presses that I have covered with cloth for china. My genius for contriving has never had full scope before but here it will find room enough. You and brother Henry are smiling at each other on the wall, Mary did not know you but neither did Aunt Bettie for she still insists your picture is more like Sophia. I have met a lady here who remembers you as a child her name is Buckner and she was a Miss Jane Fox there is also an old Mrs Graves[3] who sent her daughter to call on me and begged me to come and see her for she knew both Mother & Grandma. And I have seen several gentlemen who know all about my family. William has his library and gets an office to morrow he has been already engaged in four suits and is taking a high stand here I say this to you but I wont to any one else—they may find it out—He is one of the directors of the railroad[4] and has the greater part of the business to do, he goes next week to Lavaca on this account and as his expenses are paid and his suits wont come in for a month he is not sorry to go as he can hurry up our furniture. I cant tell you of all the kindness I receive here every week almost some one sends me vegetables or some little delicacy, this morning I had a basket filled with salad, peas turnips and lettuce and a gallon of butter milk from one lady and yesterday a dish of asparagus from another, last week I had a splendid quarter of veal and a plate of fresh butter, and so it is all the time nearly—On Thursday the 1st of May they had the Sunday School celebration[5] it was a great affair the Judge adjourned Court and the town was deserted, after marching through town the children were carried out to the San Pedro Springs about a mile out in carriages sent by the livery stables free of charge they refused to hire a single conveyance until all the children had been carried out, the US band was out and at twelve o'clock William by request made them a speech after which they had a collation served under the trees and danced until nearly night—Franc and Willie were the admiration of the company from their devotion to the little girls and their politeness to the ladies. Willie in particular was noticed to have very good taste always choosing the prettiest girls as his partners and whether he knew them or not walking up and asking them if he should have the pleasure of walking around with them I did not go out as I have not been well and was afraid of the sun. Did not Mr Barnes have the Conquest of Mexico? I see but one of your books or rather brothers among ours find that is a child's book the Magic of Kindness and if he could see the enjoyment it has afforded the children I am sure he would pardon the unintentional theft Give my love to him and tell him Mary will call his picture Grandpa The servants are all well Sam wrote to Grace[6] yesterday.

Yours lovingly

Mary

1. A rigolette was a light wrap or cap worn on the head, usually knitted or crocheted. Peter W. Hairston, "J. E. B. Stuart's Letters to His Hairston Kin, 1850–1855," *NCHR* 51 (July 1974): 291.

2. Mary Bayard Clarke was not pregnant at this time; however, son Thomas Pollock Devereux Clarke was born in San Antonio on 24 December 1858.

3. This woman might have been married to Dr. Ralph Lewis Graves, who had been born in Orange County, North Carolina. He moved to San Antonio in 1850. S. W. Pease, *They Came to San Antonio, 1794–1865* (San Antonio, Tex.: Privately printed, n.d.), 118 (hereafter cited as Pease, *They Came to San Antonio*).

4. San Antonio and Mexican Gulf Railroad.

5. The Clarke family attended St. Mark's, the Episcopal church in San Antonio. William Clarke later served as a church warden. *San Antonio Daily Herald,* 17 Nov. 1858.

6. A slave.

WINCHESTER HALL WAS ONE of Mary Bayard Clarke's long-standing friends, whom she met on her yearlong stay at the Louisiana plantation of Leonidas and Frances Devereux Polk. Hall proved a strong supporter of Mary Bayard's writings. When she died, she left a large collection of her poetry in his hands as her literary executor. He later had them published in the volume titled *Poems by Mrs. Mary Bayard Clarke, With a Sketch of Her Life by Winchester Hall* (New York: Broadway Publishing, 1905).

Hall, who served in a Louisiana regiment during the war, visited Mary Bayard Clarke in Raleigh in 1864. He described the visit in this book, saying, "He wished to see all places in the locality associated with her childhood and early life, which she willingly pointed out to him, and it was with lively interest he noted the home where she first saw light; the noble oak, under whose shade she played, the old schoolhouse where she learned her letters, the stones over which little feet pattered on the way to school; she took him to Multiflora Cottage and stood with him before the grave of her mother."

*Mary Bayard Clarke to Winchester Hall, 1856*
*Hall,* MBC Poems, *xv–xvii.*

[San Antonio, Texas, 1856]

I can no longer be considered an invalid for I eat, sleep, walk, ride on horseback, and work like a well person. The weather is so charming it is hard to stay in the house. I often resolve on Monday that I will be very domestic all the week, and get through lots of sewing, but at the first invitation to join a party and go out nutting[1] I start up like a war-horse at the sound of the trumpet, pack the children in a carriage, jump on a horse and am off for the day gathering not only pecans, but health and strength from the fresh breezes of the prairie. . . .

I have a habit, when alone, of getting up and going through the house if I hear a noise at night, and as housebreaking has been prevalent of late I always sleep with a pistol on the mantel-piece. I was awakened a night last week by a noise like the cracking of a whip, and having not even a grown servant in the house, got up to see what was the cause; just as I was about leaving my room I heard a key turned softly in the door. I made one bound to the pistol and another to the door, which I threw open and found myself within ten steps of a man who had just opened the front door, and was apparently listening to know if he had aroused any one. I did not know I had half so much of what is generally termed *the devil* in me. I had but one intense desire, and that was to kill him. I had not a sensation of fear, but raised the pistol and took deliberate aim at him; he must have see the action, for the moon was very bright, and as I fired he jumped aside so as to put the door-way between us, otherwise he must have received the charge, which lodged in the fence in a direct line from where I stood. He ran, and I after him, and it was not until I had got several steps out of the door that I remembered my defenceless condition, when I turned and ran to my next neighbor, not twenty yards off, and rousing the gentleman I rushed back to my children, who were sleeping. By the time I had assistance the robber was out of sight; and then I began to feel afraid, and sitting down with the large cavalry sabre which I had taken down from a peg in the hall after my return, I cried like a child. The fright and exposure gave me a chill and I have been sick and nervous ever since, and while acquaintances are talking of my bravery feel myself the veriest coward.

1. Mary Bayard wrote a light-hearted poem about one of her pecan-gathering expeditions called "The Battle of Pecans." Recorded in the MBC Letterbook, it is undated and consists of six manuscript pages with the inscription, "Fought on the banks of the Salado near San Antonio/Dedicated to Miss Nannie Mason."

*Barden Collection*
*MBC Letterbook [San Antonio]*

1857

*I've been thinking*

I've been thinking, I've been thinking,
Of the many happy hours,
Now scattered o're my pathway

Like bright and fragrant flowers.
I've been thinking of my trials
As of a falling snow,
Which tho' chilling to the spirit,
Hid the buds of hope below.
Of the joys and of the sorrows
Of my childhood's simple track,
I've been thinking till my spirit
Is refreshed by looking back

I've been thinking, I've been thinking,
Of my happy childish days,
When a Mother's love watched o're me
And guided all my ways;
I've been thinking of my girlhood
That sad and dreary time,
How I missed her fostering kindness
Who had faded in her prime;
There was a tender feeling
Bound her children to her side,
How rapidly we scattered,
From the time our Mother died.

I've been thinking, I've been thinking,
Of my sister's bridal night[1]
How our busy little fingers
Were trembling with delight,
Because we were permitted
To dress the lovely bride,
And wreath her hair with lillies
From the streamlet's mossy side.
How beautiful we thought her,
When those rare exotic flowers,
The Myrtle and Camelia,
She laid aside for ours.

I've been thinking, I've been thinking
Of the cool refreshing breeze,
That blows in Louisiana,
Across the Southern seas.
I seem to hear like music,

The rustling of the Cane,
And many are the memories
It calls to mind again.
'Twas there that I was married,
On that sunny Southern shore,
And my spirit has been longing
To visit it once more.

I've been thinking, I've been thinking,
Of my quiet wedding day,
How strange it seemed to marry
From my home so far away.
No sister's loving fingers,
Twined the lillies in my hair,
And tho' friends were standing round me,
My Father was not there.
But one was always near me,[2]
Who had dried my bitterest tears,
And my heart will ever bless her,
Thro' all my coming years.

I've been thinking, I've been thinking,
How happy I am now,
There's not a single sorrow
Casts its shade upon my brow.
With thee to love and cheer me,
I ask no brighter lot;
And the troubles of my girlhood,
In thy presence are forgot;
Our cherished little darlings
Are sporting by my side,
And I know to thee their Mother
Is dearer than thy bride!

MBC 1857

1. This could have been either Frances Devereux's marriage to Henry
Watkins Miller, or Elizabeth Devereux's marriage to Thomas Jones.
2. Mary Bayard Clarke's aunt, Frances Devereux Polk.

☙

*Barden Collection*
*Thomas P. Devereux to Mary Bayard Clarke*

Salt Sulpher springs[1]
Aug. 10th 1858

My Dear Daughter

Your letter of the 21st ult has had very bad luck as I only received it today it has given me great anxiety. I do not know that I can do better than to give you a very general statement. I cannot vouch for its entire correctness as I make it out from memory. I advanced Major C 5000 Dlls when he went to Texas since then I have taken up his bond at the Insurance office for 1000 Dlls I paid to his credit in bank very soon after he left 730 Dlls I have paid Mrs Ousby (now Mrs Hervey)[2] 500 Dlls & am bound to pay her 500 more in all this fall besides which I have paid the interest on all his debts certainly the greater part of them. The whole amount may be set between 9 & 10,000 dolls I have a claim upon the house & lot in Raleigh & upon the mill property.[3] The latter has been sold but I fear the purchaser is not responsible & the property will have to be taken back in a damaged state—besides which after much reflection & to still the claims of those of his creditors to whom I am not bound I have had to consent that all the other debts should be paid before mine—how this will leave me I cannot now say but if any body would take the property I hold & clear me of the debts I would very gladly submit to loose one half of my advance—I have no idea that one cent will be recovered from his fathers estate—in fact I fear they will tax him with an additional debt—but of this I know but little—I have felt greatly cramped by the advance of cash & credit which I made & which I did not expect to loose so entirely neither did I apprehend I should be so long without repayment. In justice to the other members of the family I felt bound to call upon your husband to support his family from his salary & other income leaving me to manage the North Carolina debts. It seems that nothing in Texas is available or can be made so—should the property be sold it can only be upon a credit & in that event I shall have pay all the debts & take the bonds & wait. I agree with you that it is more than useless to send negroes to Texas. I am by no means averse to your plan of taking the little children—my pride leads me to seek out an independence. I cannot at this instant do more than I have done—in all the next three months I have to pay my discharge of George's claim[4] 22,000 Dlls—between then & the month of March I have to pay including that sum 60000 Dlls & every dollar tells—but I cannot consent to your paying such ruinous interest for money. I commit much to your judgment & discretion when I say rather than submit to such sacrifices you must draw on me payable at the counting room of Mr. L. Maitland & Co. in New York—but my dear daughter you must as you value your own & your childrens property do this only to avoid such a heavy loss, and only for the necessary expenses of your self & children—should Major Clarke be able from his Texas means be able to buy your house or servants I wish him to do so without reference to my difficulties in North Carolina—but I think he ought in consideration of my releasing him from his N Carolina debts to settle it on you. I can in relation to that now do nothing "the last hair breaks the camels back" after March when my crop is sold—some collections returned & the 60,000 Dlls paid I will see what I can do—but do not expect too much—If the rail road is to be so miserable an affair as not to pay the current house keeping expenses of the officers it becomes a question whether your husband should be any longer troubled & perplexed with it. God preserve you in his holy keeping & bring you safely out of all troubles—we are all well but Mr. Edmondston & Catharine— he has had a billious attack but is recovering—Catharine looks badly & has a bad cough. All send love give mine to the children & believe me

Very sincerely &
affectionately yours
T P Devereux

1. Salt Sulphur Springs, now in West Virginia, was a well-known resort frequented by planter families. Stan Cohen, *Historic Springs of the Virginias: A Pictorial History* (Charleston, W. Va.: Pictorial Histories Publishing, 1981), 158.

2. William Clarke's half-sister Virginia Elizabeth Clarke first married John Ousby of Halifax County, North Carolina, who died in 1854. She remarried in 1854 to Peyton E. Hervey and continued to reside in Halifax County until after the war. "Clarke Family," Crawford Papers.

3. William J. Clarke's father had owned a valuable mill property in Raleigh. William J. Clarke inherited this business and ran it for a time. Murray, *Wake County,* 286–87.

4. The debt referred to involved money Thomas P. Devereux inherited through the estate of his mother, Frances Pollock Devereux. She had inherited land and slaves from her deceased brother, George Pollock. The widow and children of her second son, George P. Devereux, felt they were entitled to some of the George Pollock inheritance. They pursued a settlement through the United States Supreme Court after the Civil War. *Edmondston Diary,* xxiv, xxv.

❧

*Wootten, Moulton, Clarke Papers, SHC*
*William J. Clarke to Mary Bayard Clarke*

New York August 12th. 1858.

My Dear Wife:

Your little husband's heart fairly leaped with joy, day before yesterday, on receiving your letter of the 18th. ult., and yesterday yours of the 25th. came to hand. The glad news, that you were well,[1] sweetened all the bitterness of the account of the trials, anxieties and mortifications that you have been compelled to endure. It seems to me that at one period of my life I should have gone raving mad to know that the idol of my soul, for whom I would gladly coin my heart's blood, was enduring such things; but like an egg I have been so long in hot water that I have become hardened. But take courage my own darling, show that fortitude and constancy that my brave wife has never been lacking in! "Weeping may endure for a night, but joy comes in the morning." This will soon be over, and you will not be compelled to take a class in Mr. Cooke's school.[2]—We have been disappointed and delayed in our operations, but we have *not* "utterly failed" by a good deal.[3] I can, before this time tomorrow, close a negotiation which will satisfy our people, and enable us to build the road at about the estimate which has always been made. I had bargained with an iron company of Pennsylva. for our iron at a very fair price, as stated by Mr. Vance,[4] and they had made half of it, when the boilers of their works gave way and the delay in replacing them and getting to work again, is greater than we can prudently submit to, so as to be sure that other RailRoad Companies will not come in before us and exhaust the State Loan,[5] and hence we are engaged in other negotiations. I think we shall be thro' the most important business in a few days, and confidently expect to be home this day next month if not sooner. We find things very different from what we were led to expect when we came here. Capital is indeed abundant, but there is so much distrust and timidity in investing, in consequence of the disasters of last fall, that capitalists prefer to suffer their money to lie idle, but that must come to an end, and the tide is evidently changing. In consequence of the dishonesty of a few Northern and Northwestern Railroads, all of that class of securities are in great disfavour, this and the bad reputation of our adopted State, and the bad management and misfortunes of our enterprise in its early inception, present formidable obstacles, but we shall find a way or make one, we shall yet come out all straight at last.—Let me but get thro' with this present business, and while I occupy the presidency we shall not again be troubled for money. There has always been a set of croakers who have predicted our failure in every thing we have attempted, but still we have always accomplished every thing we have promised the Lord be praised for past mercies & trusted for those expected.

This brings me to speak of the mortification which you say you felt in applying to Mr. Maverick & Judge Paschal[6] for money. Now it is a well known fact that my salary is in arrear for nearly a year, and as I am working for a public enterprise, which is so greatly to benefit those gents., I do not see why you should feel mortified to apply for money to those who it is so well known owe me. If you need money apply to Judge Paschal, who I suppose, can get it of the collector Mr. Graves.[7]

I am sorry to learn that you have had so much trouble with Catharine[8] & about servants generally. I have bestowed no little thought on the matter but do not see how we can, at present, do better than to "float on the surface of the occasion and trust to the omnipotence of luck"—By the bye I think it is almost time that I had some luck as I have almost served out the seven years that poor Dr. Scott used to talk so much about.

As to my affairs in N.C. I don't fear but I shall be able to arrange them. I have always known, knew before I made a single move, that I must lose largely, but I have long since made up my mind to that. So much for feeling & a sense of duty etc—I almost feel like exclaiming is there a God in Heaven and these things come to pass?—But in this connnection I may remark that things are never as bad as they appear, nor so good as we expect.

Dear little Kate, how my heart throbs at the thought of her! and I am already asking myself shall I love her as much as I do her sister Mary. At all events I shall buy for her a complete outfit here as an earnest of my affection.

I expect to be able about the middle of next week if not before to send you a Bank check for $300—I am sorry that I could not send it before but so it is and I can't do better—I am well and painfully aware that many people think me a fool, and that my wife has at times thought that I was a bad manager, but I hope yet to live long enough to vindicate my claim to a fair share both of sense and prudence and management.—I don't regret that you wrote as you did to your Father. It is too much the case that he suffers out of sight to be out of mind. & you & Nora are instances of it. Property has been conveyed by me to a Trustee to secure him for a large part of what he has advanced to me and that must be considered in abatement of any statement of advances he may make. I am firmly resolved, & have long since, instructed Mr. Cantwell[9] to close the business that I may know how the matter stands, and before this reaches you the house & lot in Raleigh will be sold on a year's credit for what it will bring; the mills were sold for $3,250 sometime ago.—

This is the anniversary of the Battle at the National Bridge.[10] Many and many a time I have wished that I had died there like a brave man and been spared the sufferings I have since endured—But it seemed otherwise to the disposer of human events.—While my life endures I shall try to do my duty at the post where fate may place me.—I am rarely melancholly now, and almost fancy that I have arrived at that degree of firmness that Horace describes where his man looks calmly on the crush of matter & the wreck of worlds. For myself I fear nothing but every thing that affects you and the children is an arrow between the joints of the harness.—

Don't be cast down my darling but look forward confidently to brighter days when we shall laugh at our present troubles but may God grant that we may never forget the lesson they have taught us—

Affectionately Yours<br>/s/ William J. Clarke

Why is the birth of a child like the arrival of Havelock at Lucknow?[11]

1. Mary Bayard Clarke was pregnant with her last child, Thomas Pollock Devereux Clarke. The family had hoped for a second daughter, jokingly called Kate in this letter.

2. Oliver Dudley Cooke started a school in San Antonio to earn extra income, although he was Clarke's law partner at the time. In a letter dated only 24 January, but which was written in 1859 or 1860, Willie Clarke wrote to his aunt, Frances Miller, that "Mother is teaching my class all except greek." It appears Mary Bayard Clarke resorted to teaching for a time to help support her family. Willie Clarke to Frances Miller, Barden Collection.

3. The San Antonio and Mexican Gulf Railroad was reorganized and refinanced in 1859 under new management. *New Handbook of Texas,* 5:808.

4. This could have been William Vance or his son, James Milton Vance. The Vances were prominent entrepreneurs living in San Antonio. *New Handbook of Texas,* 6:698.

5. To encourage railroad development, the Texas legislature offered land grants to railroad companies. The land grants were then sold to finance construction costs. Clarke's concern about a competing railroad was not idle. Dissatisfied developers in Victoria sought to develop a competing line. "San Antonio and Mexican Gulf Railroad," *Handbook of Texas Online,* accessed 10 Jan. 2001, http://www.tsha.utexas.edu/handbook/online/articles/view/SS/eqs8.html.

6. This was probably Isaiah Addison Paschal, a lawyer, jurist, and legislator. He was born in Georgia and admitted to the bar there in 1830. In 1833 he moved to Louisiana, where he served in the state legislature and as a judge on a circuit court. He moved to San Antonio in 1845 and practiced law until 1847. In that year he was elected to the Texas legislature. *New Handbook of Texas*, 5:79–80; Frederick C. Chabot, *With the Makers of San Antonio: Genealogies of the Early Latin, Anglo-American, and German Families* . . . (San Antonio, Tex.: Privately published by author, 1937), 317 (hereafter cited as Chabot, *Makers of San Antonio*).

7. Nobody named Graves served as collector for San Antonio at this time. This may have been a collector for the railroad. *Mooney & Morrison's Directory for the City of San Antonio, 1877–1878* (Galveston, Tex.: Galveston News, 1877), 40–42 (hereafter cited as *San Antonio City Directory*); J. Myler, reference librarian, San Antonio Public Library, to Mrs. Graham A. Barden Jr., 9 September 1998, Barden Collection.

8. The Clarkes' Irish servant.

9. Probably this was Edward Cantwell of Raleigh, a lawyer and author who served on the board of directors for the Dorothea Dix Insane Asylum. Guion Griffis Johnson, *Ante-bellum North Carolina: A Social History* (Chapel Hill: University of North Carolina Press, 1937), 618 (hereafter cited as Johnson, *Ante-bellum North Carolina*); Murray, *Wake County*, 429.

10. William Clarke fought in this battle in 1847 during the Mexican War. He suffered a severe leg wound while completing a volunteer assignment and was cited for his gallant and meritorious service. Murray, *Wake County*, 448–49.

11. In a letter dated 5 September 1858, reproduced in this volume, Clarke solved this riddle for his wife.

*Wootten, Moulton, Clarke Papers, SHC*
*William J. Clarke to Mary Bayard Clarke*

New York August 30th. 1858.

My Dear Wife:

I have delayed writing to you for some time as I had been expecting from day to day to have something cheering to communicate, and principally from the hope that I could send you some money, but still the cry is tomorrow, & tomorrow!

Never have I been so miserable as of late, the waves and billows of trouble misfortune and disappointment seem to have rolled over me, but tho' engulphed myself I could have borne it calmly and patiently if *you* had not been involved in it. Like the sun dial I would have you number only sunny hours. Had I been drunken or profligate I could account for these pecuniary difficulties, could have expected them, but as it is it seems hard that I should thus suffer.

But tho' cast down I am not in despair, there will yet be an opening in the clouds, the storm which has raged so fiercely will intermit, if not cease entirely.

I do not think that our Railroad enterprise will by any means prove a failure, and if I should be so favored by Heaven as to carry it to a successful issue after all the despair of others so much greater will be the credit I shall gain, and so much larger will be the salary which they will be willing to pay me.

I have today signed a contract for 4200 tons of Iron at a much less price than any yet offered to us for our securities, but the people at home will have to help if they expect to have a road. The other Texas roads which are in the market with bankable paper in addition to the same securities which we offer have not been able to effect a negotiation, tho' they have offered a much larger price than we have agreed on, and it is rumoured that they will be compelled to return home without effecting any thing.

Money matters are very tight here and do not improve. The merchants never did so poor a business as thus far they have done this year.

I have for sometime been endeavoring to negotiate a loan by pledging some of our City Bonds,[1] and yet have hopes of being able to effect it. So soon as I do so I shall send you about $500—My experience of this City leads me fear that there will be delay but I live in hope.—I have no money now and have not had for sometime past or you may rest assured I should have forwarded to you.

It is very ungrateful in the directory to refuse to advance you money and I rather think there must be some mistake about it. Judge Paschal's conduct is inexplicable to me, but I am inclined to think that what he said to Phillippee was to cover his own poverty.

I hope you presented the draft to Mr. Maverick, even if he refused to pay it, as I wrote to him in the subject They will all be ashamed of their conduct yet.

I write by this mail to Mr. Mitchell,[2] prest. pro tem. and shall request him to supply you with money. I have been well nigh crazy since the receipt of your last letter, and I have thought constantly as to what is best to be done. I am ready and willing to do any thing and if my present enterprise should prove a failure surely with my education and abilities for business something will open! It really seems to me that be best thing I can do is to run this matter fully out and, if it should prove a failure, be able to show that I did my duty and my whole duty in the matter. I shall not eventually lose the money for which I have worked so hard for if the Company was sold out tomorrow, it is able to pay all its debts twice over, for in addition to the part of the road completed it owns more than one hundred thousand acres of land which must soon be saleable at some price—I feel deeply the humiliation of applying to your Father for money, but on the other hand as an offset he promised us $10,000 on 1st. January last, and the sale of my property will pay every debt I owe, and go some way towards paying the $5,000 he advanced to me when we left for Texas— Let me but get my salary and all will yet be well with us.—

There are few men of an enterprising character but have experienced at some period of their lives a back set like that I am now suffering from, but every prudence and perseverence have enabled them to come out of all their difficulties, and I do not doubt but such will be my lot. I admire your spirit which rises with the gale, and the fortitude with which you have nerved yourself to meet the exigency but I have strong confidence that the exertions and sacrifices which you, my jewel of a wife, express yourself willing to make, will not be requisite.

Had I known any thing of the little girl in N.O. I should have cast about for means to have her forwarded to you. I hope yet it is not too late. Every thing that I can do to gratify you slightest wish shall be done, and henceforth I shall be more selfish, consider my family more and cultivate them more, and not suffer any hightoned and romantic notions of generosity to induce me to hazard placing them in an uncomfortable position. Had I retained funds which have been in my hands, and paid myself regardless of every thing else you would have been spared the trouble you have had.

I will not speak of the time I shall be home for very much work remains to be done, and my Carolina business shall be settled if it takes me until Christmas.

I have been suffering martyrdom for four or five days from a bile on my nose which has been attended with a good deal of fever and a brain whirling head ache but it is now getting better—

Cheer up my darling all is not yet lost, there will yet be sunshine in our skies!

Kiss our dear children for me and tell them that Father hopes to see them before very long

Affectionately Yours,
William J. Clarke

1. The governments of San Antonio and Bexar County, Texas, each subscribed $50,000 in stock to help finance construction of the San Antonio and Mexican Gulf Railroad. *New Handbook of Texas,* 5:807–8.

2. Probably Asa Mitchell, a San Antonio lawyer who served as alderman for San Antonio in 1855 and 1856. Pease, *They Came to San Antonio,* 184.

❧

*Wootten, Moulton, Clarke Papers, SHC*
*William J. Clarke to Mary Bayard Clarke*

Sunday
New York Sept'r. 5th., 1858

My Dear Wife:

Your sweet letter of the 21st. ult. came to hand this morning, the one you mentioned in the post script to Mr. Cooke's, as having been sent to Raleigh has not been received. I was greatly comforted by the receipt of your letter, for it seems to have been written in a more cheerful spirit than I expected. I have never been more dejected than for the past few weeks but today I feel qute buoyant and the world looks brighter, why I know not. At times we feel a foreshadowing of ills to come and our spirits sink, like the thermometer at the approach of a cloud which we cannot see, why should not an unaccountable cheerfulness be, on the converse, the harbinger of good fortune. When you and my dear little ones are well, when my heart's treasures are safe, why should I be cast down? I have been unable to raise money here nor do I see how I can, but as I have been so successful in my Iron negotiation (for I have made a splendid trade) why should I despair of any thing? I can easily build the road with slight assistance at home. I can build it without any assistance. I believe I can build it with the opposition of all parties there, if they will continue the powers with which I am invested. They have no idea of the worth and importance of our charter. Give yourself no uneasiness as to my ultimately receiving every cent that is due me by the Company. They are able to pay twice over every dollar they owe. Some parties may from interested motives cry out ruin! ruin! hoping to be able to get possession of the road and franchise for a mere song, but they will be woefully deceived in their calculations.

The most painful maddening thing which I have had to endure has been the troubles which you my darling have suffered. To add to and make perfect my misery I have received no less than three letters from members of the family urging my immediate abandonment of my business and my return home. They don't state the particular reason why, but seem to think that my protracted stay is in consequence of diminished affection for you, or it may be they fear that you will elope with Mr. Cooke, Mr. Jones[1] or that bete noir James Taylor[2]—all of which are equally ridiculous. One would suppose from the tenor of their letters that I was a man of the amplest means and faring sumptuously every day and off on a pleasure trip. I have replied kindly expressing my obligations for the interest taken in me and my affairs and assuring them that I would not stay away from you one hour longer than was absolutely necessary, and reminding them of the fact which they seem to have lost sight of that, I was compelled to make a support for my family and was somewhat in the condition of the Indian hunter who could not go home without venison.—If poor James Taylor is with you, you had better get rid of him as easily as possible. If he will not take any hint you had better inform him that the state of your health is such as to render it very incovenient for him to be in the house during my absence, and if he does not then leave send his trunk to the hotel. But I doubt not that you have already disposed of him.—There is one comfort to be derived from the mortification you have experienced about money, it shows that I have appropriated the funds which came to my hands to the purposes of the road and not secured myself as I might have done regardless of consequences. I feel a deep and abiding confidence that let the event be as it may I shall neither lose money or reputation.—

I spent last evening with Ed. G. Haywood[3] & Col. Tuc[ker?][4] who are staying at this hotel. H. has improved considerably and it was a pleasure to sit and talk with them in a quiet room such as I have not for a long time enjoyed. H. does not by any means give that deplorable account of my affairs that others do & he knows as much about the situation of affairs as any one. But before very long I shall be there and see and know for myself. In this connection I will request you to direct your next letter to Raleigh. It may be possible that I shall have to return from Carolina to this city, but my present purpose is to come directly home as soon as I arrange my affairs there, so as to be there by 1st. October if not before. But *I do not wish you to say a word about this.*—I shall send Mr. Keen to Texas the latter part of this week, and he will be compelled to return here as soon as possible.—Ma[5] has either broken up housekeeping or is about doing so & will live hereafter among her children. I shall see her and arrange that if you want her she shall come on in November or December, with Charley, who intends setting in Texas—She can return home in four or five months after your confinement if it be desirable. I suppose you saw in the papers that Delia Wynne was lately married at Norfolk to Mr. Southgate.[6] Betty Otey is also married; don't that make you feel old, for it seems like only yesterday that she was quite a little child. Gov. & Mrs. Manly are in town, tho' I have not seen them on their way to the Asylum to see Ann.[7] She is in a decline and they intend taking her home, and if they cannot keep her to put her at Dix Hill[8] assylum—It is said that her hair is as white as snow. You will be surprised to learn that James Towles[9] has failed for about $60,000 and also that Jesse Brown[10] has failed. Wh[en] such skinflints fail what chance would there have been for me in Raleigh. I surely got off badly enough but if I had remained what would have become of me! T. & H. abuse R. as the meanest place on the face of the earth. I praise it as the garden spot of creation; but I am somewhat like Franc was about the porter. Oh! I believe I forgot in my last to give you the answer to the riddle, "Why was the arrival of Havelock at Lucknow like the birth of a child?" answer because the long expected sucker (succour) has arrived at last—Dr. Bethune is responsible for that—

Now dear, good darling, cheer up, away with melancholly! we are not by a good deal as badly off as you seem to think, all will yet be well and these untoward events will in the hands of a Merciful God prove great blessings as we shall see in years to come. Present my kind regards to Mr. Cooke and thank him for his letter. I shall send the lighter articles for you by Mr. K and also some presents for the children. Kiss them for

Your affectionate husband<br>William J. Clarke

I intended to have given you an account of the Atlantic Telegraphic Cable celebration which took place the 1st. inst. and was the most gorgeous pageant the most imposing ovation that was ever seen in this Country. While hundreds of thousands of people were pressing forward to catch a glympse of Cyrus W. Field I, who have somehow for a long time likened my enterprise to his, asked myself would the day ever come when I, regarded now as a visionary enthusiast, should be in somewhat the same situation and my heart replied the time will come when faith & hope and energy and endurance will have their reward. Success, when all have despaired, is doubly welcome—Never say die!

1. Not identified.

2. Not identified.

3. Edward Graham Haywood was a North Carolina state legislator and Raleigh businessman who later served as colonel of the Seventh Regiment, North Carolina Troops, until forced by his wounds to retire. Murray, *Wake County, 677*; Manarin and Jordan, *Roster of NC Troops,* 4:405.

4. Possibly Rufus Sylvester Tucker, one of Raleigh's wealthiest merchants, who later served as a major in the Civil War. Elizabeth Gregory MacPherson, ed., "Letters from North Carolina to Andrew Johnson, *continued,*" *NCHR* 29 (Jan. 1952): 118n; John W. Moore, *Roster of North Carolina Troops in the War Between the States,* vol. 3 (Raleigh: State of North Carolina, 1882), 166; Johnson, *Ante-Bellum North Carolina,* 153.

5. Catherine Hollander Clarke, William J. Clarke's stepmother.

6. James Southgate of Virginia married Delia Haywood Wynne in 1858. Both worked as teachers and school administrators in Norfolk, Virginia, until forced to close their school during the Civil War. Delia Southgate then moved to Louisburg, North Carolina, where she worked at the Louisburg Female Academy. James Southgate later joined his wife at this school, but by 1872 he sold life and fire insurance, eventually settling in Durham, North Carolina. Powell, *DNCB*, 5:401.

7. Former North Carolina governor Charles Manly and his wife Charity Haywood Manly had several children, including Ann Eliza Manly. Murray, *Wake County*, 355–56; Ashe, *Biographical History*, 3:349–56.

8. The State Hospital for the Insane in Raleigh, eventually named the Dorothea Dix Hospital, was begun in 1853 and named in honor of reformer Dorothea Dix of New York. Dix had toured the state and promoted better treatment of the mentally ill. She made a report to the North Carolina legislature in 1848, which led to state support of the asylum in 1856. Johnson, *Ante-Bellum North Carolina*, 710–13.

9. James Towles was a Raleigh businessman and farmer during the antebellum period. Murray, *Wake County*, 270n.

10. Jesse Brown, a successful Raleigh businessman, and William J. Clarke were two of the original incorporators of the Raleigh Savings Institution in 1851. Murray, *Wake County*, 272.

ᑐᕈ

*Barden Collection*
*John Devereux to Mary Bayard Clarke*

Raleigh Aug. 6th 1859

My Dear Mary

I received yours today and hasten to answer it. The circumstances as you detail them show me most conclusively that you had better leave Texas at once and I can think of no better plan than that you should return to this State. This conclusion I come to with very great reluctance on the score of your health but on that very account it is manifestly out of the question for you to go to any frontier country. You can not have there any of the comforts & conveniences which are to be had here and from the opinion of your physician I should not think that climate made a great deal of difference with you—but this is a matter which for many reasons I must decide on somewhat at haphazard and my opinion must be liable to correction by the dictates of your well considered judgement. My advice is then most unhesitatingly that you return to this state as soon as may be convenient. Sister Frances, Kate[1] or Margaret[2] will be very glad to see you at their houses until you have time to make some definite arrangement

I think the arrangement should be something of this sort—Build a house in Scotland neck[3] somewhere near Kate and let Mr Clark attend the courts in the adjoining counties—his practice will be worth something and you can from the plantations be supported at half the cash expence you now are with twice the comfort. It is very necessary for us to be as careful of the money as possible Unfortunately father's estate has never been more than half what is seemed to be & the reverses which we have suffered in the last ten years have reduced him from a rich man to one in easy circumstances only. He still owes large sums of money which I hope will be materially reduced by sales of land & negroes this fall[4] but it will not be paid in full for many years yet. Father takes more sanguine views of his affairs than I do but you may rest assured that I am right and unless he has a run of luck in both crops & prices which it is foolish to look for he will never live to pay his debts—this state of things makes it necessary that great caution should be exercised in going into debt any deeper, and causes us to use every cent so soon as it is available. We live by borrowing

Father will probably write you very soon and give you his views. In the mean time I have given mine. You must however in the end decide

We are all pretty well Margaret's recovering slowly but surely. I trust her general health may be better in future but I have no great hopes of it, her disease baffles the physicians to say what it is. The baby is very smart—she calls it Laura[5]

Love to Mr Clark & the little ones your aff'ate brother

John

All are asleep & would send love particularly

1. Catherine Devereux Edmondston, Mary Bayard Clarke's sister.

2. Margaret Mordecai Devereux.

3. Scotland Neck, in Halifax County, North Carolina, is located along the Roanoke River near the former plantations of Thomas P. Devereux and the Edmondstons. William S. Powell, *The North Carolina Gazetteer: A Dictionary of Tar Heel Places* (Chapel Hill: University of North Carolina Press, 1968), 443.

4. In 1856 Thomas P. Devereux sold 230 of "his black people" to clear himself of debt, leaving 700 slaves in his possession. One son-in-law had observed in 1856 that he hoped Devereux would use some of the money to help his children, especially Nora Devereux Cannon and Mary Bayard Clarke, who "are poor & need his aid." Henry Watkins Miller to Kate Miller, 13 December 1856, letter in possession of Mary Gibson Speer, Missouri City, Tex. (hereafter cited as the Gibson/Speer Collection).

5. Laura Margaret Devereux, the fifth daughter of John and Margaret Mordecai Devereux, was born in Raleigh on 28 July 1859. Devereux Family

Bible, in the possession of William Joslin, Raleigh, N.C. (hereafter cited as Devereux Family Bible).

∂

*Barden Collection*
*T. P. Devereux to Mary Bayard Clarke*

Salt Sulphur Aug 12th 1859

My Dear Daughter

Your letter of the 23d ult has been forwarded to me by your brother —the contents did not surprise me, for I had long suspected what you now state—the only thing now to do, is to find out the remedy. I cannot & will not say "come at once to North Carolina." that I must leave to you. the only thing that prevents me from giving at once my decided opinion for a return, is the fear of its effects upon your health. your brother as he will doubtless inform you is very clear for your return, but he I presume speaks as he looks upon it, in a pecuniary point of view—I cannot & will not take the responsibility of such a determination in respect to your health—I can only say what I can do & what I am willing to do & in doing this I *must* bear in mind my obligations to others & *must be just*—I shall not trouble you with the names—the whys & wherefores. I will simply say that just at the moment I cannot do any thing to provide you with the [fee?] [illegible] of a residence whether that residence is in Texas or North Carolina. I *may* be able to do something in the course of one or two years— I have today written my merchants in Norfolk Messrs. J M Smith & Brother[1] to the following effect—viz stoping your husbands draft upon them & directing them to honor your drafts as your convenience may suggest to the amount of 600 Dlls per annum. for this you can draw either monthly or quarterly or semi annually. At my earliest convenience I will provide you a home either in Texas or North Carolina as you may decide. but the cost of that residence or home when I pay for it must be deducted from the annual sum of 600 Dlls to the amount of the interest—Thus if the residence costs 5000 Dlls. the income will be diminished 300 & so of other sums. but I shall insist upon the property, when bought, being so settled that it shall remain yours & your childrens for your & their use & comfort forever, without any possibility of its being taken for other purposes. & to render it most secure & at the same time to enable it to be easily available for the purpose intended, it must be conveyed to me or to your brother out & out, so that it can be sold if circumstances require without any difficulty or delay as to trusts and the like.[2] now my dear daughter

I promise nothing more. I do not trouble you with my reasons. I may be able to do more but that is uncertain both as to the time & the amount.

I am my dear child in doing this fully sensible that I take a step which may jeopard your domestic happiness—since do not like to be the second person in the household. could I arrange it differently I would do so—but I cannot devise a mode in which I can effect my object as well. I must call this to your mind & beg you to be exceedingly prudent in your conduct so as avoid making [statements?] of your domestic guest. I think it best to have no concealments from your husband. but be guarded in your conduct. write me frequently & I hope to hear of your improved health. give my love to all &

Believe me your
affectionate father
T P Devereux

Anne & Susan[3] send their love

1. The mercantile firm of J. M. Smith & Brother was based in Norfolk, Virginia. Thomas P. and John Devereux, as well as the Edmondstons, used this firm regularly for business transactions. *Edmondston Diary,* 299; John Devereux Papers PC 34.2, State Archives, North Carolina Division of Archives and History, Raleigh, N.C. (hereafter cited as Devereux Papers).

2. Thomas P. Devereux was following a time-honored southern tradition in working to settle property on his daughter while maintaining control of its disposition. Married women held no property rights, and this legal coverture meant property they brought to a marriage became the property of their husbands. Devereux, unwilling to purchase a house that would become William J. Clarke's property, was insisting that he and his son, as Mary Bayard's nearest male relatives, maintain legal control of the property to decrease their and her monetary risks. Fox-Genovese, *Within the Plantation Household,* 203.

3. Ann Maitland Devereux was Thomas P. Devereux's second wife. Susan Harrison Devereux was his daughter and Mary Bayard Clarke's half-sister.

MARY BAYARD CLARKE'S GENTEEL yet faintly flirtatious negotiations with George Bagby to get her poetry published in the *SLM* provide an interesting insight into the relationship between publishers and women writers in the mid-nineteenth century. In this letter and others, Clarke took pains to portray herself as a refined southern woman who wrote on ladylike subjects and enjoyed "a delicate bit of flattery with decided relish." Publishers at that time, who were almost all male, often developed patriarchal working relationships with women authors. Women could write, but they needed to be moral and follow the Victorian code for proper female behavior. Women writers, as they became skilled in working with publishers, learned to adopt different strategies with different firms, selecting the style best suited to the particular publisher with whom they were working. Clarke chose to emphasize to Bagby her use of a nom de plume and her desire to protect her privacy, knowing this would appeal to a southern publisher embued with the South's view of women's proper place in society. For an excellent discussion of nineteenth-century publishers and women writers, see Susan Coultrap-McQuin, *Doing Literary Business: American Women Writers in the Nineteenth Century* (Chapel Hill: University of North Carolina Press, 1990).

*George Bagby Papers, VHS*
*Mary Bayard Clarke to George William Bagby*

San Antonio
Decem 16th [1860]

Dr Bagby[1]
Dear Sir

I was gratified to hear that "A View from Conception"[2] met with so warm a welcome, and in order to be in time for the Feb number send you at once a couple of translations from the French which I undertook at the request of M. Consideránt and promised to print. One is Basbiér's celebrated "Ode sur Napoléon," the other Victor Hugo's equally celebrated "Le Petit."[3] I believe they have never before been translated and as expressions of different phases of French sentiment towards the two greatest men of the nation may be interesting. I write and translate poetry con amore and should do so if I never published; but I am also anxious to get some regular literary employment in the prose line which will enable me to add to a library I am collecting for my boys. When I resided in the civilized world I regularly reviewed books for a bookseller and kept a copy of such as I fancied; but here it is impossible to make any such arrangement. I am aware that the Messenger is not in a condition to pay contributors, and that the editor is sometimes troubled for acceptable matter to fill its pages; should you therefore ever feel a desire to have any work reviewed for the magazine and are willing to entrust it to me I will gladly undertake it on receipt of the volume. I wrote critiques, which attracted considerable notice, on Dixon's Life of Penn Van Santvoord's life of Algernon Sidney, Wynne's Lives of Eminent Literary and Scientific men, The Napoloen Dynasty by the Berkly [men?] and other works that appeared about the same time.[4] I have also been in the habit of translating tales from the French, My health[5] for a long time has prevented all writing but I am now anxious to resume it and if you can give me any employment or recommend me to any one who can I will gratefully do all I can to assist you in the Messenger in the poetical line. I dont care for the money—only money's worth in the form of books, as every cent I have ever made by my pen has gone into my library

I have one request to make which I trust you will comply with, and it is that I may never appear in the Messenger except under my Nom de plume.[6] Say what you like about Tenella but nothing at all about Mrs. Clarke. When Mary Forrest[7] applied to me for a sketch of my life and selections from my writings, I wrote to her that I wished the "Public" to know nothing about me except my signature; and this feeling is so strong that I will give up writing rather than appear out of my social circle except as Tenella

Very respectfully Your
Mary Bayard Clarke

1. George William Bagby, editor of the *Southern Literary Messenger* (Richmond). Patton, *Thompson Poems,* xxi.

2. This poem was published in the *Southern Literary Messenger* 32, no. 1 (Jan. 1861): 11–13 (hereafter cited as *SLM*). The poem described the missions in San Antonio.

3. "Le Petit (From the French of Victor Hugo)" appeared in the *SLM* 32, no. 2 (Feb. 1861): 146. In a later letter to Bagby, Clarke corrected a typographical error, pointing out that one line should have read, " 'Thou will be only choked in *mine*' not wine." Mary Bayard Clarke to George W. Bagby, 12 March 1861, George Bagby Family Papers, Mss1B1463b475–482, VHS (hereafter cited as Bagby Papers, VHS). "Napoleon (From the French of Auguste Barbier)" appeared in the *SLM* 32, no. 3 (Mar. 1861): 225. The typesetter set her name at the top as Penella rather than Tenella, a mistake for which she scolded Bagby.

4. William Hepworth Dixson, *William Penn: An Historical Biography from New Sources* (Philadelphia: Blanchard and Lea, 1851); George Van Santvoord, *Life of Algernon Sydney with Sketches of Some of His Contemporaries and Extracts from His Correspondence and Political Writings* (New York: Scribner, 1854); James Wynne, *Lives of Eminent Literary and Scientific Men of America* (New York: D. Appleton, 1850); *The Napoleon Dynasty: or, The History of the Bonaparte Family. An Entirely New Work. By the Berkeley Men* (New York: Cornish, Lamport, 1852).

5. Clarke is referring to her pregnancy.

6. Clarke used the nom de plumes of Tenella and Stuart Leigh.

7. Mary Forrest, the pen name of Julia Deane Freeman, wrote *Women of the South Distinguished in Literature* (New York: Derby and Jackson, 1860).

MARY BAYARD CLARKE WROTE this article for the *New York Herald* and deliberately disguised her gender while describing the surrender of the United States Army garrison to Texas secessionists. Her husband, a member of San Antonio's Knights of the Golden Circle, participated in the seizure. Brigadier General David E. Twiggs, a career army officer, commanded federal forces in Texas at this time, with headquarters in San Antonio. The Texas secession convention, which convened in Austin on 24 January 1861, had taken steps to ensure federal army supplies remained in the Confederacy. After voting to secede on 1 February, an act ratified by Texas voters on 23 February, the convention appointed a Committee of Public Safety to meet with Twiggs to discuss terms of surrender. Committee members were Samuel Maverick, Judge Thomas J. Devine, and Philip N. Luckett. Twiggs, in turn, appointed three commissioners to meet with the committee: Major Sackfield Maclin, army paymaster; Major David H. Vinton, quartermaster in charge of the San Antonio Depot; and Captain Robert H. K. Whiteley, in command of the San Antonio arsenal. The secession convention also appointed Texas Ranger Ben McCulloch as commander of state forces around San Antonio. McCulloch immediately assembled hundreds of armed men, who marched on San Antonio and surrounded the Alamo, which was then the army depot. Twiggs surrendered on 16 February.

*Barden Collection*
*MBC Scrapbook 1, with handwritten notation "Letters to the New York Herald written from San Antonio de Bexar in the Spring of /61' By Mother"*

### INTERESTING FROM TEXAS

**The Surrender of Gen. Twiggs' Division—The Surrender of the Arms, etc., Demanded by a Committee—Major McCullough and the K. G. C.'s—The Muster of the Volunteers and the March on the Arsenal —Preparations for a Fight—Evacuation by the Federal Troops—Gen. Twiggs' Speech to the State Troops—The Union Party in Texas—Capt. Whitely, of the United States Army, in Trouble—The Pontius Pilate Guard, etc., etc.**

Our San Antonio Correspondence.

San Antonio, Texas, Feb. 17, 1861.

The week just passed has been most exciting and eventful. The Committee of Safety, clothed with plenary powers by the Convention, and representing that body during its short recess, have been in session here, with a view to obtaining possession of the federal property, which amounts to a large sum, and was guarded by only one hundred and fifty troops.[1] Of course the rumors flying about the streets were innumerable, and of every hue. It was known that the committee had demanded of the General of this department the surrender to the State of the arms, ammunition, stores, horses, mules and property of every kind belonging to the federal government then in the State of Texas; and that he had appointed a military commission to treat with them, consisting of three officers—Major Macklin,[2] Major Vinton and Capt. Whitely—the two last Northern men by birth and education. Day after day passed, and the committee and the commission were unable to agree. . . . Friday night orders were issued to those volunteer companies who had offered their services to the committee to assemble armed and equipped for active and immediate service, at the armory of the K. G. C.'s,[3] and report to Colonel Ben. McCullough. Of these there were six—four enrolled some time since by the Mayor[4] of the city—two of which, on his requisition, refused to turn out. Their services were not, as the event proved, needed; and, as they were composed principally of men known to be submissionists, who would probably, if they dared express their true sentiments, be also black republicans, it is a source of gratification to us that we were not called on to place any confidence in them. The other companies were the Alamo Rifles and the San Antonio Guard,[5] the last composed of the young men of the K. G. C.'s, who comprise in their Order many of the old Texans, and the wealthiest and most influential men of the community. Those of the Order who had not enrolled in the San Antonio Guard, under Captain Wilcox, were led by the Captain of the Castle, Major W. J. Clarke, for not a man of them was willing to be left out, and those whom the Captain had not summoned, owing either to the shortness of the time or their age, regarded themselves as defrauded of an honor.

Soon after midnight we assembled, with forty rounds of ball cartridges in our cartouche boxes, and waited for our orders, which were given at four o'clock, when, with loaded muskets, we marched quietly, without beat of drum, to our posts, near the United States barracks, on the bridges and other spots to be guarded. When it was light enough to see I discovered that every approach was occupied by Texans, a thousand of whom had marched in under Colonel McCullough and taken their positions as quietly as regular troops could have done. Sharpshooters were stationed on the roofs of all the houses which over looked the arsenal yard, where about two dozen cannon were placed. Every man expected to fight, and not one that I could see showed the least symptom of fear. It would have been impossible to man a gun, as the expert rifleman could have picked off every soldier with as much ease as they show in knocking over a deer. Hour after hour wore away, and our patience diminished in an inverse ratio to the increase of our appetites. At ten o'clock we had been six hours at our post, and, judging from appearances, were likely to remain six hours more. . . . What did it mean? If we were brought there to overawe the United States troops, would the length of our stay increase the effect produced by our numbers? . . . At twelve o'clock we caught sight of one of Uncle Sam's men emptying the hay out of his bed; others soon followed his example, and the empty sacks were packed way into boxes. It was evident a move was intended by the troops, and it looked more like a journey than a fight. A few moments afterwards we were marched to our quarters, and a special guard detailed from Captain Wilcox's company, the San Antonio Guard, to take charge of the property.

At five o'clock the United States troops marched out with their flag flying, upon which were emblazoned the names of those battles in which the regiment fought for and gallantly sustained the glory of the United States. It was pierced in many places with bullet holes, showing through what dangers it had been borne. Many of the soldiers wept as they marched away to the tune of "Red, White and Blue," and the eye of many a Texan glistened, not with triumph, but with tears of feeling. It was a mournful spectacle, and we felt we were burying our dead.

. . . .

There is not, I think, now any danger of a fight, though it is rumored there are seven companies of United States troops on the way to retake the property. They will have a merry time if they attempt it. Next Saturday the people will, by their votes, declare that the Union which has held us to the North is dissolved,[6] and the opposition which exists here must cease. Our city has been regarded as the black spot in Texas; but I think we have now wiped out the disgrace cast on us by the so-called Union party, whose leaders and spokesmen, many of them, are Northern men, or fresh from an Ohio hot-bed of abolitionism. . . . There are not half a dozen respectable Texans in the ranks of the Union party.[7] The Mayor of the city —a New Brunswick skipper—who is suspected of abolitionism; a broker, originally from Philadelphia, who has no influence except that which money always gives, and a couple of hardware merchants who originated in Maine,[8] and are not nor ever could be Southerners, either in principle or feeling, are its wire pullers. The material on which they work are the lower class of Germans and Northern mechanics, who are influenced either by their ignorance or their pockets. It has been owing entirely to the prudence and influence of the leading secessionists that these men have not had their houses burned, their property destroyed, and been forced, *nolens volens,* to leave the State. It only needed a word to effect this; but one of the most remarkable features of the whole transaction is the perfect order that has prevailed. One of Col. McCullough's first orders was to close all groceries, grog shops and drinking saloons, and, as far as I can learn, not a drunken brawl has occurred, nor any collision between the State troops and the citizens. Men who at their own expense had ridden in forty or fifty miles to fight, refused to obey any order until they had seen the committee's authorization. Capt. Whitely, of the ordinance, was charged with privately sending off arms to be shipped to New York, and several attempts were made to induce the Texans to intercept the wagons on their way to the coast; but not a man would stir until the committee signed the order. Three then rode sixty miles without dismounting, overhauled the wagons, and finding they contained the best arms manufactured for the use of the troops, brought them back last night. Since I began writing another train of wagons has been intercepted and brought in by the K. G. C's. Old General Twiggs drove down himself to inspect their contents, and was so indignant that he was heard to declare he would, if it were the last official act of his life, put the officer in chains who sent them off, unless he could explain it; for he (Gen. Twiggs) had never signed any requisition for such articles. The excuse given is that the wagons were loaded before the committee came, and were standing ready to start with the first train.

One of the companies enrolled by the Mayor goes by the name of the Pontius Pilate Guard, from the number of Jews in it; and it comes out, since all is over, that until after daylight they supposed themselves called out to protect government property from the K. G. C's who were stationed in front of them. There is little doubt had there been a fight they would have sided with the party that was getting the advantage.

The most perfect good humor prevailed between the State troops and Uncle Sam's. The troops stationed in the arsenal yard, when they discovered the company of sharp shooters on the roofs a little after daylight, rubbed their eyes in astonishment first, and when they took in the true state of the case, occupied themselves, not in making cartridges, but coffee to send up to them. . . .

1. Caroline Baldwin Darrow, the wife of one of Twiggs's military clerks, described San Antonio's siege by Texas secessionists: "In the dim light I saw the

revolutionists appearing, . . . mounted and on foot, a motley though quite orderly crowd, carrying the Lone Star flag before them, and surrounded and supported by armed men. . . . By daylight more had appeared, perhaps a thousand in all, and so great was the enthusiasm of two women who had aided General Twiggs in his arrangements that they mounted their horses, in male attire, and with pistols in their belts rode out to meet their friends. . . . By noon he had surrendered all the United States posts and stores in Texas." Caroline Baldwin Darrow, "Recollections of the Twiggs Surrender," in Clarence C. Buel and Robert U. Johnson, eds., *Battles and Leaders of the Civil War,* vol. 1 (New York: Century, 1884–88), 82–83 (hereafter cited as Darrow Recollections).

2. Maclin, although representing the United States Army, was a leading secessionist who later became chief quartermaster for Texas during the Civil War. Heitman, *Historical Register,* 7.

3. The Knights of the Golden Circle (KGC) appeared in the 1850s, organized by George Bickley. This secret society eventually blended Masonic imagery with a mixture of proslavery and states' rights rhetoric. Local chapters of the organization were called castles, and its members were knights. The golden circle encompassed Cuba, Mexico, and other areas that held potential as future American slaveholding territories. Mark C. Carnes, *Secret Ritual and Manhood in Victorian America* (New Haven: Yale University Press, 1989), 7–8. In October 1860 Bickley traveled to Texas to promote the KGC. Headquarters were established in San Antonio, and San Antonio physician George Cupples ran the order in Texas. About 150 knights assisted Ben McCulloch in forcing the surrender of federal forces in San Antonio in 1861. C. A. Bridges, "The Knights of the Golden Circle: A Filibustering Fantasy," *Southwestern Historical Quarterly* 44 (Jan. 1941): 287–302; 1860 Census, Bexar County, San Antonio, Texas: 351, Household no. 152.

4. James R. Sweet served as mayor of San Antonio from 1 January 1859, to 26 May 1862. Born in Nova Scotia, he moved to San Antonio in 1849 and established a mercantile partnership with his brother-in-law in 1850. He resigned as mayor in 1862 to join the Confederate army. "Sweet, James R," *Handbook of Texas Online,* accessed 14 Oct. 2000, http://www.tsha.utexas.edu/handbook/online/articles/view/SS/fsw11.html.

5. The Alamo Rifles and the Alamo City Guards were two San Antonio militia companies. Many of the members of each company also belonged to the KGC. Captain John Allen Wilcox commanded the Alamo Rifles, and William Edgar commanded the Alamo City Guards. Kevin R. Young, *To the Tyrants Never Yield: A Texas Civil War Sampler* (Plano, Tex.: Worldware Publishing, 1991), 43, 61.

6. Caroline Darrow recalled the excitement in San Antonio when the secession convention began to consider passage of a secession ordinance on 1 February. "Women vied with each other in distributing the little yellow ballots, on which were printed in large type, 'For Secession,' or 'Against Secession.'" Darrow Recollections, 80.

7. This description of San Antonio Unionists reflects Clarke's prosecession bias. In fact, Mayor Sweet later joined the Confederate army. Two notable German Unionists living in San Antonio were Rudolph Hertzberg and Anthony M. Dignowitz. Hertzberg, born in Prussia, moved to Texas in 1849 and opened a tobacco shop in San Antonio. He became a naturalized citizen in 1856. His strong antislavery views were shared by many other Germans in the town. Dignowitz, born in Bohemia, arrived in San Antonio during the Mexican War. He became a successful doctor and businessman, but he remained an outspoken abolitionist. He was almost hanged by secessionists in 1861 and fled the state. "Hertzberg, Theodor Rudolph," *Handbook of Texas Online,* accessed 27 Aug. 2000, http://www.tsha.utexas.edu/handbook/online/articles/view/HH/fhe65.html; "Dignowity, Anthony Michael," *Handbook of Texas Online,* accessed 27 Aug. 2000, http://www.tsha.utexas.edu/handbook/online/articles/view/DD/fdi15.html.

8. These Maine merchants were probably the sons of Judge Milford P. Norton of Maine. His three sons, Henry, Charles, and Edward, had moved from Maine to San Antonio and opened a hardware store in 1855, called Norton & Deutz. Chabot, *Makers of San Antonio,* 360.

Ᏸ

*VHS, MSS 1B1463b475–482*
*Mary Bayard Clarke to George Bagby*

San Antonio March 12th [1861]

Dr Bagby
Dear Sir

Since my last to you I have been too sick to think of reading or writing which must excuse my apparent negligence in noticing your letters; the Feb Messengers were detained merely to worry me by the PM here who is violently opposed to my husband in politics and inspects my correspondence for fear it may be treasonable.[1] Every thing is so unsettled here that I fear I shall have to leave as my health will not stand the continued excitement in which I am necessarily kept; most of my lady friends have preceded me, but aided by a new riding habit, a most bewitching Secession hat I stormed two hearts the day before I was taken sick and induced the Hon John M. Howell[2] and Dr. Henry P Howard[3] to say if I would write for, they would read the Messenger. They are both gentlemen of wealth and standing and I doubt not will long remain on your list of subscribers. I have been persecuted with enquiries from Carolina as to who [Tyed?] is, and had not the least idea myself until I heard that he spoke of Cotton Doodle and the Lone Star; I dont remember whether I ever sent those songs to you as I promised and for fear I did not put in a copy now. I also received a letter by the last mail which induced me to request that if any application is made to either you or the proprietors for information respecting the terms on which I write for the Messenger and my correspondence with you personally, you will decline giving it; perhaps no such application will ever be made and I hope not, as it is entirely a personal matter. I hope you will excuse the request and say nothing of its having been made to you. I write for three papers but not under my signature and am well paid for my prose articles which however are of such a nature as to allow me no freedom of thought and are subject to alteration, so I do not regard them as mine What I send you I write for my own pleasure and am not to be bribed into silence. My family are all strong Unionists and I am regarded as a traitor to the cause because I go heart and soul with my husband who glories in all I write; And this reminds me that your "devil" made a mistake in La Petite, the last line should read "Thou will be only choked in *mine*" not *wine*.

Hoping in spite of your state the Messenger will still bring us Secession articles and will not suffer from its adhesion to the good cause I am

Very respectfully
Yours etc
M B Clarke

1. The postmaster in San Antonio between 1856 and July 1861 was Henry L. Radaz. 1860 Census, Bexar County, San Antonio Township, Texas: 346, Household no. 51.

2. There was a John Howell who served as commissioner for the Western District of Texas during the Civil War. This may be the same man. T. R. Havins, "Administration of the Sequestration Act in the Confederate District Court for the Western District, 1862–1865," *Southwestern Historical Quarterly* 43 (Jan. 1940): 295–322.

3. Henry Peyton Howard, who moved to San Antonio at the age of sixteen, served in the Mexican War, studied medicine in Washington, D.C., and returned to San Antonio to practice medicine. He was a charter member of the Bexar Medical Society (1853) and a city physician in 1854 and 1858. He served as a surgeon and staff officer during the Civil War and later joined Maximilian's forces in Mexico. "Howard, Henry Peyton," *Texas Handbook Online,* accessed 14 Oct. 2000, http://www.tsha.utexas.edu/handbook/online/articles/view/HH/fhoay.html.

☙

*George Bagby Papers, MSS1B1463b475–482,VHS [last page is missing from*
*collection]*
*Mary Bayard Clarke to George Bagby (Richmond)*

San Antonio April 8th [1861]

My dear Doctor

Imagine De Quincy without his opium, a bon vivant without his dinner, an old tippler without his "smile," a young lady who has lost her finery on her way to the Springs or any other person equally uncomfortable
to himself and all around him, and you will have a pretty good idea of Mrs
Clarke minus a saddle horse. My private stud is confined to three horses,
a fiery brown mustang foaled on the prairie, which few gentlemen, and no
other lady can ride, a spirited full blooded Spanish horse brought from
Mexico, and a quiet little half breed, ostensible kept for *me,* but *really* for
the "Tyrant of the House" Master Tom just turned into his third year who
paces about the lot as composedly as most boys of ten or twelve, scorning
to be held in the saddle and grumbling extensively at not being allowed a
"*vitch*" Of these I have not been able for the last few weeks to catch a sight,
as Uzema, my mustang, while recruiting on the rancho, fell like other wild
young bloods into bad company, and not returning to the corral at a sea-
sonable hour was swooped off by the Camanches.[1] Queridito (or little darling in english) being remarkable for his endurance, I patriotically lent to
a Ranger[2] to follow on their trail; where on Pixie the half breed most pro-
vokingly took sick and was obliged to be turned out to grass; and "me
voila" with only two feet instead of four.

Yesterday however I succeeded in getting another mount; and riding
to the Post Office found your letter of March the 25th which with the ride
have together restored me to good humor. I am not, as you have probably
discovered by any means a "strong minded woman", on the contrary I
rather think some of that stamp would pronounce me decidedly *weak,* for
I like Michelét, and believe implicitly in the doctrines he advances in
L'amour; further I am willing to submit to any amount of petting that the
superior man is inclined generally to bestow on woman; though I do not
admit that *all* who wear pantaloons are *men,* (I always wear them myself
on horse back), and worse than all I confess to enjoying a delicate bit of
flattery with decided relish, Consequently I have no hesitation in saying I
was much gratified by your letter, and the information that La Petit
was well received by the readers of the Messenger. My incognito I only
endeavour to preserve in print, my social circle extends from Boston to

Brownsville one way, and from Cuba to Chicago the other; in it I am as well known by the name of Tenella as of Mrs Clarke, but the newspapers and public generally, have nothing to do with the latter personage, and I never see her name in print even though coupled with a compliment without feeling that my private rights have been invaded, Every gentleman, and rowdy too, is at liberty to look at Mrs Clarke as she dashes by the hotel on horseback, but that does not give them the right to look through her parlor window and watch her kiss her husband or pet her children. Mounted on my Pegasus, I soar along as Tenella and never think of the public, or if I do, dont regard their remarks as applying to me idividually and consequently am neither embarrased or annoyed by them. My father Mr Thomas P Devereux of Roanoke N C. whom you may have heard of, objects to my writing for publication either with or without a nom de plume, and if I had no feeling on the subject myself, I should keep my name out of print simply because it is disagreeable to him to see it there. I received a few days ago a letter from one of my Cuban caballeros reproaching me for not remembering Cuba in verse, as well as in prose, and reminding me of a promise I made five years ago to write something in commemoration of the death of Ramon Pinto who was executed while I was in Havana incited by the memory of old times in that lovely island, I have written the enclosed poem which as it would probably get him into the . . . [rest of letter missing]

1. Comanche raiders frequently targeted outlying ranches near San Antonio. Robert E. Lee, while stationed in Texas with the Second Cavalry, chased raiders who were stealing horses near San Antonio. Carl Coke Rister, *Robert E. Lee in Texas* (Norman: University of Oklahoma Press, 1946), 117 (hereafter cited as Rister, *Lee in Texas*).

2. A Texas Ranger.

ᔈ

*Wootten, Moulton, Clarke Papers, SHC*
*William J. Clarke to Mary Bayard Clarke*

Montgomery[1] April 26. 1861

My Dear Wife:

Knowing that you will be very impatient to hear from me I write this brief note which may possibly reach you. The Sect'y of War[2] is a very slow coach and still delays making any appointments in the regular Army except 2d. Lieut's.

Mr. Wigfall,[3] who seems to feel a warm interest in me, pressed him so hard last night that he said he would immediately appoint me a Captain if I would go recruiting W. told him that I deserved to be a Major and that he would not advise me to take any thing less, but he would deliver the message I told W. that I thought so too. W is to see him tonight again as there is very little opportunity in the day Every one tells me to hold on to my original proposition and I will get the appointment I seek. I shall wait until Mr. Conrad[4] arrives, which I expect will be tonight or tomorrow, and be guided by his advice.

N.C. is in a perfect blaze, a submissionist is hard to find.[5] In Raleigh they have raised two companies $20,000 were subscribed to equip a company of flying artillery, and $150,000 for the Confederate States. Holden[6] subscribed $2,000 for the [1st?] Co.! Hoke has issued a call for 30,000 men and they are going by Reg'ts. into Virginia.[7]

On the other hand the Yankees are pouring into the Dist. of Columbia tho' they can't get thro' Maryland.

My darling I feel so uneasy about you as I may not be able to get any money to you. If you get hard pressed don't hesitate to apply to Mr. J. Vance[8] he will not hesitate to loan you any amount you may need when he learns that I am in the army,

I shall send you money as often as I get it.—I think that a large regular army will be ordered immediately on the meeting of Congress when Mr. Cooke will have a chance.

I am heartily weary of this waiting and besides it is very expensive.— Gen'l. [Winfield] Scott has not resigned. Col. [Robert E.] Lee has and is leading the Virginians

We have not yet obtained any certain particulars respecting the fights at Baltimore—

Young Maclin[9] arrived here last evening—God bless you my heart's treasure and keep you and our dear children prays your

Affectionate husband<br>William J. Clarke

Direct your next letter under cover to sister Frances at Raleigh—

1. William J. Clarke had gone to the first Confederate capital in Montgomery, Alabama, to seek a commission in the army that was commensurate with his service in the United States Army during the Mexican War.

2. Leroy P. Walker, an Alabama lawyer, became the first secretary of war for the Confederacy. A political appointee, he resigned on 16 September 1861,

because of poor health and criticism of his administrative abilities. Mark Mayo Boatner III, *The Civil War Dictionary,* rev. ed. (New York: David McKay, 1988), 885 (hereafter cited as Boatner, *Civil War Dictionary*).

3. Louis T. Wigfall, a United States senator and Texas state legislator, was elected to the Confederate senate from Texas in 1861. A lawyer, he briefly served as a brigadier general in the Confederate army but resigned in early 1862 to become a Confederate congressman. He distrusted Jefferson Davis and tried to help William Clarke receive a higher military appointment. Boatner, *Civil War Dictionary,* 18; *Handbook of Texas,* 1:351.

4. Charles Magill Conrad practiced law in New Orleans and served in its state legislature. Elected to the United States Senate in 1842, he also served in the United State House of Representatives from 1849 to 1851. He represented Louisiana in the first and second Confederate congresses, serving from 1862 to 1864. Stewart Sifakis, ed., *Who Was Who in the Civil War* (New York: Facts on File Publications, 1988), 138; *Who Was Who in America,* 118–19.

5. North Carolina seceded from the Union on 20 May 1861.

6. William Woods Holden, newspaper editor of the Raleigh *Standard* and future governor of North Carolina during Reconstruction, quickly developed an intense dislike of the Davis administration. He led a peace movement in the state and criticized the Confederacy relentlessly. He was a personal friend of William J. Clarke. Beth Crabtree, *North Carolina Governors, 1585–1975: Brief Sketches* (Raleigh, N.C.: Division of Archives and History, 1974), 98–99 (hereafter cited as Crabtree, *North Carolina Governors*).

7. John Franklin Hoke was a North Carolina lawyer, legislator, and adjutant general during the Civil War. As adjutant general, he organized volunteer regiments for the Confederacy. He later served as colonel of the Twenty-third Regiment, NCT. Failing to win reelection, he returned to his home and served in the North Carolina Senate in 1863. In 1864 he became colonel of the Fourth Regiment of North Carolina Reserves. Manarin and Jordan, *Roster of NC Troops,* 3:xi; Powell, *DNCB,* 3:164–65.

8. James Vance of San Antonio.

9. Tom Maclin was the son of Texas chief quartermaster Sackfield Maclin. The Maclins were close associates of the Clarkes in San Antonio.

*Wootten, Moulton, Clarke Papers, SHC*
*William J. Clarke to Mary Bayard Clarke (San Antonio)*

NO. 6

Direct your letters to care of J. Edmundstone[1]
2. M's office, C.S.A. at this place I would write more
but the gent. who carries this to Tex. is about to leave—

1861

Montgomery Ala. May 15

My Dear Wife:

I have delayed writing to you from day to day with the hope of being able when I did write of being able to tell you something definite of my affairs, but day after day has passed without any result, and I have not been able to do any thing to expedite matters; nor have I heard of any one of "the noble army" of office seekers who has discovered that effective manoeuvre that would expedite matters.

Messrs Conrad & Clingman[2] and the whole Texas delegation have pressed my appointment most vigorously and even rudely but the Secretary of War, who possesses at least one of the qualities of the ass, stubbornness replies "I am not making field appointments at present, but expect to do so next week." In the mean time Congress is about to adjourn, and ever day brings in a large detachment of Virginians seeking appointments, and from long practice they have a skill in that business, which is unapproachable, and I begin to fear that no more citizen appointments will be made after those of the present day. Consequently I have on consultation with my friends concluded to accept the Sect'y's offer of a captaincy with the promise that I shall be made 1st. Capt. of my Reg't., which will secure my promotion on the first vacancy. Adjt Gen'l. Cooper[3] assures me & Mr. Conrad that he will see to it. I wrote to the Sect'y. this morning signifying my willingness to accept the nomination, and it will be sent in to Congress today. But I do not expect to serve as Capt.—N.C. is raising a *regular army* of 10,000 men and the Gov. has the appointment of the field officers and I have no doubt Ellis[4] will offer me a Colonelcy. I shall apply for leave of absence or to be detached for that command when my name will be borne on the Army rolls and at the end of the war I will resume my regular position. If I do not obtain this position, I expect to be ordered to Texas.—Out of about 100 applicants from T. the delegation united in recommending only 5. viz. one Capt. and four lieuts. Maj. Maclin's son, for his gallant conduct at the capture of the Star of the West,[5] will be commissioned 2nd. Lieut.

There is a rumor in town, which I fear is too true, that Gen'l. Sidney Johnson has been made prisoner at New York, on landing from the California steamer.—I saw Mrs. McLane & the Capt.[6] a few days ago. The old Gen'l. Sumner is fortunate in having two sons-in-law opposed to him.— I fear that Frank Bryan will prove a traitor to the South. Mrs. Williams passed through here about two weeks ago. Capt. W. had gone to Lynchburg and she raved like a crazy woman because he was not here to meet her. John Settle[7] is here and William Vance left for Little Rock Ark. last night. They are having terrible times in St. Louis and Washington city. Tell Mr. Cooke that Conn. is behaving nobly. She declares against coercion and Gov. Harry Seymour[8] refused positively to serve on the military committee. I do *not* despair of obtaining a comm. for Mr. C. Gen'l. Waul[9] is his strong and enthusiastic friend and advocate.

Darling I have many many things to tell you but there is so little certainty that a letter will reach you that I do not write as often nor as fully as I otherwise would do. I have recd. but one letter from you.

I long ardently to see you and our dear little ones, but it may be a long time before I have that happiness—I left a draft for $250 endorsed in the large pocket book in my desk (office desk) it is in a brown envellope get it cashed and use the money I shall send you a draft as soon as possible you shall have every cent of my pay that I can spare, and so soon as I am officially informed of my appointment I will notify you that you may have commissary privileges—Kiss Pet and Tom for me and embrace our noble boys Franc & Will. Respects to Mr. C. Howdy to Sam, Jane & Henry[10]— Oceans of love to my own darling from her little husband

William J. Clarke

Ben McCullock has been appointed Brig. Gen'l. in *Provisional* Army There will be no fight for a long time if at all. I don't think our folks will attack them at the north unless they invade Virg. or Maryland asks protection.

1. James N. Edmondston was a brother of Patrick Edmondston. Patrick Edmondston was married to Mary Bayard Clarke's sister, Kate. James Edmondston served as assistant quartermaster under John Devereux, Mary Bayard's brother. *Edmondston Diary*, 92.

2. Thomas Lanier Clingman, a North Carolina lawyer, state legislator, and United States senator, served as a Confederate general and in the Confederate congress. Boatner, *Civil War Dictionary*, 159.

3. Samuel Cooper, a West Point graduate, was the highest-ranking officer in the Confederate States of America. He was commissioned as a full general from Virginia on 16 May 1861, and served throughout war as "adjutant and inspector general." Boatner, *Civil War Dictionary*, 175.

4. John W. Ellis, a lawyer and superior court judge, was elected governor of North Carolina in 1858. Shortly after North Carolina voted to secede, Ellis suffered a breakdown and died from overwork at White Sulphur Springs, Virginia. Ashe, *Cyclopedia of Eminent and Representative Men*, 187; Crabtree, *North Carolina Governors*, 92–93.

5. The United States steamer *Star of the West* was a troop transport ship that sailed to Indianola, Texas, to pick up seven companies of United States troops.

The ship was seized by Earl Van Dorn and two companies of Texas militia. Boatner, *Civil War Dictionary,* 793; B. P. Gallaway, ed., *Texas, The Dark Corner of the Confederacy: Contemporary Accounts of the Lone Star State in the Civil War* (Lincoln: University of Nebraska Press, 1994), 244; "Star of the West," *Handbook of Texas Online,* accessed 20 Feb. 2000, http://www.tsha.utexas.edu/cgi-bin/web_fetch_doc?dataset=tsha.dst&db=handbook&doc_id=4498&query=star+of+the+west.

6. Eugene and Margaret Sumner McLean were good friends of the Clarkes in Texas and after the war. Eugene McLean and William Clarke had served as vestrymen at St. Mark's Episcopal Church. Chabot, *Makers of San Antonio,* 297. Margaret McLean and Mary Bayard Clarke also formed a close relationship. Captain McLean resigned his commission in the United States Army on 25 April 1861, and joined the Confederate army. McLean's father-in-law, United States Major General Edwin Vose Sumner, remained loyal to the Union. Margaret McLean kept a diary of her war experiences. Heitman, *Historical Register,* 675; C. Vann Woodward, ed., *Mary Chesnut's Civil War* (New Haven, Conn.: Yale University Press, 1981), 59n. In 1863 Mary Bayard dedicated a poem to Margaret McLean, "The Water Sprite's Bridal. *Dedicated to Mrs. Eugene McLane,*" published in the *SLM* 37, no. 1, Jan. 1863, 31–34. Clarke misspelled McLean's name.

7. John A. Settle, a former Virginian, was a San Antonio merchant who lived in the Fourth Ward. 1860 Census, Bexar County, San Antonio Township, Texas: 429, Household no. 461.

8. Clarke probably meant Horatio Seymour, governor of New York. The governor of Connecticut from 1858 to 1866 was William A. Buckingham. Boatner, *Civil War Dictionary,* 733, 859.

9. Thomas N. Waul was a lawyer and Confederate general from Texas. He later raised Waul's Texas Legion and served in the western theater of the war. Boatner, *Civil War Dictionary,* 896–97.

10. Henry was a servant employed by the Clarkes.

*Wootten, Moulton, Clarke Papers, SHC*
*William J. Clarke to Mary Bayard Clarke (San Antonio)*

No. 8.

Montgomery Ala. May 17. '61

My Dear Mary:

My heart fairly leaped with joy on yesterday, when I rec'd. yours of the 15th inst.—Quite a burden was lifted from my heart to know that you had a good stock of dimes, and I trust that God will prosper me in my endeavors to keep you well supplied hereafter. I am daily expecting to receive my commission as Capt., and to be placed 1st. on the list of capts.

in my Reg't. but the Secty. of War is an awfully slow coach and has as yet sent in no appointments in the army to Congress for confirmation, and consequently we are compelled to endure all the pangs of hope deferred, and to undergo the labor of doing nothing. This state of expectancy makes me so nervous that I find no pleasure in writing and am heartily ashamed of my wretched scrawl.—I think it more than probable that I shall be ordered to North Carolina to recruit, even should I not be detached on the application of the Gov. to command a Reg't. in the N.C. regular state army.[1] The latter position would give me a salary of about $3,000 a year, & would give me a high standing in the army when I am reduced to my regular grade on the return of peace.—Most persons think that we shall have a long war. I do not; on the contrary I believe that the delay of every day is as fatal to the north as the loss of a thousand men. Lincoln will hardly invade any of the seceding states & I do hope that we shall not provoke hostilities and stir up deadly hate, and silence every voice in the north urging reason & pleading for peace, by an aggressive act. So far thro' the whole south yankees have not been molested, while in the north the most inoffensive southrons have been compelled to flee for their lives. The thoughtless expression of the Secty. of War,[2] in his speech to the crowd, on hearing of the bombardment of Sumter, aroused and united the north. The excitement is now wearing off. They have no aggrieved honor to avenge. The public opinion of the world is against them. Bankruptcy, such as they have never known, stares them in the face, and as they see the utter futility of endeavoring to coerce the south— having every thing to lose and nothing to gain, they will soon be amenable to reason. I only fear that we will be too good friends hereafter and speedily too.

Large bodies of men are almost daily passing thro' this city some for Va. but most to Pensacola[3] We should keep their fleet engaged at the latter place as long as possible, but passion may usurp the place of reason, and a noble game may be spoiled by a false move. God forbid!

Texas will be divided into two judicial districts and Judge Devine[4] will be judge of the western. Gen'l. Waul has been quite sick, billious fever. He is now able to sit up and in a day or two will be able to attend cong. Mr. Conrad requests me to say that he did not receive one of your letters and to beg that you will excuse him for not writing at present as he is very busy. He is so absent-minded that when he walks out he gets lost and walks miles before he finds out where he is.—The chief clerk of the War office told me, day before yesterday, that my friends were very active in pressing my appointment and that no man was more enthusiastically endorsed. Clingman takes a deep interest in me. He walks about talking to himself as usual, and gesticulating with his—shoulders!—Congress will adjourn in a few days to meet in Richmond.

There is very little news in this letter, but I have a good many envellopes and they will be useless after 1st. June.

I am almost crazy to see you my darling and hope you will write me a *short* letter frequently. My coming here was absolutely necessary; for if I had not done so I would not have obtained my appointment.

Tell the boys that I shall write to them in a few days. Kiss Pet for me, tell her I hope she will be able to read and know all the catechism by the time I get home. Father never sees a piece of "tanny" without thinking of Tom. Very affectionately yours,

Wm. J. Clarke

1. William J. Clarke received an appointment as colonel of the Fourteenth Regiment, North Carolina Volunteers, on 18 July 1861. Manarin and Jordan, *Roster of NC Troops,* 7:251.

2. Simon Cameron, United States Secretary of War.

3. The excellent harbor at Pensacola, Florida, was guarded by federal forts McRee, Barrancas, and Pickens. The United States Navy Yard located there surrendered to the Confederacy on 12 January 1861, but Union troops occupying Fort Pickens refused to surrender. They were reenforced on 12 April, ensuring that the navy yard at Pensacola remained useless to the Confederacy. Boatner, *Civil War Dictionary,* 641.

4. Thomas Jefferson Devine and William Pinckney Hill were appointed judges of the Eastern and Western Districts, respectively, when the Confederate government in Texas replaced the United States district courts. *Handbook of Texas,* 1:391.

Wootten, Moulton, Clarke Papers, SHC
*William J. Clarke to Mary Bayard Clarke (San Antonio)*

Montgomery Ala. May 23d. 1861.

My Dear Wife:

There is a peculiar fitness in my writing to you today, for it is an anniversary in our history which has never passed without being remembered by me. This day fourteen years ago, I parted from you to march for Mexico; today I probably leave for North Carolina to report to the Gov'r of North Carolina for duty, as the Adjutant General on yesterday intimated that such would probably be my destination. In a few hours I expect my orders. It *may* be that before another moon has "waxed and waned" I shall see and hear "the shout, the shock and the groan of war." The same Almighty hand that covered my head in battle heretofore has lost none of its power, and his mercy is as great now as it was then. I pray for strength that I may do my duty under all circumstances, and "quit" myself as becomes the husband of a heroic woman, who would rather wear weeds for a brave man than smile welcome to a craven and a coward, who loitered at home, in inglorious safety, while his brethen and countrymen were in the tented field. If I leave no other heritage to our noble boys this at least they shall have a name unsullied by cowardice, unblackened by treachery!

But I would not make you sad, my darling, I would rather point forward to the time when *your* warrior returns with his laurels fresh and thick upon his brow, for believe me they would be, in his eyes little worth, if you could not see them—I feel a perfect confidence that I could pass unharmed through a tempest of balls. We shall meet again in God's own good time, and you shall smile again while I recount to our dear boys the particulars of my second campaign.

The young lover on leaving his lady love would have prayed good angels to prepare for his love garlands of sweet destiny amid the asphodel and the row; and that the fates, so harsh to others, might weave for her the amaranthine web of happiness and love, but the wish is cold and inexpressive when the husband looks back to years of confidence and devoted affection and feels that his wife is worthy of an affection stronger than life itself.— Pardon this little rhapsody; for my heart is stirred within me when I think of the days of gloom which have passed over you, linked to my illstarred fortunes when they should have been all sunshine and flowers.

At times my heart has been so weighed down by care my spirit has fainted so "because of the way," my faith has been so weak, that I have felt that prayer for myself was a mockery, but I have never failed to implore the blessings of Heaven, richest and choicest, on my dear wife.—I am consoled in my separation from you by the thought that I am enabled to labor effectually for you. I look back with a shudder to the long, long days when I was idle, unable to do any thing for you because no man had ["]hired" me. I now feel as if I were ascending a gentle hill with the sun in the east shining on my back and all the shadows pointing forward, and thy cheerful voice crying "excelsior."

Dear little Tom speaks that truth, for which children are noted, when he says that "it is not prayers because "fardy" is not there," for not even mother can pray as fervently for him as I do.

Pardon me again, my darling, that my heart has so strangely dilated beneath a ray of sunshine penetrating the clouds of adversity, and illuming the valley of humility, in which my footsteps have so long lingered. But has God dealt hardly with us? No. Though His ways are past finding out, still to my obscure, dim vision it seems that adversity and poverty have not been without their uses. It has proved our love, and taught us valuable lessons, though they may have been learned in bitterness and tears. The more we limit and concentrate love the more secure it is; they who widen the circle encroach upon the boundaries of danger. Wealth and fame, company and pleasure would necessarily have separated us a good deal, and numerous circumstances might have conspired to weave the icy spell of estrangement.

Truly we are led by a way we know not. The best concerted plans of mice and men ["]aft go agee." Knowledge and prudence and calculating foresight often lead more away from the path we would tread, than unreasoning folly. "Reason is a lamp which sheddeth afar a genial and general light, but leaves all around in darkness and gloom." "It is not in man that walketh to direct his steps." Like children let us strive to perform our appointed tasks leaving our support to our Father in Heaven, taking no anxious thought for the morrow!

This brings me in a very natural connection to speak of the disappointment I feel in having a much cherished plan entirely broken up. I refer to your visit to N.C. this summer.

By the circuitous route, which is the only safe one, you could travel I do not see how you can leave Tex., this summer.[1] I feel that you are as safe in Tex. now as you would be N.C. Tho' it is improbable that Lincoln will be able to penetrate that far into the South, still it is not impossible. If it rested with Virginia alone it would not be so difficult, but the men of other states in large numbers are there, and it is next to impossible.

I cannot conceive how or why Lincoln should attack Texas. To do so effectively would divert too much of his strength. It could not be done by land, and all his navy would not suffice for transports to land a sufficient force on the coast. And after he had subjugated the state what would his victory be worth?

Congress has adjourned to convene at Richmond Va. on the 20th. July next—Gen'l. Waul is about again tho' looking badly. He will not return to Tex. during the recess.—

My dear Mary, my own sweet wife. Since I wrote the above I have been to the War office & have been informed that I shall be ordered to N.C. as above. I called at the Post Office and recd. the enclosed letter.[2] I beg that you will not in any of your letters *intimate even* that you have seen it. Burn it after reading. It is like many I have recd. for more than a year past. You know me and trust in me. Your father refused to invite you to N.C. The $1,000 was a *loan* on Bonds, for $2,000, which are to be deposited for him. They may distrust you, but I know and love you better than *all* of them *put together.* I would tear the heart out of any one *not* of your blood who would intimate as much—The only remark I have to make in that connection is to be prudent, wise, discreet. But remember let who will doubt you etc., your husband's heart *surely surely unwaveringly* trusts in you.—Don't trouble yourself on that point. I am almost glad that an opportunity offers to prove how truly I confide in you, how confident I am of your love, think the same my darling of

Your affectionate husband<br>William J. Clarke

Love to all. Tell Jane that I wear her slippers every day & find them a great comfort. When you send my sash & your daguerrotype send also my prayer book

1. Mary Bayard Clarke, despite her husband's advice, traveled to Raleigh with her entire family and at least one free black servant and one of the slaves they had brought to Texas in 1855. She left Sam Taylor in San Antonio to watch their possessions. Clarke was in Raleigh by June 1861.

2. This letter from an unnamed member of Mary Bayard Clarke's family, questioning her prudence, wisdom, and discretion, does not survive.

*Barden Collection*
*William J. Clarke to Mary Bayard Clarke*

Weldon North Carolina[1]<br>Sunday Night June 2d. 1861.<br>No. 11.

My Own Darling:

I arrived in N.C., or rather in Raleigh, on Sunday morning last, and have been so much occupied since that I have waited for a quiet time to write to you. I reported to the Governor on Monday, and on Tuesday received orders to repair to this place and Garysburg, three miles distant, to muster into the service the troops. This involves the making out of three rolls for each company, and as no one knows any thing of the duty you may depend upon it I have no easy time of it; but I have entered energetically on the duty and hope to execute it properly. There are about three thousand men at the two posts. Three Regts. have already gone to Virginia, for it seems that the valorous men of the Old Dominion are deeply impressed with the value of their lives and are slow to put them in jeopardy.

I was not aware that so much stupidity existed in the world as I have seen in the last few days. Men seem to have laid aside their senses when they put off their citizen's clothes.—I can form no guess how long I shall be here, but I suppose I shall not get off for at least two weeks. Whether I shall be appointed a Brigadier Gen'l. or a Col. in the State troops seems problematical. My fitness for the position seems a disqualification. I would see them the other side of Jordan before I seek either. The "materiel" of our troops is of the first quality, but the officers are, for the most part, not fit for corporals. What do you think of Col. Duncan K. McRae of the 4th. Regt. of State Troops[2] (Volunteers for the War) which they call "Regulars"?

This is a fair sample of the appointments. It is cruel to send out our people when they cannot be properly commanded and their bravery will only make their destruction more sure. My reception has been most enthusiastic and the papers have given me flattering notices.—

I never saw any thing to compare to the spirit shown by our people, and particularly the women. If the soldiers run in battle they will not stop in N.C., for, like Noah's dove, they will not find a place for the soles of their feet on N.C. soil.

I find Hoke, Adjt. Gen'l. worked almost to death and almost every one cursing him. They cannot understand that the fault is not in him but in their miserable militia organization. Riddick is Asst. Adjt. Gen'l,[3] ranking as Col. but I am sorry to say a rival of Hoke and doing all he can to magnify all of Hoke's errors and omissions. Ellis is almost dead and seems to have lost his senses. The whole affair shows the most pitiable state of inefficiency and ignorance.

Capt. John Devereux A. Commissary[4] is stationed at this post. He blushes and protests at the title, but nevertheless is a very efficient officer, and enters spiritedly into his duties The Capt. is absent at present in Raleigh *on duty.* Of course no one would suppose that in these war times he has gone to see his very pretty wife; for Margaret is really splendid. She very kindly invited me to make her house my home during my stay in Raleigh. Anne is a very quiet interesting girl, and I learn that Kate is a splendid woman.[5]

Sister[6] was as kind as usual and received me most cordially. But Sophia,[7] whom I met at Mr. Miller's, acted most hatefully. She looks as if she was at least forty. Her tory husband after opposing the manly defence of our rights in the most childish manner, now finds himself constrained to act as a *private* in one of the companies stationed at one of the forts.

But the most amusing and wonderful thing I have heard is that your Father is the most violent secessionist and the bitterest man against the north to be found in the state. His conversion is almost as remarkable as that of St. Paul and I must tell you how it came about. It appears that old Maitland owned some real estate in Va. and that your Father wrote to Rob't. M.,[8] some months ago, proposing that it should be sold for division among the heirs. After the present difficulty occurred R.M. wrote to him saying that the *traitors* of the south had destroyed the present value of the property and he would not consent to a sale now; but that in a short time the lazy and effete population of the state would be exterminated, and the country would be possessed by "the honest, industrious & energetic men of the north" by which means the value of the property would be enhanced three fold. It is said that the Squire thereupon indulged in sundry remarks which will not be found in any edition of the Prayer Book heretofore published. And it is supposed that Mrs. D's Scotch blood alone saved her from apoplexy At all events the whole family at Conniconara are now staunch secessionists.

The thread of my epistle has been so often interrupted by company that I had almost forgotten to tell you the last family scandal. It is said "entre famille" that Maj. C. is so jealous of his wife that he has left her and joined the army, and that his not bringing her with him to N.C. is proof positive of this. Isn't this refreshing news to you?

Mr. Edmundstone was here a day or two since. He had been up to Raleigh to endeavor to get the Scotland Neck cavalry in the service;[9] but the Governor informed him that they were not receiving cavalry at present. He was very kind to me and informed me that he would send his carriage for me at any time I might find it convenient to come to see him —Sue Johnson is to be married to an *old fellow* this month. Betty Jones[10] is also to be married soon to a yankee.

About 1,000 men pass here every day—All the cabinet and officials have gone to Richmond Va.—We are expecting a fight at Manassas Gap very soon. Lincoln will not risk his Congress unless they are exasperated. England's course has had quite a calming and sobering effect on the Yanks.

Charley[11] passed through today, a private in the Raleigh Rifles, Capt. Harrison[12]—I am referred to as a military mentor for advice on any number of questions of *rank;* but I have adopted the rule to have nothing to say and have by that means avoided infinite trouble—Kiss my darlings for me and tell Tom that when fardy comes he will bring that tanny

Affectionately Your husband

William J. Clarke

1. The Fourteenth Regiment, North Carolina Volunteers (NCV), organized under the command of William Clarke at Weldon, North Carolina, in July 1861. It originally had nine companies, but a tenth was assigned in May 1862. It remained at Weldon until 18 August 1861, when it moved to Richmond, Virginia. Manarin and Jordan, *Roster of NC Troops,* 7:246.

2. Duncan K. McRae, future editor of the Raleigh *Confederate,* was appointed colonel on 16 May 1861, and assigned to the state's Fifth Regiment on 15 July 1861. He resigned on 13 November 1862, because he failed to receive a promotion. Manarin and Jordan, *Roster of NC Troops,* 4:126.

3. An R. H. Riddick was listed as an assistant adjutant general in February 1862 in the *Official Records,* series 1, vol. 9 (1883): 431. Richard H. Riddick, later colonel of the Thirty-fourth Regiment, NCT, died from wounds received at Ox Hill in 1862. Walter Clark, ed., *Histories of the Several Regiments and Battalions from North Carolina in the Great War 1861–'65,* vol. 4 (Raleigh: State of North Carolina, 1901), 155, 164 (hereafter cited as Clark, *Histories of the Several Regiments);* Manarin and Jordan, *Roster of NC Troops,* 9:251.

4. Devereux served in the North Carolina Quartermaster General's Department under Quartermaster General L. O'B. Branch The office was reorganized on 20 September 1861, and General James G. Martin was elected chief of the state's war departments. Devereux then became chief quartermaster and held this position until the end of the war. Clark, *Histories of the Several Regiments,* 1:23, 24.

5. These were two of John Devereux's daughters. Anne Lane Devereux, the oldest child, was born in Raleigh on 1 October 1843. Catherine Johnson Devereux was born in Raleigh on 28 June 1848. Devereux Family Bible.

6. Frances Miller.

7. Sophia Devereux Turner was married to Josiah Turner of Hillsborough, North Carolina. Josiah Turner served as captain of Co. K, Nineteenth Regiment, NCT (Second Regiment, North Carolina Cavalry). He was wounded on 13 April 1862, and resigned the following November. In 1863 he was elected to the Confederate congress, where he opposed the Davis administration. He later become a foe of Reconstruction and bitterly attacked its policies and supporters in the pages of the newspaper he edited, the *Sentinel* (Raleigh). Powell, *DNCB,* 6: 67; Moore, *Roster of North Carolina Troops in the War Between the States,* 2:140.

8. The elder Maitland was Thomas P. Devereux's father-in-law. Robert Maitland was his wife's brother.

9. Patrick Edmondston enlisted with other Halifax County men on 23 April 1861, in the Scotland Neck Mounted Riflemen. He later became captain of the

company, but he was discharged on 9 October 1861, following his appointment as a lieutenant colonel authorized to raise a battalion of troops. The battalion never materialized. Manarin and Jordan, *Roster of NC Troops,* 2:198, 227.

10. Bettie, or Elizabeth, was Mary Bayard Clarke's niece, the daughter of Betsy Devereux Jones. She married Hamlin Jones of Owego, New York.

11. Charles D. Clarke, William Clarke's half-brother, was then a private in the Fourteenth Regiment, NCV. He became quartermaster sergeant for the regiment on 18 July 1861. Manarin and Jordan, *Roster of NC Troops,* 7:252.

12. William H. Harrison, a captain with the Raleigh Rifles. The company left Raleigh for Garysburg, North Carolina, on 2 June 1861, where it joined the Fourteenth Regiment as Co. K. Manarin and Jordan, *Roster of NC Troops,* 5:482.

*Wootten, Moulton, Clarke Papers, SHC*
*William J. Clarke to Mary Bayard Clarke*

Weldon N.C. June 25th. 1861

My Dear Wife:

My heart fairly leaped with joy today just after dinner, when I met Col. Jones[1] of the 5th. Regt. who informed me that he had seen you, and that you and our dear children were well, and would be in Raleigh today. God be praised that you have arrived in safety! though I know you are worn out with the fatiguing journey.

At the moment of receiving tidings of you came an order from Gen'l. Gatling[2] detailing me to act as Judge Advocate to a general court Martial assembled to try two deserters.

The Court meets tomorrow and I hope will get through with its business so that I may make up and forward the proceedings and leave for Raleigh on Thursday tho' it is by no means certain. But one thing is very certain and that is I shall not delay a moment longer than absolutely necessary. I am very tired tonight and consequently do not write more at present. Kiss the dear ones for me especially Tom some of whose smart things Col. Jones has reported Love to sister & Kate & respects to Mr. Cooke & howdy to Jane

Affectionately yours
William J. Clarke

1. Joseph P. Jones was lieutenant colonel of the Fifth Regiment, NCT. He resigned on or around 24 October 1861. Manarin and Jordan, *Roster of NC Troops,* 4:127.

2. Richard Caswell Gatlin, a career army officer and West Point graduate, resigned his commission on 20 May 1861. At that time he was named adjutant

general of the North Carolina militia. He was named brigadier general for the
Confederacy on 8 July 1861, and given charge of coastal defenses. Faced with
an impossible task, he lost Hatteras and Roanoke islands and the town of New
Bern. He was relieved of command after New Bern fell on 19 March 1862.
He resigned on 8 September 1862, but he later served as North Carolina's adjutant and inspector general. Boatner, *Civil War Dictionary,* 327; Powell, *DNCB,*
2:285–86.

❧

*Barden Collection*
*Frances Miller to Mary Bayard Clarke*

[ca. summer 1861]

Dear Mary

Do not think that I lay any claim (from my always having done what I
could for your comfort & said what I could when others blamed) to a right
to give advice but just consider that in saying what I do I only feel I am
doing my duty tho I may be mistaken in my sense of it.

It is not respectable my dear Sister that you should be following your
husband to the seeming neglect of your children[1] As it now stands there is
no one responsible or seemingly there is not & as far as I am concerned I
can not let things go on so, Ostensibly they are at Bros but half the time
they are on the road & I do not know if they are with M or not As for her
I must say I doubt if she takes the slightest controll of them I can take no
such divided responsibility As long as I could hope it was for a few days I
did not object but I knew just how it would be What I propose is this, Let
me take them & *attend to them* have their washing done & give them a servants care & Mr C pay me 40$ a month half in advance then if you must
go with the regiment you can do so & not feel your children are on suf-
ferance any where This may seem mercenary in me but I have put it as low
as I can & furnish a Servant & I understand from Jane you pay her 15$ this
will not be so heavy as you will save her wagges. I regret to have to go in
to these details God knows I would take them free could I tell where to
get their support but *my* husband does not make 50$ a month yours more
than double he *can* support his children & ought when he is able then he
will be respected the present state of things is not proper Then if you
please you can go where you will but mind I have said you had better not
I am aware that this is taking great responsibility but I know you will
beleive let what will happen that I tried to do for the best as I will & to do
so that all may be satisfied I must charge for them & ask for half in advance
I do not think you ought to blame me & hope you wont.

As to Jane your proposal is a great relief[2] I shall be truly glad to get her out of the house before she is whipped & hope you will [urge?] her to go to you as quickly as possible. I do believe I am as forbearing towards my inferiors as any one but Jane I could not stand much longer Why the people in the streets will tell "how I let white children & those my absent Sister be treated by a free niger" My very blood has boiled at her treatment of Tom & language to Mary I do believe she loves them but you have lived so long with her you do not see its effects Tom is cowed Mary's worst faults the fruits of her mismanagment Bro John said he would have killed her if she had staid there & Sophia seriously told me she should board when she came down again if Jane was here as she would not allow her children to hear their kin so talked to We aint used to such my dear sister so do take Jane & welcome & leave Tom to us Of course he will fret a little but we will wean him & he will be perfectly content he is a darling so gentle & affectionate & wins his way to his uncles heart by a thousand sweet ways even if he was twice the trouble I would gladly take it to release Mary from her evil influence.

As to her she wishes to know how many are in the Mess? if she is expected to work? & when will you want her? these questions she wishes answered right off before she decides but never fear she is only coquetting she is as eager to go as you can desire I told her Friday I wished Mary Lynch sent off as I would keep no one whom I could not govern but I doubt if she not be here now had she not got vexed because I told Mary I thot she *deserved* a whipping & was tempted to gie it when she carried her off in a whirl this PM not even sending her to say farewell. Ill get on very well with Tom & the others too for I have got a house keeper & take in no more work so in Marys name let her go as quickly as she may into camp life which she is certainly more suited to than in any gentlemans family unless under more control than Ive seen her. Tom takes this & the L M also something for his Father youd better ask him for them. With love to Bro as ever

Your affectionate<br>Sister

PS I did not get the letter on time for the trunks being sent

1. Mary Bayard Clarke was visiting her husband's regiment.
2. Jane Espy, the free black woman who traveled with Mary Bayard Clarke from Texas to North Carolina, took care of the Clarke children for a time in 1861. Conflict with the extended Devereux family led her to join William Clarke's

regiment to cook for the officers of his mess. She followed the regiment to White Sulphur Springs and Blue Sulphur Springs in 1861. She stayed in Lynchburg, Virginia, for a time, when fighting became too fierce. She also nursed Oliver D. Cooke when he was wounded at Fredericksburg. When Espy became ill, William Clarke sent her to Lewisburg, Virginia, to recuperate. Clarke Papers, SHC.

&#x2767;

*Barden Collection*
*William J. Clarke to Mary Bayard Clarke*

Garysburg [North Carolina] July 14th. 1861

My Dear Wife

I have not written to you for some time as my movements were some what uncertain and I wished to let you know something of them when I did write. I am in good health but have been, and shall yet be for a few days, very busy; but expect to have more leisure after a while.

I could not leave for Richmond because so many companies were coming to this post for whom I had to make provision, and for a further reason that I did not wish to leave before the 14th. Regiment elected its officers, as the companies here, composing a great majority of the Regt., have pledged themselves to give me a unanimous vote for Colonel,[1] and to present me with the best sabre they can procure. I also think it highly probable that Mr. Cooke can be elected Major.[2]

It is the finest Vol. Regt. I have seen and is much better officered than the 5th. & 13th. who wanted me for Col. and were almost broken up when I was not elected. I will not electioneer and publickly announce that I am no candidate. I did not wish to command either of them but I am anxious to be Col. of the 14th. and have no doubt I shall be, though I have offers made me of other positions. I accepted the comd. of this post as a favor to the Military Committee and as a temporary matter.—The election in the 14th will take place on Tuesday or Wednesday and immediately thereafter I shall go to Richmond—Your memoranda shall be attended to. When I get there I shall have my account for this month made out correctly on a proper blank and send it to Maj. Maclin. It will be sufficient to pay him in full—I shall send you all I can spare out of my last month's pay and but for my board and uniform and arms would send you *all*.—

I trust that your health will improve and with it your spirits. As for myself I try to bear with composure all that befalls me but the most severe trial I have to endure is that I cannot do more for your comfort and happiness.

I have given great satisfaction as comndr. of this post, and the men tell me that it was like the sun bursting from a cloud when it was announced that I was placed in command. The appearance of things has certainly greatly improved—

A few days after my return from Richmond I expect to come to see you. We have the measles very badly here, 250 cases, but mild. We have lately had two deaths, but as a general thing the sickness is not very serious—mumps, itch, and billious pneumonia of a typhoid form which if following measles is very dangerous.

I learn that your brother intends joining Mr Edmundston's Co. I hope that he will not make any engagement until he hears from me which will be the middle of this week—Kiss Tom for me, and tell Frank & Willie that I hope they will not quarrel with Cousin Tom[3]—12 o'clock P.M. Good night darling

Yours lovingly
William J Clarke

1. William J. Clarke was appointed colonel on 18 July 1861. Manarin and Jordan, *Roster of NC Troops,* 7:251.

2. Oliver Dudley Cooke served as second lieutenant of Co. E (Lone Star Boys) in the regiment. After being defeated for reelection in May 1862, he became adjutant of the regiment on 31 July 1862. Manarin and Jordan, *Roster of NC Troops,* 7:251.

3. Thomas Pollock Devereux, the first son of John and Margaret Devereux, was born 8 November 1845. Devereux Family Bible.

*Wootten, Moulton, Clarke Papers, SHC*
*William J. Clarke to Mary Bayard Clarke (North Carolina)*

White Sulphur Springs Va.[1]
September 1st. 1861.

My Dear Wife:

We arrived here last night after a very unpleasant march in consequence of rain. We were delayed at Jackson's River by the difficulty of obtaining transportation for our baggage. I had to send out a party and impress a few wagons.

We are now encamped about 200 yards from the principal spring and but for the vicinity of a dead horse would be quite comfortable. The health of the Regt. is improving but the measles, mumps etc. still cling to us, and we have been compelled to leave some 50 men behind at different points sick. Our Major[2] was left quite sick at Covington and I doubt if he ever rejoins the Regt. a consummation not to be deplored

We are well except Jane who is complaining, but is able to be about and as she has some six or seven negro men to scold I think she will be all right in a day or two.—We saw 100 prisoners marched by our camp this morning, taken by Floyd in the fight a day or two since.—I received a dispatch from Gen'l. Floyd last night ordering me to stop at Lewisburg as there was a deficiency of provisions with him, and would be for a few days,—As I am here and doing well I shall stay for a day or two. The Gen'l. informs me that so soon as he is reinforced by my Regt. & another one or two on the march he can easily drive the invaders from the valley of the Kanawha, and that then we can go into winter quarters in Charlestown—

I have enjoyed very good health thus far tho' I have had to work like a horse—But for the glory of the thing I would much prefer to be a captain in the regular Confederate Army to commanding a Vol. Regt. I can control my officers for I have the hearts of the men. Jack Mitchell[3] joined us in Richmond and I don't think I ever saw a man more rejoiced—I shall have to caution him not to lie quite so strongly for me—There are no visitors at the Springs, and most of the public buildings are occupied as hospitals.[4]

I have been interrupted a dozen times while writing this and all my ideas have fled so I will stop—

We leave here on Tuesday and you will please write to me at Lewisburg—Give my love to all

Affectionately Your husband

William J. Clarke

1. The Fourteenth Regiment had been ordered to Staunton, Virginia, to join General John B. Floyd's Army of the Kanawha. Before Clarke reached Floyd, the southern army was attacked and forced to retire on 10 September. Clarke's regiment then joined Floyd on 11 September. The entire army retired to Sewell Mountain. Floyd left part of his force there under General Henry A. Wise. The rest of the army, including the Fourteenth, moved to Meadow Bluff, sixteen miles west of Lewisburg. Manarin and Jordan, *Roster of NC Troops,* 7:246.

2. Jonathan Evans previously served as captain of Co. F, Fourteenth Regiment, NCV. He was elected major and transferred to the regiment's Field and Staff on 16 July 1861. He was defeated for reelection on or about 16 May 1862. Manarin and Jordan, *Roster of NC Troops,* 7:251.

3. William A. Jackson Mitchell had been a quarryman before enlisting in Johnston County on 15 May 1861, as a private in Co. C, Fourteenth Regiment, NCV. He was discharged on 17 November 1862, because of being over age. Manarin and Jordan, *Roster of NC Troops,* 7:280.

4. The buildings at the White Sulphur Springs resort were used as hospitals by both the northern and southern armies. Cohen, *Historic Springs of the Virginias,* 142.

❧

*Barden Collection*
*William J. Clarke to Mary Bayard Clarke*

Meadow Bluff Greenbrier Co. Va.<br>Sept'r. 21. (Saturday) 1861

My Dear Wife

Your letters of the 6th. & 8th. inst., and the one enclosing the letters of my dear boys have been received and afforded me much satisfaction. We have made "an advance to the rear" of 21 miles, in imitation of Scipio or that famous king of France with 30,000 men. Our last march was from Big Sewell, from which place I wrote you last, 14 miles at night, part of the time in a heavy rain, over a rough very muddy road and as we had to regulate our march by the movements of the train it Iccupied [*sic*] us from 10 o'clock at night to past 10 next day

It was a terrible march and my men suffered greatly and I fear that several cases of pneumonia are attributable to that night march. To add to our troubles the evening of the day we reached this camp we recd. orders to prepare four days provisions in our havresacks and to march next morning at 3 o'clock *without tents* and only two wagons to a Regt. We expected to march to Hughe's Ferry on the Gauley River. A part of the men were up all night cooking, and all were greatly exhausted. It really seemed more than flesh and blood could bear and I really thought that our destruction was inevitable but a kind Providence ordered otherwise; before the hour appointed for the march arrived the order was countermanded and we had a day of rest. The next day we were marched about 2 miles to the Meadow River, a muddy sluggish stream about the size of the San Antonio, where we were engaged that day and the next in throwing up breast works. My Regt. was the first on the ground and worked so diligently that we finished first on yesterday, tho' some Regts. will be at work a day or two yet. We rest today, wash clothes, clean guns etc. I sincerely hope that we shall make a stand here as it is very demoralizing to troops to retreat, and my Regt. is entirely too fine a one to be destroyed in that manner. It is really an uncommonly fine body of men, and I have strong confidence that they will act creditably in any situation. The drilling, order, and appearance of the men excites universal approbation and the Va. Cols. say they don't know how Col. C. manages his men so well. The men are so much attached to me that it need only be said that "The Col. so wills it," to have it done. I could give you some really touching instances of the affection of the men as they are of daily occurrence. They say that they look upon me as their father—Many of the officers have recd. letters from home commanding them to love and obey me as such. If my officers and men understand their duty they would do it. A large part of my labor is on account of their ignorance and inexperience.

Our Adjt., Nelson,[1] had a hemmorhage from his lungs and had to be sent home. Mr. Cooke is acting Adjt. and has his hands so full that he has very little time to write letters. When I am not engaged with my appropriate duties I am overrun by company, or am with the Gen'l., who treats me with marked respect. My Regt. is by long odds the crack Regt. of the Brigade and the Gen'l. is quite proud of us.—He camps in our rear and my men are sentinels at his tent.

But for the jealousy between Floyd & Wise the battle of Gauley or Carrifax's ferry would have been the most brilliant affair of the campaign, according to the forces engaged. We killed 2 cols. and killed or placed hors de combat upwards of 1000 of the enemy and lost not a man, 27 wounded most of them slightly.—If the N. C. & Geo. Regts. had been there we should now be in Charleston in the Kanawha Valley—

Gen'l. Lee is hourly expected in our camp, he will doubtless regulate matters.[2] We are also expecting reinforcements, both of infty & art every day. I think our position very strong. We fell back from Big Sewell on account of the difficulty in obtaing [sic] supplies. We can get them more easily here. We shall, six or eight weeks hence, if we do not cross into the valley of the Kanawha, fall back to White Sulphur Springs and go into winter quarters there.

Thus far we have done very hard service and the soldierly qualities of our men have been tried to the uttermost and they have satisfied me. We have not yet had a 10th. company assigned to us. We feel neglected by N. C. and we at the same time feel that we are fighting her battles as truly as if we trod her soil for if Western Va. is overrun, western N. C. will soon thereafter share the same fate, as well as eastern Tennessee.

I am sorry that your brother failed to raise his company Four of our Lieuts. have resigned and he could have been easily elected to fill one of the vacancies. My Regt. by experience has learned that my recommendations & appointments are not only good but the best. Our Q.M. has resigned[3] and on the recommendation of the Capts. I have nominated Farrell[4] my first Q.M.—Charley Q.M. Sergt. by his industry and energy has won golden opinions—He has gone to Jackson's River with a train of wagons for supplies. Jane is quite sick at Lewisburg, 14 miles east of us, with a cold neuralgia, etc. I doubt if she can stand this climate and the unavoidable exposure.

She was greatly grieved at parting from me.—I only reconciled her by promising if I was wounded or sick to send for her immediately

Tell the boys that I shall write to them as soon as I get time, which I hope will be in a few days. They would greatly enjoy the splendid mountain scenery by which we are surrounded—

We have daily accounts of the approach of the enemy and they scare the Virginians terribly, I wish they would come. They will now have to get supplies from as great a distance as we. If there should not be a very great disparity in numbers we shall whip them badly

I don't think Gov. Clark[5] is to blame about the coast defences & I hope you will always defend him, he is a warm friend of mine. Winslow[6] is a rascal and unfit for his position—

I find our old acq. Capt. Reynolds[7] here in command of a Va. Regt. Mr. Barton formerly of S. Anto. is our Brigade Commissary. Almost the 1st. thing he said to me was to praise "The Battle of Manassas."[8] Last Sunday one of our fellows said to Dr. Wilson[9] "Dr. what is the news from Noah and the ark?" "Why do you ask such a question?" says the Dr. "Because," was the reply, you seem to be reading a very old & greatly worn paper. The Dr. replied I carry this paper to read every Sunday Mrs. C's Battle of Manassas. Tories may sneer at it, damn it with faint praise etc. but I am proud that my wife wrote it, and I don't regret that your name was at the head, put there by others—Tories and traitors may make disparaging remarks about me, I care not; hereafter when the true hearted and patriotic speak in praise of the son of N. C. who came 2,000 miles to fight with his compatriots, when my sons' blood will leap with pleasure and mantle their cheeks proudly when they say *Col.*C. of the 14th. Regt. was my father, then I shall have a full recompense for all my trials both of *mind* & body. Let us look forward hopefully to that time, let us pray our Heavenly Father to grant us to see it!

I sent my pay acct. for last month $200 to Col. Beall at Richmond, with request to forward to you. Let me know when you receive it—You shall have every third one—one goes to pay my debts—a *part* of the other for the support of your *extravagant* husband. You must remember that Mr. Cooke is on my hands and that he has not had a cent except what I have given him or paid for him. Charley has recd. no pay and has been obliged to borrow from me, but when the Regt. is paid he can and will refund— I cannot *now* advise you relative to sendg the boys to Dr. Wilson[10] for I do not know with what regularity I shall be able to receive my pay. If it can be done I wish it. My pay acct. for this month will go to Maj. Maclin. I have loaned out to my officers nearly $100 as they have recd. no pay; but they will get it in about ten days and repay—I should not be surprised if a good deal that is said about me is prompted by envy—Mr. C's health has been very good. I have had 2 turns of sick head ache, caused by eating imprudently & immoderately of heavy and badly prepared food. My gen'l health is very good and I bear the fatigue of from 2 to 12 hours in the saddle amazingly—My men are greatly surprised by my endurance. I frequently march sometimes a day oftener less and they say I am a hardened old soldier—

I have written you my darling amidst very many interruptions hence the obscurity and incoherency of my letter, I hope you will however be enabled to understand this much that I love you sincerely and shall be while life lasts, Your affectionate husband, William J. Clarke

1. Richard M. Nelson of Wayne County became adjutant of the Fourteenth Regiment, NCV, on 18 August 1861. He resigned on 18 May 1862. Manarin and Jordan, *Roster of NC Troops,* 7:251.

2. Lee arrived at Wise's camp on 24 September and assumed command on 25 September. He strengthened the defenses at Sewell Mountain and ordered reinforcements from Floyd's troops. Clarke's regiment marched to Camp Defiance, Fayette Court House, on 24 September and then to Sewell Mountain. From 17 October through 12 November, the regiment stayed at Meadow Bluff and then moved to Blue Sulphur Springs, Virginia. It was at this point that the regiment's designation changed from the Fourteenth Regiment, NCV, to the Twenty-fourth Regiment, NCT, by Special Orders No. 222, Adjutant and Inspector General's Office, Richmond. Manarin and Jordan, *Roster of NC Troops,* 7:246.

3. Burrell P. Baker, formerly a second lieutenant in Co. K of the Fourteenth Regiment, NCV, became acting assistant quartermaster on 19 July 1861, and transferred to the Field and Staff. He transferred back to Co. K on or about 24 September 1861, where he served as first lieutenant. Manarin and Jordan, *Roster of NC Troops,* 7:251, 340.

4. John Farrell of Halifax County became assistant quartermaster on 14 October 1861. He was later detailed as quartermaster of General Matt W. Ransom's brigade on or about 1 October 1863. Manarin and Jordan, *Roster of NC Troops,* 7:251.

5. Henry Toole Clark, lawyer and state legislator, succeeded Ellis as governor of North Carolina on 7 July 1861. He served until 1 January 1863, when Zebulan Vance was elected governor. Crabtree, *North Carolina Governors,* 93–94; Boatner, *Civil War Dictionary,* 156.

6. Warren Winslow, a state legislator and United States congressman, was one of three people who advised Ellis on military affairs. When Hatteras fell to

Union forces in August 1862, Winslow was one of the officials blamed for the loss. *Edmondston Diary,* 86, 86n.

7. This may have been Captain Samuel H. Reynolds of the United States Army, who resigned 28 July 1861. He became colonel of the Thirty-first Virginia Infantry during the war. Heitman, *Historical Register,* 825.

8. "The Battle of Manassas" was one of Mary Bayard Clarke's most popular war poems. It appeared in the *Richmond Enquirer.*

9. Dr. William R. Wilson was appointed assistant surgeon of the Fourteenth Regiment, NCV, about 1 August 1861. Promoted to surgeon in January 1862, Wilson served through February 1865. Manarin and Jordan, *Roster of NC Troops,* 7:252.

10. The Reverend Alexander Wilson, originally from Ireland, ran an academy in Spring Grove, Granville County, North Carolina. He served as the first principal of Caldwell Institute in Greensboro, which opened in 1836. McPherson, "Unpublished Letters to Polk," 432.

*Macfarlane and Ferguson, Richmond, Va., Papers 1860–63 (Mss4M1645b), VHS*
*Mary Bayard Clarke to Macfarlane and Ferguson (Richmond)*

Hillsborough Sept 21st [1861]

Messirs McFarlane & Fergusson
Gentlemen

In the last issue of the Messenger you very politely enquire for Tenella and express a desire to know some thing of her present where-abouts. I hope after reading this you will not regret the inquiry or consider me, as I fear the heads of departments in this state do, "a weariful woman". I have not deserted the Messenger but my time and strength are now devoted to the sick soldiers of the army generally, and of my husbands regiment particularly, "The Battle of Manassa" [*sic*] was composed in the cars while on my way to the encampment of the 14th at Weldon N C and before I had time to do more than copy it out fairly was seized by an officer of the 2d N C T, then encamped at Norfolk. he took it to his camp and read it to the officers who after giving me three cheers sent up to Weldon to request the liberty of publishing it, I had already given it to my friend the Hon C M Conrad of Louisiana, then in Richmond but of course could after such a compliment, do nothing but place it in the hands of the officer sent to make the request, and it was by him published in the Enquirer.

A day or two ago I was requested to have it printed on letter paper and sold for the benefit of the sick soldiers of the 14th Being an old contributor to the Raleigh Standard the editor[1] got it up for me in the style you see, and one of the book sellers of Raleigh offered to dispose of the copies; I have had applications for it from all parts of the Confederate States, and shall get the Edtr of the N O Picayune for whom I have written a good deal to issue it in New Orleans in the same style; and now write to request the same favour of you. I think it would sell well in Richmond if it were known for what purpose it is sold, I have not at present any friend in the city to attend to it and if you think after paying for the outlay you would incur that any thing could be realized for our hospital fund, if even only a few dollars, I should feel proud to think I had by it, not only celebrated the prowess of our brave army, but added a mite to the comfort of our sick.

I am at present with one of my sisters, and a letter addressed to me care of Josiah Turner Esq Hillsborough N Carolina, will reach me. As soon as the climate will permit I shall go for the winter to my father Mr Thomas P Devereux's plantation on the Roanoke river,[2] I shall probably have much more time at my disposal there and will gladly devote some of it to the Messenger. I am considered a pretty good proof reader, and if you need assistance in that or any other way while your corps of the office is reduced by the war, it will give me great pleasure to do any thing in my power to aid you. I spoke yesterday to Dr Reed who is lecturing for the benefit of the sick, about writing some articles for the Messenger and he has promised to send me something. While in Texas many of my short pieces were published there and in New Orleans, since my return my friends have begged me to republish many of them and if you would like them for the Messenger I will send them to you instead of the Standard Please let me hear from you soon as I shall leave this for Raleigh in about three weeks

Very respectfully
Mary B Clarke

1. William Woods Holden.
2. Conneconara.

❧

*Barden Collection*
*William J. Clarke to Mary Bayard Clarke*

Camp Defiance near Sewell Mtn.
Oct. 15th. 1861.

My Dear Wife:

Your very welcome letter of the 2nd. inst. with the copies of the Battle of Manassas came to hand on the 7th. inst. and was very cheering to me in my desolate and unpleasant situation in this wild and inhospitable country

We have now been here three weeks and our men have been sickening every day and several have died in the hospitals and in our camp at Meadow Bluff; tho' we have had only three deaths at this camp. We buried only one here and he being a hard shell Baptist I obtained the services of a preacher of that denomination from the Georgia Regt. I tho't before that "the Harp of a thousand strings" was a burlesque; but I don't think so now. I wish that I had written the sermon down & should have done so but for the solemnity of the occasion. He told the soldiers that they should deport themselves as correctly in camp as if they were at home under the observation of friends &c. & enlarged on the idea, finally he said "yes fellow soldiers you should behave as well in this country "the same similar like" of which I never have seen, tho' I have travelled up and down for 20 years preaching the gospel, as if it was a good country."

You learned from my letter of the 6th and by Mr. Cooke's letter to Frank that the Yankees gave us the slip on that day. Why they did so is a mystery as they were 15,000 strong there is little doubt. We could not follow them immediately on account of the scarcity of provisions and the want of transportation, but Gen'l Floyd is pursuing them on another road (they are on the turnpike) with 3,000. My Regt. did not go with him on account of the large number of our sick. I called on Gen'l. Lee today with Surgeon Brown[1] and represented the "hygenic" condition of the Regt., the typhoid character that the sickness assumed & that they could not stand a march and obtained permission to fall back to Meadow Bluff, 15 miles east, and shall send off three companies tomorrow, and the rest of the Regt as soon as I can obtain wagons to transport tents &c for the rest. Our sick have been sent principally to the Blue Sulpur Springs 6 miles from M Bluff. We have now only about 300 men for duty—Lieut. Wm. H. Perry[2] of Johnston County who had been sick for some time at M Bluff died there last night and we have some 30 there very sick. I think that measles and our long stay on the Roanoke together with very great fatigue and unparalleled exposure in a very inclement season has caused the sickness. Bad [illegible] & the want of flannel shirts have also largely contributed to the deplorable result. A few barrels of good whiskey would have saved many lives but we have not had stimulus even for our sick. It should be a lesson to our commanders to provide supplies and means of transporting them always before moving any considerable body of troops. Gen'l Lee is very much mortified that he has been unable to do so little but the fault was not his. He had to repair all the blunders of that mad-man Wise and to contend with a very rainy time, roads almost impassable, a sparsely settled country and a hostile or at best cowardly and indifferent local population —No man can contend against wind and tide successfully—and it is something to have caused a larger and better appointed army under the famed Rosencrantz[3] to retire precipitately. They burned several wagons, a large lot of pork and left some tents & horses. I send to the children some relics picked up by Charley on their camping ground on the top of Sewell. Now that it is all over I will tell you that Col. Ector[4] of Ga. and I offered to attack the enemy immediately in front of us and to drive them from the top of the mountn. but Gen'l. Lee would not consent. It now turns out that we should have fallen upon about 5,000 men! They were encamped on every level spot for eight miles. The 14th. & the Georgians have always been eager for a fight. I see very little chance for one this season and think that in the course of the next 2 weeks we shall go into winter quarters at Staunton, White Sulphur or Charlottsville [sic][5] or somewhere on the Railroad—

I read your poetry to Col. Lucius Davis,[6] quite a hero, and two or three other old gentlemen and they all wept. I gave a copy to Gen'l. Lee and he expressed himself highly delighted & sent his respects to you.

Oct. 16 —I wrote thus far last night amid many interruptions when my back ached so bad from leaning over a large book on my knee that I stopped. I am now in command of Floyds Brigade and shall tomorrow move my Regt. and a part of the Mississippi 20th. to Meadow Bluff. I sent off today two companies & should have sent more but could not obtain transportation—We have now had three days without rain, tho' it is cloudy & lowering today & we look for rain or more probably snow. The overcoats will be most welcome, and when the wintry winds howl, and the icy rains fall you may enjoy the comfortable feeling that by your exertions many a poor fellow is sheltered and many a life saved. The Regt. has been informed of your exertions in their behalf and feel deeply grateful to you. Lieut. Bailey[7] could not bring the box further than Richmond and we have not yet received it. It would be a great blessing to us now as we have a large number of sick and no medicine. Our surgeons are absent attending to our sick at M Bluff and Blue Sulphur springs and I have been today practicing the Thompsonian system with blackberry and poplar root bark successfully.—My impression is that the war operations during the winter will be confined to *demonstrations* on the Potomac, and active operations on the Ohio & Mississippi and the sea coast. Our Regt. should be so located in winter quarters that we may, with our Brigade, cooperate in any—

Oct. 17—I was interrupted at the bottom of the last page 1st by the arrival of the mail, bringing no letter from you however, but I hardly expected one and so far from complaining am agreeably disappointed in hearing from you so often. On my part, I hope to be able to write to you oftener hereafter, and under more comfortable circumstances. I am getting too popular at head quarters for comfort. My Major is very sick, Lieut. Col.[8] is at Blue Sulphur 6 miles from MB in charge of over 1000 sick and I without them or a Quarter Master have not only to command my Regt. but do a good deal more.

Gen'l. F. speaks of me in the highest terms as a sensible man an accomplished and energetic officer and tells the other officers "you may rest assured Col. C will do it," when he puts any duty on me. Gen'l. Lee apologised yesterday for calling on me so often, but intimated that he could find no other officers on whom he could depend. They say of our Regt that even our sentinels on post can be known by their soldierly bearing—that my camp is the best regulated of any in the division &c— I send to Frank & Willie a piece of poetry from a well worn paper I got in camp a few days ago—and to the children some scraps of envellopes picked up by Charley in the Yankee Camp on the top of Sewell. The second interruption was a visit from Col. L. Davis who informs me that a lady who had been taken prisoner by the enemy and knew the number of their forces at Sewell says that there were at least 20,000 led by Rosencrantz in person

You ask me what I wish you to send me. In reply I would inform you that your thoughtful affection has so well supplied me that I do not need any thing—I shall write to the boys when I have opportunity & with love to all subscribe myself

Your affectionate husband<br>William J. Clarke

Please let me know when and what you hear from Nora[9]

1. Bedford Brown of Person County was appointed surgeon of the Fourteenth Regiment on 18 July 1861. He resigned around 25 October 1861. Manarin and Jordan, *Roster of NC Troops,* 7:252.

2. William H. Perry, third lieutenant, Co. I, Fourteenth, NCV, enlisted at the age of twenty-one. He died at Meadow Bluff, Virginia, between 14 and 15 October 1861. Manarin and Jordan, *Roster of NC Troops,* 7:332.

3. General William Starke Rosecrans of Ohio commanded the Army of Occupation from 23 July through 11 October 1861, and the Department of West Virginia from 11 October 1861, through 11 March 1862. Boatner, *Civil War Dictionary,* 708.

4. Colonel Walton Ector of Georgia. He served in the United States Army before the war and was mustered out on 15 July 1848. He was colonel of the Thirteenth Georgia Volunteers until his death on 1 February 1862. Heitman, *Historical Register,* 396.

5. Clarke's regiment was transferred from Blue Sulphur Springs to Petersburg to recover from sickness and exhaustion. The entire regiment reassembled in winter quarters near Petersburg and named their encampment Camp Refuge or Camp Refugio. Manarin and Jordan, *Roster of NC Troops,* 7:246.

6. J. Lucius Davis was a lieutenant colonel of the Tenth Virginia Cavalry under Jeb Stuart. He was promoted to full colonel on 24 September 1864. F. Ray Sibley Jr., *The Army of Northern Virginia,* vol. 1 of *The Confederate Order of Battle,* (Shippensburg, Pa.: White Mane Publishing, 1966), 19, 238n. 186 (hereafter cited as Sibley, *Confederate Order of Battle*).

7. Lieutenant James C. Bailey of Person County was appointed first lieutenant of Co. H, Fourteenth Regiment, NCV, on 6 June 1861, and promoted to captain on 16 May 1862. Wounded several times during the war, he died from wounds on 7 June 1864. Manarin and Jordan, *Roster of NC Troops,* 7:320.

8. Thomas Brown Venable was appointed lieutenant colonel of the regiment on 18 July 1861. He was defeated for reelection on 16 May 1862. Manarin and Jordan, *Roster of NC Troops,* 7:251.

9. Mary Bayard Clarke's sister, Nora Devereux Cannon, then living in Tennessee.

*Barden Collection*
*William J. Clarke to Mary Bayard Clarke (Conneconara)*

Camp Polk, Blue Sulphur Springs
November 14th. 1861

My Dear Wife:

Since my last (6th. inst.) I recd. yours of the 2nd. and the letter to Jane which I only today found an opportunity to send to her. I was rejoiced to hear that you were well tho' I am concerned to learn that you have a cold. I dread the effect of the winter on you, but trust that you may pass thro' it not only safely but comfortably; but your strength not only of body and constitution but of endurance and forbearance will be sorely tried. As for me God be praised! my health is excellent. I never had such an appetite. You would be surprised to see me at breakfast, dinner would surprise you more, supper most. I am really getting fat. Our cooks are good and Capt. Williams,[1] the Commissary, who with Farrel the QM constitute my mess, is an excellent provider. Cooke & Adjt. Nelson mess together. It was best for C. to be with his company and our mess was too large for our table. If you could look into my tent you would see that it is quite cosy and, except in windy weather, a tent with plenty of stoves in it is quite comfortable. So far from being unhappy I have not been so happy in years and my heart is full of thankfulness, I feel that I am doing my duty and am serviceable to my country and most of all that *you* are satisfied with me. Yes! even when I was on the top of Sewell drenched with rain and pinched with hunger I was a happier man than for long weary months at San Antonio. I praise God for his goodness in changing my situation and delivering me from that trying and dependent situation.—After many delays in consequence of rain I succeeded in getting the whole of my Regt. down to this place with the exception of a few sick men who were too sick to move and their attendants.

One of them has died since, and the rest will be in a condition allowing of their removal in a few days. Our sick are almost to a man recovering but I have to be as careful with them as a mother with a set of croupy children.—We have at last recd. our over-coats and blankets and shoes. Supplies of clothing from different counties are coming in every day, and we begin to be more cheerful; but the men are frightened by the fever and as there can be nothing to occupy their thoughts, still there is a cloud over us. We have so much rain and mud that I am unable to drill often, and the men being unoccupied are very fair subjects for disease

Lieut. Snead,[2] the Iago of our Regt., has resigned and gone home. Maj. Evans is sick and, today, went to Covington. He can get my permission to go any where he chooses. He is despised in the Regt. and no one asks or cares about him—

You ask me about a Surgeon. I have recommended Dr. Wilson for (principal) Surgin & Duffy[3] (who was 2nd. asst.) for assistant—The C.S. allow but two tho' N.C. allows Surgn. & 2 assts.—As to Pierce,[4] I don't know what to say. I never thought much of him, indeed I rather thought him tainted with the rascal; but I might have been wrong. No one seems disposed to come to us. I have tried to get three and failed, and if P. gives satisfaction I feel rather disposed to recommend him for the appointment. The salary is only $600 and rations. I see by the papers that he was to leave about this time. If he has succeeded in drumming up a good supply of necessaries for us, he will be entitled to our gratitude.—I have sent wagons to Jackson's River Depot to bring up any boxes we may have there; but I fear that the box sent by Lieut. Bailey will never come to hand. I have sent by several who were passing to look for it but can hear nothing of it. Was it marked on the box or was there merely a paper on it? Capt. Dillehay[5] of Person, (Roxboro) left 1st. inst. sickly, on 30 days leave, Capt. Crockett,[6] Clayton Johnston Co. on 7th sick and scared—Lieut. O. Blocker[7] of Fayetteville should be on his way here also Capt. Lane of Johnston Co.— I mention these that you may inform any one who may ask you that these men will *probably* attend to any thing they wish to send. The wretched arrangment on the Va. railroads renders it difficult to get any thing on.

I was glad to hear of the birth of Nora's son[8] and hope that both mother and child may be spared. I fear that your Father will find difficulty in getting back home if he has not yet returned.—I see by the papers that Mr. Turner's military carreer has not been interdicted by the people, likewise that Ab. Venable[9] has permission to stay at home. How I pity a politician, how I despise one who for the sake of preferment barters away all manliness and independence!

Our present encampment is sheltered and pleasant as any place can be in this latitude. It was very bleak at Meadow Bluff. I shall reserve a description of the place for a letter which I shall commence tomorrow to one or both of the boys. I will also therein attempt a description of your mare, Lady Mary Davis, the prettiest thoroughbred you ever saw, tho' she does not now look very well having gone thro' the campaign. Bill Barrett[10] after enduring all exposure & fatigue, ten days ago fell thro' a causway and hurt his left hind ankle which caused him to fall off a good deal but he is now again almost fit for duty. He is the smartest horse I ever saw, and is a great favourite in the Regt.

It is raining again and thundering while I write. Mr Farrell arrived safely and the box from Robeson has since come with his horse & servant who had to be left behind in consequence of a break in the Railroad. I have been so busy that I have not opened the box, having indeed forgotten it. I must tell you of my luck in presents today, first a paper of molasses candy then a bale of splendid smoking tobacco, then a lot of paper and envellopes, then a N.C. ham, sweet potatoes, and some pound cake—pretty good for one day! But I omitted to state that I had two invitations to dinner one to eat chicken and squirrel pie, the other turkey, and also an invitation to tea—I have been benefitted by the mineral water at this place. I consider it equal, if not superior to White Sulphur. One can drink a large quantity without any inconvenience, it sets light on the stomach and has a beneficial effect on the whole system, I am so fond of it that I have to restrain myself, and in addition I am doubtful about the effect of sulphur in cold weather—

When I reached the bottom of the last page in the ardor of composition I had neglected my candle and it gave out, having no other in the tent as it was raing quite hard I did not call James[11] to bring me one tho' he would have gotten up and brought it most cheerfully. He is a very fine servant, intelligent cheerful and very attentive and seems strongly attached to me. I do not think him *rashly* courageous; at all events when we were marching to Sewell last time and expected a battle certainly he yielded with a good grace to my command to stay at Meadow Bluff & take care of my tent. He did excellent service in cooking and forwarding provisions; and when I sent for him seemed quite rejoiced to see me, and performed all the service for the mess which was quite onerous to admiration

Nov. 15. This is fast day but the ground is so wet and it looks so like for rain that I can have no religious services. In this connection I may state that while in Sewell Gen'l. Lee informed me that we might expect an attack of the enemy on the morning of the 4th. Sept. and to be prepared, as my position would probably be the point assailed. I told him that I did not expect it and gave him my reasons, but told him moreover that if they did come there they would get hurt. Read the Psalm (the 20th) for that day & mark its appropriateness—God is indeed with us, and as He delights to exalt those who humble themselves before Him, if we "enter His temple gates" with humility and in contrition of soul offer before him the prayer of faith his loving mercies will descend upon us like the dew of Hermon, and like the rain upon the growing corn.

Since the death of poor Charley[12] I feel that the bond to which my soul's seal is set was cemented with his blood and whoever may desert the cause, whoever may flag or falter, onward is my cry till not an inch of southern soil is pressed by the footstep of in invader.

I learn that Gen'l. Floyd is again falling back. If such be the case I am happy that I am not with him as he is in the presence of the enemy. We have never been compelled to retire in the presence of the enemy. When we marched back from Anderson's, eight miles beyond Seawell there was not a Federal in ten miles of us. We then were in the rear at a long distance from the rest of the Brigade. While at Meadow Bluff I encamped in the rear next the enemy. Here in this valley I could keep out the whole of Rosencrantz's army. I have less than 150 men for duty but could, on an emergency, "rustle up" 400 fighting men.

I am impatiently waiting a reply to my letter to Secty of War [Judah P. Benjamin] respectg. winter quarters. Tell Tom that "fardy" will send him some "tanny" when some one comes along. Kiss Pet & the boys for me.

Kind regards to your Father & Ma, love to Susy and "heaps" of it to you from

Your affectionate husband<br>
William J. Clarke

1. John A. Williams became commissary of the regiment on or about 19 July 1861. He was present for duty until his position was abolished by the Confederate congress on or about 1 July 1863. Manarin and Jordan, *Roster of NC Troops,* 7:251–52.

2. Charles H. Snead served as first lieutenant of Co. I, Fourteenth Regiment, NCV. He resigned on 12 December 1861. Manarin and Jordan, *Roster of NC Troops,* 7:332.

3. Dr. Charles Duffy Jr., an 1859 graduate of a New York medical school, began the war as first sergeant of Co. B, Fourteenth Regiment. He transferred to the regiment's Field and Staff following his appointment as acting assistant surgeon on or about 29 July 1861. Appointed assistant surgeon on 17 April 1862, he was assigned to permanent duty with the Field and Staff until he transferred to the Fifty-fourth Regiment, NCT, on or about 23 April 1864. Manarin and Jordan, *Roster of NC Troops,* 7:252; Ashe, *Cyclopedia of Eminent and Representative Men,* 2:226–27.

4. No physician named Pierce ever served with the regiment.

5. John G. Dillehay enlisted at the age of thirty-three. He was appointed captain on 5 May 1861, but he was defeated for reelection on or about 10 May 1862. Manarin and Jordan, *Roster of NC Troops,* 7:254.

6. George W. Crocket, who resided in Wake County, was appointed captain of Co. C, Fourteenth Regiment, NCV, on 15 May 1861. He was defeated for reelection on 8 May 1862. Manarin and Jordan, *Roster of NC Troops,* 7:275.

7. Octavious H. Blocker of Co. F, Fourteenth Regiment, NCV, enlisted on 1 June 1861, as first sergeant but was appointed second lieutenant on 18 July 1861. He was present or accounted for until transferred to Second Co. C, Thirty-sixth Regiment, NCT, on 15 February 1862. Manarin and Jordan, *Roster of NC Troops,* 7:301.

8. Robert Cannon Jr.

9. Abraham Watkins Venable served as a United States congressman from North Carolina from 1847 to 1853. He was elected to the Confederate congress in 1861. A. R. Newsome, ed., "Letters of Lawrence O'Bryan Branch, 1856–1860," *NCHR* 10 (Jan. 1933), 64n; Wilfred B. Yearns Jr., "North Carolina in the Confederate Congress," *NCHR* 29 (July 1952), 361, 361n.

10. Colonel Clarke's favorite horse.

11. A Clarke slave.

12. Clarke's half-brother, Charles Clarke, died at Blue Sulphur Springs on 3 November 1861, of "bilious pneumonia." Manarin and Jordan, *Roster of NC Troops,* 7:252.

❧

*Wootten, Moulton, Clarke Papers, SHC*
*William J. Clarke to Mary Bayard Clarke*

Petersburg Va. Dec. 17th. 1861.

My Dear Wife:

Hoyle says, when you are playing whist, and are at a loss what to do, play trumps, which I modify by saying when you have a leisure moment write to your absent wife: hence this letter. I am now staying at the Bolling Brook hotel, but the last detachment of my Regt. arrived today and I shall, tomorrow, go the the Model Farm 1 1/2 miles from town where my Regt. is quartered, and stay there until you come to see me when we will go to a boarding house. The citizens of Petersburg are delighted to have us here and the conduct of my Reg't. and the high reputation which they have brought with them renders them still more favorably disposed to us.—On my arrival here after leaving you I found a telegraphic despatch from Farrell Q.M. requesting me to come to Richmond. I went and staid one day. I saw Withers,[1] Myers[2] and Beall,[3] and for a moment Mr. Conrad. I am informed that I can be made Brig. Gen'l. for the asking. Old Abe Venable stopped the nomination of McRae by saying that he would not vote for any N.C. man until I was made Gen'l., others seconded him and hence McR. was dropped. I don't want to be a Gen'l. but I do want to be Col. in the Reg. Army. I have written to Genls. Floyd and Lee for recommendations and will bring all N.C. & Texas to back me, and do not doubt I shall succeed. My friends in R. (and I have some in the War office) urged me to apply for Brig Genl The devotion of my *men* to me is most touching and I receive assurances of it every day that are very affecting. We shall have quite a ceremony on giving up our number; you know that we are to be the 24th.—Daniel's[4] Regt is the 14th. He must come with his staff to receive the flag and the number. You shall be present to see it. Mr. Cooke will come on, in a few days, to see you. I cannot now say when exactly but will write you several days before hand. I hope to have him to spend Christmas week with you.—You must come to me, Darling, for I need you, I am entitled to a little rest, and while I do not feel at liberty to leave my Regt. still I may have the enjoyment of your society.—My Cousin Dr. Couch[5] and his wife are very kind and invite us to make their house our home. That I will not do, but we will pay them a visit.

I took *Cooke* to see Mary Pettigrew,[6] at Dr. Beckwith's[7] and you never saw a man so completely captivated. I must confess that she never appeared better, though she left a sick bed to see us. The Bs went into ecstacies over me and C. was quite overwhelmed. A good many NCs visit us, and by the time I see them they have drunken pretty deeply and their maudlin adulation is to me laughable but C. cannot understand it, and thinks that they are crazy about me.

I recd. a letter today from Tom Maclin, San Antonio, acknowledging the reciept of my remittance in payment of the loan.—If the Muses are proptious, what say you to a "pome" on giving up the flag and the No.?

Some of the Regts. which have lately passed thro' have behaved most disgracefully but the 14th. have on all occasions deported themselves as gentlemen.

I remained in Richmond only part of a day and consequently did not see Rachel,[8] nor did I get your sister Kate's dresses but expect to go to R. again in a few days.—I hope the Hospital folks attended to your Father's request I brought it very distinctly to their attention. I am kept pretty busy with one thing and another, and shall be, until we get our quarters finished.

This is a very stupid letter and I will close

Very affectionately
Your husband
William J. Clarke

1. Jones Mitchell Withers was a United States Army veteran, lawyer, commission merchant, and Confederate general who served throughout the war. Boatner, *Civil War Dictionary*, 944–45.

2. Abraham C. Myers, a United States Army veteran, was the Confederate quartermaster from 28 January 1861, to 10 August 1863. Boatner, *Civil War Dictionary*, 577.

3. This possibly was the Colonel Lloyd J. Beall of Richmond that Clarke mentioned in a letter to his wife dated 15 September 1861. William J. Clarke to Mary Bayard Clarke, Barden Collection.

4. Colonel Junius Daniel of Halifax County served with this regiment until elected colonel of the Forty-fifth Regiment, NCT, on or about 14 April 1862. Manarin and Jordan, *Roster of NC Troops*, 5:393.

5. Dr. C. F. Couch was a physician and founding member of the Petersburg Medical Faculty. John Herbert Claiborne, *Seventy-five Years in Old Virginia* (New York: Neale Publishing, 1904), 114.

6. This possibly was the Mary L. Pettigrew who was one of three "ladies" who volunteered their services as head nurses in Petersburg hospitals during the war. Clark, *Histories of the Several Regiments*, 4:624.

7. Dr. John Beckwith, formerly of Raleigh and a noted eye specialist, had moved to Petersburg in 1845. He was married to Margaret Cogdell Stanly of New Bern. Johnson, *Ante-bellum North Carolina*, 745; Powell, *DNCB*, 1:126.

8. This was one of Mary Bayard Clarke's nieces, the daughter of Elizabeth (Betsy) Jones.

☙

Barden Collection
Mary Bayard Clarke to Eliza Primrose (Raleigh)

Petersburgh Jan 3rd [1862]

My dear Mrs Primrose[1]

I intended writing to you before I left Conneconara but I was so hurried and so unwell I could not do so, we got here last monday and instead as I hoped of going to a boarding house and having a little quiet enjoyment with William, came to Dr Couche's where they seem trying how much they can do to make us comfortable and happy; but unfortunately I am so unwell I can enjoy nothing but my horse. I ride every day and hope it will do me good for I must be very poor company to any one just now

Your boys seemed to enjoy themselves very much at Father's and quite won his heart by their gentlemanly behavior, mine were quite reconciled to returning with them, but the parting with them was a great trial to me. I dont know what my plans will be for William seems to have none except to keep me with him which I fear he cant do long. Mr Cooke after spending a week at Father's went down to Johnson Co and will pass through Raleigh, he promised me to call on you and also on Mr Mason[2] and see how the boys were getting along, please tell him when you see him that I wrote to him and ask him to go to the office if he has not done so for I want him to attend to some business for me before he returns here. I gave the boys 50cts for pocket money and told them they must depend on you for any more they have never had much as I have generally supplied them with all they needed and I would rather they had but little at a time, and not more than your boys have. I intended making them each another pair of flannel drawers and a shirt but had not time will you please have them made I sent the material by them and also some night shirts, any thing else they need please get, and let me know before all their money is gone that I may be sure and have it replenished. I would like to have them go to sunday school and church at least once on sunday and requested Mr Mason to take charge of their sunday teaching as well as their weekly but I dont by any means object to their going with you occasionally I think children as a general rule had better attend the church of which their parents are members, but I know they will often wish to go with you and hope you will take them. If they are sick I would rather Dr Fab Hawood[3] should attend them but I hope they wont need any physician I feel very sad at parting with them and some times think I ought not to give you all the trouble of them but William is so much opposed to my leaving him and so unwilling for me to stay in Raleigh that I can do nothing else and as I know you will do *any thing* you undertake to do *well* I try to feel it is all for the best. Please give my love to them and to your boys and believe me very affectionately yours M B Clarke

PS The boys bibles were left in Texas and they have been using mine will you please get them each a good plain one

1. Eliza Primrose lived in Raleigh with her sons John, William, and Robert. The family were members of Raleigh's First Presbyterian Church. John Primrose joined Co. E, Twenty-fourth Regiment, NCT, as a private on 6 November 1862. He was promoted to ordnance sergeant on 28 June 1863, and transferred to the Field and Staff. He served through February 1865. Manarin and Jordan, *Roster of NC Troops,* 7:253, 299; Powell, *DNCB,* 5:147.

2. Reverend Richard Sharpe Mason, the Episcopal minister of Christ Church in Raleigh.

3. Dr. Fabius J. Haywood, a Raleigh physician, was the brother of Edmund Burke Haywood. Ashe, *Cyclopedia of Eminent and Representative Men,* 2:230.

*Barden Collection*
*Mary Bayard Clarke to Frank Clarke (Raleigh)*

Petersburgh Jan 5th [1862]

My dear Frank

As you are the eldest I shall write to you first and next sunday to Willie; I want you to answer all of my letters and that will give you a letter once a fortnight to write and me one once a week. I got here last monday very well (for me) but very tired and am staying with your father's cousins Dr and Mrs Couch, they have a son Emett a little older than you, a daughter just the age of sister, named Mattie and a little boy of five who plays with Tom named Jimmey; besides they have a sister of Mrs Couche's named Laura Young who lives with them. They live about half a mile from Father's quarters which is very convenient for him. I rode out to the camp last week on my new horse lady Mary, and it made me feel very sad to see the regiment looking so reduced and feeble, but so many are absent on leave, that I cannot judge correctly of them. The ladies of Petersburgh gave them a dinner on New Year's day at Poplar lawn. I went down to see the tables and saw more turkeys than I have seen all put together in six years there was enough to have dined the whole regiment and only a quarter of them were there. Father is going over to Richmond next week and wants me to go with him but I dont feel well enough to enjoy it, and would rather not go. if I do I will tell you of all the great folks I see and how they look but I am not now strong enough to enjoy sight seeing or any thing but a ride on horse back the sight of you and Willie would give me more pleasure than that of all the great men in Richmond Mr Cooke went to see Mr Mason when he was in Raleigh and told him to expect you and Willie when you write tell me frankly how you like him and what you think of him I hope you will get along pleasantly through the winter remember that it costs a great deal to keep you at school and dont waste your time I put you in Raleigh instead of at Dr Wilsons because I thought you would be happier there. I shall see you in the Spring and next August if nothing happens to prevent you will go to Dr. Wilson's you will then be older and I hope wiser. Give my love to Willie and to Mrs Primrose and her boys also to Auntie and thank her for Tom's cap which fits him very well

Dont forget what I told you about controling your temper and being kind to everybody. I want you to enquire for a letter for Mr Cooke at the PO and send it to me when you answer this God bless you both my dear boys and keep you pure. Dont forget your little sister, I know you will always remember

your affectionate
Mother
MBC—

❧

*Barden Collection*
*Mary Bayard Clarke to Willie Clarke (Raleigh)*

Petersburgh
Jan 12th [1862]

My dear Willie

I have now been two weeks seperated from you and want to see you so much, I feel as if it were two months since we parted. I am still at Dr Couch's but hope to get a boarding place this week near the quarters I am better than when I wrote Frank, for I ride on horse back nearly every day and that always does me good. Tom is very well and right bad, but so sweet when he is good. Yesterday I dressed him in his Zouave suit and put him on my horse Lady Mary, and sent him down town he rode very well and was delighted, "only James would not make Lady galop or give him a switch;" the people all ran out to look at him and seemed astonished to see him sitting so fearlessly in the saddle; he was so much pleased with the bugle on Mr Cooke's cap that he immediately begged one for his, Mr Cooke got it for him and he rides up to the quarters now and calls himself *Turnel* Clarke; the soldiers all salute him and think it is a fine joke to see him taking airs on himself. I have asked Father about your gun several times and he always promises to write about it but he is so busy he has not a moment he says to spare but if he does not get it Mr Cooke will buy you a new one as soon as it is possible to get it at a reasonable price, at present things cost so much it is like throwing away money to spend it. I hope you will write and tell me how you like Mr Mason. Study your lessons at home and dont get onto an idle way of half learning them. I feel as if I could not bear being seperated from you and Frank and want you to make good use of your time so that we may soon be together again. Give my love to Mrs Primrose and the boys and when you write to me tell me if you want any thing. Give my love to Auntie and tell her that old Dr Beckwith is very sick with errysipelas and Mrs Beckwith thinks will never recover Dr Tom Beckwith[1] is also very sick with inflamatory sore throat and they are very uneasy about him. Tell me when you write if you have been to see Aunt Margaret and how they all are out there; have you begun your scrap book yet? What do you think the Battle of Manassas was printed in Alexandria smuggled into Baltimore, set to music and sung by the ladies until the police forbid it and seized all the copies they could find, one lady told them they could never efface it from the hearts of the women of Baltimore no matter how hard they rubbed. There are a great many refugees here and one of them sent and asked me for a copy of it she said she knew they would take it from her when she passed so she left it with her sister who remained in Baltimore.

Mr Cooke sends his love and says he will write to you both before long tell Frank I am looking for a letter from him Sister has already written to me God bless you both my darling boys be very obedient to Mrs Primrose and dont forget your dear

Mother

1. Dr. Thomas Stanly Beckwith of Petersburg, the son of Dr. John Beckwith. Powell, *DNCB*, 1:126.

*Bagby Papers, MSS 1B1463b475–482, VHS*
*Mary Bayard Clarke to George Bagby*

Petersburgh Jan 13th [1862]

Dr. Bagby

Dear Sir

Some time last October or November I directed a Government messenger to deposit with you for safe keeping three boxes of hospital supplies for the 14th N C Vs and wrote requesting you to take charge of them for me. I have never been able to find out whether they reached you and write now to beg you will let me know, as I have lost sight of the messenger though by writing to the Quarter Master Gen. of NC I could I suppose find him.

I am now, Col Clarke says, commanding the cavalry of the 14th which means they have gone into winter quarters in this place, and the officers having not much to do after three o'clock put themselves—as the Spanish caballeros would say—"at my disposition" for a ride on horse back. which proves so delightful to me that I cant be tempted to leave my horse and go to Richmond even for a few days.[1] A friend of mine says the Southern women are very patriotic about sending their husbands, brothers, and lovers to the war but demure when it comes to letting their horses go. but I think he slanders us though I have not yet been tried as I left mine in Texas and have only just succeeded in replacing them with a beautiful little mare which the Col brought me from the mountains.

If you can spare time to come over I will give you a mount if you are inclined to ride and show you *my* regiment now reduced by sickness death and furlough, to about two hundred, but I really have not courage and strength of mind and body for Richmond

Very sincerely<br>M B Clarke

1. Decades after the war, Captain Charles S. Powell of Co. E, Twenty-fourth Regiment, NCT, recalled for the *Smithfield Herald* the one horseback ride he shared with Mary Bayard Clarke. Powell, who was only eighteen when he enlisted in 1861, described Mary Bayard as a "very beautiful and talented lady." He also remembered his "great surprise" when William Clarke "bade me be ready at 3 o'clock P.M. to escort Mrs. Clark on a horseback ride. My heart sank and nearly quit business for I had alwavs [sic] been a very bashful boy, had been in the society of ladies so little that I felt that I could not stand it." Manarin and Jordan, *Roster of NC Troops*, 7:293; letter from William S. Powell to Mary Barden, 12 January 1993, Barden Collection.

*Barden Collection*
*William J. Clarke to Mary Bayard Clarke*

Murfreesboro' N.C.[1]
March 3d. 1862

My dear Wife:

I have recd. your two sweet letters and they have been a great comfort to me. They breathe sentiments such as are characteristic of my true hearted noble minded and brave wife. When so many are despondent at the late reverses, when cowards are whispering with white lips the foe, the foe, they come they come, I am happy to be assured, tho' I doubted not that such was the case, that you bate not one jot or tittle of hope or confidence in the ultimate success of our cause. I am here with but a handful of men and they greatly scattered and still I feel confident that I shall be able to defend this country, for I know that a few determined men can accomplish wonders.

I have strong faith in the God of battles that He will deliver the enemy into my hands, and that I shall return to see my children a laurel crowned victor, then darling I can look into your beautiful eyes and see them lighted up with joy and pride and my happiness will be complete. I feel that God will strengthen me to do my duty and that He will shield me in the day of battle.

I am expecting reinforcements daily, and when I receive some ordnance I have applied for, I shall remove to Winton, 12 miles below this, on the Chowan, for by holding that place and stopping the enemy there, I protect the Meherrin, the Nottoway and the Blackwater Rivers.

I hope you will not set your heart on my being made General. Remember that I have neither political influence or wealth to back me, and that I remain at my post and perform my duty while others are at Richmond using every means to obtain the commission. Could I meet the enemy successfully I do not doubt I should be appointed but as matters stand I think the chances very evenly balanced, and do not suffer my mind to dwell upon it. The people down here are very anxious that I should be appointed. I was greatly gratified today to learn that the officers of the three companies of Wises Legion (cavalry) had had a meeting and resolved that if I was made Gen'l. they would withdraw from Wise and join me. The Lieut. (Bowden)[2] commanding a section of Artillery at Weldon declares that if Secty. of War will not allow him to come with me he will resign.

It is gratifying to know that one's companions in arms think him worthy even tho' he should not receive office and sooner or later it will come.

I am unable at present to advise you where to go. If you are pleasantly situated and have not outstaid your welcome why not remain where you are? So soon as Capt. Farrell arrives with money from Richmond I shall send you $100—I do not think you have been extravagant, and if you had been it would make no difference for all that I can save after paying expenses is for you, it pains me to spend money on myself; but I love to give it to you and I have no desire to know what you do with it.

I am getting things a little straight. and am not as hard worked as at first. I have ridden only twenty miles today and written only four letters tonight and I feel quite fresh now.

Present my kindest regards to Cousin Charles and Mary and Miss Laura[3] and kiss Tom for me

Affectionately Your husband

William J. Clarke

Give my love to Ma. I forgot to leave the sword and to send her the hair.[4] I have them both, and will send them when I send the money to you which I expect will be by one of my orderlies—

1. The Twenty-fourth Regiment, ordered to protect the railroad lines bringing supplies to Virginia, was moved from Petersburg, Virginia, to Garysburg, North Carolina, in February 1862. On 21 February the regiment moved to Murfreesboro. Clarke dispersed his companies at several locations in Virginia and North Carolina along the Petersburg & Weldon Railroad. Because of the confusion caused by having Clarke's troops stationed in two states, in May the regiment transferred from the Department of Norfolk to the Department of North Carolina under General Theophilus H. Holmes. Manarin and Jordan, *Roster of NC Troops*, 7:246.

2. Lemuel Henry Bowden, from New Hanover County, originally served as first lieutenant of artillery in Co. A, Thirty-sixth Regiment, NCT (Second Regiment, North Carolina Artillery). He resigned on 15 December 1862, because of ill health. Manarin and Jordan, *Roster of NC Troops*, 1:175.

3. Relatives of William J. Clarke.

4. The sword and hair belonged to Charley Clarke.

*Barden Collection*
*Mary Bayard Clarke to Frank and Willie Clarke*

Murfresboro March 19th [1862]

My dear boys

Your two letters reached me nearly a week ago and I would not have delayed replying so long had I not been first sick, and then very busy. I left Petersburg day before yesterday with Grand ma Clarke and Tom, Father sent his colored sargent[1] after us and before we could leave we had to get a pass from the Provost Marshal of the city, Martial law having been declared. We went through a gate into a yard where the cars were and as we passed were obliged to show our pass to two men with muskets, a little way further we had to show it again then when we got on the cars there was a another man stationed there who also wanted to see it; on every platform a militia man was stationed and we were guarded a mile out of town. We got to Weldon that night and staid all night Miss Pocahuntas and Mary Emma both enquired for you and sent their love. I had no servant with me and Tom was dreadfully insulted that he had to stay up stairs, he wanted to go down with the "other men" and the next morning as soon as he saw Mr Price he made him keep him until the cars came and spent the morning walking up and down the poach telling every one who asked him that he was Col Clarke going with his Mamma to see the regiment. We left there about one o'clock and got to Boykin depot at two. there we met father with a carriage and his saddle horses, after dinner I put on my riding dress and Tom sore against his will got in the carriage with Mr. Price and James My horse Lady Mary was lame so I rode a cavalry horse who had not been used to carrying ladies and kicked up his heels at a great rate, we found that the side saddle hurt his back and had to change it to Bill Barret Tom was so anxious to ride that I got into the carriage and let him ride for half a mile after which he went to sleep and slept until he got to this place—I rode all the way on horse back with Father except that half mile it is thirteen miles. I dont know how long I shall stay here but not long I think for I want to see Sister This is quite a village with two large female colleges[2] in it one a Methodist the other a Baptist Father has his men quartered in the Methodist which is the largest and we perhaps will go into the Baptist which is vacant. If he stays here until your vacation he will send for you to come and see him—You forgot to tell me how long your vacation would last I want to know so that I can make my arrangements. I sent you each a pair of boots some cloth for shirts jacket and pantaloons some socks and some marbles

Grand ma will stay in Halifax a week or ten days and when she goes to Raleigh you must go and see her I sent Mrs Primrose $40 by express to pay Mr Mason—you must tell him I had to wait after I got his bill until I could commmunicate with Father Tom has not been very well lately he has a bad cough that keeps both him and me awake at night and says the rain keeps him from sleeping, I believe he was more rejoiced at the sight of Bill Barret than of any one—He says he wishes Frank and Wee-wee would come here too. Give my love to Mrs Primrose and ask her to send any of

your socks that are worth knitting heels, or renovating in any way to Con-
noconara some time when Mosses[3] is passing Father and Mr Cooke send
love Mr Cooke says he wrote to Frank not long ago I hope he has received
the letter Write to me here and believe me

your affectionate<br>
Mother

1. This was a member of Clarke's regiment who carried the regimental flag
into battle.

2. By the 1850s, the town of Murfreesboro had two female academies. The
Baptist Chowan College opened in 1848. The Methodists established Wesleyan
Female College in March 1855. The main building of the Methodist college was
considered to be fine, being a four-story, brick building with a cupola and handsome veranda. William E. Stephenson, "The Davises, the Southalls, and the Founding of Wesleyan Female College, 1854–1859," *NCHR* 57 (July 1980): 257, 279.

3. A slave.

ॐ

*Barden Collection*
*Mary Bayard Clarke to Willie Clarke (Raleigh)*

Murfresboro April 7th [1862]

My dear Willie

I had a letter from Frank day before yesterday, but as it is your turn to
have one from me he must be satisfied with reading this until his turn
comes, which will be before very long. We are still living in Mr Smith's
house but expect to go to another this week, where we will remain until
we leave here I shall probably stay as long as Father does but I shall not
keep Sister with me all the time, and if Mr Mason gets scared, or Mrs
Primrose concludes to run away I shall have you come down, but I hope
that neither of these things will occur as it is very important that you boys
should continue at school until your session is out, and not leave before
vacation. You must be sure to take care of Mrs Primrose if the Yankee's do
come and not let them steal her chickens and destoy her garden which is
about all the harm they will do her, for I guess Lovey[1] would not care to
go to them and they would not care to steal her with all her children. Tom
has the hooping cough and is very cross and feverish with it, he does not
cough *very* hard but still it is hard enough to bring the tears into his eyes
and make him stamp his feet He hangs on me all the time and I never leave
him except to take a ride. When the weather is pleasant he rides out every
day—with Bob,[2] Mr Cooke's servant, Mr Cooke is Adjutant of the Brigade

which gives him the rank of Capt so he is now Capt Cooke, but he dont call himself so and had rather be with his company. I rode down to what is called the Devil's Elbow,[3] in the river, the other day Col Venable is camped there with five companies and a company of artillery, they have four guns and a breast work of logs and earth on a high bluff that rakes the bend of the river. I had a very pleasant ride and went into Col [Thomas] Venable's tent and rested while Father attended to his business.

Major [Jonathan] Evans is eight miles off with the rest of the regiment and as soon as we have a good day and Tom is well enough I am going to ride down there. I live almost as we used to in Texas except that I miss you boys and Mr Cooke very much, I have a sewing machine and that, with teaching sister and taking care of Tom occupies me all the morning, after dinner if Father cant ride with me I take James and ride about an hour, come home and keep Tom until he goes to sleep, have tea, then read to Sister till her bed time and after that read or write until I am sleepy. Father is in his office or drilling all day and I only see him at meals or when he has time to ride with me I am generally asleep when he comes home at night. Give my love to Mrs Primrose and when you write tell me when your vacation begins and how long it lasts tell me also if you have got the things I sent by Grand ma.

I want to see you oh so much and am looking forward to your vacation as anxiously as you are—

Good bye my darlings Sister sends love.

Your affectionate
Mother

1. A Primrose slave.
2. A slave owned by Oliver D. Cooke.
3. Companies A, E, and G of the Twenty-fourth Regiment were ordered to Devil's Elbow on the Meherrin River. Manarin and Jordan, *Roster of NC Troops,* 7:246.

❧

*Barden Collection*
*Mary Bayard Clarke to Frank Clarke (Raleigh)*

Murfresboro
April 22d [1862]

My dear Frank

As I have an opportunity to send a bundle to Raleigh I will put a letter in for you; the bundle is from Jane for Mary Lynch and you and Willie must take it to Mary Boon[1] and read Jane's letter to her. I have written it very plainly and think you can read it but you had better get Mrs Primrose to read it to you first and then before you go read it aloud to her and see if you have it right. I send one pair of stockings which is all I have done as since I came here I have been too busy sewing to knit much I went to Winton[2] Saturday as I wrote Willie I should do; we had a very pleasant ride of twelve miles Father Capt Magruder and I. we took James with us to make coffee and fix our lunch I cant tell you how it made me feel to see that deserted Village not a single soul lives there and the houses that are standing are all empty but one in which are four or five soldiers. we saw an oak tree that had been cut in two by a canon ball or a bomb shell, and hundred of marks where minie balls had hit either houses or trees, a canon ball had passed entirely through the roof of one house going in one side and out the other. There were some negroes there and before we left two of the men who had houses burnt came down to see Father and told us all about it. I ride every day so that the twelve miles down was nothing to me we had dinner there and owing to a hard rain could not leave until four o'clock but we got back before dark and found Sister and Tom very glad to see us but disappointed in not being able to go fishing they had planned to go directly after dinner and have a nice time but the rain prevented When you write to Mr Cooke which I want you to do next tell him exactly when your vacation begins and how long it will last for I want to know, you said that Mr Mason said either in May or June, the first of June will be just five months since you began; ask Mrs Primrose please to let me know if I dont owe her some thing as I want to make all my arrangements about money before I leave Father and I dont know what time he may be ordered off—or when I shall see him if he is sent away—from here—

Tom is as full of mischeif as he can be, he is very thin but other wise dont suffer much from the effects of hooping cough. Mary has not taken it and I fear wont, I wish she could have it now it is such a good time of the year and this is such a light kind. The other day Tom got mad with Mary and called her names Jane brought him to me and I told him he must tell me what he had said. You would have laughed to see him wipe his mouth and say, "its clean now Mama I wont dirty it no more" I told him he must tell me what he said but first "his head ached so bad" he did not feel well enough to talk; If he said it, it would make him cough and give him fever and then I would be so sorry. At last I told him if he did not tell I should make sister tell on him and then I would have to spank him, adding

Sister would be ashamed to tell bad words "Yes mama" said the little monkey "its too bad for you to hear you must not ask me to tell you any thing so bad"; but as he was pretty sure he would get a whipping if he did not tell me he at last whispered it and said "Now Mama dont you ever say such a bad word." Father and Mr Cooke both send love to you and Aunt Jane says when you write tell her how Mary [Lynch] is Give my love to all and believe me your affectionate

Mother

1. A slave.

2. Winton, in Hertford County, was attacked and burned by federal troops on 20 February 1862. Thomas C. Parramore, "The Burning of Winton in 1862," *NCHR* 39 (Jan. 1962): 18–31.

☙

*Barden Collection*
*William J. Clarke to Mary Bayard Clarke*

Petersburg June 14th. 1862 Saturday[1]

My Dear Wife:

I wrote you a hasty note on Monday last, just as we were about leaving for this place which we reached perfectly worn out on Tuesday 4 1/2 P.M. in a hard rain.

The Regt. staid that night in the new market house, and the next day we marched across Pocahontas bridge to the encampment on Dunn's Hill, near the Water works. We rode past the place on horseback, and if you remember a long row of cedars just before we came into the main road, where there is a fine residence owned by a relation of Mr. Dunlop,[2] just before you go down a rather steep hill, you know the very spot where we are located. We are greatly exposed to the sun, but the place is high and if any air is stirring we catch it. I am in command of the troops here, being composed of my own, the 48th. (Col. Hill) the 49th. (Col. Ramseur), & Niemeyer's Battln. and Cahoon's Battallion.[3] The orders are very strict. Only two men from a company, and four commd. officers can be absent at a time; and no officer or soldier can stay in town at night. Liquor is out of the question, and no matter how thirsty a fellow is, he must slake his thirst with Adam's ale.

It is drill, drill, all day long. I am getting well posted in the duties of Brigadier at all events, if I never receive the appointment. Gen'l. Ransom stays in town and has a pretty hard time of it as he is military governor. My Reg't. is called the veteran Reg't. and has eliceted high praise on every hand. Gen'l. R. speaks of it in high terms. The other Regts. are good, and well officered, and our Brigade is as fine a looking body of men as you will commonly see. Since I have been here I have had the offer of two companies from Va. and one from N.C., seeking to join my Reg't. But I can't take them in.—Please say to Mr. Edmundston that the cavalry com. we spoke of are attached, and were at the time I saw him; though I did not know it.

We had a grand review yesterday P.M. All the infty, two batteries of artillery, and a squadron of cavalry were out. I was in command of the whole, and was perfectly calm and selfpossessed and went thro' *every thing* without the least blunder or hesitation. My horses had not arrived, and I rode a splendid animal of Gen'l. R's who pranced and curvetted finely. My soldierly appearance and *fine riding* (!) attracted universal admiration, and at the end of the review, as I rode off the field at the head of my Reg't. the ladies sent me a beautiful magnolia. Gen'l. R. complimented my Reg't. highly on the field for their good drill, but abused the artillery, and spoke lightly of the cavalry. Capt. Williams and Farrell had no horses and were in the crowd and heard what was said about me and the Regt. and they were highly delighted.—

Sunday Henry Miller[4] was here acting as Col. Hill's Adj't. and would have been appointed but the appointment had been offered to young Gaston[5] who at first rather declined but finally accepted. H. has been tendered some position of Gen'l. [Thomas Lanier] Clingman's staff and has gone to Goldsboro' to see about it. I saw him only for a little time. It is impossible to say how long we shall be here or where we shall go. I cannot invite you to come to see me as I would not be allowed to sleep out of camp, without asking permission, which I regard (the way things are conducted) as humiliating, and I would subject myself to a refusal, perhaps to an ungracious one. I am perfectly satisfied that your visit would be any thing but agreeable, and would by no means pay.

I have been quite unwell, tho' I have been constantly on duty but if I could have gone to some comfortable house and have taken a regular course of medicine I should have done so.

I am now feeling better than I have for three weeks. I hope to escape a billious attack for I really have no time to be sick now; though I doubt if there will be any thing for us to do except to guard Petersburg.

I wept proud tears when I read the account of my heroic wife leaping into the water to rescue her Father.[6] I trust he has suffered no inconvenience from his aquatic excursion "all around the house to the back door."

If you could send my hat to me pr. Express, I could get it fixed up and should be glad to do so, as it is impossible to buy one

Farrell & Williams have tried every where, here, Richmond & Wilmington, to get one to present me. They intend presenting me the best
cap that can be obtained. It will be light blue and have as much gold lace
as any baby affair you ever saw.

I enclose you circular of an intimate friend and one of the best and
kindest men I ever saw.[7] The school is near Dr. Wilson's (surgeon) fathers
and the boys would be in excellent hands in case of sickness. A son of
Revd. Alex. Wilson informs me that his father will, most probably, not
continue his school.—I have been interrupted so often that I have entirely
forgotten what I had to say Respects to all, and kisses for the children, with
"a heap" of love to my darling from her affectionate husband
William J. Clarke Ralph H. Graves former tutor at Chapel Hill—

1. Battle lines in Virginia were shifting to the peninsula between the York
and James rivers. Union General George B. McClellan began to advance toward
Richmond, and the Confederate army under Joseph E. Johnston established a
defensive line east of the city. On 9 June 1862, the Twenty-fourth Regiment was
ordered to Petersburg and assigned to the Second Brigade, commanded by
Brigadier General Robert Ransom Jr. On 24 June the brigade moved to Richmond and reported to Major General Benjamin Huger's command. On 25 June
the Twenty-fourth saw action in the King's School House fighting and held the
line the next day against a combined infantry and artillery attack. Manarin and
Jordan, *Roster of NC Troops,* 7:246.

2. Probably James Dunlop, a Petersburg tobacco magnate. Dunlop was married to the sister of Ann Mary Maitland Devereux, Mary Bayard Clarke's stepmother. Claiborne, *Seventy-five Years in Old Virginia,* 63; Schiller, *A Captain's War,*
151n.

3. Colonel Robert Clinton Hill became commander of the Forty-eighth
Regiment, NCT, on 9 April 1862. Manarin and Jordan, *Roster of NC Troops,*
11:368. Stephen Dodson Ramseur was elected colonel of the Twenty-ninth Regi-
ment, NCT, in April 1862. He eventually became a major general but was mortally wounded in 1864 at Cedar Creek, Virginia. Boatner, *Civil War Dictionary,* 677;
Powell, *DNCB,* 5:170. Neimeyer's Battalion probably refers to William F.
Niemeyer, lieutenant colonel of the Sixty-first Virginia, which was part of
Brigadier General William Mahone's brigade. He was killed 12 May 1864. Sibley,
*Confederate Order of Battle,* 71, 290. Cohoon's Battalion was a Virginia infantry unit
originally known as the Sixth Battalion, North Carolina Infantry. Manarin and Jor-
dan, *Roster of NC Troops,* 14:423.

4. Henry Massie Miller, the son of Frances and Henry Watkins Miller.

5. Young Gaston probably referred to Hugh Jones Gaston of Wake County,
who enlisted at the age of twenty-two and was appointed adjutant of the Forty-
eighth Regiment, NCT, on 11 July 1862, to rank from 1 May 1862. He was

wounded in the shoulder and face and captured at Sharpsburg, Maryland, on or around 17 September 1862. He died in October 1862. Manarin and Jordan, *Roster of NC Troops,* 11:369.

6. Kate Edmondston described this event on 9 June 1862: "Father had a most narrow escape on Saturday night. He went upon the steps to mark the rate of the rise in the river when they, being improperly fastened, or rather not fastened at all, floated up & he was thrown backwards, striking the back of his head against the Piazza floor. He received a severe blow on the back & went down under the water. Mary, thinking he was stunned, jumped off the piazza & seized him by the shoulders & attempted to raise his head, but fortunately it was not the case & beyond a thorough wetting they both escaped unhurt." *Edmondston Diary,* 190.

7. The circular Clarke referred to was one for a school operated by an old acquaintance, Ralph Henry Graves, who was an educator in Granville County, North Carolina. Graves graduated from the University of North Carolina in 1836 and received an M.A. from the same institution in 1839. He taught at Caldwell Institute until it closed in 1850 and later became principal at the Hillsborough Academy. Just before the Civil War, Graves purchased Belmont, which stood in Granville County near the Virginia line. He ran a boys' school at Belmont until 1866. Powell, *DNCB,* 2:347–438.

*Barden Collection*
*William J. Clarke to Mary Bayard Clarke*

Camp near Drewry's Bluff July 17th. 1862[1]

My Dear Wife:

Your letter of the 15th. inst., the first I have received since I came from Petersburg on the 24th. ult., came duly to hand, and my heart was rejoiced to hear from you and our dear children. I was not surprised at not hearing from you as it was impossible in our marchings and counter marchings, for a letter to reach me. I thought I had seen something of hardship, exposure and fatigue before, but I was mistaken. We left P. with only a change of clothes and very soon were separated from that, and I went two weeks without changing my shirt. The men carried their knapsacks but had to leave them, and take only a blanket; then they had to leave the blanket and sleep in the open air, during some very cold nights, with no covering. I carried an oilcloth and a blanket behind my saddle, but on those occasions was compelled to leave my horse and sleep without any covering. The night before our last battle, the enemy shelled us so severely that we had to send our horses so far to the rear that the boys did not get to us, and Mr. Cooke and I lay together on some hickory & cedar twigs which I cut down with my knife, and we became so cold during the night that we had to hug each other to keep warm. Gen'l. Ransom is the most unfeeling brute I ever met with; but Gen'l. Huger (God bless him) is as kind and considerate as possible.—I am very thankful that my conduct has been well spoken of and that it meets with your approval. My Reg't. is praised by all for soldierly bearing and discipline, and no later than today a Virginian told me that we moved in perfect order in the charge, and that our fire on the two Yankee Regts. was destructive beyond description; to use his language we piled them. I am truly thankful, not only on the score of humanity, but selfishly, that I lost so few men, as the cowards at home had pronounced me rash and impetuous, and had predicted that I would sacrifice my men to my ambition, would pile up their bodies as stepping stones that I might climb up to honor. And lo, and behold! I have lost fewer men than any Reg't. in the Brigade, but they were nearest the enemy, and we were first in the fight, by half an hour, and left among the last.

I send you the rough notes of my report, which Gen'l. Ransom and others pronounce admirable. I don't think much of it except that it is a brief but faithful narrative.

I have been almost starved for we had nothing to eat but *very* salt bacon and crackers, with no tea or coffee most of the time. Williams, and Farrell & James were unremitting in their attentions and but for them I think I never could have gotten through. Col. Harriss[2] as usual is very sick, and Maj. Love[3] is a fool as well as a coward, and consequently I have a great deal of work to do. I am very tired and sigh for rest, rest.

I cannot resist the impression that the war is virtually over; though we are entrenching here. I think we shall remain here some time. As soon as I think that my application will be granted I shall apply for a month's leave of absence; but I fear that I shall have to wait some time.

The defeat of the enemy was disastrous beyond description, and their flight ridiculously cowardly. They threw away every thing. Men who had carried their guns one day in the flight, threw them away the second day, and the negroes say that hardly one in a hundred was armed. I have seen thousands by the road-side. I saw 15 four horse wagons at one time loaded with arms picked up & they were only a part of the wagons which were employed for nearly a week in carrying them to Richmond.

The sky was lighted up at night with the conflagration of their stores, while ever an anon a pillar of fire would shoot up into the heavens, and a loud report would show that a large quantity of ammunition had exploded. Millions on millions of property was thrown away or destroyed. I have seen a thousand dead men, and hundreds of horses lying on the same field.

A cannon ball came so near my head that the wind nearly took my cap off my head. One poor fellow, in Capt. Clark's Co., had the top of his head shot off within ten feet of me, and still I had not the mark of a ball unless my canteen strap was cut by a ball for I lost it on the battlefield and cannot account for the loss of it in any other way. I felt perfectly confident that I should escape for this text of scripture "fear not, I am with thee," was as present to my mind as if I had heard our Lord utter it.

I had no fear and my whole mind and soul was wrapt up in my Reg't. and nobly did they repay my attention.

I could give you some most touching instances of the devotion of my men to me, but the story would be tedious if made intelligible. You can tell Tom that Bill Barrett saved Father from being taken prisoner. On the night of the 25th. I volunteered to go to Col. Vance[4] with an order and got lost and went all among the enemy where I gave him the rein and he took a road directly opposite to the one I thought right. We had not gone far before a heavy firing commenced and the balls fairly rained around me; Bill carried me out like an arrow and made some extraordinary leaps. He has learned to stand fire pretty well. But Cols. generally go into battle on foot. Gen'l. Huger very kindly told us when to leave our horses. If old McGruder had not been drunk[5] we should either not have gone into the battle at all, or should have gone sooner, in which case we should have taken the battery—

I was pained to hear that dear little Willie had been so sick, and am quite relieved to hear that he has recovered. I hope they will be contented with Mr. Graves. He is a very kind man and an excellent teacher. He acted in perfectly good faith about raising his price, tho' I did not receive his letter informing me of the fact until a day or two since.

I hope that you will be able to obtain some pleasant place to spend the summer. I will send you as much money and as often as I can. My expenses are much larger than I expected. Corn meal is $3 per bushel chickens 62$^1/_2$ ct a piece, and every thing in proportion. Farrell has gone home sick, and I shall have to wait until the end of this month, when I expect to go to Richmond and draw my pay. I shall have two months due me, but I shall have to pay for a uniform which will cost about $125. I hope to be able to send you at least $150, will send more if I can.

Tell the boys that I will write out for them a full account of the battles as soon as I can. Tell Tom howdy for Father, and that Bill Barrett is very well and quite gaily; but that Tom Cooke[6] has been quite sick and we thought he would die.

Kiss Pet for me, I have a sheet of Yankee paper laid aside to write to her on. And now, darling, good bye. I long greatly to see you but must clothe myself with patience

Very affectionately your husband
William J. Clarke

1. Drewry's Bluff, also called Fort Darling, was on a bend of the James River south of Richmond. Robert E. Lee had concentrated his troops against the federal right wing and eventually forced the Union army back across the Chickahominy River. Huger's troops, which included Ransom's brigade, followed the retiring federal right wing. Ransom's brigade fought at Malvern Hill on 1 July 1862. Ransom's report of the engagement said very little about Clarke's regiment, which had been the first to support Major General John B. Magruder. During this campaign, the Twenty-fourth lost nine men killed, forty-two wounded, and twelve missing. Ransom's brigade then moved to Drewry's Bluff on 7 July. On 29 July it was ordered to Petersburg, where it encamped until returning to Richmond on 19 August. The regiment then marched to a pontoon bridge over the James River and remained there until 26 August, when the Army of Northern Virginia began moving north. Manarin and Jordan, *Roster of NC Troops,* 7:246–47.

2. John L. Harris, previously captain of Co. H, Twenty-fourth Regiment, was elected lieutenant colonel on 16 May 1862, and transferred to the Field and Staff. He was wounded at Fredericksburg and in fighting near Fort Stedman, Virginia, and was captured by the enemy on 3 April 1865. Manarin and Jordan, *Roster of NC Troops,* 7:251. He led the regiment at Sharpsburg. Sibley, *Confederate Order of Battle,* 29.

3. Thaddeus D. Love served as captain of Co. G, Twenty-fourth Regiment, NCT, until he was elected major on 16 May 1862. He served until his capture at or near Fort Stedman, Virginia, on 25 March 1865. Initially confined at Old Capitol Prison in Washington, D.C., he was transferred and imprisoned at Fort Delaware on 30 March 1865. Manarin and Jordan, *Roster of NC Troops,* 7:251.

4. Zebulon B. Vance served as colonel of the Twenty-fifth Regiment, NCT, until elected governor of North Carolina in 1862.

5. Magruder suffered from malicious gossip after Malvern Hill. According to Douglas Southall Freeman, "Rumor . . . was wagging a vicious tongue concerning him. He was accused of gross recklessness, of wild excitement and intoxication at Malvern Hill." Douglas Southall Freeman, *Lee's Lieutenants: A Study in Command,* vol. 1 (New York: Charles Scribner's Sons, 1945), 607.

6. A horse.

DURING THE PERIOD BETWEEN July and October 1862, Mary Bayard Clarke enrolled her two eldest sons in the Graves school at Belmont in

Granville County, North Carolina. She returned to Connaconara but hoped to make other housing arrangements. She visited William Clarke at some point, staying with him in Virginia, perhaps when he was ill. She definitely was in Richmond in October. She also continued writing poetry for publication, especially in the *Southern Literary Messenger*. In its October 1862 issue, she published "The Wine of Life." In the November/December issue, she published "Night Blooming Flowers," which included one of her favorite expressions used in letters over the years: "My heart hath leaves it doth not ope To every gazer's view, Its happy thoughts I give to all—Its sad ones to but few." *SLM* 34, no. 10 (Sept./Oct. 1862): 549–50; 34, no. 12 (Nov./Dec. 1862): 661.

Meanwhile, William Clarke's regiment experienced hard fighting that ended with the Fredericksburg campaign in November and December. Ransom's brigade joined that of Brigadier General John G. Walker's to form a division assigned to Longstreet's corps. The division participated in the attack on Harpers Ferry, which fell on 15 September. Lee then moved his army to Sharpsburg (Antietam), Maryland, to attack the Union army commanded by George McClellan. The Twenty-fourth lost twenty men killed, forty-four wounded, and two missing in action. Clarke missed Sharpsburg because of illness, but his regiment performed ably and won Ransom's praise. Clarke, in a letter to his wife dated 30 September 1862, described his regiment's action during the Sharpsburg engagement:

> They charged 25,000 of the enemy who had repulsed the Georgians & *Texans,* they repulsed them, they pressed them, they drove them for *two* miles. . . . Officers not of my Regt. tell me that men could not have behaved with more courage. . . . It is said that Gen'l. Ransom wept when he saw my Regt. charge for he thought that they would all be lost—

In late October, federal troops under Major General Ambrose E. Burnside crossed the Blue Ridge and advanced toward Fredericksburg. Southern troops soon moved into position on the heights overlooking the town. On 11 December the Twenty-fourth Regiment moved to the road at the foot of the two hills at Fredericksburg, extending the line held by General T. R. R. Cobb's brigade. The battle on 13 December was a devastating loss for the federal army. The Twenty-fourth lost four men killed and twenty-four wounded. Manarin and Jordan, *Roster of NC Troops,* 7:246–47, 248–49.

*Barden Collection*
*William J. Clarke to Mary Bayard Clarke (Richmond)*

Camp near Winchester Va
October 12th. 1862 (Sunday)

My Dear Wife:

I have been very busy for the last week and not having convenient opportunity for writing reproach myself for failing to write to you. Indeed the week slipped off imperceptibly and I really was surprised when Sunday came. I wrote to you by Mr. Clark of Scotland Neck directing to Clarksville and hope you recd. the letter, though there was nothing in it of special interest. I direct this to Conniconara thinking it probable that you will be there by the time this reaches that place, as I send it by private hand to Richmond, whence there is a bare possibility that it may reach you. I have recd. only two letters from you since we parted. One brought by Mr. Valk and one written previously. Gov't. officials give themselves preciously little trouble about forwarding army letters, and I think the P.M. at W. is the worst of a bad class—We are here 4½ miles north of W. bivouacked in a thick wood, doing nothing. The men have no blankets and only the clothes they have on, and many of them have no shoes. My Reg't., and indeed the Brigade, laid of their knapsacks when they went into battle at Sharpsburg, and were marched during the day a considerable distance from them as the scene of conflict changed, and when the army fell back the next night but one, they had to cross at a ford so far from them that they were compelled to leave them. It is really painful to look upon them ragged, dirty, and lousy; but they cannot help it and they are so by no fault of theirs for they behaved most gallantly. My Regt., Gen'l. Ransom says, is the one complimented so highly in the Yankee papers. Had I been with them my promotion would have been pretty sure.[1] The battle cry of the boys was "our brave Col. is very sick and away from us, let us see to it that a good report goes to him about us.["][2] They exhibit the most soldierly qualities by enduring hardships, labors and privations with cheerfulness and without murmuring Never before was there so much of laughter jest and song in camp. We have very little sickness—I wrote to you that Capt. Duffy[3] was killed at Occoquan acqueduct; I am now happy to say that on yesterday I received reliable information that he was alive on 3d. inst. and recovering. We shall probably fall back from this place towards Staunton, in a few days, as the country here cannot furnish supplies for us. The men are living on beef and flour, and our *poor* horses on hay alone. As soon as our future movements become more certain Mr. Cooke will go to Richmond and probably to Raleigh in order to obtain a suitable truss. I shall request him to call and see you. Capt. Farrell has gone for money and clothing and is expected back daily; on his return I shall send you some money. Col. Matt. Ransom[4] is quite sick, and will go home in a few days. Col. Rutledge[5] is absent very sick in Petersburg. Col. Ramseur is probably permanently disabled by his wound at Malvern, Col. Vance's Reg't. (26th) Lt Col. Burgwynn, has left the Brigde[6] and is attached to Pettigrew's—so that I am the only Col. present for duty. Gen'l. Ransom has improved in manners greatly, but my conduct towards him is the same distant, studious formal politeness, as ever, and such it will continue. But I have, I think, taught him to respect me properly.

I wrote to John Primrose, from Richmond, in full, and when we go into winter quarters which will be soon I shall send for him—I was quite concerned to hear that little Tommy has been sick but conclude that the attack was slight.

Don't be uneasy about me, I think that fighting is pretty well over for this season, and that peace will come with Spring—With love to all

Yours affectionately

William J. Clarke

1. William Clarke, despite his protestations, badly wanted to become a general. He suspected that his commanding officer, Robert Ransom, was working to have Matt Ransom promoted ahead of him. Clarke wrote to army friends and politicians, including North Carolina Governor Zebulon Vance, to see if they could help him. Vance wrote Clarke on 25 November 1862, that he would willingly write a letter in his support, but that he doubted a recommendation from him would sway President Davis. Clarke Papers, SHC.

2. Mary Bayard Clarke wrote a poem describing the heroic actions of the Twenty-fourth Regiment during Sharpsburg. Her poem, titled "The Charge of the 24th North Carolina Reg't at the Battle of Sharpsburg," was published in the *Southern Illustrated News* (Richmond).

3. George T. Duffy became captain of Co. B, Fourteenth Regiment, NCV, on 6 May 1861. On 13 February 1862, he was arrested because of a drinking episode in Petersburg. He was released but then re-arrested on 24 February. He resigned on 19 April "on account of drinking." In May 1862 he was reelected captain of the company and served until he was wounded on 9 September. He was absent or assigned light duty until 11 July 1864, when he retired to the Invalid Corps. Clarke wrote a letter of recommendation for Duffy dated 18 May 1862, which stated that Duffy, in spite of his drinking, was "incomparably the best Captain in the regiment." Manarin and Jordan, *Roster of NC Troops,* 7:266.

4. Matt W. Ransom was Robert Ransom's brother. Matt Ransom, a lawyer, state legislator, and attorney general, was a distinguished military leader for the Confederacy during the Civil War. Colonel of the Thirty-fifth Regiment, NCT, he eventually becoming a major general and served until Appomattox. Ashe, *Cyclopedia of Eminent and Representative Men,* 2:640; Boatner, *Civil War Dictionary,* 679; Powell, *DNCB,* 5:175. The aristocratic Devereux family disliked the Ransoms intensely. Kate Edmondston, writing on 16 August 1863, said, "Why cannot Mr Davis employ *gentlemen*? A open mouthed swearing braggart like Robert Ransom is no fit judge in any case, a mean bully such as he is cannot be impartial. His brother Gen Mat Ransom seems to have half the newspapers in his pay to glorify his conduct during the late advance of the Yankees into Northampton, yet he will, nevertheless, find it hard to make us at home beleive that the reason he did not follow and crush them, as he *says* he could have done, was that 'he had orders from the Sec of War not to press them.' We prefer beleiving that a man who has had his face slapped for cheating at cards & took it tamely was recreant to his duty, slow, or *even showed the white feather again, . . .*" *Edmondston Diary,* 449.

5. Henry M. Rutledge served as colonel of the Twenty-fifth Regiment, NCT, part of Ransom's brigade. In June 1862 he fought at Sharpsburg with rest of the brigade. Manarin and Jordan, *Roster of NC Troops,* 7:247.

6. Vance's regiment transferred out of Ransom's brigade on 26 August 1862. Henry King Burgwyn Jr. became lieutenant colonel of the Twenty-sixth Regiment in 1861 at the age of nineteen. After Vance resigned in 1862 to become governor of North Carolina, Ransom opposed Burgwyn's promotion to colonel. The regiment, however, elected him, and the appointment stood. Burgwyn's regiment left Ransom's brigade to join that of James Johnston Pettigrew. He was killed at Gettysburg in 1863. Powell, *DNCB,* 1:276–77.

*Frances Martin Finnerty Papers*
*Tom, Mary, and Mary Bayard Clarke to Willie Clarke (Belmont)*

Jones Spring Nov 7th [1862]

Wee Wee[1] frost is come he has bit the hickory nuts, but he aint bit me, it snowed this to morrow and I got some of it in a leaf and ate it, I am tired of Jones' Springs, we gets hickory nuts and apples, Wee Wee I want to see you, you must go to grandpa's next to morrow and bring me a whip with a leather lash; tell Mrs Graves[2] I dont get a bit of sugar in my hand and I am coming back to live with her and Emma, tell her I wrote her a letter last yesterday and am going to send her another some of these days.

Wee Wee you must send me another letter with pretty edges round it. I walk in the snow with my boots on I am going away to morrow and must pack my trunk so I cant write any more

Texas Tom

My dear Brother Willie

I am very much obliged to you for your letter to me and for the squirels skins. We are going to Raleigh to morrow to see aunt Frances and I am so glad There is no one here but Mrs Heck Mother and Dr Selden's family and there is not one soul for me to play with for all the girls are older than you we go to the iron spring when the weather is good and Mother rides a little mustang pony that kicks up. We get apples here and we roast them and the cabins are very nice but I dont like this as well as I did Buffalo. I am glad you had a nice time with the young ladies. There is a boy here named Wilson Selden who has been at Hillsborough and says he wants to go to Mr Graves' school Give my love to Emma and To Mrs Graves Your affectionate

                                                                         Sister

Dear Willie

I was very glad to get your letter telling me the $20 reached you safely so many letters have been lost from here that I was getting uneasy about it

Mary and Tom have told you all the news about this place so I will tell you some very good news and that is that Father's regiment is to be sent home, that is to N C—so we shall see him this winter

I got a letter from him to night dated Culpepper Court house, he was well I got Frank's letter to night and am sorry to hear that small pox is near you Ask Mr Graves please to have you both vaccinated at once for Dr Selden tells me it is better to repeat it. Give my love to Mrs Graves and ask her if she got a letter from me I wrote her a day or two after I got here; tell her I became quite well acquainted with Mrs Gen Lee and found her a very nice lady and she must be a christian for I never saw such resignation under affliction shown by any one as she exhibited when her daughter died.[3] I enclose a copy of some lines I wrote on the death of Miss Annie and you must give them to Mrs Graves to read when you have read them, and ask her if she or Mr Graves recognises any of the ideas. I shall only stay a day or two in Raleigh so direct your letters after this to Halifax[4] and tell Frank I will answer his as soon as I am settled, it wont be long now before I see you, you must write and tell me what day you will leave so that I can get Grandpa to send the carriage for you.

Good night give my love to Mr and Mrs Graves and kiss little Emma for me

                                                              Your loving
                                                              Mother

1. A family nickname for Willie Clarke.

2. Ralph Henry Graves married Emma Taylor of Hillsborough in 1849. They had two children. Powell, *DNCB,* 2:347–348.

3. Mary Randolph Custis Lee, the wife of Robert E. Lee, became well-acquainted with Mary Bayard Clarke while visiting North Carolina. The Lee family, forced to leave Arlington when the war began, spent most of the war visiting friends and relatives until they settled in Richmond in 1864. On 20 October 1862, Annie Lee died from typhoid while in North Carolina. Annie and her sister Agnes had been staying at Jones Springs in Warrenton, North Carolina. Mrs. Lee traveled there after learning of her daughter's illness. Annie Lee was buried in Warrenton until her remains were removed to Washington & Lee University by the family in the twentieth century. Mary P. Coulling, *The Lee Girls* (Winston-Salem, N.C.: J. F. Blair, 1987), 107–8 (hereafter cited as Coulling, *The Lee Girls*); Mary Custis Lee deButts, ed., *Growing Up in the 1850s: The Journal of Agnes Lee* (Chapel Hill: University of North Carolina Press, 1984), 109–11. The poem Mary Bayard Clarke mentions, "Annie Carter Lee," pleased the Lee family. General Lee sent the poem to his wife on 29 January 1863, writing, "I send some Copies of the verses of Mrs Clarke on dear Annie. They have been published in the Petersburg papers & some one sent me five copies. I will send a copy to Fitzhugh & one to Mary if I can." Robert E. Lee to Mary Custis Lee, Mss1L51e, Lee Family Papers, VHS. Mary Custis Lee included a handwritten copy of the poem in a scrapbook and appended a note at the end stating "Mrs. Clarke" had stayed at Jones Spring when they were there and had known Robert E. Lee in Texas. Mary Custis Lee Scrapbook, Mss1L51B65, Lee Family Papers, VHS.

4. Mary Bayard Clarke was returning to her father's plantation, Conneconara in Halifax County.

*Wootten, Moulton, Clarke Papers, SHC*
*William J. Clarke to Mary Bayard Clarke*

Camp near Fredericksburg Va.
December 1st. 1862.

My Darling:

I received your letter of 21st. ult. on yesterday and am pained to learn that some four or five of my letters have not reached you. It does really seem that Gov't. tries to make our condition as unpleasant as possible, when we cannot even communicate with our families—

I am profoundly melancholly at the prospect before you this winter. But sighing and mourning will not remedy matters. If you cannot obtain an asylum on Roanoke[1] you must elsewhere. Suppose you should write to my aunt Mrs. Frances Jasper at Lewisburg, or to my aunt Catharine Colton, Ashboro' Randolph Co.[2] to inquire for a boarding house. R. P. Dick[3] of Greensboro' might aid you. I shall write to Yanceyville inquiring—

I wrote to you to call on D. A. Barnes[4] or Mr. Nusom of Jackson for $500 left with them and to deposite it in Cape Fear Bank at Raleigh. You did not receive my letter. Draw the money and use it as I have arranged for it today.—I write in great haste to send by a man going to N.C. Kiss Pet and Tom, respects to your Father & Susy, and your sister Kate & Mr E.

Affectionately Yours<br/>William J. Clarke

1. Mary Bayard Clarke found asylum on the Roanoke River, spending the winter months with her father and his family. According to her sister, Kate Edmondston, the family initially discouraged Mary Bayard and her children from staying in their section of the country because of the threat of federal raids. 21 November 1862, *Edmondston Diary,* 303–4.

2. William Clarke's mother, Anne Maria Raboteau Clarke, had several brothers and sisters. Two of her sisters were Frances Ann and Catherine Raboteau. Frances Ann married Henry N. Jasper in 1832 and resided in Louisburg, North Carolina. Catherine first married Thomas Fuller of Fayetteville. Her second husband, with whom she lived in Asheboro, was the Reverend Simeon Colton, formerly of Springfield, Massachusetts. They were married in 1851. "Raboteau Family," Crawford Papers.

3. Robert Paine Dick of Greensboro, North Carolina, was an early friend of William J. Clarke. Both attended the Caldwell Institute as well as the University of North Carolina, and both were lawyers. Dick, who had opposed secession, became a leading Republican in the state after the war. In 1864, seeing defeat on the horizon, Dick worked with William Woods Holden in the peace movement. In 1868 he served as a justice on the state supreme court, and in 1872 he became a United States district judge. Powell, *DNCB,* 2:63.

4. David Alexander Barnes served in the North Carolina House of Commons for several terms and was a member of the Secession Convention in 1861. In 1866 he was appointed provisional superior court judge of the First Judicial District by William W. Holden. Powell, *DNCB,* 1:98.

*Wootten, Moulton, Clarke Papers, SHC*
*William J. Clarke to Mary Bayard Clarke (Conneconara)*

Camp near the Battle Field<br/>~~Winchester~~ Fredericksburg Va. Dec'r. 13th. 1862[1]

My Dear Wife

Last night at dusk I marched my Regt. on picket in the edge of W., the enemy occupying most of the town, where we remained until the battle commenced at 10 o'clock A.M. by a brisk cannonade. This continued until about M. when the enemy attacked in heavy columns and were again and again repulsed with awful slaughter. My Regt. the 24th Georgia & 25th N.C. bore the brunt of the fight. I have had only four (4) men killed outright, and thirty (30) wounded. We were in a most excellent position which accounts for the small list of casualties. Col. [John L.] Harris was slightly wounded and Lieut. Brown[2] of Barney Lanes Co.—I am sorry to inform you that Mr. Cooke received a shot thro' the fleshy part of his thigh,[3] but it is, tho' a severe still not an extremely serious wound.

I shall send him to Petersburg as soon as possible where Dr. Couch and Mrs White will take care of him.

I did not receive a scratch tho' I was necessarily a good deal exposed. We repulsed the enemy and remained masters of the field. My Regt. behaved beyond all praise and at one time checked and drove back two Regts of the enemy—Pardon my short letter for I am very tired and [illegible]—

Affectionately yours
William J. Clarke

Jackson fought about four miles on our right and whipped the enemy badly—

This is written about 10 o'clock P.M. near Fredericksburg which I've called War Station

1. The federal army, which numbered 122,000 men, reached the Rappahannock River across from Fredericksburg before Longstreet's corps arrived. Burnside, however, allowed Longstreet time to occupy Marye's Heights behind the town and establish a strong defensive position. By 13 December, when the battle began, Lee's army numbered 78,000 strongly entrenched soldiers. The Union army crossed the river and tried to take the heights. According to one source, "Federal dead were piled in front of the stone wall that ran in front of the sunken road at the base of Marye's Heights. Out of an estimated 106,000 Federals who actually participated in the attacks, 12,700 were killed or wounded. Confederate losses were 5,300 out of 72,500 engaged." The federal army withdrew on 15 December. Boatner, *Civil War Dictionary*, 310–13. On 19 December 1862, Kate Edmondston described Mary Bayard Clarke's distress before she received word that her husband had survived Fredericksburg: "Poor Mary, I do not know how she can stand it, for her husband is in Longstreet's Division which bore the brunt of the first day's engagement on Thursday, a week yesterday, & not a word from him." On 20 December, Kate mentioned that, "Mary has received two letters from her husband. He is safe & the loss in his Regt small, which is a

cause of great thankfulness to her. Her friend Mr. Cook is wounded." *Edmondston Diary*, 319, 320.

2. London Brown enlisted as a private on 31 May 1861. He became second lieutenant in Co. E under Captain Barney Lane. He was wounded in the left leg at Fredericksburg and hospitalized in Richmond. He died from his wounds on 23 January 1863. Manarin and Jordan, *Roster of NC Troops*, 7:292.

3. Cooke returned to duty on 2 June 1863. Manarin and Jordan, *Roster of NC Troops*, 7:251.

ON 3 JANUARY 1863, Ransom's brigade was ordered to North Carolina to guard the Wilmington & Weldon Railroad. The Twenty-fourth Regiment left Fredericksburg and reached Petersburg, Virginia, on 7 January. From there they went to Goldsboro, North Carolina, and on to Kenansville by 21 January. The regiment continued to march between different locations in eastern North Carolina as part of the Confederate offensive against the federal army that led to the attack on New Bern. Clarke's regiment did not participate directly in that battle. The regiment returned to Petersburg on 30 May.

*Barden Collection*
*William J. Clarke to Mary Bayard Clarke (Conneconara)*

Camp near Fredericksburg Va.<br>January 1st. 1863.

My Darling:

I had the pleasure, on yesterday, to receive yours of the 27th. ult. and was truly thankful to learn that you and our dear children were well. I am really vexed that you have not received some of my letters, as they contained brief notices of the battle as they came fresh to my mind but they as all of my letters written from the army, were poor affairs—I am still detailed as Prest. of a Court Martial and sit *every* day, commonly six hours, and return to camp perfectly worn out in body and mind. Today we got thro' sooner than usual, and hence I find time to write to you.

I have not seen any of the pieces you speak of except the elegy. I am very much pleased with that and hope that you will send me the pieces.—I am in Ransom's Brigade in a Division commanded by him, as there is a vacancy caused by the promotion of Brig Gen'l. Walker—R. has not been promoted.[1] Gen'l. Cooke[2] commands Walker's Brigade. I have not been superceded by him and have very little to do with him. When our Brigade goes in battle as a whole I command it. We were separated at Fredericksburg as I was in advance on picket when the enemy attacked us. We were at the head of the street immediately in front of Marye's hill and bore the brunt of the battle with the 24th. Georgia. We routed Meagher's Irish Brigade[3] and then they sent up their regulars and we whipped them. We engaged 13 regts. at once, and had 5 flags down at the same time. About 2,000 yankees lay dead for several days immediately in our front. We were reinforced after the second attack but did not need reinforcement, for we were able to drive back as many as could get to us.—I deserve promotion for this battle and all the army says so.—I think Ransom will be made Maj. Gen'l. and I will take his place as Brig. You will hear some stories about my mounting the breast works and shaking my cane at the Yankees and calling to them to come back, which I am sorry to say are true, but I was excited by having my Reg't. to cut to pieces two (2) Yank. regts. at the same time. I had just shot down the color corporal *myself,* and when they ran off I mounted the bank and called to them twice "*Yankees come back*", but they would not. They left 250 dead at that place every one killed by the 24th. I have the belt of one of the men taken off by me on the field as a trophy. I sent you the sword. There were six acres of dead Yanks in twenty steps of the place it was picked up in my presence. My Regt. did its full share in their taking off.

I do not think the enemy will again attack us at this place, tho' I hope they will. It is immensely strong and we are adding to its defensibility every day. I said I did not think the enemy would attack us here, but men who were so infatuated as to try it once may do so again.—I do not understand what your Father wants John Ellison[4] for, or what he is willing to pay John. I have no authority to release a soldier, but perhaps could get it done after some delay. John will go any where or do any thing I wish him—I never let him go into danger if I can help it. He brings my meals to me on the battle field—John Primrose is a clerk and does not go into battle. He is quite well and is growing every day.

I am sorry that there is no chance for you to come to see me. If I should be promoted, which is just possible, I could after a while arrange for your reception, but now every house negro cabin etc. is full of refugees—besides there are other obstacles—With love to all and a kiss for Tom and Pet

Affectionately Yours<br>William J. Clarke

I never was in better health except pain in my wounded limb.

I fear that we are located here for the winter. We shall move camp in a few days when I shall have my men to put up log houses, as it is intensely cold here Direct to Fredericksbg for the present.

1. Robert Ransom was promoted to major general on 26 May 1863. His brother, Colonel Matt Ransom, became brigadier general of the brigade on 13 June 1863. Manarin and Jordan, *Roster of NC Troops,* 7:249. When Matt Ransom received his promotion, it was over the three senior colonels of the brigade, including William J. Clarke. Frontis W. Johnston and Joe A. Mobley, eds., *The Papers of Zebulon Baird Vance,* vol. 1 (Raleigh: North Carolina Division of Archives and History, 1963–), 350–51, 168n (hereafter cited as Johnston and Mobley, *Vance Papers*).

2. John R. Cooke, formerly colonel of the Twenty-seventh Regiment, NCT, was promoted to brigadier general on 1 November 1862. Boatner, *Civil War Dictionary,* 173–74.

3. Union Brigadier General Thomas Frances Meagher commanded the Irish Brigade from New York. The brigade was destroyed at Fredericksburg. One historian described the carnage, noting, "Those who were not casualties were simply blown off their feet by the force of the volley. After a moment, single shots came back from the huddle of bodies mounded up not thirty yards from the wall at one place." Boatner, *Civil War Dictionary,* 540; Frank A. Boyle, *A Party of Mad Fellows: The Story of the Irish Regiments in the Army of the Potomac* (Dayton, Ohio: Morningside House, 1996), 217–19.

4. John W. Ellison enlisted in 1861 as a private in Co. H, Fourteenth Regiment, NCV. He was nineteen years old at the time, and he served until paroled at Appomattox Court House, Virginia, on 9 April 1865. Manarin and Jordan, *Roster of NC Troops,* 7:324.

*George Bagby Family Papers, VHS*
*Mary Bayard Clarke to George Bagby (Richmond)*

Conoconara Jan 7th [1863]

Oh dear me! How tired I am of this war, and every thing pertaining to it—especially the poetry, and the spruce blue-grey uniforms, with all the gold which ought to be *in* the pocket, displayed *on* the sleeve. Here have I been bored for three mortal hours with just such a uniform, worn by a splendid specimen of the *animal* man, six feet, and large in proportion, a treat to the eyes, but as exhausting to the mind as an air pump— and I all the time, contrary woman that I am, wishing for the sight of a wiry little fellow in a faded thread bare home spun coat—all beard and moustach and not flesh enough on his bones to get a flesh wound even at

Malvern and Maryes Hills—

But I did not sit down to tell you that I want desperately to see the Col of the 24th N C Ts, but to enclose a poem *not* pertaining to the war[1] which might as well be published as to lie in my portfolio, and to ask you a most impertinent question; and so before my courage fails I'll do it at once, and beg you to tell me on what terms you published Moyze's Addresses.[2]

I want to publish a pamphlet in just that style for circulation principally in the camps; I dont care for either good binding or paper, only legible printing. I have published one book and only one, that paid for itself and gave me a diamond ring, and I want this at least to do the first, beyond that I dont expect. I have constant applications for different poems on the war, which I have at divers times printed, and have just received a letter requesting me to publish a cheap edition of them for the benefit of our state hospitals. I am perfectly willing to do so, though I rather think the rags out of which the paper on which it will be published will be made would do the hospitals more good than the proceeds of the pamphlet. Will you be kind enough to send the enclosed to the News *it aint worth a postage stamp.*

Please send me a copy of each no. of the Messenger which contains any thing from me, I find I need it as reference, you knew I have give up my copy while wandering to my boys, and I may send you the same thing twice, and owing to the picayune management of the proprietors it cant be bought, I really believe I am in a bad humor so will bid you good night

Yours etc

M B Clarke address at Halifax

1. Mary Bayard Clarke published several poems and translations in the *SLM* in January and February 1863. Her poems were "The Water Sprite's Bridal," 37, no. 1 (Jan. 1863): 31–34; "The Leaf" and "The Snail," 37, no. 2 (Feb. 1863): 78, 116.

2. This probably refers to "The Letters of Mozis Addums to Billy Ivvins," a reprint of the humorous stories that appeared in the *SLM* 34, no. 3 (Feb./Mar. 1862): 208.

*Wootten, Moulton, Clarke Papers, SHC*
*William J. Clarke to Mary Bayard Clarke*

Goldsboro' Saturday January 17th. 1863

My Dear Mary:

Just as I predicted in my last we received orders suddenly on Thursday night to cook three days' rations and be at the RR depot next morning at 6 o'clock. I accordingly issued orders for revellie at 3 A.M. but by error in the Drum Major's watch we were roused at 2, but it was so dark and rained so hard at 5, the hour I intended leaving camp, that I did not start until past 6. We finally got aboard the cars and left about 10 A.M. and reached this place this morning at 2. By some mismanagement my Reg't. alone of Ransom's Brigade came and the rest will be along tomorrow. I am now encamped south of the town, the regt. being en bivouac, the field officers alone having tents. The wagons and baggage will be on in a few days. I was very glad to have my horse brought by the cars as he is in fine condition and would have fared badly on the journey.

I cannot at this time form the shadow of an idea whether we shall remain here or go further. I am informed that Daniels and Pettigrew's Brigades[1] are on the march to this place. This massing of troops at this place would indicate that Gen'l. Smith[2] apprehended an attack here, but I cannot think the enemy will come here if we have any considerable force to oppose them. It would be a blunder for them to attempt an advance, and the further west they go the worse it will be for them, as they leave their supplies and are liable to be cut off from reinforcements. My Reg't. is in fine condition and, God being with us, we shall give the Yankees a harder fight than in any previous battle.

I had seen "The Charge of the 24th" in the S.I. News before receiving your letter of the 8th. which is the last that has come to hand. I like it very much, and the Regt. is so delighted with it that they have bought every copy that could be found. I cannot see why any person except Gen'l. Ransom, should think it in bad taste. At any rate it will do me and my Reg't. a great deal of good—I fear that my being in Ransom's Brigade has injured my prospects of promotion, as I fear that he has damned me with faint praise, hoping to give his brother Matt. a good chance, and in addition to that he surpasses any man I know of in unpopularity, both in and out of the army, and as my promotion is in a good degree dependent on his I fear that he will not be promoted. It is rumored in Petersburg that a resolution of inquiry into his conduct will be introduced in Congress If that should be done, no matter how it results, it will ruin him; but some very censurable conduct will be made public. An officer of the 46th. has preferred charges against him.——

I most sincerely thank you for your last letter; language cannot describe how my heart has thirsted.——But I will not write more on that subject, I should hardly say more if I were with you.

You did perfectly right in sending the boys back to Mr. Graves tho' he has raised his price; but if I had any place where I could put Frank I would take him from school for a year at least. His listlessness is physical and a year's rest from study would benefit him.—I passed Ma yesterday on the cars going to Petersburg to see me. I saw her but did not have an opportunity to speak to her.

I hope during the next week to get an opportunity of coming to see you, as I want to see you beyond description. If I find I cannot come I shall send John Ellison for you; hence I await the developments of the next three or four days with impatience. Perhaps I shall have to wait until the week after. At all events I shall write you on Tuesday or Wednesday. With kind regards to your Father, Ma & Susy and also to your sister Kate and Mr. E. with a kiss for Pet and the Col. I remain

Affectionately Yours<br/>William J. Clarke

The enclosed was taken from a dead Yankee at Fredericksburg.

1. Brigadier General Junius Daniel and Brigadier General James Johnston Pettigrew. Boatner, *Civil War Dictionary,* 222, 649.

2. Major General Gustavus Woodson Smith resigned from the army on 17 February 1863, when six other officers were promoted over him. Boatner, *Civil War Dictionary,* 771–72.

*The Rebel Sock*[1]
*[1863]*
*[Published in* Poems By Mrs. Mary Bayard Clarke*]*

A true episode in Seward's raid on the old ladies of Maryland.

In all the pomp and pride of war<br/>
The Lincolnite was drest,<br/>
High beat his patriotic heart<br/>
Beneath his armor'd vest.<br/>
His maiden sword hung by his side,<br/>
His pistols both were right,<br/>
The shining spurs were on his heels,<br/>
His coat was buttoned tight.<br/>
A firm resolve sat on his brow,<br/>
For he to danger went;<br/>
By Seward's self that day he was

On secret service sent.
"Mount and away," he sternly cried,
Unto the gallant band,
Who, all equipped from head to heel,
Awaited his command;
"But halt, my boys—before you go,
These solemn words I'll say,
Lincoln expects that every man
His duty'll do to-day."

"We will, we will," the soldiers cried,
"The President shall see,
That we will only run away
From Jackson or from Lee."
And now they're off, just four-score men,
A picked and chosen troop,
And like a hawk upon a dove,
On Maryland they swoop.
From right to left—from house to house,
The little army rides;
In every lady's wardrobe look
To see what there she hides.
They peep in closets, trunks and drawers,
Examine every box;
Not rebel soldiers now they seek,
But rebel soldiers' socks!
But all in vain!—too keen for them,
Were those dear ladies there,
And not a sock, or flannel shirt
Was taken anywhere.
The day wore on to afternoon,
That warm and drowsy hour,
When Nature's self doth seem to feel
A touch of Morpheus' power;
A farm-house door stood open wide,
The men were all away,

The ladies sleeping in their rooms,
The children at their play;
The house-dog lay upon the step,
But never raised his head,
Though crackling on the gravel walk,
He heard a stranger's tread.

Old grandma in her rocking chair
Sat knitting in the hall,
When suddenly upon her work
A shadow seemed to fall.
She raised her eyes and there she saw
Our Federal hero stand,
His little cap was on his head,
His sword was in his hand.
Slowly the dear old lady rose,
And tottering, forward came,
And peering dimly through her "specs,"
Said, "Honey! what's your name?"
Then, as she raised her withered hand,
To pat his sturdy arm,
"There's no one here but Grandmama
And she won't do you harm.
Come, take a seat, and don't be scared,
Put up your sword, my child,
I would not hurt you for the world,"
She gently said, and smiled.
"Madam, my duty must be done
And I am firm as rock,"
Then, pointing to her work, he said,
"Is that a rebel sock?"
"Yes, Honey, I am getting old
And for hard work ain't fit,
Though for Confederate soldiers, still,
I thank the Lord, can knit."
"Madam, your work is contraband

And Congress confiscates
This rebel sock, which I now seize
To the United States."

"Yes, Honey—don't be scared—you see
I'll give it up to you."
Then slowly from the half-knit sock
The dame her needles drew,
Broke off the thread, wound up the ball
And stuck her needles in;
"Here—take it, child—and I to-night
Another will begin."
The soldier next his loyal heart
The dear-bought trophy laid,
And that was all that Seward got
By this old woman's raid.

1. Mary Bayard Clarke wrote this poem while staying at her father's plantation late in 1862 or early 1863. Kate Edmondston recounted the tale in a diary
entry dated 21 November 1862, stating that Mary had met a Maryland woman
who told her the basic story. Mary Bayard Clarke later set it to verse. Edmondston delighted in the tale. *Edmondston Diary,* 304–5. The poem appeared in the
*Southern Illustrated News* in 1863.

*Barden Collection*
*William J. Clarke to Mary Bayard Clarke*

Kenansville N.C. Jany 27th. 1863

My Darling:

I have been intending to write to you for the past three days, but have
so much to say that I have waited for a good opportunity to give you a connected account of some events that will interest you. That good time will
not come for I have been already interrupted since I commenced, and
must content myself to be incoherent etc.—Not to keep you in suspense,
Ransom and I have had a big blow-up, and my Reg't. will leave his Brigade
in a few days![1] It came about in this way: On Friday he left camp and rode
out reconnoitering. During his absence as next officer I endorsed passes
for the men until I found that men were arrested with passes endorsed by
me as Commdr. of the Brigade, as by Regulations and military usage I was.

I learned that he had issued orders that my passes should not be respected. Having fully established that fact, I wrote to the Adjutant General [Samuel Cooper] at Richmond requesting to be detached or transferred from his Brigde., stating that "with singular unanimity every officer and private in my Regt. concurred with me in the request." This letter has to go up thro' him, the Gen'l. comd. Division, & Gen'l. of Corps, consequently on his return to camp he saw it. He immediately caused a note to be written to me inquiring by what authority I was command. the Brigde. I replied very courteously, but firmly; and completely floored him. He endorsed on my letter that he *thought I was sick.* The only ground he had for this was that I declined riding with him that morning as my thigh was painful. Early next morning he sent for all my officers summoning them as privately as possible, and not letting me know any thing of it. When they arrived at his quarters he told them what I had written and asked each one if he wished to leave the Brigde. when all except two (2) voted to leave! Very few know of the correspondence. He is said to have been completely chapfallen and declared that he was greatly disappointed, but that he should approve and forward my petition. When the news got out among the men they were perfectly frantic with joy, and their expressions of attachment to me will never be forgotten—Thus was signally rebuked one of the meanest and most cowardly attempts to ruin me by convicting me of falsehood. His desire was to retain my Reg't. and get rid of me, as I am in the way of his brother Matt. My Reg't. has elicited the highest praise. Gen'l. Lee declared he had never seen a better one and Gen'l. Longstreet said he had never seen one so good. When we marched into Kenansville, only a few days ago, Gen'l. R. was on the side walk and pointing to the Reg't. as it passed exclaimed in the hearing of a large crowd "Gentlemen! there goes the glory of the Southern Confederacy, that is the star Reg't. of our army: G-d d-n me if I would fear to go any where with those men, they are the best fighters you ever saw" He little thought that he was so soon to lose them!

Again my darling I must thank you for your piece about the Reg't. it has done more for us than any bulletin could. It has made us the envy of the whole army and my men are as proud of their Regt. as were Napoleon's old guard, or Caesar's 10th. legion.—I have no idea where we shall go, or to what Brigade we shall be attached, nor do I much care, so I get away from modern West Point. When I think of the injustice and tyranny I and my men and officers have endured for the past eight months from that cowardly bully I feel like cursing. But I have got the advantage of him at all times by controlling my temper and acting the perfect gentleman, and, God helping me, intend still to do so until I get away from him. I expect that that happy exodus will take place about the last of this week.

So soon as I get a little settled with the new command to which we may be attached, I shall apply for a leave of absence that I may come and see you. I am almost crazy to see you and the children. Kiss the dear ones for me.

I fear that my two last letters did not reach you. I think I wrote twice to you while at Goldsboro'—There is no chance for a fight here.—I recd. on yesterday your sister Kates presents and shall tomorrow, if possible, write her a letter of thanks—

Present my kindest regards to your Father, Ma, Sue and Mr & Mrs E. My back aches terribly or I would write more. Good night darling

Affectionately yours<br>William J. Clarke

I am very uneasy about Mr Cooke. I fear that he has hectic fever and having no constitution it will go very hard with him. I haven't heard from him since we left Petersburg—

1. Clarke's regiment never left Ransom's brigade. Clarke wrote his wife on 11 February 1863, stating that "As you predicted, my petition for transfer from the Brigade has been refused" by headquarters because the brigade was in the presence of the enemy. Barden Collection.

*Wootten, Moulton, Clarke Papers, SHC*
*William J. Clarke to Mary Bayard Clarke*

Kenansville N.C. Feb'y. 6th. 1863.

My Dear Wife:

I received yours of the 31st. ult. day before yesterday, and avail myself of the leisure afforded by a rainy day to write to you. We have not yet received any news respecting our application for a transfer, tho' Gen'l. Ransom promised the officers that he would approve it and forward it immediately, but it has to go and return through the "circumlocution" route, which is not very expeditious. It is regarded as a settled matter, and having never known a similar request to be denied I have no fears as to the result.

If this does not succeed I shall try again & never stop until I get out of the Brigade. Two other Regts. Hill's (48th.) and Burgwyn's (26th.) went out in the same way last summer. I should have applied then but R.

"soft-soldered" me, and we were in active campaign. Your piece[1] has had nothing at all to do with the matter. My determination was fixed by an occurrence just after the Battle of Fredericksburg, and I was actually writing a letter to Richmond on the subject when the flare-up of the 23d. occurred. Every other Reg't. except, perhaps, the 35th (Col. Matt. R's) will follow, and they fully justify me and say that my forbearance has surprised them. The officers of the Brigade express great regret at parting with me.

This delay will necessitate a postponement of my visit to you, as I have agreed that Major Love may go home for twenty days, not wishing to keep him here waiting; tho' in reality the postponement will not be more than a week, as I could not well leave my Regt. immediately after joining another Brigade. Only one field officer can be absent at a time—Hereafter I shall apply frequently for leave as my constant service seems to be overlooked, and efficiency seems to meet with no reward, I will have as easy a time as possible. The trickery by which promotions are secured, and the favoritism displayed in the appointments are disheartening, and as it is "unbecoming" for a man to work for himself and improper for his friends or relations to assist him even so much as to move a straw out of his path, why! all we can do is sit still and trust to the omnipotence of luck. If I cannot be promoted, tho' the whole army says I deserve it, it is some comfort to see that Gen'l. Ransom and his brother make small progress on the same road. This sounds very "vigous" as Henry Miller used to say, but I cannot think it wrong to rejoice at the failures of those who endeavor to gain their ends by unfair means.—

I am sorry to hear that you are unwell, and also that you are suffering from your old disease, and greatly wish that it was in my power to accompany you to P.

I fear that your plan about Virginia's[2] house will not succeed as I think Harriet told me in August last that they had rented the house to some one. Whatever plan you adopt will meet with my concurrence; but you must remember how short my purse is.

If you write soon direct to this place, otherwise to care of Maj. Gen'l. S. G. French,[3] Goldsboro'—

Tell Tom that Bill Barrett is as frisky as a colt, and pretended to be very afraid of the drum a few evenings ago, and that he will eat ham and eggs, a fact that John Ellison thinks wonderful. With a kiss for Pet and kind regards to your Father, Ma. and Sue I am

Affectionately yours
William J. Clarke

Tell your Father that I agree with him that we shall have peace soon—
Thank Sue for the helmet which I am now wearing greatly to my comfort.
The letter of thanks I intended writing her today is necessarily deferred—

1. Her poem, "The Charge of the 24th North Carolina Reg't at the Battle of
Sharpsburg."
2. William Clarke's half-sister, Virginia Clarke Hervey of Petersburg.
3. Major General Samuel Gibbs French was in command of the Department
of Southern Virginia and North Carolina. Boatner, *Civil War Dictionary,* 315–16.

FROM THIS PERIOD UNTIL the fall of 1863, Mary Bayard Clarke tried to
find suitable accommodations for her family outside of her father's household in Halifax County. She stayed for a time at Shocco Springs near Warrenton, North Carolina, but found it too expensive. She considered
renting a house in Raleigh but the costs proved prohibitive. For a time she
hoped that South Carolina might provide an asylum, but William Clarke
questioned this idea. By September, she had stayed for a few weeks in
Raleigh but finally concluded she would have to return to her father's plantation for the winter.

*George Bagby Family Papers, MSS 1B1463b475–482, VHS*
*Mary Bayard Clarke to George Bagby (Richmond)*

Conaconara April 1st [1863]

My dear Doctor
    I have just returned from what I suppose you married men would call
—a spree—finding the mountain could not come to me, I like Mahomet
went to the mountain—in other words beat up the quarters of my "wirey
little Col" at Wilmington; after setting him and his ward robe to rights,
riding down two of his horse and spending all his ready money I concluded
to go to Richmond and see what Congress and the Cabinet were doing; I
spent three days at the Spottswood, from whence I dispatched a note to
you, which as you did not answer it, my vanity compels me to believe you
did not receive. I should have staid longer but in one mornings shopping I
spent so much money I concluded to leave, so came along with Mrs President Davis when she went south. This accounts for your having nothing
from Tenella lately. That lady is going to retire into the inmost recess of
my portfolio until she can get some better paper than this to write upon;
and now sends you the last emanation from her brain, as well as one
among the first. Ages ago I published in the Messenger then under John R

Thomson's care a poem called the Triump of Spring, it attracted a good deal of notice but was an unfinished crude production, and I afterwards rewrote it for the volume of poems I intend to publish "some of these days" and laid it away to get ripe. I have been scores of times requested to republish it but did not care to do so; the other day I received a letter from the principal of a Female school making the same request and I therefore send it to you to decide on,[1] only stipulating if you dont republish it that you send it back to me, as I cut it out of a MSS. vol, and if I dont have a printed copy to replace it I dont want the trouble of re-copying it, to say nothing of the paper it will take which is becoming a very scarce article My Muse is a dainty one, and will produce nothing worth reading if she has to use such paper as this and as it is time to begin Spring sewing I shall bid you adieu for some time, for I shall spend the summer at some watering place, probably Buffalo Springs, and do nothing in all likely hood but idle, play ten pins, and ride on horse back, Though perhaps I may be so fortunate as to get some decent paper, in which case you may here from me, I have a few sheets which I am reserving in case of an inspiration. Present my compliments to Mrs Bagby and accept my felicitations on being caught in the matrimonial noose. May you be as well taken care of as my Col is, and at the end of fifteen years of married life be as happy and contented as I am & doubt not you are at present

Very Sincerely Yours<br>M B Clarke

1. The *SLM* published "The Triumph of Spring" in vol. 37, no. 4 (Apr. 1863): 206–9.

❧

*Barden Collection*
*William J. Clarke to Mary Bayard Clarke*

Kinston N. C. April 4th. 1863—

My Dear Wife:

Your two letters have been received and were a great comfort to me, as I have been quite dejected lately, in consequence of a derangement of my liver, and needed something to cheer me. By the aid of blue mass and fasting I am now nearly well, though not entirely so. Speaking of fasting reminds me that I should tell you that the 27th. ult., which was the day appointed by the President to be observed as a national fast, was rigidly observed by my Reg't.—We had sunrise prayer meeting, and a sermon both in the morning and the afternoon. My mess observed it so strictly that the servants did not cook any supper for us, and it was nearly 9 o'clock at night before we got anything to eat.

Yesterday, being Good Friday, I was in Goldsboro' and had the privilege of attending service at St. Stephen's. The sermon was dull and heavy, but the minister read the service petty well, which makes up for many defects.

You can realize, tho' few can, what a deprivation it is to be unable to hear service. Our chaplain,[1] tho' a good and estimable man, is a poor preacher, and his prayers are of a piece with his sermons.—We left at 3 P.M. and reached here in one of the coldest rains I ever felt, through which we marched about a mile, to our present camp. I wrote to you that I intended to apply for a leave of absence. I did so on the 2nd. inst. and have just received for answer that all leaves of absence to officers, except on Surgeon's certificate of disability, are forbidden by the Lieut. Gen'l. commanding as we may expect active service. So mote it be. I have been cheated out of my leave by Gen'l. Ransom, but never mind, it will all come straight yet. I hope I shall learn never to set my heart on any thing, for then I shall not be disappointed. I am the only field officer in the Brigade who has not had a leave of absence. But it makes no difference as I have no home to go to!—

We are encamped in an old-field pine woods, and as a very cold cutting wind is blowing, it is all that we can do to keep warm. We have heard heavy guns, at intervals, all last night and today. We suppose that our folks have taken Washington, and that the Yankee gun-boats are shelling the place endeavoring to dislodge them.

I have no idea which way we shall move when we leave this place, but it is generally supposed that we shall not stay here long. If we can get at the enemy I am as ready to fight him as I shall be at any time hereafter, and so give myself no solicitude on that point.

March [sic] 5th—My Darling, something interrupted me just here, and I resume my epistle again after camp preaching today. We have heard no firing today, and therefore judge that all is quiet on the Tar. The sun glads us once more with his beams and warmth and we are more comfortable & happier. I am still quite indignant about being refused leave of absence; but there is a sweet for every bitter, the $100 it would have cost me will remain for you, and I had rather you should spend it than to spend it on myself. You ask me if the money spent when you came to see me was wasted, I answer *NO!* I never so regarded it, and now I am confirmed in my opinion. I am very sorry that I cannot see Pet and Tom, but hope that something will yet turn up so that I shall. Your accounts of them entertain me very much and increase my anxiety to see them. They must be sweet little plagues to you—I received a letter from Willie on yesterday. Mr. Cooke had been to see them, and I fear will be returning to camp this week. He is not strong enough to bear the fatigue and exposure, and it would be far better if he would stay to the end of his leave which is yet 40 days longer.——One of the privates in my Reg't., today, presented me with a meerschaum pipe which is valued at $50. A horse cannot be found good enough for me, and I have told the committee that I am in no hurry. This is especially the case in the present scarcity of provender. Bill Barrett has been a little off of feed but seems now to have regained his usual appetite. He still labors under the delusion that he is a colt.——

What determination has Sister come to respecting Kate? John Primrose was taken sick, a week or ten days ago, and has gone home. I don't think any thing very serious is the matter with him. On yesterday I received 53 conscripts from the Camp of Instruction at Raleigh, and my Reg't. now looks very large. It was before nearly half as large as Kemper's (Va) Brigade which was at this place until today. I am glad to learn from Capt. Clark, late of my Reg't., who has been on a visit to us, that the Roanoke is so well fortified. The floating battery[2] will prove a great terror to the enemy. I hope they will never attempt the passage; but if they do, I think we shall repulse them.

This has been a very unpleasant Spring, but you would have suffered more had you been in the up country, as the weather has been very severe there. I think that you can remain until the last of next month on Roanoke without any risk. I have little expectation that you can get board for less than $150 a month, even if you can get it at that. I will try to squeeze out that much a month for you, and think I can do it. If it were not for the exorbitant price of every thing my pay would be amply sufficient for all reasonable expenditures. But as things are it is a scant pattern. But we should not repine, our lot is that of seven tenths of the country. We rather have cause for thankfulness that we are as well off as we are. Mrs. D's sarcastic remarks were as foolish as they were unfeeling. I am doing your Father a service of incalcuable value, being the only one of his family actively engaged in protecting his property. The young men of wealth in our State have shown entirely too much reluctance to going into the field. Look around and see how few of them of your acquaintance are facing danger and enduring privations. The poor men are fighting for the rich, *and they know it,* and they begin to tire of bearing the beat and burden of the day, and if the feeling which prompted her remarks does not change, if the men in elevated positions do not pursue a more conciliatory course, and recognise the fact that those placed under them have rights and feelings, there will be a terrible explosion of pent up feelings, and the most disastrous consequences will ensue. I do not allow myself to speak of these things, but I cannot help seeing the current of events—If my faith in the mercy of God was not strong, I should despair; but He leadeth the blind by a way they know not, He maketh darkness light before them and crooked things straight, and He will, in His own good time, work out our deliverance. Present my respects to your Father & Ma. Say to your Father that I was greatly gratified by the account I heard of his speech at Halifax, and that I have no doubt that it has done more good to the cause than all the fighting we have had in N.C. since the war began—Kiss Tom and Pet for me. I shall write to you again in a few days

Affectionately Yours
William J. Clarke

1. Evander McNair was appointed chaplain of the Twenty-fourth Regiment, NCT, on 23 July 1862. He resigned on 3 September 1863. Manarin and Jordan, *Roster of NC Troops,* 7:252.

2. On 16 February 1862, Kate Edmondston mentioned an attempt to construct a "Fire Raft, to be turned loose when the Gun boats approach in the hope of destroying them or at least arresting their passage up the River." Patrick Edmondston was briefly placed in command of the Roanoke River defenses. *Edmondston Diary,* 119, 122, 123.

*Wootten, Moulton, Clarke Papers, SHC*
*William J. Clarke to Mary Bayard Clarke*

I commenced this letter in the Court room but could not finish it & wrote it mostly on the 14th—
Kinston N. C. May 13th. 1863

My Darling:

I was prevented from writing to you on Sunday last, as I intended, by company. On Monday I was very unexpectedly ordered by Gen'l. Daniel to superintend the execution of two deserters from Pettigrew's Brigade, who were condemned to be shot. After that sad spectacle I had no heart to write that day. On Tuesday I was engaged all day defending an officer before a Court Martial. I can get no candles so that I cannot write at night. I make these explanations that you may see that I do not intentionally neglect writing to you. There is many a time that I might write a hasty note; but I like to be quiet and undisturb'd when I commune, in spirit, with you as I do when I write to you.

This, darling, is your birth-day. May God grant you many happy returns of it, each being more happy than the preceeding!

Wharton Green[1] is here on Gen'l. Daniel's staff. He is well, and thro' him I heard from you a few days ago—

I received your two letters, written from Shocco. In relation to Frank's going to the Va. Mil. Institute, having learned that the school expenses will be $600 a years and well knowing that it will cost $100 more, settles the matter—We cannot afford the expense, and if we could it would be money injudiciously expended as, at his age, he could not derive an equivalent. For the present he had better remain with you and rest. As for Willie, even if Mr. Graves advances his price to $400 a year, we had better keep him at school. The very best thing we could do with Frank, after he has had a good rest, would be to put him into a good printing office for a year or eighteen months. He would thereby learn to spell and punctuate, and acquire habits of industry and punctuality. It might prepare him, to some extent, for the most useful and lucrative employment in the south, that of an editor. He would be more benefitted by this course, *if under the right sort of man,* than by any thing he could learn in a college or academy. He needs to digest, to settle down in his mind, what he has already acquired. I really think that he has unusual talents and endowments but he is much more likely to become a dilettanti than a practical, useful man—If I am not in an unhealthy region, and one which would affect him peculiarly on account of his residence in the up country, I would have him with me—If I should be promoted, and go to a healthier portion of country I shall want him with me. There is no peculiar call for haste in deciding on his case; and I hope before the expiration of a month to be able to visit you when we can confer, consider and deliberate on this matter—

I did not tell you about our expedition to Core Creek.[2] We went down with *eight* Regts. (4 cos. would have been amply sufficient), and tore up five miles of railroad—It rained on us terribly almost the whole time, and the men had to wade sometimes over one hundred yards in water nearly knee deep—We were gone three days—

The Yankees have lately sent out some twenty or thirty families, and it made my blood fairly boil to see them pass with their furniture and baggage, which we brought off in our Reg'tl. wagons. They were tumbled out of the cars in the woods at Core Creek and exposed a day & night to the rain Do you recollect a Lieut. Palmer[3] U.S.A. who married a Miss Jones? We saw him one night at Dr. McCormick's. Well he is now in command at New Berne, and is a much more gentlemanly man than Foster.—I fear that the Yanks will not come up here to fight us, as we are well prepared, but strike in some other direction. Gen'l. J. G. Martin has had a Brigade made up for him and his head Qrs. are at Greenville—Gen'l. Ransom may be back next week, when, if times are quiet, I shall try for a short leave for I greatly need rest & relaxation.

I saw Betty Christophers in church last Sunday, she married in Kinston —I saw Jas. Edmundston yesterday. He is Daniel's Q. M. Daniel is very polite to me, (a wonder for D.) and seems to lay stress on my opinion which he always asks—We occasionally have rumors that our Brigade will be ordered to Va. Such a thing is not probable, tho' I know Ransom will try to have it done as he is very partial to that state—

Remember me to my dear boys & tell them that I want to see them very badly, Kiss Pet & Tom for me

Affectionately yours<br>William J. Clarke

Regards to Mr Cooke if he is with you

I send you a draft on Happer, Farrell's agent at Weldon for $100— please acknowledge receipt in your note.

1. Wharton J. Green served as lieutenant colonel of the Second Battalion, North Carolina Infantry. Captured at Roanoke Island on 8 February. 1862, he was paroled and later volunteered as an aide for General Daniel. Manarin and Jordan, *Roster of NC Troops,* 3:264.

2. Core Creek was located near New Bern, North Carolina.

3. Brigadier General Innis N. Palmer commanded the Department of North Carolina for the Union army and oversaw New Bern defenses. Boatner, *Civil War Dictionary,* 616–17. He replaced Major General John Gray Foster. Boatner, *Civil War Dictionary,* 301–2.

BY THIS DATE, THE Army of Northern Virginia had begun its march toward Gettysburg, but Ransom's Brigade remained in Virginia to guard against Union raiders. On 2 June the brigade left Petersburg and marched to Blackwater Bridge, where it remained until 12 June. During this time, Robert Ransom received his promotion to major general, while his brother Matt Ransom was appointed brigadier general and assigned to command his brother's former brigade. Matt Ransom's appointment infuriated William Clarke, who, as a senior colonel of the brigade, had expected a promotion. Clarke wrote an old friend, Major General Daniel Harvey Hill, asking if he had recommended Ransom's promotion over his own. Hill emphatically responded on 19 June 1863, "*I did not recommend Col Ransom. His brother brought me his recommendation as an official paper directed to the Adjt. Genl. I told him that I would take no part in the matter & would recommend no one. . . . It mortifies me to suppose that you could believe me guilty of breach of my word. . . . I have recommended four* [North Carolina] *Colonels for promotion & as I knew would be the case, not one of them has been promoted.*" Clarke Papers, SHC.

On 20 July the brigade moved to Weldon, North Carolina, to protect a railroad bridge from federal cavalry raids. The brigade remained in North Carolina at various positions. Manarin and Jordan, *Roster of NC Troops,* 7:249.

*Barden Collection*
*William J. Clarke to Mary Bayard Clarke*

Drewry's Bluff Va. June 16th. 1863—

My Dear Wife:

Since my last letter we have moved about a good deal. On Friday we came from Ivor to Petersburg, and on Sunday we marched to this place. These moves were caused by the appearance of some gun boats in James River. They were very much alarmed in Petersburg, and well they might be, for there was only one Regt. there.

On yesterday I went to Richmond, and had the satisfaction of learning that Col. Matt. Ransom was appointed Brigadier over me. This was all done by trickery. They got me out of the way, at a position I could not leave, and had the field to themselves.

I called, with Mr. [Charles M.] Conrad, on the President[1] and plainly, but respectfully, told him what I thought of it, and the old man seemed really pained at the injustice he had done me. If a vacancy should occur, while the facts are fresh in his mind, he would appoint me, I think; but no vacancy will occur until I shall be forgotten, for I have no one to work for me at Richmond. Poor dear Mr. Conrad would do any thing in his power but he has no influence—I felt very bad at first but now I am more composed and have almost recovered my equinimity. To tell the truth I care more for the money than the honor, for the position, to a conscientious man, is one of great responsibility and labor. I hope that you will not be distressed about it. When it is best for me to receive the appointment I shall certainly get it. Of that I am as sure as I am that I live, but that does not alter the fact that a great wrong has been done me Mr. Conrad was looking better than I expected. He says that he will come to see you before long—It was really ludicrous to see how angry the old fellow got when we heard the news—I took on so that I had to take a julip with ice. I do not know whether it was mental worry, heat, or the natural goodness of the drink, but it was delicious—Mr. Cooke is sitting by me reading "No Name". He is quite well but has not yet obtained his appointment on Ransom's staff, tho' he has assurance that he will get it—

I feel very badly, even bitterly, for I have been cruelly wronged, but I shall get over it in a few days. The feeling is like one experiences after returning from the funeral of a freind; and have I not buried a cherished hope? God help us for we are truly in a pitiable condition! but I bate not one jot or tittle of hope or confidence as to the final and glorious result. Any thing is preferable to emancipation and amalgamation, and to that we were drifting as rapidly as a vessel in the current of Niagara—

Mr. Cooke has recd. yours of the 10th. mine did not come to hand—

Kiss Tom & Pet for me, love to the boys. Poor Capt. W. recd. his handkerchiefs while in an agony about his brother. Was ever any thing more sad?

I hope that my next letter will be written from the banks of the Roanoke—

Affectionately yours
William J. Clarke

P.S. Direct to Petersburg—

1. Jefferson Davis.

❧

*Wootten, Moulton, Clarke Papers, SHC*
*William J. Clarke to Mary Bayard Clarke*

Camp near Richmond July 11th. 1863.

My Dear Wife:

Since I last wrote to you I recd. your last letter, and also Willie's letter with your post-script. I am greatly relieved by learning that you are not suffering so much, and devoutly hope that, with settled weather, you will entirely recover. I think we may congratulate ourselves on having found so good a place for the boys. If it is Joseph S. Jones that they are with, they could not be in a better place. Mr. Graves's extortion surpasses any thing

I have heard of, and has lessened him greatly in my estimation. I hope the boys will learn to spell and write.

I greatly sympathise with Capt. Kennedy and his wife in the loss of their infant, and greatly fear that it is the beginning of very serious trouble between them. Poor Gen'l. Trimble[1] is reported as having had his left leg shot off; if that be so, it will kill him. I heard, today, at Brigade Head Quarters that Col. Harry Burgwyn was killed. The intelligence comes quite direct and may be considered reliable. Cantwell is taken prisoner. Gen'l. Lee's situation is far better than was reported, and so far from being cut up by the Yankee army he has almost demolished it and sent it broken and reeling to defend Washington City. Vicksburg[2] is a hard blow, and I fear that the loss of it will prolong the contest; but there is a Divinity that shapes our ends, that brings light out of darkness, and it may be that this seemingly adverse occurrence will be over-ruled to be a blessing. The President, who alone was serene amid the recent alarms at Richmond, is far from being depressed by the present position of affairs. Every dispatch which we receive from the north is more cheering than the one which preceeded it, with the exception that as we obtain more particular details we are shocked by learning that some friend has fallen. I should not be surprised if this was not the last great battle of the war east of the Alleghanies. There will probably be two great battles in the west, Grant will now press [Joseph E.] Johnston, and Rosencranz, [Braxton] Bragg, and of course there will be terrible battles.—Maj. Gen'l. Ransom is using every exertion to get us off to the northern army, and I think it highly probable that he will succeed, and that we shall not remain here more than a week longer. So far as I am individually concerned I am perfectly willing, but I dread the long and fatiguing marches for the men. I do hope that *if* a single man is killed it will be the prime mover—

Sunday July 12th. Dr. Wilson saw several officers from Gen'l. Lee's army last night, who report that he has terribly cut up the Yankee Grand army, and that his falling back to Hagerstown was to secure his prisoners of whom he had a very large number, and the wagons and artillery captured, which are now safe on this side of the Potomac. Our wounded, who fell into their hands, were mostly those who were too badly wounded to be removed. They regard the victory one of the most decisive and fruitful of the war. Good news reaches us from Charleston.[3] The enemy has been again repulsed with about the same loss as at their former attack.

Petersburg July 13th. Thus far had I written on yesterday when the drum beat for church. I attended and the chaplain had not arrived at 10thly. when one of the Genl's. aids rode up to command that we march immediately. I said not a word to the minister but waited quietly until he finished, and then gave the order, and my Reg't. was packed up and on the road to Richmond nearly half an hour before any other. They came by rail, but while we were stopping just out side of the city waiting to see if we could get transportation, Col. Magruder came along and invited me to go and dine with him at a friend's house about half a mile off. As I had had very little, except salt bacon, to eat for some time, I concluded to risk it and went, and had a royal time. The family was that of a very rich retired merchant, and every thing was of the best quality, and in profusion. While we were at dinner the Brigade was marching thro' Richmond in a furious rain. I waited until the rain was over, and then mounted my horse and crossed the river at the pontoon bridge and reached Petersburg almost as soon as the regt. Nothing was said about my absence, if it was observed. Our advent hither was caused by the appearance of Yankee gun boats in the James, at Brandon.[4] We shall be kept at this sort of thing as long as we are in this section. We like, however, to be near Petersburg, and, though I have but few opportunities to be in town, still as the country is healthy I like it too. Maj. Gen'l. Hill has been promoted and been ordered out west. Maj. Gen'l. Ransom is in command of the Dept.

I fear that your Father has met with a disaster by the freshet in the Roanoke. God grant that the Yankees may not come to destroy all that the rapacious waters have left. It is almost time for the State Home Guard to be in the field,[5] and tho' they would be unreliable soldiers for the field, they will do good service in checking raiders.

I dread to think of the thousand and one troubles you will have to encounter in going to house keeping at the present time. You will however be repaid for it when the winter comes, in some measure. If I could bear the inconveniences for you I would rather bivouac the whole winter than have you subjected again to the unkindness of your capricious and unreasonable Ma. But I know that you will get thro' it bravely and I hope that I shall be able to get a leave of absence so as to be with you when the boys have vacation, if not before.

I will send you some coffee. I should have done so sooner but I have been waiting for some safe opportunity. But now if I cannot find a way I will make one.

Mr. Cooke left us on Thursday on a three days' leave for this place. I learn that he went to Raleigh, but I am at a loss to know what for.

I will make him Quarter Master if Farrell is promoted, provided he can give the bond ($50,000), which I greatly doubt, as it is a class of suretyship that most of persons particularly avoid. I fear that he will be greatly mortified about it. He expects Capt. Clark to be his bondsman: now Clark immediately on hearing of the vacancy, before he received Cooke's letter wrote to me asking for the office himself. I have not told Mr. Cooke about this, as it is very uncertain whether there will be a vacancy

I have an opportunity of sending my letter to the P.O. so I close in haste but will write again in a few days—Love to all

Affectionately yours:<br/>William J. Clarke

1. Major General Isaac Ridgeway Trimble was captured and lost a leg during the Gettysburg campaign. Boatner, *Civil War Dictionary,* 849.

2. Vicksburg, Mississippi, fell to Union forces on 4 July 1863.

3. After several unsuccessful attacks on Fort Sumter, the North abandoned its plans of taking Charleston by naval action alone. Boatner, *Civil War Dictionary,* 583.

4. Union gunboats appeared at Brandon, Virginia, during the Gettysburg campaign. A sharp battle ensued on 9 June 1863. Boatner, *Civil War Dictionary,* 80.

5. North Carolina Governor Zebulon B. Vance issued a proclamation in June 1863 establishing the state's Home Guard to replace the militia. The state's militia law had been overruled by the Confederate conscription acts. Vance's new state defense rested on men between the ages of eighteen and fifty years who were exempt from the Confederate army because of age or occupation. Clark, *Histories of the Several Regiments,* 4:645–46, 649.

*Wootten, Moulton, Clarke Papers, SHC*
*William J. Clarke to Mary Bayard Clarke*

Camp near Petersburg Va. July 16th. 1863

My Dear Mary:

Yours of 11th. inst. has just been received, having been returned from Richmond. You speak of having received a letter from me but I am at a loss to know which of two or three, I have lately written to you, you refer to. About ten days ago I sent you a check on W. H. Happer for $125 of which you make no mention. It is necessary that the receipt of checks should be acknowledged, that their payment may be stopped in case they should fall in improper hands. I hope you will hereafter remember this—I had great misgivings about the plan of your living in Raleigh, but it seemed to be the best and most feasible that presented. I fully concur in your determination, tho' I feel great anxiety to have you as comfortably settled as possible. Every course I can think of is hedged up, difficulties are on every hand. The position of affairs is so anomalous that it is impossible for one, in my secluded position, to advise. The experienced, wise, prudent, and far-seeing seem to be little better off than the improvident, and the careless. I reckon we shall, like Dick Haywood when he was going to recitation without having prepared his lesson, be compelled "to float on the surface of the occasion and trust to the omnipotence of luck." If I could only be promoted so as to increase my income, a great anxiety would be removed. But worldly wisom and piety for once agree in impressing on us that "sufficient unto the day is the evil thereof," and tho' I should lay awake o'nights planning, scheming, and devising, I doubt if any thing would come of it. If you could only find some good country family to winter with! There are such, if we only could find them, who would be glad to have you The towns are all filled with refugees. Suppose you write to Aunt Catherine Colton at Asheboro' Randolph County, to inquire. I mention this at a venture, as possibly living may be cheap there, as it is an abundant county and not very convenient to market, consequently the people would have more for home consumption. I don't mean that you should board with Aunt as I *know* that would not be agreeable.

I am sorry to learn that the proprietor of Shocco has become so deeply infected with the all pervading spirit of selfishness. Like all dishonesty it will in the end prove injurious to him practising it. He will lose his boarders and be compelled to treat those remaining better. Apropos, I sent you on Monday, to Weldon, by Mr. Day three pounds of coffee which he thought he could contrive to get to you. I hope you have received it Use it freely and let me know when it is *about* to fail and I'll send more You may leave Nichols whenever you choose and only pay him at the rates agreed upon. He has failed to keep his part of the contract, and you only contracted to pay $50. pr. month.—

We have as pleasant a time here as we could have any where. The camp is as dry as any one could be, in this season of rain, and it is high and airy, and we have excellent spring water. We are entirely too pleasantly situated to remain here long, and will probably march on Sunday some where, as that is the day we commonly march.—We get news slowly from Gen'l. Lee, but what we get shows that our country will be clothed in mourning

Cam. Iredell,[1] & young Semmes of Raleigh are killed. It is fortunate that we were not there for the N.C. regts. suffered severely. The news saddens us but we are not despondent. There is wailing and woe in the North and they will probably, after the glorification over Vicksburg is over, begin to see that it does not and will not pay.—Three days ago I sent a scouting party out about 20 miles below this. They are still out, but I learn that they fell in with the enemy and captured *one skillet and a bag of meal.* The enemy retreated to their gun boats and spent the rest of the day in shelling the woods. No one hurt on our side. Mr. Day informed me that your Father's dams had stood the freshet, but Mr. Cooke understood your brother differently write and let me know if you have heard. Great as would be the loss I am not certain but the destruction of the low-land crops would be a blessing to the Roanoke farmers, as then there would be no temptation to the enemy to come up the river to devastate and the negroes far more valuable would be safe: But at the present time and prices a good crop is very desirable. I send a kiss for Pet in return for her rose. Tell Tom that Bill Barrett is quite well & that he is as lively as a colt. Intending to write to you again in a few days if opportunity is afforded I close by subscribing myself as ever

Yours affectionately<br>William J. Clarke

1. North Carolina regiments suffered severely at Gettysburg. Campbell Treadwell Iredell of Wake County, a twenty-five-year-old druggist when the war began, had an arm shot off at Gettysburg and died from his wounds. Manarin and Jordan, *Roster of NC Troops,* 11:273.

*Wootten, Moulton, Clarke Papers, SHC*
*William J. Clarke to Mary Bayard Clarke*

Camp near Petersburg Va<br>July 24th. 1863—

My Dear Wife:

Your very welcome letters of the 19th. & 20th. inst. were received this morning on my return from Weldon; whither we went three days ago, with all speed, to arrest the progress of the raiders who burned Rocky Mount.[1] My men were exposed without tents to the terrible rain we had at that time. Gen'l. Ransom was along but gave me the entire command of the two regts. The people there, his old friends and neighbours, did not hesitate to tell him that, while they were pleased to see him promoted, they thought that I deserved it first; and, as the conqueror can afford to be generous, he admitted it, and was most lavish of his praises. I find that the feeling is very general. I am complimented very highly for "the manly and dignified manner" in which I have borne my discomfiture. Ah little do they know how deeply I have been wounded! But eels are said to become accustomed to skinning, and our hearts become callous.

It is terribly hot, and tho' I am tired and need sleep, having been up all night, I cannot go to sleep.

You may rest easy about our Brigade going to the army of Northern Virginia. We are a part of the garrison of Richd. and shall be trotting up and down all this campaign. Besides I predict that unless Gen'l. Lee crosses again into Maryland, which is very improbable, there will be no more great battles, on this side the Alleghanies. The war in this section is dwindling down into a depredatory conflict, in which individuals are ruined, but communities suffer but little. I believe, and the impression is like a woman's conclusion not to be logically defined, that the war is rapidly approaching an end, and that end independence. It is a consummation most devoutly to be wished, war worn tho' I be, I await it with composure and patience.

I am sorry that the boys have not a higher opinion of their teacher, tho' I am far from concurring fully with them. Boys frequently think themselves fully equal to their teachers when such is far from being the case. At any rate they had better remain as the place is a good one for them to board at and saves $50. a month.—The account in the papers about my narrow escape from a shell refers to our fight at Crump's Farm near Bottom Bridge, early in the present month, of which I wrote you an account, except about the shelling, which I did not mention as it was a small affair, nor did I mention the great praise of Gen'l. Ransom for the manner in which I handled my Regt. for that was all bosh.

Faison[2] is too great a fool for you to bestow a second thought on, tho' you treated him rightly.

I have little hope that you will obtain an asylum in S.C. as all the refugees from Charleston & the sea coast are in this section of country you would like to go to.—If you can't do better how would old Mrs. Marshall in Halifax do? You must pardon me if I make some very silly and impracticable suggestions, I want to help but don't know how.

Excuse this very dull letter, but be sure to answer it nevertheless, give my love to the boys, & kiss Pet & Tom for me. Bless their souls I want to see them so badly it almost gives me the "rumatiz"

Affectionately yours
William J. Clarke

1. Federal troops from New Bern raided Greenville, Tarboro, and Rocky Mount, North Carolina, during a six-day period from 19 July through 24 July, 1863. They destroyed property and burned the bridge over the Tar River at Greenville. At Rocky Mount, northern troops burned a cotton mill, the railroad bridge, and Confederate supplies. They also destroyed the naval works, railroad cars, and supplies in Tarboro. The federal troops secured 100 prisoners, 300 slaves, and 300 horses and mules. This encouraged the Confederacy to keep more troops deployed in the state to protect its resources. *Official Records (Army),* series 1, vol. 27, pt. 2: 963, 976; John G. Barrett, *The Civil War in North Carolina* (Chapel Hill: University of North Carolina Press, 1963), 164–66 (hereafter cited as Barrett, *Civil War in North Carolina*); David A. Norris, "'The Yankees Have Been Here!': The Story of Brig. Gen. Edward E. Potter's Raid on Greenville, Tarboro, and Rocky Mount, July 19–23, 1863," *NCHR* 73 (Jan. 1996): 27. Kate Edmondston mentioned that the Twenty-fourth Regiment met federal cavalry at Crump's Mill and drove them back. 30 July 1863, *Edmondston Diary,* 444.

2. Paul F. Faison, colonel of the Fifty-sixth Regiment, NCT, also served in Ransom's brigade. Barrett, *Civil War in North Carolina,* 162–64.

*Frances Finnerty Papers*
*Mary Bayard Clarke to Frank and Willie Clarke*

Raleigh Sep 27th [1863]

My dear Boys

I have been here a week now and received your letters a few days ago, I carried Willie Primrose's to him the day I got mine; we are all well enjoying a visit from father who has run up from camp for a day or two, he goes back next wednesday, he says he has two pounds of powder for you which he thinks he can get to you in the course of a week or two; I shall have to go to Conniconara to spend the winter; I had many plans but they have all failed and Grandpa thinks I had better be there, I am very sorry that we cant do as we like, but if I go there I can afford to send you to a better school, and as Mrs Primrose thinks of sending Rob and Willie to Davidson[1] I shall try and get you in there with them; keep jogging up the Shoe maker, tell him you dont know when you will have to leave, and he must get your shoes done, dont pay any thing until you either get them all, or come away and then get Mr Jones to pay it out of the money I left with Mrs. Jones.[2] I hope you have received the book I sent you and the "Field and fireside"[3] If you go to Davidson it will be about the 1st of November before you can get off—I have some cloth to make you some jackets—very pretty, and I must have them made before you can leave me. Tom says bring him a string of chinquepins when you come; And go over to

Shocco some day and see Cousin Ellen[4] and ask her if she has succeeded in getting any homespun to make winter pants for you, and enquire all round of every body, and ask Mrs Jones if she can tell you when you can get any home spun suitable for winter pantaloons and if you can get any buy five yards, you may give as high as $5 a yard and pay for it or get Mrs Jones to do so and let me know when you have it. I am glad you have not been to Shocco but want you to go once and see about cloth. Sister goes to School[5] and is learning very well Tom says he has "education plenty for these hard times and he aint going to school just to sit on a bench and keep holding a book in his hands." Give my compliments to Mr and Mrs Jones and

believe me your<br>
Affectionate<br>
Mother

1. Davidson College, a Presbyterian school, was founded in 1837. In 1860 it had six professors and 112 students. Johnson, *Ante-bellum North Carolina,* 298. Both William and Rob Primrose attended the school at the same time as did Frank and Willie Clarke. Powell, *DNCB,* 5:147.

2. The Clarke boys boarded with a family named Jones while attending the Belmont school, which was operated by Ralph Henry Graves.

3. The *Southern Field and Fireside* occasionally published pieces submitted by Mary Bayard Clarke during the war. In 1865 she became assistant editor of the publication. According to Winchester Hall, "The connection . . . lasted only a few months, as Mrs. Clarke considered the proprietors had not dealt with her fairly." Hall, *MBC Poems,* xvii–xix.

4. Ellen Mordecai Devereux, born 17 September 1850, was the third daughter of John and Margaret Mordecai Devereux Jr. She married John Wetmore Hinsdale on 23 September 1869. Devereux Family Bible.

5. This was probably St. Mary's, founded in Raleigh in 1842 as an Episcopal academy for young ladies from across the South. The Reverend Aldert Smedes and his son ran the school. Murray, *Wake County,* 310.

*Frances Finnerty Papers*
*Mary Bayard Clarke to Willie Clarke (Davidson)*[1]

Raleigh Nov 1st [1863]

My dear little Willie

Your letter gave me great pleasure for it was not only well written but showed you were happy and improving; I think a great deal about you for you are the only one absent from me but I dont worry about you and shant as long as I can feel you are well, happy and improving. We are all well here but feeling very sad about your cousin Thomas Jones,[2] Aunt Betties oldest boy, he was wounded about ten days ago at the fight at Bristow Station, shot in the left side and we thought but little hurt, as he was able to write himself to his mother and was carried to Richmond where his wife joined him, we heard of him in the hospital there as doing well and expected to hear soon that he was able to be carried to Connaconara but yesterday we got a letter stating he was much worse and there was very little hope he could recover, Uncle John [Devereux] went on last night and we hope to hear to day how he is, I have no hope of his recovery and only trust now that his Mother got to him before he died. God has been very gracious to us in sparing our family so long, with so many exposed it is wonderful we have not before this lost some member of our family we must pray that He will keep dear Father safe. Your cousins Hamilton and Fanny Polk[3] are in town, they came down from Ashville in this State where Aunt Fanny is living on account of Hamilton's health he has had two strokes of paralasys the last brought on by his exertions in putting out a fire, some one they think a Union man set fire to the house, built a fire on the front porch and before they discovered it it had got so far under way they had great difficulty in putting it out. the next day Hamilton had a second stroke and was almost speechless he has recovered from that but walks very badly. Frank is spending the day with me I will tell him when he comes in to put a PS to this Father was well when I heard last but had been ordered to Tarborough I dont know whether he will remain there or not. Tom is very well your message came in good time as I had just had to whip him for running away—he and Dick Gatlin have got into the habit of going to Mrs White's and Cousin Tom Burgwyn's[4] with out permission and I have had to whip him several times about it Mr Conrad begged him off once and now when he does wrong he runs to him and says Mr Conrad dont let Mother whip me. Tell the boys with my love that I saw their Mother yesterday She was quite well God bless you darling

your affectionate
Mother

1. During the war, Davidson College served as a preparatory school for younger boys and disabled soldiers. Cornelia Rebekah Shaw, *Davidson College* (New York: Fleming H. Rebell Press, 1923), 105, 108 (hereafter cited as Shaw, *Davidson College*).

2. Thomas Devereux Jones was mortally wounded at Bristoe Station and died in Richmond on 6 November 1863. Kate Edmondston, in attendance at his deathbed with other family members, described his death and the grief of his widow, Martha Ann Blount (Pattie) Skinner. "I have often heard of the eloquence of greif, but never did I realize it untill then. . . . Poor young creatures! Married the 1st of last Jan., separated by the rude fortune of war five days after, to meet again & only for a few days in May & again for a few more in Oct, & then for the third & last time when she was summoned to attend on his death bed & to receive his last farewell in an Hospital. Their whole married life spent in each other's society could be compressed into three weeks!" 13 November 1863, *Edmondston Diary*, xxx, 85n, 487–89.

3. Hamilton and Fanny Polk were two of Lieutenant General Leonidas and Frances Devereux Polk's children. Leonidas Polk had moved his family to Sewanee, Tennessee, thinking they would be safer there than in Louisiana, but an arsonist set fire to their new house. Hamilton and Fanny Polk were in Raleigh in November 1863 visiting family and friends. William M. Polk, *Leonidas Polk, Bishop and General,* vol. 1 (New York: Longmans, Green, 1915), 325–27; Schiller, *A Captain's War,* 107.

4. Thomas P. Burgwyn, a brother of Henry K. Burgwyn Sr., lived as a refugee in Raleigh during the war with other members of his family. Schiller, *A Captain's War,* 13n.

❧

*Barden Collection*
*William J. Clarke to Mary Bayard Clarke*

Hamilton N.C.
Dec'r. 29th. 1863.

My Dear Mary:

I received, on yesterday, yours of the 25th. and truly sympathized with you in your disappointment at my failure to visit you on Christmas; but I found that there was a prevailing opinion at Weldon that we were about to have warm work down here about that time, and as I had been so long absent I could not do otherwise than come on immediately. On arriving here I find that the Yankees are in mortal dread lest we should attack them. I should give them grounds for their apprehensions if I had a larger force.

I left Richmond more despondent for our cause than I have ever been, as I saw deplorable evidences that the men governing and directing our destinies are unequal to the occasion.

The President is worn out mentally and physically, & Congress & Cabinet seem to have neither energy, invention or wisdom. This is the only revolution on record which has not produced a genius!

The Prest. treated me very kindly, approved of my plan and would have carried it into immediate execution but wished to know whether the troops spoken of by Gov. Vance were militia or not.[1]

If militia, the Prest. cannot appoint the Gen'l., it would "bust up" state rights, every pillar of the capitol would rock on its base and fall with appalling crash etc.

I have written to Vance and believe that he will explain the matter satisfactorily Our delegation very warmly approved my plan and I have no doubt that Smith and Bridgers[2] will press the matter. Something must be done, or the disasters you speak of will inevitably come upon this section of country. I succeeded in pretty thoroughly stirring up the Commissary Gen'l. [Lucius Northrup] and have recd. a letter of thanks from the principle Commsy. of this State.

I saw but little of Mr. Conrad. He was on the Finance Committee and very busy both day & night. He was well but looked worn and thin. I saw Wilcox[3] and rec'd. quite a budget of San Antonio news. Sam [Taylor] is well and W. pronounced quite a eulogium on him. Poor parson Jones is dead.[4] He died in Louisiana while serving as chaplain to a Tex. Reg't. Enoch Jones[5] is also dead. Flora Jones is married to the younger Yearman. Jas. Vance is going to marry Vic. Palmer—Upson is not dead as reported. Mr. Dalzel[6] of Houston has charge of the church. This is pretty much all that I heard that would interest you. It takes six weeks to go to Texas.

I saw Mrs. [George E.] Pickett in R. and Miss Lee in Tarboro' who inquired very particularly about you. I did not stop in Petersburg long enough to call on Cousin Mary but I saw Charles in the street and he told me that the family was well.

Travelling is more unpleasant than ever, and still I never saw so many persons travelling.

Has Sister been to see you? she spoke of it when I was at her house. Let me know how your sister Betsey is, when you write.

I felt very badly about not being able to send the children any christmas presents, but when wax dolls, with a ring on the finger, sell for $1,000 I could not afford it.

I hope to be relieved in about a week when I hope to be able to come to see you. Kiss Tom & Pet for me. Respects to yr. Father, Ma and Sue and believe me

Very affectionately
William J. Clarke

1. Governor Vance worked to secure a promotion for William Clarke. In a letter to James A. Seddon dated 16 December 1863, Vance described a plan to use state troops in conjunction with Clarke's regiment to defend eastern North Carolina. Vance proposed placing the state troops under Clarke's command and said, "As you will perceive this involves the necessity of conferring additional rank upon Col. Clarke. I beg leave to say particularly, that I regard him as eminently fitted for this proposed service; and generally that Col. Clarke is deserving of this promotion on account of his long and faithful services from the beginning of the war. . . . I have had the honor to recommend him to the Department before, having seen him on the field of battle." Johnston and Mobley, *Vance Papers,* 2:343–44. Clarke had journeyed to Richmond to submit the proposal to Jefferson Davis.

2. William Nathan Harrell Smith and Robert Rufus Bridgers were members of the Confederate congress from North Carolina. Smith, a lawyer and state legislator, later served as chief justice of the North Carolina Supreme Court. Bridgers, a Democrat, worked at different times as a lawyer, planter, bank president, state legislator, and railroad president. Wilfred B. Yearns Jr., "North Carolina in the Confederate Congress," *NCHR* 29 (July 1952): 361, 365; Ashe, *Cyclopedia of Eminent and Representative Men,* 2:89–92.

3. Probably John Allen Wilcox, an old San Antonio friend and fellow member of the Knights of the Golden Circle who served in the Confederate congress until his death. Young, *To the Tryants Never Yield,* 37, 38.

4. The Reverend Lucius H. Jones, formerly of St. Mark's Episcopal Church in San Antonio, actually died in 1864 from malarial fever. He had been wounded in New Mexico while ministering to wounded soldiers. A stained-glass window at St. Mark's Church commemorates his memory. Harriet Brown Moore, *Saint Mark's Church, San Antonio Texas: A Parish With Personality* (San Antonio, Tex.: Naylor, 1944), 6, 12 (hereafter cited as Moore, *St. Mark's Church*); Mary Bayard Clarke, "In Memoriam Revd Lucius Jones, first Rector of St. Mark's church San Antonio Texas, who died from the effect of a wound received while ministering to a dying soldier on the field of Glorietta," handwritten poem, Barden Collection.

5. A former associate on the San Antonio and Mexican Gulf Railroad.

6. The Reverend W. T. Dalzell. Moore, *St. Mark's Church,* 13, 14.

*Frances Finnerty Papers*
*Mary Bayard Clarke to Willie Clarke*

Conocanara Dec 31st [1863]

My Dear Willie

I hope you have had a merry Christmas and a happy New Year. I have been trying to get your pantaloons and gloves done for you and last night sent

Mrs Selly a pair of pantaloons, a box of caps, some powder, the powder horn, and some darning cotton which I asked her to send you either by private opportunity or if none occurred by express; Mr Conrad sent two pounds of shot from Richmond which I hope you have got, or will get soon. I have just finished your gloves. I knit them myself, they will be both warmer and stronger than the others which I hope reached you by mail. I did not send the "Young Marooners" because Sister wanted me to read it to her, but will send it if you would like it. I must tell you about Tom he listens sometimes, and was much interested in the account of the children carried off by the Devil-fish; the next morning he got in a pet with the tongs and called them devil-tongs, Mary was horrified and told him that was swearing, but he said it was not, for if it was no harm to say devil-fish it could not be wrong to say devil-tongs. Mary could not solve the question and asked me about it, I talked to Tom and he promised he would not say so any more, so that night when it was time to read he brought me the book and said, "Mamma please read some more about the *Satan fish*—"

I got your report the other day and was delighted with it. I showed it to Grand pa and Uncle Edmondston and they both said it did you great credit. I shall send it by this mail to Father and Mr Cooke, I hope you will continue to improve and am sure you will for you *try*, and it gives me more pleasure than anything in the world to feel that my children are well, happy, and improving. and you seem to be all three, Aunt Frances is here she came yesterday and says Franc is well and growing so fast he will soon out grow all his clothes, I shall have to put a weight on his head. I want you to save all the fur off your rabbit and squirrel skins for if carded with cotton it will make nice gloves and socks you can get it off very easily and nicely by covering the *flesh* side of the skin with a paste made of ashes and water keep it damp and you can they tell me in a few days scrape off all the fur from the other side; now dont you make a mistake and put the ashes and water on the *fur* side of the skin. you can put the fur in a bag and keep it till you come down if you have no bag I will make one and send you. If your gloves dont fit let me know and I will send you another pair, tell me also if you need socks, let me know whenever you need anything, if possible give me notice in time for I may not be able always to send what you want at once. I think you had better order another pair of shoes have them made large so you can wear them next summer.

Give my love to the boys and tell them the powder and shot are for you all three in common. Give my compliments to Mrs Kirkpatrick and

Mrs McIver[1] and tell them I am very grateful to them for their kindness to you. Auntie Sister Tom and all the rest send love May God bless my darling boy prays his loving

Mother

1. Mrs. Kirkpatrick was the wife of John L. Kirkpatrick, who became president of Davidson College on 14 November 1860. Her efforts to secure food and clothing for North Carolina soldiers earned her the accolade of being "best forager." Alexander McIver began teaching mathematics at the college in 1859 and became North Carolina's superintendent of public instruction in 1871. McIver married Mary Ann Wilcox. Shaw, *Davidson College,* 98, 116; Powell, *DNCB,* 4:151.

IN JANUARY 1864 CONFEDERATE troops commanded by George E. Pickett tried to recapture New Bern, North Carolina, headquarters for occupying federal forces. Ransom's brigade joined the column commanded by General Seth M. Barton on the south side of the Trent River, while a second column moved on the north side of the Neuse River. The third column marched between the Neuse and Trent rivers. A concerted attack by all three columns was ordered for 1 February, but the operation failed following stiff federal opposition.

By mid-February the regiment was encamped near Petersburg but soon returned to North Carolina. Four of the regiment's companies raided sections of eastern North Carolina. The remainder of the regiment moved with the brigade to Franklin, Virginia, and then back to North Carolina, at which time the detached companies rejoined the regiment. Ransom's brigade proceeded to drive a federal force down the Dismal Swamp Canal to within twelve miles of Norfolk. On 4 March Ransom's brigade moved toward Suffolk, driving northern troops from that town on 9 March. The brigade held the town for two days before moving to Weldon on 2 March. Manarin and Jordan, *Roster of NC Troops,* 7:249.

*Frances Finnerty Papers*
*William J. Clarke to Mary Bayard Clarke*

Weldon Feby. 7th. 1864

My Dear Mary:

I arrived here this morning with the Regt. in good health, but wearied by the loss of a nights sleep. We have rendered very efficient service and undergone great hardship during the past week. We advanced on Newbern by the upper Trent road and were to have crossed Bryce's Creek within two miles of N. but found it too strongly fortified. The expedition failed thro' mismanagement, and from want of brains. A part of my Regt. was subjected to a heavy shelling on Monday morning and I had one man from Person killed and one officer (Lt. Long)[1] wounded but not mortally & two privates bruised by shell. We were under Gen'l. Barton—The column between the rivers was led by Genl Pickett. They carried the post at Batcheller's creek, took about three hundred prisoners, arms clothing &c. Col. Shaw[2] was killed & one private, about 20 wounded. The boats destroyed one large gun boat. This ends the expedition to Newbern, but we are not done with it. We will take the place yet.—I am sorry to see that you are so despondent, on the contrary I am in good spirits. I have not a shadow of doubt that we shall in a reasonable time gain our independence and that I shall be not only a Brigadier but a Major Gen'l. You will be gratified to learn that no officer is spoken of more or in higher terms of praise than your little husband. We came to a creek and were brought to a stand. I rode to the front and saw the condition of things, and offered to build a bridge in two hours. Gen'l. Barton said it would take eight hours and seemed to doubt if I could do it at all; but consented that I should try. I went to work having no tools but axes, and buit [sic] it at night in a little over one hour, and crossed over every thing without the slightest accident.

I have no idea how long we shall be here but will write to you in a day or two. I am very much in need of a horse. Let me know if Bill has recovered and if he has not if I can get the use of Tom Jones's horse until Bill gets well or I can get a horse. I don't expect to need him more than a month, if so long.

The Cape Fear Bank at Raleigh refused to take my money on deposite, so that you will please destroy the check I sent you. I have however sent one hundred and fifty ($150) to your brother for you—I sent it last night by Q.M. of 25th. Regt. and you can draw on him for it. Please say to your Ma that I took a glorious drink out of the bottle she gave me, in front of N, after lying all night in the rain, with no covering except the trees & without fire, and that her blankets were a great comfort to my poor fellows Present my rspects to your Father, Ma, & Sue, & kiss Pet and Tom for

Your affectionate husband

William J. Clarke

Please send my tooth brush if you have an opportunity.

1. Alexander M. Long of Person County enlisted on 6 June 1861. He was promoted to first lieutenant in 1862 and served until hospitalized in Richmond,

Virginia, on 15 May 1864, with a gunshot wound in his right thigh. He returned to duty before 1 January 1865, and was wounded in the left arm at Fort Stedman, Virginia, around 25 March 1865. He again returned to duty and was paroled at Greensboro on 17 May 1865. His pension application indicates he was also wounded at New Bern on an unspecified date, which may be the action recorded in this 7 February 1864 letter. Manarin and Jordan, *Roster of NC Troops*, 7:320.

2. Colonel Henry Marchmore Shaw. *Edmondston Diary*, 549, 785.

*Frances Finnerty Papers*
*Mary Bayard Clarke to Willie Clarke*

Coniconara
Feb 23d [1864]

My dear little Willie

Your sweet letters are such a comfort to me they come like bright smiles to my heart and I look for them as the pleasantest event of the week; I hope you have got your pantaloons by this time as Frank writes they have left Raleigh, I sent them up a little after Christmas. I have just had another visit from father he came quite unexpectedly walking from Halifax,[1] he is stationed two miles from Weldon now and hopes to be sent back to Hamilton. John Primrose was very well and so was Mr Cooke. We have had some terribly cold weather and of course I had rheumatism but it is gone now. Miss Sarah Dunlop and her little Sister Mattie[2] are here Sister is delighted at having a companion so near her own age and they have nice times together. They all laughed when I read them about the old woman shooting at the young man. Tom says he wont go seranading if thats the way they treat people, the other day I told him to bring me some wood out of the passage, he replied "Mamma I cant its too big for me lift" Father went for it and I said Oh you lazy fellow "Thats not laziness, said he laziness aint not doing what you cant—its not doing what you can—" I thought it a very good answer, dont you? You need not fear I shall make my self sick writing I promise you I wont I have finished what Mr Lincoln would call "a big job" and am going soon to begin another I'll tell you all about it some of these days but you must not tell not even Rob and Willie.

Miss Nettie Spruill[3] is dead, she died day before yesterday and is to be buried to morrow in the Scotland Neck grave yard. Sister is not well, her head is very sore and—if it dont get better I shall take her to Raleigh to see Dr Haywood she has been out to Scotland Neck to see Dr Hall[4] and he did her a great deal of good but he is too far off to attend her regularly. Frank writes that Mr Cooke had to go to Raleigh to get his coat mended and to get a new one made poor fellow a new coat now a days costs a fortune to a Lieutenant I suppose you got my last letter and father's in it. I will write again soon it is very late and I must say good night my darling— Did you see the improved Texas song[5] in the last Messenger—and what do you think of the change I'll tell you some time how I came to make it

Your loving Mother

1. Kate Edmondston noted on 16 February 1864, that, "About dinner time came Col Clarke having walked from Halifax! Mary should be complimented by such an instance of devotion." *Edmondston Diary,* 526.

2. Sarah and Mattie Dunlop were nieces of Ann Mary Devereux, whose sister was married to James Dunlop.

3. Nettie Spruill was the daughter of Mrs. and Mrs George Evans Spruill. She died of consumption after months of suffering. 24 February 1864, *Edmondston Diary,* 530, 530n.

4. Probably Dr. A. S. Hall of Halifax County, who also attended the Edmondstons. *Edmondston Diary,* 253n, 366, 647.

5. This was probably "The Flag of the Lone Star," which Clarke originally composed in 1861. She rewrote it in 1863 and published it in the *Daily Herald* (San Antonio) and the *SLM.*

THE TWENTY-FOURTH REGIMENT participated with Ransom's brigade in a series of assaults on federal troops in North Carolina. On 9 March the brigade forced federal defenders at Suffolk to evacuate the town. In April the brigade moved to Tarboro to join General Robert F. Hoke's attack on Plymouth, North Carolina. Ransom's brigade participated in heavy fighting on 18 and 20 April. Clarke's regiment captured one of the federal flags, which he presented to Governor Vance and the North Carolina General Assembly.

Hoke then began preparations to retake New Bern, but in May he received orders to move to Petersburg to counter federal forces under General Benjamin F. Butler. Hoke's command, including Ransom's brigade, left for Virginia. The Twenty-fourth fought at Drewry's Bluff from 12 through 16 May. William Clarke, badly wounded at Drewry's Bluff on or about 15 May, was hospitalized and took no further part in the regiment's military actions. Manarin and Jordan, *Roster of NC Troops,* 7:249–50; George Little to William J. Clarke, 28 April 1864, Clarke Papers, SHC.

*Frances Finnerty Papers*
*Mary Bayard Clarke to Willie Clarke*

Raleigh May 8th [1864]

My dear Willie

Your two letters reached me this morning, as I have been out of town since last tuesday, I went down to Kinston hoping I could see father but he left the day I got there. And camped that night five miles out of town. I staid until I heard the attack on Newbern was abandoned and the troops ordered to join Gen Lee in Virginia I am truly glad father is out of it at present for every hour nearly brings us news of some death and the fight seems to be a desperate one; the Yankees have cut the telegraph wires between Weldon and Petersburg and burnt Stony Creek bridge so you will probably hear the news as soon as I shall for it must all come by Danville and Greensboro. I dont like what you say in your letter at all and fear you are getting into a bad state of mind. My dear child you can no become a christian all at once than, you can become a mathematician without study and practice and I think the cause of your bad feelings is want of exercise and too steadily thinking on one subject Frank writes me that you take no exercise beyond a short walk every day and that you do not look well. Now I want you to try my plan and that is to say your prayers night and morning and dont think about not loving the Savior enough but simply try as your catechism tells you "to do your duty in that state of life to which it has pleased God to call you." you can best show your desire to be a true christian by striving to do your duty and this continued excitement evidently prevents your doing it you cannot study and keep well while your mind is so upset, God does not require us to be in a constant state of fervor but He does require us to show our love and reverence by doing the duties He lays upon us and your present duty is very plain you should be guided by your father and Mother who are both opposed to these religious excitements. and do not believe a person must go through a state like that in which you describe Robert Primrose to be in before they can become christians God is not opposed to any innocent pleasure and believe me darling when I tell you that it is not the way to please Him to deny yourself these. Frank writes me that he has not seen either Robert or Willie Primrose laugh since he went up there it cant be good for you to live in this state of excitement and much as I should dislike to do so I must take you from the school if it is kept up for I know that your health will suffer unless it is stopped, and what is worse you will get false views of religion that may injure you for life. I beg you then my dear to stop all this at once

—read your bible and say your prayers night and morning and try in all things to do as you think right and dont fret any more about not loving the Savior enough as long as I thought it was doing you no real harm I was willing you should please yourself but I am getting anxious about you and would rather you should stop these religious talks and praying through the day until your mind is in a healthier state. Dont you know when you study too long you seem to get stupid and cant understand things that are as plain as possible when your mind is fresh? it just so now your mind has been unduly excited and your body sympathizes and you are depressed and think you dont love the Savior enough. Just take Mother's advice, and as I used to say "put your book up Willie and run about a while till you are fresh"—so I say now stop this until you get over your fatigue and can look at it sensibly—I send you father's last letter containing an account of the battle at Plymouth and some envelops. I will send some slate pencils if I can get any. Tell Professor McIver I will send the money for your april board as soon as I can communicate with father you see what he says—Now I want you to promise me you will associate more with the other boys take more exercise and read amusing books in your play hours till you are better. I got two hats for you from Plymouth but nothing but two hand grenades from the battle field. One of which I gave Dr Haywood the other which was Aunties she says you can have but its too heavy to send by express to you. Write me again soon and tell me how you are I shall be anxious till I hear from you Your loving

Mother

❧

*Frances Finnerty Papers*
*Mary Bayard Clarke to Willie Clarke*

Raleigh May 18th [1864]

My dear Willie

Your letter has just reached me and I hasten to reply and tell you that I only meant to *advise* you as to what was best for you to do in my opinion, I leave the matter to your own judgement as long as it goes no further than you write me it has; I am sorry that poverty compels me to leave you where you are until the end of the session, if I could afford it I should at once send for you to come home where I could see for myself, but we have no home. I dont like revivals or what is generally called "getting religion" but I dont say you must not go to Professor Rockwells[1] or attend the prayer meetings you must decide for yourself as I cannot be with you and may God guide you aright my darling. As to the presbyterian catechism any one who could tell you that "it did not teach doctrinal principals but only the Word of God" did not tell you the truth, I object decidedly to your learning it, or to your reciting your own catechism to the person who told you so. I would rather see you a Roman Catholic than a Presbyterian any day, and dont fear your becoming one, but I do fear from your letters that you have contracted mistaken notions about the duties of christians and shall be glad when the time comes for you to come back to me.

When you go to the prayer meetings remember Mother does not think it best but is willing to leave it to you. She had a great deal rather you would pray to yourself in secret and use your prayer book or the words of the prayers in it, but I dont say that you must do this, or must not do that, God never intended religion to unfit us for the duties of this life, and to withdraw from association with those around you because you fear to hear an oath is like the hermits monks and nuns of the Roman Catholic church, my advice would be rather to show by your manner and example that you disliked it and try to make religion pleasant not distasteful to those who do not feel as you do. I know you think you are not excited unduly darling, but your letters show you are; write to me freely and always feel that though I may not agree with you I sympathize with your feelings, and wish to know all about them; where would be the use of telling me what you do and feel if you did not know that in my answers I gave you my true views and opinions on what you tell me. I regard your present state of mind as morbid and shall wait patiently till it passes away only begging you to do nothing publicly. I did not need the testament as I have a bible which I can use Sister and Tom are busy with chickens and the garden Col. [Winchester] Hall is still here Tom goes to school to cousin Lizzie[2] and is learning very well. My cough continues very troublesome Father is I suppose in Petersburg I have not heard from him since a week ago to day as the mail does not come through Give my love to Frank and tell him when he writes to send me the certificate of the $100 he funded Write me again soon darling and believe me your loving

Mother

1. Reverend Elijah Rockwell arrived at Davidson College in 1850 to take the chair of chemistry and natural philosophy and stayed until 1868. A graduate of Yale University, he studied theology at Princeton and Columbia seminaries. During the war, either Rockwell or John L. Kirkpatrick, president of the college, conducted an hour of "singing, prayer, and exhortation." Rockwell resigned from

Davidson to become president of the Presbyterian-affiliated Concord Female Seminary. Shaw, *Davidson College*, 61, 70.

2. Cousin Lizzie was Elizabeth Collins Miller, the wife of Henry M. Miller.

WILLIAM J. CLARKE RECEIVED a "Shell wound Causing Compound fracture of left Scapula," according to a statement signed by surgeons E. Burke Haywood and H. E. Fisher on 2 June 1864. On 3 October 1864, a board of medical examiners stated that Clarke's application for assignment to light duty was approved, noting they found him to be "suffering from a wound inflicted by a large fragment of shell on the left Scapula, or shoulder blade, causing compound fracture thereof, with loss of a portion of the bone. That his left arm is almost entirely disabled, and that he is suffering from general debility, that said wound was received near Dreweys Bluff Va on the 15th day of May last, and that in consequence thereof he is, in our opinion unfit for Active duty in the field and will not be able to resume his duties in a less period than three (3) months, but is able to do light duty." Clarke Papers, SHC. On 28 January 1865, North Carolina Surgeon General Edward Warren and surgeon Richard B. Haywood, two of the physicians who attended Clarke in Richmond, pronounced, "his recovery has been slow but gradual; and though still incapable of assuming active duties in the field, we do not regard him as permanently disabled—" Edward Warren and R. B. Haywood, 28 January 1865, Clarke Papers, SHC.

*Frances Finnerty Papers*
*William J. Clarke to Mary Bayard Clarke*

1864
Richmond, Sunday, May 22

My Dear Wife:

I wrote you a long letter on yesterday, which I hope you received. Tom Devereux has just called to inform me that he leaves for R. tomorrow morning and I employ a half hour of sun-light to inform you that I am doing fully as well as ever a man in my condition.

Drs. Warren, Dick Haywood & [blank] called to see me this morning & were pleased at my condition: tho' Dr. W. says that he cannot see how it failed to kill me instantly.

I ate a heavy dinner today, broiled ham, do spring chicken, irish potatoes Lettuce, straw berries and iced milk—The family are very kind, and do not seem to like my talk of leaving this week. But I feel that I must get on to see you and the little band who would have truly mourned had I fallen

I do not often suffer acute pain, but I dread the slow depressing painful process by which lost flesh and bone must be replaced.

I shall leave this on Wednesday or Thursday—

Give my love to sister and tell her that I think of her frequently and would send her some smart message but my mind is yet clouded.

Kiss for Pet & Tom

Affectionately yours<br>
William J. Clarke

☙

*Frances Finnerty Papers*
*Mary Bayard Clarke to Willie Clarke*

Raleigh June 2d [1864]

My dear Willie

I have delayed replying to your letter until I could tell you that father was here; he arrived yesterday morning looking very pale and thin from loss of blood but able to sit up and walk about, the wound is on the top of the shoulder blade about the length of my little finger and the Dr says nearly as deep as the length of my hand; there is no inflamation and all the pieces of bone have been taken out but Dr [Edmund] Burke Haywood says it will be two months at least before he can use his arm or go back to the field, so you and Frank will have a chance of seeing him. I am much obliged to you for your nice long letters they are a great comfort to me; I have no objection to your joining the bible class but beg you not to take any more studies as I think you have more now than you can well manage if you are to give any time to preparing a lesson I would rather you should not undertake it as I think your sunday bible lessons are enough for you in the way of study though I dont say you must not join the class I am not with you to see for myself and can only advise you. I dont like all this getting up of revivals and immoderate praying and bible reading as the reaction which is sure to come after the excitement is apt to bring real religion into contempt and I fear that more than anything else. I read some where of a hermit who was too good and pious for this wicked world and was constantly praying to be taken out of it, at last an angel appeared to him and told him to cut down the Palm tree at the door of his hermitage and make a rope of it so that he could draw him up to heaven the hermit was so anxious to get away that he worked so hard at the rope that he stopped all but his regular daily prayers and from ceasing to pray to be taken out of this world and regular employment regained his happiness, and when the angel appeared the second time and told him to take the rope for a girdle and make a ladder to heaven by the fulfilment of his duties to the rest of mankind instead of moping and praying to be taken out of a world into which God had sent him, he was convinced of his error and was satisfied that God knew better what was best for the world than he did and would rather be served by the faithful fulfilment of duty than by incessant prayer I often think of the alligory when I hear of people neglecting evident duties to "get religion" Give my love to Frank and tell him to write me and his sister, Tom was delighted with your letter and will write and answer it.

I must tell you of the impudence of a Yankee chaplain at Plymouth. he came to Gen Hoke and said "Gen I hope I shall be allowed to retain this box of theologocal works given me by my friends from the North" Certainly sir said Hoke carelessly taking up one. they seem a handsome collection, opening a Scotts family bible—But what did he see there but Josiah Collins'[1] name, and on looking further found the whole box full had been taken from libraries of gentlemen down there "You infamous rascal said Gen Hoke how dare you dishonor the livery of Christ with such a lie?["] ["]Oh they were all given to me but my friends got them in Carolina!!["] I have just written another Song to music which I will send you as it will be published in Richmond. Father sends love he will write you when he feels a little Stronger

Your loving Mother

Ill send your summer clothes next week

1. North Carolina planter Josiah Collins Jr. owned Somerset Plantation and was one of the state's largest slaveholders. Johnson, *Ante-bellum North Carolina,* 485.

*Frances Finnerty Papers*
*Mary D. Clarke to Willie Clarke*

Raligh June 6th [1864]

Der brother

Father is here

he came thursday morning at sunrise. The doctor said if it had been a littel lower it would have killed him, or if it had hit him in the head

I have eigteen chickens, I had nineteen but wone died, he had the gaps, and he was a little better, and the cow steped on it.

beleive me
your affectioate

sister Mary

[on back by MBC] Father is about the same walked out yesterday

Willie

❧

*Frances Finnerty Papers*
*Mary Bayard Clarke to Willie Clarke*

Raleigh June 18th [1864]

My dear Willie

Your long letter has lain unanswered from day to day, first because
I waited to get the money to send you and then because I was so unwell;
this cool weather keeps me feeling very badly all the time, it also makes
Father's wound stiff and sore and keeps him from gaining strength; but he
is not going back and I am thankful for that day before yesterday I dressed
his wound myself, the bandages hurt him and I took them all off and put
them back again he said as well as the Dr could have done—I am glad you
have plenty of strawberries, we have had very few though there seems to
have been plenty in town but they sold for from three to four dollars a
quart getting towards the last to [bud?]—and I did not feel willing to give
so much for well people I like to hear of your going after them and amusing yourself in harmless ways—much better than the gloomy way Robert
Primrose talks I declare I dont know the boy, if he were mine—I should
feel that no benefit of education could ever make up for the injury that has
been done him; he used to be a pleasant cheerful boy now his face is as long
as my arm and he talks about nothing but religion which is to me very
convincing proof that he has not the real religion of Christ. If my cheerful
bright faced Willie were to come home to me as much altered as he is I
should be not only very sorry but very angry with those who produced the
change in him. I had a letter from Mr Cooke the other day enquiring about
you boys—his PO is Richmond he says he wants you both to write to him.

I send you $50 which is all I can spare at present, let me know how
much you have left after you and Frank have paid all your debts. I hope the
box has reached you before this and you like the clothes, I did not send you
any pantaloons because I thought you had enough but if you want a pair of
white ones write to me and I will have them ready for you when you come
down.

I send you the first No of Marguerite[1] keep the papers and bring them
to me when you come home. Tom and Mary go after mulberries very
often with Mr [Patrick] Winston Tom is entirely alone as there are no
boarders here but Col Hall. Mrs Bowen went away the other day; Col Hall

leaves day after to morrow as he has been exchanged and goes to Gen Polks head quarters Aunt Bettie and Cousin Rachel are here but go down to Grandpa's next friday when there will be no one here but our family; I wish I had it all here You must be sure to let me know what day you are coming for they ask $5 to bring a trunk from the depot and I will save $10 by having some one to meet you. Oh I wish it was to morrow you were coming. Do plait some [plumes?] to make Tom a sunday hat. I have made him one out of the straw you gave me last year which he has nearly used up already. With much love to Frank believe me your affectionate

Mother

1. "Marguerite or Two Loves" was a serialized story about Creole life that Mary Bayard Clarke wrote for *Field and Fireside* (Raleigh).

*Frances Finnerty Papers*
*Mary Bayard Clarke to Willie Clarke*

Raleigh July 20th [1864]

My dear Willie

Your letter and Franks reached me this morning. I had been well laughed at for my mistake about the date, the way it happened was that I looked at the Mercury which comes out a week before hand and say [*sic*] 18th on it. I hope you get the beginning of Marguerite. I send you the second number to day the other day I sent you a story written by Mrs Cress of Set I hope you get it Father is about the house again but is very feeble and suffers with his shoulder some days very much; the house is full of Petersburg refugees who have run away from the shell and the Yankees I have great compassion for women and children who run away and a greater contempt for men, there are three strong men here who have left their homes to be defended by braver men and are quietly waiting here until it shall be safe for them to go back I should be ashamed to own them if they were my brothers or sons. a man who wont fight when his own hearth is threatened is not worth the powder and shot it would take to kill him I suppose you have seen the account of Uncle Polk's death,[1] it is very very sad he was killed instantly by a stray cannon ball it is a great loss to us for he was a good general, he was Frank's God father and if he could write a letter without any bad spelling in it I should tell him to write to Aunt Fanny but I am really ashamed to have her see his letters; tell him I say that no body but a paddy from Ireland would spell sure *shure*. I dont by any means wish to mortify him but only to laugh, scold, and poke at him till he spells better. I am so busy I have not time to write many letters so I shall here after write one to you and the next to Frank

I shall enjoy eating some blackberries of your picking very much I am giving a dollar a quart for them, or rather for Dew berries for father. he has no appetite and seems to enjoy them more than any thing else. Mr Conrad is here, he came yesterday morning to see us and wants me to go to Charleston with him but I cant leave father. I dont care what plait you make for Tom's hat indeed he dont need it as I have enough of that you plaited last summer. I thought you had pantaloons enough for this summer but if you have to borrow from Frank I had better have some more made for you you did not tell me whether the jackets fitted you. I have no doubt my dear boy you will be a christian but I dont want to see you such an one as Robert Primrose and am glad he is no longer with you. Sister sends love and Tom says write him a letter. Give my love to Frank and believe me your

loving Mother

1. Lieutenant General Leonidas Polk died during the Atlanta campaign on 14 June 1864, at Pine Mountain. Boatner, *Civil War Dictionary*, 657–58.

*Frances Finnerty Papers*
*Mary Bayard Clarke to Willie Clarke*

Raleigh Jan 17th [1865]

My Darling Willie

Your letter reached me yesterday and almost made me cry to think of you so far off from us all and so lonely—I want to write you to come right back but that would be foolish so we must both bear it till the end of the session then if you still feel lonely you can come home and go to Mr Lovejoy I will leave it entirely to you. I was very anxious about you that rany day for fear you would start to Davidson and very glad when I heard you had staid over at Mr Dewey's; the storm that day did so much mischief that we are still suffering from the effects of it, there has been no mail from Richmond since consequently I have heard nothing from Frank, except that he was to stand his examination[1] on the 10th I have been acting as clerk for Major Daves[2] for one or two days, five in all and made $25 which I shall send you for pocket money, I am trying to get a permanent position in Col Mallett's[3] office as he has permission from the Sec of War [John C. Breckinridge] to employ lady clerks If I do you are to have all I make to pay your board which will be however only $150 a month. I would rather you should have it than any body in the world, when you write tell me if you have a room mate and who he is, and how you get along; we[4] are all well Legislature meets to day but only one of our boarders has come and if a great many do not get in in the western train this morning there will not be a quorum

Tom is looking out for Col Bryson[5] and Mr Crawford[6] because they both promised to bring him some apples. What do you think I found the little monkey doing yesterday, smoking a pipe as cooly as if he were twenty years old Dr Love gave it to him and he stuffed it full of paper and set to work to smoke You can guess I scolded them both well and told Tom if he ever did such a thing I would switch him well. I suppose you have heard that Fort Fisher has been taken, Wilmington will go next[7] and then I believe the enemy will march right up here, but you must not be uneasy if they do and you dont hear from me for I shant try to run away they wont stay here long and I shall stick it out I have seen too much misery and suffering among refugees for me to be willing to run off from home not knowing where to lay my head and perhaps have to camp out and get my death of cold. Dont be uneasy about me I shall get along very well Auntie and Miss Mary are going to stay too. If you can get a lamp chimney for Auntie send it to Mr Dewey and ask him to send it by some one passing or to pack it carefully and send by express if they will take it.

There is no news to tell you, I never see Charlie Snow[8] or any of the other boys, but when I do will ask them to tell me all that is going and try and remember it for you. I enclose your report, it is a very good one and does you credit

All send their love Col Hall keeps bothering me so I cant write any more. Good bye my own darling boy. I love you dearly and want to see you so very bad

Your loving<br>Mother

I have just got the enclosed letter from Frank his first did not come

1. Frank Clarke joined the Confederate navy as a midshipman at the age of thirteen, serving on several ships, including the *Patrick Henry, Tennessee, Chicora, Raleigh,* and *Torpedo Boat No. 3.* He fought in the Battle of Mobile Bay and at City Point, Virginia. Allen Johnson and Dumas Malone, eds., *Dictionary of American Biography,* vol. 4 (New York: Charles Scribner's Sons, 1930), 150–51 (hereafter cited as *Dictionary of American Biography*); Powell, *DNCB,* 1:380; William N. Still Jr., *The Confederate Navy: The Ships, Men and Organization, 1861–65* (Annapolis, Md.: Naval Institute Press, 1997), 117 (hereafter cited as Still, *The Confederate Navy*).

2. Graham Daves, a lawyer who lived in Raleigh and served as Governor Ellis's private secretary before the war, joined the Twelfth Regiment, NCV (later

the Twenty-second Regiment, NCT). He served as adjutant of the regiment until April 1862. After serving under General Joseph E. Johnston in the western theater, he returned to Raleigh and resigned his commission. He then joined Raleigh's Conscript office in a clerical capacity until 7 July 1864, when he became an aide-de-camp on the staff of Lieutenant General Theophilus Holmes in Raleigh. He served until March 1865, when he was transferred to Hoke's Division. He surrendered at Greensboro on 26 April 1865. Ashe, *Biographical History,* 6:184–86.

3. Colonel Peter Mallett of Fayetteville, a merchant in New York City before the war, returned to his home state to raise a company of infantry. He served as captain of the Third Regiment, NCV, until appointed assistant adjutant general with rank of major in 1862. He oversaw the drilling, subsistence, and distribution of conscripts in the state and was generally known as the Commandant of Conscripts. He was made colonel in November 1862, but the appointment was not confirmed by the Senate. In December 1862 Mallett fought at the battle at Kinston, where he received a wound that disabled him for months. After the war, he returned to New York as a commission merchant. Manarin and Jordan, *Roster of NC Troops,* 2:697, 3:511; Johnston and Mobley, *Vance Papers,* 1:175n. 4.

4. The Clarke family was staying with Frances Miller in Raleigh.

5. Samuel C. Bryson served in the Twenty-fifth Regiment, NCT. He was promoted to lieutenant colonel of the regiment on 17 May 1862, and remained on active duty until he was wounded near Petersburg on 17 June 1864. He resigned on 10 December 1864, because of disability from his wounds. Manarin and Jordan, *Roster of NC Troops,* 7:355.

6. This might have been James G. Crawford of Macon County, who served in the North Carolina House of Commons from 1865 to 1867. Otto H. Olsen and Ellen Z. McGrew, "Prelude to Reconstruction: The Correspondence of State Senator Leander Sams Gash, 1866–1867, Part II." *NCHR* 60 (Apr. 1983): 220n. 48.

7. Fort Fisher fell to Union forces on 15 January 1865. Wilmington fell on 22 February.

8. Charles Snow was the thirteen-year-old son of T. H. Snow, who owned a "steam mill" and lived in Raleigh. 1860 Census, Wake County, Raleigh Township, North Carolina: 63, Household no. 532.

*Barden Collection*
*William J. Clarke to Mary Bayard Clarke*

Officers' Prison Barracks[1]
Fort Delaware, Del.
March 29th. 1865.

My Dear Wife: A transport lies off the island, which is 40 miles below Philadelphia, and it is probable that some 200 of the 1800 officers, here confined, will be sent south to be exchanged, and I avail myself of the opportunity to inform you that I and Mr. Cooke are well. I have written to you by flag of truce but I have little hope that my letters will reach you by that channel of communication. I have requested officers going off by special exchange to write to you from a memorandum given them and hope that you have heard from me through them, though the letter would be at the mercy of our wretched mails. We are far more comfortable than I thought possible in our condition. Dick Cooke[2] supplies his brother with funds and Frank Bowen supplies me, and as the Sutler is allowed to sell us provisions we live quite well for half a dollar a day. A Lieut. cooks for me, another washes my clothes. If I had a good bed I should be quite comfortable: as it is, we are as comfortable as you were at Happer's Hotel. The regulations of the prison are strict but I cannot say that they are to be condemned. We have to submit to annoyances and insolence, which are galling to a sensative gentleman, but *many* of our officers are not gentlemen; indeed one of the most disagreeable things, I could complain of, is being thrown in contact and unpleasant proximity with rude, coarse men, with whom I have nothing in common. On the other hand there are a good many highly cultivated courteous gentlemen here, with whom I have pleasant association. My bunk-mate is a Col. [Charles H.] Simonton, 25th. S. C. Infty. I have become oppressively popular without any exertion, and am chief of my Division, No. 28—am greatly respected and promptly obeyed. On last Sunday I read service and a sermon in a Division near ours, and on my return to my own Divis. was invited to take whiskey and quite a sumptuous dinner with the gamblers—If this is not being all things to all men I do not know what is! My health has improved and I am in better flesh than when I left home, but it will be a long time before I am able to take the field again. My shoulder pains me occasionally in bad weather but I am recovering the use of my arm far better than I ever expected.

Our rations are of good quality but very scant, only about 10 ounces of bread and six of meat: allowance is only made for two meals a day. We are tolerably well supplied with books, and get the Phila. Inquirer every day, except when our troops have gained an advantage over the Yankees. We place very little reliance on its statements; but I have been in great fear that you have had a visit from the rascally invaders. Our affairs wear a very gloomy aspect, and it would really seem that the end is not far off; but I do not despair; our cause is just, and that is a tower of strength, but our Prest. is not the right man in the right place, we have not made the best use of our means and failure and discomforture have followed as necessary results. If we could get rid of the incubus, far gone as we are, we might yet succeed. Che sera, sera! If we are to be subjugated I am glad that I shall leave to my children the proud satisfaction of saying that their father used his utmost exertions to avert the disgrace and calamity. Eight millions of men so lost to every generous and manly principle as to submit to be deprived of their rights without a struggle would deserve to be not only subjects of a despotic government but to be a mark of scorn and opprobrium to the whole world. As it is, if we fail freedom will shriek when our last battle is lost, and Liberty will flee from earth. The prisoners are still hopeful and defiant. As long as there is any reasonable hope of success I, if alone, will contend, The cowed appearance of the people of the North fills me with painful apprehensions, and leaves little hope of peace and quiet except in our independence. The negroes and deserters are in a most deplorable condition—Mobocracy & fanaticism are in the ascendant and the carnival of blood will not end when the southern armies shall lay down their arms.

I send you Lieut. Broughton[3] of Raleigh, a power of Atty. to draw my pay and allowances. I shall send you others from time to time. I want to see you very badly: to hear from you would be a great satisfaction. Write to me every week or two, perhaps I may receive some of the letters— Give my love to sister Kiss Pet and Tom for me, and do not let them think of me as in a gloomy prison or looking through jail bars. I hope to get home in May, and feel quite confident on the subject.—It is not certain but this letter may be taken from the officer by whom I send it, therefore I am more brief than I otherwise would be. When you write to Frank and Willie give them my love and tell them that they are constantly in my thoughts, and now, my own darling good by for the present—

Affectionately your husband

William J. Clarke

1. Clarke and Oliver Dudley Cooke were both captured at or near Dinwiddie Court House, Virginia, on 5 February 1865. Clarke was trying to rejoin his regiment when federal cavalry overtook him. Manarin and Jordan, *Roster of NC Troops,* 7:251. Fort Delaware in the Delaware River was considered by southerners to be one of the worst northern prisons. Boatner, *Civil War Dictionary,* 673. Kate Edmondston noted Clarke's capture on 16 February 1865, writing, "Sad news of the capture of my brother in law, Col Clarke . . . & when captured was on his way in an Ambulance with another officer to Petersburg. At Dinwiddie C H they were overhauled by the enemy in a manner most unexpected to them both & hurried off to Yankee instead of Confederate Head Quarters. I fear the

confinement will go hard with him, for his health is delicate & his wound still open & from its position on the shoulder blade he needs the services of an attendant to dress it. I am deeply sorry for poor Mary. Her distress must be very great." *Edmondston Diary,* 666.

2. Members of Cooke's family lived in Connecticut and New York and were able to help him while he was imprisoned.

3. First Lieutenant Gaston H. Broughton of Wake County was wounded and captured at Gettysburg on 3 July 1863. Originally confined at Fort Delaware on 6 July 1863, he was transferred to Johnson's Island, Ohio, on 18 July. Broughton moved to Point Lookout, Maryland, early in 1864, but he was returned to Fort Delaware on 23 June 1864. He was released from prison on 12 June 1865, after taking the oath of allegiance. Manarin and Jordan, *Roster of NC Troops,* 7:506–7.

GENERAL LEE SURRENDERED the Army of Northern Virginia on 9 April 1865, and federal troops under General William T. Sherman occupied Raleigh on 13 April. Mary Bayard Clarke, her daughter, and youngest son Tom were living with her widowed sister, Frances Miller, at the time of the occupation. Clarke and her family prepared for the impending catastrophe by hiding valuables, continuing to feed and nurse departing Confederate soldiers, and comforting each other in a time of great stress. Raleigh, with a population of about 4,800 in 1860, faced an occupying federal force of roughly 85,000 men. Clarke and her friends feared that Raleigh would face pillaging and burning, as towns in Georgia and South Carolina had experienced. Clarke, undoubtedly anxious for her family, her imprisoned husband, and her friends, nevertheless critically observed the actions of her acquaintances while recording their conversations for future use in articles she would publish in 1866. After the federal forces arrived, Mary Bayard Clarke embraced the opportunity to learn more about the officers in Sherman's forces. Her southern prejudices remained strong, but her determination to learn more about the people and the events unfolding around her led her into protracted conversations with Sherman's officers. To the mortification of family members, she found several whose company she enjoyed. Clarke also used her acquaintances in the Union army to find out when her husband would be released from prison and to probe northern minds to find out their opinions about the former Confederate states and their leaders.

At some point, Willie Clarke arrived in Raleigh from Davidson College. One account states that he served in the North Carolina Quartermaster's Department, commanded by his uncle John Devereux, in the

early months of 1865. To augment family resources after Raleigh fell to
Sherman's troops, he and his brother Tom sold pies and lemonade to federal soldiers. Frank Clarke, a midshipman in the Confederate navy, did not
return for some weeks. When he finally reached Raleigh, he joined Willie
in selling groceries to federal troops and in other business enterprises.
William Clarke's half-sister, Julia Clarke Fisher, writing to William at Fort
Delaware in June 1865, mentioned that "Mary and the children . . . were
well, . . . the boys had bought out a sutler, and was doing well, what a comfort they must be to their mother."

Mary Bayard Clarke, meanwhile, worked with the Raleigh publishing
firm of W. B. Smith & Co., writing articles and serving as an editor for
*Field and Fireside.* Other newspapers received articles from her, and her
publishing efforts began to turn away from poetry to political essays. She
avidly followed political discussions and she wrote articles analyzing events
in the state. In August 1865 the New York *Daily News* published four of her
articles, in which she sought to reassure northern readers that the South
accepted the end of slavery and the preservation of the Union. This particular paper was one of the leading Copperhead newspapers in New York
City in 1866. Mary Bayard Clarke carefully selected papers she felt would
publish her work, and this paper together with the *Old Guard* (New York)
printed many of her articles.

Despite Mary Bayard Clarke's political solidarity with the Conservative
faction in the state, her continued interactions with northern officers led to
an estrangement from Frances Miller and other family members. Forced to
leave her sister's boardinghouse during the summer of 1865, Mary Bayard
Clarke found lodging in a boardinghouse run by an old friend, Mrs. John B.
(Harriet) Bobbitt of Raleigh. Julia S. Fisher to William J. Clarke, 22 June
1865, Clarke Papers, SHC; "Southern Correspondence," *New York News,* 10,
14, 25, 29 August 1865, MBC Scrapbook 2.

*Barden Collection*
*William J. Clarke to Mary Bayard Clarke*

Field Officers' Barracks
Fort Delaware, April 29th. 1865

My Dear Wife: Yesterday afternoon I was a happy and a proud man,
for your letter of the 13th. inst. came to hand. Mr. C. also received yours
of the 16th. They were a gleam of sunshine which warmed our hearts

and wreathed our faces with smiles. I felt like rushing out and reading it to every acquaintance. All honor to her who taught you to write, and glory to God who gave me such a wife! John Bryan[1] also rec'd. a letter from his sister. G. Whiting[2] was brought here a few days ago from Johnson's Island. We are all well, Barringer,[3] Beevers,[4] Day, the Bakers[5] of my Regt. and those I have mentioned. Mr. Cooke is looking badly & is quite unwell from an attack of cholera morbus caused most probably by eating too much at dinner yesterday. We had been permitted then to receive money for the 1st. time since the death of Prest. Lincoln,[6] & had a better dinner than usual. My health is pretty good, and I manage to keep in pretty good spirits, though I would like a little old Nick Williams.— I want to see you & our dear children beyond description—I have thought a good deal of it & it strikes me very forcibly that my best plan would be to go immediately from New York to Texas—Hard work & self denial are before me and I feel straitened until I enter upon my labor. By being upon the ground, when business opens, I should occupy quite a favorable position. I should take a vessel to some T. port. What does your *judgment* say to this? We must, for the present, ignore & disregard feeling & sentiment. I am glad that Willie is with you. I am anxious about Frank, but too many real evils press on us for me to anticipate trouble. We are in the midst of great excitement & bitterness of feeling. The oath[7] has been tendered to us, and more than half of the officers have agreed to take it, for which they are bitterly denounced by the nonjurists. I am in the latter class, but I do not feel called upon to join in the clamor, for it seems that "that is the complection to which we must all come at last," but I will wait for developments of events. I rec'd. a very kind letter from Sue Johnson a few days ago. She has rec'd. yours of 15th. Feby. They express a willingness to do any thing for me. Julia [Fisher] writes to me constantly. She is well but from her accounts of Kate I fear she will never be raised. Give my tenderest love to sister. I would write to her but the restrictions on correspondence render it so distasteful to me that it is with the greatest difficulty I can bring myself to write a letter. Add to this the uncertainty of its being rec'd & it requires nerve to take up a pen. Kiss my daughter for me & my noble boy Tom. Tell Willie that father's trust and faith in God do not fail him even in this dark hour. Be of good cheer darling wife. God bless you

Your affectionate husband William J. Clarke

Col. 24th. Regt. N.C. Troops

1. Second Lieutenant John S. Bryan served in Co. K of the Fourteenth Regiment, NCT (Fourth Regiment, NCV). He was captured in May 1864 and transferred to Fort Delaware on 23 June 1864, from Point Lookout, Maryland. He was released on 16 June 1865. Manarin and Jordan, *Roster of NC Troops,* 5:482.

2. This might have been George M. Whiting of Wake County, captain of Co. C, Forty-seventh Regiment, NCT, who was captured, imprisoned, and died from disease contracted while in prison. He was incarcerated at Johnson's Island as of 30 March 1864. Clark, *Histories of the Several Regiments,* 3:84, 4:701.

3. Rufus Barringer became a Confederate general of cavalry in 1864 and was captured on 3 April 1865. He was imprisoned at Fort Delaware until his release. Boatner, *Civil War Dictionary,* 46–47.

4. This was Charles W. Bevers of Wake County, who served in Co. K of the Fourteenth Regiment, NCT (Fourth Regiment, NCV). He was captured at Sharpsburg, Maryland, in September 1862 but was exchanged in October of that year. He rejoined his company early in 1863 but was captured at Winchester, Virginia, and confined at Fort Delaware until released on 17 June 1865. Manarin and Jordan, *Roster of NC Troops,* 5:482.

5. Burrell P. Baker, Janadius H. Baker, and Richard S. Baker, all serving with the Twenty-fourth Regiment, NCT, were captured on 25 March 1865. Originally confined at Old Capitol Prison in Washington, D.C., all three were transferred to Fort Delaware on 30 March 1865. Each was released on 17 June of that year, after taking the oath of allegiance. Manarin and Jordan, *Roster of NC Troops,* 7:251, 340, 341.

6. Lincoln was shot on 14 April 1865.

7. This was an oath of allegiance required of Confederate prisoners before they could be released from federal military prisons.

*Barden Collection*
*Frances Miller to Mary Bayard Clarke*

[ca. June 1865]

Dear Mary

Do not take what I say as a threat do not take it as unkindness & above all do not as you have done return this & say you have not read it as you must do it to shape your course & I shall feel certain you have

God knows I do not wish to hurt you you ought not to take advantage of my delicate situation with regard to you for you know how much pleasure it would give to a large number of our family if they could say "they have parted in anger" & I sincerely wish this house to be as much your home as Kate [Miller Baker] or Lizzie [Collins Miller]—But it must be on the same terms Neither, would ever have offered to have told me

"I could not help their receiving who they pleased that this was a boarding house & could be closed" those were your words tho not in connection yesterday before C.G¹ Now such may be the fact, but I do not chose to be so hampered; & I tell you I can not & will not permit the recurence of yesterdays incident It is against my taste an outrage to my children & above all in my view (mind you in my view & I have the right to have my notions respected & my house hold regulated accordingly [crossed out in original: not that I would [arogate?] to myself any right to protect him over his wife)] it is an insult to Bro William while he is in a northern prison to have his wife entertain for 4 hours one of his jailors Not that I would imply *you* would not be as jealous of his honor as *I* only we think differently & you ought to humor me. "If I have no influence over you", you should remember your promise to do as I wish if you think as you said "I cant help myself" pause & think how easy I could (but at what expense!!! & nothing but your persistence in disregarding my feelings & injuring me will force me to it) write to Father, & tell him that you were his daughter, & he must take you under his eye till you could be restored to the protection of your husband as your conduct was compromising me If you knew but half of how I have been blamed, for none will beleive what you boast that I have no influence you would not wonder that I am driven to this

I know we must receive them some times & be decently polite but my dear Mary you & I can certainly manage to do that so they will not repeat willingly I feared youd put it on the ground of injuring [sic] to my house dont—just be polite to those who are paying me & Ill manage be fore such a thing as happened yesterday should again occur I would become a refugee. I realy fear GB [George Baker] would take Kate away fearing she might be implicated but do not take this as a threat it was not so given & I would no more take it from one of my children than I would give it to you Pray let us live in peace you are over sensitive as to my wish to [rule?] you & your age you wont beleive if I say I dont but cant you give up & have Faith that I love you & yours next to my own & only equal to Sister B But Mary I have pride & what is done in my house I am answerable for in the eyes of the world even tho "I do keep a boarding house & Col Granger knows it" Be advised by me dont receive him or any other like, & dont speak to them from your window on familar footing & believe me my dear sister I speak with all charity & love dont wish to threatten dont wish to wound only to let you know how I feel

your affectionate sister

1. This was George F. Granger, colonel of of the Ninth Maine, Third Brigade, Second Division, part of the Tenth Army Corps of the Army of the Ohio, commanded by Major General John M. Schofield. Granger also served as commander "of the Post at Raleigh" for a time in 1865 and was honorably discharged on 13 July 1865. Boatner, *Civil War Dictionary,* 351; William Tecumseh Sherman, *Memoirs of General W. T. Sherman* (New York: Literary Classics of the United States, 1990), 826; *Official Records (Army),* series 1, vol. 46, pt. 2:748.

❧

*Barden Collection*
*Mary Bayard Clarke to Frances Miller*
                            [n.d., reply to ca. June 1865 letter from Frances Miller]
My Dear Sister

My position as your guest places it utterly out of my power to do any thing *but* submit to your requirements. and I beg leave to say that I will do so with the best grace in power. The *spirit* of my remarks to both you and Kate have been so much misconstrued that all explanation of them would be idle I can only simply apologize to you for them. The kindness of your acts to me and mine must ever out weigh the harshness of your words though you have written what will sink deep and remain long.

When I can maintain my composure I will again join the family—until then I beg you to excuse me and not impute my retirement to any but the true motive

❧

*William J. Clarke Papers, SHC*
*Mary Bayard Clarke to William J. Clarke*

Raleigh June 19th [1865]
My Dear William Your letter by Lt Jordan was delivered to day and a few moments after Willie sent up yours of the 10th [Provisional Governor William Woods] Holden has been applied to and recognized your claim on him, *said* he would do all in his power for you but we know if he had you would be at home now; we are all well, keeping house in Mrs Bobbitts house near the fair ground as I wrote in my last, Willie gets $50 a month as clerk.[1] Frank is in business on his own account, he says he will take you and Mr Cooke both as clerk for a week and try which suits him bests, but he really cant afford to employ you both, he says as the negros are free and lording it over their masters he dont see why school boys should not have the same chance, he made $20 clear last week we want to send you some

but every body advises us against trying; a school is hopeless *everybody* is teaching and *nobody* learning Willie says come home and sit in the cool and smoke just as much as you want to and he will work for both. Dear little fellow I believe he likes nothing better than to work for me, he certainly is the best boy I ever saw. Frank is growing so fast he is not strong he is taller than I am. Mary is housekeeper and hen wife; sells me a dozen eggs a week. Tom goes for milk and sweeps the walk for which I pay him five cts a week, I get a little writing occasionally but make more by sewing. Lanah[2] has concluded she is too delicate to do my work, and decided to *board* and support herself by going out by the day she leaves the 1st. of July but there are plenty to be had for from three to four dollars a month so I shant suffer. Yours affectionately

Mary B. Clarke

PS. Mrs Christophers says write to Franklin Bowen, he has written inquiring about you—(Care of *Foy & Bowen*—Exchange Philadelphia.) Yours of April 29th just here

1. Willie Clarke worked in a lumber and grocery business between 1865 and 1867. Powell, *DNCB*, 1:380.

2. An African American woman who worked as a servant in the Clarke household.

᎓

*Hall,* MBC Poems, *xviii*
*Mary Bayard Clarke to Winchester Hall*

Raleigh
[August/September] 1865

I leave home at 9 o'clock and write in the office[1] until 2. I review new books, write to correspondents, select matter, and write articles for the paper. I have a large quiet room, comfortably furnished, with carpet and curtains, and am treated as a decided, and much-to-be-made-of addition to the establishment. My salary is paid weekly, and I generally leave home with the children when they go to school, and return when they do. I do not feel they are neglected.

My old Texas negro servant,[2] hearing I was sick and needed her, came back to me, and my family are now all together for the first time in four years.

1. Mary Bayard Clarke worked as assistant editor at this time for *Southern Field and Fireside,* which had offices in Raleigh. This letter, which indicates that her

entire family was together again, must have been written in August or September 1865. William J. Clarke was released from Fort Delaware on 24 July 1865.

2. Jane Espy.

THIS ARTICLE, THE LAST OF four Mary Bayard Clarke wrote for the New York *Daily News* and signed as L S, enunciated the concerted effort on the part of southerners to convince the North that the South accepted its defeat, was ready to rejoin the Union, and that slavery, although finished, had been a positive good for enslaved African Americans. Clarke's arguments echoed those found in articles she wrote for the *Old Guard* and other newspapers. In this particular article, Clarke derided former secessionists who chose to denounce the war and its supporters. The editor of the *Daily Progress* (Raleigh) mentioned in the article was John L. Pennington, who cautioned against electing former rebels to state or national offices. Pennington worked with North Carolina's provisional governor William Woods Holden, whom President Andrew Johnson appointed on 29 May 1865.

One of the most pressing issues for North Carolinians concerned the status of newly freed African Americans. Few white southerners believed former slaves were entitled to citizenship or the right to vote. Former slaveholders also doubted that blacks would work without coercion. The Freedmen's Bureau, established in the state by July 1865, excited particular suspicion. North Carolina whites believed the bureau made African Americans dependent on government handouts. In actuality, bureau head General Oliver O. Howard reported that the number of rations he issued in North Carolina declined from about 215,000 in July 1865 to 137,350 in September of that year. He also pointed out that many of the recipients were white women and children who had been widowed and orphaned by the war. Only 5,000 freedmen out of 330,000 received government aid by September 1865. Clearly, many African Americans had found employment, although their interactions with former slaveholders were not as smooth as the following article suggests. Determined to maintain control, white employers frequently fired blacks, refused to pay them fair wages, or physically attacked them. When the freedmen in the state issued a call for a Freedmen's Convention, to be held in Raleigh between 29 September and 3 October 1865, many whites were alarmed. The convention, with 106 delegates, strongly supported the right of blacks to vote and argued for improved educational and employment opportunities for their race. Overall, the tone was moderate and thoughtful, but the initiative shown by African Americans angered many whites.

Holden issued a proclamation on 9 August 1865, ordering an election to select delegates to a state convention. Those who had voted before the war, had been pardoned for war activities, and had taken the oath of allegiance could vote for convention delegates. There were fourteen excepted classes of North Carolinians, who could not vote unless they received a special pardon from President Johnson. Elections were held on 21 September, and the convention convened on 2 October. It abolished slavery, repudiated the war debt, and declared the ordinances of secession null and void. The convention also called for the election of a North Carolina governor in November, as well as a state legislature and representatives to the United States House of Representatives. The new state legislature would then select two men to serve in the United States Senate. Initially, both William and Mary Bayard Clarke allied themselves with the Conservative Party in the state, which hoped to gain readmission into the Union without accepting black citizenship and voting rights.

*MBC Scrapbook 1, Barden Collection. Article written in 1865 for New York* Daily News *[MBC inked in top margin.]*

NORTH CAROLINA CORRESPONDENCE. General Kilpatrick and Reconstruction—The Editor of the Progress and His Antecedents—Loyalty of the North Carolinians—The State Convention—What it Will Do—Soldiers to Return as Civilians—The Negro and Labor—Treatment of Prisoners at Fort Pulaski—Call for Investigation—Negro Convention, etc.

[Correspondence of The New York News.]

Raleigh, Aug. 29, 1865.

General [Hugh] Kilpatrick has written a letter, it is said, to some one in Washington to the effect that the President's reconstruction policy is premature, by at least four years, for that the people of North Carolina and the other Southern States are in such a frame of mind and state of heart that it will take at least that length of military rule to prepare them for the management of their own affairs. The Progress newspaper of this city fully indorses the General, and adds that he (the editor)[1] "would prefer continued military rule to a State Government to be controlled by the leaders in the rebellion." This is a great mistake of the General's, the more to be regretted that in so much as it shall influence the mind and conduct of the President and of Congress, it will seriously injure a great community, who, whatever may be their feelings and opinions of the past, are as loyal in their purposes toward the Government as any State north of the Potomac. The General has no political ends to serve, and if he has written any such letter, doubtless stated what he believed to be true, having been misled by just such men as this editor of The Progress, who, having been a violent secessionist before the war, a volunteer in the "rebel army" during the first twelve months, a true and consistent supporter of the war, so far as he can be true and consistent, and so long as the war promised to be successful, is now a self-nominated candidate for the convention, and, some say, will offer himself for Congress. His blatant professions of loyalty, after such a record, and his brutal abuse of his old friends, have utterly disgusted both Governor Holden and the United States officers here; and his despair of obtaining any office in the new State Government leads him to utter these slanders upon a loyal people, who, whatever may be their political differences, agree in condemning and distrusting him. I have conversed with men of every class and from every part of the State, and am confident that there is no disposition on the part of the people of North Carolina, rich or poor, original secessionists or original Unionists, to dig up the dead bodies of slavery and secession and attempt to resuscitate them. No well informed person really thinks so, and none pretend to, except a few, who, expecting in this great social revolution to rise into power and influence, are disappointed to find that the people will not transfer to them the confidence which they once reposed in their old leaders. The people of this State will bear with equanimity the losses, both pecuniary and political, consequent upon the war; and would to-day, I believe, if that would facilitate their rehabilitation, adopt the constitution of any Northern State which does not allow the negro to vote; and there are some who even go so far as to favor negro suffrage, though I believe there is no paper in the State which advocates it. The feeling of the people is: take away the military, let us have a State Government, and we will give up everything, even to the election of Holden for Governor; but don't force the negro or the editor of The Progress upon us. The Convention, which assembles in October, will come together in this spirit, and with the determination to throw no obstacle in the way of the early reorganization of the State Government. There will be a short session and great unanimity of action, and the result will, I believe, be satisfactory to the Government at Washington and all reasonable people at the North.

The charge that the people of this State show a disposition to ill-treat the negro is equally false with the other. No laboring population in the world was ever so well fed, well clothed, well treated generally, and, as a consequence, so happy and so prolific, as the slaves of the South. The sudden rupture of the relation existing between them and their masters has not yet destroyed the mutual good feeling. In most cases they remain with their old masters on stipulated wages, either in money or a part of the crop. Many of those who left at first have returned, and many more wish to. Most of the complaints which come before the Freedmen's Bureau prove, on investigation, to be without foundation. The employer of the South who performs his part of the contract, has less cause of complaint than the same class at the North. But this question of labor, after all, is the great question, to which every other is subordinate. Will the freedman work? If he will, then the prosperity and wealth of the South will soon be unexampled. If he will not, then what?[2]

The force which has been stationed here for some time has left for the North, or is about to go. The present garrison is much smaller, consisting of a part of the Twenty-eighth Michigan and the One Hundred and Twentieth Indiana.[3] Captain McIver is commandant of the post and provost marshal. Of those who have gone, many, before leaving, declared their intention to return, buy land, and show us how much better the negro will work as a freedman than he has a slave, and how these "old fields" can be made, by a proper system of agriculture, to smile with plenty. Some one has said that the man who causes a blade of grass to grow where one never grew before, deserves well of his country; but monuments of brass and marble would be feeble testimonials of the merit of that man who shall teach us how to persuade the freedman to work; We can make him work if you will let us; but you who maintain that he requires no compulsion, "come over and help us."

The experiments on Mr. Davis's plantation and elsewhere don't turn out well; and those who know the negro and his history say that he never has and never will work except under the driver. But as it is a given up fact that the Southerner knows nothing about the negro or his management, perhaps if a native of a New Hampshire manufacturing town will honestly buy a worn out North Carolina plantation, he may succeed with Cuffee when his old master fails. By all means let him come and try.

So Captain Wirz has been put on his trial, and the treatment of Federal prisoners of war at Andersonville is to be investigated, and Captain Wirz hanged.[4] Cannot the field for examination be extended so as to embrace

Fort Pulaski, and evidence be taken of the treatment of certain Confederate officers at that post during the Winter of 1864–65? The Secretary of War may object; but quite a number of his fellow citizens would like to have that matter investigated and the same punishment meted out to him, if guilty, as is to be inflicted on Captain Wirz. Put upon the stand the commanding officer at Fort Pulaski at that time and propose these questions to him: 1. What were the rations issued to the prisoners under your charge? 2. By whose orders did you issue those rations? 3. Were the prisoners allowed to purchase of the sutler or to receive food from their friends? On such a trial sketches as vivid as any photographs might be produced of the physical effects of a forty day's diet on six ounces of spoiled meat and one pickle per day. Then let evidence be taken to show how many of these prisoners, after they were brought back to Fort Delaware, died in hospital of scurvy and other diseases. Put the surgeon of that post on the stand, with Brigadier General Schoepff, the Hungarian commandant, and Captain Ahl, his adjutant, and if the truth can be gotten out of them under oath, ascertain why, when there was an abundance of vegetables on the island, these same officers were suffered to die of scurvy for want of them? Let the investigation be thorough. Let it cover the whole ground. Let all the facts be brought to light. Let the orders from Washington to the commandants of the different military prisons and camps be published. In a word let the treatment of Confederate prisoners of war at Fort Pulaski, Point Lookout, Fort Delaware, Old Capitol, Elmira, Johnson's Island and elsewhere, be made the subject of close inquiry. When that trial comes on there will be found witnesses to take the stand, who in their testimony will give dates and names with a frightful and unimpeachable accuracy.

The following notice appears in The Newbern Times:

Newbern, N. C., Aug. 22, 1865.

A call for a Convention of the colored citizens of North Carolina, to meet in Raleigh, N. C., in October next (day to be named). Object of the convention, to promote the welfare of our people. Those favorable to the call will send in their names to Post Office box No. 177, Newbern, N. C. A. H. Galloway.[5]

If the convention assemble, your correspondent will be present and give a correct account of the proceedings.

L. S.

1. John L. Pennington edited the New Bern *Progress* and predicted an early southern victory as the Civil War loomed. On 20 September 1861, he was commissioned first lieutenant in a Craven County battery of heavy artillery, but

he resigned on 17 July 1862, because of ill health. He moved his paper to Raleigh after New Bern fell to federal forces and renamed it the *Daily Progress*. During the war he advocated peace without reunion, and he criticized the Davis administration. At the end of the war, Pennington announced that his paper would give "cordial support to the views and principles of the great National Union Party," which was the forerunner of the Republican Party. He soon left North Carolina and President Grant named him governor of the Dakota Territory between 1874 and 1878. Powell, *DNCB*, 5:67.

2. Mary Bayard Clarke's father, Thomas P. Devereux, echoed the thoughts of many former slaveholders when he wrote in 1866 that "the Negro is but an overgrown child" who could not be trusted with the vote or to work without being controlled by white men. T. P. Devereux to Jonathan Worth, 20 October 1866, General Assembly Session Records 1866–67, State Archives, North Carolina Division of Archives and History, Raleigh, N.C.

3. Both of these infantry regiments were part of the occupying federal forces in North Carolina following the war. By August 1865, more than two thirds of the northern forces in North Carolina had been discharged. In September about 9,000 soldiers remained, 3,972 white troops and 5,296 black troops. By October 1866, fewer than 2,000 solders remained in the state. *Official Records (Army)*, series 1, vol. 47, pt. 3: 610; Roberta Sue Alexander, "North Carolina Faces the Freedmen: Race Relations During Presidential Reconstruction, 1865–1867," (Ph.D. diss., University of Chicago, 1974), vol. 1: 136 (hereafter cited as Alexander, "North Carolina Faces the Freedmen").

4. Andersonville Prison, a Confederate prison in Georgia, became notorious after the war because of the death rates suffered by federal soldiers imprisoned there. Rations given to prisoners matched those of Confederate soldiers in the field, but death rates soared because of poor sanitation, crowding, exposure, and inadequate diets. Captain Henry Wirz was the Andersonville commandant. Boatner, *Civil War Dictionary*, 15.

5. Abraham H. Galloway was an African American leader born in North Carolina. During the war he worked as a spy in the state for the Union army. A brilliant political leader, he worked before and after the war to organize freedmen and to secure equal rights and protection for them under the law. He and James Henry Harris led the Equal Rights League in the state. David S. Cecelski, "Abraham H. Galloway, Wilmington's Lost Prophet and the Rise of Black Radicalism in the American South," in *Democracy Betrayed: The Wilmington Race Riot of 1898 and Its Legacy* (Chapel Hill: University of North Carolina Press, 1998); J. G. de Roulhac Hamilton, *Reconstruction in North Carolina* (Gloucester, Mass.: Peter Smith, 1964, reprinted with permission of Columbia University Press from 1914 edition), 147, 150 (hereafter cited as Hamilton, *Reconstruction in North Carolina*).

⮫

*Barden Collection*
*W. B. Smith & Co., publishers of* Field and Fireside *to Mary Bayard Clarke*

Field and Fireside
Book Publishing House
Raleigh, N.C., Octr 4, 1865

Mrs Mary B Clark
Raleigh, NC
Madam:—

We will publish your volume of Poems[1] and will give you twenty per cent of nett profits upon first edition, twenty five per cent of nett profits upon second edition and thirty three and one third 33⅓ per cent of nett profits upon third edition; the first edition to consist of not less than 3000 three thousand copies and the second and third editions of not less than 5000 five thousand copies each, all the proceeds accruing from sales of this work upon each edition respectively to be applied to canceling cost of publication of each edition respectively until the same is restored to the publishers after which the division of profits according to rates herein agreed, will be made weekly between author and publishers unless otherwise ordered by the author

The publication and sale of the three editions herein specified to be entirely in publishers possession and controle, after which the copy right to recur to the author and to be hers forever

We are Madam

Very Respectfully
Your Obt Servts
Wm. B. Smith & Co

1. This was *Mosses from a Rolling Stone: or Idle Moments of a Busy Woman,* published in 1866 "for the benefit of the fund raised by the ladies of Winchester (Va.), for the Stonewall Jackson cemetery of that place." Hall, *MBC Poems,* xix.

*Mary Custis Lee Scrapbook, Lee Family Papers, Mss1L51b65,VHS*
*Mary Bayard Clarke to Mary Custis Lee*

November 4, 1865

Mrs Robert E Lee
Dear Madam

Will you allow me to offer you a slight tribute of love and veneration for your noble husband, in whom I feel that I, as well as every other native-born, and true-hearted Southern woman, have a right to glory.[1]

I dare not venture to send it to him, but take that liberty with you, knowing, that, as every true wife should, you must take pride in the honours which crown his revered head.

Hoping that your health has improved since I last had the pleasure of seeing you, and that of your daughters continues unbroken, I am dear

Madam very sincerely

Yours

Mary Bayard Clarke

Raleigh. NC.

November 4th 1865


1. Mary Bayard Clarke enclosed her poem "General Robert E Lee" with this letter. In August 1866 she published "General Lee at the Battle of the Wilderness" in *The Land We Love,* published in Charlotte by James P. Irwin and edited by former Confederate General Daniel Harvey Hill.

*William J. Clarke Papers, SHC*
*Sam Taylor to William J. Clarke*

San antonio Texas December 6 1865

My deare Master I take this oppotunity of wrighten you a few lines to Let you know I am well at pres and am very anchus to see you and the famly or to her from you all ti is true the Curlard peple has bind mad free by the united States but my master I do give you my Sincere thanks for myne for you could of Sold me long before that happen if you wish tho my Deare master I am a long ways from home and Sum times out doose and Sum times in a house just as my Chanch offer I would by me a Small lot but the peple ask from 2 hund and fifty to 3 hundred dollars and my deare master I thaught if I could get you wright to Mr Mavrate [Samuel Maverick] you might get him to let me have a pec of ground Chapper than I Could get it I would like to know if you are Coming out here

plese remember me to Mistress and all the Children and my Mother and all my friends San antonio is full of life as when we forst Came here I have your trunk Still with me which my Mistress pack before She left here

I wish to here from you very murch and as Sun as you wright to me in Care of W. D. Cotton I would wright more but not knowing whether you will get this or not I will Close

by your umble Servent Samuel Taylor

Barden Collection
Mary Custis Lee to Mary Bayard Clarke

Lexington December 7th 1865

you will pardon me my dear Mrs Clarke for not replying sooner to your interesting letter when I tell you I only arrived in Lexington a few *days* since I have never forgotten our acquaintance made in my time of sorrow & your beautiful lines upon my darling Annie have been often perused with many tears both by her Father & myself—& appreciated by a large circle of friends who knew & loved her. Those contained in your letter are even more valuable as *poesy* & you may be sure I appreciate & respond to the *sentiment*—I did feel certain that had my husband been the honoured instrument of bringing our glorious struggle to a successful termination a grateful country would have crowned him with honour & glory but that defeated & shorn of his position & the ability to do any thing for [our independance?] he should meet every where with so much consideration was beyond my fondest hopes. He begs me to say how much he feels gratefied at being honoured by your pen & to present his kindest regards to yourself & husband whom he remembers very well—He is much occupied with his duties here[1] & we are all happy once more to have a home which is being made very comfortable thro' the kindness of many friends—Shall I not hope to have the pleasure of seeing you & yours here when the season renders the mountains attractive I should be very glad to welcome you to our House. I am sorry to say that my disease is much worse than when I saw you as I am unable now to walk at all without crutches, but I enjoy very much seeing my friends Agnes [Lee] is in Richmond & I have only Mildred [Lee] with me my eldest daughter [Mary Lee] being in Baltimore She unites with me in love to you—

Yours most truly & gratefully

M C Lee—

1. Robert E. Lee became president in 1865 of Washington College in Lexington, Virginia, where he stayed until his death on 22 October 1870. Coulling, *The Lee Girls,* 108–9.

Barden Collection
Mary Bayard Clarke to Miss Deane, care of J T Heath Esq.
Liverpool & London Insurance Office, New Orleans

Raleigh Feb 23d [1866]

My Dear Miss Deane[1]

    My book is out and I hoped to send you a copy by this mail but John Bryan[2] has served me a scurvy trick and refuses to allow me but one copy for myself, and not one to distribute to the press, so I shall have to wait until I can get orders enough to enable me to buy at whole-sale and sell at retail. this will leave me copies for my own use, I intended to have sold six copies for the benefit of the fund to protect the graves of our dead about Winchester but have adopted another plan which will check mate John H Bryan Jr I hope. Is it not awfully unromantic to be cheated by an old lover? You will see my advertisement in the Picayune please get me all the orders you can, I buy through a third person at $66^2/_3$d cts a copy, and sell at the same price the publishers do, one dollar; but I must pay cash for what I get so I shant buy until I get orders. Please write me at once and tell me all the queer customs you can think of among the Creoles[3], I am writing a novel scene laid in Louisiana and I want to make it as life like as possible Tell me particularly about weddings for of course I must marry my hero and heroine. All are as usual Sophia expecting, and poor Nora also. Brother John is in a low state of health and we are all anxious about him Miss Deane has not that Roanoke property been a curse instead of a blessing? but for it Ma would not have married father and but for it brother would not be sick. I am in hopes of leaving Raleigh before long. William has gone into a partnership with a firm in New York[4] who advance the money for the purchase of a saw mill which he and Mr Cooke are to manage. I want to go and live there, but as yet have not got him to say I may; it is in a lonely spot and not very healthy in the fall, but as much so as Scotland Neck where Kate lives. I hate to have him staying there half the time and only running home saturday night, so I am trying to convince him it is better for us all to stay there ten months and board the other two, than for me to stay here with the children and he to go down monday and come back Saturday it is only two hours and a half ride on the rail road and I shall be awful jealous of it if I cant be there too. I think we have been separated enough during the last four years. But he knows how I hated Conniconara and cant bear to take me into quite as lonely a place where we must live very roughly, but I tell him Coniconara to a young girl and a home of her own to a settled woman are too widely different things. I hate country life, I have no health for its pursuits and enjoyments and love a little society but in the present state of affairs these are but feathers—and to go where we would not always be worried about the Almighty dollar is my first desire.

I am waiting to catch the mail and can hardly see so excuse mistakes and believe me yours lovingly

Mary

[Endorsed] Miss Deane

Care of J Y Heath Esq

Liverpool & London Insurance Off.

New Orleans

1. Mary Bayard Clarke's former tutor.

2. John H. Bryan, one of the publishers with the firm of William Smith & Co., was the son of New Bern attorney John Heritage Bryan and an attorney in his own right. Sometime after the Civil War, he moved to Brazil and lived there until his death. Emma Morehead Whitfield, comp., *Bryan / Smith*, vol. 2 of *Whitfield, Bryan, Smith and Related Families* (Westminister, Md.: privately printed, 1950), 166–67.

3. This story, titled "Chalmette," was serialized in *Field and Fireside*. The installments ran from 16 December 1865, to 3 March 1866. Clarke, however, was critical of the way the publishers had handled the story, feeling they had injured her reputation as an author. She sought legal assistance to regain copyright of the story. After legal mediation, Clarke regained copyright to the published story as well as to any future additions she might write. She severed her employment with the firm at this time. William B. Smith and Co. to Mary Bayard Clarke, 6 January 1866, Clarke Papers, SHC.

4. Powell, *DNCB*, 1:381–82.

 తు

*Barden Collection*
*General Robert E. Lee to Mary D. Clarke*[1]

Lexington Va;

14 March 1866

My dear Miss Mary

I have received the book of poems by your mother,[2] which you so kindly sent me.

They afford me double pleasure; having been written by her, & given by you; and Carry me back to the pleasant days, when I Saw you both in San Antonio.

I am much gratified that you still remember me; and hope the time is not distant when I may again see you; and that you will have in me the Same Confidence as then.

I must ask you to say, to your mother, that I greatly enjoy her poems, & to present to your father my friendly Compliments.

To both, to you & to your brothers, I send my sincere regards.

Praying that the blessing of Heaven may be showered upon you

I am respt & afft

yours

R E Lee

Miss Mary Clarke

1. This was the Clarkes' daughter, Mary Devereux Clarke.
2. *Mosses from a Rolling Stone; or, Idle Moments of a Busy Woman.*

*Barden Collection*
*Mary Custis Lee to Mary Bayard Clarke*

Lexington 15th March [1866]

I received your kind note with the little Book my dear Mrs Clarke which I value highly both for your sake & its own merit will you be kind enough to send me 5 copies for some of my friends for which I enclose $5.00 If you will have them put up & directed to Genl Lee by National Express they will come *free* of charge I suppose Miss Mary will be so charmed to receive the Genl's letter she will scarcely care to have a message from me But you may tell her that I am sure a young lady of her age so thoughtful & *provident* of the future, will make a good wife & Mother & that her *grand*children will be worthy of her—I have a son of 21 years[1] who has just gone to work on his farm where there is only an overseers house in which he lives & who is so lonely he declares he will marry any woman who will build him a house & come & take care of him Now ask Miss Mary if she cannot save up a sum for this charitable purpose the only obstacle in the way is I fear his patience will not last till she is 16. I am so busy this evening I must write you a short letter. I am sorry to tell you that I do not improve at all in my powers of locomotion yet I seem to have full occupation for all my time & thoughts.

we have quite a comfortable home for the present where I should be very happy to welcome you should you ever feel disposed to penetrate into these mountains—I hope your town Raleigh is recovering from the direful effects of the war.

Beleive me yours most sincerely

M. C Lee

Mildred unites in special love she is the only daughter I have with me at present

1. After the war, Robert E. Lee Jr. farmed lands left to him by his grandfather in King William County. Coulling, *Lee Girls,* 107–8.

∽

BRANTZ MAYER (1809–79) WAS a lawyer and United States Army officer who had known the Clarkes before the Civil War. Born in Baltimore, Maryland, he served as secretary to the United States legation to Mexico from 1841 to 1844, and he was a founder of the Maryland Historical Society. During the Civil War, he served as a brigadier general of Maryland volunteers from 1862 to 1863, as a paymaster from 1863 to 1867, and was breveted lieutenant colonel of volunteers in 1865 for faithful and meritorious service. He retired as a full colonel on 15 June 1875.

Mayer published several books and greatly admired the writing of Mary Bayard Clarke. He wrote a poem titled "To a Lady with an Apple" in her letterbook while on board the steamer *Eclipse* somewhere on the Mississippi River around 1855. In the poem he said, "more daring still, in Eden / If you plucked it from the tree, / I'd have tempted death and sun / Adam-like to *take* from thee!" He and Mary Bayard Clarke exchanged several letters in 1866, during the early stages of Reconstruction. Although her letters to him have not survived, he answered questions she raised and engaged in a spirited debate with her on Reconstruction in the South. Clarke's son Frank visited the Mayer family in 1866, and she visited them in Baltimore in 1868. In addition to the letters published here, Mayer also wrote to Clarke on 5 and 16 April, 9 May, and 9 October 1866. *Who Was Who in America,* 340; Heitman, *Historical Register,* 699.

*Barden Collection*
*Lieutenant Colonel B. Mayer to Mary Bayard Clarke*
Baltimore Md. 26 March 1866.
My dear Mrs Clarke,
    I am really quite flattered by your remembrance of me in the gift of the Charming little volume which has gathered up the poems you have scattered among us for so many years. I think I suggested this to you as due to your reputation and to your friends, and I am glad to see you have performed the duty, though very, *very* sorry to hear the Cause you gave for it. The war has, indeed, Stricken many homes with great suffering, in all quarters of the United States. You, of the south, are not the *only* sufferers.

The trail of battle has passed *broadly* over many parts of Maryland and Pennsylvania, marked by physical desolation; but there is *hardly a family* into which death has not been brought by it, at the North. It is the natural, inevitable, result of war, and we can only hope that experience, that Stern teacher of wisdom, will hereafter enforce peace, and speedily produce a true restoration of Union feeling throghout our beloved Country. Do not think, my fair and valued friend, that time, trouble, and war have at all dimmed my very agreeable recollection of you and yours, or my kindliest sympathies for you. Though in the Army, we—(the Northern officers)—have always striven to subdue personal animosities rather than encourage them. Of course, manhood, resents insults,—silly, wonton, or studied,—at all times and in all sections,—but I think we may safely say that we have never "thrown the first stone." Some of my dearest friends, &, *one,* the very loved Companion of my youth, are, and have been, in the south during the whole war. We very seldom heard from, or, of them; but, thank God, their lives were spared, & most of them have Come out of the fire with comparatively little diminution of fortune or estate. Of Course you will do me the real justice to think I *often equired for you,* from friends who had been in Texas—supposing you still there; but none of them had heard of you or the Colonel. The *only* trace I had of you during the Conflict of arms, was your poem on the death of Miss Lee, which was copied in the papers with your signature. In it I recognized the well known marks of Tenella. Pray give me some account of your adventures. Following your husband "in an ambulance" or "riding with him at the head of his regiment," you must have seen much of actual warfare, and I dare say many a "lyric" was suggested and now lies either in embryo, in your heart, or, in ink, in your portfolio. The war gave birth to many fine poems. I have quite a collection of Rebel Verses—many of much merit, and nearly all of *much fire,* which were written and published in Maryland between May 1861, and 1865. I should like to show them to you. I have been in the Army since the spring of 1863, and it is probable that I will remain in it, at least, another year. I want, if possible, to go to Europe in 1867, with my family. I have *three* daughters married, & you will imagine *how old* I am getting— when you hear I have *two* grand children. May I not hope, however, to see you once more before that time, or, may you not go abroad like so many of you "wicked rebels" have already done? Be assured it will give me true pleasure to meet you either here or there and to refresh the memories of our agreable journey in the "Eclipse" along the "Father of Waters." On you,—fair women of the south,—rests a great responsibility in restoring our country. You know your influence over mankind and "a word to the wise" is sufficient for such a woman *as you are*. Noah sent forth *the dove* to get the olive twig—*and she got it!* Are you living permanetly now-a days, in Ralegh N Carolina, or do you intend to go back to Texas? From all I have heard of the state of things there *during the war,* I am surprized you left it, & must suppose *you* Were so very belligerent that you could not keep your hands off of us! Was that just the truth? Texas does not seem to have suffered much except on its *fringes.* Some of our Baltimore friends, who have farms there, write quite *prosperously* indeed, and say they have retained all their work people, who, after a little deliberation, have gone into the field as of old,—do their tasks comfortably & faithfully,—and are paid regular wages. How much more sensible is this than what I find ocurring in Virginia, when the planters sit idly with folded hands, talk politics and make faces us, with the expectation of the "restoration of slavery" after the next Presidential election! How vain, how besotted! There's about as much Chance for the restoration of that devil as there is of the draining of Niagara. If one thing has been settled by this war, my dear dame, that *one* thing is slavery. There *can* be no more of it, There *ought* to be no more of it; and our best duty now is to think of reorganizing labor by the blacks, and at the same time, of making that labor as intelligent as possible.

But, my dear Mrs Tenella, I did not sit down to write "politics" to you & hope you wont consider what I have said more than as a *friendly word for Aid* from a noble woman, who, wherever she is, *must* exercise unbounded influence over all who come within the sway of her Charmed circle. Do all you can to make this people *one* again. You can't exist unless we are *one* again. I know it.—

Since I saw you some years ago I took a fancy to making a complete collection of *letters* of the Signers of the Declaration of Independence; (*autographic.*) Can you help me with some of *your Southern ones,* or *direct me into a Channel in which I can obtain my missing ones by exchanges?* If any thing occurs to you favorably in this way, I will send you a list of my *duplicates* which I will offer to any souhern Collector bitten by the same mad dog. I have good autographs of nearly all the signers except the following, whose names I commend to your kind enquiries:

| N. Carolina | Georgia | S. Carolina |
|---|---|---|
| W. [William] Hooper. | B.[Button] Gwinnett | T. [Thomas Heyward] Hayward Jr. |
| Jno. [Joseph] Hewes. | Lyman Hall | T [Thomas] Lynch |
| Jno [John] Penn. | Geo [George] Walton. | A [Arthur] Middleton |

The only fault I have to find with your delicious little volume is that you have *not set your gems more worthily.* You should have *had them printed in Boston,* (if you could have brought that little rebel muscle in your bosom to permit it——); and had *them published* by Ticknor and Fields. I hope to see them there yet.

Remember me kindly to the Colonel, to whom you have been playing the good wife, & who, I hope, has not been suffering much from the Drury Bluff fights. Receive my truest regards for yourself & believe me always your Sincere friend

B Mayer (*Lt Col USA*)
Mrs Clarke. Ralegh, NC.

Have you a spare autographic letter or note from *my old friend* Bishop Polk?

*Barden Collection*
*Lieutenant Colonel Brantz Mayer to Mary Bayard Clarke*

Baltimore 3rd April 1866.

My dear Mrs. Clarke,

If you ever needed to be "converted," as you seem to think you do, it would be a glorious and delicious privilege to any one to be allowed the duty of attempting the work. But, my dear Madam, I have been one of those faithless sinners, who don't believe in sending "Missionaries to the heathen"; and as I have never contributed a cent for the redemption of pagans, I certainly do not mean to undertake the task of bringing a Christian woman back into the Union fold. Your recounted smartnesses quite charmed me and a very appreciative person to whom I took the liberty of reading them; but they struck me, as I daresay they did the persons to whom you addressed them, as showing how clever a person Tenella was, but, what a pity she allowed *just a little* spice of bad temper to get the better of her good taste![1] In fact, why dont you keep yourself out of the kitchen altogether so as not to get into the neighborhood of that dreadful "teakettle" which you describe as boiling over so wrecklessly,——though you gel[?] your delicate little body on top of it,——and scalding everybody else——save yourself!——But *badinage* aside, I was very glad to have the pleasure of receiving your letter of the 29th March, and to see that you were as full of vitality and spirit as ever, and that there was a probability of your coming this way to visit your Sister——whose name and address you omit.[2] It gives me and my family great pleasur to see and visit any Southern friends, to whom we know our intercourse would be agreeable; but

we are Cautious in our efforts to be friendly, being surrounded in Baltimore by so many idiots of *our own state* who pretend not to know Mary-
landers who had courage enough not to be intimidated by them into
rebellion. It is due to you to say that I opposed the Southern scheme
openly from the begining, and was anxious to avoid war if possible; but
when you began with the farce of Sumpter (÷the farce—alas! *before* the
tragedy,÷) there was no longer a doubt of your meaning,—or rather, of
the meaning of the *Chiefs,* who have led your Southern people by the nose
to the slaughter block and to utter ruin. We sympathize with you sincirly
and tenderly in *your mistake,*—the result of a temper which was so excited
that it could easily be misled and as easily used. That you are brave, who
doubts?—that you fought well, who denies?—that you were whipped,
who contradicts? And such being your precedents and your predicament,
let us no longer make mouths at each other but see how we can, out of
sorrow and *mutual* misfortunes, educe the *best qualities* of each section for
the *best interests* of all quarters of what is, by the decrees of God & Man,
to be hereafter & forever one Country.—Sense, Sense, Sense,—is what
we want—now-a-days, and not sharpness, smartness, or scolding. No one
is such a fool as to imagine that people who have been fighting one another
for four years are to rush into each others arms, with a yell of joy! But we
are *all too impatient for immediate results;* and, indeed, it is natural we should
desire to be restored to our normal conditions, for, luckily, (unlike the
Mexicans) we are unused to revolutions.

And so you all want to emigrate "to Mexico": that is your "Eldorado".
what do *you* know about it? *I do* know about it, having lived there & studied the country & the people thoroghly. It is'nt a country for you, or *your
children,*—to whom you have duties, independent of your selfish wish for
a temporary refuge from imaginary wrongs. I should think you had enough
of "revolutions", without going to a land of which "revolutions" is the
Chronic malady; & which, in addition, is now threatend with the establishment of a Franco-Austrian despotism[3] under the guise of "stability"!
What sort of a ruler for *an American born freeman,* think you, is the scion of
the "House of Hapsburg."!! Nay—my dear dame—think better of it, and
rather go back to your old Texas, which should be near enough to Mexico, in climate and productions, to suit your tropical heart. I will begin to
believe you are a "rolling stone" in something like fact as well as poetry.
Roll on, however, as long as you will, especially if the rolling, as usual, will
keep the moss off of you for many a long year yet to come.

There is part of the 8th United States Infantry to be stationed immediately in Raleigh, all of whose officers I know, and some of whom I esteem.

Major Worth[4] (son of the late General Worth) you will find to be a very clever gentleman. The Lieut Col of the detachment, Eddy,[5] is rather a rough person *in appearance,* but has an *excellent heart and good discretion.* If you get into any trouble, I dare say these gentlemen will be found friendly in any emergency. As to myself, I dont know yet whether I will remain in the army, &, if I do, where I will be stationed,—having been at this post for three years. I should like, of course, to be near so charming a lady as dame Tenella who condescends to promise "*harmonizing with me individually*";—for, if I go south, I suppose I shall have to encounter much *brusquerie,* or to live in barrack seclusion until better days arrive. I hope you will let me know your Sister's Name and residence in Baltimore; or rather, if she Should desire to know us, that she would be so kind as to send her card to No. 16. McCulloh Street, where it will give us real pleasure to visit her.

I am really obliged to you for your promise of Bishop Polks *autograph letter,* and for your efforts in my behalf with Gov [David Lowery] Swain, or with any Gentleman who is willing to *exchange* autographs and to whom I will cheerfully send a list of my duplicates. I have a very rich Collection of American and European Celebrities, and want to Complete, if possible, my series of Signers of the Declaration of Independence, and to add to my list of *eminent* General Officers (of both sides) of the late war of 1861–5.

When I begin to write to you I, some how, go on, insesibly covering an immense quantity of paper (—with very bad writing)—very pleasantly for myself, but, doubtless, very boreingly for you. If you think so, pardon the selfishness which brings back so many delightful memories of our old *Sympathetic* intercourse. Do you believe in the doctrine of "elective affinities?" I sometimes recognize it *on my side,*—as well as that of "natural repugnancies"; and I believe I once, on board of the Eclipse, told you that I rather discoraged those "affinities" unless they could be *perfected,* & that I also, described my idea of their *only perfectability*! Alas, therfore, why do we *seem,* in this world, to have so many elective affinities, and so little prospect of even an approach to their perfection!

But the bottom of the paper tells me to stop, yet leaves me space to tender you my sincerest wishes for your health, welfare and happiness, and to hope, that you will, before long, pay the hinted visit to Baltimore, when we will, surely, be so delighted to welcome you.

With kind rembrances to the Col I am truly your friend

B Mayer<br>
Mrs Clarke<br>
Raligh, NC.

1. Mary Bayard Clarke wrote a letter to Mayer on 8 April 1866, in response to this one. In it she apparently described the hostility she was encountering in Raleigh because of her association with Union officers stationed in the city. Mayer wrote Clarke on 16 April, praising her for dropping the "saucy, petulant tone" in former letters and applauding "Mrs. Tenella Clarke's natural garniture of right-thinking independence." He felt that her letter showed more sense then all the correspondence he had seen from the South, but he admitted there was "a Shadow, nevertheless, [that] accompanies all your wisdom in the reflection that your fair friends condemn you for your independent judgement!" He added, "I sympathize deeply with many Clever men, whom I know to be patriotic, & who, I think, would act patriotically in Congress, if admitted, but, I would not vote to morrow to admit them, after the receipt of such a letter as your last showing the bitterness of your kindred & townsfolk *to you*—for what?—because you dared to be human! I speak very plainly to you, because I recognize the *truth* of what someone said to you as flattery or, at least, as a compliment; that 'Mrs Clarke is a person who makes revolutions.'"

2. Elizabeth (Betsy) Devereux Jones.

3. Some former Confederates moved to Mexico and South America after the war. England, Spain, and France had invaded Mexico in 1862 to collect claims against the Mexican republic. England and Spain withdrew, but Napoleon III of France controlled a puppet government there. He placed Maximilian, brother of the Emperor of Austria, on the throne in Mexico. Napoleon withdrew French troops from Mexico on 5 April 1866. Maximilian refused to leave and was executed by Mexican authorities in 1867. James A. Padgett, ed., "Reconstruction Letters from North Carolina, Part 2, Letters to John Sherman," *NCHR* 18 (July 1941): 282n (hereafter cited as Padgett, "Reconstruction Letters from North Carolina").

4. William Scott Worth of New York was breveted major for gallant and meritorious service during the Virginia Campaign on 9 April 1865. He retired in 1898 as a brigadier general. Heitman, *Historical Register*, 1:1061. Major Worth was the son of General William Jenkins Worth.

5. This may have been Asher Robbins Eddy of Rhode Island. He served in the war and was promoted to lieutenant colonel on 6 June 1872. He was breveted a lieutenant colonel and colonel on 13 March 1865, for his service during the war. Heitman, *Historical Register*, 1:396.

MARY BAYARD CLARKE TOOK full advantage of the incidents and people she met in occupied Raleigh following its capitulation to Union troops on 13 April 1865. Using information from conversations, letters, and notes, Clarke wrote three articles describing Sherman's occupation of Raleigh for the New York City serial *Old Guard,* a periodical that lauded the South and claimed on its masthead to be "Devoted to the Principles of 1776 and 1787." In these articles, Clarke recounted how Raleigh's citizens coped with the fear of approaching northern troops as well as the reality of the northern presence. Her articles illustrate how many white southern planter women viewed Sherman, his troops, and the growing interference of federal regulations in their lives. The articles, published between April and June 1866, offer a model of Clarke's writing style. She used quotes and dialogue to draw readers into her story, and she cultivated northern audiences by including southern propaganda that described the South's planter class as benevolent and genuinely concerned about the plight of its former slaves. Her work reflected the myth perpetuated by many southerners that portrayed slaves as being happy and contented with slavery. Clarke firmly adhered to southern orthodoxy on the abilities, intelligence, and honesty of African Americans, as she and others of her class sought to reassert white control over the freed men, women, and children in the state.

Another point of interest is that Clarke sometimes annotated copies of the articles in a scrapbook she kept of her writings. In the Sherman articles, she identified some of the citizens and Union officers anonymously quoted, and many of the anonymous sources she quoted actually referred to herself. In the following article, the first in the series, Clarke's penciled identifications are included in square brackets exactly where she pencilled them in her scrapbook. Although none of these articles carried her name as author, she inked in "M B Clarke" at the start of each scrapbook article.

In addition to the Sherman articles, the *Old Guard* published several other items authored by Clarke: "The South Expects Every Woman To Do Her Duty," "A Tribute to the 'Beast,'" "Uncivilized Warfare," and the poem "Battle of St. Paul's." These articles and others she wrote for miscellaneous conservative papers through early 1868 marked a major development in Clarke's career as a professional writer. In an age when many women writers, both north and south, concentrated on romantic literature, Clarke turned increasingly to prose articles that discussed political events of the day. She saved every article she wrote and relished her accomplishments, despite ongoing struggles caused by a limited income and family tragedies. When her husband shocked everyone by joining the state's Republican Party in 1868, Clarke found many of her old avenues to publication closed. Undaunted, she explored new topics and thereby encountered social, cultural, and intellectual differences that subtly altered her southern view of the world. Although never able to shake her prejudices or the enjoy-ment she took in being a southern lady, Clarke began to raise questions about women's education, their work for equal pay, and her own religious beliefs.

*MBC Scrapbook 2, Barden Collection*
*Old Guard 4, no. 4, Apr. 1866, 226–32.*

### GENERAL SHERMAN IN RALEIGH.

It was a bright, sunshiny spring day in the month of April, when the news reached Raleigh that General Joseph E. Johnston would, with his whole army, pass through the town that day, on his way to unite with Gen-eral Lee. Every one who had a spark of patriotism, and a pound of bacon, set to work cooking provisions for the weary and hungry soldiers, who had so long, and so gallantly held at bay a force so greatly their superior in everything but courage, and spirit to do, dare and endure. All felt that the enemy must take possession of the town, and prepared themselves for the fate of Columbia, Fayetteville, and other places in the path of the destroyer. Yet only a few wise and far-seeing ones were despondent as to the final issue. "Overcome, overpowered, out-numbered, but not conqered," was the universal cry. The knowledge of the horrible outrages committed by Sherman's army prepared all minds for the worst; it was useless to run away, for there was no place of safety except in the front of Johnston's retreating army; so it was generally decided that all the gentlemen, likely to be taken prisoners, should leave the place, trusting to work their way back when the enemy should have passed, while the women and children remained to gather up the fragments and save what they could from the general wreck.

It was a time which tried mens' metal, and ,womens' temper, and brought out the true characters of all *white* persons; the black population did not yet dare to throw off their mask, or were really, as was usually the case with them, swayed by the prevailing tone of the white, and felt for the time what they expressed.

The whole population of the town turned out into the streets, and stood at their gates offering provision to their weary defenders, which the soldiers took from the hands of the ladies without pausing in their march.

It was indeed a touching sight to watch those worn, weather-beaten soldiers as the ladies waved their handkerchiefs, handed out bread and meat, tobacco, or any little luxury the strict blockade had allowed them to procure.

"But I don't like to take it from you, ladies," was frequently heard from the roughest-looking men among them.

"Never mind; we don't want it as much as you do; we will give John-ston's boys everything we have." Or, "take it, take it, the Yankees will destroy it if you don't," was heard on all sides.

"Yonder's a soldier aint got no hat," said a little boy to a group of ladies who stood at the gate of one of the largest houses in town, ministering to the "grey jackets."

"Here, run take him mine," was the quick response of one of them, pulling off a little jaunty straw hat, trimmed with black velvet, and adorned with a plume, as she spoke. [Kate Baker][1]

"No, no!" shouted the soldiers, "Johnson's [*sic*] boys don't rob the ladies, God bless them;" while the soldier laughed, and said, "I could not think of robbing you of it *now;* but wait till we whip Sherman, and then I'll come for it."

Suddenly one of the ladies, turning her back on the soldiers, threw up her hands and said, in accents of the deepest sorrow:

"My God! This is the funeral procession of the Southern Confeder-acy!" [MBC]

"What do you mean?" they all exclaimed.

"*Lee has surrendered to Grant!*" was the reply, in a low, distinct voice.[2]

"Impossible!" broke from them all. But it was too true. A telegram had just been received to that effect, and the news had been whispered by a gen-tleman passing, who had paused for a moment on the side-walk. [Henry Burgwyn][3]

Never can I forget the faces of those half dozen ladies, as they gradu-ally took in the full meaning of these terrible words, "*Lee has surrendered to Grant!*" It was as though each one had just heard of the death of her near-est and dearest, and stood face to face with a terrible calamity.

Tramp, tramp, tramp, all day long did those grey coats pour through the town, receiving food and encouragement from the inhabitants, who fully expected to be themselves homeless and houseless in a few days.

"God bless you, ladies!" said one poor fellow, "God bless you! We are too tired to cheer, or we would give you three times three."

Far into the night the dull sound of many feet, and the rumble of wheels were heard; few thought of sleep, for we knew not at what moment the enemy would be upon us. Gov. Vance had sent a deputation[4] to meet General Sherman and surrender the place to him, requesting protection for private property; but no one knew the issue of the movement.

General [Joseph] Wheeler and his staff were still in town, and we knew when he left that the Yankees could not be far off. All the afternoon his cavalry had been riding yelling through the streets, having broken into the Commissary and Quarter-Master's depots, and sacked them, on the ground that if they did not, the Yankees would. Occasionally, one would pass loaded with hoop-skirts, one of which he would whirl round his head, and dash at any lady he chanced to meet. Sometimes a package of stockings, or pocket handkerchiefs, would be tossed into a group by a cavalry-man riding by at full speed, who would exclaim, "Take them, ladies! take them! The Yankees will get them if we don't."

Now, as the Confederate States Government certainly never provided such articles for the use of its soldiers, there is doubtless some truth in the numerous stories in circulation respecting the depradations of "Wheeler's men," and many in Raleigh said truly they had suffered more from them than from the enemy. But these were individual cases; there were many desperate characters among our cavalry, and all deeds of violence committed by men in grey jackets, on horseback, were laid without inquiry to "Wheeler's men." It is well known that there were numbers of Yankee spies[5] who passed through the country disguised as "Wheeler's cavalry," and many a robbery committed in lonely country places may be laid to the door of rascals who for their own purposes passed for what they were not.

By three o'clock in the morning we had bid adieu to every Confederate soldier, and instead of going to bed, retired to dress for the "sacking of the town."

"I mean to put on every white skirt I have," exclaimed one lady, "for the Yankees tore up all the ladies' and childrens' clothes in Fayetteville, and as I don't know when I shall get any more, I will keep these, if possible."

To have heard them, no one would have supposed them unprotected females preparing to save what they could from a lawless soldiery. They were more like school-girls dressing for a masquerade. Stockings, collars, pocket-handkerchiefs, and all small articles were hung on hoop-skirts, and artistically fastened with pins, so that they should not drop off at unexpected times, and two days after, a lady in the street raising her skirt to pass a muddy spot, displayed unconsciously a whole wardrobe thus secured, which she had not felt sufficient confidence in the honor of General Sherman to restore to her drawers.

We had been for a whole week, like an immense flock of magpies, hiding and burying our valuables; but now we were dressing to support the dignity of the Southern Confederacy, in the absence of our fathers, brothers, husbands, and lovers; and right nobly did we "swell" for the occasion. Two at least of each article of underclothing was put on, beside the loaded hoops, and when dresses obstinately refused to meet over those "double tides," we pinned them together, and covered all deficiencies with our cloaks, religiously martyrizing ourselves until bed-time next night, by carrying around half our wardrobes, and wearing our cloaks, furs, and hats, that we might not be in the forlorn condition of some of our Fayetteville friends, who were literally left with nothing but what they had on; and, not having taken precautions similar to ours, had not a change of clothing.

It was laughable, when the danger was over, to see the unearthing and bringing to light of the hidden and buried articles. One young lady had carefully buried her best bonnet, to find it, after lying a week in the grave, a perfect paste; another threw her silver down a well, and a third planted her spoons and forks in a parsnip bed, and fortunately discovered a soldier just in the act of pulling up the parsnips. The politeness with which she offered to give him some "much better than those," and the suavity with which she seduced him from the garden to her store-room door, was amusing to those who knew the reason.

Another lady quilted four dozen forks and spoons into a petticoat which she wore day and night, while diamond rings, and wedding rings, breast pins and bracelets, were sewed into the wadding of dresses and under-bodies.

"Your diamonds will certainly be the things nearest to your heart when the Yankees come in," said a Confederate officer to a lady whom he saw employed in thus securing her jewelry. "Literally nearer than husband or child."

Many forgot where they had secreted articles, and some to this day have never discovered them; others called in the assistance of the "bummers," who, by order of their officers, in a very short time discovered the "cache."

Most of the ladies carried pistols, resolved to kill at least one man in defence of their jewelry.

All agreed to offer but passive resistance to the destruction of household furniture, provisions, books, clothing, etc.; we determined to bear the knocking in of barrels of sorghum over our parlor carpets, the ripping open of beds, to be stirred into the mess with lard, meat, oil, spirits of turpentine, and everything else that came to hand; for we knew this was a favorite amusement of Sherman's brave soldiers. Had not our sisters, cousins, and friends, borne it before us? Had they not even borne more? Yes—their ear-rings had been torn violently from their ears, their wedding rings taken forcibly from their fingers, and their broaches snatched from their bosoms.[6] It was here that we decided to resist with the determination of lionesses.

Whether we should have been transformed into sheep in the presence of the danger, was never proven, for, as a general rule, our tongues were the only weapons[7] we had occasion to use. Nothing could be more perfect and thorough than the discipline of General Sherman's army, *when he chose it should be so;* and the conduct of his *men* in Raleigh was

"Confirmation strong as holy writ"

of the falsehood of the assertion so often made by his *officers,* that the diabolical outrages committed by the Federal army in Columbia, Fayetteville, and other towns, as well as in their whole line of march, could not be prevented.

Savage Sherman will forever stand in the estimation of southern people beside Beast [Benjamin] Butler, and Austrian [Julius] Hayneau; he had not the first conception of civilized warfare, and allowed his soldiers to vent the spleen he could not pour out on General Johnston, on the defenceless women and children who had the misfortune to come within their reach. He verified his motto, "WAR IS ESSENTIALLY CRUEL," and openly avowed that he did war upon women and children; justifying his conduct by saying the South could never be conquered until the spirit of its women was broken.[8] "I will destroy your homes, desolate your country, starve your children, and, if necessary, hang your women," was his language to the wife of one who had been his brother officer and friend. It was not the plundering of his soldiers which has placed Gen. Sherman in the unenviable position he will ever hold in the estimation of Southerners—that was expected; but it is the firm conviction that the wanton destruction which marked his war path like that of the savage, was a part of his system, and done by his orders, which has rendered him the object of deep, bitter, and burning hatred wherever he has gone. There is not a particle of this feeling towards General Grant; he is regarded as an enemy to the South, but as an honorable, civilized one, whom, when the "passion of contest" is over, we can greet as an equal. But Gen. Wade Hampton spoke the sentiments of his countrymen towards Sherman, as well as Kilpatrick,[9] when he refused to take the proffered hand of the latter, asking "how he dared offer his hand, red with the blood of his countrymen, and black with the ashes of their bones, to any southerner."

It is not my purpose to relate the public events of the first few weeks after Sherman's occupation of our town—they are too recent to need repetition in a paper intended simply to portray the sentiments and acts of private individuals, mostly of the female sex; so I will return and take up the thread of my narrative at the entrance of Kilpatrick, who, marching up the principal street, came very near losing his life by a shot from a drunken cavalry man, who, discharging his pistol, put spurs to his horse and attempted to escape, but was caught and hanged after trial by a drumhead court martial.

It was pouring down rain, and forlorn indeed was the appearance of the van-guard who took possession of what might have been a city of the dead from the welcome they received. We afterwards discovered that Sherman's army had regarded Raleigh as a strong Union place, where they would be gladly welcomed, and were bitterly disappointed when they marched in, at the closed doors and silence of the inhabitants. Guards were posted as rapidly as possible in all the houses, but in many instances they arrived too late to save the owners from the "bummers," who grumbled no little at being disappointed of their expected plunder.

Never can I forget our feelings at the first sight of the blue coats. We had no confidence in General Sherman, and could not for days bring ourselves to believe that we had escaped the horrors of Columbia. Gradually the painful conviction grew on us that all was lost. Johnston's surrender[10] followed Lee's, and we felt that for the rest of our lives we must either live under Yankee rule or abandon our homes. Gladly would we have given up all, houses, furniture, clothing and jewelry, for the privilege of still struggling on. But it could not be, we were under the iron heel, and submission was all that was left us; and right nobly and royally have the people of the South submitted to what they feel is inevitable. Holding firmly to the political creed of their forefathers in 1776 and 1787, that the right of all governments is based on the consent of the governed, they seceded from the Union they had agreed to with the northern States, and boldly took up arms in defense of what they then and now believe to be their rights. By noble deeds of valor on many a hard fought field, and as noble acts of self-denial in thousands of homes, they have given proof of the sincerity of their declarations, and the earnestness of their purpose. After four years of unavailing war, they agreed with their leaders and brothers in arms that the time had come to lay down the sword and return to their desolate homes. As men of honor should, they contended to the last for what they believed to be their rights; failing, they yielded, and being men of honor, will abide by their terms of surrender. More than this an honorable enemy should not desire. It is idle to attempt to force them to say and feel they were wrong. They were right. They feel it, and will not deny it; they walk erect with unblushing front, unconscious of any cause of shame, with a sorrow in their hearts which casts its shadow on their faces, but with truth on their lips when they take the oath of allegiance to the United States. They are loyal *subjects* of that government, which, by keeping their representatives out of Congress, prevents their becoming loyal *citizens.* The women are as submissive as the men; they believe that as ladies they have certain inalienable rights, such, for instance, as declining the visits and attentions of all gentlemen not agreeable to them, whether they wear blue coats or gray; but when this right is denied to them, they meekly submit for the time, and acknowledge that the force of circumstances obliges them to be polite outwardly, when in their hearts they are saying very naughty words.

"You have the matter in your own hands," said one to a United States officer in authority, who was complaining of the young ladies refusing to receive the friendly advances of himself and brother officers. "Issue an order that any lady who refuses to receive the attentions of a Federal officer, on receipt of a written order to that effect, shall be imprisoned for a week." [MBC to Col. Grainger][11]

"Would you obey such an order?"

"Certainly; send any officer or private in Sherman's army to me, with such an order from you, as commandant of the post, and let him ask me to ride out with him, and I will not only go, but also pin the order on my hat, that all my sister rebels may profit by my example, and be equally submissive."

"I rather think," replied he, shrugging his shoulders, "that he would enjoy that ride."

Even the school girls, while submitting outwardly, claim the right to make faces, as some of them proved to Gen. Sherman's satisfaction.

Gen. Howard[12] was camped in the grove of St. Mary's school, and knowing coffee to be a great luxury, politely sent a bucket full of it with his compliments to the young ladies of the school. They knew that the principal would not allow them to return it, but not one of them would taste it, though there was nothing they desired more except candy. Every morning, when the United States flag was raised, they rushed to the windows and drew the curtain, that they might not look upon it. Had no notice been taken of this demonstration they would soon have tired of it, but Gen. Howard gladdened their hearts by making them martyrs to their cause. He sent in word to the principal[13] that unless all such expressions of dislike to the United States flag were stopped he would close the school.

Col. Granger, of the Ninth Maine, pursued a more sensible course when he was commandant of the post. Some such "so-called" impertinence coming under his notice, he replied, when asked if he intended closing the school, "no indeed; let the little doves flutter, they can't hurt the eagle. If I desired to punish them I should rather order the school to be kept open during vacation; to close it would only be punishing the principal, and giving the young ladies a holiday."

By dint of lecturing and preaching, the principal finally brought his flock of doves under such good discipline that when Gen. Sherman called a few days afterwards he was charmed with the polite reception they gave him; so charmed, that after saying adieu, he must needs turn at the bottom step for a parting bow. Unfortunate movement! They were one and all making such mouths as only angry school girls can make, while some more daring ones were absolutely shaking their pretty little fists at him. He told the story himself. I wonder when he did so if he thought of Macaulay's lines on Sextus:

> "On the housetops was no woman
>     But spat at him and hiss'd,
> No child but screamed out curses,
>     And shook its little fist."

(*To be continued.*)

1. This was Mary Bayard Clarke's niece, the daughter of Frances Miller.

2. Lee surrendered on 9 April 1865. Jefferson Davis telegraphed General Johnston in Raleigh telling him of Lee's surrender on 10 April. *Official Records (Army),* series 1, vol. 47, pt. 3: 777.

3. This was probably Henry King Burgwyn Sr., a relative and old family friend of the Devereux family. He and his wife were in Raleigh at the time of Sherman's occupation. Just before the federal army entered Raleigh, Mrs. Burgwyn moved her family and some furniture to the home of John Devereux, Mary Bayard Clarke's brother.

4. During the morning of 12 April, Governor Vance met at the state capitol with former governors David L. Swain and William A. Graham to compose a letter

to Sherman surrendering the city and the state. Swain and Graham were appointed commissioners to take the letter to Sherman. They were accompanied by Dr. Edward Warren, the state's surgeon general; Colonel James G. Burr of the State Guard; and Major John Devereux of Vance's staff. The commissioners' train was first halted by Confederate troops and shortly thereafter by federal cavalry. The Union soldiers finally took the delegation to Sherman, who agreed not to assault the city. Meanwhile, Vance vacated Raleigh for Confederate lines to the west late that evening but left a letter for Sherman asking that the city's and state's government records be spared. Jerry C. Cashion, comp., *Sherman's March through North Carolina: A Chronology* (Raleigh: North Carolina Division of Archives and History, 1995), 66–69 (hereafter cited as Cashion, *Sherman's March*).

5. Scouts for Union General Oliver Otis Howard "dressed in Confederate uniforms" to spy on Confederate soldiers. Cashion, *Sherman's March*, 9.

6. Kate Edmondston noted in her diary that a friend of the family, Mrs. Isabella Huske Williams, who lived in or near Fayetteville, had fled her home after Sherman's troops arrived there. She then stayed with Frances Miller in Raleigh. Huske was robbed and "treated with great personal indignity, her wedding ring torn from her fingers, & the earrings from her ears, & a pistole placed at her head she was forced to show the wretches where she had concealed her silver. When she left her house they were preparing to fire it." 19 March 1865, *Edmondston Diary*, 679–80.

7. White southern women of all classes freely expressed their anger toward Union soldiers in words and actions. The Yankees were easy targets for these displays, however, because Union officers and enlisted men were unlikely to retaliate against white women, especially if they belonged to the middle or upper classes. Women recognized and took advantage of this immunity. Drew Gilpin Faust, *Mothers of Invention: Women of the Slaveholding South in the American Civil War* (Chapel Hill: University of North Carolina Press, 1996), 196–99, 201–2. One story handed down in different branches of the Clarke-Moulton families underscores how members of the former planter class taunted northern troops. After Lincoln's assassination, General Schofield proclaimed a day of mourning for 31 May 1865, by Special Order No. 76. Statues on the capitol grounds in Raleigh had been draped in black crepe as a sign of mourning. Supposedly, eleven-year-old Mary Devereux Clarke and a friend filled a basket with red roses and went to the capitol to place the flowers in the folds of black crepe. They initially ignored comments from a sentry, who said that he was glad to see rebels mourning for Lincoln. After all the flowers were placed, however, Mary D. Clarke reportedly exclaimed, "You old fool! Don't you know red and black are mourning for the devil?" The two girls ran, but the sentry caught them and brought them before the provost marshal. This official allegedly sentenced both girls to several weeks confinement in their yards. Grandchildren of Mary D. Clarke recall hearing this story from older family members.

8. In September 1864 Sherman said, "You cannot qualify war in harsher terms than I will. War is cruelty, and you cannot refine it." John G. Barrett, *Sherman's March through the Carolinas* (Chapel Hill: University of North Carolina Press, 1956), 16 (hereafter cited as Barrett, *Sherman's March through the Carolinas*).

9. Wade Hampton was a Confederate cavalry general who joined General Johnston in opposing Sherman's advance through the Carolinas. He thoroughly detested his main cavalry opponent during this campaign, Hugh Judson Kilpatrick. A good officer, Kilpatrick was viewed as a controversial and immoral man. Charles Van Doren, ed., *Webster's American Biographies* (Springfield, Mass.: G. & C. Merriam, 1974), 449 (hereafter cited as Van Doren, *American Biographies*); Barrett, *Sherman's March through the Carolinas*, 235; Boatner, *Civil War Dictionary*, 459–60.

10. Johnston surrendered to Sherman on 26 April 1865.

11. One of the federal officers in Raleigh whom Mary Bayard Clarke especially liked was George Frederick Granger, colonel of the Ninth Maine. Granger, who enjoyed his repartee with Clarke, carefully recorded the reactions of the southerners he encountered, and what he saw concerned him. He shared his thoughts in a letter to Thaddeus Stevens, a Radical Republican congressman from Pennsylvania, on 11 January 1866, deploring the actions and sentiments of white southerners and their unwillingness to help the freed slaves. He dismissed their complaints about blacks' dishonesty and unwillingness to work and observed "that the South is *not loyal,* No, not Even Conquered." Although an admirer of many things he saw in Raleigh, he added he would never live in the South as a northern man unless there was military protection. Padgett, "Reconstruction Letters from North Carolina, Part 1, Letters to Thaddeus Stevens," *NCHR* 18 (Apr. 1941): 171–95.

12. Brigadier General Oliver O. Howard was named commissioner of the Freedmen's Bureau on 12 May 1865. Boatner, *Civil War Dictionary*, 413–14.

13. Episcopal clergyman Aldert Smedes.

*Barden Collection*
*Lieutenant Colonel Brantz Mayer to Mary Bayard Clarke*

Baltimore 23d April 1866.

There is *one* thing, my dear Mrs Clarke, or, (if you will) My dear *Miss Tenella*,—(I cant think a muse *married*,—) there is, at least, *one* thing, I repeat,—that the government of the US. is doing for you that you cannot complain of, and it is the rapid regularity with which it is transporting the mails,—and the lucubrations of us males and females,—betwixt North Carolina and Maryland. The mail service, evidently is in capital condition; for, behold! here have I this Monday morning, at 9 O'clock, your charming letter of the 19th before me and read. It is a profoundly interesting and an exceedingly valuable letter,—for, if you do'nt care to send me, as I hoped you would, the photograph of your face, it conveys to me the photograph of your mind, and I confess it is one that pains and grieves me beyond expression. But, before I say a word in response to its sadder parts, let me Cordially thank you for your kindness and that of Governor Swaine in sending the Autographic note of the Pater Conscriptus. It supplies a gap in my collection which I feared would perhaps remain unfilled. . . . The letter from my old friend the Bishop,—(for, once upon a time, we were very Good friends, *episcopally,* in Nashville, during my early life,—) will come in good time whenever it may reach me.

    . . . .

    Your letter, I say again, has made me very Sad. There should be wisdom beneath the brows that are crowned with thorns. But, I fear the thorns will, rather exultingly and ambitiously, be self-driven into the brain, than allowed to be lifted either gently or surlyly from your heads. I would gladly return to the charge & endeavour to convince you (if I thought I would be of any use) that there is no "bitterness" among the northern people towards you;—that they do'nt "*hate*" you;—that their object is *not* to oppress, degrade and ruin you. There are no such sentiments among the people. Living in the midst of Unionists of all kinds, and observing the radical classes as well as the *moderates,* I have no hesitation in declaring that the main desire of all is to secure *peace* and *loyal government* for the future,—to restore *all* civil rights as soon as these are guarantied, —and in fact to restore the Union on the substantial basis of the Constitution. The misfortune is that the *unrepresentative* classes of both sides are the only ones that generally come in Contact, and their discussions are founded,—(—aye, and have been *since this time last year*—) upon a series of alleged wrongs like those detailed in your letter. A spirit of *generalization* has characterised all reports made *to* you and *from* you; & the consequence is that both sections think there is more ill feeling extisting [sic] than is really the case. What you complain of, is the natural result or sequence of war,—its logical "quod erat demonstrandum,"—and all you have to do is to adopt the dignified course you so much admire in General Lee, and make the South stop dwindling from a warrior into a Scold. I would gladly argue, reason with,—nay beseech you—if I thought that word of mine could avail for your welfare, but "Ephraim is joined unto his idols—let him alone"; & you *will* not & I *can* not mend the broken ring.

I should be sorry to see you accept the position of the old conquered provinces of the Roman Empire, (to which you so *historically* allude in your letter;) for, surely, my dear dame, you forget that the provinces Rome Conquered were "*barbarian*" provinces, in an age when Greece and Rome were the only Civilized nations. Would you have our "military colonies" in your midst? What would become of your beloved "States", for which you are so willing to surrender the glory of your *nation*? Why did you "*Confederate*", the moment you thought you were (as States) out of the old Union? Would'nt South or North Carolina be a glorious independent nation? You were wise, I think, to get under the Wings of a big chicken as soon as you got rid of the Eagle; &, although your rooster Crowed and clawed like a bird of mettle, I ca'nt help thinking you made a bad exchange But, not a word more of quarrelling—though you do it so beautifully. If I continue the discussion, I know you will tell me a dozen equally good stories of "Yankee rudeness" & "Yankee rapacity," and Freedman's Bureau misbehavior. What could I say to you in reply? Nothing but what I have already said. "I dare say they are true—they are very bad,—I am sorry for them,—I am not surprised at them,—I saw as bad things in Maryland and Pennsylvania during the war when you set our Maryland youngsters, who had gone into your army, to burning, plundering, stealing, rifling trunks, consuming railway cars with fire & their occupants with them;—I think the burning of my friends Bradfords house & the turning his family out into the fields horrible; nay I dont approve the stealing of—silver forks, and Mrs. _____ silver pitcher, at Chambersburg, a very reputable thing for Colonel _____ who hung it to his saddle bow. I dont, indeed, like all or any of these things recounted by you or me;—but dear madam all of these *are war,* &, for God's sake dont let us go on, like simpletons, making war over & over and over "for the 100 years" you predict, in conversation & on paper, in speeches and in politics." That we can reunite, live together, and be proud of *Our Nation,* I am quite sure, for there is not a prouder people in the world than the English, and *that* united people survived the follies of Charles, the raids of Cromwell, and the horrors of its Revolution.

If you do me the favor to write to me again, (which I sincerly wish you to do, and by [leave] to express the *hope* that you will,) I promise my future Correspondence will never touch on the sad topics that have hitherto annoyed you. I wrote only because I thought you *would believe* what I said when I told you what was the true *purpose* and the true *feeling* of the *people* of the North. I thought you were too much a woman of the world to confound the *people* with the politicians; and that you were, also, too good a Christian not to believe in Eternal Justice and its final success. Your letter, as you say, was *not* "Tenella". Pray, let your next be "Tenella"—*the* Tenella I knew in New Orleans and on the Mississippi, and *especially* in Baltimore. If you remove from Ralegh, pray also inform me of your address, if you care to hear from me again, and be so kind, when you see Governor Swain to thank him for his valued gift. I was glad you liked and recognized the likeness. It seems, therefore, that I dont *look* so old as I really am. But I am not altogether decrepit. I hope, too, you wont abandon your visit to Balto, & that you will give *us* a little of yr time when you Come hither.

Truly your friend

BM.

Do'nt omit your photograph next time!

Emily Mason of Virginia, a devout Catholic, had worked as a Confederate hospital matron during the war. In 1866 she began compiling a book of southern war poetry, which was published in 1867. A second edition, issued as *The Southern Poems of the War,* was published in 1868 by John Murphy & Co. of Baltimore, Maryland. Mason collected southern poems to celebrate the Confederacy and to raise money to educate the orphan daughters of Confederate soldiers. In the preface to the first edition of her book, she stated, "I have another design—*to aid by its sale the Education of the Daughters of our desolate land; to fit a certain number for Teachers,* . . . to provide for the women of the South (the future mothers of the country) the timely boon of education. Many of these children are the orphans of soldiers, from whom they have inherited nothing but an honorable name." In the preface to the second edition she recorded the assistance she had provided to needy southern girls: "I have provided for the maintenance and education of twenty-five Southern girls, and I trust that the sale of another edition will enable me to accomplish as much more." [October 1867]

Mary Bayard Clarke endorsed Mason's efforts, working to obtain clothing and the names of needy young women who would be eligible candidates. A review of Mason's second edition, which appeared on page 91 in the May 1867 issue of *The Land We Love,* stated that "she has six pupils from North Carolina, who are being educated out of the proceeds of this book." Clarke also allowed several of her poems to be published in the book under the names of "Tenella" and "Mrs. M. B. Clarke." Her poems in the second edition were "The Battle of Manassas" [80], "The Battle of Hampton Roads" [131], "The Rebel Sock" [275], "Lines on the Death of Annie Carter Lee" [302], "General Lee at the Battle of the Wilderness" [386], "The Chimes of St. Paul's" [396], and "General Robert E. Lee" [418].

Efforts such as these by southern women to help others of their class reflected the change in southern women's self-awareness during and after the war. Before the war, planter women confined themselves to their families and homes. During and after the war, many planter women, faced with poverty and diminished prospects for marriage, were forced to join with others of their social class to promote better education and job opportunities for women. Mary Bayard Clarke's involvement in this fledgling network of southern women marked a significant step in her development after the war.

*Barden Collection*
*Emily Mason to Mary Bayard Clarke*

Tappahannock
July 10 [1866]

My dear Mrs Clark

I return from Maryland to find yr kind letter & thank you very much for yr prompt & cordial response to my request. My friends Miss Manly & Miss Gaston with whom I was staying prompted me to write sure of the result but you are far more generous than I had any right to expect though in Common Cause & Common Sufferings have made us *Sisters*—The book will probably come to me by the next stage from Richmond as I have written for it—and have also written to some of the "Editors" to make honorable mention of it & of the good object for which it is sold. Mrs Graham (Miss Gaston's sister) is a rich woman & a most patriotic one—devoted to her "old North State" & will I am sure aid you in getting subscribers in her neighborhood—I have two poems upon Genl Polk—Mr Flash's fine lines[1] & some "In Memoriam" beginning "Peace troubled soul["][2]—& since I wrote you a full & good copy of yr Battle of Manasses is sent me—I am sure you will find I have a fuller collection of poems than has yet been made & I shall have great pleasure in sending you my vol—& hope you will help to circulate it —I shall make it very cheap that it may reach all our poor people—the Soldiers especially—to whom it is dedicated that it may help to keep alive in them the memory of our "rights" & our "wrongs"—of our glorious past—

My nephew Maj. Rowland[3] who is with us now was in the Same Brigade with Col. Clark—& speaks of him as all do who know him—in most admiring strains He says he has also the pleasure to know you—He was on Genl Robt Ransom's staff—

And now to tell you of a great & *Mournful pleasure* I have just had—I have seen *our President!*[4] Spent the *4th July* with him in Fort Monroe! pressed to my lips his poor emaciated hands & wet them with my tears—Saw the iron *cage* which confines him & heard & saw some of the indignities practiced upon him which he bears as only *one other* has ever done—He whom he resembles in that he bears the sins of *us all* in his own person & bears without a murmur to be "scorned derided—insulted" He is of course very feeble—his voice very weak—but he is cheerful—wonderful in conversation—so full of thought & wisdom that every sentence is like an aphorism & we felt like Dr. Craven[5] ready to run out & *set it down* that all might hear & read—By the way *that book* is full of inaccuracies as you may perceive—It is written by Col. Halpin ("Miles O'Reilly")[6] who was on Hunter's staff & hence he makes Mr Davis praise that vile & bloody man—of whom Mr Davis really says "Hunter is simply *a brute*"—I once thought him a consciencious man though radical—but he is entirely changed—

Dr Craven furnished *facts* no doubt, but the writer messed them up to suit his own views & the taste of his readers They say the book is finely written & must do good in the North—as it creates great sympathy for "our Chief" Mr Davis is allowed now to receive every thing Sent him. Every thing Sent to *her*[7] reaches him—Send yr *book* it will please & touch him—At nine A.M. he is permitted to go to the casemate where his wife & child are—& spend the day but at six a bugle sounds the guards appear & with a look of mingled patience & agony he is consigned to solitude bolts & bars—Three Sides his little room in "Carroll's Hall" are of iron bars where walk three sentinels—gazing upon him *in bed*—reading—writing—*washing*—dressing—A bright light from two great lamps shines in his eyes, which with the changing of the guard—the "Challenging" passersby & the noise of the soldiers who inhabit the house effecually banishes the *drowsy God* & must eventually wear him out. There is an order prohibiting the soldiers from touching their Caps to him & an officer must sit in his presence without removing his hat!—This gives you some idea of the petty malice of Genl (!) Miles[8]—the Commandant who is a young vulgar looking *fellow* of 26—a *volunteer* Genl & was a *Carpenter* in *Mass*—!—Since the 5th Art. have been Sent there Mrs D. says their Condition is much ameliorated—The young officers are kind & polite in spite of Genl Miles & the ladies have all called her Some of them are very Southern in Sentiment—Dr Cooper's[9] wife is a Virginian & he is most kind to Mr Davis—It was through him we were admitted—

Think of those odious soldiers having until now spoken of Mr Davis as "Jeff"—Taking him his meals & *poking* them through the grate with "Jeff here's yr dinner"—

I must tell you an incident which will (I hope) fire yr *poetic soul* for my benefit—The president told it in these touching words—"Walking one day on the ramparts I spied a poor half starved cur lying in the grass. I thought here are two poor friendless dogs—we should join Company— motioning to him he came feebly licked my hand—followed me home & from that day has never left me will suffer no other hand—not even the baby's to caress him["] I forgot to tell you the contents of that chamber in Carroll Hall which the papers said was "fitted up comfortably" for the "illustrious prisoner"—a very narrow Iron bedstead & *very* thin mattress —a wooden stool on which rests basin & pitcher—a wooden table & wooden chair! Comfort?

Again thanking you for yr kindness—& praying yr son to be prompt in his copying I am most truly yr obligd

Emily V. Mason

I send to yr son a bit of grass gathered by Mr Davis *own hand*—4th July 1866—on the Ramparts Fortress Monroe—with many thanks for the trouble he takes for me[10] Please send me some lines to Genl Lee I have not one poem to him

And please ask yr niece for the poem I spoke of which I hear is *so good* I will not publish *her name*. I send to her a bit of the grass to *tempt* her— to *bribe* her—[11]

1. This was Henry Lynden Flash, whose poem "Polk" appeared on page 371 of Mason's book.

2. This poem, written by Fannie M. Downing in 1864, was titled "In Memoriam of Our Right reverend Father in God, Leonidas Polk, Lieut-Gen., C.S.A." It appeared in Mason's book, pages 375–76.

3. Thomas Rowland served as an assistant adjutant general in Brigadier General Robert Ransom's brigade. Manarin and Jordan, *Roster of NC Troops,* 1:173.

4. Jefferson Davis.

5. Dr. John Joseph Craven wrote *Prison Life of Jefferson Davis. Embracing Details and Incidents in His Captivity, Particulars Concerning His Health and Habits, together with Many Conversations on Topics of Great Public Interest* (New York: Carleton, 1866). He served as physician to Davis during his captivity in Fortress Monroe from 25 May to 25 December 1865.

6. Charles Graham Halpine was a Union officer and author born in Ireland. He wrote under the name "Pvt. Miles O'Reilly." His poem "Sambo's Right to Be Kilt" appeared in the New York *Herald* in 1862, after General David Hunter

organized the first troop of black soldiers to be mustered into federal service at Hilton Head, South Carolina. Halpine served on Hunter's staff. Boatner, *Civil War Dictionary*, 367–68; William Hanchett, *Irish, Charles G. Halpine in Civil War America* (New York: Syracuse University Press, 1970).

7. Varina Howell Davis.

8. General Nelson A. Miles commanded Fortress Monroe when Davis was imprisoned there after the war. Hamilton, *Reconstruction in North Carolina*, 225; Carol K. Bleser, "The Marriage of Varina Howell and Jefferson Davis: 'I gave the best and all my life to a girdled tree,'" *Journal of Southern History* 65 (Feb. 1999): 22–23.

9. This was possibly George E. Cooper of Pennsylvania, who served as a Union surgeon during the war. Heitman, *Historical Register*, 326.

10. The grass still exists in the Barden Collection.

11. It is possible that this is the poem "The Fall of Fort Sumter, April, 1861," written by "A. L .D." of Raleigh, North Carolina. One of Clarke's nieces was Annie Lane Devereux, a daughter of John Devereux. The poem appeared on pages 38 and 39 of Mason's book.

THIS ARTICLE APPEARED IN the *Old Guard* 4, no. 8, Aug. 1866, 479–83. Although Clarke had it published under her pseudonym of Stuart Leigh, she inked in her initials in her scrapbook copy and added, "Written at the request of Governor Vance." Clarke also signed her full name at the end in blue ink.

*MBC Scrapbook 2, Barden Collection*

## "THE SOUTH EXPECTS EVERY WOMAN TO DO HER DUTY."
### [BY A LADY OF NORTH CAROLINA.]

There is no evading or denying the fact that the women of the Southern Confederacy were the unrecognized "power behind the throne," during its whole existence. Mr. [Secretary of State William Henry] Seward, General [Benjamin] Butler, and General [William T.] Sherman, all, by their bitter persecution of them, tacitly acknowledged them to be a latent force which must be overcome before the South could be conquered. These leaders knew well that although the southern women did not in person wield the sword, or enter the legislative halls, their steady, unchanging influence did more to fill the ranks of the Confederate army than all the edicts of its Congress, or acts of its Conscript Bureau. Hence the endorsement by the Executive of General Butler's notorious order in New Orleans, and General Sherman's policy in his march from Atlanta to

Raleigh. On this account were young girls taken from their homes, by order of United States army officers, and set down penniless, destitute, and without protection, miles from any habitation, and forbidden, on pain of imprisonment, to return to their fathers' houses. For this reason were southern homes desolated, and helpless women and children turned out without food, shelter, or any clothing but that which they had on at the time, by the "bummers," who acted under General Sherman; and for this reason did that General adopt as his motto, "War is essentially cruel," and act on it.

Nobly and bravely did the daughters of the South meet this persecution. Up to the day of General Johnston's surrender their voices were raised for war—war until the rights of the South were acknowledged, and her freedom secured. Their tongues, sharper than two-edged swords, were mercilessly turned against all deserters, shirks, and "bomb-proof officers;" while no sarcasm was too cutting, no scorn too withering for the man who was suspected of being "a Unionist."

They equalled the women of Poland and Hungary in their enthusiasm and devotion, and excelled them in persistent opposition to, and hatred of those whom they regarded as the oppressors of their country. Many a poor fellow, whom the final surrender caught in a northern prison or a Confederate hospital, hesitated to take the oath of allegiance which would have at once procured his release, although he knew there was no longer a Confederacy to be true to, because he did not know "what the women at home would say to it."

History shows that in all stubornly contested civil wars, women have been more bitter and uncompromising than men. And why? Simply because they are women, and seldom let the head dictate to the heart. Where one woman acts from policy, one thousand act from impulse.

The southern women have proved themselves worthy to be the wives and mothers of the brave men who fell upon our battle-fields, or, crushed and broken hearted, still drag on a miserable existence with a sorrow at their hearts which no individual prosperity can heal.

What higher praise can we accord them than this?

We think they will themselves unanimously reply, "None."

Why then, oh, sisters, who have so nobly won a glorious reputation, will ye not be constant to it, and still share the burden of your statesmen and warriors? We are crushed, conquered and ground down in the dust, and your fathers, brothers and husbands, bitter as it is to their proud spirits, must bow their heads to the yoke, and, for your sakes, dear ladies, submit unresistingly to many an insult which their blood boils to resent.

We hear on every side, from the northerner and the southerner, that the conduct of the southern women towards the United States army officers stationed amongst us is tightening the chains and increasing the weight already pressing so heavily upon our unhappy country.

Your own trusted and beloved leaders will tell you that it was no idle threat which that whiskered young army officer uttered the other day when you refused to pass through a gate which he held open for you, and drew aside your skirts to avoid the contamination of his touch, till he ground his teeth, and said under his breath, "some one shall suffer for this." Yes, not only some one, but many a one, will suffer because you wounded that man's vanity. And what good did your rudeness do you, your friends, or your country? None. But sooner or later it will do all three much harm. "But," you exclaim, indignant at the shadow of blame being cast upon you for any expression of hatred or contempt exhibited to a "Yankee officer." "how do I know he is not the very Captain who set up the likeness of my dead mother as a target for his men to shoot at, and himself rummaged my aunt's drawers and stole her jewelry and lace, while some of his men were stirring the contents of her pantry into a 'Douglas larder' on her parlor carpet, and tearing my cousin's clothes to pieces before her eyes. For aught I know he is the very man who had my grandfather's vault broken open in Newbern, and my uncle's coffin taken out and used to send the remains of his Colonel back to New England, while he had not even the decency to bury the bones he sacrilegiously displaced?"[1]

My dear young lady, it is not only possible, but probable, that he has done all this, if not to your relatives, to some other southern family. But what then? Why warm into life with the fire of your indignation the snake that is "scotched" by the cessation of hostilities? Never unnecessarily irritate a venemous reptile when you are not strong enough to crush it; give it as wide a berth as you can without exciting its rage, and pass as though you did not see it. But, my dear Miss Amelia Jane, while we are supposing, let us suppose also that he is the identical officer who, when General Sherman took up his quarters for the night in the house of your other aunt, who lives in South Carolina, and took from her every pound of meat, and every quart of meal she had, leaving her without food for herself and children, or a teaspoon to administer medicine to her almost dying child; let us suppose, I say, that this very Captain whom you insulted yesterday, is the officer who put a guard at the door where your cousin lay sick, and assured your almost distracted aunt that although he could not protect her from General Sherman, he could and would from his men; and shortly afterwards smuggled in two pieces of bacon and a bag of flour which he had been obliged to steal from the pillagers, and cautioned her to secrete under her bed, while he drew from his pocket half a dozen spoons and told her to keep them hid on her person until the whole army had passed. Should this prove to be the case, would you not regret that you had unnecessarily mortified him? Certainly you would, or your heart is unworthy of your beautiful face.

"But," you exclaim, "because all of Sherman's officers are not brutes, would you have me welcome them as friends?"

By no manner of means, my indignant and unreasoning beauty; but because some of these officers are brutes, is that any reason why you should forget you are a lady?

"General! do you touch your hat to a negro?" asked one of his officers of the great rebel General George Washington, on seeing him return the salute of a servant. "Would you have me allow him to excel me in politeness?" was the mild but pointed reply.

We ask you the same question, gentle and high-bred southern lady; will you allow a "Yankee officer" to excel you in courtesy? Certainly you will not.

"And so, I suppose you expect me to receive graciously and as though they gave me pleasure, the attentions of every butcher, baker and candle stick maker who wears a blue coat with shoulder straps upon it? I must walk with him, dance with him, entertain him when he choses to call upon me, and perchance, as some renegades have already done, marry him when he condescends to do me the honor of offering his hand? I'll do no such thing; the sight of that uniform causes me to shudder, for it reminds me that we are conquered. Every ring I see on the finger of a United States army officer, every pin I see in his scarf, every article of jewelry he displays, I imagine torn from some southern woman by violence, or stolen from her wardrobe. When he takes out his watch, I wonder what South Carolina gentleman it belonged to? There goes a Brigadier General in a barouche with two blood horses which he boasts of having 'picked up in Georgia.' No, I will have nothing to do with them; I shake off the dust from my feet when I happen to step in the foot-print of one of them, and gather up my skirts to show my horror and disgust at their unmanly conduct. I care not that this or that officer is a high-minded, honorable gentleman; he represents not a single individual, but a class who have disgraced humanity, and he must suffer for being in bad company. While our State is under a military despotism, our ex-President a prisoner, and every newspaper filled with accounts of the trials of Confederate officers for simply obeying the customary laws of civilized warfare, I will make the officers of the United States army who are stationed here feel that no true-hearted southern woman will associate with them."

Calm your just and natural indignation, my ruffled fair one, and listen to the words of reason as spoken by your own ex Governors, Senators, Generals, and the men of the country generally. Make the United States' officer as uncomfortable as you please, but do it so as not to disgrace yourself and your country; do it in a genteel, lady-like way, and you will cut him far more severely than you possibly could with rudeness, and yet not leave him one single good cause of complaint against you. I am not pleading for him but for you, pleading with you for yourself.

Give the next one who holds open a gate for you to pass through a "thank you," as you would any other stranger. If your ex-footman or your ex-maid were to offer you their politeness, would you not thus acknowledge it? Certainly you would, for you are a lady. Well, do not the radicals of the North say that the late war was waged to put them and the negro on the same footing, socially and politically? Now, although you may reasonably think there was a way to accomplish this, without the shedding of so much blood, by simply letting them go their way while we went ours, still, though they would not agree to this, and have got the best of us in the fight which we entered into to gain our point, is that any reason why you should desert your principle? Certainly not; stick to it; go your way individually, if you cannot politically, and let them go theirs undisturbed by the flirt of your Balmoral skirt.

The United States army officer has, by force of arms, won the right to stand on the same platform as that now occupied by your late servant. In God's name let him enjoy the fruits of his victory. You cannot avoid coming in contact with him sometimes, and if you really wish to punish him, not as an individual, but as a member of a class, take the advice of an old beau and a true southerner, and be so sweetly amiable, so interestingly agreeable, or so sparklingly attractive, so bewitchingly fascinating, and yet so crushingly and overpoweringly polite and indifferent, as to make him long for the delights of your society, and regret that "some how he can never get one inch beyond the formal politeness and stiffness of a first introduction with those charming southern ladies, with whom it would be so pleasant occasionally to spend a social evening." Don't draw down the corners of your mouth and turn up your nose until you look almost ugly, and then knock the fellow flat with a rude act or speech, because if you do he'll get up "blazing angry," and as he can't now imprison you in revenge, he'll hurt some of your friends. If he is in the Negro Bureau,[2] he will decide the next case that a negro brings before him against the white man, without caring whether the negro tells the truth or not, indeed he will be rather glad of an opportunity of showing that his *ipse dixit* can make you, through your countrymen, uncomfortable. Or worse still, if he is on a military court, he will say as that Judge Advocate did the other day, "While the southern women are so confoundedly impertinent, I'll do what I can to hang the men." Or, at the very least, he'll feel and say you are "no lady, and he don't care to know you." But just give him a glimpse of Paradise, and keep him, as Congress is doing our Representatives, "out in the cold," and you will not only punish him but preserve your own self-respect.

Should he politely offer your uncle an apple in the cars, and say, "won't the young lady take one?" don't turn your back on him as if you did not hear him, when he can't help knowing that you did, and oblige your respected relative to stammer out an impromptu fib, and say, "she's rather hard of hearing," and force him to stoop over, and in a loud voice ask, "my dear, will you have an apple?" because that hurts your dear uncle's feelings far more than it does the officer's. Just say politely in the first instance, "No, I thank you, sir," and then look placidly out of the window, as though there was not an army officer within a mile of you. If you pursue this course, he will feel that you have given him to understand, in a lady-like way, that you desire neither his apple nor his conversation.

Don't say now, my silenced opponent, "The men must come in contact with them, but we women need not."

You did not shrink from bearing your share of the privations of the war; you cheerfully gave up not only luxuries but comforts, and taught your fair, and heretofore, rather idle fingers to work for the soldiers; you knit socks for them; you made shirts for them, and sent out from your sewing-bees some of the most remarkable pantaloons that were ever manufactured by mortal hands; you tore up your nice soft linen and sent it to the hospitals, wearing negro shirting in its place you went, yourself, into the hospital and attended to the sick and wounded. You gave yourself heart and soul to the Southern Confederacy, gloried in its success and mourned over its defeat as only a true woman could glory and mourn; and will you now shirk its humiliations? Will you leave your lovers, your fathers, brothers and husbands to bear their burden alone? Or worse, will you, against their reiterated entreaties, increase that burden? They do not ask you to compromise either your dignity or their pride; they would be deeply mortified did you welcome and entertain a Federal, as you do a Confederate soldier. All they ask is that you will not, by a childish and useless exhibition of a natural and commendable feeling, sink your country still deeper in misery and render it ten times harder for them to struggle under the heavy load which God in His wisdom has seen fit to lay upon them.

Oh, my noble and patriotic country-women! look up to, and follow the example of our great and glorious General, Robert E. Lee, greater, if possible, in his day of humiliation than in his hour of triumph. He stands pre-eminent before the world, first among its Christian gentlemen; has he stooped his grandly proud head one hair's breadth since he surrendered to Gen. Grant? No! Nor has he sullied his fair fame with one discourteous act or word towards his opponents.[3] Let him be your guide in defeat as he was your star in the hour of triumph; and like him, so act and speak as to wring from your conquerors, whether they will or not, that respect which generous spirits spontaneously yield to dignified misfortune.

STUART LEIGH.

[Mary Bayard Clarke]

1. There apparently was some truth to this story. On 26 January 1870, the Raleigh *Sentinel* published an article that quoted a letter written during the war by Edward R. Stanly to Senator Charles Sumner. Stanly, appointed by Lincoln as military governor of North Carolina, observed Yankee excesses in occupied New Bern and stated that "They literally robbed the cradle and the grave. Family burying vaults were broken open for robbery; and in one instance (the fact was published in a Boston paper and admitted to me by an officer of high position in the army), a vault was entered, a metallic coffin removed, and the remains cast out that those of a dead soldier might be put in the place." Hamilton, *Reconstruction in North Carolina,* 94n–95n.

2. Freedmen's Bureau.

3. Robert E. Lee advised Confederate soldiers returning home to forgo bitterness and to be loyal citizens to the United States. Charles Bracelen Flood, *Lee: The Last Years* (Boston: Houghton Mifflin, 1981), 29 (hereafter cited as Flood, *Lee: The Last Years*).

*William J. Clarke Papers, SHC*
*Mary Bayard Clarke to Frank Clarke (Baltimore)*

Atlantic House[1]<br>Beaufort Sep 2d [1866]

My Dear Son

I did not get your letter time enough to write to you in Raleigh before the third, but sent you a message in Auntie's[2] in case you had not left. I am glad you enjoyed yourself there and feel sure you did not give any body particular satisfaction by getting into a scrape or I should have heard of it; it will be very different in Baltimore[3] there you will be looked on as a man and not regarded as a boy so I hope the knowledge that you are perfectly free and accountable only to your self will make you feel your own importance and act accordingly Remember it is the principal of your father's property you are now spending and lay it out so as it will be an investment for life time, work hard and play hard but dont the play interfere with the work get all the good you possibly can out of your money and your stay in town and make no acquaintances you will be likely to feel ashamed of here after; it is very important for a young man to have acquaintances of standing and respectability in a place and you may conclude here after to live in Baltimore so I hope you will be careful as to the acquaintances you form there. I would like to have you find out Dr Warren and call on Mrs Warren[4] she is a nice lady and may introduce you to some nice girls, of all things be particular in your female associates while you are polite to all do not be intimate in any but the best families *socially* You will find after all that ladies and gentlemen will be most agreeable to you in the long run. I enclose you a letter of introduction to Col Brantz Mayer he is an old friend of mine and an old resident of Baltimore. I have not the No of his house but you can easily find it out I send one also to Mr Sheppard Bryan[5] an old schollar of your father's deliver them both in person and if they are out leave your card with your name and address Francis D Clarke 530 West Lexington St if they invite you to their houses go *once* for politeness and after that consult your own taste I dont think I can pay your hand writing a higher compliment than by telling you I at first thought your letter was from father and said "What is William doing in Raleigh" Willie is well but seems to have a dull time except when fishing there no boys at all here and only two girls. I have been sick ever since I came down and have a slow fever that weakens me very much you did not tell me whether you had gotten over your chills or not, if not take some medicine or rather consult Dr Warren at once. Give my love to Aunt Bettie cousin Rachel and Frank [Jones] write to me as soon as you enter the college and tell me what you are doing write every Sunday to some one of the family direct to me at the Atlantic House till you hear otherwise and let me know if you want any thing.

Your affectionate<br>Mother

1. The Atlantic House, a popular seaside resort, was washed away in a storm in the 1870s.

2. Elizabeth Devereux Jones lived in Baltimore with her children and operated a boardinghouse. Her daughter Rachel also taught to help the family's income. Frank Clarke stayed at her home while attending a business college in the city.

3. Mary Bayard Clarke closely monitored the career plans of her two sons after the war. Recognizing the depressed economic conditions in North Carolina, she did not want either of them working at jobs that would not lead to better opportunities. For a time, both Frank and Willie worked in a small country store, which neither enjoyed. By 1866 Frank was attending a business college to prepare for a job in a mercantile firm in one of the larger cities. His mother, while supporting his plans, worried about the people he would meet. She urged him in this letter and in one dated 17 October 1866, to "make your *friends* in the same rank of life as your self; *acquaintances* you must have in all ranks—but I want you always to feel at liberty to bring your friends home with you." Clarke Papers, SHC.

4. Dr. Edward and Elizabeth Cotton Warren.

5. William Shepard Bryan graduated from the University of North Carolina in 1846 and received a master's degree from that institution in 1850. He moved to Baltimore in the latter year and became a distinguished lawyer in that city. Powell, *DNCB*, 1:264.

CORNELIA PHILLIPS SPENCER OF Chapel Hill, North Carolina, was active after the war in memorializing the Confederacy and in opposing Republicans and Radical Reconstruction. The daughter of a professor at the University of North Carolina, she wrote *The Last Ninety Days of the War in North Carolina,* which was published in 1866. In it she recounted the fall of the Confederacy in North Carolina and Sherman's depredations in the state.

Spencer, too, took an interest in helping the orphaned children of North Carolina's Confederate soldiers. She and Clarke exchanged occasional letters concerning their work to help these children.

*Cornelia Phillips Spencer Papers, North Carolina State Archives, Raleigh, N.C.*
*Mary Bayard Clarke to Cornelia Phillips Spencer*

Keoco Mills Oct 1st [1866]

My Dear Mrs Spencer

I wrote you from Morehead City in reply to a letter from you in which you said that Miss Sally Mallett would like her eldest neice to go to Miss Mason's care this fall, I presume as I have received no answer to this letter that she has either changed her mind or you have made all necessary arrangement with Miss Mason's agent, and though I have intended writing bad health and other causes have prevented my doing so. Just before I left Morehead City Mrs Henry Bryan[1] (whose Mother was a Miss Biddel) begged me to write and enquire of you the ages of the children and their names, she says her cousin Mr Sam Biddel, I think, was Col Mallett's most intimate friend, and she believes would be glad to educate one of them himself. I could not tell whether there was a boy among them or not, and she is anxious to know as if there is she declares Mr Biddel shall educate him; She is an energetic and determined little woman and I dont think these poor orphans could have a better or truer friend than she would be to them. I have been prevented writing since I got home by a hemorrage from my lungs which has left me weak, and being forbidden to speak—more than is absolutely necessary—I am, like the frenchman's parrot, that was'nt a parrot you know but an owl, and though he did not speak kept up a terrible thinking; and now that I am back in my old seat ready for my fall work but unable to do it as yet, I will let out a few of my thoughts on paper and perhaps—accomplish something. I will be very much obliged if you will give me the information Mrs Bryan desires as soon as you can. I shall not leave home again probably—for some time so please address as before to Boon Hill and believe me very sincerely

Your friend

Mary Bayard Clarke

PS—I have made enquiries respecting Miss Buie but can find no one who knows anything of her beyond what she published herself in the Sentinal

1. Henry Ravenscroft and Mary Biddle Norcott Bryan, who were married in New Bern on 24 November 1859. Powell, *DNCB*, 1:254.

*Barden Collection*
*Mary Bayard Clarke to Frank Clarke (Baltimore)*

Raleigh Oct 22d [1866]

My Dear Son

I received your letter enclosing the sample of paper last night, I like it very much but cant get it at present, there is some hitch about lumber and money cant be got, I am very sorry about your clothes, I thought your drawers would last till cold weather and dont like the idea of your not having a new coat but I have not a cent of money just now and must wait till I can get some from the Old Guard. you shall have the first that comes in,

I have been worried to death getting a cook and housekeeper but can hear of neither. I am almost in dispair negroes are plenty but as soon as one hears it is in the country they cant go on any terms I sometimes think of writing to aunt Bettie to see if she can get me a house keeper but then I think she would not be satisfied to live at Keoco and the cost of getting her would be too great.

I am real provoked with you and am going to read you a lecture you have been writing some nonsense to one of the boys in town, I cant find out who, about going to the green room and getting acquainted with the actresses and divers other things that boys when they first get to themselves are apt to do and be afterwards ashamed of—Now you know how Raleigh is and how little it takes to raise a story and they have it all over town that you are "weeding a wide row—," very dispated and instead of attending to your business and going to the College at night are running after actresses and all such ungentlemanly amusements; and my lecture is dont *write* such things as can be perverted to Raleigh boys for they will tell of them and then they are exagerated and made much of—Auntie[1] is already sighing and shaking her head and old Dr Mason has been hoping you will not be led into bad company and dissipated habits and lectures *me* on allowing *you* to go to the theatre, Now you know that I want you to enjoy yourself and see no harm in your going either to the theatre, or once in a way to gratify your curiosity behind the scenes but I dont want you to have the reputation of being fast any more than to be really so and I think if you would write fewer letters to Raleigh boys and be more careful what you say in them it would be better for you. I was surprised when I heard you had written to Ransom as no good can come of such associations you are the son of a gentleman and should choose your correspondants and friends from the sons of gentlemen, and remember you can enjoy life and not tell of all you do—be careful of your reputation and if you do go to see actresses behind the scenes—and tell of it—make it appear that it was only an accidental thing and not what you were in the habit of doing.

Mary sends love and says she did answer your letter but will write again soon. Give my love to all and direct your next letter to me at home for I shall leave here day after to morrow—

Your affectionate<br>Mother

1. Frances Devereux Miller.

ॐ

Wedding portrait of William J. and Mary Bayard Clarke, 1848. William Clarke is pictured wearing his Mexican War uniform. Daguerreotype by Charles Doratt of Raleigh. Barden Collection.

Thomas Pollock Devereux, ca. 1860s, from a photograph taken by John W. Watson of Raleigh. Courtesy of Laura Hobson, Memphis, Tennessee.

Miniature of Catherine Johnson Devereux, Mary Bayard Clarke's mother. Courtesy of Robert Cannon Hobson, Nashville, Tennessee.

Mary Bayard Clarke's grandfather, John Devereux Sr. An Irishman and Charleston merchant, he married Frances Pollock of New Bern, North Carolina, in 1790. Portrait in the possession of Mary Gibson Speer, Missouri City, Texas.

Portrait of Henry Watkins Miller of Raleigh, a prominent lawyer and state legislator who married Frances Devereux. Portrait in the possession of Mary Gibson Speer, Missouri City, Texas.

Portrait of Frances Devereux Miller, Mary Bayard Clarke's eldest sister. Portrait in the possession of Mary Gibson Speer, Missouri City, Texas.

Carte de visite of Frances Miller, ca. 1870s. Photograph by Edward
Gerock, North Carolina. Barden Collection.

John Devereux Jr., Mary Bayard Clarke's sole brother, shown in his Confederate uniform. Photograph courtesy of the North Carolina Division of Archives and History, Raleigh, North Carolina.

Margaret Devereux, the wife of John Devereux Jr. and a member of the prominent Mordecai family of Raleigh. Carte de visite. Barden Collection.

Catherine Devereux Edmondston, one of Mary Bayard Clarke's sisters and a writer. Her Civil War journals were published in 1979 by the North Carolina Division of Archives and History as *"Journal of a Secesh Lady": The Diary of Catherine Ann Devereux Edmondston, 1860–1866.* Photograph courtesy of the North Carolina Division of Archives and History, Raleigh, North Carolina.

Honoria or Nora
Devereux Cannon,
Mary Bayard Clarke's
closest sister. Barden
Collection.

Robert Hines Cannon, a
physician and the husband
of Nora Cannon, from a
daguerreotype. Courtesy
of Laura Hobson, Memphis,
Tennessee.

Three of Nora Cannon's daughters, who often visited the Clarke family in New Bern. Left to right: Honoria or Nonie, Katie, and Sadie Cannon. Courtesy of Laura Hobson, Memphis, Tennessee.

Sophia Devereux Turner, a younger sister of Mary Bayard Clarke. She later was committed to and died in the Raleigh insane asylum because of an addiction to morphine. Photograph courtesy of the North Carolina Division of Archives and History, Raleigh, North Carolina.

Josiah Turner, the husband of Sophia D. Turner and a political foe of William J. Clarke. Photograph courtesy of the North Carolina Division of Archives and History, Raleigh, North Carolina.

Susan Devereux, the half-sister of Mary Bayard Clarke, was born to Thomas P. Devereux and his second wife, Ann Mary Maitland Devereux. Carte de visite in the possession of Mary Gibson Speer, Missouri City, Texas.

Frank Devereux Clarke was the eldest son of William J. and Mary Bayard Clarke. Carte de visite taken by photographer James C. Sleight of New York in the 1870s. Barden Collection.

William or Willie Clarke, the second child of Mary Bayard and William J. Clarke. This tintype was taken by E. A. Weed, a photographer in New York, while Willie attended Columbia Law School in the 1870s. Barden Collection.

Mary Devereux Clarke, the only daughter of Mary Bayard and William J. Clarke. This carte de visite was taken by Rufus Morgan in New Bern in the 1870s. Morgan later married Mary D. Clarke. Barden Collection.

Thomas Pollock Devereux Clarke, the youngest child of Mary
Bayard and William J. Clarke. Photograph ca. 1860s. Barden
Collection.

Lithograph that William J. Clarke brought back from Cuba in 1855 showing the execution of Ramon Pintó. The original inscription states, "Ejecucion de D. Ramon Pintó en la Habana, á las siete de la manana del dia 22 de Marzo 1855." Barden Collection.

Rare Civil War camp scene found with the papers of William J. and Mary Bayard Clarke, possibly depicting a company in Clarke's Fourteenth Regiment, North Carolina Volunteers. It shows enlisted men sitting in front of a common tent. Based on the uniforms, caps, and leaves on trees, this image probably was taken in the summer of 1861. Barden Collection.

"Before and after" cartes de visite of William J. Clarke. The first was taken early in the Civil War. The second, taken in Philadelphia, shows Clarke after his release from Fort Delaware prison in 1865. Both, Barden Collection.

Front of the Louisiana House, the Clarkes' home in New Bern. William J. and Mary Bayard Clarke are at the porch railing. The other individuals are not identified. However, the young woman at the foot of the steps probably is Mary D. Clarke. Between 1873 and at least 1875, the Clarkes employed a black woman named Martha as their cook and housekeeper. Other servants who appeared in letters were Betty and Debbie. The photograph was taken by Rufus Morgan in the 1870s. Courtesy of the North Carolina Collection, University of North Carolina at Chapel Hill.

Tintype of Mary
Bayard Clarke, ca.
1860s, probably taken
after the Civil War.
Barden Collection.

Rufus Morgan,
the husband of
Mary D. Clarke.
A photographer by
profession, he died
in California after
eating poisonous
mushrooms.
Barden Collection.

Mary Clarke Morgan, tintype, ca. 1870s, taken after her marriage to
Rufus Morgan. Barden Collection.

Frank D. Clarke, taken during his tenure as superintendent of the Michigan School for the Deaf, ca. 1883. Cabinet photograph by C. S. Seabolt, Flint, Michigan. Barden Collection.

Thomas D. Clarke. This photograph was taken in Flint, Michigan, ca. 1880s, when he visited his brother, Frank D. Clarke. Cabinet photograph by C. S. Seabolt, Flint, Michigan. Barden Collection.

Wedding photograph of Willie Clarke and his bride, Bessie Howerton
Clarke. Cabinet photograph by Gerock, 1886. Barden Collection.

Mary Bayard Morgan, Mary Bayard Clarke's granddaughter and the daughter of Mary and Rufus Morgan. After her marriage, she became a professional photographer in North Carolina using the name Bayard Wootten. Barden Collection.

Mary Bayard Clarke. This Chicago photograph probably was taken during her stay there in 1877. Barden Collection.

William J. Clarke, ca. 1870s. The cabinet photograph was taken by
Rufus Morgan, Goldsboro, North Carolina. Barden Collection.

George Moulton, the New
Hampshire immigrant who
married the widowed Mary
Clarke Morgan at Mary Bayard
Clarke's deathbed in 1886.
Barden Collection.

Mary Morgan Moul-
ton, taken about the
time of her marriage
to George Moulton.
Cabinet photograph
by Gerock of New
Bern, ca. 1886.
Barden Collection.

# I've been Thinking

I've been thinking, I've been thinking
   Of the many happy hours,
Now scattered o'er my pathway
   Like bright and fragrant flowers.
I've been thinking of my trials
   As of a falling snow,
Which tho' chilling to the spirit,
   Hid the buds of Hope below.
Of the joys and of the sorrows
   Of my childhood's simple track,
I've been thinking till my spirit
   Is refreshed by looking back

        ◦

I've been thinking, I've been thinking,
   Of my happy childish days,
When a Mother's love watched o'er me
   And guided all my ways.
I've been thinking of my girlhood
   That sad and dreary time,
How I missed her fostering kindness
   Who had faded in her prime;
There was a tender feeling
   Bound her children to her side,
How rapidly we scattered,
   From the time our Mother died.

*William J. Clarke Papers, SHC*
*Mary Bayard Clarke to Frank Clarke (Baltimore)*

Keoco Nov—20th [1866]

My Dear Boy—

Your letter has just reached me and I cannot tell you how happy it has made me to feel that you were willing to do what I wished in this matter; after writing you your father told me he had written you to come home and had sent you the money to do so, I hope you get it in time to leave with your Aunt Sue [Devereux]—but if you have not I cant let a mail pass without writing to you. Your Father is in such a state of mind that I cannot speak to him again on this subject, Frank he has never been himself since he was in prison for more than a little while, I dont mean that he is out of his mind but his mind is weakened and he is very irritable,[1] you are old enough now to share this trouble with me and help me hid it from the world and the other children as long as possible. I hope it will be only temporary and will not say anything more now but when you come home we will talk it over; he says he has written you to come home at once and sent you the money—my only objection to the plan was the expense and the fear that if you did come home you would not get off in time for the best time for getting a situation in New York. Your father has some idea about your studying something I dont know what under him this winter and not going to New York at all, I do not say to you to fly in his face and go—but I do say as he has taken this notion and written you positively to come home at once to come and talk to him and see if you cannot get him to agree to your not wasting another year here—If you can only get to New York in time I will be glad of an opportunity to see you for I do want to so much and had you gone to New York without coming home I was resolved to go and see you. but you can now see us all and I will try and hope you may yet be in time. Your father said he had sent you money but I do not know whether he has or only thinks he has because he intended to do so and cant ask him If he has not you must write to him; if you will let me know exactly what you owe and need if he has not sent it I will put it down "Mother I need so many dollars["] and I will get it for you.

Your loving Mother—

1. In later years, references in family letters to William J. Clarke's irritability increased and probably reflected his growing addiction to alcohol. He continued to suffer severe pain after the war from his wounds, and it is possible that alcohol helped to dull the pain.

*Barden Collection*
*Fanny Downing*[1] *to Mary Bayard Clarke*

Charlotte N.C. Feb. 5. 1867

My Dear Mrs Clarke,

I have been thinking a great deal of you lately, and your kind letter just received, seems as if it had come in reply to these thoughts. I have been talking of you too, on paper, and only three days ago was writing of you to a distinguished South Carolinian, who has never met you. Telling how much he would enjoy such meeting, that is if he is capable of enjoying the most brilliant conversational powers that I certainly, have ever listened to, and telling him—do not scold me—of those sweet eyes, which one told me not very long ago, no one could "look at and not love."

I am so sorry to hear of your continued ill health, and trust your "enjoyment" thereof may exceed mine. Did they have me in the "Sentinal"? I did not know of it—I hope I was well treated.

Let me thank you for the pleasure you give me in even trying to assist you in the work so dear to us both. I will make my appeal to several of the Merchants here, this afternoon, and if I do not send you a "bundle" it will not be my fault.

I do not know Miss Mason at all, and never thought of sending her poems from the same cause which prevented my correspondance with Mr. Simms—excessive weakness.[2]

You are very kind to speak of my poems as you do, and I thank you. I regret so much that you have not written much, well knowing how greatly we outsiders have lost.

General Hill was tête â tête—piece á piece rather, with me for a morning, some two weeks ago, and he showed me a manuscript poem, signed by the name we all love to see, and which well deserved "Auto-cratical" approbation.

I have some idea of having my two or three thousand "lines" cast on the waters of popular opinion, but c'est séla!

You will think Capt. Waring[3] transformed by matrimony, when I tell you he has never been to see me since his marriage! I met him at a party last week and we had a pleasant little chat in the old style.

Madame was not present, being at present [in my opinion] a case for the offices of the Humane Society.

Have you made Swinburne's acquaintance yet? I received him yesterday, and find it some what difficult to leave him.

He is a carnivorous creature with an insatiable appetite for blood, uses some ugly words, is or pretends to be an infidel, repeats himself half a dozen times in as many verses, yet there is a charm, a music, a ring about his poetry that haunt me.

His "Laus Veneris" is a condensation of "Tannhauser", and the theme is the same, only treated more savagely—Woman the author of all evil, from Eden and apples down to Venus and the H[?]ssel! Heaven save us from such "praise!" Are we not poor persecuted lambs?

I think the winter has broken and that the "Triumph of Spring"—do you *know* how exquisite that poem is?—is about to be established.[4] In that case, I hope you will forsake the "Swamps" and return civilization and Raleigh, as I may there hope to see you, a visit to that City being among my plans for the Spring Campaign.

I shall send your card to Capt. W. and your bundle, should I obtain it, to Mrs Miller.

I write in the greatest haste, as I ought to be dressing for dinner, but I feel, that like my self, you prefer what children call "a try so" letter to one copied from the "Correct Letter Writer's Guide".

With my respects to Colonel Clarke and regards to Mary, General Lee's bright little favorite, believe me

Yours truly<br>Fanny Downing

1. Frances Murdaugh Downing, born in Virginia, was a noted southern author. She married Charles W. Downing in 1851 and moved to Florida. She published both prose and poetry pieces, frequently using the pseudonyms of Viola or Frank Dashmore. *Who Was Who in America,* 155. Downing was one of Mary Bayard Clarke's fellow contributors to *The Land We Love.* She also worked to help the orphan girls Emily Mason placed in schools to receive training as schoolteachers.

2. Mary Bayard Clarke had urged Downing to send some of her poems to Emily Mason for inclusion in Mason's compilation of southern poetry. Although Downing indicated she had not sent poems to Mason, she soon got in touch with the other woman because more than a dozen of her poems were included in Mason's second edition.

3. This probably was Captain Robert P. Waring, who served as captain of Co. B, Forty-third Regiment, NCT, and later served as adjutant general with the Second Brigade. Clark, *Histories of the Several Regiments,* 3:2; 4:6, 66.

4. This poem was written by Mary Bayard Clarke.

ABBY HOUSE, WHO LIVED IN Franklin County, North Carolina, sprang from the state's yeoman class. Poorly educated but strong in her convictions, she fiercely supported the Confederacy while freely castigating its leaders and some of its policies. She died in 1881, and her grave marker carried the inscription, "Angel of Mercy to Confederate Soldiers."

Eight of House's nephews served in the war. She tended to their wounds and, when required, ensured that their bodies were returned home for burial. She also nursed wounded soldiers near the front lines in Virginia. When she was not traveling between North Carolina and Virginia, she collected food and clothing for the soldiers. She particularly admired North Carolina Governor Zebulon B. Vance and felt entirely comfortable walking into his office in the state capitol without invitation to demand his help. She proved equally fearless in forcing her way into the offices of the Confederate elite such as Jefferson Davis and Robert E. Lee. When House's health failed, Confederate veterans in Raleigh found a cottage for her in Raleigh to ease her final days.

Mary Bayard Clarke was the first to record House's exploits when she published the article "Aunt Abby The Irrepressible" (1867). The first part of this two-part series appeared in *The Land We Love* 3, no. 1, May 1867, 63–70. The second part appeared in vol. 3, no. 2, June 1867, 124–29. Clarke relished her conversations with the profane and energetic Abby House. In addition to interviewing House, Clarke also researched her subject by writing to people who crossed House's path during the war. As shown in the letter below, she contacted the Lees. She also wrote to Zebulon Vance to hear his recollections of the "inevitable" Abby House. Billy Arthur, *The State,* Apr. 1995, 13–14; Powell, *DNCB,* 3:210.

*Barden Collection*
*Mary Custis Lee to Mary Bayard Clarke*

Lexington, 22d—February, [1867]

By quite a coincidence my dear Mrs Clarke I had just mailed a letter to Mrs Mason in Raleigh & sent you a message when yours arrived. I immediately questioned the gentlemen as they severally entered my room concerning Miss Abbey House, & A Gustus[1] seemed to have a *lively recollection* of her & his efforts to keep her from annoying Mr Davis, gave her credit for her good feelings & all her efforts to serve the soldiers during the war & the Genl said he recollected her perfectly & that no doubt she was entertained in his tent tho' he does not remember sitting *at table* with her, that she seemed to have an *unusual* number of relatives among the N Carolina soldiers & that he very possibly signed that furlough in the night as he signed *many* for her, but hopes you will tell her that this is the most *inaccessible* place in the world & that she would encounter great fatigue & difficulty in reaching here I told both the gentlemen that had she been a young & pretty girl they would both have had many anecdotes to relate concerning her, to which the Genl very readily assented but A Gustus, who is very reticent on all subjects declared he had told me all he knew, I have no doubt you will make a very amusing article & as he takes the "Land we love" I shall look out for it Have you seen Miss Emily's Book It has been very successful—She is in Baltimore now bringing out a second edition & expects to go to Europe in the Spring with Miss Emily Harper a rich Catholic friend of that place who is to pay all her expenses for the pleasure of her company—Do you not envy her? or are you perfectly satisfied with the wilds of North Carolina,—My youngest son [Robert E. Lee Jr.] who has recently spent a month in Baltimore where he was much entertained in that luxurious city—said they were much surprised to hear him declare he was *homesick,* as his home is a *mere shelter* from the storms being all that the Yankees left on his place & he lives there *all alone,* generally he says wearing his overcoat to keep his *back* warm, while in front he is roasting before a blazing fire but he fully subscribes to the words of the song, "Be it ever so homely there's no place like home" I wish I could have a home feeling here, but like the Exiles I am always yearning for the dear home of my youth² though perhaps it would be a greater trial than I imagine to witness its desecration & desolation Have you seen Mr Barrow Hope's poem at the grave of my Annie, If not I will send you a copy It is very sweet I think, pure & exalted, I cannot tell you what a tender feeling I have for the State that so cherishes her remains & her memory. once I thought I would like to remove them at some future time now I think I would prefer they should remain there Indeed we can never forget how freely that State sent forth her sons to battle for our cause They seem too to have suffered most severely for the hospitals were filled with their sick & wounded, I wish I could furnish you with some incidents for your Muse but I saw very little of my husband during the war & in those very rare visits he seemed to prefer leaving the Camp & its associations behind him, though the subject was interesting to me & now he never [?] to it

I was quite struck a few days since on reading the old Testament I think Deuteronomy to see the rules that a man should not be required to go to war the year he was married but should stay to comfort & cheer his wife & recollected how many of our Men were forced to leave their wives, some the very day after marriage with out any assurance of their safety or comfort how many were unable even to return to those weary with illness

& hope long deferred to see those so dear to them, & necessary to their very existence yet they did not complain, Oh if this exalted & self deny-ing patriotism had continued to the end what might not have been? we shall one day know *why* we *failed*—& why the wicked are now allowed to triumph over us. We can only pray that their joy may be of short duration & that we may come out of the furnace of our affliction purified & refined. We read in the papers the most heart-rending accounts of the destitution within your State & further South which I hope are exaggerated, If true all the funds that have been raised to alleviate it must be almost as the drop in the bucket, you perhaps saw the story that was in all the papers last sum-mer of a little child that had followed the yankee camp & was left by them I had an application from a friend in N York to adopt a southern orphan and immediately wrote to the address given "Mrs D. W. Jones Photogra-pher Smithfield N C.["] I enclose you her reply as you may be able to ascer-tain some thing about this child, if the family are still unwilling to give her up &c I have no doubt I might procure something to aid them in sup-porting her It is a most interesting case & I would like you to take care of Mrs Jones letter & return it to me at some convenient time The Genl desires to unite with me in kind regards to you & all your family especially Miss Mary Tell her my son Rob is still sad & lonely on the banks of the Pamunkey—

I have written you quite a long letter would not the story of the little Malvina furnish you with material for your ready pen to enlarge upon Thank you for the poetry it was quite touching & Genl Lee says he doubt-less when he lifted his hat *felt* those sentiments if he did not utter them[3]

Beleive me yrs truly & affec'ly<br />M C Lee

I am still unable to walk tho' on the whole more *comfortable* this winter

1. George Washington Custis Lee, the eldest son of Robert E. and Mary Custis Lee.

2. Arlington.

3. This is a reference to Clarke's poem "General Lee at the Battle of the Wilderness."

*Wootten, Moulton, Clarke Papers, SHC*
*Zebulon B. Vance to Mary Bayard Clarke*

Charlotte N.Ca<br />6th March 1867—

Mrs Clark

   Madam,

   On my return from Edenton court[1] Monday last, I found your letter concerning Mrs House requesting that I would give you some reminescences of her &c—I am sorry that time will not permit me to do so as fully as I could desire, but the letter to which you refer I think I can give from memory, with the attendant circumstances—

   She was universally on the pad, from Raleigh to Richmond, the army & every where else, and managed to travel without money—the conductors were afraid of her tongue (many brave men you know are afraid of that weapon) She had two nephews in the army by the name of Dickenson, for whom she was always asking something—On one occasion she came to me & said her nephew Marcellus D.—was in the hospital at Richmond and "was a gwine to die, shure, if he didnt get away from thar, to whur sumbody could nuss him" and promised me solemnly that if [I] would get him a sick furlough of 30 days that she would return him at the end of the time *dead or alive*! Upon this I applied for the furlough, & gave my personal pledge that he should promptly return—She put off to Richmond with it & soon Aunt Aggy [*sic*] & Marcellus came home rejoicing. It had all passed out of my mind, when lo! at the end of 60 days into my office popped Aunt Aggy; she took a seat & stuck her feet on the fender without a word spoken. "Well" said I, "you took Marcellus back didnt you?" "No I didnt" said she, "that child's got the wust coff ever you seed —and Ive cum to git you to write 'em that he aint able to go back" "The mischief you have! How do I know that"? "Why *I* tell you so; do you dorr to spute my word?" "Well but *I* dont know it; *Ive* not seen him, and I cant certify to anything which is not within my own knowledge, & besides I am not a doctor." "But they'l believe anything you tell 'em"—"Yes but I cant tell them a lie"—"Taint no lie I tell ye! If you could see that boy coff it would make you sick! Shet up with yer foolishness, and just write to 'em as I tell ye, tell 'em *I* say he aint fitten for to go back"—"Well well," said I in despair, "Who shall I write to?" "Write to Gineral Lee, I dont want no botherment with some of these officers"—I seized a pen and wrote about as follows—

*General,*

   The ubiquitous, indefatigable and inevitable Mrs House, will hand you this—She asks me to say, that *she* says that her nephew Marcellus of— Regiment N C T, now at home 30 days over his time on sick leave, is still unable to return to duty. She says he has a most distressing "Koff". I have not graduated in medicine, nor have I seen this patient, but judging from the symptoms as detailed by Mrs House I venture the opinion that Marcellus —like his great namesake—has his thoughts "bent on peace"—I fear that the air here is too far south for his lungs and earnestly recommend the more salubrious atmosphere of the Rapahannock—and that when comfortably established there he be made to take for his "Koff" a compound of Sulphur, Saltpetre & charcoal to be administered by inhalation, copiously. I should be happy to learn of the result of this prescription—I have the honor to be General, Yr obt sevt. Z B Vance—"

I read it over to her in a loud and pompous tone—she was greatly delighted & slapped me on the shoulder, saying, "Lord bless ye honey, thats it, why could'nt ye a done that at fust, without all this fooleshness"? As I folded & addressed the letter I said to her that there were many people in the army who didnt like me & perhaps some of them would make fun of my letter, & if so she must let me know—"Jist let em *dorr* to laugh at it" said she, and with many thanks she left me—

In a couple of weeks she came into my office again with a very long face indeed—"What luck Aunt Aggy"? said I, "did you get Marcellus excused?" "Lord bless you honey, it didnt do no good. I carried your letter to Ginral Lee, & he read it, but they tuck him, bless your heart they tuck that child back, jist the same as if you hadnt a writ that letter"!! I expressed my concern of course and added, "I hope Gen Lee didnt make fun of my letter, did he?" "No" said she, he begun to laugh once, but I tole him to dry that up, and he read it through very solemn and said it was a mighty smart letter"—

This is all that I can give you now—If I had time—which I have not— my heart is too full of sadness & concern for the awful situation of the country as well as my own, to enter fully into the humorous. Mrs Vances health is very feeble, and the approaching reign of terror and abolition of our courts makes the prospect of supporting my helpless family very gloomy indeed. Tell the Col to save a place for me on his saw mill!

With kindest regards to him, & trusting to hear from you again when convenient—believe me dear Madam to be

Most Sincerely & resply
Yr obt svt.
*Zebulon B. Vance*

1. After the war, Vance settled in Charlotte, North Carolina, to practice law. He remained heavily involved in Conservative politics.

❧

MARY BAYARD CLARKE WROTE a series of articles in 1867 and 1868 under the name "Betsey Bittersweet," which attacked and ridiculed Radical Reconstruction, Republicans, northern troops, and the efforts by blacks to secure their rights in North Carolina and the South generally. In March 1867 the United States government had passed over President Johnson's veto the Military Reconstruction Bill, which divided the South into five military districts. Each southern state was expected to convene a convention to amend the state constitution, to give blacks the vote, and to ratify the Fourteenth Amendment. At the same time, certain categories of southern white men were disfranchised. In North Carolina, the state's Republican Party formed in March 1867. These developments provided ready fodder for Clarke's conservative pen.

Clarke exploited southern speech patterns in the Betsey Bittersweet series by trying to write in a vernacular style to approximate the speech patterns of semiliterate white women. Clarke paid close attention to the people she met from all classes and listened for differences in speech patterns and pronunciation. This interest in the speech of lower-class whites also appeared in her "Aunt Abby" series, which was published in *The Land We Love* in 1867. The style and tone of these articles imitated the popular "Bill Arp" newspaper articles written during the Civil War and Reconstruction periods by Charles H. Smith. Smith's articles, written in southern vernacular and bitterly anti-Republican, remained respectful of different classes of southern whites. Clarke's Bittersweet series, like Smith's, contained social commentary wrapped around southern speech patterns and a love for story-telling.

The Bittersweet series proved especially popular in the South, although at least one article appeared in the *New York Day Book* (18 Mar. 1867). This article contained an extremely funny account of the interactions between Raleigh women and Union troops occupying the city in 1866. Clarke, observing the determined efforts of her peers to annoy northern officers, astutely noted what angered women.

> They all 'on em know'd the southern wimen hated the very sight o' the stars and stripes, and 'sted o' being satisfed with having it over the State House, and over the Government House, . . . they must needs grind it into us by stretching on it . . . over the side walks o' front street, to Force the gals to walk under it. Lord bless your soul, Mister Editors, didn't they have sense enough to know that nothing pleases a woman better'n persecution of her? . . .

Well, the wimen all vowed they would cross the street whenever they come to a flag, and most on 'em did. You'd er thought it was Christmas, and they'd all bin a drinking egg-nogg, from the zig-zag way they went first to one side and then to 'tother. I thought they'd all on 'em er staid at home as could do so; but 'stead o' that, it seemed like they was every one on 'em bound to go up or down street a dozen times that day. I didn't go out myself, but I sot at cousin Jane's winder. . . which was rite oppersite whar some officers lodged, and they had hung a flag clean across the pavement, and sot a watching the galls as they passed, and er marking down every one on 'em as wouldn't go under the flag. Lord bless you, how delighted the galls was at the black looks!—But bime by, a young man come 'long in a Majer's uniform, looking mighty spruce and nice, and he tuck off his hat as perlite as possible to two young galls as was a passin', and had turned out inter the street, jest before he met 'em, to keep from going under the flag; and arter they passed, he went on a sorter smiling to hisself till he got to the flag, when he tuck up his coat tails a mincing like, and went clean out inter the middle o' the street like as if he had skirts on, and was a holding 'em up to keep 'em from tetching of a Yankee; the officers on the piazza they jest laughed and hollered, and he walked up the steps and says, "that's the way the sweet little rebels does." "Yes," says one of 'em, "did you ever see such a pack o' fools in yer life?"—Ses he, "I think you all bigger fools for getting mad with school-gals and wimmen for not walking under the flag, than they is for not doing so." Ses I to cousin Jane . . . "them's the senserblest words ever I heard from a Yankee yit." "Yes," ses she, "that hurts me a sight woss than arestin' of the gals." "Yes," ses I, "if thar's one thing hurts a woman mor'n another, 'tis to feel a man thinks her anger ain't no 'count, and she's nothing more en a child to be humored in her whims, when thar ain't nothing hurtful in 'em."

The *Sentinel* (Raleigh) and the *Southern Home Journal* (Baltimore) carried most of the Bittersweet stories. Clarke clipped the published versions and pasted them into a scrapbook, but she did not always note which article appeared in a particular paper. Most of the articles alluded to local events and political figures, some of which defy explanation.

Clarke's handwritten version of "The Union Washing Machine" is published below. In the salutation she mentions "Mister Hill." This referred to former Confederate General Daniel Harvey Hill, editor of *The Land We Love*. Hill, however, declined to publish the article, scribbling on the manuscript version that it was "too rebellious" for his paper. Clarke found no difficulty in having the *Sentinel* publish it in 1867. MBC Scrapbook 2, Barden Collection; James C. Austin, *Bill Arp* (New York: Twayne Publishers, 1969).

*Barden Collection*

"The Union Washing Machine."
Betsey Bittersweet

Newbun, North Carliner

Dear Mister Hill

I 'spose, being as how you's in the publishing line yourself, you reads all as is printed, and has seen the letters I've been a writing to Mister Editers of New York, and knows that I'm so bad subjugated that I wont call no-body Gineral who dont wear a full dress United States army uniform; so I wont waste time 'pologizing for Mistering of you; Sence you've come out and declared you was loyal to green backs I jest holds out the right hand o' fellowship, and in the words of the poet says "Here's another——" and whats more'n that, I'm a right down riggerler Unionist too, none o' your Holden-Fontlord unionist, but a up and down *mash-in* Unionist. My ole man, whose allers a talking in unbeknown tongues, says we hev got to go back inter the union—*no-lans yo-lans*—which I take it means confiscated o' our lands and none an'em our'n, but Betsey Jane, thats my darter you know, says it means *willy-nilly*—which is french for whether we want to or not. She's high eddicated, Betsey Jane is, having bin a spell to Docter Smedies siminary,[1] and I gives up to her considerable in the litter-ary-line——, but she cant hold a candle to me in the cleaning up one——, and thats what I sot down to tell you. Ef we's got to go back inter the Union I wants all my sisters in afflicshun, whose half worried out'n their lives and whole worried out'n ther tempers, to turn mashin Unionist at wonst, and send off the freed ladies o' colour they's a paying for *not* doing of ther washing and git a UNION WASHING MASHIN, and a UNION CLOTHES WRINGER, and a UNION CLOTHES DRYER. So out o' pure love and kindness to them, and a desire to do ther souls good as well at their bodies, Ive writ a ditty advising on 'em to do so. Betsey Jane corrected the spellin, and pinted it she sed, but seems to me twas pinted enuff when I give it to her, and aint no sharper now, but then I want eddicated by Docter Smeides' siminary. Them as likes it can go on with the AMERIKIN MANGLE—I dont rickomend it, seems to me them as is a ready ironed, to say nothing 'bout being muzzled, dont need no mangling; and both the AMERICAN MANGLE, and the down right one—Lord bless my soul! I meant the UPRIGHT one, is too expensive for sich poor folks as us——. And I dont like SHERMAN'S WRINGER nether, it haint got no cogs, and squeezes ruther too hard. Some folks ses the WORLD'S DRYER is better'n the UNION DRYER, 'cause it performs revolutions, but that's the very reason I dont 'prove of it. Revolutions is apt to put things out o' order ginerally, and, if they dont run smooth, ends in being nothing but rebellions, and all we Southern women knows as how in this here "great rebellion"—so called—a sight o' clothes has bin tore up, and we cant afford the ware and tear of the WORLD'S DRYER if its gwine to rebell insted o' revolutionizing, as it will be full like to do—if a freed lady o' colour has the handling of it. So I dont advise none but the UNION MASHINS, as you'll see when you've read my ditty.

Now Mister Hill dont you let your devil—you've got one in the Land we Love havnt you?—get the better o' you and print that word wrong—; for my ole man sas as how *have his corpis* is suspended, and the next thing arter that will be a having er herse; and if Mister Jeemes Fontlord—hears as how I've writ you that the North Carliner Unionist is a dirty set, and oughter be run through a mashin and wringer, and then left higher and dryer—than he'll be when the *vox populi nux vomica* of his coloured friends has swaged down inter a whine; the fust thing I know, I'll be in jail with my funeril appinted and old Handy Lockett,[2] the undertaker of the Mongrel Convention,[3] engaged to see that *my* corpis is suspended too—. So praying that the Devil may be cast out o' The Land we Love without rending of it, and that the Sickles[4] of the reapers-of-the great harvest may'nt cut you down, I remain your constant reader and well wisher

BETSEY BITTERSWEET

PS. Betsey Jane says as how I oughter a writ it *vox populi vox dei;* but I knows better en that, for I heard a Texan Unionist say wonst afore the war—, "My friends I tell you in the words o' that great Mexikin proverb—, *vox populi-nux vomica*" and I reckon he knowd.

*[Hill's notation on the manuscript, made when he declined to print it]*
Too rebellious my friend

Mr Sickles Aunt Abby is splendid—would like to have a bushel of the same sort Im too unwell to write Pray excuse pencil scribble

Respectfully,<br>D H Hill

*[Published version found in the Raleigh* Sentinel*]*
*A UNION DITTY.*
DEDIKATED TO HER SISTERS IN AFFLICKSHUN BY BETSEY BITTERSWEET.

The AMERICAN MANGLE we have been thro',
And tho' we come out of it pressed ruther flat,

The Reddykills said we still would'nt do
an so SHERMAN'S WRINGER they added to that.
But Lord bless yew, sisters, dont heed 'em, I pray,
Of one thing we none on us have any doubts,
That it can no longer be treason to say,
If we did'nt see-seed, we some how saw sprouts.
By a long "course o' sprouts" we are out at the toes,
The elbows and pocket, and now we must try
How best we can save our money and clothes,
Or the next Yankee patent will squeeze us quite dry.
SHERMAN'S WRINGER of hearts?—don't wring us of bread,
So Stevens[5] is fixing to patent, next fall,
The Plantation Wringer of purses instead,
To leave us no need for a DRYER at all.
As they won't leave us out, we've got to go in,
And I'm for a Union dont need so much soap,
The great UNION WASHING AND WRINGING MASHIN,
Which offers poor house-keepers some little hope.
My Betsey was told by a Yankee o' late,
If she'd say just exactly how much *she* had lost
By the freeing o' niggers and bumming o' plate,
He'd open his pocket and pay the whole cost.
But Betsey she sed, it could'nt be done,
Salvation was worth far more'n his cash,
And she was afeard for her there was none
From losing her temper and speaking so rash.
Mr. Hill he is loyal to greenbacks and sich,
And I'm for the Union, so mind what we say,
Get a washing mashin with a WRINGER, for which
You wont have salvation, but money, to pay.
For I, Betsey Bittersweet, tell yew in rhyme,
A saving o' money, a saving of clothes,
A saving of labor—and saving of time,
Is a saving of temper as well as of those.
You can put all the darkies to wielding a hoe,
For washing is no more than running "a SINGER,"
And ladies of color may weed a wide row,
If we've this mashin and a DRYER and WRINGER.

Where can yew get 'em? Of *J.Ward & Co.,* 23 Cortlandt Street, great New York city, And now I have told yew all that I know, and so ends the Bittersweet's sole Union Ditty!

1. St. Mary's Academy, Raleigh.

2. Handy Lockhart, a North Carolina African American, became an officer of the Colored Educational Association of North Carolina. There was also a Handy Locket, a Wake County cabinetmaker, who attended the State Equal Rights League meeting in Raleigh in October 1866. Alexander, "North Carolina Faces the Freedmen," vol. 1:379n. 1, 405n. 4.

3. Clarke's reference to a mongrel convention indicates that black and white delegates jointly attended. There were several Republican organizing conventions in 1867 that included blacks. There was also the state's Constitutional Convention in 1868, which ratified Radical Reconstruction measures.

4. General Daniel Edgar Sickles was military governor of the Carolinas from 1865 through 1867. Boatner, *Civil War Dictionary,* 760.

5. United States congressman Thaddeus Stevens of Vermont.

Cornelia Phillips Spencer and Clarke exchanged occasional letters concerning their work to help children orphaned by the war. The Mallett referred to in this letter was Lieutenant Colonel Edward Beatty Mallett of the Sixty-first North Carolina Regiment, who was killed on 21 March 1865, during the Battle of Bentonville. He left a widow and five children, who had fled New Bern in 1862 when it fell to northern troops to seek refuge in Chapel Hill. Mrs. Mallett's health failed after her husband's death, and she also died. Her friend, Cornelia Phillips Spencer, described her death and the children's plight in her book, *The Last Ninety Days in North Carolina,* 73–75. Ashe, *Biographical History,* 3:401–5; Richard L. Zuber, *North Carolina During Reconstruction* (Raleigh, N.C.: Department of Archives and History, 1969), 63–65; Manarin and Jordan, *Roster of NC Troops,* 14:651.

*Cornelia Phillips Spencer Papers, North Carolina State Archives, Raleigh, N.C.*
*Mary Bayard Clarke to Cornelia Phillips Spencer*

Macon House
Morehead City [North Carolina] Aug 2d [1867]
My Dear Mrs Spencer

Your letter was forwarded to me from home and reached me last night. I am indeed pained to hear that there is no hope for our University, but I have feared for some time that it was doomed, and felt it could never recover under Gov. Swain's management and am not therefore surprised at what you tell me; bad news seldom surprises me now. I am sorry to hear such accounts of your Mother's[1] health my own heart trouble is a slower death than that which the physicians warn you of in her case, but I think there is as little hope for me, though I have improved since I came down to the sea side.

As soon as I got your letter I began devising some way of fitting out Col. Mallett's daughter and think I can assist in doing it; I took Mrs Bradley Johnson (Jennie Saunders)[2] into my confidence as she had told me she was in some way connected with the Malletts, and between us I hope to do something, Jennie has as you know just lost her father and is in mourning and she tells me will see if she cannot find some coloured dresses suitable to be altered for a school girl. I think I can get some inexpensive dresses and other articles from a gentleman who has done much to help me in these matters, he has a large dry goods store and I need not mention to him for whom the articles are intended, so there need be no delicacy on Miss Sallie's part in accepting what I can procure, I am a terrible beggar for "Miss Mason's children" and have helped in this way fit out others; travelling expenses must be provided for in the same way I suppose, and I shall go to work at once and see what I can do; Please write me and tell me at what time Miss Sallie would like her neice to go to school—and give me the address in full of the gentleman who has charge of Miss Mason's affairs, I have it at home but no one there can get the letter for me; I will write him at once if Sallie is to go this fall, as it may be necessary for him to look about for a vacancy for her. Please find out whether a Catholic School would be objectionable, they are generally the best and as they are endowed can afford to take the girls for nothing, Most generous have they been in their kindness, for they say they have suffered nothing pecuniarily from the war—and their Church desires to assist those who have. I know nothing of the vacancies since Miss Mason left—Impress on Miss Sallie that what I gather except from those who like Mrs Johnson and my self are interested in her neices for their parents sake, will be collected in Miss Mason's name and none will know for whom it is intended, further, than as I said before, "it is for one of her children," I inferred from your letter that next spring would be the time most agreeable for Sallie to leave her aunt and therefore have taken no steps about it hoping Miss Mason would have returned by that time but she wrote should it be desirable to send her before her return I was to apply to the Rector of St Paul's church Baltimore

Very Sincerely—your friend

Mary Bayard Clarke

1. Judith V. Phillips.

2. Bradley Tyler Johnson, a Maryland native, married Jane Claudia Saunders of Raleigh, North Carolina, on 25 June 1851. Powell, *DNCB*, 3:293–94. Her father, Romulus M. Saunders, for whom Jane was in mourning, died 21 April 1867. Powell, *DNCB*, 5:285.

❧

*Wootten, Moulton, Clarke Papers, SHC*
*Emily Mason to Mary Bayard Clarke*

Newport Ky
Jany 7th [1868]

My dear Friend

Yr letter addressed to Lex. Ky. followed me here, and I the more regret the delay as I have been most anxious to bring some influence to bear upon Col. Wm Johnson[1] Charlotte N. C. Prest. of that R. R. to get free tickets on his Road for the two children nieces of Jas. Dudley of Marion C.H., S. C. who have been waiting some time to get on to Wheeling Va where a School awaits them—in which one child is taken gratuitously & I pay for the other—My plan is this—While I *wait* for money from my book & from other Sources, I *beg* in Every School I know of or encounter —Catholic—Episcopal—Presbyterian—Methodist or Baptist for my daughters to be taken gratuitously—which leaves me only their clothing & travelling expenses to provide—& this much puts me "to my triumph" especially as R.way charges are so enormous! So far I have provided places for Eight children but have not yet been able to get them to their Several destinations—The Catholics are most prompt to meet my wishes— as they say—they can best afford it—as they do not have to pay their teach- ers—& they are universally—Southern in sympathy—only yesterday the German Sisters of Notre Dame in Cinna—(who have a fine School)[2] agreed to take *two girls* for two years—even providing their clothing! & I am raffling some bracelets to get the money to bring them on from Stafford Co Va—out of a family of six motherless girls—"*barefoot* & in rags!"—yet of the best blood of the Old Dominion

Jany. 8th

Since writing the above I hear from St. Louis that the friends to whom I wrote there have provided for 10—or 12—of my children in good schools & I think the Southern relief Ass. of that city will provide them clothing—I have not yet selected the girls for these places If you know of any girls clean, & needy of good family & willing to be instructed to teach—let me know—I think you may, (if you please) notice my 2d Edition or rather notice the fact of the popularity of my scheme—my first Edition (3000 vols.) sold in less than three weeks & I am hurried by Murphy[3] to put the other in print by the 10th He cannot fill the orders he has—I have the 2d Edition nearly ready & if you have any thing to add please send it without delay to Murphy & Co—I thank you for the offer of Mosses & yr other poems—Tell me the address of yr publisher & I will write him about it.—If you notice my forthcoming Edition please say that it is enlarged & improved—with many additional poems—It is now of 456 pages to which I add about 80 pages of new matter taking out 67 pages of the original vol.

I write in haste as I am just on my way to Balt. & very busy Have you seen Gilmore Simmes[4] vol. It disappoints me—& is not *here* thought equal to mine I don't think he has one of yrs & *not one* of Col. Hawkins'[5]—*Do* tell me *candidly* what you think of mine & write directly *any hints* you may have for the 2d Edition—Should I have a preface to 2d Edition—*or how?* Say it for me! in haste aff. yr oblgd

*E. V. Mason*

1. William Johnston, a lawyer from Charlotte, North Carolina, served in the state's secession convention in 1861 and ran for governor against Vance in 1862. In 1849 he became president of the Charlotte and South Carolina Railroad Company and the Atlantic, Tennessee, and Ohio Railroad Company. He operated his railroad lines during the war, but much track was destroyed. In 1865 he began rebuilding the lines. Powell, *DNCB*, 3:310–11.

2. The Sisters of Notre Dame was a Catholic charitable organization and teaching order run by women who devoted "their lives to saving from misery and degradation the children of those who cannot or will not perform a parent's duty." The children they helped were female. According to an 1874 issue of *Catholic World*, the Sisters of Notre Dame had "the care of 20 houses, in which there are 431 boarders and over 1,200 day scholars, besides about 14,000 pupils attending the free schools." "About Several Things," *Catholic World* 9, no. 50 (May 1869): 277; "The Female Religious of America," *Catholic World* 19, no. 111 (June 1874): 362–75.

3. John Murphy & Co., a publishing firm in Baltimore, Maryland, published both editions of Mason's book, *The Southern Poems of the War, Collected and Arranged By Miss Emily V. Mason, of Virginia.* The second edition appeared in 1868.

4. William Gilmore Simms, a South Carolina lawyer and author, edited the *Southern Quarterly Review* between 1849 and 1856 and became a leading southern novelist. *Who Was Who in America*, 484.

5. Colonel W. Steward Hawkins of Tennessee was "a genial poet and gallant soldier" whom Emily Mason greatly admired. He was captured in 1861 and imprisoned throughout the war at Camp Chase in Ohio. While imprisoned he wrote many poems, which were published and enjoyed by readers in the North and South. After his release from prison in 1865, he "returned home to die." Mason ensured his poems were published in her collection of southern poetry. Emily V. Mason, comp., *The Southern Poems of the War* (Baltimore: John Murphy: 1868), 204, 366, 369.

THE STATE'S CONSTITUTIONAL Convention met from 14 January through 17 March 1868. The convention, controlled by the state's newly formed Republican Party, included delegates elected by thousands of African Americans as well as white voters. One of its primary tasks was ratification of the Fourteenth Amendment. The Raleigh *Sentinel*'s reporters were eventually banned from covering the proceedings, which they persisted in calling the "So-Called Convention."

The Conservative Party derided the convention's black members and began a white-supremacy campaign, initiated by William A. Graham's speech on 5 February. This speech clearly drew the color line and signaled the start of a ruthless campaign against carpetbaggers, scalawags, and black leaders in the state. As the violence increased, several secessionist Democrats turned to the Republican Party because they feared another war.

*MBC Scrapbook 2, Barden Collection*
*Letter From Betsey Bittersweet*

Raleigh, N. C. Feb. 21st [1868]

*Dear Mister Home Journal of the South:*
I aint writ to you sence the Constitutional Convention (so-called) met in Raleigh to set on an egg that they will addle in spite of all their cackling; for to tell you the truth, all my spare time has been tuck up a-trying to sense the reports we outsiders git of their doings. They haint done nothing yet but talk about *per diem;* (you understands Latin, so I don't translate;) but they haint made it clear whether the niggers wishes to be dyed white, or the so-called whites wishes to be dyed black. Jim Harris,[1] a 'spectable nigger, mattrass maker before destruction, said in the last convention he set in along of the Tom, Dick, and Harry's that I wrote you about, that he "want ashamed of his color, and he hoped that that there white man as wanted all distinctions of colored dropped from 'de archives of gravity' wasn't ashamed of his;" for you see Jim is cute enough, he is,

when he's put up to a thing, and somebody put him up to believing that if the white men, who met to converse with their friend and their brother, the nigger, in a sociable way, wasn't ashamed of their colored, they was of their company, and didn't want it known abroad generally that there was any niggers in that convention. But Jim's got sense enough to know that Mr. Plato Durham aint platonic, and that he and Mister John Graham,[2] and the other Conservatives of this so-called Constitutional Convention aint met for peace but for war, and mean to give the Radicals jestice if it is in their power to do so; and, like the Irishman whose lawyer promised to see that he had jestice, that's jest what they don't want. And I can tell you, Mister Home Journal, that the fight lays between the Conservatives and the niggers, for the white Radicals in this convention aint got sense enough even to be the puppets of the X. P. G., Mr. W. Holden, and the niggers have, and is accordingly elevated to that dignified position. When that nigger Carey[3] said he wanted "to be put down in the de archives gravity," and to get there according to true Radical rule, began by destroying the gravity of his hearers, Jim Harris got mad, he did, because the *Sentinal* published jest what Carey said, insted of dressing of it up like the *Standard* done, and saying "the sense of what Mr. Carey said was, &c.," so he pitched into the reporters, and said he was "tired of being reported by irresponsible striplings who put the words down jest as they come out of a fellow's mouth, before the P. G. had time to correct 'em." When I read this I jest made up my mind to come right straight to Raleigh and hear for myself what they really was a-doing. My ole man axed me how I was a-going to hear for myself. Ses he, "No 'spectable woman kin go to that there convention. The Yankees, when they talk about social equality means it for us, not for them. They is ready enough to howl about Southern folks excluding the niggers from the galleries, but ketch one of them a-setting beside of a nigger. Why in their schools the marm is always stuck upon a platform, and when one of 'em takes a notion to go to the convention, and I take it its only the nigger school-marms who ever does go, the X. P. G. [William Woods Holden] orders them seats on the platform behind the speaker's chair, and escorts them to it. And I just ask you if you think he's a-going to allow you, Betsey Bittersweet, to put your foot on that there floor." Ses I, "Ole man, a woman can pull wool over the eyes of a man, even if he is an X. P. G.; and if I choose to do so, I'll make him escort me to the platform same as if I was a school-marm." Ses he, "And ef you does I'll apply for a divorce the very next court." I never sed nothing more, but the next day I walked into the room whar he was, in a short-tailed dress, with a red wig on, and the hair all skewerld on the top of my head, with a little hat the size of a saucer stuck on in front, and a pair of green specks on. He laid down the paper he was a-reading, and ses, "Betsey, have you tuck leave of your senses? You look as if you was ready for the lu-nat-ic assilum instead of that there men-a-gery at the capital." I didn't say a word, but I pulled out a false nose some of the boys had at the masquerade—a long, prying sort of nose—and I fastened it on under the specks, and drapped a blue veil over my face, and then I ses, "Would you know me if you was to meet me in the streets?" Ses he, "No more en I would a nigger school-marm." Ses I, "And no more will the X. P. G., for that's what I am, a nig-ger marm on her travels, anxious to hear the debates in a convention of the wisdom, learning, and ability of North Car'liner. The Southerners will all be glad if I am satisfied with listening, and don't want to take a part; and as for the Radikils, they will think, no matter what I do, its all for the glory of God and to make money. So I am a-going to report for the *Southern Home Journal,* and not be dependant on no 'irresponsible stripling,' nor on one that reports in kid gloves 'nother." Ses he, "Well, jest go to the depot by yourself, will you? for I wouldn't be seen escorting you through the streets of Newbern for nothing." The conductors didn't none of 'em know me, neither did the hotel porters and the omnibus drivers. They all know ole Miss Bittersweet; and when I go up to Raleigh it's "how d'ye, Miss Betsey? how's ole marster? Give me your bag; you always goes up in our 'bus. You's a-gwine to Miss Jane's, aint you?" and so on. But this time they all tuck me for a marm, and I was so delighted I wouldn't go to Cousin Jane's, but drew up to a boarding-house, and tuck a room. And now you may depend on hearing the truth about the convention, 'thouten they adops Plato Durham's last amendment afore I get there. Somebody moved to adjourne tother day, and Plato he jumped up and moved an amendment, which was that they adjourne *sine die;* and do you think one of the blackest Radicals didn't second the motion, and if it hadn't been for Mr. Rodman[4] they would have adjourned themselves out of existence, which is a catastrophe devoutly to be wished for.

And so no more from your

Special reporter,
BETSEY BITTERSWEET.

1. James Henry Harris, an African American politician born in Granville County, North Carolina. He was apprenticed in 1840 to be trained as a carpenter and later went to school in Oberlin, Ohio. He received a commission in 1863

to help raise the Twenty-eighth Regiment of U.S. Colored Troops. Harris returned to Raleigh in June 1865 as a teacher for the New England Freedmen's Aid Society. He quickly became a leader in the black community, serving in the North Carolina Freedmen's Convention in 1865 and 1866 and as vice president of the National Equal Rights Convention of 1865. During Reconstruction he became a charter member of the state's Republican Party and served in the 1868 Constitutional Convention. He also was a state legislator for several terms. Powell, *DNCB,* 3:53; Alexander, "North Carolina Faces the Freedmen," 1:78–79.

2. Plato Durham, a Confederate captain during the Civil War, gained political prominence as a Conservative politician and white supremacist during the 1868 Constitutional Convention. He and John W. Graham were the main Conservative leaders in this strongly Republican convention. Hamilton, *Reconstruction in North Carolina,* 254; Lancaster, "Scalawags of North Carolina," 299–300.

3. Wilson Carey was one of the black delegates to the 1868 North Carolina Constitutional Convention. Hamilton, *Reconstruction in North Carolina,* 254, 258.

4. William Blount Rodman was a lawyer from Beaufort, North Carolina, who joined the Republican Party in North Carolina after being an ardent secessionist Democrat before the war. Rodman, although opportunistic enough to hope his Republican connections would lead to an appointment on the state's Supreme Court, also believed that black citizenship and suffrage were inevitable consequences of freedom. He hoped to moderate the influence of the more radical Republicans in the state while leading the state toward reconciliation with the North. Lancaster, "Scalawags of North Carolina," 279, 285.

MARY BAYARD CLARKE WROTE this article around same the time as her Betsey Bittersweet article of 21 February 1868. The difference in tone between the two articles reveals much about Clarke's advocacy of the Conservative cause. She opposed giving blacks the vote, she supported the white-supremacy campaign outlined by William A. Graham, and she stressed the need for political peace between former Whigs and Democrats to achieve success against Radical Reconstruction. It seems unlikely that she knew at this point that her husband, disquieted by the Conservative leadership and doubting their willingness to provide him with political office, would be willing to court Republican leaders and friends.

William J. Clarke, a former Democrat, had a long history of political conflict with North Carolina Whigs. The same men he had distrusted before the war now dominated the Conservative Party. Clarke tried to work with them by giving speeches and criticizing the "Miserable puerile and vile speeches" of Republicans.[1] Nevertheless, Clarke's respect for party leadership waned.

Other factors influenced William Clarke's disaffection from the Conservative Party. He had taken an oath of allegiance in 1865 to obtain his release from a federal military prison. Clarke took his promise of loyalty to the United States seriously, and he slowly became convinced that Conservative politicians could lead the state into armed conflict with the North. Clarke hoped, too, to obtain a judgeship somewhere in the state. He apparently received little "encouragement" from the Conservatives, despite his wife's efforts to promote the Conservative program.

After the statewide elections in 1868 that resulted in a resounding defeat for the Conservative Party and the election of William Woods Holden as governor, the ascendancy of the Republican Party in the state seemed irreversible. Clarke reevaluated his options, writing on 27 April, "The Conservatives are badly beaten. I regret that I had anything to do with a party, with whom I had so little in common. Ardently do I hope for the organization of a new party where a Democrat can have some chance."[2] Clarke soon approached the Republicans, hoping his friendship with Holden, Robert Dick, and other North Carolina scalawags would lead to a judicial appointment. It was a fortuitous moment, because many scalawags were trying to stem the influence of northern carpetbaggers within the state's Republican Party. The scalawags hoped to moderate some of the extreme reforms being proposed by the northern faction while preserving peace. To obtain these ends, they needed to control party leadership. As explained by Robert Dick, the scalawags sought leaders "who are known to the people, and who established a character for devoted loyalty in the fiery ordeal of the rebellion.——" Clarke, a former Confederate colonel, fit this mold and would have been an attractive addition to the scalawag fold.

By June, Clarke was socializing with Republicans, although he faced "political persecution and social ostracism."[3] In July the Republicans approached Clarke about editing their newspaper, the *Republican,* although nothing came of this. Nevertheless, Clarke wrote with satisfaction that "The Republicans seem to be rallying to me. God knows I need help and encouragement."[4] On 26 July Clarke gave his first, and well received, Republican speech to a large crowd. He justified his actions in his diary, writing, "God knows that none but patriotic just and humane motives influenced me."[5] No documentary materials exist to indicate how or when Clarke informed his wife about his decision to join the Republican Party, but it undoubtedly caused her considerable anguish.

❧

*MBC Scrapbook 2, Barden Collection*
*"For the Journal of Commerce." Signed in ink "C." in scrapbook, ca. Feb. 1868*

On Wednesday, the fifth day of February, 1868, a body of delegates, representing the respectable portion of the people of North Carolina, went into Convention[6] in the city of Raleigh to organize a steady and determined resistance to the radicals, both Northern and Southern, who are attempting to force negro supremacy upon them. It was one of the most intellectual, as well as intelligent, public bodies that ever met in that place; for it was an assemblage containing the leading men of the State, irrespective of all former political differences, who went "ready," as their President, the Hon. William A. Graham,[7] said in his opening speech, "to trample under foot all party distinctions of Whig or Democrat and unite to avert the impending evil of negro supremacy." Here were seen old line Whigs shoulder to shoulder with true blue Democrats, anxious to bury the hatchet of political warfare, and smoke together the calumet of peace that they might more effectually unite with each other; and, as the Hon. Thomas Bragg[8] truly remarked, "the Democratic party of the North— to resist their enemies in every lawful manner—face to face—foot to foot—and go down—if fall they must like true men. By the side of the Hon Charles Manly,[9] sat the venerable Weldon N. Edwards,[10] he whose voice had been raised with such effective power in the convention of thirty-five, "unfit to use his own words—'from extreme age to take an active part in the business of the convention, but coming simply to signify his approval of it, and his desire to connect his fortunes to the same barque as that which held those—be they good or bad—of the Anglo-Saxon race."

It was a source of regret to many that he was not nominated as President of the Convention. The able speech of Mr Graham would have been quite as effective from the floor, as from the chair; and it would have been most appropriate for the contemporary and bosom friend of Nathaniel Macon, to preside over the cordial Union of the two political parties who have, since his day, divided the State of North Carolina.

Mr. Graham's opening speech exceeded the expectations even of those who knew his abilities. Clear, forcible, and argumentative—covering the whole question with the accuracy of the Lawyer and the enlarged and comprehensive views of the Statesman; it rose like a Doric column in a Grecian temple—severely simple, but complete in all its parts—without ornament beyond the chaste dignity of its diction, but impressing all who heard it with a sense of strength as concentrated and perfect to render any other adornment superfluous.

The coldness of the marble however was as preceptible as its grandeur and strength. The statesman and the lawyer were clearly defined, but nothing was seen of the man. He spoke to the head, and not to the heart; recognizing the intelligence of his hearers, he appealed to that alone, and it responded with applause to the arguments addressed to it. But there was no enthusiasm in the speaker, and consequently none was excited in the audience.

Side by side with the Doric of Mr. Graham, rose the Corinthian column of Zebulon B. Vance; appealing to the hearts of his hearers by many a homely simile, or laughable anecdote, which, like the toys gathered by the affectionate nurse, and placed in a basket on the tomb of her beloved young mistress, were not only tokens of a warm and kindly heart, but became, when wreathed with the Acanthus leaves of genius, an appropriate capital to a column equalling the Doric in strength, and surpassing the Doric in luxuriance of adornment. Every word that he uttered came, so evidently, directly from his heart that it went as directly to the heart of his hearers; the very tones of his voice as he said, after describing the old black cook skimming the scum from the boiling pot, "and I don't think I exaggerate when I say I have stolen a thousand biscuits from her," brought down the house. It was a touch of nature that convinced his black as well as white hearers, that he spoke but the truth, when he said that he had nothing but the kindest feelings towards the negro; and that while he would unflinchingly stand up and do battle for the supremacy of the white race, he would ever be found the champion of the black, should they be threatened with oppressions, or denied their civil rights before the law.

One great source of power in Governor Vance's speeches is his forcible application of Scripture to the subject under discussion. Nothing could have been more effective than the manner in which he said, after describing the horrors of negro supremacy, should it be established; "It will be too far then for us to go up to Jerusalem, to sacrifice at the temple, and a calf will be set up amongst us and they will say (Here he turned and pointed to the negro gallery,) 'These be thy gods, Oh Israel.'"

As we listened to these speeches and looked on this assemblage of the gentlemen of North Carolina, we thought with sadness of one of her most brilliant sons, whose voice were it not silent in death would have rang out in trumpet tones to sustain this effort made by the white men of the State to avert the black wave of barbarism; which ever rolls in the wake of the

Radical party, while it domineers over the South. The speech of Henry W. Miller, had he been living to make one would have risen an Ionic column between the Doric of Mr. Graham and the Corinthian of Governor Vance. Lighter and more graceful than the former, yet less luxuriantly fanciful than the latter, it would have rendered the temple of North Carolina's eloquence complete; and shown even more clearly than was demonstrated on this occasion, that she has among her sons the wisdom to conceive, the strength to sustain, and the beauty to adorn.—Peace be to his ashes.

. . . .

But though N. Carolina has lost her Badger[11] and Miller, her Ellis and Morehead[12] the meeting of this Convention proves most satisfactorily to all who saw it in session, that there are still left among us men who will not sit quietly by and see their native State given up into the hands of "the Holdens and the Harrises." The stars are indeed already paling before the sun, and darkness giving way to light.

C.

1. Entry of 11 March 1868, Clarke Diary, SHC.

2. Entry of 27 April 1868, Clarke Diary, SHC.

3. Entry of 28 June 1868, Clarke Diary, SHC.

4. Entry of 20 July 1868, Clarke Diary, SHC.

5. Entry of 26 July 1868, Clarke Diary, SHC.

6. This was the Conservative Convention, which convened to outline its opposition to the Constitutional Convention and Radical Reconstruction, particularly the Fourteenth Amendment.

7. William Alexander Graham, a prominent North Carolina attorney and leading Whig politician, twice served as North Carolina's governor. He also served as a state legislator, United States senator, secretary of the navy under President Millard Fillmore, and as a Confederate congressman. He became a leading opponent of Radical Reconstruction until his death in 1875. Ashe, *Cyclopedia of Eminent and Representative Men,* 2:161–63; Crabtree, *North Carolina Governors,* 84–85.

8. Thomas Bragg, a lawyer and a Democrat, served as governor of North Carolina and as a United States senator. He became the attorney general for the Confederate States of America in 1862, serving until 1863. Ashe, *Cyclopedia of Eminent and Representative Men,* 2:115–16.

9. Charles Manly served as North Carolina's last Whig governor from 1849 to 1851. Ashe, *Biographical History,* 6:349–56.

10. Weldon Nathaniel Edwards—Democrat, lawyer, and secessionist—served in the state's House of Commons. He succeeded Nathaniel Macon as a United States congressman and served for eleven years. He continued his political career as a state senator and was speaker of the state's Senate. He was a delegate to the

Constitutional Convention in 1835 and the Secession Convention in 1861. Johnston and Mobley, *Vance Papers,* 1:195.

11. George E. Badger, who died in 1866, was a prominent Whig attorney who served as a superior court judge in the state, as secretary of the navy under President William Harrison, and as a United States senator. He retired in 1855 and returned to Raleigh to practice law. *Who Was Who in America,* 34.

12. John Motley Morehead was a major promoter of internal improvements in the state. An attorney, he served as a Whig in the state legislature, in the 1835 Constitutional Convention, and as governor from 1841 to 1845. He served as a delegate to the Confederate Provisional Congress from 1861 to 1862. Powell, *DNCB,* 2:321–22.

❧

*Barden Collection*
*John R. Thompson to Mary Bayard Clarke*

17 Lafayette Place:
New York City—
21 May 1868.

*Confidential*
Dear Madam,

Judge Requier[1] has been kind enough to send me your letter of the 15th. addressed to his care.

You would have done wrong if you had hesitated about writing to me, or supposed that I could feel indifferent to your literary success. My only annoyance in receiving your letter is that I can really do so little to assist you. I am myself without regular employment, living as a Bohemian, without influence, coldly treated by publishers and editors, and earning a most precarious subsistence by hap-hazard correspondence. This I say *entre nous* and simply to explain my inability to render you any substantial aid. And now for practical suggestions.

1. A. F. Crutchfield,[2] formerly editor and proprietor of the Petersburg Express, is about to start a literary weekly paper in Richmond. I have grave doubts as to its success, but he is a man of uncommon energy and may carry it through. More than this, I believe him to be a man of strict integrity. Whatever he promises he will perform. To lose no time, I have written to him, advising him to negotiate with you for a serial story to run through several months of the paper. I have hinted to him that he must expect to pay for it at the rate of $5 a column upon receipt of the Ms. If he *does* write to you, and you are willing to try it, you might make a definite bargain for a certain specific sum for the *use* of your story, reserving to yourself the right of publishing afterwards in book form.

2. The volume of poems. Banish the thought at once and forever from your mind, as holding out any promise of pecuniary return. No poetry pays expenses, but Longfellow's, Titcomb's (trash) and, perhaps, Saxe's. Send all your unpublished poems (retaining copies of them) as soon as possible to the magazines that pay—Lippincott's, Harper's, Galaxy, Northern Monthly, Putnam's, Peterson's, etc. etc.[3] If one declines, try another. You might even send to the Atlantic Monthly, with a private note to the Editors explaining your friendly relations with Major Winthrop. Do not speak of me in writing to them, as they hold me in great disfavour.

3. Have nothing more to do with papers like the Sou. Home Journal, The Leader, and the like. A more beggarly, disreputable lot I never had to deal with. These are the starvelings who bring Southern literature into contempt. But if you are inclined to try the stately style of the Quarterly Review, it would be worth while to submit something to Professor Bledsoe's work in Balt.[4]

4. If you could contrive to please [Robert] Bonner of the N. Y. Ledger (you smile at this) it would be a fortunate Coup. He likes material adapted to the most ordinary comprehension, but he pays very liberally.

You will excuse, I am sure, the freedom with which I have written to you, my sole object being your advantage. Deeply regretting the necessity which impels you to look to literature for support and with my best wishes for your success, I am

Yours most truly,
Jno. R. Thompson.
Mrs. M.B. Clarke.

1. Augustus Julian Requier of Charleston, South Carolina, published plays and poems, practiced law, and served as district attorney for the Confederacy. *Who Was Who in America,* 438.

2. A. E. Crutchfield was editor of the *Petersburg Express* during the war. He started *Literary Pastimes* in Richmond, and Mary Bayard Clarke contributed several articles to it. Edgar E. Folk and Bynum Shaw, *W.W. Holden, A Political Biography* (Winston-Salem, N.C.: John F. Blair, 1982), 144.

3. Clarke went on to publish a variety of items in several of these papers, including poetry, book reviews, and prose articles. She was paid for some of her work, but at times the payment consisted of the books she was reviewing.

4. Albert Taylor Bledsoe, a lawyer, journalist, educator, and Methodist minister, edited the *Southern Review* (Baltimore) from 1867 to 1879 and ran a school in Baltimore that the Clarkes' daughter later attended. *Who Was Who in America,* 60; Frank L. Mott, *A History of American Magazines 1865–1885,* vol. 3 (Cambridge, Mass.: Harvard University Press, 1938), 382–83 (hereafter cited as Mott, *American Magazines*).

❧

THIS POEM APPEARED IN *The Land We Love* 5, no. 2 (June 1868): 117. According to Willie Clarke, it was his mother's personal favorite of all her poems, and its images reflect her life. The happiness found in her poems from the 1850s had withered into "Nothing but ashes and dust." Winchester Hall, *MBC Poems,* 148–51. She republished the poem in the *Signal* (Raleigh) on February 11, 1880.

## Under the Lava

Far down in the depths of my spirit,
Out of the sight of man,
Lies a buried Herculaneum,
Whose secrets none may scan.

No warning cloud of sorrow
Casts its shadow o'er my way,
No drifting shower of ashes
Made of life a Pompeii.

But a sudden tide of anguish
Like molten lava rolled,
And hardened, hardened, hardened,
As its burning waves grew cold.

Beneath it youth was buried,
And love, and hope, and trust,
And life unto me seemed nothing—
Nothing but ashes and dust.

Oh! it was glorious! glorious!
That Past, with its passionate glow,
Its beautiful painted frescoes,
Its statues white as snow.

When I tasted Love's ambrosia,
As it melted in a kiss,
When I drank the wine of friendship,
And believed in earthly bliss;

When I breathed the rose's perfume,
　With lilies wreathed my hair,
And moved to liquid music
　As it floated on the air—

To me it was real—real,
　That passionate, blissful joy
Which grief may incrust with lava,
　But death alone can destroy.

'Twas a life all bright and golden,
　Bright with the light of love;
A Past still living, though buried
　With another life above—

Another life built o'er it,
　With other love and friends,
Which my spirit often leaveth,
　And into the past descends.

Though buried deep in ashes
　Of burnt-out hope it lies,
Under the hardened lava,
　From which it ne'er can rise,

It is no ruined city—
　No city of the dead—
When in the midnight watches
　Its silent streets I tread.

To me it changeth never;
　Buried in all its prime,
Not fading, fading, fading,
　Under the touch of time.

The beautiful frescoes painted
　By fancy still are there,
With glowing tints unchanging
　Till brought to upper air.

And many a graceful statue,
In marble white as snow,
Stands fair and all unbroken
In that silent "long ago."

It is not dead, but living,
My glorious buried Past!
With its life of passionate beauty,
Its joy too bright to last!

But living under the lava—
For the pictures fade away,
And the statues crumble, crumble,
When brought to the light of day;

And like to dead-sea apples
Is love's ambrosia now,
And the lilies wither, wither,
If I place them on my brow.

And so I keep them ever
Far down in the depths of my heart,
Under the lava and ashes,
Things from my life apart.

The Clarkes' financial problems multiplied during 1868, when Frank Clarke incurred several debts while working for the North Carolina Railroad Company and helping his brother with a store in Selma. The railroad company suspected Clarke of misusing company funds. Josiah Turner, president of the railroad company and a political foe of William Clarke, approached Clarke in June to tell him Frank was behind $1,000 in his accounts. Clarke, horrified by this "Sickening, maddening thought," worked with Frank and Turner to salvage the family's precarious finances. On 24 June Clarke received the "crushing intelligence that poor Frank has been dismissed from his position on the Railroad."

The Clarkes lost the Selma property to settle the railroad debt, and finances tightened. Mary Bayard Clarke again turned to her writing and editing to earn additional income. She wrote to Winchester Hall in 1868 that, "I am busy editing my paper, the *Literary Pastime;* corresponding with two others; contributing to two magazines; and translating a French novel; added to which I am composing the libretto for an opera, and writing Sunday-school hymns at five dollars apiece."[1]

Republican friends helped the Clarkes as well. Mary Bayard Clarke worked as a secretary to one of the state supreme court justices. Governor William W. Holden wrote to William Clarke on 2 November 1868, to offer him a judgeship on the superior court when August S. Seymour resigned.[2] The Raleigh *Standard* announced the appointment on 11 November 1868.

Frank Clarke moved to New York and eventually taught school with Oliver Dudley Cooke at the New York Institution for the Deaf. Clarke taught in this profession for more than forty-three years and became a leader in the development of teaching techniques for the deaf. He also earned a master's degree in civil engineering from Columbia University and married Cecelia Laura Ransom, a teacher at the New York school for the deaf, on 24 September 1873. Together, they moved to Little Rock, Arkansas, where Frank became head of the Arkansas Institute for the Deaf in 1875. After seven years there, they moved to Cecelia's home state of Michigan and Frank assumed control of the Michigan School for the Deaf.

*Wootten, Moulton, Clarke Papers, SHC*
*William J. Clarke to Mary Bayard Clarke (probably in Raleigh)*

New Berne[3] July 17th. 1868.

My Darling:

With a candle flaring so badly that I can hardly see, and the weather so awfully hot that I cannot exclude the air, I sit down to write you a few lines to let you know that I am quite well, and that I send you by Express the wine, and that the whiskey will come when I can get it.—Every thing down here is as stagnant as the dead sea, and will be for the next six weeks, It seems like a month since I saw you, and when I was with you I was so little myself that it does not seem like a reality—It is doubly unfortunate at this time that I am not busily engaged, that my mind was not occupied with other than sad thoughts.

I can't hear from Texas though I have written again and again. I go to the Post Office every evening only to be disappointed—I can't hear from Bates tho' Sadler, whom I saw on Sunday last, says that I shall have the information I desired and which was promised six weeks ago—I sent Frank some goods he ordered and have just rec'd a letter from him informing me that they had been received, and one of the best letters he ever wrote to me. He seems desirous of taking up some studies and inquires for 1st. vol. Paley and Watts on the Mind.

When do you send Pet to Dr. Smeedes?[4] And when do you go to Kittrel's? Give my love to the wench and tell Tom I am so lonely without him that I wish he had not come down, and that the boys are enquiring about him every time they meet me.—Mrs. Moore and Sophy[5] were greatly surprised that you did not receive their letters and Mr. M. says he knows they wrote.

My Masonic Address[6] was a great hit, and if you had seen the great gratification of a young countryman, on receiving a copy which he applied for, you would have been convinced that there was sincerity in their admiration. I send you an extract from Quarterly Review for your edification. I wish I had a thousand dollars to send you

Affectionately yours
William J. Clarke

1. Hall, *MBC Poems,* xix.

2. William W. Holden to William J. Clarke, 2 November 1868, Clarke Papers, SHC.

3. William J. Clarke practiced law in New Bern in Craven County, which became a popular place of residence for several leading Republicans in the state. Perhaps Clarke found their companionship preferable to the animosity he faced from old friends and family in Raleigh. In fall of that year, he became a trustee of the New Bern Academy.

4. St. Mary's Academy in Raleigh.

5. Sophie Moore was the daughter of William P. and Mary Ann Jones Moore, a farmer and distiller. 1870 Craven County Census Index: 109, 4th Ward, no. 2; Elizabeth Moore Collection no. 322.34, Manuscript Collections, J. Y. Joyner Library, East Carolina University, Greenville, N.C.

6. According to William Clarke's 1868 pocket diary, he began work on his Masonic address on June 8 and delivered it on 24 June at a Masonic parade in New Bern. Although he felt at that time that he "failed greatly in delivery," on 26 June Charles C. Clarke of St. John's Lodge, No. 3, wrote Clarke to thank him "for the instructive and eloquent address you delivered on the anniversary of St. John the Baptist; and to request a copy for publication in the papers of the city." Clarke Papers, SHC.

❧

*Barden Collection*
*Sophia Devereux Turner to William J. Clarke*

Hillsboro [July 1868]

My dear Brother,

For dear you will always be to me in spite of political tenets I hear you are a Radical in other & in plain terms a Scalawag

I have refused to believe it! And I determined to ask you whether with the noble & high strung wife you have and the Daughter whom I know So well you love better than life its-self. You are determined to make them the sufferers for what I will only believe is a political freak. Can You bear to think Your Darling Daughter shall be cut off in school from the only associates that she is born to mingle with? cut off too by the epithet "*Scalawags Daughter.*"[1] Oh Brother I know you dont agree with them & now the abominable outrageous article "*Work*"[2] must give you cause sufficient & excuse for coming out from their midst You are a gentleman in the fullest sense of the term—Think of your lovely Daughter in the arms of such a wretch as Rodman Jones. Sherard & Jenkins if you are one of them you give your consent to their throwing their arms around that Pearless wife and Darling Daughter and consent to conduct that even Shameless as they are they only publish in a Dash_____. Do not feel angry with me I feel ever grateful for the welcome your fireside gave me in my chilled & unhappy girlhood.

Do let us, in our poverty and down trodden condition, Do let us cling together of course I am too ignorant of Politics to attempt to influence You politically—but—all I ask is you should spare the Poor little Daughter the bitter Suffering she is daily undergoing

Give her back the feeling which no scalawag's Daughter can feel that her father is her pride & her joy & that it is his pride & joy to do nothing which disgraces her. Do no be angry but believe me I am your true friend &

Sister Sophia

1. Sophia Turner's prediction turned out to be true. Mary Devereux Clarke, enrolled in St. Mary's School for Young Ladies in Raleigh, found that some of her cousins and friends would no longer speak to her. In a letter dated only "St Marys 1st," but written in 1868, Mary wrote her brother Willie that, "We have 68 scholars now and some of the ugliest and worst girles that it was ever my fate to meet with. I did not know how bad girles could be till I came up here. One of the accomplishment that I have acquired is to [be] the most acomplished in that line." Wootten, Moulton, Clarke Papers, SHC.

2. The *Standard* (Raleigh), a Republican newspaper, published an editorial titled "Work" that encouraged scalawags and carpetbaggers to approach southern women and "don't hesitate to throw your arms around their necks now and then, when their husbands are not around, and give them a good——." The article infuriated many readers, and there were threats made against the newspaper's proprietor, who quit the paper. Hamilton, *Reconstruction in North Carolina*, 369–70.

*William J. Clarke Papers, SHC*
*Mary Bayard Clarke to William J. Clarke*

Raleigh July 21st [1868]

My Dear William

I received your letter last night and have just put up the names to send Mr Crutchfield—with a sketch of Governor Vance[1] which Judge Osborn[2] says is Capital, Vance never sent me any material so I picked up what I could find from the members—and Mrs. Spencer's book, for Crutchfield had advertised it and *something* was necessary——; I suppose he will send you some more prospectus I have distributed all but a few. Please find out what I ought to pay for the postage of Mss——, they make me pay here full letter postage but what comes to me is open at the ends and only charged newspaper rates, they say at the office that it is only *book* Mss that can go for newspaper postage

Mrs. Margaret Preston has sent me her poem of Beachenbrook[3] it is smooth and sweet, but has little or no force in it. I suppose the first No of the Pastime will be out by the first of August. I hope Mr Williams will invite me before long to honor his house with a visit so that I can see you, but I really dont care to spend money going about, Judge Jay Bird[4] is to get me a free ticket on the NC, and I think I ought to have one on the Atlantic Is Whitford[5] still in place?

Coleman and Jenkins[6] have taken the bit in their teeth and are both resolved to have clerks of their own choice Independent of politics, Coleman means to have *me* if he can accomplish it, and I think I can get Willie a place in his office also, Jenkins says he gave the treasurer's bond *not* the party, and he is treasurer of NC and means to have the best clerk to be had, and not undertake to run his office with raw hands and no heads——, so he keeps Bain[7] still with the proviso that *when* his *son* a boy of eighteen or nineteen—*can* take his place he is to give it up which as Judge Osborne says wont be in four years——. Coleman says he has not mentioned my name but only said he means to inaugurate the system of female clerks but the leaders all pitched into him at once and said I had Judge Reade[8] crazy on that subject and *he* had caught the infection I told Coleman if I could be the means of opening such a field of labor for our women I would be only too happy to do it, that my position was such that I could take the initiative and people who at first would say that it was a piece of my excentricity and independance would in a few weeks be seeking places

Judge Jones[9] is also for it and says hundreds of thousands are saved by having female clerks in Washington. Coleman says I can be his clerk and librarian too, if I can it will help the income very much and keep the children at school. Judge Reade has great influence and will help you get any place you wish to have, is there any that you could take that would not interfere with your practise?

Pet *pretends* she dont like Dr Smeedes but I see she does and will soon admit it, she came home on friday and returned Sunday afternoon The music alone will keep her there.

Yours Affectionatly

Mary

I believe I wrote of the safe arrival of the wine—did I not? thank you for it—

1. Mary Bayard Clarke published "The Hon. Z. B. Vance" in *Literary Pastimes.*

2. James Walker Osborne—lawyer, jurist, and politician—was a Whig before the Civil War and served on the state's superior court from 1859 until 1866. Thereafter, he represented Mecklenburg County in the state senate. Ashe, *Cyclopedia of Eminent and Representative Men,* 2:201–2.

3. Margaret Junkin Preston was a prominent author whose book of poetry *Beechenbrook, a Rhyme of the War* appeared in 1865. *Who Was Who in America,* 424.

4. This was Mary Bayard Clarke's nickname for superior court judge Albion W. Tourgee, one of the leading carpetbaggers in the state.

5. Colonel John Dalton Whitford and his family were neighbors of the Clarke family in New Bern. Whitford had served as New Bern's mayor, as a state legislator, in the Confederate army, and was cofounder of the successful shipping and commission merchant firm of Whitford, Dill, and Company. Powell, *DNCB,* 6:187–88.

6. Republican William Macon Coleman was elected state attorney general in the April 1868 election. David A. Jenkins, a noted scalawag, served as state treasurer from 1868 to 1876. Lancaster, "Scalawags of North Carolina," 296, 297.

7. Donald W. Bain had served as chief clerk to the state treasurer. William Woods Holden, *Memoirs of W. W. Holden* (Durham, N.C.: The Seeman Printery, 1911), 48 (hereafter cited as Holden, *Memoirs*).

8. Mary Bayard Clarke became supreme court Judge Edwin G. Reade's clerk or secretary. Reade roomed with Frances Miller when the court was in session and came into frequent contact with Mary Bayard Clarke. He deeply admired her and her literary abilities. He sought to have her hired as the state's first woman librarian with the court. Clarke's sister and other Raleigh associates were appalled by these developments, and the uproar eventually forced Clarke to withdraw her name from consideration for the post. It also led to a long-standing breach with Miller and other relatives.

9. Superior court justice Edmund W. Jones of the state's second district.

EDWIN G. READE PROVED a catalyst in Mary Bayard and William Clarke's lives during Reconstruction. Reade, born in Person County in 1812, had worked hard after his father's death to support his family and to receive an education. He read law from books he borrowed from another lawyer and was admitted to the bar in 1835. A Whig for many years, he became a highly respected lawyer and jurist. He served briefly in the United States Congress but disliked politics and opposed secession.[1]

Late in the war, Reade served in the Confederate congress and on the state's superior court. While in the Confederate congress, he opposed many of Jefferson Davis's policies and advocated peace with the North, which cost him his congressional seat when he ran for reelection. Nevertheless, his views on the Union and the need to seek readmission shaped his actions as North Carolina adjusted to defeat and reunion.

In 1865 Reade was a member of the constitutional convention and was elected to the state's supreme court, serving until 1879. Conservatives and Republicans respected him, although his strong support for Reconstruction earned him enemies. When he stayed in Raleigh during court sessions, he frequently boarded with Frances Miller. There he met Mary Bayard Clarke and quickly developed an interest in a woman he described as *"the most gifted poet in the state."* He explained his political philosophy to her by saying, "I am opposed to all that is radical in the Republican & Conservative parties;—& there is much that is radical in both." Writing on 20 July 1868, he asserted that his "devotion to my country, my government, my home, was with me a *passion.*" He tartly added, "because I speak of my country, my home, my Government & its flag, in terms of endearment, those who are simple suppose that I mean them for party. One of the Raleigh papers, especially, has been fed on spoiled beef & whisky until you may smell it across the street, & it is almost as malignant as it is imbecile. . . . I am sure, my just & generous friend, that *you* will not misunderstand me."[2]

Reade continued to court his newfound friend over the succeeding years. He hired Mary Bayard Clarke as his secretary, he successfully promoted the appointment of her husband as a judge, and he loaned money to the Clarkes for the purchase of a home in New Bern.

Did Reade fall in love with Mary Bayard Clarke? He definitely felt a keen affinity for her company and freely acknowledged his sentimental feelings for her. Frances Miller and others in the family questioned the propriety of the relationship. Reade's wife, Emily Moore Reade, by his own admission, became curious enough about "Mrs. Clarke" to question him about her in the middle of the night. Reade and Clarke visited Washington, D.C., at the same time, and Reade took great delight in guiding Mary Bayard Clarke through the capital. Still, there is no indication that the relationship developed into anything beyond friendship. Mary Bayard Clarke, for her part, found it useful to court a respected member of the supreme court who possibly could help her family. Although she expected initial criticism for accepting Reade's offer of a salaried position outside the traditional boundary of home that most southern women of her class preferred, the ferocity of the attack that came from Frances Miller caught her off guard. The allegations Frances made during the heat of Reconstruction battles eventually caused Mary Bayard to write Miller that, "I can no longer believe in the existence of any sisterly affection in your heart." William Clarke, not overly enthusiastic about Reade personally, never questioned his wife's judgment or integrity and bitterly resented the insinuations made against her. The suspicions and hurt fueled by the politics of Reconstruction tore this southern family apart.

*Wootten, Moulton, Clarke Papers, SHC*
*Judge Edwin G. Reade to Mary Bayard Clarke*

Roxboro July 28th 1868
Mrs Mary Bayard Clarke,

My Dear Madam:

I received, on yesterday, your letter of 24th with its enclosure of the poetry on the Swallows. The poetry is very sweet—but more of that some other time.

I approve every sentiment & word in your letter. I do not know whether it does the greater honor to your head, or to your heart. Any one might be proud of having written it. And any one would be gratified at having received it. The thoughts were just, the style elegant, & the language such as

"Virgins might use & Angels hear"

No one of your friends will be more delighted than I, if your literary pastimes shall be appreciated by the public, & shall be an easy & agreeable occupation to yourself; & if your graver labors shall win for you the fame which you so richly deserve: & if both together shall be a source of income & of independence.

It was thoughtless in the gentleman whose name you mention so forbearingly, by a careless word to mortify you, by any allusion to the necessity, which we all feel now, to labor. I am proud that you had the good sense to show, that you consider labor, not as a shame, but as a praise. It is a praise. Who is of any worth without it? Labor, either with the brawn or with the brain, is all that makes the world better for one's having lived in it. Idleness is never creditable, & is innocent only in so far, as it is too lazy to do mischief. He who has only a vicious heart, a nervless arm, or an atomic brain, does best when he does nothing. Let *him* be idle. Let *him* be ashamed of his vicious, drivelling, or slavering displays. But the world has its claim upon virtue, strength & intellect: & it is both a pleasure & a duty for those who have them, to use them,—to labor. I mean it not as fulsome, but as just praise, to say, that you are blessed with these beyond the common lot. Be proud of them. Use them. And every one whose good opinion you ought to prize, will put his hands under you & raise you up. And any one who would bear you down, will be beneath your contempt. I would not exchange the satisfaction of knowing, that by industry & virtue—labor—& by these only, I have attained to any little honor or position which I enjoy, for much greater honor or position, which fortuitous circumstances might have cast upon me. Mrs. Genl. Lee in her letter to you, & of which I am as proud as you are, says: "I am sure I had rather make my living by my pen than by any other means." That was spoken like a woman. What would the sneers of a million of struts & blockheads weigh against that! Mrs Lee is a queen among women, & so is Mrs Clarke. And I am glad that they are friends of each other.

Did I ever tell you that I am fonder of the society of ladies than of gentlemen? This I say not in gallantry but in truth. Men chew & spit, drink & gamble, fight & gouge, swear & swagger; & I do not practice any of these. I do not deny that they are very considerable accomplishments & it may be that, because I do n[ot] possess them, I feel some embarrassment in the presence of those who do. I will not say that they are decidedly repulsive; but—& this is an anomaly because of the negative qualities which I possess; they are not strongly attractive. The ladies have none of these accomplishments; but they have what are nearly as good, decency & gentleness. And these so molify my own stern nature, that I feel the necessity of their influence. And in Mrs Clarke above all others, I have found so much of refinement without effeminacy, strength without coarseness, friendship without treachery, & piety without cant that I esteem my friendly relations with her, the most pleasurable & profitable, that I have ever formed. And it shall be my constant care that nothing shall ever disturb them.

Most respectfully & affectionately

E. G. Reade

1. Ashe, *Cyclopedia of Eminent and Representative Men,* 2:58–60; Powell, *DNCB,* 5:184.

2. Edwin G. Reade to Mary Bayard Clarke, 20 July 1868, Clarke Papers, SHC.

THE REPUBLICAN STATE CONVENTION was held in Raleigh on 16 September 1868. The party endorsed Ulysses S. Grant and the Republican platform. North Carolina Conservatives had met in August and endorsed Democratic nominees Horatio Seymour and Francis P. Blair. The ensuing election campaign further aggravated political passions, and many Democrats left the Conservative party because they distrusted its leadership. Edwin G. Reade joined the Republicans at this time, as did former Confederate General Rufus Barringer. William Clarke also joined the migration. He wrote in his pocket diary on 2 September, "The prosecution is hot, the pressure great, but I pray for strength and wisdom to bear it and stand up valliantly for the right." He attended the district Republican convention and delivered a speech on 8 September, and he attended the state convention in Raleigh and dined with its leaders at Governor Holden's official residence. An article in the *Weekly Standard* (Raleigh) described Clarke's 8 September speech and his reasons for joining the Republicans. Noting that it had been a slow and painful process for Clarke "because in coming to this conclusion he would be forced to sever ties that were dear to him, and perhaps give pain to those whom he had always loved and honored," the article added that Clarke "could not have been treated worse had he become a Turk and donned the Turban. But he had not acted rashly—it was because he loved his country better than party, that he was found to-day in favor of the election of Grant and Colfax." The article stressed Clarke's Confederate war record, his belief that "no true soldier fires a shot after he has surrendered," and his assertion that the Conservatives had raised "the cry of white man's party . . . because they wanted to keep the colored man in slavery."

*Barden Collection*
*Frances Miller to William J. Clarke*

Sept 6th 1868

Dear Brother

Will you let me use the privelege of more years to give you a little advice also the well known fact that lookers on see more than players & being rather behind the scenes I learn more from Radicals than is generally thot From all these I learn that you will be doing a very unwise thing not to come up to the Conv on the 16th[1] If you do not you may lose all the advantages you may gain from them & as by your speech last week you have openly taken their side the Dem will not thinke you less a Rad I have no idea than any thing of this kind influences you doubtless it is some other engagement but; pray put all else aside, In the long run nothing you can have to do, is as important as giving the Rads this proof of your sincerity & depriving some of their party of the handle to use against you which they most assuredly will be glad to have The constant remarks of the most prominent ones are "we will not permit any shirking a man must show us & the world that he considers himself one of us politically & socialy" If you dont, they will use your name & influence & never pay & tho I would not for a breath thinke or imply you did it *for* pay; yet you ought to take the place you are entitled to So please think no Court or business is as important & come I shall be very much disappointed if you do not & besides a word for myself I want you to help fill my house my expense are heavy & I have nothing coming in & depend on those two days to carry me thro a month Daughter Mai[2] too, will be much disappointed she has just come to be kissed before going to Church & says "Tell Father *please please please* come I have looked forward to it so long & now Mother aint here[3] he must not let that disappoint me & give him this report & ask him please send it to Mother & tell her to send it to F & W" I give her words But I must not forget another matter I began my letter for Marys bill to Sept 3rd is one hundred & twenty five dollars ($125) & I must have that sum to pay for my coal by the 20th or I shall have to borrow at heavy interest so please try & send it at least by the 25th if indeed you wont come but I do hope you *will,* & stop the predictions of those who say "old associations will be too strong for him" & making my words good when I say "Bro never did any thing he was ashamed of & he will come if he can & tell the Gov I say so" Mr Browne says Mai grows prettier between every Friday

your loving Sister

1. Lancaster, "Scalawags of North Carolina," 327, 329, 332–33; Clarke Diary, 2, 8, 16 September 1868, SHC; *Weekly Standard* (Raleigh), 9 Sept. 1868.

2. A nickname for Mary Devereux Clarke.

3. Mary Bayard Clarke was in Baltimore to promote *Literary Pastimes* and to do research for articles. She stayed with her sister, Betsy Jones.

∂

*Barden Collection*
*Judge E. G. Reade to Mary Bayard Clarke*

Roxboro Sept. 7th 1868

Mrs Clarke:

I have been wanting to write to you for some time, but I am too nervous to shoot on the wing, & I have been waiting for you to light. I infer from your last letter, that I may fire at Baltimore, with some chance of winging my bird.

No: I do not think you "weak" for being mortified at the bad treatment of those you thought your friends, on account of your supposed politics. I never thought you weak about any thing, & it is a weakness to be indiferent to the opinion of others. I do not doubt, that the unreasonable prejudice will wear away of itself. And I think it fortunate, that you can be absent until the storm blows over. It is often wiser to bow like the fragile reed,—I did not say Reade—than to stand erect like the sturdy oak, & be uprooted by the storm.

Altho you cannot be indiferent, yet do not allow yourself to be depressed by it. *They* "cut" *you*! Why, bless their dear little cimblin heads & pug noses, what if they do! Is the queen dependant upon her court, or they upon her for recognition? clearly the latter. But still, let the queen be considerate, & seem not to know of their impropriety rather than to punish their impudence. Poor cimblin heads! Umph! Whew!

And you have gone North! Well, I hope you will not be so much on the wing as to be wearied, nor yet suffer yourself to be *eager*. And I hope you will find a thousand friends to make you very hapy. But, I am right sure, you will weary yourself in,—what is so natural & habitual with you,—trying to make every body else hapy, to the entire negation of yourself. knowing this, I am selfish—not to say cruel enough, to ask, for myself, a share of your profusion. Business will take me to Washington City about 1st October, probably a few days sooner or later, & will detain me there some week or two. It will be a leisurely business, not occupying so much of my time that I cannot be reasonably gallant. And it will be such business as my secretary can aid me in. Now then, after you have well drank of that which is worse, elsewhere, will you not come to the fountain—the Capitol —& drink of that which is better? or, after having given others the brim, will you not come & give Washington the dregs—there are no dregs— of the pleasure of your society? You shall have the freedom of the City, in the sense that you may share my crusts as long as you may choose to sit with me at table. I will show you all that is to be seen.—The most magnificent Capitol in the world, with its splendid marble halls & mirrored walls; its speaking statuary—Discovery, The Savage, Civilization, War, Peace, Youth, Education—Progress, Art,—Agriculture, Liberty— Hancock, Washington, Jackson; its gorgeous paintings—The Embarcation The Landing, The Surrender at Yorktown; its large select & elegant Library. Then the Patent Office with its world of the curious & useful. Then the Navy Yard & Armory, with their grim faces & giant arms. Then the Treasury with its full vaults, & you may actually put you hand—ough! upon 100 000 000 of gold, & upon 1000,000,000 of currency! Oh me! fix you some side pockets, And then I will point you to the clear warm sun, & turn your face to the fresh pure air, & direct your eyes to the broad rich land. And then with pride I will whisper to you, *this* is my "Home" of which I have sometimes spoken. And my gifted poetess Tenella, & my patriotic Chevaliere Bayard, will be less appreciative than is her want, if she do not respond, It is my Home too. And then, on the rich sofa of the Parlor of your inn, you may prattle as much as you please. And when you are weary you may retire & dream that you can be hapy in spite of the sickly hate of Ignorance, & that you can make others hapy, as well.

Will you come to the Capitol?—to our "Home"? Come. Do come, Please come.

But whether you come or not I shall always be most respectfully & affectionately your friend.

E. G. Reade

❧

*Barden Collection*
*Mary Bayard Clarke to Willie Clarke*

Washington City Oct 11th [1868]

My Darling Willie

Your letter of the 2d has just been forwarded from New York. I am glad you have at least $20 certain and shall try all in my power to get you away from Selma. I have suceeded in getting Frank a good openning and now I am going to turn all my energies for you. I went yesterday to see the President [Andrew Johnson] to get permission to copy Governor Vance's letter book—but you must not tell any body what I went for. Col Wheeler[1] told me I could not succeed but I told him to let me do the talking and I would, we had to wait an hour with some twenty or thirty others in an antechamber and Col Wheeler kept telling me loud enough for every body to hear that I would fail, at last I sat down and drew up a petition and told him to hand that to the President to endorse if, as he said, I would have to go to the war office At last we got in and you would have laughed to have heard me talk, I only staid ten minutes and though he said positively at first that he could not, it ended in his endorsing my petition in the strongest manner, telling me he was proud of me as a North Carolinian, giving me an immense bouquet and himself escorting me to the door and handing me out to the amazement of the outsiders. It was funny to see the surprised looks as I passed with my petition in a great official envelope endorsed "War Office" in one hand and my bouquet in the other and Col Wheeler laughing and saying "let a woman alone for doing it up brown when she starts" Every body turned round and looked at me and the fact that the President had given me a bouquet and walked to the door with me stamped me as somebody at once. We then went to the War Office but old [John M.] Schofield was hateful, and I flourished my bouquet and said President Johnson had given it to me and wished me success —and talked again till I got permission to come back on Monday and if there is nothing objectionable in what I wished to copy I am to be allowed under the supervision of an officer to copy it Meanwhile I have a letter from Gen [George] Stoneman to Schofield and I am going to make him either let me take the book to Baltimore or give me a free pass over the road for ten days—so that I can come over every morning and return every evening—to Sister Betsey's

I am very tired and want to see you all dreadfully but I shant come back till after the election for it is better I should not you must send this letter to father I wrote him the other day but he will like to hear how I got along with the President. Tell him I had my usual luck was taken for a dashing young widow and the President even asked me how old I was—and said he did not believe I had two grown sons. I went the other night to see

"Uncle Tom's Cabin" acted, and laughed till I was afraid I would be mobbed it was worse than a burlesque for the negroes all talked broad Yankee and Topsey said "hadnt oughter" I dont go out at night much it is bad for me if it is chilly for my throat is very troublesome but the houses here are so much better built than ours that I dont feel the cold as I do at home I have not sat by a fire yet nor felt the need of one even to dress by— and in Carolina I know I should have suffered for one by this time—Write to me and direct to Baltimore care of Wm. T. Jones 219 W Baltimore St and believe me

Your Loving<br>Mother

If Frank has not left tell him to hurry up and get here soon—for I shall leave on thursday

1. John Hill Wheeler was a historian, diplomat, and lawyer. He served as state treasurer, in the state House of Commons, and as United States minister to Nicaragua. He had several books published on historical subjects. *Who Was Who in America*, 573.

*Wootten, Moulton, Clarke Papers, SHC*
*Mary Bayard Clarke to Willie Clarke*

Baltimore Oct 21st [1868]

My Dearest Willie

I received your letter to night and was very glad to get it, I cant tell you darling how much I dislike to have you left alone at Selma and how anxious I am to get you away from there I think I can accomplish it by the 1st of January if not before, and I am glad you feel about it as you do. I know Sunday is a long day and if you could only come to me that day I would be so glad; for I feel the want of you my boy as much as you do of me and I shall never rest till we are together again; I think I have done something by coming away from Carolina and I hope to do more yet.[1] I shall be at home soon and come and see you. I got a letter from Frank to night which I enclose but you must say nothing about it except to Father for I dont wish it known he has gone till it is settled he will stay. I have not been out at all here for I have been quite unwell ever since I came, I took tea at Mr Mayers last night and enjoyed it very much, but I dont think I will go there to stay, I am not well enough. I went to see two editors yesterday and got some work—from them, as usual they took me for a gay widow, and thought I was very pretty Capt Lewis' son was in the office and told what they said after we went out. I have a book for you, it is the second edition of Miss Mason's poems of the war presented to me by the Publisher it has the Rebel Sock in it and I said as soon as I got it that you should have it. I shall go to Richmond next week or the last of this I am not sure which and then home; write to me next sunday and mail to the Care of Mr Crutchfield Box 129—Richmond—and tell me if I can stay all night in Selma, I dont know yet whether I shall go to New Berne or Raleigh first. Aunt Betty and Cousin Rachel both send love to you and say they wish they could see you Cousin Frank's wife is very pretty but she is not well now—has been in bed for two or three days; Give my love to Dash and tell him to be a good dog. I shall have a great deal to tell you when I come home, I hope you get the Pastime and read my letters in that. Good night my darling boy—if I can only get you comfortably fixed I shall be so happy and I am trying to accomplish it

Your loving<br>Mother

PS—Send F's letter to father when you have read it

1. One of Clarke's errands in Baltimore involved finding a school for her daughter Mary, whose unhappiness at St. Mary's became acute after William Clarke joined the Republicans. The Clarkes investigated a Baltimore school run by Albert Taylor Bledsoe, an editor familiar with Mary Bayard Clarke's work. He wrote Mary Bayard Clarke late in 1868, assuring her there was an opening at his school starting in January 1869. He reduced the tuition from $500 to $400 for the Clarkes, but he urged her to "say nothing about this; as others pay five hundred, as all except yourself & one other personal friend pay 500." A. T. B. to Mary Bayard Clarke, 30 December 1868, Barden Collection.

*Wootten, Moulton, Clarke Papers, SHC*
*Mary Bayard Clarke to Willie Clarke*

New Berne Wednesday<br>[ca. November 1868]

My Dear Willie

I got here safely and found father waiting for me at the depot, he is well and so is Tom and I hope we will soon be settled. I have been very busy since I came and have rented half of a house near Mrs Carroway's[1] and will board with her. I have a parlor—, two good bed rooms and one attic room so you can come and see me when you like and find a room if you will send me furniture for it, I want you to get all my sheets pillow cases towels etc *that you dont want to use* and all my mattresses and pillows and bolsters, my tea kettle that dont belong to the store, my old dominia [?] coffee pot my tea pot (if I have one)—and every thing you dont want to use and pack them up to send to me *Dont send anything you want to keep yourself* I want my sofa but you had better not send the chairs until the 1st of January as I can get along without them. Write to me and let me know what there is, if I remember right there are two bed-steads with mattress and pillows Dont send till I write you, only get them together see what there are and let me know. Is my rag-carpet there and is the carpet that used to be on the parlor floor at Keoco still in existence I may put that on one bed room floor. I think I will stop over one train with you and go on to Raleigh on the freight next morning then I can see what I want. I shall take tea at my rooms—and need cups saucers plates and knives, and my waiter but I wont take anything that you need—You had better send down any books you dont wish to keep as they will be safer here. Father has— thirteen scholars—already, he gets $1200—no matter if he has none at all, and then so much more for every scholar.[2] Tom goes to him and seems to like it, his vacation will be July August and September so I can have him out of the sickly country in these months. Would you like to go to West Point,? you know you need not remain in the Army and you will get pay all the time you are there—I think I could get you appointed to enter next June—as Perrin Busbee is in the navy[3] I dont see why you should not be in the Army as a cadet. write and tell me what you think of it but dont mention it to any one else—

Your loving Mother

I pay $10- a month for my house $20- for father and myself and $10- for Tom making $50- for board $10- for house rent and $5- for washing—

1. This was probably Mrs. D. T. (Sarah A.) Carraway, listed as a boarding-house keeper in the 1870 census. Eula Pearl Beachamp, comp., and Jo Ann E. Murphy, ed., Index to "1870 Census Craven County North Carolina" (New Bern, N.C.: New Bern–Craven County Regional Library, 1999), 281, 4th township, no. 293 (hereafter cited as 1870 Craven County Census Index).

2. Clarke served as head of the New Bern Academy until 1870, when he resigned to serve as a superior court judge. Powell, *DNCB,* 1:381–82; Mary Ellen Gadski, *The History of the New Bern Academy* (New Bern: Tryon Palace Commission, 1986), 116–17 (hereafter cited as Gadski, *New Bern Academy*).

3. Perrin Busbee, before becoming a cadet at Annapolis, had tried to get an appointment to West Point with the assistance of Governor Jonathan Worth. On 23 April 1866, Worth wrote to B. S. Hedrick in Washington, D.C., explaining

that Busbee came from a worthy Raleigh family, that his mother was a widow, and that Busbee had never served in the Confederate army or navy, being only six-teen years old in 1866. Jonathan Worth Letter Book, January–July 1866, PC49.7: 356–57, North Carolina State Archives, Raleigh, N.C.

*Wootten, Moulton, Clarke Papers, SHC*
*Edwin G. Reade to Mary Bayard Clarke (New Bern)*

Raleig Feb. 1. '69

Dear Mrs Clarke:

Your letter & enclosures came to me this morning. I beleive implic-itly, all that you say, & I sincerely thank you for the warning. I cannot account for the course of the person to whom you allude. If as you say, & as I do not doubt, I have unconsciously been the object of hate & intrigue, & if under such circumstances I have been made to appear wrong, it will at some time, if not now, commend me to the indulgent consideration of one who I know is not an enemy, & to whom I am, & as long as I live will be, a friend.

Your allusion to alleged confidential conversations which I have had with Mrs. M[iller] & to the quotation from my letter to you, as evidence that I had showed it to her, satisfies me that I have been grossly misrepre-sented to you. And it makes it indispensible that I should explain. Until a few days before I wrote that letter, I had not had a word of conversation with Mrs M. except occasionally in a general way, since last summer. For reasons which you know, I had avoided it. A few days before the letter, Mrs. M. applied to us for the Librarianship for Mr. Baker.[1] I sent her word that it was usual to make a formal written application. She said she did not know the form, & I wrote a form for her. It occurred to me that from that she might infer my support, & be disappointed. I went to her parlor & told her, that she must not so infer, & that I would state frankly that I had no reason to beleive Mr. Baker could get it—that we were pledged to Mrs. Clarke. She said she knew you had wanted it, but that she supposed you had abandoned it. I told her that the last I heard from you, you did want it, & that I could vote for no one else. The next sunday morning, she told me at the breakfast table, that she desired to see me before I went to church. I called at her parlor, & she said, that your freinds were outraged at the idea of your appointment, & were determined to leave no means untried to prevent it—that they had requested her to make an appeal to me, & if that failed, to write to her father. Much was said, & with such feeling, that I thought I ought not to disregard it. She said If I did not promise to write to you before I went to church, she would write that day to her father. I asked her to authorize me to write to you to come up, so that we could explain, but she refused. I went to my room & wrote to you the letter, & sent it to Mrs. M. to read & to send to the mail. We had a long conversation in which I labored to remove prejudices which were apparent, & I thought I had succeeded, but I can see how much I was mistaken. Mrs. Clarke, *This is all.* You remember that I told you, that I had had a talk with Mrs. M. & that as soon as I could I would explain, but I did not want to worry you immediately upon your arrival, & I saw so little of you, that I did not explain at all, Please, *please* do not think ill of me about that, or about any thing else. Nothing is left for me but to say that if I have offended in any thing I beg your forgiveness. I never said a word to any human being about you, & never will, except in kindness & praise.

Please let all the past go.

If the explanation in the particular named is satisfactory, or if there is any thing else you would have me explain please say so.

I beg you to beleive that I have not mentioned the matter of the letter to widen the breach which I know exists between you & Mrs M. Indeed my hesitency in mentioning it at all, was to avoid that effect, but I could not have you to suppose, as I inferred from your letter that you did, that I had plotted with any body to your mortification. Please do not speak of it, & I will try in the future to guard against the evils of which I was unconscious.

I uncomplainingly submit to the conclusion of your letter. It is right. I will write to you when I think I can interest you. And whatever may be the circumstances of the future, there is no being in the world outside of my own home, that will have more of my respect, admiration & affection.

E. G. Reade

The last letter from Lizzie sends love to Mrs. Clarke. It is very tender— please accept it with mine.

1. Frances Miller's son-in-law, George Baker.

*William J. Clarke Papers, SHC*
*Samuel Taylor to William J. Clarke*

febury 15 1869 San antonio Texas

Deare William I recived your Letter to day and I Could hardly relize my name on the back of your letter I often thought you had turn me luse in a wile Cuntry and did not Care which end of me went famast and I can tell you that the worst end has taken the lede of both of use tho Deare Sir you are more able to Sture your Boat then I am I am from hand to math Sum times I get a little work and my wife takes in washing and that is all we do I often go out in the Cuntry to work and has to walk back 15 and 20 miles which at this time I has Surch pains in my ankles I hardly Can worlk I often get Letters from mother but not any from you Dr. Cuples was telling me somthing a baught you a yeare a go I has not of you Sence untill this Letter go here by S.Y. Newton

Mr Henry Lewis is here but he hardly know what a Sobber day is he is worse then when went to North he told me he was gorn to hunt up your Books but I think thee Cant be found during the war I had all your law Books car rage dawn the new archnewl by jurge divines in the Care of Mager Mackeen and when the war ended the Canfederate Came back here and urn up side down the went in Stoes and braken every thing the wanted and went out and I think the went down where your Books was and destored them all your furnitur was Sold oxian [auction] I wrote you ward I Cauld not take Care of them So you wrote Thomas Macklen to Sell all and take Charge of me So he lold [sic] all at oxian excepe the fedder Beed and turn post Beed stieed which Thomas Macklen Sold at privet Sale to Old Mrs Adams who Mr jones moved in the house of after Mrs Mary left San antonio I know nathing more of any thing I give my wagers to Mr jones as long as the Stade here which he pade a deat you owed to Sam bady her 15 dollars I lent to jaine and he went to arozino with jenral Sibble [Henry H. Sibley] the I give sam to Thomas Macklen and he dide then I give Som to the old man Macklin and then I keep 300, 50 dollars which I has a baught 300 hundred dollars now in Confederate money the peple talk of putting me in the ware which I had to wark for a little of any thing to keep out Som times I would get 2 1/2 dallars a weeke I worke So hard un till now I Cant See these letters with out Spects

I was Call in the Court hause with Mager Macklen to give account of the railrode Books wich the peple thaught the rail rode Books was with your law Books the Mager told in the Cout house Som body Came to him and got your Books from him by your ordor but he did not know who it was and for I my Self put all your Books in his Charge and now he do not know what had became of them nor me

it is Surch a Sursprizen thing for me to wright to you I am a fred you Cant wrede my hand wright plese remember to Mrs Mary and all the Children I was So glod to her from you

My Deare Sir you do not know what a time I had after you and Mrs Mary left her

I Cant Speel good a nufe to wright as I wish

I has one little Boy by the name Samuel 2 years and a half old I lost a little boy in novmber it lived one day and night and dide

Our winter has bind like the forst winter we moved out her

nothing more hoping to her from you a gain

your Samuel Taylor

I hope you will excue my bad wrightin for you did not give me any Scoaling

*Barden Collection*

*Frances Miller to William J. Clarke*

March 2nd 1869

Dear Brother

I did not answer yours received some time since because I did not know how "to hold out the Olive Branch" I knew I had done nothing but what Mary forced me to, by refusing to act in my house as I had a right to ask her & I could not go back from my resolve that she must not continue doing as she had done. I have said nothing to injure her, in deed nothing on the subject I could avoid, & had she not refused to come to the house, her not staying here would not have been noticed. Mrs Haywood told Nora[1] her only reason for not wishing her was the fear that I would not like it. The remark reported by M Magee turns out to be only, that "I said to Dr H, I was not going to consent to Judge Rs building on my lot" which Dr H told Mr M, Judge R must not think of doing for it would result in injury to Mrs. C In all this I can see nothing but kindness to Mary In passing, I will say, that *His Honor* told me, he did not know what Dr H aluded to, as *he had never thot of proposing to add to or build* Mary may see by this how much he can be depended on

Now my dear Bro I think all this very foolish as far as it is allowed to break up sisterly intercourse. I have borne it quietly till now, because I heard from Mary regularly thru Judge R & occasionly from Mai thru Mr B; but I do not want to live so; & I hope time, has led Mary to better thoughts; as to her excuse that "you would not permit her to come" we all know, & appreciate your kind indulgence to her; & are sure she can have her own way in that as in every thing else

I can not take back any thing as to the facts, & my action, based on those facts, but I see no reason why, now I can receive Mary as a visitor, she should not come. Kate E[dmondston] will soon be here on a visit to Margarette [Devereux] When I know the exact time I will write to her begging her to come, in the mean time do not answer this but think it over

& your answer I can learn in the acceptance or rejection of that invitation. This is but the answer to yours If you consider it, "The Olive branch" I shall be very glad, but if not I am sorry to say it is all I can do toward healing a breach which has cost me much pain I think I have a right to feel as if I was not treated well as regards my darling Mai. Of course you have a perfect right to prevent my intercourse with her; & I have no wish to make the child judge between her parents & I. But Mary told me, she wished me to make no difference, & brot me an *opened* letter which implied I was to answer it. I did, sending her the articles she wrote for, (the letter was put in the box of m[?] in the hat box with some of her books & the Spread) Yet she complains thro Mr B of my neglect & silence. Now I think *that* letter should be given her; & she told that I can not write her; as of course I can not; after my little birthday gift & the few words accompany, were returned & as I do not think it best to send the explanation thro Mr B May I hope you will give her so much of an explanation that she will not feel that her "Old Auntie" who has never treated her otherwise than as an own child had suddenly lost all love for her? Understand I do not ask that she may do, or write *any thing* only be set right in her thoughts

Another thing If you & Mary have heard I said any thing against her you should not have told Mai, at least on the word of a half crazy fool She wrote B that Mr P said this, & this Now he is simply a liar—& his lie bears it on the face No one would have said to him, they could not board Mrs C for any such reason. even if they had, had the reason which they never had, they would have kept it back & given some other excuse—I know they were excuses but they were based on the talk of the men boarding with me last summer & getting out from them

Had Mary done as I begged, staid quietly with you this winter, it would I think have been far best—but that is a matter of opinion & each can keep their own

If you have a right to complain of what you heard *I* said—do you not think I may, of your giving out that I treatted Mary so, because of your change of politics? Now *I* simply said "*I dont believe Bro ever said so*" Please try to think fairly over this & let the result be as it will never fail to beleive that I am & ever will be to you both, a

true & loving Sister

1. Nora Devereux Cannon had left Tennessee by this time to educate her daughters in North Carolina. She stayed with the Edmondstons much of the time before securing a teaching position at St. Mary's in 1872. *Edmondston Diary,* 728, 738.

❧

*Barden Collection*
*William J. Clarke to Frances Miller*
*[This is a copy made by Mary Bayard Clarke of letter sent to Frances Miller]*

New Berne March 27th 1869

My Dear Sister

When I wrote you that the olive branch must be held out by you, I was under the impression that in a moment of anger you had refused to allow my wife to board with you, and had written that letter in which you said she had "abused your hospitality, and you would not be glad to see her in your house if she persisted in going to Raleigh," also adding that you wished your correspondence with her to cease. Hoping and believing that when cool you would see and feel the necessity of apologizing and retracting these harsh expressions I simply wished to let you know that though we felt deeply agrieved still "our thoughts were turned for peace." But as in your letter you justify your conduct and say I am foolish to allow it to make a breach between you and my family, no other course remains for me but to say that I must submit to be regarded by you as foolish—The leniency of my controul over my wife seems to give you offence. I am happy in being able to say that, however self willed you may regard her, that she never disregards a decided wish of mine. I felt compelled to instruct her as to the course she should pursue when she went to Raleigh, and I should have felt aggrieved had she accepted your invitation coupled with the insinuation that she should accept it *for her own sake*. I write these things in sorrow, and not in anger, for my heart melts when I remember that in days past you have treated me and mine with very great kindness and affection: because of this, I have borne much from you in silence that I would have warmly resented in another, but were you my own mother, I would say in the most decided manner you must stop. I cannot be mistaken as to my duty in requiring that my daughter and her mother must *outwardly* stand on the same footing with you. I returned your present to her as a means of saying this in the most positive manner, and also to show you that I am firm in the determination which I have more than once expressed to you, that I cannot and will not submit to your interference in my family affairs. Your letter to my wife was read to Mary and I told her that it was my wish that all intercourse between you and my family should, for a time at least, cease She was afterwards told that your officious interference in the matter of the librarianship, as reported by Judge Reade would prevent her from going to Baltimore. She acquiesced in my decision cheerfully and has entered the academy, of which I am principle, as a scholar. Though she deeply regrets the course you has seen fit to pursue towards me, she has no idea that you have ceased to love her, and I have carefully avoided everything tending to exasperate the feelings of my children towards you—I shall consume no time in contradicting any reports you may hear of expressions in regard to you. I think of you as of a very dear friend who died to me recently and I never mention your name. A similar course of conduct on your part is the only favour I shall ever ask of you, while I shall be your well wisher and friend—

(Signed)
William J. Clarke
Copy of letter to Mrs. H. W. Miller
March 27th. 1869.
Examined & found correct—
[This portion is in WJC's handwriting]

ॐ

*Barden Collection*
*Frances Miller to William J. Clarke*

March 30th [1869]

I am very very sorry my dear Bro In all I did, I feel now, as then confident that I acted for your, for Mary, & for Mai's best good. I was actuated by no feeling but love for all If I wrote Mary I did not wish her to write me it was not what I intended; I ment *on that subject,* How could I? when Mary's letters were next to my own children's the greatest comfort I had I am unfortunate in the use of my pen for you seem to have taken offence at my using *foolish* I ment it in no offensive sense as I hope you did not the word "officious"—I was honest in thinking Mary no longer wished the Librarian's place—did not know I had, or was, using influence against her; & this is the first of my knowing that you considered yourself agrieved by *that.* But I must be honest in saying I should have acted as I did for I knew how it would wound my Father, & heard so much of what would never reach your ears, showing how her having it, would be regarded Still; I said what I thot true, when I told Judge R I thot she had forgotten, or did not know it was necessary to with draw her application It need not prevent Mai's going to Baltimore Mr Browne is ready to perform what he promised

Mary told me she did not wish Mai to know of the matter I think if she was shown any letter of mine she should be told *I* never wished or intended to close our correspondance Of course I do not desire or expect your children to keep up an intercourse that would be disrespectful to their Mother. I only said I could not feel willing to have Mary with me under certain circumstances At all other times under all other circumstances I shall be very glad to see her, for my dear Bro do you not know that she is my favorite sister that my love for you can bear no comparison with that of any other Bro in law? I long to hear from you all, & wish; as you decline all intercourse you had, at least in yours, told me how she was. I am homesick, & heart sick for her I never shall regard *you* "as dead to me" but will ever live in the hope that this cloud may pass & shall ever hail with pleasure the least rift in its blackness, standing ever ready to prove to you all that my love & interest is unchanged & that I am

Your affectionate<br>Sister

Now please if you dont like what I have written do not think I mean unkindly I have not one feeling of anger & will never again think of the hard things you have written

❧

*Barden Collection*
*William J. Clarke to Kate Edmondston*[1]

[1869—after March]

I was greatly surprised as well as pained by your letter to Mary. I regretted the necessity of going to Raleigh in my short vacation on imperative business, as I knew that you would be there, and that I should be unable to see you; for I did not think it practicable to meet you elsewhere than at Sister Frances's house; and, in consequence of her very singular and unjustifiable conduct towards Mary, I am determined never again to enter her doors, unless she complys with the simple terms of reconcilliation I have proposed to her long since, and which she has persistently refused hitherto. This estrangement is very painful to me but it has been her act. We have stood only on the defensive We have never returned railling for railling. We both cherish in tender recollection her many kindnesses to us and the love of long years, and both wonder and moan her strange conduct. Self respect requires that I should take a firm stand in this matter, & having shaped my course after calm deliberation I shall not swerve from it.

I assure you that I wish to see you very much and my failing to call on you was from no want of affection but from necessity, as I did not see how I could see you except at Sister's without exciting remarks. I hope to see you at my house before your return to Roanoke

1. This letter was not signed and is a copy, in William Clarke's handwriting, of a letter he sent to Kate Edmondston. Why Clarke kept such close oversight of his correspondence with his wife's family is unclear. Perhaps, fearing the information would be circulated and misrepresented in Conservative circles, he wanted a record of what actually transpired between himself and his various in-laws.

❧

*Wootten, Moulton, Clarke Papers, SHC*
*Mary Bayard Clarke to Willie Clarke*

New Marlboro[1]
Berkshire Co Mass
July 14th [1869]

My Dear Willie

I have now been a week here and have some idea of the place so I will write and describe it to you. First it is but half the size of Goldsboro— I should think, for in the village there are only about twelve hundred inhabitants, but as there are half a dozen villages the same size within a radius of twelve or fifteen miles the country seems to me thickly populated. We are very comfortable and have good fare except meats which as Mr Cooke says are sent by God while the devil provides the cooks, we have breakfast at quarter past seven always very good though father would object to the cold bread, *potatos* and *lettuce* are always served at breakfast and generally strawberries, I eat oat meal porridge and brown bread and drink milk of which we have plenty, the butter is also delightful and abundant and I never saw such nice battercakes and waffles but they are never brought on the table till the last just like a desert, dinner is at half past twelve and I never care for it but every thing is very nice except the meat which is cooked to death, we have tea and milk both for dinner and desert every day—strawberry short cake is a nice dish that I never saw before; for tea we have always two kinds of cake but nothing hot but the tea. I never saw more delightful bread both white and brown or more butter & milk so I get along very nicely we have tea at six and every body goes to bed by nine, there are three or four ladies very nice ones here two of whom have children at the Institute[2] a school for boys and girls both just opposite the hotel, think of a boarding school for boys and girls together! would not Mr Smeedes go crazy. Dr Rising the physician of the village is the father of one of the teachers who is a friend of Mr Cooke's and Frank's he is a very nice young gentleman and comes every day or two to take me out to drive and if I cared to I would go every day but I dont gain strength very fast and prefer setting in the piazza to driving with a gentleman to whom I have to talk. I have written twice to father—in my first I sent you a neck tie, and in my last wrote for you to receipt for any money that might be sent to me from Raleigh and keep it for your own use for I abuse Frank every day about your clothes which though nice of their kind are not what I wanted you to have

I spilt all my arsenic the other day and Mary kept my Strichnine with her in New York so I have only had it since she came up she regrets she did not spill that too and wont hear of my taking it but I do regularly and the potash also I am about as I was before my last attack except for weakness but I have no strength and a hundred yards is a long walk

Would you like a situation as teacher in the new school of articulation? write decidedly yes—or no—I think I can get a place for you and would prefer it[3]

with love to father

your loving
Mother

1. The town of New Marlborough, in Berkshire County, Massachusetts, became a popular summer resort during the late 1800s. Mary Bayard Clarke had traveled there to rest and visit with Frank Clarke and Oliver Cooke.

2. The South Berkshire Institute.

3. Frank Clarke hoped to have his brother Willie join him in New York to teach at the New York Institute for the Deaf. In a letter dated 30 July [1869], Mary Bayard Clarke replied to a letter from Willie stating that Frank was sorry to hear Willie intended to stay in North Carolina. Eventually, Willie did join his brother at the institute, teaching there for three years while working on a law degree from Columbia, which he received in 1873. Ashe, *Cyclopedia of Eminent and Representative Men*, 2:126–27.

*Barden Collection*
*Frances Miller to Mary Devereux Clarke*[1]

Sept. 19th =69

Oh Mary my child your letter has greived me. It were best not to answer it, but if you thought yourself old enough to write such an insulting letter, you had better have the truth

Your Mothers conduct was in my eyes not what it should have been as the wife of a man in the prisons of those with whom she was associating on friendly terms You may remember too how you greived & wept over it & I did "threaten" if she did not *in that,* change; (not if she did not do exactly as I said in all things) I must put her under Fathers charge—

I never said, or thought, or acted, as if you Mother was "bad" God forbid that I should have thot so; for I love your Mother & you next to my own

I told her "the world was talking of her intercourse with Judge R & saying I was countenancing & abetting her in it, that my sons were remonstrating with me declaring their wives should not come to my house if I continued to permit it." "That *we* could not act as others might, the eyes of the world were on us, I begged her to give it up, money might be too dearly earned, showed her how it might be continued under my roof without scandal." I told all, she meant no harm, I defended, I do, defend her. She, neer for a breath thot I thought her "bad" I hoped she would give it up; but she braved me, & the world & there was nothing else left me. Ask yourself was there?

I do not blame you, for defending Mother, but for the tone & anger of yours to me, your second Mother. & remember I have never asked you to my house save with your Mother when the offending cause was away & I wished her, to be here with her sisters; & that I might say to the world "I did not think your Mother "*bad*"

Not the least of the many kindnesses I have tried to do you was saving your Mothers reputation Had she taken my experience that *The World could not be braved* She would not have had to fore warn her Father of reports against her, Nor would her relatives & frends be now called on to deny that your Father had sent her from him. This is what you now have to lie under When told Auntie has made this up it is not true do not beleve it I would not dceive you, nor would I for worlds darken your young life with it but you force me to it, you must open your eyes & see what I would have saved you from Remember I here state & in the strongest terms I can—I never thot ill of Mother. I always loved & stood up for her she is my favorite Sister Yr Father my best loved Brother-in-law I only wished to stop her in conduct that every friend she had was saying was most imprudent & if you are as old as you wish to appear you will in your heart agree to it if not with age will the conviction come. As our circle of loved ones narrow around us every such blow as that you have delt me is harder to bear up against I love you my child still dearly tenderly & nothing consoles me but the beleif that you did not compose only copied it but by so doing you endorsed it & I must defend myself from another by warning you that should you again wish to address me it must be under cover to a medium who will assure me it is such a communication as you should write to

your greived & agreived<br>
Aunt<br>
Frances

PS I can not understand why my last angered you so All you accused me of doing & saying I had done before you wrote me first from Mas Did you think so meanly of me as to beleive I would, to get your love or company retract conduct based on the highest sense of duty & persisted in with greater pain than any act of my life

1. There is a "draft" version of this letter by Miller identified as "Copy of my answer" that differs slightly in language from the letter actually sent. The copy is also in the Barden Collection.

❧

*Barden Collection*
*Frances Miller to Mary Bayard Clarke*

Jan. 23rd 1870<br>
Sunday A.M.

dear Mary

After two rebuffs I will not again force myself on you, but will be glad if you will come to see me

If you are thrown with my children by your own course or by accident of course you will receive polite respect but you must not expect attention from them otherwise for they feel it would be disrespect to me

Your affectionate<br>
Sister Frances

Please keep this [note on back of letter]

❧

*Barden Collection*
*Mary Bayard Clarke to Frances Miller*

Blair House Monday Jan 24th [1870]

My Dear Sister

Your note of yesterday was not one to be hastily answered, and as this is a crisis which will affect our future lives you must excuse me if I refer to things which I hoped need never be mentioned between us again. More than a year ago you refused to receive me as a boarder, giving as a reason for doing so that your son and son-in-law would not allow their wives to be under the same roof with me unless I pursued a course of conduct dictated by you. Believing you spoke in momentary anger, I, by my husband's advice, simply stated that I would procure a room elsewhere, You then wrote me, "if you persist in coming to Raleigh I will not be glad to see you in my house," I again accepted your decision and did not go to your house, and my husband wrote you that what I did was "not only with his consent but his approbation" he told you that he could not submit to any further interferrence in his family and distinctly stated that until you promised him not to interferre again our intercourse must cease. This promise you would not give, and again interferred, and by so doing gave him deep offence, for he regarded your conversation with Judge Reade about the librariarship as a deliberate and wanton insult. I wrote you this, and sent you a copy of Judge Reade's account of that interview. You offered no explanation, and no apology——, but on the contrary in a letter to my child last fall—repeated the insult you had offered me before—and justified your conduct. Sister that letter to Mary my husband will never forgive, and he is now only anxious to avoid ever setting eyes on you again—I am not—till I read that letter I believed you loved me, but the scales then dropped from my eyes and in grief and sorrow I say to you that I can no longer believe in the existence of any sisterly affection in your heart, for if you loved me you would feel that such a letter to my child though it might have been penned in momentary anger could not be put slightly aside and atoned for only by an invitation to visit you——. Had I been dying and you in your desire to save my life had given me a dose of medicine that produced instant death would you not mourn your act, even though at the time you believed it for the best. Sister this may be a similar case—though I do not say it is—but I do say—that until you can bring yourself to express regret—not to me but to my husband—for your past course and give him the promise he requires I shall obey his wishes respecting our future intercourse. This is the last appeal I shall ever make to you, if you cannot bring yourself to write to my husband "I regret the past and will not again interfere in your family" on your head rests the blame if we are for all our future lives strangers instead of Sisters. Please do not answer this for though I should receive a visit from you were you to make it, I could not return it until assured by my husband that he is willing I should do so

*Barden Collection*
*Frances Miller to William J. Clarke*

July 20th 1870
Now William do not be angry & throw these aside without attention

Think what other motive could I have in taking the trouble to copy them but the desire to clear my self in your eyes of intentional wrong

Mary has accused me of blackening her in her child's eyes says you have so accused me. Read this & see if justice to me does not demand a retraction of *that*. You may regard my conduct & the letter as all wrong but you can not I feel sure, persist after reading Mai's letter & mine, in refusing to permit Mary to come to my house as you see by the extracts from hers she writes me you have.

I learn you have spoken with bitterness of my not upholding your wife after you upheld me Please think a moment there was no such chance allowed me she would not come & be upheld Remember there never was a question of her well or ill doing I have never called her conduct in question save as regarded its effect on me She might be what she, & you pleased, but while with me she must to a certain point regard appearnces This you called interrference & had a perfect right to withdraw your wife from it, but I can not see in it any cause for a quarrel nor will the world think that, all. When Mary again visits Raleigh let her return my visit made Jan 69 & so end this public scandal.

I shall never say more to you of it at your pleasure but do not again put down our coldness to politics it is not just to me

If inclined to be angry look at the date of this remember all we then felt I have never failed to remember it Try & think the best of one whom you used to regard as

a loving Sister

PS I forgot to tell you that Hoke desired his regards & regrets that he did not see you that he might be down again in August & hopes to meet you

POLITICAL EVENTS IN North Carolina approached a crisis between July 1869 and 1871. Although Governor Holden seemed to have the upper hand with a Republican legislature and support from the Grant administration, his enemies launched a counterattack that ultimately unseated him. The Ku Klux Klan spread rapidly and committed brutalities with impunity. The violence led Holden to declare several counties in a state of insurrection by December 1869. Then, on 26 February 1870, the KKK murdered a black leader in Alamance County and state Senator John W. Stephens in the Caswell County Court House.

In June 1870 Holden decided to send troops into Alamance and Caswell counties. He organized two regiments, one under the command of

Colonel George Kirk and the second under the command of William J. Clarke. This began the Kirk-Holden War. In an order to Clarke dated 11 June 1870, from Adjutant General A. W. Fisher, Clarke was appointed to the "2nd Regt. Vol. Infantry" with the understanding that the appointment was "only temporary and after the K.K. are quieted you are to be commissioned Maj. Gen. 1st Division State Militia." According to J. G. deRoulhac Hamilton, Clarke helped Holden plan his strategy against the KKK, meeting with Holden and political friends on 8 June 1870. Clarke then went to Washington, D.C., to meet with President Grant and obtain federal aid. By 19 July, Clarke, with "two companies of negro troops from New Bern, arrived in Raleigh and encamped there" to protect Holden from potential attack. On 25 August 1870, Clarke received information that the "Arsenal was to be attacked this afternoon." Although no violence erupted, tensions in the city remained high.

Interactions between the Clarke family and their Conservative relatives were further exacerbated when Holden arrested Clarke's brother-in-law, Josiah Turner. Turner had used the pages of the *Sentinel* to publish unrelenting attacks on Holden and his allies. On 3 August 1870, Turner taunted Holden, calling him a "white-livered miscreant" and daring Holden to arrest him. Turner also wrote that Holden's followers had shot "powder in the face of Mrs. Turner, [and] threw a five pound rock in her window which struck near one of my children." Turner closed this essay by signing himself "Yours with contempt and defiance . . . Josiah Turner, Jr." Holden arrested Turner, but the courts freed him. Turner returned in triumph to Raleigh to continue his diatribes against the Holden administration. By December 1870, with new elections and the legislature in the hands of the Conservative faction, Holden faced impeachment proceedings. He was impeached on 22 March 1871, and barred from any future state office. The redemption of North Carolina from the hands of the Republicans had begun with a resounding victory.

*Wootten, Moulton, Clarke Papers, SHC*
*William J. Clarke to Mary Bayard Clarke*

Raleigh Aug 21st. 1870

My Dear Mary:

I wrote to you last Sunday from New Berne informing you that I had gone down to see about the Academy business. I found that it was not certainly known whether the Peabody fund would be continued, tho' from the letter of Dr. Sears it was supposed it would.[1] They were expecting to hear from him soon, when a meeting of the trustees would be called, of which I would be notified. I tried to get a meeting while I was in N. but there was not a quorum in town I spoke to some of the Trustees about Willie[2] and sent an application for him to the Secty. He seems to be in good favor, and if we can get a full meeting will I think obtain the situation.

I rec'd yours of the 11th. on my return, on Tuesday night. Since that time I have been very busy and the heat has been intense and almost overpowering.

The political excitement increases rather than abates. Mr. Turner was taken before Judge Brooks at Salisbury and released as the State denied the right of a U. S. judge to interfere in the matter, and would not show cause for his arrest. He is expected here next Thursday, when there will be a great turn out. The rest of the prisoners were brought here and are being examined before Judge [Richard Mumford] Pearson. I am told by counsel for the State that the evidence is very strong and that the developments will be startling If Judge [George Washington] Brooks is correct in his position then your hope for an empire is realized, and state rights is a fossil idea.

I think we are now about arriving at a climax, and that, after a little, matters will be more quiet. I do not fear that Holden will be unable to show that he had abundant cause for the course he pursued.

At the earliest practicable moment I will either come to you or send for you to come to me; but your presence here at this time would be very disagreeable to you, and that would render me unhappy. I am far from being very jolly as it is. I want to see you and the children very badly, and I need rest and quiet. I wrote you that I would send you some money on the 20th. I should have done so but the Pay Master was absent when I returned, and has not yet come back; when he does I will be able to remit.

I am anxious about a school for Pet. I cannot think it possible that the expenses are as enormous as you state, when I see men of limited means sending two or three daughters to school. My salary as Judge will enable me to clear about $2,000 a year.[3]

If Willie was only of age I could get him into one or two good places worth from $1200 to $1500—Much as I should miss him I sometimes think that it would greatly benefit him to spend a year or two in the north, in contact and association with a higher civilization than we have. How long will the vacancy in the Institution be open? I expect Judge Reade here tonight.—I enclose a letter for Frank's information. I should have sent it sooner but I mislaid it. Mrs. Young, who boards at this hotel, returned last night and inquired very particularly about you.

I have a great deal to say to you about the split between me and your brother, but I will not write it, as one does not know into whose hands a letter may fall. I am glad that, like the diffirence with sister F., it can be ascribed to politics.—

By the way, are you French or Prussian? I feel like a Hebrew tonight and as I am sleepy will say good night

With love to all

Affectionately yours<br>
Wm. J. Clarke

1. After the Civil War, George Peabody of Massachusetts created the Peabody Fund to aid education in the South. The Republican trustees of the academy applied for funds and obtained them. This increased the school's enrollment to its highest ever. The fund continued to support the academy until August 1876. Dr. Barnas Sears was an agent of the Peabody Fund. Gadski, *New Bern Academy*, 119, 128.

2. Willie Clarke, who had taught at the New Bern Academy for one year, was applying for the job of superintendent of the academy.

3. Holden planned to appoint Clarke to the Superior Court to complete the term of Charles Randolph Thomas. Lancaster, "Scalawags of North Carolina," 297.

↺

*Wootten, Moulton, Clarke Papers, SHC*
*Mary Bayard Clarke to Willie Clarke*

New Marlboro<br>
Aug 27th [1870]

My Dear Willie[1]

As I have written once to Frank I write now to you though I owe him a letter too but you must be like sister about the toddy and "dib him half." first did you have to take Mary's trunk to New York or did you leave it in Barrington? Next did you get a letter I enclosed you from your father, and last we are all well and hope this will find you etc—

I have had another letter from Mr Woodbridge asking me write a "*poam*" and I have "writ" one[2] and I want you to make your lazy little buddy get it by heart and do himself justice as a speaker, tell him if he chooses to say anything else he can but he must wind up with this, and must speak "Slowly and audibly," make him practise it before you till he can read it beautifully for I want him to make a ten strike he being our "oldest hope"

I am to be sung by the choir and am to be "some" on the occasion so look out and do your best

I had a letter from Mrs Stanly[3] last night she says all the girls are out of town and all the boys well Mr and Mrs Pool[4] have taken Mr Forbes school, if you dont take the "cad'my" I mean to sent Tom to them. I have decided on Baltimore and Dr Bledsoe for Mary as his charges are $250 a year *less* than Lespinasse's and no outfit required, If I could I would take Lespinasse's but I cant afford it. Let me know what you have decided to do when you do decide. Enjoy yourself as much as you can and with love to Frank

believe me
Your loving
Mother

Mr Cooke wrote to Mr Peck asking for a place for you for fear it might be filled if you dont wish it you can decline when it is offered as soon as you are of age your father says he can do something for you

1. Willie Clarke was visiting his brother Frank in New York to assess whether he wanted to teach at the New York Institute for the Deaf.

2. Jonathan Edwards Woodbridge, a descendant of Jonathan Edwards and a relative of Mary Bayard Clarke, was one of the organizers of the Edwards family reunion held in Stockbridge, Massachusetts, on 6 and 7 September 1870. For the occasion Woodbridge asked Clarke to write a poem, which was read by Frank Clarke. In 1871 remarks from the event were published, including Frank Clarke's comments and his mother's poem. *The Memorial Volume of the Edwards Family Meeting at Stockbridge, Mass., September 6–7, A.D. 1870* (Boston: Congregational Publishing Society, 1871), 158–61.

3. Esther Stanly taught the primary department of the New Bern Academy between 1870 and 1873. Gadski, *New Bern Academy,* 121–22.

4. Colonel and Mrs. Stephen Pool briefly supervised New Bern's parochial school. Stephen Pool later served as editor of the New Bern *Journal of Commerce* from 1866 to 1876 and helped to found the North Carolina Press Association. He also published in New Bern *Our Living and Our Dead* between 1873 and 1876. In 1874 he became superintendent of public instruction for the state, serving until 30 June 1876. He moved to New Orleans, Louisiana, in 1877. Powell, *DNCB,* 5:120–21.

TURNER'S ATTACKS ON HOLDEN and his men included printed allegations in the *Sentinel* against William Clarke. Turner repeatedly maintained that neither Holden nor Clarke had a legal right to organize and enlist a military force in North Carolina. On 25 June 1870, he accused Holden's troops of threatening the lives of his wife and children. On 23 August, Turner asserted that Clarke, Kirk, or any of their men would be held responsible for "any thefts or robberies they have committed, for any rapes, murders or arrests they have made, in fact for every thing the people have suffered from their conduct."

*Wootten, Moulton, Clarke Papers, SHC*
*William J. Clarke to Willie Clarke*

Raleigh Sept. 9th. 1870.

My Dear Willie:

Yours of the 4th. inst., postmarked 6th., came to hand this morning, and I was glad to learn that you were well, and enjoying yourself. You made only one orthographical error, that of writing, awhile (for a short time), as two words, thus "a while." I think that it was quite an undertaking to row 45 miles, and if the weather was any thing like as hot, with you as it has been with us, it must have been quite a sudorific job. You had a good opportunity to see some of the finest scenery in our country, and will have a more correct idea of it than the tourists who survey it from the deck of a steamboat through the smoke of a Havana

I am approaching the end of one of the most disagreeable services I ever performed, and I thank God, that, with every thing to irritate almost to madness, I have done nothing to be ashamed of. I have borne calmly brow-beating, and villification; though I must confess that if the courage of some men had equalled their impertinence, it might have been different. Entering upon the service with the best, the purest, the most patriotic motives, and running counter to the prejudices of a large portion of our people, I felt that the "mens sibi conscia recti," must sustain me, and that, like Bacon, I must wait for time to vindicate me. There have been follies and great improprieties on our side, but I had nothing to do with them, and would have prevented them had I known of them. On the other hand, it amazes me to see gentlemen, held in reputation for wisdom and honor, defending and making common cause with murderers and heinous malefactors. The Sentinel has become the most mendacious sheet I ever saw. The attempt to ostracise me, made by many whom I never suspected capable of such meanness, I treat with contempt; though it is exceedingly unpleasant to be placed in antagonism with men to whom you are attached, and whose friendship you value. The root of the whole matter lies, in the deep hatred to the U.S. government, and prejudice against the negro, whom, if they cannot reinslave, they are unwilling to invest with any political rights. The Republican party only contends for loyalty to the government and justice to individuals. Gov. Holden strives, as in duty bound, to execute the laws, and every good and true man should stand ready to assist him. This is the head and front of my offending. The men who would drive the negro from our state are aiming a dagger at our prosperity, and the progress of years will make it apparent.

On Monday, I caused to be paid off all of my Reg't., and mustered them out of the service, with the exception of part of a Co. I remain, until the latter part of next week, in service attending to final settlements; then I go to Johnston Court: then the 1st. week in October to Wayne, to try the Lenoir Ku Klux. My thoughts and feelings have been so much engaged in the service that I was engaged in that my mind has almost run to waste; but I hope to get back again to habits of thought, study, and business.

I am glad that you had an opportunity of attending the opera. Such things do very well, occasionally, but I agree with you that they foster sensuality as much as they refine and cultivate the taste. I also agree with you that Dr. Bledsoe's will be a better place for your sister than some other schools which were spoken of, no amount of head learning could compensate for loss of delicacy, and I would rather have her unlearned than forward. You will be sorry to learn that your friend [Rufus] Morgan has been very sick with typhoid fever, I learn that he is now in New Berne and is convalescing. It has been very sickly in N. though not many persons have died.

The summer has been intensely hot. I never before had the cutaneous eruption, called the heat. The crops are generally good, and a few bales of cotton are already in market. The fruit crop has been very abundant, and the restrictions on stilling having been greatly lightened a good deal of apple and peach brandy will be made.

Tell your Mother that I am ashamed of myself for writing for her to come here on the 17th: to stay as long as she pleases, and that to compel her to do so I will not send that money to Baltimore as I intended, and told her I would do.

Give my love to Frank, and tell him that I had no idea that he would make you so much of a *row*-dy.

I doubt if any thing has been done about the Academy in consequence of absence of the Trustees. I'll go down next week and see about it, and let you know.

With love to all

Your affectionate father<br>Wm. J. Clarke

❧

*Wootten, Moulton, Clarke Papers, SHC*
*Nora Cannon to Willie Clarke*

Hillsboro Dec 6th [1870]

My Dear Boy

You have been most shamefully used by your Aunt Nonie and so "deeply convicted" does she feel that she can scarcely summon courage to write you "*ever any more*" as Mat[1] says But indeed I am not entirely to blame for my whole time, mind, & body have been kept on the stretch ever since the receipt of your last letter before which time I did not know how to direct to you. first Mr Edmondston & your Aunt Kate went to Augusta to attend the Agricultural Congress leaving me in charge of the house and plantation Just after they left a most fearful religious excitement broke out among the poor ignorant negroes there were two grand rascals who were at the head of it declaring that "Christ had entered into their bodies and that they only uttered the words of the Lord & did his work;["] they refused to work & ordered the other hands to quit the field and go to the woods to pray and some times the cotton baskets would be left in the row for an hour or two while the negroes were scattered around in the woods praying. At last I lost all patience and ordered the two ring leaders either to go to their work or leave the plantation and not come on it again till Mr E came home enforcing my command by telling them that "my commands must be obeyed whether the Lords" were or no" & "if they were seen on the place they should have a quick trip to the next world for I would shoot them as if they were mad dogs" After this I had less trouble as they took me at my word but I could not sleep at night for fear they might fire the Gin house which was full of cotton I used to spend half the night at a window which overlooked the gin & stables there were 3 gin houses set on fire in the neighborhood within the three weeks & I was very much afraid Mr E's would be but I let it be known that I was on watch every night and fortunately no one ever came around it. I had determined to shoot the first person I saw in the lot at night and you know I am a bag shot. Then after two weeks absence your Aunt Kate & Mr E came home & were both taken sick, your Aunt Kate was so ill that I had to sit up for three whole nights & three more I dozed and slept by the fire All these "stirring events["] have prevented me from writing you of your cousin Kate's engagement to John Primrose though I daresay Willie Primrose has written you of it They will be married on the 11th of January here at your Aunt Sophia's [Turner] house where I am to stay with all the children till after the wedding & then go to your Mothers (D[?]).

And now to show me that you have forgiven me for my long silence I want you to get me a nice lady's traveling trunk as large & nice as you can get for $10.00 & have it marked Miss K. A. Cannon N.C. and send it to me here at Hillsboro I have not the money to send you now so I must ask you to lend it to me I have been very much hampered in buying her wedding outfit by the fact that my house rent is not due till the first of January[2] in fact had it not been that Brother Josiah got credit for me in Raleigh till the first of Feb I could not have bought any thing for her The trunk I am going to give her over and above the $100 I set aside for her trousseau and you must be sure not to give more than $10 for it that is as much as I can afford Do not punish me for my long silence by not writing me again I will try and do better in future Good bye your loving

Aunt
Nonie

1. Mattie Cannon.
2. Nora Cannon still owned the house in Sommerville, Tennessee, that she and her husband had received as a wedding gift from her father, Thomas Pollock Devereux. She rented out the house to help with family finances.

*Wootten, Moulton, Clarke Papers, SHC*
*Emily Mason to Mary Bayard Clarke*

225 N. Fremont St. Balt.
Decr. 11th [1870]

My dear Mrs Clark

Yr. letter should not have been so long unanswered had I been in the City on its arrival, but I have been on a sorrowful pilgrimage to my old home or rather to the *site* of my old home in Va

It mortifies me immensely to tell you that I have not been able to find the mss. for which you ask. Are you *sure* I did not return it to you? I was so pressed by business of every Kind before going away that I cannot remember about it distinctly, but conclude it must have been left with the papers I left behind with my nephew—I shall look still further amongst these I remember taking it to Kelly & Piet who promised to look it over with the view of publishing it for me—Mr Kelly has been away & Mr Piet promised he should look for it as soon as he returns—It may be that he has it—

Thank you for yr. Kind welcome & for the interest you express in my "work"—I have been successful beyond my most sanguine expectations—

Eighteen of the girls whom I have been educating have gone back to their homes prepared to teach & give *unqualified* delight to their parents & friends—For these I have managed to pay *a little* & in most cases I have clothed them—While in Europe I sent home 14 trunks & boxes of clothing & raised a good deal of money—Besides that I have sold my "Journals" —& "sketches" to great advantage—My "two months in Spain during the late Revolution" published in the Cath. "World" of N. York (a most admirable literary magazine) brought me $250—So you see how fortunate I have been—& how God has aided my efforts. I am still *up to my eyes* in work—am going to N. York in Jany to publish two novels translated from the German & a book of French poetry (selections from the best authors of this century) for the use of schools—I have also two translations (novels) from the French—on hand—and am engaged to write a child's History of Genl Lee—

With all these "irons in the fire" I hope to finish the education of several other children whom I have yet "*on hand*"—& then shall I be ready to sing the Nunc Dimittis—But Holy Simeon lived a few years after He sung this!

I reciprocate yr desire for our meeting *face to face* & hope you will be here before I go to the North I shall try to see yr daughter before you come—I used to know Dr Bledsoe very well & liked him much. most truly & affy yrs

Emily V. Mason

❧

*Wootten, Moulton, Clarke Papers, SHC*
*Mary Bayard Clarke to Willie Clarke*

New Berne Dec 22d [1870]

My Dear Willie

I received your letter a day or two since and am glad you like the book—I do very much; by diligent canvassing, Henry Duffy has sold *three* copies, but he hopes before Christmas to sell a dozen. Mrs Lehman has written a notice of it for the Standard which I will send you when it appears; also for Forney's Washington Chronical; send me all that you see as here I see nothing Tom is about the same as when I wrote yesterday to Mr Cooke, the Dr thinks he will not have typhoid fever but I cant be easy about him, tell Frank I got his letter to Tom last night after he was in bed and put it away to give him with the engine on his birth day, he will be delighted as he wants a camera and I wont let him have it so the engine will be just the thing, I expect it is at the PO. now, it would not go in the box, and they sent word there was some thing too large to go in the box, though why they did not send it I cant tell. Mary writes that the book is very much admired by her circle and Dr B is charmed with it;[1] she says she went to high Mass the other day and a sister stopped her and told her she, (*the nun*) read *all* my poetry. Mary did not know her, or know that she was known to be my daughter, and the little monkey never asked who it was. Miss Mason has lost the Mss of Chalmette but thinks Kelly and Piet may have it, so I have written Mary to go down and raise a gentle howl over its loss and incite them to search for it, it may turn up as the Governor More-head Mss did. There is no news that I know of except that another deluge is coming, Holden is impeached, the legislature has passed a bill for convention and it goes to the people who will probably vote for one and then we will be all turned up again, no money in the treasury and increased taxes. George Baker[2] has taken Sister's house and advertises for boarders she had but five and accuses father of trying to ruin her. [Rufus] Morgan has not returned yet, but report says he will be back next month and marry Miss Fanny Dissosway[3]—Mrs Stephenson and Delia are expected daily, and Stephen Pool is waiting to see the latter before he leaves for New Orleans. Tell Mr Cooke Dr Charles Duffy came to see me yesterday and enquired after him very particularly, he thinks of settling here; if he does I shall send for him as I dont like Dr Hughes's practise, he is attending Tom but if I had known before I sent for him that Dr Duffy was in town I would have had him. We are to have a masquerade New Year night that they say will be very grand—Give my love to Frank and tell him to write to me

Your loving<br>Mother

PS—When you see Mrs March tell her I never had any thing to do me so much good as those baths and Mr March ought to try them

1. Mary Bayard Clarke's ambition to have another book of poetry published was realized with the publication of *Clytie and Zenobia; or, the Lily and the Palm, A Poem,* published in New York by E. P. Dutton and Company in 1871. It was sixty-five pages long, including notes. Albert T. Bledsoe reviewed the publication in his journal the *Southern Review* and lauded it as "enriched with the inventions, of the gifted authoress." MBC Scrapbook 2, Barden Collection.

2. Baker was Frances Miller's son-in-law.

3. Fanny Disosway, the daughter of Israel Disosway, was a special friend of Willie Clarke. Her brother Billy was a frequent visitor at the Clarke home and

held a warm regard for Willie's sister, Mary Devereux Clarke. However, Mary D. Clarke eventually married Rufus Morgan.

*Barden Collection*
*Margaret J. Preston to Mary Bayard Clarke*

Lexington, Va.
Dec. 28th '70

My dear Mrs. Clark,

Within a few days I have recd, thro' your Publisher I believe, Your beautiful gift of *Clytie and Zenobia,* and I write now to offer my thanks for so acceptable a memento. I don't think You have ever written anything more graceful; it is pervaded throughout with the fervid fancy and opulent imagery of the East—and coming to me just at the same time with Whittier's last Poem *Miriam*—wh. is an Oriental story, like Yr' own, I could not but realise how much more delicate *Your* handling and elaboration of such a theme is than his.—And the *getting up* of Yr' volume is simply exquisite. Could a jewel be more appropriately set?—I trust that the book will make its way so successfully that it will "put money in Your purse," which is certainly more than I expect of *my* recent volume. I sent You a copy, wh. I hope may have reached You. I shall be glad to hear that those ogres, the Critics, deal very gently with the tender *Clytie* and the proud *Zenobia.* I don't think our Southern readers are at all quick at recognising home talent. The *Northern* press has been kinder far to me, as Yet, than the *Southern.* If N. P. Willis[1] occupied the chair Editorial yet, wouldn't *Tenella* be sure of his graceful and unstinted homage? I am fully aware that literary talent counts for more North of "Mason-and-Dixon", than South. Is not that Your experience? Were you ever so heartily praised as in *The Home Journal?*

With best wishes for the New Year, believe me, dear Mrs Clark most faithfully Yrs

Margaret J. Preston
Mrs. Mary Bayard Clark—

1. Nathaniel Parker Willis published the *Home Journal,* a popular periodical during the nineteenth century. He died in 1867. Fred Lewis Pattee, *The Feminine Fifties* (New York: D. Appleton-Century, 1940), 115–16, 253, 256–57, 259, 260.

*Barden Collection*
*Mary Custis Lee to Mary Bayard Clarke*

Lexington 11th Jany [1871]

I should have acknowledged the receipt of your sweet little volume long since my dear Mrs Clarke but for many hindrances & the uncertainty how to direct to you I have forgotten your former direction & shall have to send to the Post master in Raleigh with a request to him to forward this letter to you as I do not know any one there except Mrs Mason & have not heard from her for so long a time that I do not feel certain about her I read the poem all through as soon as I opened it, with much pleasure & was delighted to be recalled to you again in such a pleasant way I hope you will write & tell me all about yourself & family for it seems a very long time since I heard aught of you. I know you have mourned with me in our irreparable bereavement,[1] which even yet I can scarcely realize. I might have been better prepared for it, had not my eyes been blinded & had I not refused to listen to his forebodings of an early death, for humble & [consistent?] Christian as he had been for many years, yet for the last 2 he had evidently been fast ripening for glory—& that fatal night, when just as the terrible storm commenced he entered the house & was taken speechless his whole bearing as he sank into his chair was one of the most sublime resignation. Perfectly conscious yet unable to express his feelings I saw that he felt his hour had come, there was no restlessness or attempt to struggle with his fate, but a perfect calm as he sat upright in his chair awaiting the arrival of the Doctors & as soon as they had administered some remedies & placed him in a bed brought into the room the bed from which he never rose, he turned over to sleep as gently & quietly as an infant & slept almost continuously through the storm which raged for two days & nights & which seemed to wail for the sorrow which was to befall us, when roused for he was allowed to sleep hoping that rest was all he needed, he greeted us all with a kindly pressure of the hand but never smiled & rarely spoke, save in his dreams & they were of those terrible battle fields. He never enquired for the absent ones or missed them from his bedside, never asked for any thing but took what was offered him, He had evidently done with earth & was calmly & gently sinking into rest, once when Agnes urged him to take some medicine he said very plainly "Tis no use" & when he was so much better Dr Barton[2] said you must now get out & ride your favorite grey he shook his head very emphatically & looked up to Heaven. I love to think of him there & not in the cold silent grave. At the last after about 36 hours of insensibility with one long deep sigh his spirit took flight to those Mansions of bliss which are open to the faithful on earth, to the Rest, prepared for the weary & heavy laden—Had he lived to be the Deliverer of our beloved South, he could not have been more beloved & respected & the fame which he never sought or courted will follow his name through ages to come I am content, though life seems very dreary now. I have given you these particulars feeling that you would be interested in them & would pardon me if I indulged in some womanly expression of pride for one whom all delighted to honour My daughters unite with me in Kind regards to you and yours Affecly Mary C Lee

I will venture here to express a hope that the South will continue to patronize our College here in which Genl Lee was so deeply interested— I hope my son will be able to carry out his views & wishes concerning it I send you a little picture which you must keep for one of your children

1. Robert E. Lee died in October 1870 after suffering a stroke. Family letters about his death mentioned the terrible storms described here, as well as his troubled memories. After Lee's death, George Washington Custis Lee assumed presidency of Washington College. Coulling, *The Lee Girls,* 108–9; Flood, *Lee: The Last Years,* 256–57.

2. Howard Barton was a Lexington physician who became a friend of the Lee family. He and another physician attended Lee during his final illness. Flood, *Lee: The Last Years,* 191–92, 223.

❧

*Wootten, Moulton, Clarke Papers, SHC*
*Mary Bayard Clarke to Willie Clarke*

New Berne Jan 28
1871

My Dear Willie

According to my promise I dont write to Mr Cooke, but to you though I have nothing particular to say. I hope you had a pleasant journey, I have been in bed most of the time since you left as I only kept up while I had you and Frank with me, I caught your trouble and have rheumatism but fortunatey not in my right arm but in my left. I thought so much about you boys and now I am wondering if you are safe at the Institution and how Mr Cooke is, give my best love to him and tell him I say dont be imprudent for I do worry so over him that I am selfish in wishing him to get well as it will relieve me so much. Sister continues about the same looks very badly and the children run her nearly crazy as even I have to confess that Tom is really bad since he has had Bob to domineer over[1]

Nonie [Cannon] still suffers greatly she has not been down stairs for two days and as I cannot get up I have not seen her Dr Duffy says it will be some time before she is well. Mrs Lehman and Allie are both sick Mrs Stevenson ditto and the weather so bad that I suppose half the town are sick too Dont forget your promise to write and tell me just what you think of Mr Cooke. They have passed a bill setting aside the two Special Courts for Lenoir and Craven through the house—if it passes the Senate it cuts us out of $200—but I hope it wont pass though father seems to think it will—I am sorry to see the Conservatives Stooping to such meanness as they are guilty of every day in the legislature—they can say nothing of the Republicans that cannot be said of them with equal truth now, and I fear are going to act so as to throw us back under military rule, they have ousted two Republican Senators because a body of US troops were in the County at the time of election and put in Democrats for the purpose of securing Holden's conviction. If the election was fraudulent on that account for them it certainly was for the Democrats under the same circumstances—Well it only proves what I have always said "the party in power is always corrupt" Mary sends love and says Allie got sick because you left and so did she, She says tell Cousin Dud to make haste and get well so he can read a letter from her—

Your loving<br/>Mother

1. The Clarkes were entertaining Nora Cannon and all of her children. In addition to the Clarkes' two children, there were Bob, Sadie, Nonie, and Mattie Cannon.

*Wootten, Moulton, Clarke Papers, SHC*
*Mary Bayard Clarke to Willie Clarke*

New Berne Feb 3d [1871]

My Dear Willie

Your two letters were received in due time and relieved my mind considerably—I would have written before but I have been so unwell and worried out, mentally and physically, I could not do so—The weather has been horrible, and we could not let the children go out of the house for more than a week except at long intervals for a short time; Sister and Tom were both half sick, and "As cross as two old bears," Nonie whole sick, and the sweetest, most patient little thing on earth; she is "Beth" in "Little

Women" all over——; the rest were well and restless and you can imagine
my troubles when I tell you that from the time I got up till I got them all
in bed at night it was, "Mama cant I have this",——"Mama please let somebody do that——", while my usual refuge, the sofa, always had a sick child
curled up on it, and when clear tired out I would think of stealing off
to my own room for a rest, a snort from father would notify me that he,
like Dicken's Baby, was "simmering between the blankets" after dinner, for
the weather gave him neuralgia and the Legislature shut down on his
special courts here and in Lenoir, and cut him out of $200, so he was
another "Bear" to be borne with. Mary does not get any better, and the Dr
has changed the medicine and put her on horse back——, we got one of
Eubank's ponies about the size of a Newfoundland dog and this evening
she is going for her first ride, if she is thrown it will be no more than falling
off of a chair, but judging from appearances the pony wont go fast enough
to hurt her.

Tom is looking worse than ever and has headache all the time, I sent
Bob and Saidy to School and he is very anxious to go but tried it one day
and had such a headache he had to give it up, he Studies his Latin at home.

I was interrupted just here with a petition that Mama would come and
see the pony, I went and found the saddle so much too large it would not
and could not be put on him so as to be safe, I sent Jack with it to the sad-
dlers and he was pitched over the rats head, and Nathan Davison[1] ditto so
I concluded it was best for sister to let that little animal alone, and next
week I will try and get her another. Do tell Mr Cooke that I would write
to him if you had not forbidden it, but I mean to do so next time and
enclose to you and then you can read it to him and not let him have it. Tell
him I am too tired to have an idea, and the only quiet I get is when I am
out walking. Certainly my place of punishment will be Pandemonium I
dont mind fire, as Mrs Adams used to say, but noise and confusion sets me
crazy and housekeeping breaks me down I thought I had a good servant in
Martha but she cant remember any longer than I am telling her and is as
easily confused as I am, and when confused utterly useless——for head
work. Tell Mr Cooke I have been obliged to call in Dr Duffy and he comforts me considerably for he tells me Mrs Huntly saved my life, and my
present troubles are only temporary for I have not lost what I gained under
treatment, only was not long enough under it. Give my love to Frank and
tell him I intended writing to him on his 22d birthday——but I was very
unwell and could not do it. I hope now the weather is good I will enjoy Aunt

Nora's company some—what a pity she has such a lot of children so young —She sends love to you boys and says tell Mr Cooke she is as anxious to see him as I tell her he is to see her—

Your loving
Mother

1. Nathan Davidson was the son of Elias and Charlotte Davidson of New Bern. 1870 Craven County Census Index, 97, 2nd Ward no. 86.

*Barden Collection*
*Mary Custis Lee to Mary Bayard Clarke*

Lexington 4th February 1871

Last night I received by mail my dear Mrs Clarke your sweet little poem on the silk as well as the others on paper, your letter had reached me a few days previously. I think the poem headed "The [illegible]" is very fine, I have sent it to be published in our College paper to which I suppose you would not have objected. They talk here of having all the eulogies & poems etc published in a volume to themselves but I do not know how soon they will be able to accomplish it—they would fill a very large one.

I regret very much to learn of the burning of your church in these hard times[1] & am sorry not be able to give any material aid, but I always consider it a duty not to withhold any *mite,* I enclose $10.00 from myself & some of my family among them my daughter Agnes I have a very tender feeling for your state, where I have experienced so much Kindness & where the remains of my dear Annie have been so honoured, If possible I will send more in time but we have all been struggling hard to collect means for our repairs to our church here, which is in such a dilapedated condition as to be scarcely fit for use & otherwise the people here, especially the Episcopalians are so poor & have been called on for so many purposes this winter I do not like to apply to them. However I will show your circular to our pastor Dr Pendleton & see if any thing can be done further—I hope this peace on the Continent while it will release thousands there from all the sufferings of what seems to me the most unnecessary war[2] will help our poor South a little in raising the price of cotton. It does seem to be reviving yet I suppose there is much destitution that does not meet our eye, while we have food & raiment let us be content tho, few appreciate releif from *destitution*

It must be a great source of pleasure to you to have your children gathered into the fold of Christ your sons must be very young Professors,

I did not know the Deaf Mutes were ever taught further than to read &
write, but truly this is an age of progress, Tell Mary as you would not give
her *your* picture I must send her mine taken about 6 years since & from a
porcelain type which accounts for its looking so young I was arranged in
this pensive attitude by a young cousin of mine who is very artistic in her
tastes & the vase of flowers was photographed from Nature—I have had
some photographs taken since but should I ever live to be 80 they could
not look older so that I prefer to use this one

I hope you receive handsome renumeration for your writings which
must fatigue you very much if you do not feel well, I have had so many letters to acknowledge in the last 2 months & my hand somewhat rheumatic
that I have feared I might suffer the fate of a certain Mr George Prentess of
Louisville of whom perhaps you have heard as he is really a fine poet, whose
thumb became so affected by constant writing he could not hold a pen for
many years before his death which I think occurred during the war. I can
only find any comfort save in the kindness & sympathy of friends & the
mercy of my Heavenly Father in constant occupation & trust I shall never
be deprived of the power to use my hands & eyes as my other limbs are
almost useless to me. My daughters desire to reciprocate your kind remem-
berances I send mine to all your household & beleive ever most truly

your friend<br>Mary Custis Lee

1. New Bern's Episcopal Christ Church caught fire on 10 January 1871, and
burned completely. The fire began across the street in Hahn's Bakery, and sparks
flew over to the shingle roof of the church. A new church building was conse-
crated on 23 May 1875. Gertrude Carraway, *Crown of Life: History of Christ Church,
New Bern, N.C. 1715–1940* (New Bern, N.C.: Owen G. Dunn, 1940), 177–80.

2. The war between Prussia and France, which ended with a Prussian victory in 1871.

*Wootten, Moulton, Clarke Papers, SHC*
*Mary Bayard Clarke to Willie Clarke*

New Berne<br>April 21st [1871]

My Dear Willie

I received your last letter on my return from Beaufort [North Caro-
lina] where I went to look for board as you proposed. Such a time as we
had, I can hardly think of it with out laughing, but I will tell in due order.

Father and I went on Thursday evening so as to take the freight back on Friday and not stay two nights,

Mr Nash went with us as he had a little business and did not wish to go alone. I thought of Miss Davis where we boarded you remember, but Sister cast longing eyes towards the Atlantic House where all the fun would be, and so I compromised and engaged board at Mr Lowenbergs. Mrs L is a sister of old Dr Duffy and they live about one square from the Atlantic House and a square from the plank walk so—

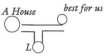 our party will consist of Jennie Mabrey and a nice bright little musical woman a Mrs Hall wife of one of the officers of the cutter, board $25 a month for grown folks $12 for Tom and a servant whom we cant do without you know at such a place. We will fill the house and Sister can go to as many hops as I am willing for her to attend and have as many beaux as she likes with out killing herself; board at the hotels is $40 a month, and they wont reserve rooms for us so the little girl, being very reasonable, is satisfied to be out of the rush on consideration of having a brother to take her down into it and surf bathing and not being dependant on her beaux—

All this settled by ten o'clock and Mr Nash being through his business proposed we should kill time by going to see a Whale on Shackleford's banks.[1] So we chartered Ben and Frank who both enquired after you and started on

*My First Whaling voyage*

I did remark to Mr Nash that I hoped we should not see the elephant instead of the whale, but he was so confident that he inspired me; our program was to see the whale, then go to the fort[2] and dine, and from there to Morehead[3] to take the cars at five o'clock.

We had a delightful sail and landed on the inner side of the bank. Here my heart misgave me and I asked if I had to cross those sand hills, "Oh just a little way, there's a good path" Misses, said that deceitful Ben who armed with a bottle of water and a glass walked a head to show the way, Half a mile we trudged through the sand and I began to demur for we were going down the beach not across. "Ben when are we going to cross?" Right now Misses and into the bush we plunged single file, Ben leading. Five fences did I scramble over and no sign of the Atlantic, suddenly the path ended, and a blank sand hill rose before me the artfull Ben having surged a head so that I had to scream at the top of my voice "Ben how much farther "Dont you hear the surf Misses we just got to go over this hill and we'll see the breakers." I dragged on another mile, two miles, three miles—

(*so I thought*[)] for I did hear the surf. I surmounted that hill convinced the whale was just the other side. When I reached the beach I was exhausted, but I looked for the whale, and Mr Nash thought it was just round that head land and if I would stop and take a drink from Ben's bottle, with a little from his, I would soon get there. Ben the artful was by this time out of hearing but a shout from Mr Nash brought him up with that bottle, but I did not feel like taking any thing on hearing from Ben "we were most there," another mile, and yet another I trudged, and then in the dim distance about five miles off Mr Nash pointed to the Whale—a large black mass on the beach, I was encouraged, I saw the whale and I boldly struck out on the five mile heat encouraged by remnants of the carcase of one killed the week before which were scattered along the beach. The black mass grew larger—it loomed—but it began to look suspiciously like a boat, it was—a boat—or rather the hull of a sailing vessel high and dry— but from beyond it we could dimly see men passing with great black things on their shoulders which were pieces of blubber cut from the whale with the Skin on looking like lard done up in enamel cloth At last we reached the spot—but alas for the Whale who was not! that piece of blubber was the *very last* cut and nothing but a disgusting mass without form or shape was left of what had been a whale! There I colapsed—sat down on the boat and said meekly "if any body was to ask me now what I would like I should say something out of Mr Nash's bottle"

I did not even retort when Ben asked me if I was tired, and said I had walked "nigh upon three miles!!" I knew it was "nigh upon" twenty but I did not *say* so for I had seen the elephant if not the whale, and I simply turned to Mr Nash and said "What went ye out into the wilderness to see?" I got a rib of whale bone from the creatures mouth for Tom ordered four of his ribs for Mary to make arches for her arbor of, and then took the back track supported by Mr. Nash on one side and Father on the other. In an hour we reached the boat which, the tide having risen, was some distance from land Ben picked me up remarking Hm—Miss Clarke you used to be the lightest one I had to tote but you's a good lift now." I thought of Mr Weller and Mr Pickwick but I only said Mr Nash I am not equal to dining at the fort "put me in my little bed as quick as possible," and so the sail was set for Morehead where I determined to lie down till the cars left— and reflect on the wonders of the deep Alas! Frank spoke up—"Judge I duno 'bout that bed nor dinner nether at Morehead they is repairing the hotel and no body lives thar" so we sailed for the fort and called on the sutler for something to eat and to drink in the shape of crackers and cheese and ale and then went to Morehead and I slept ten minutes in the car and dreamed I was after whales. By nine o'clock we were home and if ever I was tired I was then and have been ever since. When you come down *perhaps* we'll go for another whale, I dont know of any books I particularly want you to bring just bring any you think of that are new and keep your money to begin on next fall; your whole trip ought not to cost over a hundred dollars $50 for two months board $30 passage to and fro—$20 for incidentals And now good night for I am tired of that whale in more senses than one Love to Frank

Your loving<br>Mother

1. Shackleford Banks is located on North Carolina's Outer Banks. It is a sandy island between Core Banks and Atlantic Beach.

2. Fort Macon, at the tip of Atlantic Beach, overlooks the entrance to Beaufort harbor. It is now a North Carolina state park.

3. Town located on the mainland just across from Atlantic Beach, North Carolina.

ಎ

*Wootten, Moulton, Clarke Papers, SHC*
*Mary Bayard Clarke to Willie Clarke*

New Berne<br>May 26th [1871]

My Dearest Willie

I received your letter, telling of the mean way the Seniors behaved at the Commencement, last Wednesday and think with you that some notice ought to have been taken of it; I am truly glad you have some rest and shall count the days now to the end of the session for Oh I do want to see you so much.

We have had a meeting of the State Medical Society[1] here and your letter came in the middle of it the people of New Berne did not put themselves out much to entertain the Drs and as Father was away I had to do double duty, and as I was just out of a headache found it rather tiresome; we asked Dr Dick and Dr Burke Haywood to stay with us but the latter was pledged to Dr Hines[2] and only dined with us, Dr Dick staid from Monday to Thursday and would have staid longer but for sickness in his family, he enjoyed himself very much, and of course fell in love with a nice little lady is staying with us, and who is very musical, a Mrs Hall whose husband is a lieutenant in the Revenue Service, she has set up an organ in the back parlor and keeps Sister up to her music in a way I could not do; she is very bright and full of fun she will go with us to Beaufort and hopes you will like her. Dr Dick told me a great deal of Raleigh news—he says Uncle John's girls are not popular because they are so stuck up and spiteful, Lou [Root?] is not married nor likely to be, Ark Royster's brother Wisconsin[3] is getting quite a reputation as a Dr and doing well Dr Dick thinks Auntie is very anxious to make up but is under Kate Baker's Lizzie Miller's and Kate Primrose's rule and they are all three as bitter as gall against Father.

Sister is well and glad not to go to Tarborough she is as usual flirting I think Johnnie Hughs[4] is pretty high up at present in her good graces—Big Dis' stock has gone down though they are good friends yet. Give my love to Celia and Bella[5] I wish I could see them and I hope you will take them out rowing very often it will do you all good Father is as usual away—, next week is Carteret to and then he is through

Good bye  Your loving<br>Mother

1. The North Carolina Medical Society became active in the state when the 1848 state legislature created a medical board to examine and evaluate the qualifications of doctors in the state. A group of doctors met in Raleigh on 16 April 1849, to organize the professional society. Only doctors who had graduated from an approved medical school and who had practiced for at least five years in the state could be admitted to the society. A Medical Examining Board was established between 1858 and 1859, and in 1858 the society began the publication of its *Medical Journal of North Carolina*. Johnson, *Ante-bellum North Carolina*, 758–59, 760–61, 762.

2. This probably was Peter Evans Hines, a prominent Raleigh physician who graduated from the medical school at the University of Pennsylvania in 1853. He served as a Confederate physician and medical director, and after the war he returned to Raleigh. He was president of the Wake County Medical Society, the Raleigh Academy of Medicine, and the North Carolina Board of Medical Examiners at different times during the 1870s. Powell, *DNCB*, 3:146–47.

3. The family of James Daniel and Mary Ashley Royster resided in Raleigh, North Carolina. Each of the couple's eight children was named after a different American state. Wisconsin Illinois Royster served during the Civil War as a Confederate mail clerk in Raleigh before transferring to Dr. E. Burke Haywood's Raleigh hospital to work as a surgeon's assistant. In 1866 he attended the Bellevue Medical School in New York City and graduated two years later. Wisconsin Royster returned to Raleigh in 1870 to set up his medical practice. His brother Arkansas Delaware Royster became a prominent local businessman in Raleigh

who established Royster's Candy Company following the Civil War. Barrett, *Sherman's March through the Carolinas*, 250; Ashe, *Cyclopedia of Eminent and Representative Men*, 2:238–39.

4. John Hughes was a New Bern attorney and president of the National Bank. *Chas. Emerson & Co.'s Newbern, N.C. City Directory* (Raleigh: Edwards, Broughton, 1880), 69 (hereafter cited as *1880 Newbern City Directory*).

5. Celia Laura and Isabella R. Ransom were daughters of Alexis Ransom of Kalamazoo, Michigan. Both taught at the New York Institute for the Deaf, where Frank and Willie Clarke taught. Frank Clarke married Celia Ransom in 1873. *The Michigan Mirror Memorial Number* 40, no. 2 (Flint, Mich.: Michigan School for the Deaf, 23 Oct. 1913), 8 (hereafter cited as *Michigan Mirror*).

*Wootten, Moulton, Clarke Papers, SHC*
*Mary Bayard Clarke to Willie Clarke*

New Berne
Nov 20th [1871]

My Dear Willie

I have written to both the others and now it is your turn. I hope you were not uneasy about me in the blow which was terrific but I was too sick to care for it. I am just getting up again, for I was weakened a good deal but every body says I look so well I think I must be better only I dont know it. Father came home Saturday night and said I did not *look* as well as I did the first night I got here but I *feel* better

Sister is as great a belle as ever the parlor has at least one beaux in it every night, but oftener two or more, Lulu[1] creates a sensation among them she is thought a great beauty and even Mr John Missilear[2] pronounces her a "beautiful girl" and you know his opinion is unanswerabl; he asked permission to call and be introduced and invited her to go to the theatre tomorrow night. There is a masquerade Wednesday night and Sister is stitching away to go as Edith Plantaginet with Willie Dissosway as Kenneth. Lou thought at first she would go in character but changed her mind and goes with me in her own character to look on and see how others do before she takes part herself. There is but little news to tell you Charlie Slover and Emma Ellis[3] have made up and will be married next month. Both the Misses Cobb were married last week on the same night Miss Sue Branch is married to a Mr Jones and Dink Heartt is to be married to Miss Annie Dewey who lives at the corner below the Mayor's office She spent last summer in Raleigh and it was made up then.

The church is nearly finished and we will be in it by Easter. Dr Bates is to be married to Mrs Downney[4] the widow, Miss Mary Whitford[5] and Miss Mary Manly[6] have come home for good—Col Whitford has bought Miss Naney Smith's house opposite Dr Smallwood's,[7] and I believe that is all—Give my love to Frank and Mr Cooke I hope you will write me sometimes but I know that you are very busy—and shall not expect you to write often.

Sister and Lou send love and with much from me—believe me your loving

Mother

1. An unidentified friend who was visiting from the North.

2. John Louis Henry Missiliar, a store clerk and family friend. *1880 Newbern City Directory,* 80.

3. A Charles Slover appeared in the 1870 census as a retail grocer. Emma Ellis Slover was the daughter of Benjamin and Eliza H. Ellis. Eliza Ellis was a widow who lived near the Clarke family. *1870 Craven County Census Index,* 97, 1st Ward no. 88; *1880 Newbern City Directory,* 56.

4. Henry G. Bates, a New Bern physician, married Ann M. Downing. *1870 Craven County Census Index,* p. 84, 1st Ward no. 59.

5. Mary Whitford was the daughter of Colonel John D. Whitford of New Bern. Powell, *DNCB,* 6:188.

6. Mary Manly was a daughter of Mathias Evans Manly of New Bern, a lawyer, state legislator, and superior court judge. He also served on the North Carolina Supreme Court from 1860 until the end of the Civil War. A Conservative politician, he continued his law practice in New Bern and acted as a county judge after being defeated for the supreme court during Reconstruction. Padgett, "Reconstruction Letters from North Carolina," 297n.

7. Edward F. Smallwood was a New Bern physician. *1880 Newbern City Directory,* 93.

☙

*Wootten, Moulton, Clarke Papers, SHC*
*Mary Bayard Clarke to Willie Clarke*

New Berne Jan 3d<br>1872

My Dear Willie

I received your sweet Christmas letter last week but I gave Frank the right of primogeniture as I could not write two letters at such a busy time, and wished to tell you all about both Christmas and new Year—Of course you have read his letter so I wont go over the Tournament, but only say that the girls were so used up that they were as cross as tired children usually are, and I had to say if they were not less languid they should not go out any more for some time. I had invited Mr Morgan to pay us a visit and would not hear of his going before New Year's day, and it was not hard to keep him for I think he enjoyed every moment of the time and quarreled and made friends with one or the other, every ten minutes. Father got home Saturday night and New Year's day began with a hard rain before breakfast but was bright and clear by nine o'clock, *the children,* which includes Morgan, had draped the parlor with evergreens and I set my table in the little room just in front of the folding doors, it looked very pretty and so did the girls, I had invited Mrs Hall a pretty young lady staying at the hotel to spend the day with us, and some others to come in in the evening, I had chicken salad, pickled oysters, sandwitches, a large bowl of apple toddy, another of Whiskey punch, and two decanters of Wine. We had forty five calls and would have had many more but for a rain that came up about two o'clock, and prevented some of the old fogies from turning out, also my young ladies from coming to tea, but we had a very merry evening as about fifteen of the boys were here and supper was given till twelve o'clock, No one was the *worse* for drinking but some were very amusing among them Willie Whitford who came three times to show me he was not tight and discussed suicide most learnedly, Green Bryan was very devoted and Bennie was happy, altogether it was quite a success and if we said once we did fifty times "it only wants the boys to be perfect" I did indeed wish for you both for that season—but when I thought of what these boys were all doing and their prospect for life I was glad you were not living here—Willie Whitford is studying law with Mr Charles Clarke[1] and often says he could learn twice as fast if he was where he could hear lectures and have your advantages Morgan is making money but says he hates his business[2] and wishes he could get out of it—Bennie[3] still drives the Express cart and acts as clerk Big Dis is with Mr Berry and studying chemistry to be a good apothecary he has only one night in the week and invariably spends that here or with Mary somewhere else, he is a case, and so is George Guion and Ed Smallwood[4] and the little lady says she likes them all equally—and will take the first that comes for a walk or a party but none for life. John Roberts has cooled off Delia got jealous I believe of his attentions to Mary and took Willie Whitford in his place which sent him off to a Miss Evans for comfort since sister would not give it to him. The girls send love. Lulu says she has started to school today and dont like it a bit but wishes you were here, Sister says tell Willie she will write to him when she get rested and the news is that Mark Dissosway[5] has had a quarrel with Mary Dunn[6] and has flown off to Georgie Wallace, that Miss Duncan is in town and if you dont look out George Guion or Bennie Bryan will cut you out. Mary Whitford is not popular (she says). I think she is carrying on with Lon Moore[7] and the young men dont like it. Allie Lehman is not visited by the young gentlemen she is not at all popular and I think it is the way her mother behaves. Good night

Your loving Mother

1. Charles C. Clark was a prominent New Bern lawyer and Conservative politician. He also served in the state legislature before and after the war. In 1854 he married Fannie Howard, and they had four sons and four daughters. Powell, *DNCB,* 2:371–72.

2. Rufus Morgan worked as a traveling photographer, taking photographs on commission and selling them to the general public.

3. Benjamin Bryan worked as a clerk at the Southern Express office. *1880 Newbern City Directory,* 46.

4. This was probably a son of Dr. Edward F. Smallwood. *1880 Newbern City Directory,* 93.

5. Years later, Mark Disosway's daughter Myrtle married George Clarke Moulton. Their daughter Mary Moulton Barden is co-editor of this volume.

6. Mary Dunn was the daughter of Margaret Dunn. 1870 Craven County Census Index, 82, 1st Ward no. 82.

7. Leonidas J. Moore was a twenty-five-year-old lawyer in 1870. He practiced law in New Bern for more than forty years and died in 1903. He eventually married Betty Terry of Virginia. 1870 Craven County Census Index, 90, 1st Ward, no. 159; *1880 Newbern City Directory,* 81, 107. Archibald Henderson and others, *North Carolina Biography,* vol. 4 of *North Carolina: The Old North State and the New* (Chicago: Lewis Publishing, 1941), 115.

*Barden Collection*
*Robert Dick to Mary Bayard Clarke*

Raleigh NC<br>Febry 4th 1872<br>Mrs M. Bayard Clarke.

My Dear Friend

I had nearly finished the labors of the week and was in the midst of an opinion about writs of sein facias and judgments quando when I received your letter. It came like a gleam of sunshine after a cold and stormy day.—

It also made me think of another simile.—Your cheerful spirit and sparkling thought was as exhilerating as a glass of champagne and I enjoyed it greatly, altho' the association of ideas was not very appropriate for a temperance man.

I regret to learn that you are compelled to quit *brain work* but I feel assured that the fountains of the heart will become full of beautiful affections and sympathies, which will in due time gush forth, and sparkle in the sunlight of genius. I do not regard myself as using the language of compliment when I express the hope and speak the voice of all the lovers of the true and beautiful in literature.

Since I last saw you I have become a thorough womans rights man, and gave into domestic bankruptcy at home. I have surrendered every thing to my wife, and now I am in a delightful condition of freedom without independence. I shall advise Judge Clake to do the same thing when I see him for I am decidedly pleased with this "new departure" It may be that Judge Clark will say that he does not need my advice, and claim to be my illustrious predecessor in this new line of policy.—

I have forgotten to thank you for your kind invitation, and now do so most sincerely.—I cannot say when I will be in your city. This will depend on future arrangements made by my friend Mr Lehman.—I have promised my friend Miss Allie to be at her disposal, and I must stay where my friends may place me.—It is not my purpose to deliver a strictly temperance address.—but I expect to read a lecture on the "Anglo American" I will be sure to visit you and we can talk fully about "the books" and many other pleasant things

I will not leave here before the 10th of March, and cannot go to Newbern before April.

Present my kind regard to Judge Clarke,—and my sweetest affections to the little sunny-hearted Mary.—

In haste
With high esteem,
Your friend
*Robt R Dick*

❧

*Barden Collection*
*Mary Bayard Clarke to Willie Clarke*

New Berne
Sunday [March 31, 1872]

Dear Willie

This is Easter Sunday and I have been disappointed in getting to church as I have one of my miserable headaches and am adorned with a beladonna plaster on my temple. Father adjourned court over Good Friday and we went to church but being late could not get a seat, it was the first really spring day we have had and the long walk in my winter clothing without any rest was too much for me and I got home with a headache which steadily increased till I had to go to bed with it I am up to day but feeling very shaky. I dont understand what you mean by Allie Lehman's marrying the butcher I did not know there was one named Tom Powers; this man has been here a long time but he is not *now* a butcher; may have been for aught I know, he is now U S Assessor and every body speaks well of him, he is good looking and desperately in love but I dont know if she is engaged or not as I see very little of her Mary does not like her and she does not like Mary—except when you and Frank are here—Did you get one of the enclosed circulars? I have one of the originals so did not care for it. I hope I shall be able to see you next fall but I am getting doubtful even of that and it is a great disappointment I dont know what we will do or where we will go—I should like to send Sister off and stay here quietly but I know I cant do that, there is no further news of the Supreme Court for Father, I dont believe he will get it, and I think he is becoming doubtful himself.[1] Lulu goes home by the next trip of the Zodiac and I shall send your sheets then, but how will you get them? She will not stop in New York and she cant express them to you. Shall she leave them at Murray & Ferris? if so I had better get a bill of lading for them and pay freight as they will be safer. Dont you need drawers? if so let me know and I will make you some tell Frank of it. Father feels more and more disappointed about his engagement, I never saw him take any thing so much to heart, he curses his poverty which obliged him to let you boys be where you are, and indeed I cant but agree with him that all the troubles we have ever had have been caused by poverty and when I think of them it is not to be wondered that I hate to see Frank take this burden on his shoulders. Mary is better but still far from herself I am going to let her go to see Jennie next month she will be on a plantation and quiet.

Aunt Kate has published an essay in pamphlet form called "Morte d'Arthur and its effects on the Chivalry of the South" or something like that.[2] I will send you a copy when I can get one she sent me one but never told me she had written it, I guessed it and Aunt Nora confirmed my suspicions, it is very bitter and just at present very ill advised

There is no news Beaux are devoted Bill Ellis being the favoured one at present because he sends flowers and takes her out on horse back She is looking so badly it makes me sad but she says she is not sick only weak

Love to Frank and Celia

Your loving<br>Mother

1. Thomas Settle Jr. resigned his position on the North Carolina Supreme Court on 24 March 1871, and left the state to serve as the United States minister to Peru. He returned to North Carolina in 1872. Caldwell reappointed Settle to the state's supreme court on 20 June 1872. Jeffrey J. Crow, "Thomas Settle Jr., Reconstruction, and the Memory of the Civil War," *Journal of Southern History* 62 (Nov. 1996): 689–726.

2. Catherine Edmondston wrote and anonymously published *Morte d'Arthur* in 1872. What may be the only surviving copy can be found in the Barden Collection.

৵

*Wootten, Moulton, Clarke Papers, SHC*
*William J. Clarke to Willie Clarke*

New Berne June 23d. '72

My Dear Willie:

I have not written to you for so long a time that I fear that you think that I have either forgotten you, or that I have forgotten how to write.

I have just finished a very laborious circuit, both as to the number and the difficulty of the causes I have tried. My general health has improved, and I hope to be able, in my vacation, to read a good deal of law, on the "recubaus sub tegmire fagi" principle, so that I shall return to my labors in the fall better prepared to discharge my duties, with credit to myself and profit to the community, even if I should not be promoted to the Supreme Court bench, of which I stand a good chance, to fill a vacancy caused by the appointment of Judge Dick, U.S. District judge.[1] I was in Raleigh last week and my chances were considered the best of all spoken of and my friends of this section are pushing my claims, but I have not set my heart on it, and tho' I feel myself far better qualified than most of the persons spoken of, still I do not *feel* as if I should be appointed; tho' I feel that it is but justice to myself, and my family, to assert my pretentions to the office. It is at least gratifying to be generally spoken of as worthy and qualified for so high an office.

Your sister and Mrs. Hall accompanied me, and were delighted with their visit. The Devereuxs called on Mary Your Aunt Nora is in Hillsboro' and I saw nothing of your Aunt Frances and her family.

Raleigh is very sickly. The city has improved so that you would hardly know it. I am sorry that I cannot say the same of New Berne. Boon Hill is improving rapidly, and almost every other place except this.

Your Mother is counting the days until you come. The Terry[2] leaves tomorrow (Monday) at 6 P.M. and we hope you will be able to return on her. She has been detained by a strike among the dock hands.

The political cauldron is boiling vigorously, and every stump is occupied by a speaker, to whom (if the newspapers are to be believed) Demosthenese could not hold a candle. The Republicans will carry the State ticket by a large majority, and I think they will have a majority of the legislature, and also of the Congressional delegation, and the State will go for Grant in Nov. by a heavy majority.

Mary has just returned from church with half a doz beaux among them is your friend Wm. Disossay who is well—Morgan was not in R.—

This leaves us in our usual health. I have just learned that the Terry will leave N.Y. on Saturday next, so you can make your arrangements accordingly.

With love to Frank and respects to Mr. Cooke, I am

Affectionately yours

Wm. J. Clarke

1. Robert P. Dick resigned his position on the North Carolina Supreme Court in 1872 after President Ulysses S. Grant appointed him judge of the United States District Court for the western district of North Carolina. Powell, *DNCB*, 2:63.

2. The steamship *Ellen S. Terry* followed a regular route between New Bern and New York.

*Wootten, Moulton, Clarke Papers, SHC*
*Nora Cannon to Willie Clarke*

Raleigh Aug 6th [1872]

My Dear Will

Your letter was most welcome and would have been answered sooner but for the fact that there were several girls here who had come from home without their sheets & pillow cases & by taking the job I could make a dollar or two so I have been every afternoon hemming sheets instead of writing to you but I knew that you would excuse me as I have given up in despair making any money by my pen and am obliged to do what I can with my machine. Your letter gave me a great deal of pleasure as well as some pain; you cannot tell how grieved I was to learn that Katie had come away from Beaufort without calling on her Aunt Mary and showing her that she had determined to be friends with her Mother's sister and friend even tho she had to abandon the quarrel of her Auntie[1] which I told her she was not called on to take up. I can only say "I am sorry deeply sorry" and assure you that I am in no way to blame, and feel hurt at the fact that my daughter should disregard her Mother's wishes and show disrespect to those whom *she* loves and who have been so kind to her. Do not I beg think her conduct is any indication of my feelings, and therefore let your love for me fail I had anticipated so much pleasure in hearing Sis Mary's praise of my Grand child that I could hardly help crying when I heard that she had not seen her Believe me Willie when I say that my heart ached and I almost regretted not sending Nonie down with Kate for I know she would have gone to see her Aunt Mary at once You should have heard her tone of voice when she exclaimed "*Why Sister*!!! did not you go to see *Aunt Mary,—Mothers sister!* when you were right there where she was!!![*"*] But enough of this enough for me to say I find out that my children are not governed by their mother's expressed wishes as I hoped they would be and I must only say to you all "Love me as I love you."

We are all quietly settled here at work I teaching and Sadie & Mat learning, Nonie's health is so feeble that Dr Haywood tells me not to bring her here for a while, she is now at her Sister's and goes next week to her Uncle John's; she is just about as she was when you met us at the depot at New Berne except that she does not suffer from Rheumatism and her spirits are *generally* better though at times she is very low spirited

Give my love to your Mother and Father & tell them that they *both* owe me a letter for I *answered* the letter from your Father *which I never got* and wrote a note to your Mother telling her I had received & read & remailed her letter to your Aunt Sophia. I wish I could see you my dear boy but suppose I shall have to wait till next winter for if I live & nothing unforseen happens to prevent I shall spend my winter vacation at your Father's house Sadie and Mat the only ones with me send much love to you one and all. Good bye remember what I have said about continuing to love me and believe me ever your affectionate Aunt

Nonie

1. Kate Cannon Primrose remained actively engaged in the feud between Frances Miller, the "Auntie" referred to above, and William and Mary Clarke.

&#x223D;

*Wootten, Moulton, Clarke Papers, SHC*
*William J. Clarke to Mary Bayard Clarke*

Goldsboro' Sunday night
[ca. November/December 1872]

My Darling wife:

I cannot go to bed tonight without writing to you. I was very low last night; I felt disappointed, injured, sore. I had buried a great hope; a tower, like Babel, erected by unreasonable hope, had fallen, and I felt crushed.[1] Today, sunlight is on my soul, and I can thank God for all the blessings I enjoy; and say "Thy will be done" as to things I hoped—

I think of what I have, not of what I wish. While you and the children are spared to me, while I occupy an honorable position, with an income sufficient to support us decenty, and comfortably, I feel that there is no room for repining. No one knew how sad and sore my heart was, and, as if to console me, last night more than one person told me of the high regard the people had for me and the great satisfaction my administration, as judge, gave. My great hopefulness astonishes me, on self examination, perhaps it is "a sign of a revival," I dont know, but I only hope you could feel as hopeful as I do, and as contented and as happy—I am glad I was not with you in my despair, and low spirits—But that has all passed, and we are engaged in a Railroad suit, in which I shall give a great opinion.

Church today, splendid singing; fair sermon; horrible reading; pretty and well dressed women; good dinner; wretched supper—A fair number of visitors, *who did not* disturb me in my *Sunday* (Sunday spelt with a capital) nap—

I don't think that after reading this letter you can be at a loss to know whence Pet derives her *genius* for correspondence. Write me a little love letter to let me know that you are not in the dumps—Give my love to all

Affectionately yours
*Wm. J. Clarke*

1. Apparently Clarke was referring to Thomas Settle Jr.'s appointment to the North Carolina Supreme Court, although the appointment officially occurred on 20 June 1872. In a letter dated 8 December [1872], Mary Bayard Clarke wrote to their son Willie that, "all our cake is dough respecting the Supreme Court judgeship Caldwell has reappointed Judge Settle after giving Father's friends reason to think he intended to appoint him." Wootten, Moulton, Clarke Papers, SHC.

❧

*Wootten, Moulton, Clarke Papers, SHC*
*Mary Bayard Clarke to Willie Clarke*

New Berne
Dec 8th [1872]

Dear Willie

I received your letter the day after I sent off my last to you and have such a headache I can only acknowledge it and tell you all our cake is dough respecting the Supreme Court judgeship Caldwell has reappointed Judge Settle after giving Father's friends reason to think he intended to appoint him, but there is no use talking of what cant be helped. You dont say a word about your shirts. did Celia give them *all* to Frank? its just like her if she did for I believe she'd give him her eyes—if he wanted them but you just tell her from me if he is good looking he dont need a thousand shirts. Have Tom's been sent to him, he never would think to mention them

Mrs Stevenson said the other day I might as well tell the truth about Celia for Mark said he knew she was either your sweetheart or Frank's and she wanted to know which was in love with her—, I said you were devoted to her, then she wished to know if you were engaged or going to be to which I replied that I did not believe it would ever come to any thing seeing Celia was engaged to another Gentleman in New York whereat she expressed great disappointment saying she liked her so much she hoped one of my boys would get her and then she would come down here some-times to see us again. Allie Lehman sends her love and says you owe her a letter and she wishes you would pay up, I think there is no doubt about her and Powers being engaged.

Aunt Nora comes down to morrow with all her girls—so I shall have a housefull—Father and I have moved to the garret during her stay—My head aches so I must stop love to Frank and Celia and tell Frank he might write to me sometimes if he is in love.

Your loving
Mother

I sent a check for two dollars in my last—dont send it back.

❧

*Wootten, Moulton, Clarke Papers, SHC*
*Mary Bayard Clarke to Willie Clarke*

New Berne
Jan 1st [1873]

A Happy New Year to you my dear Willie and many thanks for your pretty present which reached me last night, they are beautiful and also useful—Father thinks he is going to get one of them in the dining room to hold matches for his pipe but he is mistaken I am going to put one in the parlor and one in my bed room. His pipe did not come but will be here I suppose to morrow Tom has been much better but to day has another headache and looks as white as a sheet but the Dr says it is only weakness now as the fever is broken, poor Charlie Bates has never been out of bed yet but Ed Berry like Tom keeps up only ailing all the time. There is no news to tell you except that I have been to a party and danced with all the Jews in town![1] Mrs Davison sent her little boy over after tea one night last week to ask me to come over and spend the evening as they were going to have some music so father staid with Tom as I had declined going so often and said he would come for me at half past ten, when he did he found us in full blast and *I,* your respected Mother, sailing down the room with Emanuel's longest nosed clerk! the Misses Radcliff[2] were the only Christians or Americans in the room beside me—and I said that they would think I was "stuck up" if I did not dance so I stood up intending to walk through a quadrille but it was bitter cold and as there were no carpets I found dancing warmed me and I kept it up. When father got there he, like an artful dodger, instead of saying he had come for me, regretted he could not get over earlier being detained by business!! and went to flirting with Mrs Hahns[3] the bakers wife—; at twelve o'clock we had a nice supper and went home about one to find Tom had never stirred. I am to receive calls to morrow and Allie comes over to help me and I guess we will have all the Germans in town for they professed themselves so complimented at my going to a German party—Give my love to Frank and tell him now he is well I shall begin to scold if I dont hear from him. Father sends love and thanks for your letter he only got home last night but has a week's rest

Your loving Mother

1. North Carolina's Jewish population came primarily from Germany. The 1870 census indicated that about 300 Jews lived in the state, mainly in cities and larger towns. Harry L. Golden, "The Jewish People of North Carolina," *NCHR* 32 (Apr. 1955): 203n, 211n.

2. Sarah and Irene Radcliff were the daughters of Samuel Radcliff, who owned a saw mill in New Bern. *1880 Newbern City Directory,* 87.

3. Meyer and Amealin Hahn moved from Baden, Germany, to New Jersey. They later moved to New Bern and opened a bakery on Pollock Street. 1870 Craven County Census Index, 83, 1st Ward, no. 52.

❧

*Wootten, Moulton, Clarke Papers, SHC*
*Nora Cannon to Willie Clarke*

New Berne Jan 5th/73

My Dear Will

Your letter was duly received and before I leave the [illegible] of Craven" I will answer it and tell you how we are getting along. Your Mother I am sorry to say is *completely disgusted* with me first as I told you before because I will not have my hair put up on the top of my head & secondly because I will compose "*dogrel parodis*" on every thing that comes into my head and spout them out at her while we are sewing and lastly because Mr Leonidas J Moore having had the good taste to fall desperetely in love with your sister Mary; for some unknown reason (as he supposes) is all attention and affection to me whom he has taken for the best confidante in the world and I will not obey her (your mother) and "put Mary on her guard" but just laugh and say "Leon Moore is big enough to take care of himself and as I say and believe is too old a bird to commit himself when he finds out the little lady wants "none of him" but if he is not "it will not *kill* him to be thrown"

In the mean time if there is any truth in the saying "laugh and grow fat" I shall become as stout as Mrs John Hughes for it is *such fun* first will come a *note* to your mother with a present of a Mocking bird!! then a note to Mrs Hall "also a few apples" then a law paper to Father! between each reminder the gentleman "putting in an appearance" as I believe you lawyers say. He gave Miss Mary a beautiful New Years present of a silver Cake Basket thereby raising the wrath and indignation of "the boys" Big Dis, Green Bryan, [illegible] to hire a body guard for fear they might way lay him on his way up here some night. The other night I nearly expired at Big Dis;—Mr M & myself came into the parlor at Mrs Davidson's where the girls were having dance and had to stand for a moment looking for a chair Big Dis rose from beside Mary & gave me his seat & Mr M after standing a moment beside me turned off when Big Dis said I give my seat to *you* with pleasure but *Leon Moore* shant have it for *I am as big a man as he is*"!! I do wish you could [torn] in on us and see the [black?] looks the boys give him & how he will then come & *devote* himself to me, bending over &

speaking low to make it appear he is saying "something sweet" all this so that when he gets the mitten from Mary he can say "I went there to see Mrs Cannon" well knowing that no one could be so absurd as to suppose that he had any "*designs*" in doing so as I am old enough to be his mother What he will do when I leave which will be on Wednesday next I do not know. Oh I forgot to say that his "tribbins" to me come in the shape of nur [torn] & putting us to sleep every night that he is here.

Still I have had a *glorious* four weeks holiday and have enjoyed *every moment* of it to the full.

Clem got jealous & brought big Brother "Basil" to drive Leonidas off but lo & behold! his big Brother pitched in for himself & Clem had to hurry up & propose for himself for fear he would have to fight the big Brother. "Go it Bar go it Husband I dont care which beats" as the old woman said

Mary says she can only spare time from the care of her beaux to tell you she loves *you* dearly

Mattie says I must [torn] you "she thinks her book is the prettiest of all["] and I believe I agree with her though the others were beautiful

Good bye when I write next it will be from the Academic shades of St Marys to which place direct your next to your loving but Mother says *naughty*

Aunt Nonnie

∾

*Wootten, Moulton, Clarke Papers, SHC*
*Mary Bayard Clarke to Willie Clarke*

New Berne Jan 12th [1873]

My Dear Willie

I received your letter last Wednesday on my return from Goldsboro where I went with Aunt Nora on her way to Raleigh, she and the girls said they had enjoyed every moment of their stay and I am truly glad they did, for I was too unwell to enjoy it myself and feel really relieved at having a quiet house again, I wrote Celia all about the trip and as I know you read each other's letters I wont repeat but go on with the tale, on Thursday evening the redoubtable Mr Moore called as usual but did not see Missie, for as soon as she heard father say "good evening Mr Moore" as he opened the front door, she bolted out the back parlor and up stairs leaving me to fib for her and make out she had a headache, she vows she's tired of him, says there is *so much* of him she cant bear him for more than an hour a week, and would not marry him if there was no other man on earth, and yet she wont put the boys out of their misery, but keeps them believing she likes Mr Moore, because she says she is not going to let them think that *they* can dictate to *her*. Mrs Hall is invaluable now as we propose whist when he comes which is quite a relief—

evening—Interrupted here by a ring and the gentleman himself appeared—My motto about Mary's beaux is "a fair field and no favor" so I left him in posession and went to see Mrs Stanly who is a strong Phifer[1] woman, when I got back I had to lie on the sofa to laugh, for it seems he proposed a walk to the grave yard, where all the New Berne beaux take their lady loves, and sister, mindful of Clem's exploit there last week, said she would have to go there some day whether she wanted to or not and prefered another direction whereon he launched out on the subject of her health,[2] said she only needed red blood and he wished she would consent to have a vein tapped in his arm and his blood transfused into her veins, in dead earnest he went on to urge the operation and Missie's account was so ludicrous that I have done nothing but laugh since I got back. I wish you were here to enjoy the fun for as I dont believe Lon Moore is really in love I dont feel any compassion for him. Perhaps I shall be punished by seeing you in love hopelessly, I hope not, for I am looking forward to your coming home and bringing your wife to live with me when Mary deserts me, Celia is to come and stay whenever Frank is where she cannot be with him but I dont mean to let you go, once I put my hands on you, you are to live with Father and me till you have "so many children you dont know what to do" Father is so glad to hear you think of coming home to settle he would have written to you himself but had to go to Raleigh last week and only got home Friday, this morning he left to hold a Special Court in Pitt Co and wont be back for two weeks—Love to Frank and Celia, I hope Frank is better by this time, Your loving

Mother

I wrote to Celia last week Mrs Whedbee (Miss Lizzie Manly) and Miss Maria are at the Fifth Avenue Hotel. Miss M says to go to see her.

---

1. This unidentified suitor of Mary Devereux Clarke resided in Charlotte, North Carolina. To her parents' relief, Mary D. Clarke later broke off her correspondence with him.

2. Mary Devereux Clarke suffered from an illness identified in one family letter as "chlorosis," which left her weak and listless. Chlorosis, a form of anemia, was common in adolescent girls.

❧

*Wootten, Moulton, Clarke Papers, SHC*
*Mary Bayard Clarke to Willie Clark*

New Berne
Feb 2d [1873]

My Dear Willie

I received your letter of the 26th in due time and enjoyed your account of the slide down the hill though I had to hold my head when I laughed for fear it would split with the neuralgia; we have had a taste of your weather and for two weeks Mrs Hall Mary and I have all had neuralgia, not violently only just miserably and we have done nothing but sew and play casino, it affected my eyes so I could not read and tho I could run the sewing machine I could not thread the needle, Father is still at Pitt court but we expect him home to morrow and I am glad we are all better before he comes, Aunt Nora wishes to know if you got her letter telling about the fun going on here, she is back at St Mary's as school begins on the 25th—

What do Canaries cost? I have no idea and she is so anxious for one that I mean to get her one some time when I can afford it. I have not forgotten that I owe you ten dollars and shall pay my debts soon. Frank pokes a good deal of fun at me about my secret correspondence with you and is evidently as curious as a woman, Missie too is sure I have been telling some of her secrets so I have uttered a declaration of independance and informed them both that I loved all my children *differently,* and I am glad to say that they all have distinct individualities and what I say to one is not intended to be stereotyped for the benefit of the family, you all feel you can say things to Mother you wont say to anyone else and I am not going to be cheated of my rights and intend to feel that I can say and write things to you that I would not tell Frank and Mary and ditto, ditto, ditto. You dont all look exactly alike and it is not strange you should not feel alike, think alike, and act alike, you three eldest are grown, and though I may be a class or two a head of you in the school of life it does not follow that you are all to do and think as I do, I am intensely individual in my thoughts and sentiments but I dont set up for infalibility and insist on my children fitting into my nitch and I wish they would not try to put each other on to a Procrustean bed and insist on all thinking feeling and acting "as they ought to do" but would make up their minds to differ yet not disagree.

Live your own life is my motto but I was brought up to think I ought to live some body elses life and must take my opinions—and feelings as I did my clothes when a child, they were cut and made properly and I must wear them—

I have always tried to avoid this with you children and I should as soon think of making you all like the same things to eat as of insisting you should all think alike or—scold because you did not, no two human beings were ever more unlike in character than you and Frank and of course you are going to hold different opinions but do please my dear Willie start in life with the conviction that God intended men to think differently and to feel differently and dont think that because people dont agree with you they are necessarily wrong—. because a great many good people think its a sin to go to the theatre it dont follow that we should be bad people because we go there and enjoy it; a great many people think as Homes says "they are very pious when they are only dispeptic.["] I say my religion suits me and I love it but that is no reason it should suit any body else. I have suffered so much from intolerance on every subject that I dread to see it in my family and the first symptoms of it are an unwillingness for any two to have something together or any one to have *any thing* they dont tell the others—and I have mounted a pinacle and declare to you all that I regard you as my equals—but—beyond a certain point—I dont mean to be bossed by any body, nor do I intend to attempt to boss—any of my children I mean to have secrets and to keep secrets—such as they are—from and with you all. I have told you about Phifer because I thought [torn] I have not told Frank because I saw no need to do so—and you were quite right to keep my secret and I hope you will continue to do so Missie suspects me but I shut her up by telling her she and I had secrets and she need not expect you and I would not have them.

I gave Frank a hint in my last to the effect that he had better not make fun of the afore said gentleman and I hope he'll take it for he is coming here before long and sister has—not bully-ragged me—but just set up and looked pale and sick at me, till I have let her write to him in reply to another letter from him the contents of which she keeps a dead secret from me beyond the fact that he's coming soon. I had no notion I was writing such a volume you may read part of it to Frank if you like but dont you *ever* give my letters *always* to *any body.* you may give an occasional one but I want to feel I write to *you* and not to all of you children at once, when I do that Ill say "dear boys"

Yours lovingly
Mother

❧

*Wootten, Moulton, Clarke Papers, SHC*
*Mary Bayard Clarke to Willie Clarke*

New Berne
Feb. 16th [1873]

My Dear Willie

I received your long letter last night and thank you for it. I am glad to hear your friend is out of danger and hope she will have no draw back in her recovery. I wish I could agree with you about Frank's engagement, but I cannot, I regard it as very unfortunate, but being inevitable I shall not add to the sorrow it gives me by opposing it. A woman can say to a man "I must break my engagement with you because my parents dont like it" but a man cant say that to a woman without doing a dishonourable act, and I would rather suffer any thing than feel one of my sons had acted dishonourably to any one, but more particularly to a woman. Personally I have no objection to the young lady for you know I only know her through you boys— she struck me as decidedly lady like, agreeable, and pretty, but she is too old for Frank and he too young in my judgement to marry any woman I have not changed my opinion in the least but I think only of my children's happiness I do not think it will add to Franks happiness to marry and have a family to support with nothing but his daily labor to look to, all the ills and sorrows of my life have come either directly or indirectly from poverty and I cannot see Frank take this burden on him without groaning in spirit, but he has taken it and I shant add to it by expressing an opinion that must give him present pain and can do no good either now or in the future. He has decided for himself and says now to me Mother I bring you this woman as my future wife, and I say to him and to her—I receive her as such and she shall be a daughter to me, but I have cried my self to sleep every night since I got his letter. I have not seen your Father as he did not come home Saturday but I sent the letter to him and told him what I had decided on doing—he wrote that he felt just as I did, but as we could do nothing it was best to try and feel that it might not be as bad as we feared. Tell Frank to write to him, for he feels very sore that it has all been settled without his knowledge I dont mean you should tell Frank this last or how I feel—, I have written him, *and truly,* that his happiness is my first wish, its no use to tell him I think he has done a foolish thing, because he cant undo it, The young lady is not to blame and I wont hurt her feelings by letting her see how we feel—if Frank marries her she shall never know from me that I dont like it and I know you wont tell her, but this settles any coming North next Summer I dont wish to do so now I am afraid I could not conceal my feelings and I dont wish to show them I am not surprised he could not conceal his, I am not angry, or mortified, I am only deeply grieved because I think he has made a mistake, You say he has made his engagement public, ask him from me not to write his Southern friends of it till there is a prospect of his immediate marriage

I dont want to be asked questions about it, I dont want them to find out that I dont like it. I will get use to it before he can marry disappointment is nothing new to me it has met me at every turn for so many years that I have ceased hoping almost for myself and hope only for my children, I can still hope for their love and that I may not worry them or render them unhappy is the effort of my life, so I dont mean to say any more about Frank's engagement being disagreeable to me but set my teeth and make the best of it and all you must say to him and Celia is simply "Mother will never oppose it she believes everybody should marry to suit themselves"

I must close for we have company Give my love to them and come what may believe you will always find a loving heart in the bosom of your

Mother

❦

*Wootten, Moulton, Clarke Papers, SHC*
*Mary Bayard Clarke to Willie Clarke*

New Berne
March 5th [1873]

My Dear Willie

I will write your birthday day letter so that you will get it on the 7th if possible as I know I shall not feel in good spirits then, as it is a sad anniversary with me since my dear Father died on it. I sent you some of Morgan's prettiest views——, that is I sent them to Frank to give to you, I wrote him a long letter which I hope he got but I gave it to a man desperately in love to mail, and have since thought I was rash. And now I must tell you what I am sure you will be glad to hear. Sister has become convinced that he[r] Beaufort admirer of last summer is not the kind of man she ought to marry, and has of her own accord sent back all his letters and broken off the correspondence. I hope it will never be renewed but I confess I look with fear and trembling on the posibility of his coming in person to plead his cause.

Morgan left last Monday positively refusing to take *No* for an answer; he says he can make $2000 a year over his expenses and will wait as long as she remains single for her, I dont know how it will end; personally I would as soon she married him as any man I know it would not be a brilliant but it would be a safe match for her, his plan is to start a peach farm in the mountains where the fruit is never killed by frost, take views—and increase his stock of negatives all the time, and in the winter live in New Berne never letting sister be here after May or before a killing frost—, I am selfish in wishing her to take him, I know for it would leave her so much with me and yet take her out of this climate when it is sickly—but I tell him I will neither make nor mar a match, that all I say is that he shall have a "fair field and no favour"

Her health is miserable and getting worse, she now neither sleeps nor eats well, and Dr Duffy is evidently anxious about her, write to her often and cheerfully—even if you have to leave me off occasionally and tell Frank to do the same, let him read this letter and then let us all drop the name of Phifer from our memory—, and never mention him to her; to abuse him will rouse her pride I dont believe she ever really loved him, she only fancied she did—, she has not been crossed or talked into breaking it off, she simply heard he gambled and was not safe I dont know as it so— but I never liked it and am glad it is ended without leaving any bitterness in her heart towards any of us for breaking it off—I think she feels a little sore at having been cross with you about him, so be more than usually affectionate to her. Father has just written he is not well enough to come home between Wilson and Wayne Court so I must go up to see him on Saturday and Spend Sunday and Monday with him

Your loving<br>Mother

ↄ

*Wootten, Moulton, Clarke Papers, SHC*
*Nora Cannon to Willie Clarke*

St. Mary's March 23d [1873]

My Dear Willie
. . . .
. . . . I agree with you entirely in your views and opinions as to a man's *making his* own fate; and though in a less degree a woman can do the same thing but you know that I believe firmly in "the divine rights of *men*["] and while I admit that women have *three rights* I contend they have no more these are 1st to be as *bewitching* and pretty as they possibly can, 2d always to have a nicely laid table with a nicely cooked meal on it ready for the coming man & 3rd *always* to have the buttons sewed on his shirts. Now any

woman who does exercise these three rights & never flags will be happy. Of course if there is no Man coming home she must necessarily take on herself part of the man's work and rights & resign her own;—Understand, I mean by *bewitching* not only to the eye but to the mind by cultivating her Intelect and to the heart by fostering the amiable qualities of her disposition God help the man whose wife lets her mind go to waste and shelters herself behind "*housekeeping duties*" But enough foolishness for one time even from your foolish but loving Aunt

Nonie

❧

*Wootten, Moulton, Clarke Papers, SHC*
*William J. Clarke to Willie Clarke*

New Berne April 6th. 1873.

My Dear Willie:

This is the 25th. anniversary of my wedding day, and though I ought to have gone to Onslow today, still I determined to do, what I have rarely done, sacrifice duty to inclination, and stay at home. I am happy to say that your Mother, who has been quite unwell, during the past week, and confined to her bed, was able to be at the very quiet dinner we had, no one out of the family, except Mr. Morgan, being present.

We thought much of you boys, and the tears were in Mother's eyes when she spoke of you, and I felt myself rather blue on the subject. We also received intelligence this morning that Mr. Hall had been detached from the cutter and would probably leave in the course of a month. If it had not been Sunday possibly we might have received some presents; as it was we received a butter knife from Morgan, and a beautiful set of castors from Mr. & Mrs. Hall.

I am now over the most difficult part of my circuit, having just finished Court, in this County, which the members of the Bar declare was the most pleasant court they ever attended. But I am very tired of the judgeship, and wish that I could retire. If I could support my family, for one year, I am satisfied I could make more money at the bar, and get it too, than I can *clear* by the judgeship. But I see no other prospect, and what can not be cured must be endured.

With reference to the inquiries you make relative to privileged communications I have only to say that the rules laid down in Starkie or Phillips are strictly observed in both states.

Joy on the Admissibility of Confessions 57 page, in notis, "Our law, (Eng) utterly disowns any attempt to make a clergyman of any religious persuasion whatever, divulge any confessions made to him in the course of religious visits, or for the sake of spiritual consolation, as subversive of the great object of punishment, the reformation and improvement of the offender.["] Law Library vol. 40. But the general rule is that "confessions, made in cosequence of persuasion by a clergyman, not with any view of temporal benefit, is admissible".

With reference to attorneys, I have seen, in Texas, the Court refuse to receive the testimony tho' the atty. was willing to testify.——The English Courts jealously guard the communications & knowledge of a client's affairs obtained by his atty. This extends to business existing & in contemplation.

I regret that I can give you so little assistance in this matter; but I do not doubt that you will do very well.

Now I am going to tell you something that you must not mention in your letters home, nor tell any one but Frank, and he must, for the present, keep dark and that is, Morgan, last night, proposed to your sister and was accepted, and I have given my consent. Though I would not have chosen him myself, still I could not refuse. I pray God that it may turn out well! The happiness, and success in life, of my children is the chief object of my life.

We are now having hot weather, the thermometer stood today, in the shade 90°

Tell Frank that I rec'd. his letter and that I will write him next week when I expect to be at home.

Give the enclosed to Mr. Pollok.

With love and kind regards to all

> Your affectionate father
> Wm. J. Clarke

❧

*Wootten, Moulton, Clarke Papers, SHC*
*Mary Bayard Clarke to Willie Clarke*

New Berne April 13th [1873]

My Dear Willie

I received your letter last night and was thinking of writing to you when it came, but I was so broken down I concluded to go to bed instead; we have had another terrible fire, the last was nothing to it, it broke out in Emanuel's store or behind it, and swept from there both ways so that from the National Bank round to Mr Patterson's house there is not a shed standing. Both Wenstein's stores went as the woodden cornice on the brick store caught and they could not reach it, for the heat was so great that the artesian well at the church corner could not be used and the engine hose would not reach to the river till the fire got to Patterson's. Mrs Mark & Mrs Meadows barely escaped with life, as Mark's store was on fire when he woke, his wife had not time to do more than stick her feet in her slippers and run out with her children and except the clothes that happened to be at the washerwomans saved nothing Hahn's bakery was burnt, Augustine's store and stock, Marks, Emanuel, old McLachlin, Goldsmith, Ulerich, Kosmenski, Mrs Dunn, Dr Hughes, and Mr Davison with Wenstein and Meadows——, but the worst is that Mrs Primrose who owned half of Meadows store has lost all but the house she lives in, Misses Custis who owned Ulrich's house had no insurance neither had Mrs Dunn. Over twenty houses were burnt and seven families. Meadows, Marks, Ulrich, Mrs Dunn, Henry Pool who rented half of Mrs D's house, Boni Augustine over his father's store, and Dr Hughes were houseless. Oh it was awful to see them I just ran about the street crying because I could not help them. Mrs Marks and her children are quartered on Mr Hahn and I have two young Jews sleeping upstairs, I sent for Mary Dunn to take half of sister's room but she was with Mrs Baxter, and I am busy now making clothes for the seven Ulrich children.

Morgan saved Patterson's house, that was next to Dr Hughes' and they blew up the Dr's Office and got the hose in the river at the foot of Middle street and it was just long enough to play on the ruins and Patterson's House. We were in no danger as the wind did not set towards us but Mr Lehman was and Augustines house was on fire twice. Henry Pool had just gone to house keeping but he and Mrs Dunn saved most of their furniture the Baptist Church was on fire twice but was saved Mr Nash got his hand very badly burnt blowing the house up but there were no serious accidents I cant write any more I am so tired and heart sick at all this trouble that I cannot relieve. Father is at home this week and sends love Sister Continues to improve I hope to see you next month love to Mr Cooke and Frank

Your loving<br>Mother

❧

*Barden Collection*
*William J. Clarke to Mary Clarke Morgan*

New Berne Jan'y. 4, 1874

My Dear Daughter:

As I leave on Friday next to hold a special term of Robeson court, I seat myself to write you a few lines merely to inform you that, tho' you have been away for almost two months, I have not forgotten you; which may be set down as a remarkable instance of memory! Your Mother's health has so greatly improved that she is able to sit up most of the day, and to go to the table. She is looking very pretty in spite of her sickness, and with returning health her spirits have improved. My prescription, powdered charcoal, has done her more good than any thing she has taken for her dyspepsia.

Mr. Cooke left on 1st. inst. and Willie on the 2nd. Willie will stand for his license tomorrow. He is splendidly prepared, and I doubt not will make a fine lawyer. I joked him about his examination until I really think he became nervous, for you never saw any one study so hard.

Your Aunt Nora with Mattie are with us. N. seems in good spirits tho' she has a good deal to trouble her. John Primrose has broken up housekeeping and gone to Mrs. Miller's to board. He is out of business, and does not exhibit any inclination to do any thing. It is very sad to see a young man of so much promise, and capabilities acting so.[1]

We spent last Wednesday evening with Mrs. Lehman, and enjoyed it greatly. Mrs. Stevenson was there and full of fun. I never saw Mr. Cooke laugh so much. Willie did not go, but pegged away at his law. I never saw Miss Allie look so well. She played Dixie for Mr. C.

Frank is still with us and will probably remain for ten days to come. He is very anxious to see Mr. Morgan. I am sorry that he left his instruments behind, as I wanted him to survey a little tract of land I design leaving to you. It begins at a stake on Greenland's icy mountains and runs south to a palm tree on India's coral strand. I reckon you have heard of it before. Tom will go north with Frank. I don't think he is yet entirely reconciled to your getting married and going away. Don is so fat that he can hardly strike a gallop. New year's day and Christmas were unusually dull. Very few persons rec'd. Well, I believe I have given you all the news such as it is—We are having delightful weather, tho' my wounds keep me very nervous, and your Mother's sickness depresses me greatly.

Present my kindest regards to Mr. M. and believe me

Your affectionate father

*Wm. J. Clarke*

Chemistry not chymistry—

1. John Primrose suffered from alcoholism and died an early death, leaving Katie Cannon Primrose a widow with a young child.

*Barden Collection*
*William J. Clarke to Mary Clarke Morgan*

New Berne, June 28th. 1874

My Dear Daughter:

I have been so "riled up", and absorbed by Judicial election matters that I have failed to write to you for some time. Suspense as to that matter is now over, and my mind is at rest. I withdrew my name and [Augustus S.] Seymour rec'd. the nomination, but I immediately declared myself a candidate.[1] I was rec'd. with the wildest enthusiasm, while S. was treated with great coldness. Most of the delegates, after the adjournment, came to me and pledged themselves to support me, the leading Republicans throughout the district have done the same, while the majority of colored voters, even in New Berne, are warmly for me. I have no doubt that I shall beat him 2,000 votes if no Conservative runs, for S. has no personal popularity. The unscrupulous and tricky Yankees have, almost to a man, worked day and night against me. While I was off attending to my court business they were scheming and plotting against me, but I shall give them a lively time. Yesterday I went to Trenton and made a speech which produced a fine effect.

Your mother says you are troubled for something to read. I am sure you have regretted not taking Rollin with you, and if it was not so bulky I would send it to you by Sophie Moore.

I am rejoiced to learn that your health is restored. I was very uneasy about you. Give my love to Mr. Morgan. I find that Willie has written to you, so I will close this dull letter

Your affectionate father
*Wm. J. Clarke*

1. Clarke failed to receive the Republican nomination for judgeship of the Third Judicial District and later lost his reelection bid. The Republican Party, dominated by northern men, frequently awarded party positions to fellow northerners. Clarke bitterly resented this and staged a vigorous campaign as an independent Republican candidate. In a printed election appeal, he recalled his years of service as judge and denied that he was a "bolter from the party" because he refused to accept Seymour's claim to be the sole Republican candidate. He added that Craven County Republicans were controlled by men "who are not natives of

North Carolina" and who were interested only in the spoils of office. Clarke Papers, SHC.

❧

*Barden Collection*
*William J. Clarke to Mary Clarke Morgan*

New Berne, June 6. 1875

My Dear Daughter:

I received your letter and was greatly gratified to hear from you, though I have delayed answering it principally because I have been very busy and also absent from home. I am now in better health than when you were with us, and if I were not so much troubled about your mother, and money, I should be quite cheerful.

Your mother is improving though she is still quite weak, but she is in better spirits, and has a tolerable appetite. Mr. Patterson[1] was here, at the Convention, and visited her frequently, and his conversations seem to have had a favorable effect on her. Through him a reconciliation was effected with Miss Kate Carroway; and an explanation with Mr. Forbes.[2] Today the latter came and administered the holy Communion to your mother, the rest of the family, with Nora, joining. Frank and Martha partook for the first time. It was a solemn occasion, but I trust that we all felt that it was "good for us to be there." I hope and believe that this sickness has been greatly sanctified to your mother, and that her eyes are opened to errors in belief and feelings, which have been a source of great disquiet to me. Association with the realists and pantheists of the North, had caused her to entertain doubts of the efficacy of prayer; which destroys all comfort in religion.

There is great talk about Mr. Forbes' resigning, but I have little doubt that it will end in smoke. Possibly he may be induced to take an assistant, but that will be the full extent of all the clatter. I have not opened my mouth on the subject.

Your Aunt Nora writes that she will be here on Friday next, and I cannot say that I shall be glad to see her, as it will worry your mother, when she so much needs rest; and besides the girls will expect us to give some entertainments, which they will be disappointed about, as I cannot afford the expense. Nora will, I hope, return to Raleigh with me on 18th. inst. when I go up to attend the Supreme Court. She is rather difficult to entertain, and don't seem to have enjoyed her visit.

The ladies in our neighbourhood have been very kind, and have almost worried your mother with attentions.[3] Willie is very assiduous in his attentions to Miss Sophia, sends about a cart load of flowers to her each week, and stays there until 12 o'clock about every other night—This reminds me to give you a caution about talking about Lon Moore. Somehow I feel doubtful about his marrying the young lady, and it will be well that he may have no cause to think that you had any thing to do in breaking it off.

Frank is doing next to nothing, and I feel very sorry for the poor fellow, for he seems willing to work.

I want to see you very badly, and we speak about you frequently, and wish that you were with us. The late attack of your mother was not more severe than others she has had, but she was so enfeebled that she succumbed to it. I saw Judge and Mrs. Reid last week, and they both inquired particularly about you—Tell Tom that he need not be surprised if he gets a letter from me before long. With respects to Mr. Morgan & Miss Lou

Your affectionate father
Wm. J. Clarke

1. George Patterson, born in Boston, Massachusetts, attended the University of North Carolina and became an Episcopal clergyman in 1856. He taught in church schools and provided religious instruction to slaves living at Josiah Collins's Somerset Plantation in Washington County. During the Civil War, he served as a chaplain. After the war, he worked at two Episcopal churches in Wilmington, including St. James Episcopal Church from 1870 to 1881. J. G. de Roulhac Hamilton, "George Patterson: North Carolinian by Adoption," *NCHR* 30 (Apr. 1953): 191–99.

2. Forbes was the Episcopal minister in New Bern.

3. Mary Bayard Clarke had suffered another of her frequent ailments. Her poor health worried her enough that she drew up her will on 6 July 1875.

AFTER WILLIAM J. CLARKE lost his reelection bid for the superior court judgeship, the Clarke family experienced economic problems. William Clarke and son Willie opened a law practice together, but little cash circulated in New Bern and they found it difficult to collect legal fees. In addition, during the next few years, William Clarke's alcoholism deepened, alarming the entire family. Mary Bayard Clarke again used her pen to supplement the family income. Her writing also gave her the opportunity to travel and leave behind the strains imposed on her marriage.

The majority of her writing concentrated on newspaper articles and book reviews. She still wrote poetry for her own enjoyment, but newspaper articles had a better chance of being sold for hard cash. Mary Bayard Clarke wrote for Appletons, Harpers, and a number of other newspaper publishers within and without the state until her health failed in the 1880s. The money she earned never provided the level of support she had hoped, but her energy and intellectual development blossomed during the late 1870s as she encountered new people and new ideas. She wrote to her old friend Winchester Hall in March 1876 that, "I review for Harper, Appleton, Sheldon, Scribner and Hale, but get only copies of the books from the publishers. Sometimes I can get pay for a review, but not often. I would give it up, but the reading matter keeps me from utter despair, by interesting my mind." [Hall, *MBC Poems,* xxi] Despite the low pay, her pride of authorship remained strong. She clipped and pasted her articles into scrapbooks, usually without a clear indication of date or which paper had published them.

*Barden Collection*
*MBC Scrapbook 2: unidentified book review by Mary Bayard Clarke. Christian Reid's novel was published in 1875, dating the clipping to that year.*
[1875]

LITERARY GOSSIP.

Appleton & Co. have lately issued a literary cookery book under the title of "BREAKFAST, DINNER AND TEA," which contains, besides three hundred practical receipts for family use, much curious and interesting information in relation to the gastronomic habits and peculiarities of all ages and nations. Whether viewed practically, poetically, or historically, cookery is a subject of general interest to the ladies, for, as Owen Meredith truly says,

> "We may live without poetry, music and art,
> We may live without conscience and live without heart,
> We may live without friends and live without books,
> But civilized man *cannot* live without cooks."

We are inclined to think that when Dr. Johnson said of his friend, Mrs. Carter, that "she could translate Epictetus, and make a good pudding," he decidedly preferred the latter accomplishment to the former, in as much as he could himself do the translating, but could not make the pudding. Until the millenium of the "emancipated woman" comes, when the streets, according to the old "Irish poet," shall be paved with loaves of bread, and little pigs ready-roasted shall run through them crying 'come and eat me,' women must at least superintend the family cooking, and the book before us is especially intended for the entertainment, as well as the assistance, of those orderly housekeepers who are also well informed and intelligent women.

. . . .

We cannot say as much for the next one we take up from Appleton—"A QUESTION OF HONOR"—by Christian Reid, which is the longest and poorest novel we have seen from this author. As a story it is *nil,* having neither plot nor interest; the characters are poorly drawn, and in the last degree commonplace; the conversations are rapid and tedious, leading to nothing and without the sprightliness of repartee which characterizes "A DAUGHTER OF BOHEMIA," which is by far the best novel Christian Reid has ever written, eclipsing VALERIE ALYMER and all the others from her pen, and leading us to hope for something at least as good, if not better, in *A Question of Honor.*

A lady novelist told us once she always made her husband translate her slang into the language that would have been really used by the characters she was depicting, which gave them such a veri-similitude that a captious critic said, after reading one of her books, that she must keep strange company for a refined woman, or she could not know what word to put in her characters mouth. If the authoress of A QUESTION OF HONOR had consulted some lawyer friend in the same way, we think he would have told her that any lawyer, who knew enough to get a license, would have taken old Mr. Burnham's deposition to be used *de bene esse,* and not have risked an important law-suit on which the interest of her novel hinges on the life of a man in his ninetieth year. We could, however, overlook this defect if there was anything of interest in the book to redeem it.

M. B. C.

ᴓ

*Barden Collection*
*Reverend George Patterson to Mary Bayard Clarke*

University of the South
Sewanee, Tenn. August 14th 1875

My dear Daughter—

You may berate me for my silence as much as you chuse—& I will not open my mouth to reply—If, however, you can pardon my *apparent* neglect I shall be truly thankful—The fact is, I have been very busy ever since the reception of your kind letter of June 7th—And then the hot weather unfitted me for every thing save what was just before me—

I thank God for His great mercy in bringing you out of that fearful attack wh was coming upon you when I was in Newbern—May He still vouchsafe you his grace—for increased strength to resist the effects of the disease until your work is completed, & may He then take you to rest with the Saints in Paradise—But more than all do I thank God for giving you the victory over yourself—This is 10,000 fold better for you than bodily health or strength—Better be weak in flesh than weak in spirit—You have followed the will of our blessed Master—& the self-denial—& subjugation of your will to another, will surely bring you a blessing—God grant that you may still go on in the good work—Count then upon my love, prayers & entire sympathy with you as you bear your Cross after the God Jesus. Now that you have seen your own lawful priest & recd his ministrations—you will be enriched with Sacramental Grace—No matter—tho' you do not wish his services—yet receive them in spite of your earthly will—& there will be a grace given you for life, for death, & for life everlasting—Be sure to send for Mr Forbes—at regular times—& heed what he says—You must not go to the services of the Roman Obedience[1]— They will do you great spiritual harm—We believe that their worship is idolatrous—if it be so—& I am sure that it is. You wd be injured by participating with the Romans in their worship, wh is entirely subversive of the Faith of the Catholic Ch—Excuse my great plainness of speech—but it is for your good that I say it—If God does not give you strength to attend the public worship of the Ch—be patient—& submit—& God will give you a multiplied grace—"They also serve, who stand & wait." Wait *there* where God hath placed you—& you will be no loser. I do hope that you have improved in health—Day by day do I mention your name in my prayers—The poems you sent me—are both of them very beautiful— The 1st—"Prayer" is highly meritorious—The 2nd—"Prayer to the B. V." wd be equally so if it were only doctrinally orthodox—I always read after you with pleasure, & almost always with profit as well as pleasure—

You may ask what I am doing here. At the last Convention held in Newbern I was elected Clerical Trustee to the University of the South—& here I have been in attendance on the meetings of the Board—I wish I had the time to give you a detailed afc—of what I have seen & heard here—It wd interest you hugely—I start for home on Monday pm—& hope, D.V., to reach Wiln by the 1st Sunday in September—Love for the Judge & your children— With love, prayers & Blessing for you my dear Child—I remain, as ever,

Yr Faithful Father in Ct—

Geo: Patterson:

1. Mary Bayard Clarke's grandfather John Devereux had helped to found St. Paul's Catholic Church in New Bern and gave $500 to help build the church building. Clarke did not follow Patterson's advice on avoiding contact with Catholics. She cherished her friendship with the local priest and studied a variety of religions. Steve Worsley to Mrs. Graham Barden Jr., 27 November 1982, Barden Collection.

*Hall,* MBC Poems, *xxi*
*Mary Bayard Clarke to Winchester Hall*

[New Berne, New Year's Day, 1876]

I wish I could say I was well, but I have no hope of ever being better. I am one of those doors that hang long, but will always creak. Any sudden or unusual tax on my strength, or any anxiety or worry, upsets me entirely; and the worst is that people who see me, only when I am at my best, think one-half my ill-health imaginary, and the other half only the indulgence of my own whims—that I can do what is agreeable to me, but can not do what is not; simply because I won't. I can't keep house or sew, without being laid up in a few days; and it is impossible for me to get any writing to do that will pay and enable me to hire the work done. So I am generally either trying to do it, or repenting that I have tried. I sometimes despair and wish for the end, for I am so tired of it all. The new year seems but another link, added to a heavy chain. So here I am tired—rusting instead of wearing out—the old year closes sadly, and the new brings no hope of anything better.

In June 1876 Mary Bayard Clarke traveled to New York and Philadelphia to cover the Centennial celebration of America's 100 years of existence. She wrote a series of entertaining articles covering the Fourth of July celebrations in New York City; well-to-do residents of Riverdale, New York; Anna Leonowens's American visit; and the Centennial Exposition in Philadelphia. Her topics also explored women's rights and work and scientific discussions on the evolution of man. Many of the Centennial articles, which she clipped and pasted into a scrapbook, were written for an unidentified North Carolina paper. The articles reveal how good a writer Clarke was and also hint at her gradual rejection of many traditional attitudes held by southern women of her class. Clarke capitalized on her northern sojourn by meeting publishers and investigating how far a career in journalism could carry her. It was a pivotal year in her evolution into a professional journalist. She continued to explore journalism in 1877, especially concentrating on publications in Chicago that hired women editors and reporters. By the end of 1877, Clarke returned to North Carolina when her income failed to support all her expenses in Chicago. Nevertheless, she continued to write for a variety of newspapers and publicly advocated many platforms she had adopted in the North, especially with regard to improving work opportunities for women and providing them equal pay for that work.

❧

*William J. Clarke Papers, SHC*
*Mary Bayard Clarke to William J. Clarke*

Norfolk Saturday
[June 1876]

My Dear William

As Capt Southgate[1] has given me leave to use his desk and we dont leave for several hours I will write you a letter instead of a PC. I have already written one to the Times so will say nothing except that it has been delightfully smooth. Capt. S. is a brother to Delia Wynn's husband, and when he found I used to know his sister Mariana who married Dick Wynn after Annie Spencer died, he was very chatty and pleasant; told me Mr Roboteau had not been heard of for three years and Mrs R is with Delia. Tell Willie Mrs Williams turned out not to be Mrs Williams but Mrs Powell, having been married last month, she wishes to pass her baby off as this husband's child and came near getting in to a difficulty by doing so; as she told the cook and stewardess she had been married two years and some negro woman aboard who knew her and not heard of her marriage told them she was not married to the man as they had known her longer than that, the Stewardess was about to put her out of the lady's saloon saying she was not fit to stay with me but I fortunately found it out before they spoke and said I knew Willie would not have introduced her to me if she had been an improper character. So Will has done her one more service than she knows of for I would not let her feelings be hurt, she had an out side state room and her husband got mad because he was not allowed in the saloon and would not let her stay so I had the whole to myself which I preferred as the children were troublesome though she was not. Eliza the chamber maid made a bed on the floor and slept in there so I might not be alone if I needed anything at night.

Tell Celia it was very undignified but I could not help laughing at her description of Mrs Kinney and the way she took her off which was inimitable. The lady has embalmed her memory all along the rout and poor Mr

Kinney is considered a martyr. She made a terrible fuss on board of the Wyanoke because some ladies who had been on board two days had seats at the table she wished and the purser would not move them; then she found that the settee in Mrs Dennison's stateroom was full six inches longer than hers and complained that her son in law had telegraphed for *the best* accomodations and she ought to have that room. Miss Lossie Grist is to be married on Tuesday to a Mr Clark of Tarboro whom she never saw till she went there to convention, he would not trust her to wait longer and as she only had to get a dress and he promised to take her to the Centennial she consented, it seems she has quarreled with Fanny Clarke and wishes every body to know her beau is no relation to Fanny the Capt says he thinks she is marrying very well; it is not a son of Gov Clark Tell Ce I have provision enough for a week she was so bountiful I get my breakfast because I felt it best to have some hot coffee but did not need to do so for provision

I felt very much depressed when I left and thought of Mr Lehman but I feel to day as if I should live to get home and find you all alive God grant I may—yours

lovingly<br>Mary

PS Capt S's pens and ink are not first class if his fare is—

1. Southgate was captain of the steamer *New-Berne,* which sailed regularly to New York. His brother James Southgate and his wife Delia Haywood Wynne Southgate both were former teachers and school administrators. By 1876 the Southgates lived in Hillsborough, North Carolina. Powell, *DNCB,* 5:401.

*Barden Collection*
*MBC Scrapbook 2: unidentified newspaper clipping, second of seven in Mary Bayard Clarke's Centennial series.*

New York, July 5th, 1876.

I have often heard old soldiers speak of the confusing effects of being for a long time exposed to the noise of battle even when not engaged in it, and I know now what it is, for I have spent the last twenty-four hours literally under fire. The small boy assisted by his big brother, has had possession of the city since sunset on the third,[1] when he began his bombardment of crackers and fire works which has been kept up without intermission till this morning when there is a partial lull in the noise. Could ladies with safety go on the streets? was the question to be settled, looking out of the window the answer was "certainly not," as a perfect hail storm of fire was raging in all the cross streets, while Broadway and the Avenues were packed with a dense mass of people all rushing to Union Square to obtain places to see the procession enter at mid-night, hear the six hundred sing the hymn of rejoicing and the band play "Hail Columbia" and other patriotic pieces. I meekly assented when it was pronounced by the gentlemen dangerous for even the scant drapery of pin backs to be exposed to the fire and the crowd, but had not the slightest intention while assenting to of submitting. I had dined the day before with some of the leaders of the National Woman's Suffrage Association,[2] and knew my rights—and wrongs—and though I had no desire to vote I determined to see and hear, so, when the staid middle aged members of the party retired for the night proposing to hear the mid-night chimes from their pillows, a party of irrespressibles quietly slipped out the front door and braved the storm of fire, determined to make a night of it. The ladies all shrieked when I appeared in a water proof [torn] alster buttoned down to the feet with the hood drawn over my head. It was not a becoming costume I must admit, neither was it very comfortable; serene in the depths of my ugliness I listened to the louder—or rather shriller shrieks which pierced the air as the sparks began to fall thicker and thicker, and exclamations of "Oh dear I am burning" "take care of your skirts," "Oh my hat's on fire," and so on were heard on every side. But when I saw a policeman tear a handful of curls from a lady's head in his efforts to put them out, I rose superior to all minor considerations and absolutely triumphed and gloried in my unbecoming rigg, when [torn]ed the crowd could not be distinguished from one of Worth's dresses,[3] so tight was the jam. I shan't attempt a description of the procession, it was immense and over two hours in passing the Mayor who stood on Madison Square to review it; some of the transparencies were very handsome, and the fire works were magnificent, but the decorations of the city generally, except among the Germans, were tasteless, consisting of innumerable flags tied to the shutters or strung all over the front of the buildings. Everything was of course red white and blue, and General Washington looked sternly or placidly from the windows of a thousand houses, now blandly—smiling and then darkly frowning, according to the skill of his delineators. Decidedly the handsomest transparency that I saw was an immense one, covering the whole of the front of a seven or eight story building on Madison Square, representing the Statue of Liberty[4] which the French Government is to give to the United States, placed somewhere near the entrance of New York harbor.

The pedestal [is] to be one hundred feet high, on which the figure of Liberty, also one hundred feet high, will stand gazing, with blazing eyes, by night [torn] lamps within the head will be lighted, either out towards the sea or down on the city, it is not yet decided which way Liberty will look, whether approvingly on America or longingly towards France.

At mid-night the chimes of Trinity and St. Paul's rang out, but the effect was entirely destroyed by the noise of the cannon and the ringing of the other bells. Had the burst of noise come first, and the clear music of the chimes followed, like the "still small voice" after the storm, it would have been far finer, as it was no one could distinguish the tunes played; and only those near hear the music of six hundred voices that sang. Beethoven's hymn, "The Heavens are telling the Glory of God." But those who were near enough to hear it as I was, can never forget the grand effect, and it was a great pity that all squibs, fire crackers, rockets and shouting could not have been hushed until it was over. But small boy of America is not only irrespressible, but tireless, and though out in full force all night long he kept up his fusilade all of the next day, and was ten times louder than ever on the night of the 4th by which time the fire engines were dashng through the city at full speed steam up and sparks flying to put out some fire caused by a misplaced rocket or cracker. The day was breaking when I emerged from my water proof and dropped on my bed. Decidedly night processions are at this season more to be desired than day ones, and it was a good idea to begin celebrating the nation's high day at mid-night instead of day break. But the general feeling to-day is one of relief, the housekeepers are relieved from their fear of fire and thieves, and the public generally from the fear of accidents. The absence of all drunkeness is a marked feature of this fourth, I did not see an intoxicated person on the streets, and except from the danger of fire a lady might safely have walked unattended through the illuminated parts of the city and the adjacent streets.

We are all on the *qui vive* to-day to hear the result of a conspiracy, gotten up by some of the Sprightly Suffrage ladies, to burst like a bomb shell on the demonstration in Philadelphia and protest that the whole celebration and all the speeches about liberty, equality, independence etc., is a fraud and delusion, since one half of the American nation was still taxed without representation. The programme was to procure tickets of admission to the platform for as many of the leaders as possible, and then for Mrs. Lucretia Mott, as the orator, or Mrs. Stanton if Mrs.

Mott could not from her age and infirmities, to rise, after the reading of the Declaration of Independence, and solemnly protest on the continent injustice of men to women by denying them the right to vote. But as the morning's papers make no mention of any such protest I suppose it was not carried out.

Like the man who could dispense with the necessaries of life, provided he was abundantly supplied with its luxuries, I am willing to let my rights take care of themselves, provided only I can retain my privileges as a woman. But I suppose I am neither patriotic nor progressive, for I hate pop-crackers, and don't want to vote, and, if I don't regard the celebration of the 4th and the Declaration of Independence as a fraud and delusion, I certainly feel, when I look at my peppered water proof burnt in twenty minute places and remember the din and disturbance of yesterday, glad that the glorious Fourth—like Christmas comes but once a year—and a Centennial but once in a hundred years.

M. B. C.

1. New York City began its Centennial Independence Day celebration on 3 July 1876. The festivities included a torchlight parade and midnight gathering at Union Square; decorations on the city's homes, businesses, and public buildings; a parade with 25,000 marchers; and elaborate fireworks and musical events. Brooks McNamara, *Day of Jubilee: The Great Age of Public Celebration in New York, 1788–1909* (New Brunswick, N.J.: Rutgers University Press, 1997), 138–39.

2. The National Woman Suffrage Association, led by Elizabeth Cady Stanton and Susan B. Anthony, staged lectures and demonstrations in support of woman suffrage, including a counter demonstration at the official 4 July 1876, celebration in Philadelphia. Mary Bayard Clarke interviewed women associated with the women's movement to evaluate their platforms, including members of New York's Sorosis, a leading club for women. Her cousin, Lillie Devereux Blake, also was an active campaigner for women's rights in New York and nationally. Mary Bayard Clarke greatly admired Blake and agreed with many of her views on women's receiving equal pay for their work and a better education to prepare them for employment. Clarke never admitted, however, to desiring the vote for herself or other women. Robert C. Post, ed., *1876: A Centennial Exhibition* (Washington, D.C.: National Museum of History and Technology, Smithsonian Institution, 1976), 173 (hereafter cited as Post, *Centennial Exhibition*).

3. Charles Frederick Worth was an English fashion designer who ruled Parisian fashion during this period.

4. The French began work on the statue in 1875. It was shipped to New York City in 1885, and the official dedication occurred on 28 October 1886.

❧

*Barden Collection*
*MBC Scrapbook 2: unidentified newspaper clipping, third of seven in Clarke's Centennial series.*

### From our own Correspondent.

Riverdale, July 20th, 1876.

. . . .

The women's rights women carried out their programme in a quiet way, but the New York papers made no mention of it. Immediately after the reading of the Declaration of Independence by Gen. Lee, Miss Antony rose very quietly and advancing to Mr. Terry said, "I present you with a protest from the Women of America." Mr. Terry bowed and took the parchment tied with red white and blue, and the ladies immediately began distributing copies of the "Declaration of Rights of the Women of the United States" drawn up in the form of Articles of Impeachment against the rulers of the United States, for violation of the fundamental principles of our government. I really had no idea how vast and deep were my wrongs as a woman until I read the document, a copy of which I send you, and found I am denied the right of Habeas Corpus and trial by jury of my peers, and am taxed without representation. All ladies—no, *women* who desire to sign this declaration of rights can do so by sending their names written on their paper to be pasted in the book. But with their names they are requested to send one dollar, at least, for the good of the cause, with as much more as they feel inclined to give, to the National Woman Suffrage Parks No. 1431 Chesnut Street, Philadelphia.

There is one thing which the Woman's Rights movement has done that all must approve of, and that is the improvement they have effected in the lives of the shop girls of New York, who formerly were over worked and greatly imposed on by some of the employers. Now their position is much easier, and one of them told me it was owing to the hue and cry raised by the Women's Rights ladies whenever a case of oppression was brought to their notice. They have also opened new employments for women so that teaching, keeping boarding house, and sewing, are no longer the only occupations in reach of women who are obliged to work for their living instead of marrying for it. . . .

M. B. C.

❧

*William J. Clarke Papers, SHC*
*Mary Bayard Clarke to William J. Clarke*

New York Thursday
[August 1876]

My Dear William

I feel as if I wanted to keep a journal and tell every thing as it occurs for fear I shall forget some thing. I wrote you from Norfolk, and Celia from this place, telling her how warmly I was welcomed, and how pleasant it was. I am now comfortably settled and feel as much at home as it is possible for me to be out side of my own house. I like the room I have now better than one I had last, as it is one flight higher, is cooler and more quiet; I have an apparatus for making coffee over the gas light, and get up as I did at home and by the time I am dressed my coffee is ready for me and I have a quiet time to write till half past seven, when we have breakfast

I spent yesterday with Dr [Charles] McCormick and I cant tell you how sad it made me to see him so broken in body and shaken in mind; he is a feeble old man, tottering about on a stick cross, bitter and hateful in speech, all of which covers a sorrowful heart, he seemed glad to see me but was so changed and cold at first that it was very painful to me to be with him——, but after the first interview he broke down and told me all his troubles. It seems all his family side with Mrs Wells, as she now is, and not one of them speak to him, Mrs [Margaret] McLean says she hears he is very rich and has grown very stingy, she told him very plainly he ought to make a will and leave me comfortably off, and his reply was "I shall take care of Mary——" but I fear it is all *intention* whether he will act on it I dont know. Schofield wrote the department asking to have him kept in here as his mind had failed so he——Schofield——did not want him out in California. Dr demanded the letter, went to another Dr. and got a certificate and is to be sent back with the rank and pay of a Colonel, so he is capable of making a will—*but will he?* I should have no sentimentality about cutting out his relatives, neither should I hesitate, if I had occasion to do so, to tell him frankly I wish he would provide for me, but unless he speaks first *I cannot* suggest it, he is queer and irritable, and seventeen years absence make me cautious of offending him, but he has grown—stingy I can see that. Gall the optitian[1] has examined my eyes, and says they are in a critical state, and I must be careful of them, so I shall not use them by gas light at all; the old fellow has taken a fancy to me, and not one cent will he charge for advice or new spectacles, has fitted me out with a new pair instead of simply replacing the broken glass, and says——"you comes to me every now and then and I sees these eyes has good glasses for themselves. While you stays, and if you minds me you will not go blind of one eye; if you dont you does;" as he *Tells* me nothing, and has the reputation of being a good occulist,——I think his advice disinterested, and "minds him" quinine he objects to my taking as he says it aggrivates the trouble which is an affection of the optic nerve caused by bad health *generally,* and headaches *particularly* he has given me, not stronger glasses, but deeper tinted ones ——and they suit me very well——. I think my next letter will be to Will as I count Frank and Celia as one, and send you two for every one I send others. Make Tom write when you dont feel like it and dont get sick for if you do I shall come home

Yours lovingly
Mary

Evening. I wrote this, letter before breakfast and kept it out to the last moment and will tell you what I have been doing all day. Went first to Wilcox & Gibbs and got the promise of an exchange for $15 cash; told them I would not pay a cent cash, and now they have the matter under consideration; Next went to Appletons and arranged to get any of his books at cost, one third off, so tell Frank he may take as many orders for Appleton, Harper, or Hale as he likes, as they will let him have from one, to any number, but he had better send through me if he gets any orders this summer. Went to Harpers where I was made much of, saw the Editor of the Weekly and talked extensively, then went and lunched at the Tribune office with Bayard Taylor,[2] a fat, red faced, sea-captain-looking poet!! you'll read my *public* account, this is my private——, Spent an hour very pleasantly and then went into the Surrogate's Court with Mr Underhill,[3] and was kept waiting till I rebelled and said I was accustomed to be waited *on* by a Judge, and not to wait for one——, where at the lawyer's laughed sent the Judge word to hurry up, and he did hurry and dismissed them to play, as the case should not be tried, Spent an hour with Hale and came home to find your letter and take a bath——am glad you are going to Morehead. I wonder who has the good taste to puff you in the Times. Cant guess! I shall go to Philadelphia next week probably——mean while, *"wait for the waggon"* or my published letter

Yours lovingly
Mary——

1. Joseph Gall was a New York City optician with an office at 21 Union Square. He worked between 1868 and 1879. Alice Reingold, reference librarian, New-York Historical Society, to Mrs. Graham A. Barden Jr., 14 November 1998, Barden Collection.

2. Bayard Taylor was a noted nineteenth-century poet, educator, and diplomat. He published several books of verse, managed the literary department of the New York *Tribune,* and taught German literature at Cornell University between 1870 and 1877. In 1878 he served as the United States minister to Germany. He was no relation to Mary Bayard Clarke. *Who Was Who in America,* 520; Frank Luther Mott, *American Journalism: A History of Newspapers in the United States through 260 Years: 1690 to 1950* (New York: Macmillan, 1950), 270.

3. Edward F. Underhill of the firm of Underhill, Boynge & Adams, was a law reporter with offices located in the Tribune Building in New York City. Mary Bayard Clarke stayed in the Underhill home while in New York. In a letter to her son Tom, written on 14 August 1876, she explained that the Underhills had left on a trip and she was in charge of the house, silver, and herself, which she thoroughly enjoyed. At this time Tom worked for a New Bern printing business. His mother, monitoring her youngest son, added in her letter, "I hope my dear boy you wont lose your good manners and grow rough because you are in the printing office, remember I am very proud of my boys and dont want the youngest to fall behind, keep your good manners and . . . dont run down at the heel and get careless." Mary Bayard Clarke to Thomas Clarke, 14 [August] 1876, Clarke Papers, SHC.

❧

*William J. Clarke Papers, SHC*
*Mary Bayard Clarke to William J. Clarke*

New York
August 8th [1876]

My Dear William

I have received your two letters, one this morning and thank you for them. I hope you may be appointed but you know I am always a Thomas, doubting instead of believing, I am afraid your delicacy was misplaced, and it would have been better to have said either yourself or through a friend, to B. "I will get you nominated if you will appoint me." I dont believe Person is honest in his support of you, and am sure Reede is not, Holden I think is. I dont like your ending of Custer[1] but will consider it—none of the papers will publish it, why I dont know as I did not ask any payment. Mr and Mrs Underhill leave this week, I shall go to Riverdale but make this head quarters so dont change the direction of my letters—I have been very busy this week but dont make much not more than enough to keep going. As for Dr McCormick I dont know what to say except that he is *queer*. The other day we went out together, he is so infirm he likes to have me go with him in the street cars, he stopped at the headquarters in Houston Street, and instead of taking me in and giving me a seat while he transacted his business, he said "Just walk up and down for a few minutes." I did not exactly like to refuse and had only walked twice when he came out and said "I have to go up stairs and came to tell you so you might not be surprised." of course I supposed he would only be another few moments and perhaps I would have to walk twice as long——, Instead of which I walked for *fifteen minutes,* and then got wrathy, and finding a porter sent my card up with the information that I had gone home, and I took the next car, two hours afterwards he came in a carriage to see me and I would not go down stairs, but sent word I was sick; the next day he came again and then it came out that he forgot all about me, and went to see a sick man, got in a quarrel with another Doctor and I might have waited the two hours in the street. I get him books, and wait on him, run around and do his errands for the sake of old times and past kindness, but I would not stand him even on these considerations were I not convinced that he is not himself, his mind is perfectly clear on business and science, but blurred on ordinary daily occurrences, and clear gone on the question of North and South, he is rabid against all Southerners, as such, but I dont know as he is personally so against his friends though he may be

I had the unexpected pleasure of meeting Lucia Polk,[2] now Mrs Chapman, the other day, her husband is a broker in New Orleans. She had lost every vestige of good looks, and looks as old as I do only has no grey hairs; She says Mr Conrad often talks of me—he also had a slight paralytic attack this past spring. Meck's [Polk] family are at Saratoga yet but he has returned. I send Tom a toy that Mr Underhill brought home the other day it is called Love's Telegraph and he can whisper sweet things to the girls across the room please tell him to take the enclosed note to Mrs Bryan she asked me to see about a piano for her. I have to send a lot of books to Dr Duffy this week—I get them at whole sale price for him. I wish you coud see the Radiometer[3] that I spoke of in my last letter to the Times I never rested till I found it and there is but one place in the US they can be had that is at Galls where I get my spectacles and he showed it to me and explained it all—I send a note to Celia, I am sorry she leaves before I get back—but perhaps it is best. I am glad you are better and hope you will continue so——

Yours lovingly
Mary

1. George Armstrong Custer's fight at the Battle of the Little Big Horn occurred on 25 June 1876.

2. This was one of the daughters of Leonidas and Frances Devereux Polk.

3. An instrument used to measure or detect radiant energy.

ॐ

*Barden Collection*
*MBC Scrapbook 2: unidentified newspaper clipping, fourth of seven in Mary*
*Bayard Clarke's Centennial series.*

### The Centennial[1]

[From our own Correspondent.]

Philadelphia, September 3rd, 1876.

. . . . I have been impatient to get to the Exposition since the 4th of July glorification was over, but both Doctor and occulist have said "No— not till cooler weather—wait till September," and now I find, from those who are here and have borne the heat and burden of the Centennial day, that I have lost nothing good, and missed much evil and weariness of spirit by waiting. Things are now really in order, errors have been discovered and rectified, all the articles are unpacked, and in place, and for the next two months the Exposition, or as it is universally called the Centennial, can be seen with much less weariness, both of mind and body, and—what is of more importance at a far less expense than at any previous time. . . . I have been here since the 1st and find I am just beginning to take it in its length, width, depth, and height, and am now ready to settle down to the investigation of special departments. Having passed the gates we at first agreed to keep together and see the sights in company, but I soon rebelled at this arrangement, and determined to "go it alone" even if I did, as was prophecied "get euchred," and miss the best parts for want of some one to point out the particular beauties I ought to see; but then I did not care for those particular beauties perhaps, and did care for some particularly tiresome ugliness. So, acting on the principle that a Centennial without independence was not at all the thing, I agreed to meet the whole party at half past five in front of Memorial Hall, and went off to make a day of it. We had first all together taken the car ride round the grounds, and I then discovered where the newspaper building was, and determined to deliver my credentials as a correspondent there, and get free of the establishment. Over eight thousand newspapers are taken in, and any one can go in, ask for a paper from home, and get it with a comfortable seat in a cool room to read it, while up stairs are convencies [*sic*] for writing, and quiet, for all newspaper correspondents who present their letters to Geo. P. Rowell &

Co.[2] I next went to the Judge's Hall, where Governor Hawley,[3] the President has his office, to deliver my letters of introduction to him, some private, and some official, but finding him temporarily absent, I attacked the
main building single handed and alone, and at the end of an hour was mentally and physically exhausted, and found I must adopt a plan and adhere
to it, if I wished to see to advantage. So I contracted for a rolling chair, and
was fortunate enough to get a most intelligent helms-man, who soon
found out my special taste and stopped at interesting objects saying, "and
sure now it is this that will jist plaze you." After three days hard work Sunday came, and I feel now that I have some idea of the whole and am prepared to enjoy it in detail. . . . Correspondents, after three or four days of
red-tapeism, are furnished passes, on which must be put the regulation
photograph of the holder of the pass. Such a pass entitles the holder to a
return ticket should he or she wish to leave the grounds and return that
day, but no others can get return tickets; . . . To give a detailed account of
even the most interesting objects would require a volume, so I shant
attempt it, I shall not even begin with the old time things, but with something which a hundred years ago would have been not only unheard of, but
considered impossible to be in existence, the Woman's Rights Department, modestly called "The Women's Pavilion," where money seems to
have been expended in the most useless manner by the ladies of New York
in a banner that cost $2,000, and is utterly unfit for all the purposes of a
banner, as it does not wave but hangs stationary from the walls, and though
*given* by women there is no evidence that it was *made* by women, and consequently it has no right to be where it is, in a department devoted to the
work and invention of women. I was much more interested in the
improved griddle greaser, invented by Mrs. Sherwood—*not* the author of
"Little Henry and His Bearer," and the "Lady of the Manor," but a practical
housekeeper who had greased her fingers—and burnt them too, and now
offers the result of her suffering to her sisters in the shape of this patent
improved griddle greaser, which shows its face beside a patent dish washer,
a kind of revolving drum that turns round and round in the boiling water,
with the cups and saucers inside, and saves the hands of the dish washer,
an old-fashioned mop does as well.

Mrs. Romberge,[4] a female dentist, shows the teeth she has pulled, and
the teeth she has manufactured, and there are some crayon drawings from
the Cooper Institute Female Art School, but, with these exceptions,
beside the head of Charlotte Cushman[5] by Miss Stebbens, and a plaster
"Eve," there is nothing in the building but the ordinary exhibits of any

Agricultural State fair, and it would have been better for the reputation of the women, as artists, to have let their productions pass with others of the same kind in the general collection but the "cause," I suppose demanded a separate building for "women's work,"[6] her best and most enduring work can never be exhibited for truly it is "never done." . . .

M. B. C.

1. The Philadelphia Centennial Exposition, the first of its kind in the United States, featured an international fair that required ten years of planning and cost more than $11 million to complete. It covered hundreds of acres, had 30,000 exhibitors, and admitted at least 10 million people. Buildings that generated much interest included Machinery Hall, Government Building, Women's Pavilion, Japanese Building, and other exhibits by foreign countries. The iron-and-glass Main Building alone covered twenty acres. The exhibits by foreign countries were housed in separate sections within the Main Building. The exposition also showcased the work of women in the United States. It was an eye-opening experience for Mary Bayard Clarke and other visitors. James D. McCabe Jr., *A Centennial View of Our Country and its Resources* (Philadelphia: Hubbard Brothers, 1876), 1232, 1241; Post, *Centennial Exhibition,* 13–15, 173.

2. George P. Rowell published *George P. Rowell's and Company's Newspaper Reporter and Advertiser's Gazette* in New York between 1868 and 1884. He also published the first annual collections of statistics for newspaper circulation. Mott, *American Magazines,* 6, 565.

3. Joseph R. Hawley, a newspaper publisher, former congressman, and public speaker from Hartford, Connecticut, was elected president of the Centennial Commission that organized the Exposition. Post, *Centennial Exhibition,* 11.

4. Annie Ramborger had attended the Pennsylvania College of Dental Surgery. Post, *Centennial Exhibition,* 169.

5. Charlotte Saunders Cushman was an acclaimed American actress who died on 18 February 1876.

6. The Women's Pavilion actually included a much more varied selection of exhibits on women's work in medicine, business, science, journalism, and literature, all areas of great interest to Clarke. In addition to featuring inventions by women, the exposition highlighted women typographers, authors, and a women's journalism club, the "76 Club." On return visits, Clarke gained a deeper appreciation for the women's exhibits. Post, *Centennial Exhibition,* 169, 171.

*Barden Collection*
*MBC Scrapbook 2: unidentified newspaper clipping, fifth of seven in Mary Bayard Clarke's Centennial series.*

[From our own Correspondent.]
THE CENTENNIAL.
Rowell's Newspaper Building, Centennial Exposition.

September 7th.

I have been here now nearly a week, and feel that I am just beginning to take in the length and breadth, the height and depth, of this mammoth undertaking. To retain all the new ideas I have acquired I feel that it will be necessary to have a story added to my brain, a kind of mansard roof stuck on top of an old North Carolina house; for the present arrangement will never hold the new material. I am writing now at Rowell's Newspaper Building, where pens, ink, paper, and envelopes are furnished gratis to all press writers. Mr. Lobo, the Superintendent of the Press Building to whose kindness I was recommended by General Hawley, who has done everything for me that I could desire, offered me accomodations for writing in his department, but I find it much more quiet here, and come daily to arrange my ideas and set them down before they escape me.

"Why has not your State made some effort to be represented here?"[1] is a question that meets me at every turn, and I can only answer "Why indeed?" I spent this morning with Mr. M. E. Hyams of Statesville, N. C., who is the only exhibitor from our State that I have yet seen, and is, I believe, the only one here; Mr. Hyams is a South Carolinian by birth, but a North Carolinian by adoption, he is a botanist, and represents the firm of Wallace Brothers of Statesville, wholesale dealers in medical roots, herbs, barks, etc., and sits in a little room inside the Main Building, the walls of which are composed entirely of specimens put up in glass. He has 265 specimens of medical fruits in glass boxes, 80 of medical flowers, 137 of medical woods, nicely labeled, 631 medical plants, giving their medical properties, 290 mosses, 106 mushrooms, and over 500 more medical substances in glass boxes and jars, all from North Carolina, and all valuable in medicine and commerce. It cost this firm over $3,000 to prepare their exhibits, and when I asked, confidentially, whether they thought they would realize that amount, Mr. Hyams replied he had no hesitation in saying that he had already received foreign orders that would more than cover it. I was glad to hear that they were to be granted a first-class prize and diploma. They certainly deserve it. Mr. Hyams took me to the exhibit of the Western North Carolina Land Company in Agricultural Hall, which was hastily gotten up, and, though showing only the products of the lands of this Company, is very creditable to our State, and might with very little more expense have been largely increased and shown the products of the whole State. The gentleman in charge of it was very polite, and told me the exhibit attracted considerable attention, it has in it 72 varieties of wood in natural state with duplicates planed and highly varnished, some of which for cabinet purposes are as beautiful as any foreign woods. The mineral exhibits here do not show a tithe of what our State produces; the fexible sand-stone attracts a great deal of attention, so do the fine specimens of Samarskite a mineral only found in the Ural Mountains and in Western North Carolina. A book is kept here for visitors from our State to write their names in, and I noticed the names of Dr. George Slover and F. M. Agostine from New Berne, and also that of Mr. Edward Stanly of Rahway as having been formerly from New-Berne. I have met Judge Seymour and his wife, Mr. Rufus Tucker and daughters of Raleigh, and Mr. Jenkins son of Treasurer Jenkins, but the old North State seems as poorly represented by her sons and daughters as by her exhibits. It really made me indignant to go into the Kansas and Colorado State buildings and hear people talking about the beautiful exhibition of woods from those States, when I *knew* that, had she chosen to exert herself, North Carolina could have made a far better show in woods and minerals than either of these States, and probably than any other, certainly quite as good a one; while in wheat she could have equalled the best show here. . . . I must not forget one thing from North Carolina in the Woman's Pavillion, and that is a handkerchief worked by Mrs. Mary Lucas of Charlotte, which compares well with the other contents of the case, though it is the work of a lady over eighty years of age and done without spectacles.

On a more thorough examination under the pilotage of Mrs. Caldwell I find there is more in this department than I supposed at first. In company with General Hawley, who had never been over it, I did the building the other day, and found that the steam engine,[2] which prints the paper published by the ladies, and does all the steam work of the building, is entirely managed, from the making of the fire in the morning to shutting off the steam at night, by a young woman under thirty who sits in a little brick building attached to the Pavillion as neat and clean as if in her parlor, and seems no more troubled to manage the engine than she would be to regulate and use a cooking stove; she told me it was not near such hot work as that of a kitchen. People come up and look at her through the window, but most seem afraid to trust themselves inside for fear of being blown up; one lady sat looking so long without speaking that the *engineeress* at last asked her if she was interested in steam engines? "No," she replied with a weary sigh, "I never could understand *chemistry,* even when I studied it at school, and I don't see how you can remember enough of it to turn them screws and wheels at the right time," shs [*sic*] added "I hope you won't git blowed up," in a tone that implied "I know you will." Secretary Bristow,[3] who was of our party, in company with Mr. Murat Halsted of the Cincinnati Commercial expressed himself much pleased with a desk for reading rooms and offices invented by Mrs Styles for the purpose of utilizing all the space, and condensing it as much as possible. This lady has also invented and patented a swinging inkstand, that prevents all ink spilling. To-morrow General Hawley is to introduce me to the commissioners from Japan, China, India, and other far away countries, and I am to go over their departments under their escort and see all that is to be seen if that is a possible thing.

Before closing let me suggest that we begin *now* to prepare for the French Exposition of 1880, and have our State represented there for what she really is, her minerals and her woods, her cotton and her wool, her grain and tobacco her fruit and vegetables, if we wish to bury [*sic*] capital and emigrants to our homes.

M. B. C.

1. The Ladies Memorial Association of Wake County provided a flag for the Centennial celebration to honor the state's contributions during the American Revolution. The banner actually was created by the Reverend Johannes Adam Simon Oertel, a noted artist. H. G. Jones, "A Banner for the 'Yankee Celebration,'" *The State,* Jan. 1984, 24–25.

2. In the Women's Pavilion, where all the exhibits were made or operated by women, a Canadian woman named Emma Allison ran a steam engine that powered several looms and a printing press used to print the journal *New Century for Woman.* Allison's occupation attracted much attention. When visitors questioned her about safety issues, she replied that the steam engine required less attention than rearing children and was less tiring than cooking over a hot stove. Post, *Centennial Exhibition,* 17, 165.

3. Benjamin Helm Bristow served as United States secretary of the treasury under Grant from 1874 to 1876. *Who Was Who in America,* 74.

*Barden Collection*
*MBC Scrapbook 2: unidentified newspaper clipping, sixth of seven in Mary Bayard Clarke's Centennial series.*

[From our own Correspondent.]
## The Centennial, Huxley, etc.

New York, September 24th, 1876

I left Philadelphia in order to spend the past week in New York and hear Huxley's[1] three lectures on Evolution, the expectation of which has kept the whole literary scientific and religious world on the *quivive* of expectation ever since they were announced to come off. Reserved seats for the last two weeks were not to be had at any price, and the fortunate holders of tickets were among the envied. I reached Chickering Hall on the night of the first lecture about half past seven, and found the stairs blocked with eager seekers for seats, as tickets for those not reserved were sold only at door. Looking up the line I recognized the President of the University, Hon. Kemp Battle,[2] and after a tight squeeze through the crowd came on Professor Kerr and Dr. Phillips waiting inside. The house was crammed every night by an intelligent audience who, on the third night generally expressed themselves as much disappointed because there was nothing said to shake their religious belief, or indeed in any way to affect it. We all expected either to be converted or called to combat assertions on the evolution of man from a lower order of creation, but not a monkey did we see or hear of, and so clear, forcible and logical was the argument that it would be the heighth of presumption in the man or woman not up, or rather deep in geology and fossil remains to doubt, much less dispute anything advanced. It was all good, probably all true, but it was not what the audience wanted, nor was it what the clergy warned us not to believe or give ear to. It was evolution backward for we were clearly shown that the original horse had five toes or fingers and now has but one great middle finger with a hoof for a nail. I found it quite possible to believe every word the learned gentleman uttered and yet remain an Episcopalian, indeed I had read and accepted all he told us long ago—accepted it as possible, and a thing to be settled by the scientists not the religionists, was only intensely disappointed that it was the horse and not man where evolution was traced by diagrams, showing the fossil remains found in Europe and America.

To originate an hypothesis is one thing, to show that it is not only a possible but a probable one, is another, but to *prove* it to be true, is a totally different thing from either of these. Darwin did the second with regard to the hypothesis of evolution, and, after hearing Huxley, most of his audience felt it was, and always would be, an impossibility for any human being to do the third. The circumstantial evidence of the fossils in favor of evolution is stronger than any produce yet against, but here, as elsewhere, man finds "thus far shalt thou go and no further." in his investigations of nature; and those of us who are content to take the Bible, for its ethics, as an inspired book must feel the deeper we go into science, that no man by searching can "find out God." . . . Before going back to Philadelphia I have promised to spend an evening with Mrs. Leonowens[3] the author of the English Woman in Siam; her account of life in that country carries one back to the days when the Bhamins were most flourishing, and makes one feel, when combined with the Indian exhibit I mentioned in my first letter from Philadelphia, as if they had really been to the place. I dined in the New England log house the day before I left the Exposition, and could hardly realize that there were people who had never seen cotton-cards, a spinning wheel, or a quilt in a frame; but the crowd at the door of this house is so great that a policeman stands at the gate to keep them back, and only admit so many at a time. Inside it is just such a house as may be found any-where in North Carolina, only the articles furnishing it are more battered and ancient than those found in our log-cabins, and very many of them are historical. Over the mantle piece hangs an old flint lock gun, a powder horn, a turkey wing, some bundles of sweet herbs and the inevitable and ever present almanac. Beside the fire place is the quilting frame, and a young girl dressed in the costume of 1776 sits slowly quilting a patch work quilt which, like Penelope's robe, never gets done.

"Did they crimp their hair in those days?" I whispered to her.

She looked up and laughed replying "I'm sure I don't know."

"I'd vow they did, if I were you, for it looks very pretty under that high crowned cap."

"What is this?" asked a fashionably dressed lady—just then—"An old-fashioned ironing board, is it not?" For, to take up as little room as possi-ble, the quilt was rolled up till not wider than an ironing board. "Is this an old time bustle?" asked another, taking up an old-fashioned green silk *caleche,* worn by our grandmothers to keep their high crowned caps intact as they went out to tea. On the bed in one room is a quilt that was stamped in France shortly after the Declaration of Independence, on it America is represented as laying on the altar of Liberty a number of medallions each bearing the likeness of a signer of the Declaration; the likenesses are all good. Here too is shown the writing desk of John Alden, and a number of old books, one that I looked into having been printed in 1618. . . .

M. B. C.

1. Thomas Henry Huxley, an English biologist and evolutionist, supported Darwin's theories of evolution and publicly lectured on Darwinism. He traveled

to America in 1876 to continue his lectures while attending the opening of Johns Hopkins University. Huxley's 1863 publication *Evidence of Man's Place in Nature* discussed primate and human evolution, to the consternation of many.

2. Kemp Plummer Battle, a lawyer and former state treasurer, became president of the University of North Carolina in 1876, serving until 1891. The Professor Kerr and Dr. Phillips mentioned in this article were University of North Carolina professor Charles Phillips and state geologist Washington C. Kerr. Robin Brabham, "Defining the American University: The University of North Carolina, 1865–1875," *NCHR* 57 (Oct. 1980): 437n, 441, 447–48, 452n.

3. Anna Harriette Leonowens, immortalized in the play and movie *The King and I,* wrote two books about her experiences in Siam, *The English Governess at the Siamese Court* (1870) and *The Romance of the Harem,* the latter first published in Boston in 1872. She came to America to promote her books, which generally received favorable notices in America. Susan Morgan, ed., *The Romance of the Harem* (Charlottesville: University Press of Virginia, 1991), ix. Clarke interviewed Leonowens and published "An Evening in Siam" in the *Sunny South* (Atlanta) in 1876. MBC Scrapbook 2, newspaper clipping.

*Barden Collection*
*William J. Clarke to Mary Clarke Morgan*

New Berne, Oct. 8th. 1876.

My Dear Daughter:

My conscience is very sore about my neglecting to write to you for so long a time; but I do not like, at any time, to write letters, and this past summer has been the most wretched time of my life. I never was so poor, or lived so hardly. I never took in so little money, in the same length of time. The last month Willie and I did not receive quite $50; though we have a good prospect of doing much better this month. We have lived as economically as possible, and eaten the cheapest and coarsest food. Tom has at times gone almost bare-foot because I could not raise money to buy him a pair of shoes. I have been thankful that your mother was absent, for I felt these things keenly, and if she had been here I almost think I should have gone crazy. I did not write to you because I did not wish to infect you with the gloom which pressed so heavily on my soul. As I would not communicate the small pox to one of my family, so, when they are unable to assist me, I would not distress them with my troubles. It is some consolation to know that my difficulties have not been peculiar. We have done about the best paying practice of any lawers in this city. There seems to have been a money famine. I not only have not had money myself, but I have not seen others have it.

I have been reading very closely, and now feel that few members of the profession have a greater fund of legal knowledge. When business improves this will yield a rich harvest.

The health of the town has been very good the entire summer, and we have had very few deaths. I am sorry to say that Mrs. Judge Green now lies very low. How thankful I am that your mother could go, last summer to New York, and have the very best medical treatment, or her condition might have been the same! She has steadily improved in health, and has enjoyed herself, [torn] has all been done on $30, for I could raise no more to give her. She got a free pass for her connexion with the newspapers, and that has been her passport every where. She will return after the election. I do not wish her to come before that time, as Willie is a candidate, and I fear that something unpleasant might occur.[1] Willie is nearly through with his canvass, and has given great satisfaction to his party-friends. Of course there is no apprehension of his defeat, as we have a majority of 1,500 in this county. The Republican party will, I have no doubt, carry the presidential election, and I am very hopeful about our electing Settle and the State ticket.[2]—I must tell you something about Willie, which is to be a profound secret. He is engaged to be married to Katie Street![3] I only knew it a few days ago. She is a nice girl, and it is a good family, and I trust that they may be happy [torn] I like it much better than his penchant for Sophie Moore.

The equinoctial storm was very severe with us, but it did not do much damage in town. It relieved us, in a great measure, of mosquitoes, and relieved us entirely of apprehensions of yellow fever.

Celia and Frank are boarding with Mr. Peet. Their address is Station M. as it formerly was. I sent you Daniel Derunda and the numbers of Harper's Magazine containing the portion not printed in volume Keep them carefully as the magzs. belong to Frank—Hoping that you and your little family are well, and with a thousand kisses for Mary Bayard, I am,

Your affectionate father<br>Wm. J. Clarke

F's mother is well I saw her a few days ago—

1. William E. Clarke followed in his father's footsteps to become a prominent Republican leader in New Bern and the state. He served two terms in the state house and four years in the state senate. Ashe, *Cyclopedia of Eminent and Representative Men,* 2:126–27.

2. Thomas Settle Jr. lost the gubernatorial election to Zebulon Baird Vance.

3. This engagement never occurred. Willie Clarke married Sarah Elizabeth (Bessie) Howerton, the daughter of William Howerton, on 23 February 1886. Katie Street was the daughter of S. R. Street, proprietor of the Gaston House in New Bern.

*Barden Collection*
*Inland Monthly Magazine (July 1877): 69–71. Mary Bayard Clarke inked in her initials on her copy.*

### Woman in Journalism.[1]

There is no subject more interesting to the public, just at present, than the problem of woman. Even those who are bitterly opposed to "Woman's Rights" and "Woman's Suffrage," have sometimes to think of woman's wrongs and woman's sufferings, and are obliged to admit that there are many more women who must support themselves than are required to fill the ranks of teachers, seamstresses and boardinghouse keepers—occupations that may be called the three R's—reading, 'riting and 'rithmetic—once considered all that was necessary for woman's education. Every day opens wider the gate that admits woman to the green pastures of business—a gate whose bars have been all the more slowly withdrawn because they were bars of prejudices—which were supposed to be principles. Speaking from our own experience, we must say that we believe the majority of thinking and practical men, who are opposed to the letting down of these bars, honestly believe it will be detrimental to woman herself to admit her to the sweets of making money, unless it is imperatively necessary that she should support herself, because they fear it will injure her for the highest duties of her life—those of a wife and a mother. But all women are not wives, and many who are, never become mothers; not that I am by any means willing to admit that the duties of the domestic relations are necessarily not well performed by a woman of business; on the contrary, we maintain that a woman is a better wife, or mother, for being competent to understand the business of her husband, or her sons, even if it should never be necessary for her to take an active part in it. She has a brain as well as a heart, and while home duties fill the one, the other often cries loudly and vainly for sustenance.

But it is better to give her this training in youth, while she has the comfort and protection of a home, than to wait till, deprived of both, she is thrown ignorant and helpless on the world, it may be with a bare pittance, or it may be with nothing between her and starvation but a superficial knowledge of a few accomplishments, an ability to do her own sewing, take care of a home—which she has not—write a letter, cook a dinner, or get up laces?

How often do we hear such fathers say, "I will give my girls the best education that money can get, so that they may teach, if thrown on their own resources"?

Very good, as far as it goes; but why not carry the principle into something else, so that if the "army of martyrs," called teachers, has no place vacant in its ranks, they may be able to do something else with equal skill? Why restrict them to the three R's, when they are capable of winning diplomas in some higher and better paying business?

There are liberal-minded men who say, "Because we fear that contact with the world of men may expose our daughters to temptations from which they are sheltered at home."

There is, at the first glance, apparent reason in this objection, but on a closer inspection we see the fallacy of the argument, for the ranks of the fallen show the truth of the old maxim, "An idle brain is the devil's workshop." Give a woman some occupation in which her ambition to make either a fortune, or a name, can be gratified, at least, by the attempt to do so, and she is far safer than if she had no outlet for her vanity, except in becoming a social queen, or the leader of fashion in dress. Half the flirtations, which bring either ruin or unhappiness to women in their train, begin in sheer idleness.

Found schools, ye rich men, where your daughters can be trained to business, just as you establish institutions where they may be taught music and dancing, drawing and painting, French and German. She can drop her business knowledge, if necessary, as easy as she does her music, after marriage, and be none the less womanly for having the ability to take care of herself should it ever become necessary for her to do so.

There is no profession to which woman is better adapted than that of journalism. The physical labor of it is not half so trying as that of sewing, either by hand or with a machine, nor the mental half so wearing as that of teaching. It requires quickness of comprehension, facility of expression, and a talent of "cramming" rapidly on any given subject, more than strength of mind or profundity of learning to become a good editor. These qualities women often possess in a greater degree than men; while for gossippy news-letters, detailing little items of interest, she lays him in the shade entirely.

And here let me pay a well-merited tribute to the liberality of the journalists of the United States generally, and more especially those of Chicago, on the woman question. While she has had to fight her way by years of endurance and resolute persistence into the medical profession, and is still virtually excluded from the legal, she has been cordially welcomed and promptly recognized as a co-laborer in the field of journalism. Individually, she has doubtless had her trials and rebuffs, but the gentlemen of the press have never made common cause to exclude her from their ranks, but accepted her; first, it is true, as a spoilt child, playing at being one of them; next, as a useful assistant; and, finally, as an equal.

Just here we will quote a paragraph from the *Baltimorean* of July 14th, which expresses the stand taken by the INLAND MAGAZINE on this question. It is headed—

"Woman to the Front."

"There is an increase of at least twenty-five per cent. in the last fifteen years in the number of women supporting themselves in this country, especially in the large cities. But it is noticeable that this change is due to what women have done for themselves rather than to what has been done for them; and it is to be noted also that the increase has not been in consequence of any loud-voiced agitation in favor of women's rights, but in spite of it. The plain fact is, that the war left large numbers of women who had hitherto led domestic, dependent lives, obliged to work or starve. In consequence, they have quietly taken up all kinds of occupations, many heretofore considered impracticable for their sex. They have gone into artistic work of every kind, from designing stoves to high art painting. They are skilled nurses, dentists, photographers, and in some of the cities the whole retail trade is in their hands. They are horticulturists, hotel-keepers, stock-raisers. They have pushed their way into every position in a newspaper office, undertaken every kind of manufacture done by hand. All this too by the class of women who work with least noise or boasting. They deserve, in short, the name of good citizens, as any man would who honestly plods his way to a settled income by a self-respecting life.

The way to increase and help this class of women is to give them the instruction which a workman would receive, the protection which he would not need, and then leave them to enter the market precisely as he must do. Good work, good wages; sham work, poor wages, with no question of sex, is the inexorable rule which is bringing confusion out of this much debated question."

I do not know whether this emanated from one of the editors or was contributed, but I do know that the course advised has been pursued, by one at least of them, ever since the war. Before that time Southern women had made no effort to progress farther than the three R's. Shortly after it, A. F. Crutchfield, now the senior partner of the *Baltimorean,* started a weekly paper in Richmond, Va., called the *Literary Pastime,* taking Mrs. Mary Bayard Clarke, of North Carolina, as his assistant, which position she filled, until the paper was merged into the *Baltimorean.*

There are business colleges all over the United States for young men, but Chicago has the honor of founding the first school of journalism for women.[2] As yet it is an unweaned babe, but it bids fair to become a thriving child. It was started by the ladies of the "Inland Club," and is designed to instruct women in practical *versus* theoretical journalism. Pupils are nominated by members of the club, and pay an admission fee of $5, which entitles them to instruction in all the branches taught, they giving their services to the school during their stay. If not residents of Chicago, suitable board and lodging are found for them outside of the school. If they desire to become printers they are put at once to the compositor's "case" and taught all the details necessary to carry on an office. If they wish to become journalists, they are instructed in proof-reading, interviewing and reporting; made to prepare editorials on the question of the day, write letters from different points, and get up news items, and make selections from other papers. Short-hand and wood engraving will be added as soon as the funds will admit.

Any one, whether a lady or a gentleman, a resident or non-resident of Chicago, can become a life member of the club on payment of $25, which entitles him to nominate one pupil every year for admission to the school, who will remain till dismissed with a certificate of her ability. Southern gentlemen of means—if there are any such left—could not make a better use of their money than by becoming life members of this club, and sending some woman from their own locality to be entered as a pupil in the newly-founded School of Journalism, and thus opening another field for woman's labor in the South, where as yet there are so few occupations in which she can find employment either for her head or her hands. I appeal to the gentlemen of the press to continue their generous assistance to struggling woman by spreading the fame of this school far and wide, so it may come to the knowledge of all who need its aid. All letters, either of inquiry or for admission, should be addressed to Mrs. Charlotte Smith, "Inland Club" Rooms, Chicago, Ill.

1. Women found many jobs open to them in the field of journalism. With better education and good writing and editing skills, women worked as reporters, editors, and typesetters. Still, critics of women working outside the home remained both North and South. Clarke's essay urging women to seek employment represented a major departure from the beliefs of her social peers in North Carolina. Mott, *American Journalism*, 405–6.

2. The 1870s saw an effort to establish a school of journalism for women in Chicago. Clarke's reference to it here is briefly corroborated in a 1911 obituary for Martha Louise Woodworth Rayne that bears the subtitle, "Founder of First School of Journalism in the World and Author of Many Short Stories." Rayne, born in Halifax, Nova Scotia, wrote for the *Chicago Tribune* and other papers, including *Century*. She also worked in collaboration with Clarke on the Chicago serial *Current Thought, Literature, Fashion, Society and Home Topics.* The Inland Club, under Charlotte Smith and named for her *Inland Magazine,* reflected Smith's interests in training women in the practical aspects of journalism. Whether Rayne actually founded the Chicago school is open to question, given that Smith's career as a professional journalist dated back to at least 1872. *Chicago Tribune,* 9 Apr. 1911; clipping from Emily Clark, assistant librarian, Chicago Historical Society, to Mrs. Mary M. Barden, New Bern, 4 June 1996; Kenny J. Williams, *Prairie Voices: A Literary History of Chicago from the Frontier to 1893* (Nashville, Tenn.: Townsend Press, 1980), 375.

*Barden Collection*
*MBC Scrapbook 2, unidentified newspaper clipping by Mary Bayard Clarke.*

## LETTER FROM CHICAGO.

### TREMONT HOUSE, July 24th, 1877.

MESSRS. EDITORS:——The strike is on Chicago[1] and we are sitting quietly awaiting the consummation; thanks to the vigilance and forethought of the authorities there is but little apprehension of mob violence; troops have been concentrated here, cannons placed so as to rake the streets if necessary, and the police force largely increased. All day yesterday the excitement, though suppressed, was intense, and we felt as if on a volcano. Bands of strikers paraded the streets armed with sticks, and went from factory to workshop trying to induce all workingmen to suspend labor and render the strike general. Sometimes they succeeded and sometimes they failed, but no violence was offered, and except around the bulletin boards of the newspaper offices there were no crowds gathered. The Mayor advised women and children to keep out of the streets, and shut up every drinking saloon. About half-past five I left the office of the *Inland Magazine*[2] to go to dinner at the Tremont House, and was struck with the absence of ladies on the street, and the expression on the faces of most of the men. I wished to stop at the office of the *Chicago Post,* where I drop in occasionally for a chat, but had to give it up, owing to the crowd round the door intently studying the bulletins in the window, which were added to from time to time as news was brought of the closing of some factory or place of business. I next tried the *Inter-Ocean* but with no better success; I could have forced my way in, for the crowd would have parted for me, but I did not care to make the attempt and went on to the Tremont, which I found packed and jammed with passengers from the trains, some of whom could go no further, and some preferring not to do so but to weather the storm here, rather than run the risk of being detained at some wayside station further on. Every room in the house was filled before dark, and dinner was kept going till all the hungry crowd were fed, for the Tremont, under Mr. Wilcox, is equal to any emergency. Having eaten my dinner I began to think what it was best for me to do, as my room is about two squares from the hotel, and I had no desire to be caught there. No meals being furnished in the house, I should be obliged to depend on coffee, made on my little lamp stove, and dry crackers for breakfast, should it be impossible to get out the next day. I felt sure Mr. Wilcox would find me a place if I decided to stay, but then I did *not* feel sure it was necessary to do so, and decidedly objected to being separated from my belongings if it was not. My finery carried the day, and I returned to my lodgings to find them entirely deserted. There are never any gentlemen in the house except between the hours of 10 P. M. and 7 A. M., and I did not know whether the ladies had fled or not; but not even a cat was on the premises. Going back to the outer door, after making this discovery, I stood outside till a couple of policemen passed, and quietly calling them in asked them if it would be safe for me to stay; they assured me it would, as fire was all I had to fear, and the house was surrounded with fire-proof buildings, having Hooley's Theatre just back of it, and a bank on either side. So I lighted the hall lamp, made fast the door, and sat down to wait, determined if some one did not come in by bed-time to go to the Tremont for the night. In about an hour the landlady came; fearing she might be besieged next day, she had been out to lay in supplies, for, like her lodgers, she takes her meals out, and has no conveniences for cooking in the house. Together we determined to "hold the fort," and stick to our plunder. She had eggs, butter and canned meat, with plenty of bread, and I had a kerosene stove in my room over which we could cook a comfortable breakfast if necessary. The other ladies had fled, but the gentlemen came dropping in until 12 o'clock, and we slept quietly all night, to be roused next morning with the cry of "Extra News," "Extra *Post,*" "Here's your *Times,*" and so on, from the newsboys who are reaping a rich harvest of nickels and three cent pieces. Order reigned in the streets, and Tremont was quietly feeding its thousand guests, when I went down to my breakfast at 8 o'clock and meekly received a scolding for not staying all the night before. As Mrs. Smith, the proprietor and editor of the *Inland Magazine,* is absent I thought it best to go early to the office, a press of work having obliged us to take in three or four new men, of whom we knew nothing; I found them all at work, though the strikers were going round to the large establishments of every kind trying to induce workmen of all descriptions to leave. As I sat in the editorial room correcting proof, one of the printers brought in an inflammatory handbill, addressed to the "Working men of Chicago," calling on them to rise against "the aristocrats," and beginning "will you still remain disunited while your masters rob you of all your rights?" and laid it on my desk. I read it through, and quietly handing it back to him said, "you had better tell them there is no master in this establishment—only a mistress, who has too much business of her own to attend to just now, to mind other people's." He went away laughing, and I went on with my work, tlll [*sic*] suddenly a terrific yell burst out in the street, and the cry came up that the police were firing on the strikers in Twenty-Second Street. But the shouts, on listening more attentively, did not seem to be in the voice of anger, and were mingled with loud clapping of hands, and in a few moments we could see from our windows, which are in the third story, the advance of a company of United States troops who had just arrived from the West, and were marching down Madison street, greeted by shouts of welcome from the citizens, who have organized in squads to assist the police if necessary. "That knocks the strikers into a cocked hat," said one of our men, pointing to the troops. "*For a time,*" was the reply of another, and they went back to their cases, while we ladies, three in number, continued our work, having agreed beforehand we would be as calm as May mornings, and if we were afraid not to show it. But really there seems nothing to fear, here in the heart of the business portion of the city; on the out skirts, where the factories and machine shops are, there may be danger, but I cannot get up a scare beyond the fear of being obliged to close the office for want of printers. I did not leave it till we closed at six, when I went to dinner at the Tremont. If I had been born a man I should certainly have ordered a bottle of champagne, for I was tired out, but being only a woman consoled myself with tea.

I don't know when you will receive this, as I did not get THE OBSERVER to-day and am not sure if the train goes through, but I think, with our printer, that the backbone of the strike is broken and order will soon reign once more.

M. B. C.

1. The Baltimore and Ohio Railroad strike of July 1877 affected many American cities, including Chicago. For the first time, the president called in the United States Army to stop the riots, which was done with little trouble. Clarke's article on the strike was written for an unidentified North Carolina newspaper.

2. *Inland Monthly Magazine* of Chicago and St. Louis, Missouri, was published by Charlotte Smith, an editor, publisher, reformer, and economic feminist. According to L. U. Reavis, the *Inland Monthly* "won a leading position in the best of literary publications of the West, and brought to its support some of the best talents of the country." Dains and Sadler view it not as a woman's magazine, as Mott stated, but "a regional, general interest magazine, containing articles on politics, philosophy, and economics in addition to poems, serialized fiction, and articles focused on the South and West." Clarke worked for Smith as an editor and writer in Chicago. Mott, *American Magazines,* 95–96, 572; L. U. Reavis, *Saint Louis: The Future Great City of the World, with Biographical Sketches of the Representative Men and Women of St. Louis and Missouri,* centennial ed. (St. Louis, Mo.: C. R. Barns, 1876), 756–57; Mary K. Dains and Sue Sadler, eds., *Show Me Missouri Women: Selected Biographies,* vol. 2 (Kirksville, Mo.: Thomas Jefferson University Press, 1993), 51–52.

*Barden Collection*
*MBC Scrapbook 2, newspaper clipping,* Current Thought *1, no. 1, Oct. 1877, 1.*
Current Thought
*Literature, Fashion, Society and Home Topics*
### "Woman North and South."
By Mary Bayard Clarke.

Oliver Wendal Holmes says that religion is a matter of latitude and longitude, and the same may be said of the characteristics of woman. They are fundamentally the same; and she is developed into the varying types of the sex by her surroundings. As a class, the Northern and the Southern woman differ materially; but climate has quite as much to do with this difference as social surroundings. That the Northern woman is physically the

stronger, is owing to climatic influence, that she is mentally more independent to social. It is a mistake to suppose the Southern woman naturally
more indolent than the Northern; but she is undoubtedly softer and more
yielding, with far less independence of thought and action. She is less given
to striking out for herself, and more apt to take her opinions, as she formerly did her property, by inheritance. She does and thinks as her mother
and grandmother, because they so did and thought; questions neither her
religious nor her social teaohings [*sic*]; is more conservative, slower to
change, and less enquiring than her Northern sister; she does not care for
her rights, because she is satisfied with her privileges; but the softness of
her manners often covers an indomitable will, which leads her to cling to
her prejudices and elevate them into principles.[1] She does not reason on
them herself, and will not listen to reasoning from any one else. She is not
the bar of iron, but the cushion of down. Richard Cœur de Lion's sword
could cut the first in two, but by Saladin's scimeter could divide the last.
She is a devoted wife and mother, a kind and thoughtful mistress, but after
marriage is apt to ignore all social duties but the grand one of hospitality.
She regards a woman's club, whether a literary, artistic, or social one, as a
monstrosity, and leaves all work and amusement outside of home to her
husband, brother or son, except the societies of her church. In her home
she is generally queen regnant, and her husband only king consort. He
interferes far less in the management of domestic affairs than the Northern husband; is more affectionate and more tender, considering it a disgrace, not to her but to him, if his wife engages in any occupation for the
purpose of making money, and a dire misfortune if his daughters are
obliged to work, out of the family circle. Consequently girls are seldom
trained even to teach. They are educated, as their parents say, so that *if necessary* they can teach, but they are never *trained* to any occupation till the
necessity is on them. How bravely and nobly they can meet such necessity,
the records of nearly every Southern family since the war will show. The
Southern man does not wish his wife, sister or daughter to be self-supporting; not because he is jealous of her rivaling him, but because he feels
that it is his right, as well as his duty, to be the bread winner. There were
before the war fewer sudden pecuniary reverses South than North, and
most persons could live as their fathers did before them, and were generally content to do so. But all this is changed, and the Southern woman
grows yearly better adapted to the great social and domestic change in her
circumstances produced by the war. Necessity is forcing her to be more self-
reliant and more self-supporting. In the South there are few large centres

and much less attrition of mind against mind than in the North; the people are homogenous and slower to change, and public opinion is much less fluctuating. The Northern woman who wishes to strike out for herself in business, has ten times the advantages of her Southern sister. She is from climate physically better fitted to work hard, both with her head and her hands. When she goes into shop, or factory, or business of any kind, whether it be literature, art, medicine or law, she has not to brace herself against public opinion, and is not made to feel that she is regarded by others as having socially lowered herself, as the Southern woman is, until she has become a success. The very women who were hardest in their judgment of Susan Dimock,[2] when she first went to Zurich to study medicine, were the proudest of her success after she was established in her hospital in Boston, and the North Carolina Medical Association, when she applied for admission to the Society, unanimously elected her, without a single utterance against the vote.

It is the custom now to sneer at the "chivalry" of the South, but that very sentiment, while rendering it harder for a woman to break through old customs, most heartily sustains her when she has successfully done so. Northern women had an idea that before the war Southern women did little or nothing, but had troops of servants at their command, who performed every office for them, even to putting on their shoes and stockings, and dressing their hair daily, and so they had; but the very woman who indulged in the luxury of a well trained maid, who never thought of folding her own dress or shawl, and would send a servant up stairs twenty times a day to get her handkerchief, her fan, or her keys, carried those same keys continually, and gave out all the family supplies for twenty or thirty persons, and if she lived in the country, frequently superintended the spinning, weaving and sewing for the plantation. The Northern housekeeper, with one or two servants, could form no idea of the duties and cares of a Southern, with from ten to twelve, of all ages, from a month old infant to a grandmother of three-score. While the Southern woman, knowing nothing by personal experience of the compactness of a Northern house, the many labor-saving contrivances, and the conveniences which save time and render many servants superfluous, was too apt to regard a Northern woman, who did her own housework and assisted in the cooking, as necessarily a drudge. But the abolition of slavery is gradually bringing the Southern woman to the Northern method of housekeeping, and obliging her to look out for some other method of earning money than teaching or taking boarders. Then, too, the population of the North, being so much more dense than that of the South, more women are forced to earn their own living here than there. Except in the large cities, even shop girls are rare, and there is nothing in the whole South corresponding to the intelligent factory girl of New England. Commercial and manufacturing countries are always more progressive than agricultural. Whether this progress is in a desirable direction is a question of opinion, but the fact remains the same that they do not stand still, and it is to be hoped that now that the South has been forced by outside pressure to move, that the women of the two sections may approach nearer to each other, for each may learn something by doing so.[3]

1. For a useful discussion of North Carolina women from the former planter class and their reactions to the need to work, see Jane Turner Censer, "A Changing World of Work: North Carolina Elite Women, 1865–1895," *NCHR* 73 (Jan. 1996): 28–55. Censer notes there is disagreement among historians over the role these women played following the war, but her nuanced evaluation of women by age as well as class provides an important perspective on how women coped after the Civil War.

2. Susan Dimock was North Carolina's first woman doctor, although she never practiced in the state. Dimock was born in Washington, North Carolina, in 1847. She was introduced to medicine by a local practitioner. Following her father's death, Dimock and her mother moved to Sterling, Massachusetts. There, Dimock pursued a medical career at the New England Hospital for Women and Children in Boston. When Harvard University refused to admit her for formal training, she went to Europe to study. In 1872 the North Carolina Medical Society made Dimock an honorary member. In that same year Dimock returned to Boston to serve as resident physician at the New England hospital. In 1875 her steamship sank while sailing to Europe and Dimock drowned. Powell, *DNCB*, 2:70.

3. In the MBC Scrapbook 2, Barden Collection, Mary Bayard Clarke pasted an undated newspaper editorial from a later issue of *Current Thought,* probably published around November 1877. The editorial mentioned Clarke's assertion that "women in the South are, through necessity, beginning to be self-reliant and progressive." It praised Clarke and expressed hope that her influence on other southern women would encourage "rapid growth among women." The editorial closed by expressing the opinion, "Should the Southern women grow as rapidly as we of the North have done, they will soon be solving their own problems."

৵

*Barden Collection*
*MBC Scrapbook 2, unidentified newspaper clipping [1877] by Mary Bayard Clarke.*
Woman As a Worker.
By Mary Bayard Clarke.

"Why is it that so many avocations suitable to women are entirely given up to men?" we asked a gentleman, who was lamenting the inability of educated and refined women to support themselves except by the wearing occupations of teaching, sewing, or taking boarders, incurring the censure, or at best receiving but the cold tolerance of society for doing so.

"Because of the inefficiency of woman," was the reply that startled us, coming, as it did, from one who believed in women, and was desirous of giving them every advantage in the race of life.

Instantly we bristled up in defense of our sex, and wished to know if Madame [Charlotte Irene Denman] Lozier and Susan Dimock were examples of the inefficiency of women as physicians, or if Caroline Herschel, the discoverer of eight comets, and Mrs. Mary Somerville, both of whom were enrolled as members of the Royal Astronomical Society of London, were inefficient astronomers; or if Angelica Kaufmann or Rosa Bonheur were failures as artists, or if Miss [Mary] Carpenter, the sister of the distinguished Dr. Carpenter, or Miss Whately, the daughter of Archbishop [Richard] Whately, both celebrated, the one for her labors among the women of India, the other for her work among the fellah women of Egypt, were specimens of the inefficiency of women; or if the term could in any way be applied to Florence Nightengale, whose executive ability brought order and comfort out of the chaos of the Crimean hospitals, or to Fanny Kemble, Charlotte Cushman, Henrietta Sontag, Louise Kellogg, or any of the other stars of the dramatic and musical world; or, coming nearer home, to Mrs. Tupper, of Des Moines, the queen of apiarians, who, by her practical experience, has become an acknowledged authority in bee culture, and is quoted in the best bee journals of America, to which she has been a constant contributor. Growing bolder as we talked, we widened the circle, and asked if the lace-workers of Honiton, the watch-makers of Geneva, and the thousands of women in France and Germany, who engage in business of manufacturing on their own account, were not a convincing proof that it was not the inefficiency of woman that kept the sex in America tied, by prejudice, to a few unremunerative employments.

To our surprise, instead of being overwhelmed by our proofs, he boldly declared they were all in his favor, and asked if Madame Lozier and Miss

Dimock had not gone through exactly the same training and course of study as any male practitioner; if Caroline Herschel, had not, from her earliest youth, devoted all the energies, both of her mind and body, to becoming her brother's assistant, and worked day and night, with no other object in view except, as she herself expressed it, that of "becoming a serviceable tool for his hand;" if Rosa Bonheur had not studied anatomy, and dissected subjects, as well as learned the art of mixing and laying on colors; if Fanny Kemble and Charlotte Cushman had not both spent years in patiently laying the foundation on which the structure of their fame had been built, and if every musical star had not gone through a long course of study and practice before they attained the zenith of their fame? After which he utterly quenched us by asserting that every European woman who went into trade or business of any kind began just as a man would, and prepared herself for what she intended to be a life-long, not a mere temporary, occupation, till something better presented itself, instead of spending her youth in acquiring habits both of mind and body, which totally unfitted her to compete successfully with man in the very occupations to which, with proper training, she would be better suited than he is.

"But why are American women, as a rule, more inefficient than Europeans?" we asked; ["]can they not also be trained to work systematically?"

"Not for a generation to come," was the discouraging reply, because it will take at least that time to modify the prejudices of society and enable the working woman—we use the term in its largest sense as including all who in any way work for remuneration—to live more in accordance with the laws of nature, and adopt a costume that does not in some way hamper every motion. Until we can have healthy women we cannot have efficient workers; and the dress worn by women is one great reason why they do not, as a general rule, enjoy the same relative health as a man, and are entirely shut out from many of the higher avocations in which he engages.

Formerly, a dress which prevented all labor was the distinctive mark of a gentleman; the embroidered waistcoats, laced coats, lace frills, powdered wigs, and swords worn by gallants, rendered them as useless for work as the long skirts hoops, tie-backs, or high-heeled shoes of the women of today do her. Woman in her present costume, cannot compete successfully with man as a worker in any but the purely sedentary occupations of life, and, until she shall have independence enough to assume one which will give free play to her muscles, either for strength or quickness, she need not hope to do so. The sweeping skirts of a female chemist would be out of place and terribly in the way among chemicals in the laboratory, and are equally hampering to the apiarian, obliged to be out in the early dew and to follow her bees through bush and brake when they have swarmed. One-half of the physical ills brought on females by protracted standing might be averted were they not obliged to support the weight of their skirts, and more than half the weariness consequent on bee-keeping, horticulture, the preparation of medicinal herbs and drying of fruits, all employment in which women can successfully engage, would disappear if Mrs. Grundy[1] would allow her to wear a suitable costume while at work.

But the working woman is not willing to be recognized as such by her dress. She does not hesitate to put on mourning and say to every passer-by, by her dress, "I cannot go into the gay world at present because of reasons which prevent;" and the gay world pats her approvingly on the back and says, "the ball room is no place for crape, come to us when you can lay it aside, but keep away while you are obliged by custom to wear it."

Why not say the same of her working dress, when it is necessary that it should be worn on the street?

Take for example a male and female newspaper reporter. The first is best paid, because he must be ready at any moment to snatch up his hat and coat and be off, it may be for an hour, it may be for a week; if caught without time to run home for his bag, he buys a clean shirt, if necessary, brushes his clothes and his boots, uses a pocket-comb, and comes out from his toilet ready for action. How can the woman, whose hair must be puffed and crimped, whose hat must be held on by an elastic, and who must don an overskirt and an underskirt, and hold her train up with one hand as she waddles along in her tie-back and French heeled boots, expect to compete successfully with him? Or, we will suppose both required to attend a fashionable wedding or evening entertainment where it is necessary they should appear in full dress; and then think of the time consumed and the thought and labor required to get up the lady compared with that for the man. We once heard an authoress of some reputation say she had spent brain force enough, in contriving one new costume out of two old ones, to have produced a first-class article for the *Galaxy*. Too poor to order one ready-made, as a man does a suit of clothes, she thought to economize by doing the work of a dressmaker herself, growling all the time at Mr. Grundy for not allowing her to go to her work in a dress, suitable for labor, which she could have ordered at a fixed price.

In Europe, where there are strictly defined classes, a woman who works never thinks of competing in dress with the woman of leisure, and however tasteful she may get herself up when off duty, never hesitates to wear a dress suited to her work when engaged in it.

"If you will go down into the office and take a desk there, I will raise your pay one-fourth," we once heard a stenographer say to one of his lady amanuenses, who took down in short hand and reproduced in long, ready for the copy-press, the testimony taken by him in court, working often at his house till twelve or one o'clock, and rising, as often, at four or five. To our surprise she positively refused the offer, and gave as a reason that she could not bear the weariness consequent on working all day in the dress it would be necessary for her to wear in an office and in the street going to and fro. "At home," she said, "I put on a loose wrapper and slippers and can work twice as long as I could in my street dress." Had she been a French woman she would have devised a suitable dress and worn it in the street and at her work; persons seeing her, however, would never have taken her for the wife of a millionaire, as they might some of our lady workers from their get-up. There is no reason why a working dress for a woman should be any more masculine than the present style, and, were a number to adopt one, it would soon cease to attract any more attention than a mourning suit now does. Let the skirt be short enough to hang clear of the ground, say reach only to the top of the boot, be suspended from the shoulder, giving full play to the lungs and not dragging on the hips; over this a loose sacque, buttoning to the throat, with sleeves and arm-holes large enough to allow free use of the arms; a hat with a brim broad enough to shade the eyes and the back of the neck; stout shoes with broad heels, placed where nature designed them, instead of in the middle of the foot, and only high enough to raise the hollow of the foot just as nature raises it in a perfectly formed one. Such a costume might be made coquetish and becoming, and yet leave the wearer free in every muscle. For some employments it might be necessary, while at work, to wear a shorter skirt and remove the sacque, which could be done with as much propriety and as little loss of time as the taking off and putting on of ordinary out-door wraps. . . . In this dress, with the same training given them as boys and men receive, there is no occupation engaged in by her father, brother or husband, from which a woman need be excluded. The wife of a European peasant works in the field at as hard labor as her husband. Rising in the social scale, man does less and less physical labor, and his wife and daughters would also do less. Whether such labor is desirable for woman, except in cases where it is necessary to keep the wolf of hunger from the door, is another question, and one into which we do not propose to enter. We simply wish to impress on the minds of those women who desire to compete with men in any avocation, the necessity of first being trained to work as men are, and next of adopting their costume to their work, so that it shall in no way impede the free action of the brain, the body and the limbs.

We once visited a cheese factory, owned by a joint stock company of New England farmers, where the whole work was done by one woman and two half grown men; on our way we overtook the manager, and entered the factory with her. She was dressed as any other well-to-do farmer's wife might have been, but in five minutes had dropped her outer skirt and sacque, and appeared in a skirt reaching half way down the calf of her leg, pantaloons and short sacque, with loose sleeves that could be rolled up to her shoulders. In this costume she went to work, weighing the milk brought in, testing its richness, and going through the whole process of cheese making, working the curd with her hands and arms immersed in the vat, as she said it was only in that way she could judge the temperature. We spent the whole day, from nine till four, with her, saw the whole process, even to the turning of the cheeses made the day before, which was done under her eye by the boys. There was nothing she did not do, or superintend, and when we asked if it was not very hard work, she replied, "Not half as hard as cooking and washing, or superintending a farm house; for when I am through, my work is done, and I can change my dress and rest. . . ." Shortly after this, at a social gathering in one of the farm houses, we recognized our friend of the factory, dressed in a good black silk dress, a fashionable cap, and lace collar and sleeves, and overheard her discussing George Elliott's last novel. She had been trained from her youth to work systematically, and had no trouble in adapting herself to the position she held, and no unwillingness to wear a suitable costume while at work, though amply able to don her silk and lace, and discuss a novel after work hours. She had competed successfully with a man, even in a business requiring strength of muscle and constant standing. . . .

1. Clarke referred to Mrs. Grundy and Mr. Grundy to describe society and its dictates.

THIS LETTER INTRODUCES one of Mary Bayard Clarke's cherished correspondents, Dr. Nathan W. Abbott, a New York physician then living in Chicago, Illinois. Abbott, who died in 1880, was the friend of several women writers in Chicago, which is where he met Clarke in 1877. Abbott saved Clarke's letters to him, which were returned to her following his death. The correspondence provided Clarke with a rare opportunity to exchange thoughts and opinions freely with someone who adopted a more open attitude than Clarke generally found in North Carolina. According to one account of Abbott published after his death, "In modes of thought he was large-minded and liberal. It was at his office that the Chicago Philosophical Society was organized, and, along with the Rev. Dr. Thomas, he has been from the beginning one of its warmest and staunchest supporters." Clarke and Abbott discussed religion, science, health, literature, and more. She even urged him to visit her in New Bern while her husband was out of town, with her husband's full knowledge and consent. Abbott declined this offer, but his friendship and encouragement helped Clarke to endure many of the trials that were to follow.

*Barden Collection*
*Dr. N. W. Abbott to Mary Bayard Clarke*

Chicago Dec 23d 1877

Mrs. Mary Bayard Clarke
New Berne N.C.
My Dear Mary

Your good letter of the 2d inst is not entitled to the treatment it has received at my hands. I am every way truthful when I say words cannot express the satisfaction your letters give me. They are literary, refined, sweet and philosophical. I would give thousands if I had the ability to express my views as you have on paper. I have for some reason sought for and read more of your productions since you left than I had done before. If you ever again ask me to read a vol. of your poems I will not reply as I did on a former occasion. Alas! how many prizes we lose by not taking the tide at its flood. Your letters seem to breathe a depth of thought and warmth of feeling which I little dreamed of when first we met. Your kind expressions in regard to Mrs Leonard[1] whom I admire as much as you do, and your sensible, philosophical and charitable sentiments, and expressions in regard to Mrs. [Charlotte] Smith are worthy to be engraved on the tablets of the memory. Goethe has somewhere said that if one would save up the choice sentences in letters from friends, one would finally have a store of valuable thought and expression which could not be equalled in any other way. I thought I would so treat your letters, but I find I have to save the whole letter, and so I have preserved them. They are sacred. I do however read portions of them to Genl. Buford.[2] One of the beautiful expressions in your first is, "there is a love which is an inclination of the intellect and not a passion of the heart" etc. In your last they are too numerous to mention. All these things render your letter deserving a better fate than it has received at my hands. In other words it should have been answered sooner. But I seem to have been unusually busy of late. And even now I have time only to write you hastily and imperfectly, as I start in a few hours to visit my brother in the state of Mich. and will not be home until the 2d of Jan. Hence I have to write you rapidly and you see the result. There is much that I would like to say that must be left unsaid. During the past week I spent an evening with Mrs. Leonard. Your ears must have burned for we talked much about you. She read me some of her manuscript. I think her philosophy well founded, although some of it may not be practicable now nor for a long time to come. She is a woman of a good heart and a lover of humanity. I am glad that you think well enough of my scribbling to read such portions to your family as you think would interest them. I hope I may sometime become acquainted with the entire family. I know your husband is a man of good sense or he never would have found you.

The Inland drags its slow length along. It has less life than when you were here. Mrs Brainard is what I would call local editor. Miss Dolson is in Wis. and has been for several weeks, I have not seen Mrs Smith for three weeks. I find in your first letter a sentence which to this hour is to me an unsolved riddle. It is this "I will confess I did not like you one bit at the first of our acquaintance, but that now seems so long ago that I can smile at the delusions into which I was led by Mrs Smith and acknowledge them without a blush." A word of explanation will put me out of my misery. The Thanksgiving poem[3] was published on that day in the Tribune. I sent you three papers. Did you get them? I have not been around to have this last one published. I will as soon as I return from my trip. Please write me soon, so that I may receive it soon after my return. I hope to see you in the spring, and then I will go for that kiss. I am so sorry that timidity overruled my great desire. Please remember me kindly to your family and accept for yourself my sincere love.

I am as ever yours<br>N W Abbott

Dear Mary—I never told you that my right hand is crippled, from much writing years ago. Hence you must not Judge my character by my chirography

1. According to an unidentified and undated newspaper clipping Clarke pasted into a scrapbook, "Mrs. Cynthia Leonard, humantarian [*sic*] and free thinker" was

a writer, lecturer, and supporter of women's rights. The clipping noted that "[Leonard] has yet lent a helping hand to many workers, and her name is indissolubly connected with Chicago journalism. She was the originator of the Chicago *Sorosis,* the first woman's paper published in this city, and president of the society of that name." After Clarke left Chicago, Leonard separated from her husband. Clarke wrote to Leonard and her daughters thereafter, but Leonard soon blamed Clarke for the disintegration of her relationship with her daughters. Clarke, writing to Abbott in her own defense, explained, "If I were guilty of the charges brought against me by my friend I should deserve her extreem displeasure. I can imagine no greater treachery than setting children against their mother under the guise of friendship, and I am sure I would resent such an act more even than interference between myself and my husband." Clarke added, "that it is an unpardonable impertinence for any one, but a blood relation, to interfere in family differences." MBC Scrapbook 2, Barden Collection; Mary Bayard Clarke to Nathan Abbott, 30 July [1878?], Barden Collection.

2. Napoleon Bonaparte Buford, a West Point graduate, served during the Civil War and attained the rank of major general. He died 28 March 1883. Heitman, *Historical Register,* 260.

3. Written by Mary Bayard Clarke.

*Barden Collection*
*Mary Bayard Clarke to Dr. Nathan Abbott*

Newbern
May 16th [1878]

My Dear Doctor

I should sooner have written to acknowledge your kind letter but have delayed hoping I could tell you that I had arranged to spend the summer in Chicago, but day by day my prospect of being able to do so grows less, and I fear I shall have to give it up altogether for want of funds. You can form no conception of the dearth of money in this section; with a good practise and more work than he can do, my husband has found it impossible to collect a tenth of what is due him, and I am unwilling to go so far from home unless I was *sure* of funds in case I failed to support myself, as I did last summer; Mrs Rayne writes me she can pay me nothing for my work of the past winter, so it will not do to depend on getting work after I reach Chicago; I am very much disappointed but it cant be helped unless you can find a situation for me that will pay my board, I care for nothing more than *that,* as I shall be in funds by fall when the crop is made, which is here like the coming in of the whale-ships, the only time when money circulates.

I should not care so much if my Doctor did not object so seriously to my staying in this climate during the summer just at present, he says I am at a point of life,[1] which you can understand, when I need all my strength and vitality to meet the demands made on me, and ought not to stay where I have an additional drain in the shape of malarial influences. I think I ought to have married a Doctor he would always have been sure of *one* patient, and, as my Doctor is kind enough to say, of an efficient assistant; I dont care for the *practical* part of your profession one bit, but I do love the *intellectual* portion of it, and have just completed what would have been a task to any one not so inclined, for I have spent two weeks writing an elaborate paper on Diphtheria, from the rough notes of Dr Duffy who delivers the opening address on this subject at the State medical convention that meets this week in Goldsboro. I have done so much of this work for him that, man like, he takes an ell whenever I give an inch, and this time coolly informed me I had been all the year reading Tyndall and Pasteur and Bastian on the germ-theory of disease and spontaneous generation, and could hunt up authorities as well as he could and string his notes together better than he could Of course after such a compliment I was going to do "my level best" for him, and together we have got out a paper of fifty six pages of the full size of this whole sheet, he doing the head and I the hand work, and I feel fully posted on Diphtheria and told him I could condense those fifty six pages into one sentence, namely, "We dont know what causes Diphtheria, and we dont know how to prevent its genesis and spread, neither do we know why it kills or how to prevent its doing so, we can only watch each case and treat each as its symptoms may lead us to think best, and are never certain we are doing good and may do harm. It is certain it sometimes originates *de novo* and equally certain it is sometimes conveyed from one patient to another." The Dr said I had about hit it but he thought the association would prefer my elaboration to my condensation. I am glad you liked my article on "Servetus" Mr Frothingham wrote me quite a complimentary letter, but I liked yours best and so did my husband, he is away a great deal now and I am entirely alone for days, and find writing my only resource, I dont mind the work, in fact like it, but it is discouraging when I know how much there is in me to feel I must rust, rather than wear out. I return your slip, I was interested in the account of your triumph, but confess I dont see how you achieved it, this playing with fire is a dangerous business to the unscientific.

Do you ever see Mrs Leonard now? she will not write to me, why or wherefore I cant imagine, she wrote me a long letter telling me Hattie[2] had left home and how worried Mr Leonard was, she spoke kindly of him and said she was sorry for him, and I had not an idea of any thing wrong, except the chronic uncongeniality between them which I hoped they had agreed to let lie like a sleeping dog. I feel very much hurt at Mrs Leonard's persistent silence, it was some time before I could think it any thing but accidental—If you know of any cause of offence she has against me do let me hear the truth, for I love and admire her, and nothing but malicious misrepresentation can account for her total loss of interest in me. I shall not write again unless I hear from her, not because I am offended, but because I fear to intrude; Mrs Rayne sent me the slip from the paper and Mr Leonard wrote me of the present arrangement, I have also heard from Hattie and Nannie, the last seemed much distressed. I have had an invitation to join a summer excursion to Europe that would be charming but requires $500 in gold. I intended to have gone had all things worked out as we expected last fall, but as it is it is out of the question. I shall be alone all summer nearly, as William & Willie are "right bowers" in a general election and will doubtless be both either working for some office themselves or to get some other Republican in, I hate elections, all the old bitterness rises up in them and Republicans here need expect no mercy socially, I think I'll get you to advertise in the Tribune for a situation for me; William says unless I get a divorce and advertise to fill the place of wife to some other man, he cant recommend me either as a Dr's, lawyers, or clergyman's assistant, he often tells me—or used to, that my vocation in life was not work but to sit up and look pretty and entertain company, he thinks now I can write, and *knows* I can sew, but laughs at my cooking and house keeping, for the first time in my life I am without a house keeper, and I dont take kindly to it and cant teach a cook when I dont know how to cook anything but oysters and coffee, pickles and preserves, I am well up in the fine arts of house keeping but Oh the drudgery! that gets me in the *small of my back* and I have *struck* work.

I did not know how true that last sentence was for company interrupted me and I have been in bed for two days unable to raise my head from pure prostration and loss of strength in one of my old attacks of hemorrage. I cant do more now than close this hoping I may some time or other get that kiss which seems to receed instead of approach nearer to yours most affectionately

Mary

1. This reference to the onset of menopause, oblique as it is, reveals the candor Clarke felt in corresponding with Nathan Abbott.
2. Hattie and Nannie Leonard were Cynthia Leonard's daughters.

❧

*Hall,* MBC Poems, *xxii.*
*Mary Bayard Clarke to Winchester Hall*

New Berne
1878 November

—I have been on a spree of reading and writing. In three days I wrote five poems and two news letters. I will be merciful and send you one of the last when printed, which will contain one poem, the other four will keep until printed, when you will get them in broken doses. My son Willie says I have literary delirium tremens, for, of course, I have a headache, which I impute to mince pie and Thanksgiving, and the Doctor to my brain, which is shaky. He threatens me with congestion of it if I don't stop reading and writing for a while. I am having bronchitis pretty badly this fall, and that always keeps me out of company, as talking is tiresome—consequently I read more than usual; have just finished a new history of the French Revolution epoch, by Van Laure, and "Idols and Ideals," by Moncure B. Conway—a perfect mine of literary jewels, from which I have stolen a handful and reset in rhyme, which is the cause of three of the five poems.

❧

*Barden Collection*
*Dr. N. W. Abbott to Mary Bayard Clarke*

N. W. Abbott,
Physician and Surgeon,
Office, 145 South Clark Street,
Chicago, Nov 28th 1878

Mrs Mary Bayard Clarke
New Berne N.C.
My Dear Mary

Your good letter of the 18th inst came in due time. I was very glad to hear from you as I expect always to be. The Gen [Buford] has not since yours was recd asked me whether I had recd a letter from you as he has often done before. I had my plan laid out. It was to read part of it to him and say that the other was strictly personal and private and would not be interesting to him. I can reply to only a small portion of your letter, for I am going to write you a long essay in corroboration of one of your points. But I take issue with you when you say of Christianity, "It is true so long as men believe it to be true and no longer." Men believed for a long time that the sun revolved around the earth, was it ever true? For a long time men believed in witchcraft. Was there any truth in that belief? The Mormons today believe Joe Smith dug up golden plates on which was written the mormon bible. Is it *true* simply because they happen to so believe? But enough of this. You again say "I believe religion like every thing else is the result of evolution and all changes in it must be gradual." I am in entire accord with you on this point, as I am in regard to dogmatism of which you speak so truthfully. And to convince you that we are in harmony on these points, I take the liberty to inflict upon you a long extract from a lecture I delivered before the Phil Soc five years since. I trust you will pardon me for I really want you to know how nearly we harmonize. Man is a religious animal. If we define religion, as *devotion, worship;* it is very nearly approached in the affection of the dog for his master; but if we define religion, to mean a *feeling out* for the unknown; a searching of the *heart* and of the *intellect,* for the *unseen*—the *spiritual* the unknowable,—a sentiment beautifully expressed by the Psalmist "lead me to the rock that is higher than I" and in Raphael's last and best work of art "The Transfiguration" in which is conveyed to canvas, the yearning of every soul in weariness and grief, for higher than human help; for the language of the picture is "Look up"; then we have a something that is common to all races of the human family, and which has no corresponding faculty in the lower animals so far as we know. If we were ask a dozen present to define the term religion, no two would give the same, or any thing like the same definition. Hobbs says "Superstition is religion out of fashion and religion is superstition in fashion." Another would say, religion consists in living and walking sincerely in all the ordinances of the church: another that it is love to God and to man: another faith in our Lord Jesus Christ, and so of many others. All of which embrace more or less truth. If we ask a dozen or more botanists present to describe either by word or with the artists brush a leaf from the forest, we will have before us, perchance as many different descriptions or paintings as there are varieties in the forest. . . .

. . . The religions of the historic world are as numerous and as varied as the leaves of the forest, and like them perform necessary functions in the economy of nature. The intellect may be misquited. The conscience perverted, as it is sure to be if the education is wrong. It then becomes an engine of evil instead of good. The religious faculty however, is a gift from the Creator. And to this principle of seeking something *higher* than ourselves, this stretching forth our hands toward an unseen real; to this attempt to bridge the chasm that divides between actual and ideal is due much of the progress and *developement* of the race.

Philosophy perhaps seeks more, to solve in pure thought. Religion embraces more the affectional and emotional. Any taste or faculty we have, may be perverted; but the condition is not so hopeless as when there is no faculty. This religious faculty is as old as history and for aught we know as old as man. . . . All religions voice the same great hopes and ideas. If we may carry our figure a step further, it will apper that the vine dresser often finds the vine so over grown with foliage that the *light* is excluded, and the vine rendered unfruitful. It then becomes necessary to prune off the foliage in order that light and vigor reach the fruit. So religion may out grow a man's intellectual strength, and overshadow his other faculties so as to render him not only *useless* to his fellow man but a curse to his race; having zeal without knowledge, he then becomes a bigot. In the horticultural world, the quality of the fruit depends upon culture, light and heat. In the religious world the quality of the fruit depends upon culture, light and reflection. . . .

. . . Thus you see by the above long but I trust not altogether uninteresting extract from my lecture on "Science and Religion" that you and I are very near together. Now I cannot close here for it is too abrupt.

I hope you will criticise what is here said freely. You always do it with such a loving hand, that the cuffing seems rather a luxury than otherwise. My Dear Mary are we never to meet on this side the great ocean of eternity? I hope we may meet I think if you were to spend another summer here I could appreciate you. I will send you the Sunday papers occasionaly. They are about the only ones that are worth sending so far.

I shall send you a copy of the Herald of the 16th inst and a slip from a former one giving the history of a "trip to the moon" in which the tall philosopher, Gen Buford, and Mr Hertig are referred to. I believe one or two more articls on the same subject will appear. The writer is a Mrs Kirby who came here soon after you left. She is quite brilliant in conversation. She seems to know much of your literary ability, although she has never seen you. She came from Davenport here. She knew Gen Buford while he lived at Rock Island. I am pained to know that a shadow is thrown over your life through the illness of your sister.[1] I find it is a general rule that sorrows increase as life wears away. Give my love to your family. And if this letter does not frighten you by its great length, I hope you will write me as convenience permits. We have had no cold weather here yet. I have heard nothing from Mrs Leonard since she left here. Good night. I am as ever Yours

N W Abbott

1. Sophia Devereux Turner had been hospitalized in the Raleigh insane asylum because of her addiction to morphine.

⇔

*Barden Collection*
*Mary Bayard Clarke to Dr. Nathan Abbott*

Newbern
Dec 12th [1878]

My Dear Doctor Abbott

Your nice long letter was brought me by my husband as I lay on the sofa gasping for breath with the remark—"here darling is something I know will make you feel better;" and so it did; it was very good of you to take the trouble to copy so much of your lecture, I enjoyed it very much and have read it several times and mean to steal from it as soon as I am able to write an article.[1] I admit your correction, I used the term "true" too loosely, I meant that as man, as you well say, "is a religious animal," that the religion he *fully* believed and *accepted* was the best for him while in that state of intelligence, just as the large ferns were the best growth for the earth at the time they covered it; but when man does not *fully* accept and believe a religion, but is reaching out for some thing higher and better, he is sure to find it. Hence I would never undermind *any faith* except by cultivating the reason and intelligence, and leading every man by environment and adaptation gradually on. While I would have perfect freedom of speech and the press, let it do its own work, dont take away the scaffolding till the building, so far as it has gone, is firm. If people never have doubts, never question the truth of the faith they are taught, I never would interfere with them; some do not because they never think of the subject, others because, as Holmes says, they are "excellent little wretches who amount to nothing in the sum of a nations intellectual life" If a man picks up a book or hears a lecture or a sermon in which there are truths new and startling to him advanced, he is much more apt to be influenced by them if they are brought forward apparently without any wish to shock prejudices which he believes to be principals. If he is a man of any force, though he may never accept, he does not denounce the belief or opinion so advanced; but oftenest the seed lies in his heart and germinates, it may be years afterwards. I know by myself that I now fully accept and highly value beliefs that ten years ago would have shocked me, because I have come to them by thought and reading, gradually; but I love the old out grown beliefs as we do old homesteads round which cluster a thousand memories—I dont wish to go back and dwell in mine but I dont want to see it turned to a factory, pull it down as useless but dont desecrate it. I have been reading Conways "Idols and Ideals," do get it, I will send you with this one of his gems that I have reset in rhyme. What can be more decided than his essay on Christianity but what more delicate and poetic? I told you I was reading Chadwick's "Bible of To Day" Well I sent to my rector and got a whole library of orthodox books to read the other side, and lying here I have read faithfully and candidly, and all that I have read shows me that for me it must be "Rome or Reason" It cant be Rome so I have quietly rejected the whole fabric of Inspiration, the immaculate Conception, the Trinity, and a personal God as one phase of religion which I have passed and cannot go back to.

I am suffering just as I was last fall with a fearful cough only worse, in as much as it does not yield as heretofore to the gradual effect of the mild climate. It is bronchitis combined with constant, though not violent, pain in the back of my head just above the neck, I cannot take opium in any shape and nothing else relieves the cough, except for a few moments, except whiskey which I cant take on account of this pain in my head. I am fifty (I tell you the truth)—my next birth day—, but show not the slightest sign of the usual change at that age—, I fear when it does come I will go off as many of my family have in rapid consumption, I see my Doctor fears it too, all our plans have been changed by this attack for it is useless for me to try and live in Raleigh, which in winter always disagrees with me, so, instead of giving up my home here we have decided to keep it up and let my husband go alone to Raleigh and come occasionally to see me till warm weather, when I will go up and board there all summer, but not take a house as proposed; the difference will be that instead of leaving him in summer to keep house alone, he will leave me in winter to do so, and I will go to him in summer instead of to some Northern city or watering place. So I cannot answer your question of when we shall meet, for I shall have to practise economy and cant afford to go off at pleasure. Now Doctor I have never thought of how you stood pecuniarily, but have rather inferred—that you were comfortably off and as you speak of building houses—I am confirmed in this belief, so why cant *you* take a holiday and come and see *me*? You dont know my husband or you would know that his heart always opens to all who esteem, love or admire me, and that to please me is to please him. But you ought to know me well enough to know I would not ask you to come if it would not be agreeable to him. He goes to Raleigh the first of January, so does my son who is in the legislature and my son in law in Goldsboro goes to California,[2] leaving my daughter and granddaughter with me; so we shall be two grass widows in a large house and you shall have study and bed room and do just what you please; I think you could pass a few weeks here very pleasantly, and as you have never been south see something new—William will come down and so will Willie occasionally and they both want to know you. My husband lets me do just exactly what I please in every respect except where my health is concerned, then he says good wives are too hard to get to be killed, and grows tyranical and despotic, which I allow until he seriously inconveniences me when I call in the Dr and convince him I am right. I believe in making those who love us happy if possible—and so does he,—so the largest liberty is allowed, neither expecting the other to do more than *observe the proprieties* and avoid scandal. He would let me go to the moon with you if I could, and never ask any thing except that I should be taken care of and allowed to do as I please; but as we cant join the Y[?] P and his friend in their trip lets have a little moon all to ourselves down here, I will give you oysters game and fish in abundance and you shall scold me as much as you like.

I have at last written Gen B. and sent him a poem on "Humility" which he will show you doubtless. I send you one from Conway appropos to what we are writing of.

Yours lovingly—Mary

P.S. I sent you a paper with an account of my last appearance in public, I took cold then and have not been out of the house since

MBC

1. Clarke later wrote a poem titled "Religion" based on Abbott's letter.

2. Rufus Morgan moved to California to start an apiary business near San Diego. He planned to bring his wife and children out after the business was established successfully. The Morgans' first child, Mary Bayard Morgan, had been born on 17 December 1875. She later became famous as a photographer under her married name of Bayard Wootten. The second child, Sam, was born while Rufus Morgan was in California. Jerry Cotten, *Light and Air: The Photography of Bayard Wootten* (Chapel Hill: University of North Carolina Press, 1998).

*Barden Collection*
*Mary Bayard Clarke to Dr. Nathan Abbott*

[December 1878]

"Plagarism" my dear Doctor "is like theft among the Spartans only a crime when detected"; this is my favorit theory for I do steal so much and always confess when sure to be found out if I dont. I told you I should steal from that beautiful extract you sent me and here is my feather from the Peacock's tail which I give to you to do what you please with. I wrote it to night and send it hot from my brain.

I still continue very unwell and my Doctor is uneasy about me for I have such regular fever and such prostration with bad nights and cough that I do nothing but read and write I suppose the fever excites my brain for Willie—my son, says Mother has *poetic tremens,* I have written a long review to day of Chadwick's *Bible Of To Day* and am not equal to a letter only the poetry just bubbled out and I send it with these few words. I am living on cod-liver oil whiskey oysters and beef-tea So you see my Doctor dont mean to let me starve to death, Opium I *wont* take in any shape and nothing else stops the cough—I sit up half the night because I am so weak and miserable in the morning after tea I get brilliant and poetic—if it is so simply to set others ideas to rhyme—Good night Yours lovingly

Mary

‿◦

*Barden Collection*
*Mary Bayard Clarke to Dr Nathan Abbott*

Newbern Jan 19th [1879]

My Dear Doctor

I received your letter a week ago to day and was really disappointed to find I had no prospect of seeing you—I had not thought I hoped to do so till I found by the blank I felt that there was some hope in my heart.[1] To day my daughter received a Postal from her husband saying he had called on you as I begged him to do. I suppose he told you I was still half sick, and I hang just where he left me, too good for nothing to write or sew, and only able to read. Mary and I are alone and to keep her spirits up I drag out to meals but I have not left the house yet, and vibrate between the sofa and my arm chair; just as I think I am getting a little strength the fever comes back on me, not high, only continuous for a day or two, and I feel as if I was slowly but surely settling into invalidism

I cant realize I ever wrote a line of poetry or did any thing but "lie around loose" like the milk, my cough is better but has by no means left me, In short I want shaking up if the weather was good I would run away to New York but its not to be thought of

I had not noticed the anachronism in my last, Of course it is wrong, please make the alteration and add the stanza I sent you in my last

Creeds, dogmas fables myths and all
Shall crumble and decay,

> But Love the kernel live when faith
> The husk has passed away.

Somehow I fancied Gotama and Confusicious before Moses though as soon as I read your letter I saw my mistake. I have been two days writing this. I *hope* I shall see you again in this life though I see no present prospect of it as I shall not be able to leave home for a long time if ever again. They say I have not consumption because no one ever had it who believed they had. Consequently as I think I have it I am free from it but exceptions prove the rule

I will rally perhaps with spring and may live some time but I believe my death warrant is signed and I have to keep up till my daughter is over her pregnancy and confinement which we expect in July—This is a miserable excuse for a letter but it is all because you make me believe you care some thing for me that I write of my trouble

> My happy thoughts I give to all
> My sad ones to but few
> Yours lovingly
> Mary

1. On 7 January 1879, Abbott declined Mary Bayard Clarke's invitation to visit her in New Bern. He also critiqued her poem "Religion," which she had sent him in December 1878. Delighted to have Clarke set his lecture to poetry, he wrote, "I little thought when I rose one night, three years since, at eleven oclock and wrote sixteen pages of that lecture, before three in the morning, that a beautiful and very intellectual woman in N.C. would ever think any of the lines then hastily written were worthy of her notice, much less her time and thoughts in transposing them into a beautiful poem. When I read the 3d 4th 6th 7th and 10th stanzas, I find my own thoughts so much more beautifully expressed it brings the moisture to my eye." He firmly corrected her statement, however, that Confucius and Gautama Buddha followed Moses chronologically.

*Barden Collection*
*Mary Clarke Morgan to Rufus Morgan*

Sunday
Jan 26/79

Dear St.Rufus

Baby's last feat was to come down stairs one morning & scold her Grandma & tell her it was her "terlessness" (carelassness) that her garters were lost. The way the little lady gave it to her Grandma was amusing. If Mother had been three & Baby fifty she could not have acted differently.

The little one is in great trouble tonight One of the Bryan boys came by & threw a stone at Dash which struck him He howled very pitiously; Mother opened the door, he rushed in the parlour & had a fit or something. I like to have had a fit too, he was hustled out in a hurry The last heard of him he was in the back yard rushing round like wild. He has either died or gone off, have not been out to see. Baby's trouble was that she could not feed him to night. She is not at all well, coughed almost all last night, so neither of us got much sleep. I have felt very badly all to day but took Gib[1] to church. She seemed to like it very much. This is the first time I have been since I got here. I got me a nice green & black wrapper & will make it this week. All of my clothes are getting too tight, but I think it is because I am so much swollen, my rings are very tight. Seems to me I am swelling sooner than with Baby. I have one piece of good news for you. Fada has been appointed Clerk of the Court here & will come home Tuesday. Mother is not at all pleased with it but I think beggers should not be choosers. Willie comes down tomorrow & I suppose will bring the money. Tom sent me a [illegible] says trade is very dull & he has had two or three bills for you, but can't collect those you [torn] Mother sends her love [torn] says do you want the "Commonwealth" sent regularly? Gib sends love. Good bye darling, I can't tell you how I miss you My last postal was from Devil's Ridge. Mr Patterson asks after you very often I dreamed last night you were kissing me & I woke up to find Baby patting [my face?] She talks a great deal about you

Your loving<br />little Wife

1. Alice Gibson Person, nicknamed Gib, was one of Rufus Morgan's nieces. Her parents were Alice and Joe Person.

*Barden Collection*
*Mary Bayard Clarke to Dr. Nathan Abbott*

Newbern March 12th [1879]

My Dear Doctor

I have been hoping you would write, and laying down yards of that pavement which is said to cover a hot place, by intended every day to write to you to morrow, when I felt stronger, or had not so much to do; or was not so tired out; I have never recovered my strength though my cough is "scotched," not killed, and I am going about again, always however wanting strength and health. I feel as if I had been struck by the sword of the magician Velent, and if I shook myself would fall apart, every body says "how you have improved,["] and I feel as if I were a humbug for not being worth some thing, when in reality I am nothing but a cracked bowl, fine enough china, but useless except for looks; I am convinced this cough has reached way over to the end of my life and cut off a piece there, if it has not killed me now; I am awfully lazy, and hence I have not written much of anything, only read and thought, I send you a mixture of Emerson, Chadwick and Sir Walter Scott, for which I can find no name, I sent it Chadwick and asked him to name the child, but he says the only name he can think of is "Exit Jehovah," which wont do at all—Did you ever have the poem I stole from your lecture printed, I have not seen it or heard from you since I made the correction you suggested about Moses.

31st You see my dear Doctor I tried to write, but was knocked down before I had finished my letter by the news of the sudden death of one of my sisters,[1] who had not two weeks before written begging me to take care of myself saying she had had a bad cold all winter and knew how hard it was to get over one. They were all far more anxious about me than about her, when she suddenly sickened with congestion of the lungs and died in less than a week, my phisical strength seemed to leave me under the shock, I could not shed tears, but I just sunk down and kept my bed unable to sit up—I received your papers and enjoyed them, sending one in return which contained an extract from a Baltimore paper of an article, or rather part of one, I wrote on Dr John W Draper, I received a letter of thanks from the Dr and another work of his, the one I was reviewing being his Scientific Memoirs on Radiant Energy I also marked a notice of my husband's appointment as Probate Judge of this County an office worth about $2500 a year which as yet has only brought him a law suit as the old officer refuses to give up the office on the ground that the Commissioner had no right to turn him out So as yet we are no better off—except in expectations. Have you ever read Conway's "Idols and Ideals" if not do so if you can lay hands on it I think you would like his essay on Christianity which is in it I did not know what you meant when you said once to me that you were not a Christian as you did not believe in Christ I know now—that you do believe in all that Christ taught as applicable to this age and are *better* than most Christians—The book is published by Henry Holt and Co New York I have illustrated my copy with poems from the text will send you some as I publish them adios MBC

1. Betsy Devereux Jones.

❧

*Barden Collection*
*Mary Clarke Morgan to Rufus Morgan*

New Berne
Dec 7/79

Dear Big Baby

I have had two letters from you since I wrote one was forwarded from F. & the other directed here. Both had V's in them. Thank you very much for them Now I will pay some of my Debts & I can't tell you how glad I am. All the folks have been very good but I hate to owe a darkey. Pride I suppose. I will write you as soon as I hear from the 17.50. I can't get it without a duplicate & it seems to me the P. O. master at San Deigo is taking an awful time to send it. Don't you think he is? I can't tell you how glad I am that you have some shoes. It surely worried me to think you were out of them. I will send the socks soon. I am very glad that the ferns are going to do well. I thought it was a very small thing when you first wrote of it. Had no idea there was any such business. What kind of picture are they? I would like to have you send one to Dr or Mrs Person. They were very kind to me when Bayard was sick & I could not make any return then. I will lay the matter of Tom's going before the folks but shall neither encourage or discourage it. I would like to have him go myself as I think he would do well out there but as you had a failure this year I think the folks are rather out with Cal. & they have got to decide for them selves. Tom is crazy to go. The paper will be printed by some one else & not by Fada, he is only editor.[1] I don't know yet who will take the printing Fada says he will want Tom as a clerk. I do hope the paper will be a success but Fada is not the man he was ten years ago. His irratability[2] has grown on him greatly in the last year. If he is making any thing he may improve & I think he will. If it don't succeed may the Lord have mercy on us. I will see about that Mrs. Woodson. I don't think Will will bother himelf about Tom & I can't blame him. When do you think I can come? I want to begin to talk about it so they will get use to it. Will it be by April? I should not think March would be a good month on account of the children. I do wish you could see Sam, he is a splendid fellow. Looks eight months at least instead of five. We have him in short clothes now but not near enough made to keep him clean. I have been in such a hurry all this week that I have hardly time to sleep. Had nothing that was fit to go in the street & had to fix up all three at one pop [sone?]. I swaped off my last winters dress to Mother for a black one & fixed that up. I will not get any thing for myself this winter but a calico but the little one are obliged to have some things. I have made a bill at Baker's (Allie Baker) You were too far off to consult you before hand. Betty & Ham Jones are with us & will stay a month any way, perhaps all winter if he can get enough to do. They pay board. Willie runs the house & take entire charge of the house keeping Mother has nothing at all to do with it. I suppose Willie would have credited me if I had asked him but I did not & Fada was head of the house last winter. Will gets what I want & I have nothing to do with the bills. It was not that way last winter & I prefered to take my ten for the house to giving it to Fada. At Present I am just as busy as it is possible for me to be but that won't last for more than a month. I have been talking to Mother about my going out to Cal. & she wants me to wait till June & says if I do & she possibly can she will come with me. I don't want to wait that long & shall not if it is possible for you to send for me sooner I do want to see you so dreadfully bad. This has been a very very long year to me

Your loving<br>little Wife

1. William J. Clarke became editor of the Republican newspaper the *Signal* (Raleigh), which began publication in December 1879. Powell, *DNCB*, 1:382.

2. This word alluded not only to irritation but to Clarke's increasing dependence on alcohol.

MARY BAYARD AND WILLIAM CLARKE worked together to write an inaugural address, "To The Ladies" of North Carolina, in the opening issue of the Republican newspaper the *Signal.* The article explicitly stated that "woman was created for some nobler and higher purpose than 'to suckle fools and chronicle small beer,'" and asked for the active support of its women readers. The article, excerpted below, provides an interesting insight into the Republican Party's views on women and those held by the Clarkes.

Signal *(Raleigh) 1, no. 1, 24 Dec. 1879, 1.*
To The Ladies.

With respectful obeisance to the ladies of North Carolina, we desire to say, that it is our earnest hope to secure their approbation of our journal, as we shall attempt to make it acceptable to them. We do not intend to address any remarks to them of a political character; thought we feel fully satisfied that we could demonstrate that the Republican party has heretofore been, as it will continue to be, the best friend of our women. The party which gave liberty to the slave would be sadly derelict if it left the wives and daughters of America in bondage. We shall demand that woman shall be treated as the comrade and equal of man; that the disabilities and obstacles which debar her from the prosecution of certain pursuits to which God and nature have adapted her; whether imposed by law or custom—shall be removed, and that, disenthralled, she shall have perfect freedom in "the pursuit of happiness" or the gratification of a laudable ambition, or the acquisition of wealth in many ways she is now precluded from. It will be our endeavor to educate public sentiment on many of these matters, which have been, hitherto, sadly neglected by the press of our State.

. . . .

∻

*William J. Clarke Papers, SHC*
*Mary Bayard Clarke to William J. Clarke*
*[ca. January 1880]*

Sunday Night

My Dear William

I reached home last night having spent a day in Kinston—I distributed several papers—and heard the Signal well spoken of, but people generally seemed to think that in becoming an editor I had lost all the feelings of a woman, for a dozen said to me—"his success is certain if he will only— let whiskey—alone." Your opponents are counting on your inability to do this, and my heart died within me, for I felt that John Richardson was right when he said "—Oh if the Judge could only know what a difference *one* drink makes in him he would never touch it." Oh William this is *your last* chance in life, and I cannot tell you how heart sick it made me when I saw you were taking whiskey before breakfast, and realized how excessively irritable you had grown; not only to me—for I have become accustomed to that—, but to every-one who approaches you. I know you think me a fool on this subject, but when I thought of Mrs Grissom who *is* almost one on *all* subjects, and remembered how she, as I told you, could keep her husband from taking it even when he needed it, I felt I would be willing to be indeed a fool—if I could have as much influence over you; and sadly remembered the time when you used to tell me that if it made *me* even unhappy you would not touch it, though I might be foolish about it. It does make me—more than unhappy—for it makes—me miserable, hard, and bitter, and I shudder when I think of the intense disgust that overpowers me at times and what it may lead me to.——Doubtless I am to blame for the loss of your love——, for I have lost it——, and I dont appeal to it any longer, I only tell you that Willie asked me if you were drinking, and I told him a deliberate story and said *no*——, at which he seemed relieved——, for he had heard you were,——and said to me "Mother you had better understand at once——that this is father's *last chance,* and if he drinks *at all* he is gone,—— for I shall make no effort and speak no word for the paper unless he abstains entirely." I know this will make you angry——perhaps you wont even read what I have said——but as you said about Mary's writing to Mr Morgan last summer——, "A wife has a right to speak her mind to her husband and tell him when she thinks he is not treating her as he should." I shall not come up to Raleigh again, for——I felt I was a restraint on you—— as I *cannot* conceal my feelings on this subject.

Mary says she is going to California alone in April if Mr Morgan sends the money for her to do so——so I shall not go to New York though Col Whitford told me again that he would get me a pass——if I wished it.

Mr Hale told me to tell you he liked your paper better than any he had seen in North Carolina——far better than *"Hale's Weekly"*——said it was—— good from beginning to end——John Long says——"as usual the Judge is going for the women and he had hit between wind and water in doing so" I enclose a scrap from the Kinston paper——that shows you hit there—— perhaps you have seen it. Tom is not well and in doubt what to do he has been offered the place of foreman of the "Democrat" office I oppose his taking it even temporarily as he has one week's work *secure* at Richardsons——

By the way send the Signal for six months to John Richardson Newbern——he paid me a dollar on the cars.——and says he means to take it regularly but Christmas left him poor——I send a receipt in your name to him to night. Bayard sends love to "Dampa["] and says tell him I sleep in his place now——.

Hoping you will take this as it is intended I am your loving wife *Mary*——

*MBC Scrapbook 1, Barden Collection*
*Mary Bayard Clarke article,* Signal *(Raleigh), 3 Mar. 1880*
LETTER FROM THE EDITOR.

HUMPHREY HOUSE,
Goldsboro, Feb. 22. [1880]

Having run up here in the interest of the SIGNAL, we are happy to state that Wayne will make up the club called for by our chief, and Lenoir be not found wanting. Now, if the ladies of North Carolina will take the same interest in their half of our paper as the gentlemen assert they will do—*should it prove a success,* we may, possibly, make it one. But it will be impossible for us to do so, if each stands off and waits for it to become one, without making any personal effort to increase our subscription list. We have often been urged to start a literary paper in North Carolina, by gentlemen of standing, who believed we could establish one, but have felt that the time had not come when a family paper could maintain itself, simply on its literary merits, however readable it might be made. Hence the union of the "Woman's Exchange" with a political paper, to give it a pecuniary ballast sufficient to float it till such time as it can "go it alone," without danger of being "euchered." If the women of North Carolina will help us *now,* in the "dark days," this can be accomplished, and we appeal to all who desire to see such a paper in existence to come to the rescue, and make up clubs; promising to those, who object to the politics of the other side of the sheet, that we will, if they desire it, send them, for one dollar per annum, only the first and fourth pages, leaving the inside a blank— on which they can write their own political creed, and change it as often as the candidate for any political office shall be "the man after their own heart," or otherwise. We have never made any personal appeal for support, but have received many encouraging words, and would cheerfully canvass among the women of North Carolina for it, if we had the time and the means.

Having for eight months successfully conducted a woman's paper in Chicago, we feel competent to do it in North Carolina, with the help of the latent talent that lies hid in many of our women, simply because they have not the courage to put pen to paper for publication.

We spent Sunday in Goldsboro with one of our old Chicago friends, who urged us to return there, and resume work in that city, with brighter prospects of success than before. But to do so we must give up a home in North Carolina, and we are not willing yet to do this. . . .

ᗄ

*Barden Collection*
*Mary Clarke Morgan to Rufus Morgan*

New Berne
March 14/80

Dear St. Rufus

. . . .

I did take you by what you wrote. That you could not come for me till Sept. & that you thought I would have to stay till then. You ought not to have written Mother so cause you know how she is. Dinah will not go with me & I am sorry she ever said any thing about it. I was very much in hopes she would. I may be able to get another & will try. Willie is not here now has gone to Raleigh & will hardly be back for three weeks. I don't think he can do a thing in the way of letting you have any money He as just as much as he as can do to get on now. That Clerkship cost him 310. & he only made the last payment last week.[1] He has *all,* every single thing that is gotten for the house, to pay for & help Fada besides. That paper is going to fail, you see if it don't. He wrote me last summer he owed you about 120 & since then I have had 20. from him, & five months board. The month I was confined there were three servants, two nurses & a washerwoman so I think there ought to be something extra on that month. When you think of that; he will not owe you much if anything. Fada did not pay one single bill. I don't want to feel that they have been at any expense for me & my babys. . . .

Your loving
Wife

Monday Sam is a great deal better this afternoon & I guess he is all right now

1. In a letter dated 30 March 1880, Willie Clarke wrote Rufus Morgan about his father's clerkship, stating, "I have spent about $150.— on father's contest. We have got a peremptory order from the Judge, and I think father will get possession of the office shortly. It is tiresome work waiting; but when he gets in he is settled for life. At least for as long as he wants it on a comfortable salary." Barden Collection.

RUFUS MORGAN'S LAST LETTER to his wife was dated 4 April 1880. He died shortly after it was written from eating poisonous mushrooms. His business partners, the Woodsons, wrote a letter to Mary Clarke Morgan on 5 April informing her of her husband's death. She received both letters on the same date. She opened her husband's letter first. She then opened the Woodson letter and fainted after reading its contents. It was a devastating blow to her both emotionally and financially because it left her dependent on her parents and brothers for shelter and help in rearing her family.

*Barden Collection*
*William J. Clarke to Mary Bayard Clarke*

Raleigh, April 26th. 1880.

My Dear Mary:

    I feel that you will very naturally expect a letter from me by this mail, and I would not willingly disappont you; but I am perplexed as to what to say. Like Job, I feel that in the great troubles which darken our household, "miserable comforters are ye all." The image of our poor grief-stricken & crushed daughter is constantly before my eyes. I wake at night and think of her. I rise early, and all day long she is before my eyes. I should have come home, but I have no words of comfort to utter, & I should be uneasy all the time, fearing that I was neglecting my duty in my last venture.

    Times are awfully dull with the Signal, but my faith is unshaken that it will be a success.

    Both Tom & myself are in better health and I hope it will be reflected in the paper. At this time of "slack water," before the turn of the tide, I have to be very cautious, as from my location, I am the organ of the party, hence I have to be very cautious about my editorials, and make them brief.

    I am sorry that Willie has suffered so much with his thumb. The biting was a most unmanly & cowardly act, and every one condemns Etheridge.

    I thank you for your letters informing of Mary's condition.

    Hoping to be able to write you some good news before long, I am as ever

Very affectionately<br>Wm. J. Clarke<br>Love to Mary, & kisses for the children

MARY BAYARD CLARKE WAS hired in 1880 to edit the Oxford Orphan Asylum's paper, the *Orphan's Friend,* by asylum superintendent John. H. Mills. The asylum, which was a project of the Masons in North Carolina, relied on donations from across the state to augment its income. The paper kept readers informed of asylum achievements and needs. Clarke, while working on the paper, observed areas under Mill's management that she thought needed improvement. When she voiced her criticisms, Mills peremptorily removed Clarke from her job, using the excuse that the paper did not make enough money to warrant its continuation as a weekly. Furious, Clarke carried their debate into the public arena. Clarke clearly considered her work as that of a professional journalist and objected to her treatment and that of teachers at the asylum. Mills, if he had hoped to silence Clarke's objections by removing her from the editorship, soon learned that he had underestimated his opponent. A literal war of words ensued. Mills eventually became personal in his attacks, referring to Clarke's "peculiar" views and her health problems. Clarke did not get back her job, but her insistence that she was a professional journalist and her vigorous in-print denouncements of a southern man provide interesting insight into Clarke's self-confidence as well as her views on women, work, and education.

*Barden Collection*
*J. H. Mills, Orphan Asylum, to Mary Bayard Clarke*

Orphan Asylum,
Oxford, N. C., July 28, 1881

Mrs Clarke:

The Dr advises me to free myself from anxieties as far as possible. I feel the necessity of following his advice. The O. F at present brings in so little and costs so much that I see no way but to change as indicated in our article inserted to-day. You will not therefore be needed next month. I will settle with you to-morrow.

With sincere esteem
J. H. Mills

ಞ

*Barden Collection*
*Mary Bayard Clarke to John Mills (fragment)*

[ca. July 1881]

as the wife of a mason and a member of the editorial profession I hereby record my protest against the treatment I have received from you. I came here at your request as a favor to you and when I asked you on hearing Miss A would not return how long you wished me to stay you replied "as long as you can". I at once told you on what terms I would remain till frost and you said you must consult the GM. before replying. Finding you had not written to Mr Grainger[1] ten days after this, I asked and obtained your permission to write to him myself. His reply was just what I expected it would be—that he left the matter in your hands. he also wrote you the same thing I handed you his letter to me as soon as I received it and had my work not suited you or my terms were too high it was your duty to have told me so then and not as you did, allow me to give up possible positions to remain here with you

In consideration of the state of your health I could overlook this; but no matter how sudden your determination to stop the weekly paper nor what the cause of that decission you had no right to allow me to hear of it first as you did by accident—through an editorial sent not to me as the editor but to one of your printers with directions to set it up and send the proof to you. I believe masons of the state will sustain me when I say as I do, that such conduct was unworthy of a mason much less one in whom they have reposed such a trust as they have put in you hands

1. H. F. Grainger was grandmaster of the Masons in North Carolina.

THIS ARTICLE MARKED THE opening salvo of Mary Bayard Clarke's public criticism of the management of the Oxford Orphan Asylum by John Mills. Clarke expressed particular interest in having the female students receive a practical education rather than just learning to read and write. This perhaps reflects the difficulties encountered by her own daughter, Mary Clarke Morgan, who had received an education considered suitable for a young lady; she could read, write, play the piano, and speak French. When it came to earning a living, however, Mary Clarke Morgan found herself ill-fitted for securing a good job. Based on her experiences in Chicago, Mary Bayard Clarke felt that women from all classes could be trained to work in a variety of venues, given the opportunity to do so.

Clarke's article elicited an angry response from Mills in an article published October 1881 in the *Oxford Literary and Educational Monthly.* Clarke clipped the article and pasted it into one of her scrapbooks (Scrapbook 2, Barden Collection). Mills stated that he had "no idea of engaging in a controversy with any woman," but he added that it was "my misfortune not to be able to accommodate many who are in urgent need of servants." Warming to this theme, he said that he did "'repudiate the Idea' of reducing children to slavery, because their parents are dead. I also 'repudiate the idea' of placing orphans in the social position of those lately in slavery. When slavery was abolished, the social position of the slave was abolished also. Yet it seems that some people can not realize the fact." Despite his assertion that he was not engaging in controversy with a woman, he concluded his column by criticizing Clarke's "peculiar views," about which "several prominent friends complained," and then pointedly added that "Mrs. Clarke has thought proper to attack our management, and to disparage our orphans in a public newspaper, just as we are struggling to erect a new building for the boys." He urged anyone with concerns to direct them to the Grand Lodge of Masons, the "wise and good men" of which would give them "respectful consideration." Mills confidently delivered a challenge to Mary Bayard Clarke: "Let one of our girls cook a biscuit, a pie, a pig, and a chicken, and let Mrs. Clarke do the same. Then let Col. [Leonidas L.] Polk decide which is better. If the orphan's cooking be not preferred, then I will make Mrs. Clarke a present of a basket of stale bread and a box of tea."

❧

*MBC Scrapbook 2, Barden Collection,*
Oxford Literary and Educational Monthly.

For the Farmer and Mechanic
## One of the State Charities. Is Properly Managed?
Bellevue Springs, Sept. 26. [1881]

"What is the end and aim of the Oxford Orphan Asylum?" is a question which is being very freely discussed since Mr. Mills' statement, in the last dying speech of the *Orphan's Friend,* of the terms on which he will put out the girls old enough to leave the institution, and his appeals for aid appearing in most of the State papers after the collapse of his own especial organ. As the *Farmer and Mechanic* has such a wide circulation perhaps it may reach some one capable of giving a satisfactory answer to this question, interesting not only to the voters but to every woman of our State. Is the Asylum, like a "Home for the Aged," intended as a mere charitable institution where little children can be comfortably cared for and taught to read and write, and at the age of fourteen be put out into families, the heads of which will treat them as their own children and pay from five to ten dollars a month for the privilege of doing so? or does it aim higher than this, and propose, not only to care for its inmates as children but to fit them to earn their own living and become producers instead of mere consumers? If the first then there is nothing more to be said, as it answers its purpose; for it would be hard to find a hundred and fifty children in any charitable or State institution who would show by their personal appearance that they are as kindly and well cared for, and are in the main as healthy and happy as these orphans. They are too as a general rule as well advanced in the rudimental branches as the children of their age who attend the common schools, being kept in the school rooms every day, Saturday and Sunday excepted, from nine to twelve, and from two to five.

Mr. Mills advertised girls over fourteen as good house-keepers, for whom he required ten dollars a month, and girls not so good who would require some looking after, for five dollars a month. Now will some mason ask him if these girls have been taught under a practical house keeper, to make bread, get an ordinary meal, do up a shirt or a dress, and take care of family supplies; or under a seamstress to cut and make their own clothes. There has not been either matron or house keeper employed at the Asylum for three or four years, and from my personal knowledge, acquired by a month's residence in the institution while editing the *Orphan's Friend,* I can safely say there was not during that time a single girl in it, who knew enough of cooking, house-keeping, scouring or laundry work, to enable her to retain a position as house-keeper in any well regulated family for a week.

All the cooking it is true is done by the children, with elder girls over them as house-keepers, but these so-called house keepers could not cook, nor could they wash and iron, all the laundry work being put out of the institution and, so fearful is Mr. Mills that each girl will not get her full quota of school room teaching, that the cooks are constantly changed, and it was the standing joke at the teachers table, where I sat, that we would certainly exhibit the biscuits at the State Fair and take the premium for the very worst ever made; as for eating them it never entered into our heads to do so.

Mr. Mills says that the funds will not admit of teaching the boys trades, and scornfully repudiates the idea that he is fitting the girls to be "servants to the rich!" Is is [sic] derogatory to any woman to know how to cook, wash and iron, or make her own clothes? Or, if necessary, is it derogatory to her to do this work? If not why does not Mr. Mills employ a competent matron and house keeper and have these girls so taught? I am standing up for them and their best interest, when I say, if he cant afford to pay all, he had better dismiss two of his young lady teachers and keep half the girls out of the school room half of every day under competent instructors in these branches. Old aunt Abby House told President Davis, "he was trying to do more than God Almighty intended any man to do, for he was trying to be President and all the Secretaries too," adding, "the Lord knows it is enough for one man to be President of these Confederate States." So say I of Mr. Mills, it is enough for him to be Superintendent of that Orphan Asylum without trying to be the house-keeper and matron too. He is an admirable Superintendent, the materials he supplies for cooking are good and abundant, but I never sat down to the table at the institution without thinking of the Spanish proverb—"God sends the meat and the Devil sends the cook"—I write in no unkindness to him, but in justice to these orphan girls, that they may be taught to earn an honorable living by the labor of their hands instead of being unfitted, as they now are, for work of any kind.

M. B. C.

❧

*MBC Scrapbook 2, Barden Collection*
*Clipping from the* Farmer and Mechanic *(Raleigh)*

For the FARMER AND MECHANIC

*Mrs. Clarke's Reply to Mr. Mills.*

(*See outside page.*)

Bellevue Springs, Nov. 2 [1881].

The last number of the *Oxford Literary and Educational Monthly,* contains an article from Mr. Mill in reply to mine in the *Farmer and Mechanic,* on the management of the Orphan Asylum. I am sorry he did not see fit to publish it in the same paper in which mine appeared that all who read one might read the other. He opens by saying that I "discuss a question not open to discussion," and adds: "the Orphan Asylum belongs to and is managed according to regulations adopted by the Grand Lodge." Granted? But do not the voters of the State pay the subsidy given by the Legislature to the Asylum, and do not the women of the State contribute largely to support of the Institution, not only by keeping alive the interest in it, but by actual donations of clothing to the Orphans? Certainly they do, and therefore, I or any one else have a right to call public attention to the Asylum and its management.

In reply to my assertion that a practical housekeepor [*sic*] was needed to teach the girls, Mr. Mills says, "Some of our girls are worth ten dollars a month, *especially those whom Mrs. Troy, of Company Shops, has trained in the art of cooking.*" Granted again, for Mrs. Troy's reputation as a housekeeper is of the best, and could she train all these orphan girls, they would be indeed valuable members of any community. But she never had had but two when I wrote, and if the girl could be properly trained at the Asylum why did Mr. Mills send her these two? Mr. Mills says: "The late Mrs. Robards was a wonderful worker and we gave her too much to do. The work is divided as it should have been before."

Now if the work was too much for one "wonderful worker," how can it be well done when divided up among the teachers who are in school from nine till twelve, and from two till five? For the place of nurse at the hospital is filled by a teacher who does her full quota of work in the schoolroom, and consequently can have no time to properly and systematically train the girls so that they will be able to fill positions as either housekeepers or assistant housekeepers.

Mr. Mills proposes that Col. Polk[1] be appointed to eat a "biscuit, a pie, a pie, and a chicken" cooked by one of the orphans, and another biscuit, pie, pig and chicken cooked by me, and then decide which is best, promising, if I win he will present me with a basket of stale bread and a box of tea.

I decline the contest for two reasons, first, Col. Polk's life is too valuable to be risked in this rash manner, for no matter which side won, *he* would suffer. Then, though I have never been a dyspectic, I should certainly be one for life did I eat that basket of stale bread, if it be made at the Asylum? The box of tea is I grant a temptation, and if he will promise it shall be black, and bought of no one but ———— in Raleigh, I will compromise by offering to cook a biscuit, a pie, a pig, and a chicken, for Mr. Mills to eat, confident that after a long seasoning of such cooking as he sets before his teachers he cant be hurt by mine.

But there is one thing about which Mr. Mills, like the boy who wanted two throws at mumble-the-peg to his brothers one, has "the very badest remember" I ever saw. He says "ugly words passed between Mrs. Clarke and the housekeeper." In justice to the housekeeper, I positively deny this. She never gave me an ugly word while I staid at the Asylum, and all my "ugly words" were spoken to Mr. Mills himself. Doubtless they did sound very ugly to him, for I told him plainly he had no right to tamper with the health of his teachers by setting such badly cooked food before them.

As I have no wish to make this discussion a personal one, I shall take no further notice of Mr. Mills personal allusions. I only desire to stand up for the good of these orphan girls, the boys I leave to the men. I dont care whether they are taught trades or not, but I repeat the Masons of the State do not realize that these girls are taught absolutely nothing by which they can make a living when they leave the asylum, . . . Many of these girls have mothers, who, if poor and unable to send them to school, would at least teach them to work. . . .

He throws himself back upon the orders of the Grand Lodge, but no one knows better than he does, the deservedly high estimation the Grand Lodge has of his capacity as a superintendant, and one word from him as to the advisability of employing a housekeeper and training the girls more in cooking, laundry and house work, and less, if needful, in mere book teaching would meet not only with attention but assent from the gentlemen of that body. Let him try it. M. B. C.

1. Leonidas L. Polk was a journalist, politician, and leader of the Grange, who helped to organize the state's Department of Agriculture in 1877 and served as its commissioner until 1880. He later started the *Progressive Farmer* in 1886 and was a founder of the North Carolina College of Agriculture and Mechanic Arts in Raleigh, now North Carolina State University. He also led the North Carolina Farmers' Association, later the Farmers' Alliance, serving as its president in 1889. Powell, *DNCB,* 5:110–11.

&

*MBC Scrapbook 2, Barden Collection*
*Article on the Oxford Orphan Asylum.*
NEWBERNE, N. C., Dec. 25th [1881].

A Merry Christmas and a Happy New Year to you and your readers, dear "News," and my best thanks to your senior, It was he who so amusingly endorsed, with his approval, my course in what he calls "the duel"[1] between Mr. Mills, of the Orphan Asylum and myself. No, I could *not* expose Col. Polk's life so rashly, more particularly as the question was not a personal one, for what do the people of North Carolina care whether *I* can cook or not? But they do care whether these orphan girls, whom they carry so lovingly in their hearts, are taught *anything* by which they can get a respectable living when they leave the Asylum; and they ought to care whether the ladies, who so untiringly devote themselves to their instruction, are treated with simple JUSTICE. The only streak of Woman's Rights which I have, beyond that common to the sex, a firm belief in the right of every woman to have her own way about her own affairs, is a strong and unshaken belief in the right of every woman who works for payment, to receive as good treatment in a business point of view, as if she were a man. This these ladies do not receive from Mr. Mills, but they dare not complain, for they hold their positions by his *ipse dixit* alone. One of them in a private letter to a friend says, "Mrs. Clarke puts it in the mildest possible form, for the teachers are often forced to buy food, or get it from their friends, as it is served either raw or burnt up, and is seldom fit to eat." So, behold me a champion for Woman's Rights—to strong coffee and well cooked food—but, more than all, to the rights of these girls to the education which the patrons of the Orphan Asylum believe they are receiving, but of which they are defrauded. . . .

1. In an undated clipping found in Clarke's Scrapbook 2 in the Barden Collection, the *Raleigh News* or possibly the city's *Daily News* ran an article titled, "A New kind of Duel, or something of that Character." In the article, the editor noted that the controversy stemmed from "what might, could would of should

be taught to the girls of the Asylum in the way of cooking, or housekeeping." Declining to offer an endorsement to one side or the other, the editor did note Mills's "gastronomic cruelty" for "wishing to inflict upon an honest and unoffending citizen, a first class case of dyspepsia." Slyly calling the challenge "a new feature of the code *duello,*" the Raleigh paper applauded Clarke's refusal to engage in the challenge as a "calamity . . . averted, . . . by the goodness of a woman."

*Barden Collection*
*William J. Clarke to Mary Bayard Clarke*

Goldsboro' Sunday night
1882 Jany 15

My Darling:

That incomparable paraphrast, Watts, paraphrasing the last verse of St John's gospel says, "nor could the scroll contain the whole, though stretched from sky to sky", And just so equal space and voluminousness would be necessary should I attempt to tell you how much I love you, and how worthy I think you of my devotion. I went to church today and feverently prayed God to be merciful to me a miserable sinner. Can it be that loving one's wife is a sin? The ascetics think so, or at least say so. I can't believe it. Yet why are we, so linked in heart, "comrades of mind and soul" separated?—Darling, that last visit to New Berne has nearly ruined me. I am so unhappy without you, that the separation seems to me more than I can, or ought to bear. The most earnest prayer of my heart is that, in some way, it may end. I do not think that the mercies of God are clean gone from me, but He certainly seems to be slow to hear my prayers. "Labor is prayer" & the past week has been one of uncommon labor. We are beginning to acquire a great reputation, and though the immediate results are not seen still the harvest will come.

I have not heard directly from Willie for a week, but I learn incidentally, that his trip has been very successful. I enclose Frank's letter. I wish that I could believe that he had squared the circle, invented perpetual motion, &c. Perhaps it can be done but I am incredulous. Let us wait and see. In our day and generation we have seen many strange things.

Think about an old fellow, approaching the grand climacteric, writing a love letter! Well his heart is so full of love for you that he must write love or not write at all. Give my love to Pet & the children.

Your affectionate husband
Wm. J. Clarke

P.S. I hope to write you an acceptable financial letter during the week.

⁓

THE REVEREND MORGAN DIX discussed in the following book review by Mary Bayard Clarke was the nephew of Dorothea L. Dix, the American educator and humanitarian reformer. He served as pastor of Trinity Church in New York City and during the late nineteenth century published many books, including *Lectures on the Calling of a Christian Woman and her Training to Fulfill It*. This book, published in New York by D. Appleton and Company, was based on a series of lectures he delivered "during the season of Lent" in 1883.

Lillie Devereux Blake, author of the second book under review, was Mary Bayard Clarke's cousin and her congenial friend. Before the war Clarke had known Lillie Blake, who was from New York, but it was after the war that the two developed a closer friendship. Blake gained national prominence as a champion of women's rights and served as president of the New York State Woman Suffrage Association from 1879 to 1890 and as president of the New York City Woman Suffrage League between 1886 and 1900. Clarke, whose background and tastes resembled those of her cousin, learned a great deal from cousin Lillie. Clarke's "pen portrait" of Blake serves equally as well as a description of Clarke herself.

Although Clarke never supported the woman suffrage movement advocated by Blake, it is interesting to speculate whether Clarke would have moved in that direction if she had not died in 1886. Both women strongly supported equal pay and improved working conditions for women. In an article titled "A Women, Amen!," written for the *Farmer & Mechanic* (Raleigh) and dated 16 May 1883, Clarke again alluded to the Blake book and urged North Carolina women to buy it. Clarke promoted the hiring of women as principals in the public schools and urged improving the salaries of female teachers. She pointedly used the South's argument that woman's place was in the home to ask, "If every perfect home should . . . have a father and a mother, so it seems to me every School Board of Trustees should be half of them women when the schools are for girls as well as boys." She acknowledged the resistance to this notion by many in the state, but Clarke had a rejoinder for that as well: "I remember one such [man] saying to me once that he objected decidedly to the higher education of women, that the 'Three R's' was all sufficient for the best woman in North Carolina. Looking at him meditatively from head to foot, I replied, 'When I reflect on the narrow-mindness of some of the men with whom they will have to spend their lives, I am not prepared to say you are entirely wrong.'"

*MBC Scrapbook 2, Barden Collection*
*Mary Bayard Clarke book review [1883]*

Two books have been simultaneously laid on our table to be gossiped about "*The Calling of a Christian Woman, and her Training to Fulfill It,*" by the Rev. Morgan Dix, S. T. D., rector of Trinity Church, New York; and "*Woman's Place To-Day,*" by Lillie Devereux Blake.

As the last mentioned is a reply to the first it is most appropriate that they should be read together, but in reading them it should be remembered that the lectures which they contain are addressed to two distinct sets of women, or rather that Dr. Dix addresses a small portion of the women of to-day, as he begs his readers to remember, in reading his book, that it was written for his own people and in the line of his pastoral work. The majority of the women of Dr. Dix's parish are fashionable New York society women, eminently superficial, generally wealthy, and, as individuals, knowing but little of any life beyond that of their own and similar circles in other large cities. Mrs. Blake on the contrary addresses, and defends against Dr. Dix's wholesale assertions of immorality, infidelity and neglect of home duties, the whole mass of the women of America.

Dr. Dix is a pessimist of the gloomiest kind; he believes that the world is at its worst, that religion is becoming nothing and going nowhere, that modern thought is fast reaching "the point at which man rids himself of the last vestiges of faith in God, or love or fear of God, and seeks to erase the name of God from the page of human knowledge, and to banish God finally from society and the world."

In proof that the last and worst times are on us he refers to the state of Russia, Germany, France and England; "the secularization of the English Universities," "the progress of democratic ideas in England,[']" and, worse than all, the existence of the Broad Church School in England, which stands, according to him, "but a very few inches outside of the portals of the house of scepticism and infidelity."

When we read this wholesale slander against men like the late Dean Stanly, Canon Farrar, Bishop Colenso and the late Professor Maurice, we are no longer surprised at the writer's utter inability to see the force of any argument that opposes his own pre-established prejudices. For all this simply means that Dr. Dix is what Mrs. Blake calls him, "an animated fossil," who stands on the same plane as the Rev. John Jasper, of Richmond, and cannot admit that the world moves.[1]

What does the secularization of the English Universities mean? The throwing wide their doors to admit all English citizens, whether Quakers or Baptists, Jews or Unitarians; it is the removing of all religious disabilities, so that a man may now enter them even if he can not subscribe to the thirty-nine articles. The progress of democratic ideas in England means simply that republican ideas are spreading rapidly, not only there but over the whole world, while the Broad Church School[2] which contains the saintliest and the purest men of the age, men who like Bishop Colenso with the native natal population make the cause of any wrong that comes in their way of duty their own cause, is a magnificent bulwark against the narrowness of both the Evangelical and High Church Schools.

Dr. Dix thinks women incapable of logic; they cannot, according to him, see the force of an argument that is against their preconceived ideas. If this is a characteristic of the sex, then is the Rev. Doctor the most complete "old woman" who ever wore a gown.

We have only touched on his ideas respecting women. They are those of a respectable relic of the middle ages, and Mrs. Blake uses him up so entirely that it is needless for any other woman to "hit him now that he is down." He is, as his opponent says, "a theological Rip Van Winkle," living only in the past, resolutely shutting his eyes not only to the future but to the present, outside of the wealthy circle to which he preaches. Little chinks of light do however sometimes stream through the painted glass window behind which he sits, and through one of these he discovers with dismay that the position of woman has changed, that she has advanced from the seclusion of the past, and some of them actually have their names printed in the newspapers—their full names—like men!

Mrs. Blake says: "It is true that Dr. Dix highly approves of marriage for women and dwells so much on the importance of their training as wives and mothers that he evidently thinks young ladies have nothing to do after leaving school but walk into some convenient church and be married to some good husband, who is regularly provided for every woman as soon as she reaches a suitable age." The Doctor admits that many women have no homes, but says they are exceptions whose unhappy cases do not make against the line of his argument. "An airy way of dismissing the facts in the case," says Mrs. Blake, who then proceeds to show that in "New York city alone there are to-day 400,000 women over twenty-one and unmarried, either maidens, widows or divorced wives, which is about one-third of the adult female population. When you add to these the many women who are obliged to support not only themselves but their husbands, you have so large a number of women who cannot expect to find homes or a support in marriage, that only one who stood in 'an early English attitude' would think of considering woman's position to-day without having some thing to say in regard to this constantly increasing army of unmarried and unsupported women."

"Man's is the outer life, woman's the inner," says Dr. Dix: "It can not be her duty to go down and strive in the streets."

"Ah!" says Mrs. Blake, "but it is not only the duty but the necessity of many women in every community to earn their living by leaving their homes, and striving to make for themselves a place in the world; and at what fearful disadvantages are these women placed by the teachings of just such men as Dr. Dix!"

"Women are laboring in our schools at one-half or one-third as much pay as men, who do no better work, toiling in our shops for a wretched pittance, and running sewing machines at starvation wages! The picture is a terrible one in some of its aspects."

"But for all these struggling souls Dr. Dix has not one word. The whole sole, solitary training of a woman must be for the home, which, considering the facts of the case, is about as sensible as if all young men were to be educated for the ministry, with the absolute certainty that there would never be pulpits enough for them to preach from. And even when women are married, may it not be desirable for them to have some art, some trade or profession, by which they may earn what will make their homes more complete and their lives happier? Machinery has taken from women all their old avocations—spinning and weaving, knitting and sewing; the occupations that once filled up all women's time and made their services of industrial value, have been taken from them by the inventions of the last century. Even the potting and pickling and preserving that were once done at home, are now done at factories, and unless a woman has an unusually large family of children she will have much leisure time, which might be profitably employed if only fair opportunities in life were open to all."

It is just here that Southern women, since the war, can sympathize with the Northern "Woman's Rights" movement; their efforts to open new occupations for women, and see that they are paid a man's wages for a man's work is about the only point, as a general rule, in which they touch the conservative Southern woman's heart. As a mass we do not trouble ourselves about the ballot; "what shall we eat and drink, wherewithal be clothed?" is pressing us down.

Say the Northern Woman's Rights leaders, "unless you become a political power by means of the ballot, you must always struggle with overwhelming odds when you are forced by circumstances to make and support your own homes."

And how many of our Southern women have been forced to support their own homes since the last war, who would gladly have followed Dr. Dix's advice and lived lives of "Peace, prayer, retirement!" Such can appreciate the force of the argument in Mrs. Blake's book and the want of it in Dr. Dix's.

We think if the good Doctor could have enjoyed with us the privilege of spending a week in Mrs. Blake's family[3] he would be convinced that it does not necessarily follow that, because a woman "comes before the public" in her efforts to support herself and her children, she has no love for home and necessarily neglects her husband's comfort and her children's training. Mrs. Blake as a girl was one of that circle to whom Dr. Dix addresses his lectures, a wealthy society woman. His graphic picture of the career of a fashionable girl who leaves school at eighteen and achieves what is called "success" in society is a pen portrait of her; she had "the ambition to appear clever and brilliant, the desire to say bright things, to banter and jest and make repartee," which he so much deprecates, and having also the ability to do and to be as well as to appear, she—to use a slang but nevertheless expressive term—"wed a wide row" in society. She married early and was left a widow with two little girls, her husband having run through all her property and that of her widowed mother. Here she may be said to have taken up the burden of life, for though she married a second time, she had before doing so achieved pecuniary independence by her pen, and has ever since her second marriage continued a bread-winner as well as a bread-dispenser for her family. Her husband, who is devoted not only to her but her two daughters by her first marriage, whom he adopted as his own, did not seem when I last saw him to be any more hen-pecked than the majority of good husbands are. They lived in a flat at that time, and to avoid the necessarily close and constant contact of an Irish servant girl in their confined quarters, mutually agreed not to keep one, Mrs. Blake and her daughters with a gas stove doing all the cooking that was not done out of the house. Both of the young ladies were at that time teachers in the public schools, going out of "the retirement of home" to earn their living, wishing, as one of them said to me, "that mama would not work so hard, now that we can help her."

Mrs. Blake deals her opponent a telling blow when she reminds him of the labors of his own aunt, Mrs. Dorothea Dix, after whom the Insane Asylum at Raleigh is named, another one of those women, who came out into the world and did something for the good of humanity, whom it was our privilege to know intimately and esteem highly. . . .

1. The men mentioned in this paragraph were writers and theologians during the nineteenth century. A. P. Stanley served as dean of Westminster in the Anglican church. Frederic W. Farrar was an English writer who became canon of Westminster Abbey in 1876. John Colenso, who died in 1883, served as Anglican bishop in Natal, which is now South Africa. Professor John Frederick Denison Maurice served as professor of English literature and modern history at King's College, Cambridge, and wrote for many literary journals. The Reverend John Jasper of Richmond probably referred to the Reverend John Jasper who lived between 1812 and 1901. He published a book in 1882 entitled *"The Sun Do Move!" The Celebrated Theory of the Sun's Rotation Around the Earth* (New York: Brentano's Literary Emporium, 1882). A later edition of the book states "He Stands on Scripture and Tells Why He Believes the Earth Is Square."

2. The Broad Church movement in the Church of England emerged in the mid-nineteenth century. The word "broad" reflected its views on church doctrines and the need for social reform. Its influence transformed elements of the American Episcopal church.

3. Blake's first husband had died and left her penniless with small children to support. She began to write to earn a living. She married next Grinfill Blake, but she continued her work and maintained an active professional life until shortly before her death.

ஃ

*Hall,* MBC Poems, *xxiii*
*Mary Bayard Clarke to Winchester Hall*

New Berne, November 1883

My death warrant has been read to me. I shall not, probably, die soon, but I live under sentence of death and almost in a cell, for I have had a stroke of paralysis, affecting all my left side. The Doctor says from brain trouble. I write while I am able to tell you this myself. I can drag myself around the house, and talk after a fashion, but I will never go in public as I am now, and I have no hope of being better. I will write as long as I can, and always be the same—no, not that, I *can't* be the same Mary Bayard ever again.

ஃ

*Hall,* MBC Poems, *xxiii–xxiv*
*Mary Bayard Clarke to Winchester Hall*

New Berne, December 1883

"The grasshopper is a burden," or I would have written to you before. They say I will get over it, but I *feel* I never shall. The Catholic priest came to see me the other day—a good, old Irishman, who thinks me the best of heretics, and I think he did me more good than any one else. 'Be the same woman ye were? No! ye've no right to expect that,' and then with tears in his eyes, he patted me on the shoulder and added: 'But there's plenty left in life for ye to do, and enjoy yet, if ye can't be first and foremost and go at things with a rush, as ye have done.' This is the truth I am trying to bring home to myself, and I wish my children could make up their minds that mother is not going to get over it, but may live for years as she is, and had best try and adapt herself to circumstances.

&part;

*Hall,* MBC Poems, *xxiv*
*Mary Bayard Clarke to Winchester Hall,*

New Berne 1884 April

Post yourself on tricycles. I see ladies are using them, and I mean to try if I can get about on one; I have not the slightest desire to do so, but know I had better do so, if in my power.

I cannot tell you how much I enjoy my caligraph. I could not write now without it, as for ten days I have had gout in my right hand; I can use it with either hand, or rather with one finger of either hand.

&part;

*Hall,* MBC Poems, *xxiv–xxv*
*Mary Bayard Clarke to Winchester Hall,*

New Berne April 1885

I am stronger than I have been since I had the stroke, but my head is so confused, and my memory so much affected I can do little or no brain work. An hour of it tires me more than a day of it used to do. I have even lost my power of reading, for more than a short time, without rest. I have just finished 'The Life of George Eliot,' by her husband, Mr. Cross, and am delighted with it, but the magazines and papers are about all I am equal to now.

&part;

*Hall,* MBC Poems, *xxv*
*Mary Bayard Clarke to Winchester Hall*

New Berne November 1885

I am very much interested in the Ethical Culture Movement,[1] and have just finished a review of Weston's Lectures on it. Have you seen them? I have very little time for either reading or writing now, and feel very rusty, but sometimes I rouse up, and write a letter or read a book, though generally my time is taken up with sewing, housekeeping and attending to my sick husband.

1. The Ethical Culture Movement was founded by Felix Adler in 1876. It consisted of a mixture of religious and educational theories and claimed to have been "inspired by the ideal that the supreme aim of human life is working to create a more humane society." See Pat Hoertdoerfer, "A Brief History of the Ethical Culture Movement," from the AEU Core Curriculum, Teacher's Handbook, found at the Brooklyn Society for Ethical Culture Web site, accessed 9 Sept. 2000, http://www.bsec.org/info/history.html.

GEORGE MOULTON TRAVELED from his native New Hampshire to New Bern to visit the grave of his cousin, who had been buried in the town's National Cemetery during the Civil War. Moulton was also interested in scouting out business prospects in the area. During his visit, he met the Clarke family and developed an interest in the widowed Mary Clarke Morgan. Mary Bayard Clarke, aware that her husband was dying and that her own health was precarious, nurtured the romance in the interest of her daughter's financial future. She sent letters of inquiry to New Hampshire to determine if Moulton's character was good, and she sought to verify his financial standing. Satisfied with the answers she received, Clarke overlooked Moulton's educational and social shortcomings in the interest of economic stability. Moulton liked Mary Morgan's children, he liked the town, and he decided to stay. This letter was addressed to his sister, who still lived in New Hampshire.

*Barden Collection*
*George Moulton to Mary Josephine Graves*

New Burn NC
Dec 27—85

My Dear Sister

I though you might look for a letter the ferst of the wek so I write I recived yours teling about the recept of the money well I am going down to the Coste if nothing in Providence prevents Tuesday to be gone a weeke or 10 days and may go befor I get a letter from you if I am whare I can write Sundey shall do so I have not kiled mey birds as yet but hope to this week I like bording my self better than bording the folks are to kind to me all to grate to last long they will Send me up my diner or supper and insist on my taking it yet I wish they would not I hired a man preach to day from Mass at the Bapist Church am going to Spend the afternoon out with a Widdow ladie by in vite a geting acquanted full fast enough I think dont you then the young ladie at the House It is colder now than ever but I have my door open. I have seen Charlies Grave there is a mistake on the Stone it is marked Charles F in Sted of C T the grounds are vary nicely keep with white marble Slabs and Shade trees and our Flag always to the breeze I have seen Onions 6 inches in hight also Cabage & Turnip Farmers are preparing ground for Peas now. I recd a lettr from Cosin Warren B this week and his Picture also well I hope you are well now try to keep from geting *cold* and get well if you can write as before to New Burn N C

Affly Bro<br>Geo Moulton

I wish you A Merrie Chrstmas & *happy* new *Yeare*

❧

*Barden Collection*
*William J. Clarke obituary,* Daily Journal *(New Bern),* 26 Jan. 1886[1]

**DIED,**

January the 23d, of paralysis of the brain, Hon. William J. Clarke, aged 66 years.

Judge Clarke was born in Raleigh, N. C. Aug. 2d, 1819, graduated at Chapel Hill and entered on the practice of law in his natice place. At the beginning of the Mexican war he entered the U. S. A. as Captain of Infantry, was severely wounded at the battle of the National Bridge and breveted as Major for gallantry in that and other actions, served till the close of the war, when he was pensioned by Congress.

In 1848 he married a daughter of the late Thomas P. Devereux and resumed the practice of his profession in Raleigh, forming a law partnership with Patrick H. Winston, afterwards Supreme Court Reporter. He was for several terms of the Legislature elected State Comptroller or Auditor, which office he held until his removal to Texas in 1857, on account of the health of his family. He resided in San Antonia until the beginning of the late civil war, when he returned to North Carolina and was appointed Col. of the 24th N. C. Regiment, in which capacity he served during the war. He was severely wounded at the battle of Drury's Bluff, having his shoulder-blade shattered by a fragment of shell. He was captured by the Federal troops before Petersburg and held a prisoner in Fort Delaware till after the close of the war. Shortly after which he settled in New Berne, where he resided to his death.

He was elected to the State Senate in 1870, but did not take his seat, resigning it on his appointment as Judge of the Superior Court before the meeting of the Legislature.

He was a ripe scholar, a genial and courtly gentleman of the old school, and made and kept many warm friends who will regret his death.

Notwithstanding the very disagreeable weather, Judge Clarke's funeral was attended by a large number of our citizens on Sunday evening. The services were conducted by Rev. V. W. Shields. The underbearers were Mr. W. H. Oliver, Col. Jno. D. Whitford, Hon. C. C. Clark, Hon. A. S. Seymour, Hon. George Green, Hon. C. R. Thomas and Messrs. Henry R. Bryan and M. DeW. Stevenson.

1. The same edition of the paper also carried an "In Memoriam" for Clarke. Typical of many Victorian eulogies, it described his kind heart and his willingness to comfort the afflicted and distressed. It also recorded that Clarke was buried in the Cedar Grove Cemetery in New Bern.

*Barden Collection*
*Nora Cannon[1] to Mary Bayard Clarke*

January 29th/86

My Dear Sister

Your letter reached me this morning and I cannot tell you how my heart has gone out to you all day! and how I have wished that I could be with you in this dark hour of your life, It is as you say hard to think that his death was the best thing that could happen, & yet it was so and when we remember his gentle nature & his uncomplaining patience under the severe sufferring which was his for many years past, it does not need the remembrance of the dark cloud which over shaddowed his last months to convince us that death was to him a joyful release, even tho to those who loved him as we did it is hard, bitter hard to say "Thy will be done!"—

I am so glad that I paid you that visit last summer and had so many pleasant walks & talks with him—Do you remember the afternoon we spent together in the Cemetary? I have often thought of it, & of his remarks since he was taken sick—Oh my sister none can sympathize with you more than I can whose heart has been wrung and almost broken in the same way & yet not in the same way either for *you* had the blessed privlege of ministering to & waiting on him whom you loved & have lost while I!—

I know that this blow has fallen with terrible force on Mary who had always worshiped her "Fada" and who in a letter received from her a short time since spoke of him so affectionately—

I do hope soon to hear from some of you again and that you will write oftener than you have done heretofore, for as Death lessens the number of our family, those who are left should cling closer together—You & I & Susy are the only sisters left now[2] of the family—& tho separated by distance let us be near in love & keep each other posted as to our affairs—

We are all well except Mattie who has been in poor health all the fall & winter She & Nonie both join me in love & tender condolence to you and the children—I shall send your letter to Sadie by the same mail that carries this to you, tho she will not get it till Monday morning—

God bless & keep you all & when your heart almost breaks with lone-liness & longing for the "Sound [of his voice?] which is mute" may He com-fort & strengthen you is the prayer of your loving

Sister Nora

1. By this date, Nora Cannon had returned to Tennessee to live with her son and daughters while working as a county superintendent of public education in Fayette County. She won reelection to this office in 1886 and served until her death in 1888.

2. Kate Edmondston had died in January 1875 and Elizabeth (Betsy) Dev-ereux Jones passed away in 1879. Sophia Turner died in September 1880, and Frances Devereux Miller died in August 1881.

*Barden Collection*
*Judge Robert Dick to Mary Bayard Clarke*

Greensboro

Jany 30th—86

Mrs Mary Bayard Clarke
My Dear Friend

I have just received a copy of the Daily Journal, informing me of the death of my friend Judge Clarke

He has been my constant friend for near fifty years. When I heard of his death I felt that one of the *ties of earth* was broken. I use the words "ties of earth" and not the "ties of life"—for life is immortal and its fond ties are never broken but link us still to departed friends and loved ones in the Heavenly Home.

Judge Clarke was a pure and noble man and I sincerely believe that he never did any wilful wrong to a fellow man.——He met the duties of life bravely and did them well, and now he rests from his labors, and has received his reward of eternal blessedness and joy.

I assure you and your family of my deepest sympathy

Most Sincerely<br>
Your Friend<br>
*Robert Dick*

ও

*Barden Collection*
*George Moulton to Mary Josephine Graves*

New Burne N. C.<br>
March 10 –86

My Dear Sister

I recived a letter from you Sunday and will try to answer allthough I cant write you so long a letter you wrote me yet I will try to tell you how I am Suituated just now you will be Surprised But I will tell you Marys Mother is vary Sick Monday A.M. She had a Second Shock of Parrilas. and is in vary critical condition yet her mind is cleer—and She is vary ancious that we be married imeadately as She wants to see us married before She dies and Mary consents to if She Says any more about it may take plase to day or any time I have the weding Ring all ready in case it must come But Mary wants to wate untill the first of June the time *Set* for my part I am ready only I *need* a new *Coat* and a little money for I have Shiped off to Boston a lot of Potatos and not had any return as yet from them Mary is to have the house they now live in so we will have a home. but the first of June I shall take my wife home I do wish I had 10 or $15.00 jus now. If I had known of this I could have ben prepared for it

The Dr says Mrs Clarke must be gratified in every thing she wants for there is vay grate dange of inflamation of the Braine if She is not. Dear Sister I know you will love May She come from one of the first familie of the State her father was a proment Lawyer and judge of the Supeior Cort. if you could Send me a little by mony order. I can pay you as soon as I here from my Potatoes in Boston Plase write me soon the Ring is plane gold She is an Episcopallian and that Servis requres a Ring—I wish it was over with for the ceromy is lengthy have to kneel Twise 2 times and repet a

Prayer and repete all the cerom good by now Sister I shall goe at noon to see if it is to be to day will tell you if is is tomorow

Affly Bro George

it is so funie to me to think I am about to be 2 in sted of an old batch any longer

❧

*Barden Collection*
*George Moulton to Mary Josephine Graves*

New Burne N.C
March 14 –86

My Dear Sister

I know you will be surprised when you get the letter I sent you yesterday A.M. Now I am vay hapy to tell you that you have one of the *Sweetest Sisters* that one could ever wish for if did not think so you know I am such an old batch that I should have refrained. Now dear Sister Cant you congratulate me on having a dear good companion. We have 2 Children to start life with Bayard & Sam. B. is 10 in the 17 of last Dec and S. 7 next July and *Mrs Moulton* is 32.[1] and you know my age is 44 So much for that. now I will tell you about our mariage wich took plase yesterday (A.M. 11) in the Sick room and by Mothers bed side She giving Mary away the weding owing to the *extream Sickness* of *Mother* was strickly Privet[2] only the Dr a Mrs Stanly a Miss Beary & Mr Willis out Side of the family which consist of Mr & Mrs Wm E. Clarke Mr Thomas Clarke and you humble servant & family people are vary much execised over the mariage but I guess they will servive it the Serimony was vary impresing to me I think the Knot securely tide the Knot was tide by Episcopal cerimony had to kneal during a part and wer marrid with a Ring each of us had to repeate the serivis I like it though it most took my breath away dont it seeam funey that you old batch Brother should have done Such a thing. Mrs Clark is not expected to recovr from her illness. there is much solisation for her recovry and I hope she will soon My Dear Wife is nerly worn out now taking care of her it is quere to me but a reality Sam allready calles me Paps and it is so funnie we have no cards but I hope my friends will not forget me. Did you get my letter asking for the lone of some money please $15.00. I am out of funds and dont know what I shall do with out any dont Expect to here from Boston jest yet. Please reply to this with out mention the money

Affly, Your brother

Geo

1. After Mary Clarke Morgan's marriage to George Moulton on 13 March 1886, she bore three more children: George Clarke, Warren Raboteau, and Celia Clarke Moulton.

2. According to the wedding announcement in the Raleigh *News and Observer* dated 16 March 1886, "The marriage was solemnized . . . at the bedside of the bride's mother, Mrs. Clarke, who lies stricken with paralysis. The marriage tie was thus bound at her request."

*Barden Collection*
*George Moulton to Mary Josephine Graves*

New Berne N.C.
March 21 –86

My Dear Sister

I recived you two last letters this A.M. with the money order of $15.00 for which accept my gratitude. I need it vary much I lost by Freezing therefore am crampt, but what I handle here pay a better proffit than the same would pay at home. I hope MAM will come out all right as well as the little one Mary is writing by my side to some of her friends I sat up with Mother a part of last night and have a cold & head ache to day neither of us have much spare time to write allthough Willie and his bride[1] also brother Thom help take care of her have to feed her with a sponn & lift here up & down there seams to be a gradual sinking away Mary sends her love and says she is trying to make me a good wife and when I tell you how much I reget I could not have meet her years ago, and, married her you will know that she is "a *good Wife*"

Bayard goes to school while Sam projects about for amussement.— the weather is like May fine warm growing. Peas are 6 in high Onions also new E R Potatoes as large as hens Eggs greens abundant Mrs Flanders Sent me $5.00 as a weding presant wasnt that *nice?* I here Warren has comenced to build. had a letter from Geo A Hatch this week. Must close loving—

Brother Geo Moulton

I shall send a coppy of the Raleigh Paper with notis of my marirage for the News letter to Print . . .

1. William E. Clarke married Sarah Elizabeth (Bessie) Howerton on 23 February 1886. The only child Mary Bayard Clarke failed to see married was Thomas, her youngest son. Thomas Clarke, married to Lottie Clarke, died in Washington, where he successfully served as superintendent of the Washington

State School for the Deaf and Blind from 1906 to 1920. H. William Brelje and Virginia M. Tibbs, "Part III: Coming of Age, Thomas Pollock Clarke, 1906–1920," in *Washington State School for the Deaf: The First 100 Years, 1886–1986* (N.P.: privately published, 1986), 19–23.

∽

*Barden Collection*
*George Moulton to Mary Josephine Graves*

New Berne N C
March 31 86

Dear Sister

I expect a letter from you tonight but will write you the Sad intelegence that Mrs Clark died this A.M. at 7 9 week ago death took awy her husband. and with in that 2 marriages have taken plase in this Same family rather a remarkabe ocorance I think Mother pased away vary quitely but was some time dieing funeral is tomorow A.M. at 10. Oclock It have poared in torance all day but I hope it will be plesant in the moring. . . . Byard is neere me now She is a beautifull Girl of her age I think.—I have closed my shop

Good bye with love
Bro Geo Moulton

∽

*MBC Scrapbook 2, Barden Collection, unidentified newspaper clipping*
### IN MEMORIAM
"Just as I am—without one plea,
But that thy blood was shed for me,
O, Lamb of God I come."
Sacred to the memory of
**Mary Bayard Clarke,**
who died in Newbern, N. C., on Wednesday, March 30th,[1] 1886, in the 58th year of her age. Mrs. Clarke was the widow of the late Judge W. J. Clarke, and a daughter of the late Thomas P. Devereux.

For many months she had suffered from attacks of Paralysis, and although her suffering was acute, she bore it with fortitude.

Mrs. Clarke was a gifted woman, she had received a very high education, and her literary attainments were of high order.

It is not of these, however, that the writer wishes to speak. It is to bear witness to, and to place upon record her goodness of heart, her kindness of disposition, and her ever willingness to relieve distress

It was around the hearth-stone of the afflicted, at the bed-side of the sick, and wherever there was sorrow that the kindness and sincerity of her disposition shone so bright.

Hers was no sudden call. The Silver Cord was not cut hurriedly, nor the Golden Bowl broken in an instant. The Cord was gently untied, the Golden Bowl melted away, as the light fades away from the firmament at the coming of the evening shades.

> "Just as I am, thou wilt receive;
> Because thy promise I believe—
> O, Lamb of God, I come."

Newbern, N. C.                                                                                                        O.

1. According to George Moulton's letter dated 31 March 1886, Mary Bayard Clarke actually died on 31 March. She was buried next to William J. Clarke in New Bern's Cedar Grove Cemetery.

# Appendix

Letters Written by Mary Bayard Clarke Printed in this Volume

| Place | Date | Written To |
|---|---|---|
| Raleigh | October 31, 1854 | John R. Thompson |
| Matanzas [Cuba] | March 7, [1855] | Patrick A. Winston |
| [Havana, Cuba] | March 24, [1855] | Frances Miller |
| Port Lavacca [Tex.] | January 30, [1856] | Frances Miller |
| San Antonio | February 7, [1856] | Frances Miller |
| San Antonio | February 14–15, [1856] | Frances Miller |
| San Antonio | May 5, [1856] | Frances Miller |
| [San Antonio] | 1856 | Winchester Hall |
| San Antonio | December 16, 1860 | George W. Bagby |
| San Antonio | March 12, [1861] | George W. Bagby |
| San Antonio | April 8, [1861] | George W. Bagby |
| Hillsborough | September 21, [1861] | Macfarlane and Ferguson |
| Petersburg | January 3, [1862] | Eliza Primrose |
| Petersburg | January 5, [1862] | Frank Clarke |
| Petersburg | January 12, [1862] | Willie Clarke |
| Petersburg | January 13, [1862] | George W. Bagby |
| Murfreesboro | March 19, [1862] | Frank and Willie Clarke |
| Murfreesboro | April 7, [1862] | Willie Clarke |
| Murfreesboro | April 22, [1862] | Frank Clarke |
| Jones Spring [N.C.] | November 7, [1862] | Willie Clarke |
| Conneconara | January 7, [1863] | George W. Bagby |
| Conneconara | April 1, [1863] | George W. Bagby |
| Raleigh | September 27, [1863] | Frank and Willie Clarke |
| Raleigh | November 1, [1863] | Willie Clarke |
| Conneconara | December 31, [1863] | Willie Clarke |
| Conneconara | February 23, [1864] | Willie Clarke |
| Raleigh | May 8, [1864] | Willie Clarke |
| Raleigh | May 18, [1864] | Willie Clarke |

Letters written by Mary Bayard Clarke (*continued*)

| Place | Date | Written To |
|---|---|---|
| Raleigh | June 2, [1864] | Willie Clarke |
| Raleigh | June 18, [1864] | Willie Clarke |
| Raleigh | July 20, [1864] | Willie Clarke |
| Raleigh | January 17, [1865] | Willie Clarke |
| [Raleigh] | [June 1865] | Frances Miller |
| Raleigh | June 19, [1865] | William J. Clarke |
| Raleigh | [August? 1865] | Winchester Hall |
| Raleigh | November 4, 1865 | Mary Custis Lee |
| Raleigh | February 23, [1866] | Miss Deane |
| Beaufort | September 2, [1866] | Frank Clarke |
| Keoco Mills [N.C.] | October 1, [1866] | Cornelia Phillips Spencer |
| Raleigh | October 22, [1866] | Frank Clarke |
| Keoco Mills | November 20, [1866] | Frank Clarke |
| Morehead City [N.C.] | August 2, [1867] | Cornelia Phillips Spencer |
| Raleigh | July 21, [1868] | William J. Clarke |
| Washington, D.C. | October 11, [1868] | Willie Clarke |
| Baltimore | October 21, [1868] | Willie Clarke |
| New Bern | [ca. November 1868] | Willie Clarke |
| Berkshire Co., Mass. | July 14, [1869] | Willie Clarke |
| Blair House [Raleigh] | January 24, [1870] | Frances Miller |
| New Marlboro [Mass.] | August 27, [1870] | Willie Clarke |
| New Bern | December 22, [1870] | Willie Clarke |
| New Bern | January 28, 1871 | Willie Clarke |
| New Bern | February 3, [1871] | Willie Clarke |
| New Bern | April 21, [1871] | Willie Clarke |
| New Bern | May 26, [1871] | Willie Clarke |
| New Bern | November 20, [1871] | Willie Clarke |
| New Bern | January 3, 1872 | Willie Clarke |
| New Bern | [March 31, 1872] | Willie Clarke |
| New Bern | December 8, [1872] | Willie Clarke |
| New Bern | January 1, [1873] | Willie Clarke |
| New Bern | January 12, [1873] | Willie Clarke |
| New Bern | February 2, [1873] | Willie Clarke |
| New Bern | February 16, [1873] | Willie Clarke |
| New Bern | March 5, [1873] | Willie Clarke |
| New Bern | April 13, [1873] | Willie Clarke |
| New Bern | [January 1, 1876] | Winchester Hall |

| Norfolk | [June 1876] | William J. Clarke |
| New York City | [August 1876] | William J. Clarke |
| New York City | August 8, [1876] | William J. Clarke |
| New Bern | May 16, [1878] | Nathan W. Abbott |
| New Bern | November 1878 | Winchester Hall |
| [New Bern] | [December 1878] | Nathan W. Abbott |
| New Bern | December 12, 1878 | Nathan W. Abbott |
| New Bern | January 19, [1879] | Nathan W. Abbott |
| New Bern | March 12, [1879] | Nathan W. Abbott |
| [New Bern] | [ca. January 1880] | William J. Clarke |
| [New Bern] | [ca. July 1881] | John H. Mills |
| New Bern | November 1883 | Winchester Hall |
| New Bern | December 1883 | Winchester Hall |
| New Bern | April 1884 | Winchester Hall |
| New Bern | April 1885 | Winchester Hall |
| New Bern | November 1885 | Winchester Hall |

## LETTERS WRITTEN TO MARY BAYARD CLARKE PRINTED IN THIS VOLUME

| Place | Date | Written By |
| --- | --- | --- |
| Salt Sulphur Springs | August 10, 1858 | Thomas Pollock Devereux |
| New York City | August 12, 1858 | William J. Clarke |
| New York City | August 30, 1858 | William J. Clarke |
| New York City | September 5, 1858 | William J. Clarke |
| Raleigh | August 6, 1859 | John Devereux |
| Salt Sulphur Springs | August 12, 1859 | Thomas Pollock Devereux |
| Montgomery | April 26, 1861 | William J. Clarke |
| Montgomery | May 15, 1861 | William J. Clarke |
| Montgomery | May 17, 1861 | William J. Clarke |
| Montgomery | May 23, 1861 | William J. Clarke |
| Weldon | June 2, 1861 | William J. Clarke |
| Weldon | June 25, 1861 | William J. Clarke |
| Garysburg | July 14, 1861 | William J. Clarke |
| [Raleigh] | [summer 1861] | Frances Miller |
| White Sulphur Springs | September 1, 1861 | William J. Clarke |
| Meadow Bluff [Va.] | September 21, 1861 | William J. Clarke |
| Camp Defiance [Va.] | October 15, 1861 | William J. Clarke |
| Camp Polk [Va.] | November 14, 1861 | William J. Clarke |
| Petersburg | December 17, 1861 | William J. Clarke |
| Murfreesboro | March 3, 1862 | William J. Clarke |

Letters written to Mary Bayard Clarke (*continued*)

| Place | Date | Written By |
|---|---|---|
| Petersburg | June 14, 1862 | William J. Clarke |
| Drewry's Bluff | July 17, 1862 | William J. Clarke |
| Winchester | October 12, 1862 | William J. Clarke |
| Fredericksburg | December 1, 1862 | William J. Clarke |
| Fredericksburg | December 13, 1862 | William J. Clarke |
| Fredericksburg | January 1, 1863 | William J. Clarke |
| Goldsboro | January 17, 1863 | William J. Clarke |
| Kenansville | January 27, 1863 | William J. Clarke |
| Kenansville | February 6, 1863 | William J. Clarke |
| Kinston | April 4, 1863 | William J. Clarke |
| Kinston | May 13, 1863 | William J. Clarke |
| Drewry's Bluff | June 16, 1863 | William J. Clarke |
| Richmond | July 11, 1863 | William J. Clarke |
| Petersburg | July 16, 1863 | William J. Clarke |
| Petersburg | July 24, 1863 | William J. Clarke |
| Hamilton [N.C.] | December 29, 1863 | William J. Clarke |
| Weldon | February 7, 1864 | William J. Clarke |
| Richmond | May 22, 1864 | William J. Clarke |
| Fort Delaware | March 29, 1865 | William J. Clarke |
| Fort Delaware | April 29, 1865 | William J. Clarke |
| [Raleigh] | [June 1865] | Frances Miller |
| Raleigh | October 4, 1865 | W. B. Smith & Co. |
| Lexington | December 7, 1865 | Mary Custis Lee |
| Lexington | March 15, [1866] | Mary Custis Lee |
| Baltimore | March 26, 1866 | Brantz Mayer |
| Baltimore | April 3, 1866 | Brantz Mayer |
| Baltimore | April 23, 1866 | Brantz Mayer |
| Tappahannock | July 10, [1866] | Emily Mason |
| Charlotte | February 5, 1867 | Fanny Downing |
| Lexington | February 22, [1867] | Mary Custis Lee |
| Charlotte | March 6, 1867 | Zebulon B. Vance |
| Newport [Ky.] | January 7, [1868] | Emily Mason |
| New York City | May 21, 1868 | John R. Thompson |
| New Bern | July 17, 1868 | William J. Clarke |
| Roxboro [N.C.] | July 28, 1868 | Edwin G. Reade |
| Roxboro | September 7, 1868 | Edwin G. Reade |
| Raleigh | February 1, 1869 | Edwin G. Reade |
| Raleigh | January 23, 1870 | Frances Miller |
| Raleigh | August 21, 1870 | William J. Clarke |
| Baltimore | December 11, [1870] | Emily Mason |

| | | |
|---|---|---|
| Lexington | December 28, 1870 | Margaret J. Preston |
| Lexington | January 11, 1871 | Mary Custis Lee |
| Lexington | February 4, 1871 | Mary Custis Lee |
| Raleigh | February 4, 1872 | Robert Dick |
| Goldsboro | [November/ December 1872] | William J. Clarke |
| Sewanee [Tenn.] | August 14, 1875 | George Patterson |
| Chicago | December 23, 1877 | Nathan W. Abbott |
| Chicago | November 28, 1878 | Nathan W. Abbott |
| Raleigh | April 26, 1880 | William J. Clarke |
| Oxford | July 28, 1881 | John H. Mills |
| Goldsboro | January 15, 1882 | William J. Clarke |
| [Tennessee] | January 29, 1886 | Nora Cannon |
| Greensboro | January 30, 1886 | Robert Dick |

### ADDITIONAL LETTERS WRITTEN BY WILLIAM J. CLARKE PRINTED IN THIS VOLUME

| Place | Date | Written To |
|---|---|---|
| Havana [Cuba] | March 31, 1855 | Frances Miller |
| San Antonio | February 24, 1856 | Frances Miller |
| New Bern | March 27, 1869 | Frances Miller |
| [New Bern] | [1869] | Kate Edmondston |
| Raleigh | September 9, 1870 | Willie Clarke |
| New Bern | June 23, 1872 | Willie Clarke |
| New Bern | April 6, 1873 | Willie Clarke |
| New Bern | January 4, 1874 | Mary Clarke Morgan |
| New Bern | June 28, 1874 | Mary Clarke Morgan |
| New Bern | June 6, 1875 | Mary Clarke Morgan |
| New Bern | October 8, 1876 | Mary Clarke Morgan |

### MISCELLANEOUS LETTERS PRINTED IN THIS VOLUME

| Place | Date | Written By | Written To |
|---|---|---|---|
| Jones Spring [N.C.] | November 7, [1862] | Mary and Tom Clarke | Willie Clarke |
| Raleigh | June 6, [1864] | Mary D. Clarke | Willie Clarke |
| San Antonio | December 6, 1865 | Sam Taylor | William J. Clarke |
| Lexington | March 14, 1866 | Robert E. Lee | Mary D. Clarke |
| Hillsborough | [August/ September 1868] | Sophia Turner | William J. Clarke |
| Raleigh | September 6, 1868 | Frances Miller | William J. Clarke |
| San Antonio | February 15, 1869 | Sam Taylor | William J. Clarke |

Miscellaneous letters (*continued*)

| Place | Date | Written By | Written To |
|---|---|---|---|
| Raleigh | March 2, 1869 | Frances Miller | William J. Clarke |
| Raleigh | March 30, [1869] | Frances Miller | William J. Clarke |
| Raleigh | September 19, 1869 | Frances Miller | Mary D. Clarke |
| Raleigh | July 20, 1870 | Frances Miler | William J. Clarke |
| Hillsborough | December 6, [1870] | Nora Cannon | Willie Clarke |
| Raleigh | August 6, [1872] | Nora Cannon | Willie Clarke |
| New Bern | January 5, 1873 | Nora Cannon | Willie Clarke |
| St. Mary's [Raleigh] | March 23, [1873] | Nora Cannon | Willie Clarke |
| [New Bern] | January 26, 1879 | Mary Clarke Morgan | Rufus Morgan |
| New Bern | December 7, 1879 | Mary Clarke Morgan | Rufus Morgan |
| New Bern | March 14, 1880 | Mary Clarke Morgan | Rufus Morgan |
| New Bern | December 27, 1885 | George Moulton | Mary J. Graves |
| New Bern | March 10, 1886 | George Moulton | Mary J. Graves |
| New Bern | March 14, 1886 | George Moulton | Mary J. Graves |
| New Bern | March 21, 1886 | George Moulton | Mary J. Graves |
| New Bern | March 31, 1886 | George Moulton | Mary J. Graves |

## Articles Written by Mary Bayard Clarke Printed in this Volume

| Title | Date | Where Published |
|---|---|---|
| "Interesting from Texas" | February 17, 1861 | *New York Herald* |
| "North Carolina Correspondence" | August 29, 1865 | *Daily News* |
| "General Sherman in Raleigh" | April 1866 | *Old Guard* |
| "The South Expects Every Woman To Do Her Duty" | August 1866 | *Old Guard* |
| "The Union Washing Machine" | 1867 | *Sentinel* |
| "For the Journal of Commerce" | [ca. February 1868] | *Journal of Commerce* |
| "Letter from Betsey Bittersweet" | February 21, [1868] | *Southern Home Journal* |
| "Literary Gossip" | [1875] | Unidentified newspaper |

| | | |
|---|---|---|
| Untitled | July 5, 1876 | Unidentified newspaper |
| "From our own Correspondent" | July 20, 1876 | Unidentified newspaper |
| "The Centennial." | September 3, 1876 | Unidentified newspaper |
| "The Centennial." | September 7, [1876] | Unidentified newspaper |
| "The Centennial, Huxley, etc." | September 24, 1876 | Unidentified newspaper |
| "Woman in Journalism." | July 1877 | *Inland Monthly Magazine* |
| "Letter from Chicago." | July 24, 1877 | Unidentified newspaper |
| "Woman North and South." | October 1877 | *Current Thought* |
| "Woman As a Worker." | [1877] | Unidentified newspaper |
| "To The Ladies." | December 24, 1879 | *Signal* |
| "Letter from the Editor." | February 22, [1880] | *Signal* |
| "One of the State Charities. Is Properly Managed?" | September 26, [1881] | *Farmer and Mechanic* |
| "Mrs. Clarke's Reply to Mr. Mills" | November 2, [1881] | *Farmer and Mechanic* |
| Untitled | December 25, [1881] | *Raleigh News?* |
| Untitled Book Reviews | [1883] | Unidentified newspaper |

## Poems Written by Mary Bayard Clarke Printed in this Volume

| Title | Date | Where Written |
|---|---|---|
| "I've Been Thinking" | 1857 | San Antonio |
| "The Rebel Sock" | 1863 | Conneconara |
| "Under the Lava" | 1868 | Raleigh |

## Miscellanea

| | | |
|---|---|---|
| Obituary, William J. Clarke | January 26, 1886 | *Daily Journal* |
| "In Memoriam," Mary Bayard Clarke | March 1886 | Unidentified newspaper |

# Bibliography

## Primary Sources

*Manuscripts*

Bagby, George. Family Papers, Mss1B1463b. Virginia Historical Society, Richmond, Va.

Barden, Mrs. Graham A., Jr. Collection. New Bern, N.C.

Clarke, William John. Papers, 1819–86, no. 153. Southern Historical Collection, Wilson Library, University of North Carolina at Chapel Hill.

Cooke, John Esten. Papers, 2nd 82:G. Special Collections Library, Duke University, Durham, N.C.

Denison, George. Family Papers. Manuscript Division, MMC–0249. Library of Congress.

Devereux Family Bible. In the possession of William Joslin, Raleigh, N.C.

Devereux, John. Papers, P.C.34.2. North Carolina State Archives, Division of Archives and History, Raleigh, N.C.

Finnerty, Frances Martin. Private manuscript collection. Brevard, N.C.

General Assembly Session Records, 1866–67. T. P. Devereux to Jonathan Worth, 20 October 1866. State Archives, North Carolina Division of Archives and History, Raleigh, N.C.

Hobson, Laura. Private collection. Memphis, Tenn.

Lee Family Papers. Mss1L51b65, Mss1L51c. Virginia Historical Society, Richmond, Va.

Macfarlane and Fergusson Papers, Mss4M1645a1. Virginia Historical Society, Richmond, Va.

Reid, David S. Papers P.C.1.8. State Archives, North Carolina Division of Archives and History, Raleigh, N.C.

Speer, Mary Gibson. Private collection. Missouri City, Tex.

Spencer, Cornelia Phillips. Papers, P.C. 7. State Archives, North Carolina Division of Archives and History, Raleigh, N.C.

Turner, Josiah. Papers no. 730. Southern Historical Collection, University of North Carolina, Chapel Hill.

U.S. Census, Bexar County, San Antonio Township, Tex., 1860.

U.S. Census, Craven County, New Bern Township, N.C., 1870, 1880.

U.S. Census, Wake County, Raleigh Township, N.C., 1850, 1860, 1870.

Worth, Jonathan. Letter Book, January–July 1866, PC49.7: 356–57. State Archives, North Carolina Division of Archives and History, Raleigh, N.C.

Wootten, Moulton, and Clarke Family Papers no. 4805. Southern Historical Collection, Wilson Library, University of North Carolina at Chapel Hill.

*Periodicals and Newspapers*

*Catholic World* (Paramus, N.J.), 1869, 1874.

*Current Thought, Literature, Fashion, Society and Home Topics* (Chicago), 1877.

*Field and Fireside* (Raleigh), 1866, 1867.

*Galaxy, A Magazine of Entertaining Reading* (New York), 1877.

*Inland Monthly Magazine* (Chicago), 1877.

*The Land We Love* (Charlotte), 1866, 1867, 1868.

*The Michigan Mirror Memorial Number* 40, no. 2 (Flint, Mich.: Michigan School for the Deaf, 23 Oct. 1913).

*New Bern Republican,* 1868.

*News and Observer* (Raleigh), 1886.

*North Carolina Standard* (Raleigh), 1868.

*Observer* (Raleigh), 1877.

*Old Guard* (New York), 1866.

*Orphans Friend* (Oxford), 1880, 1881.

*Raleigh Register,* 1877.

*San Antonio Daily Herald,* 1858, 1859.

*Sentinel* (Raleigh), 1865–70.

*Signal* (Raleigh), 1880, 1881.

*Southern Home Journal* (Baltimore), 1867, 1868.

*Southern Literary Messenger* (Richmond), 1853, 1854, 1855, 1861, 1862, 1863, 1864.

*Weekly Alamo Express* (San Antonio), 1861.

## Secondary Sources

*Published Books*

Ames, William E. *A History of the National Intelligencer.* Chapel Hill: University of North Carolina Press, 1972.

Ashe, Samuel A., ed. *Biographical History of North Carolina from Colonial Times to the Present.* 8 vols. Greensboro, N.C.: Charles L. Van Noppen, 1905–17.

————. *Cyclopedia of Eminent and Representative Men of the Carolinas of the Nineteenth Century, with a Brief Historical Introduction of South Carolina by General Edward McCrady, Jr., and on North Carolina by Hon. Samuel A. Ashe.* Vol. 2. Madison, Wis.: Brant and Fuller, 1892.

Austin, James C. *Bill Arp.* New York: Twayne Publishers, 1969.

Barrett, John G. *The Civil War in North Carolina.* Chapel Hill: University of North Carolina Press, 1963.

———. *Sherman's March through the Carolinas.* Chapel Hill: University of North Carolina Press, 1956.

Blake, Katherine Devereux, and Margaret Louise Wallace. *Champion of Women: The Life of Lillie Devereux Blake.* New York: Fleming H. Revell, 1943.

Boatner, Mark Mayo, III. *The Civil War Dictionary.* Rev. ed. New York: David McKay, 1988.

Boyle, Frank A. *A Party of Mad Fellows: The Story of the Irish Regiments in the Army of the Potomac.* Dayton, Ohio: Morningside House, 1996.

Brelje, H. William, and Virginia M. Tibbs. "Part III: Coming of Age, Thomas Pollock Clarke, 1906–1920." In *Washington State School for the Deaf: The First 100 Years, 1886–1986.* N.p.: privately published, 1986.

Buel, Clarence C., and Robert U. Johnson, eds. *Battles and Leaders of the Civil War.* Vol. 1. New York: Century, 1884.

Burke, Pauline Wilcox. *Emily Donelson of Tennessee.* Vol. 1. Richmond, Va.: Garrett and Massie, 1941.

Carnes, Mark C. *Secret Ritual and Manhood in Victorian America.* New Haven, Conn.: Yale University Press, 1989.

Carraway, Gertrude. *Crown of Life: History of Christ Church, New Bern, N.C. 1715–1940.* New Bern, N.C.: Owen G. Dunn, 1940.

Cashion, Jerry C., comp. *Sherman's March through North Carolina: A Chronology.* Raleigh: North Carolina Division of Archives and History, 1995.

Cecelski, David S. "Abraham H. Galloway: Wilmington's Lost Prophet and the Rise of Black Radicalism in the American South." In *Democracy Betrayed: The Wilmington Race Riot of 1898 and Its Legacy.* Chapel Hill: University of North Carolina Press, 1998.

Chabot, Frederick C. *With the Makers of San Antonio: Genealogies of the Early Latin, Anglo-American, and German Families.* San Antonio, Tex.: privately published by author, 1937.

*Chas. Emerson & Co.'s Newbern, N.C. City Directory.* Raleigh, N.C.: Edwards, Broughton, 1880.

Claiborne, John Herbert. *Seventy-five Years in Old Virginia.* New York: Neale Publishing, 1904.

Clark, Walter, ed. *Histories of the Several Regiments and Battalions from North Carolina in the Great War 1861–'65.* 5 vols. Raleigh: State of North Carolina, 1901.

Clarke, Mary Bayard. *Clytie and Zenobia; or, the Lily and the Palm, A Poem.* New York: E. P. Dutton, 1871.

———. *Mosses from a Rolling Stone; or, Idle Moments of a Busy Woman.* Raleigh, N.C.: W. B. Smith, 1866.

———, ed. *Wood-Notes; or, Carolina Carols: A Collection of North Carolina Poetry.* Raleigh, N.C.: Pomeroy, 1854.

Clinton, Catherine. *Fanny Kemble's Civil Wars*. New York: Simon and Schuster, 2000.

Cohen, Stan. *Historic Springs of the Virginias: A Pictorial History*. Charleston, W. Va.: Pictorial Histories Publishing, 1981.

Cotten, Jerry. *Light and Air: The Photography of Bayard Wootten*. Chapel Hill: University of North Carolina Press, 1998.

Coulling, Mary P. *The Lee Girls*. Winston-Salem, N.C.: J. F. Blair, 1987.

Coultrap-McQuin, Susan. *Doing Literary Business: American Women Writers in the Nineteenth Century*. Chapel Hill: University of North Carolina Press, 1990.

Crabtree, Beth, ed. *North Carolina Governors, 1585–1975: Brief Sketches*. Raleigh: North Carolina Division of Archives and History, 1974.

Crabtree, Beth, and James W. Patton, eds. *"Journal of a Secesh Lady": The Diary of Catherine Ann Devereux Edmondston, 1860–1866*. Raleigh: North Carolina Division of Archives and History, 1979.

Craven, John Joseph. *Prison Life of Jefferson Davis. Embracing Details and Incidents in His Captivity, Particulars Concerning His Health and Habits, Together with Many Conversations on Topics of Great Public Interest*. New York: Carleton, 1866.

Creecy, Richard B. *Grandfather's Tales of North Carolina History*. Raleigh, N.C.: Edwards and Broughton, Printers, 1901.

Crow, Jeffrey J., and Robert F. Durden. *Maverick Republican in the Old North State: A Political Biography of Daniel L. Russell*. Baton Rouge: Louisiana State University Press, 1977.

Dains, Mary K., and Sue Sadler, eds. *Show Me Missouri Women: Selected Biographies*. Vol. 2. Kirksville, Mo.: Thomas Jefferson University Press, 1993.

deButts, Mary Custis Lee, ed. *Growing Up in the 1850s: The Journal of Agnes Lee*. Chapel Hill: University of North Carolina Press, 1984.

Devereux, Margaret Mordecai. *Plantation Sketches*. Cambridge, Mass.: Riverside Press, 1906.

Faust, Drew Gilpin. *Mothers of Invention: Women of the Slaveholding South in the American Civil War*. Chapel Hill: University of North Carolina Press, 1996.

Flood, Charles Bracelen. *Lee: The Last Years*. Boston: Houghton Mifflin, 1981.

Folk, Edgar E., and Bynum Shaw. *W. W. Holden: A Political Biography*. Winston-Salem, N.C.: John F. Blair, Publisher, 1982.

Foner, Philip S. *Business & Slavery: The New York Merchants & the Irrepressible Conflict*. Chapel Hill: University of North Carolina Press, 1941.

Forrest, Mary. *Women of the South Distinguished in Literature*. New York: Charles B. Richardson, 1866.

Fox-Genovese, Elizabeth. *Within the Plantation Household: Black and White Women of the Old South*. Chapel Hill: University of North Carolina Press, 1988.

Freeman, Douglas Southall. *Lee's Lieutenants: A Study in Command*. 3 vols. New York: Charles Scribner's Sons, 1942–44.

Gadski, Mary Ellen. *The History of the New Bern Academy*. New Bern, N.C.: Tryon Palace Commission, 1986.

Gallaway, B. P., ed. *Texas, The Dark Corner of the Confederacy: Contemporary Accounts of the Lone Star State in the Civil War.* 3rd ed. Lincoln: University of Nebraska Press, 1994.

Green, Rena Maverick, ed. *Samuel Maverick, Texan: 1803–1870.* San Antonio: privately printed by Rena Maverick Green, 1952.

Hall, Winchester. *Poems by Mrs. Mary Bayard Clarke, With a Sketch of Her Life by Winchester Hall.* New York: Broadway Publishing, 1905.

Hamilton, J. G. de Roulhac. *Reconstruction in North Carolina.* Gloucester, Mass.: Peter Smith, 1964.

Hanchett, William. *Irish: Charles G. Halpine in Civil War America.* New York: Syracuse University Press, 1970.

Heitman, Francis B. *Historical Register and Dictionary of the United States Army, From its Organization, September 29, 1789, to March 2, 1903.* Vol. 1 Washington, D.C.: Government Printing Office, 1903. Reprint, Urbana: University of Illinois Press, 1965.

Henderson, Archibald, and others. *North Carolina: The Old North State and the New.* 5 vols. Chicago: Lewis Publishing, 1941.

*History of the Confederated Memorial Associations of the South.* New Orleans: Graham Press, 1904.

Holden, William Woods. *Memoirs of W. W. Holden.* The John Lawson Monographs of the Trinity College Historical Society Durham, North Carolina Series. Durham, N.C.: The Seeman Printery, 1911.

Johnson, Allen, and Dumas Malone, eds. *Dictionary of American Biography.* Vol. 4. New York, Charles Scribner's Sons, 1930.

Johnson, Guion Griffis. *Ante-bellum North Carolina: A Social History.* Chapel Hill: University of North Carolina Press, 1937.

Johnston, Frontis W., and Joe A. Mobley, eds. *The Papers of Zebulon Baird Vance.* 2 vols. to date. Raleigh, N.C.: State Department of Archives and History, 1963–.

Klement, Frank L. *Dark Lanterns: Secret Political Societies, Conspiracies, and Treason Trials in the Civil War.* Baton Rouge: Louisiana State University Press, 1984.

Lefler, Hugh T., ed. *North Carolina History Told by Contemporaries.* Chapel Hill: University of North Carolina Press, 1934.

Manarin, Louis H., and Weymouth T. Jordan Jr., eds. *North Carolina Troops, 1861–1865: A Roster.* Raleigh, N.C.: Division of Archives and History, Department of Cultural Resources, 1966–.

Mason, Emily V., ed. *The Southern Poems of the War.* Baltimore: John Murphy, 1868.

May, Robert E. *John A. Quitman: Old South Crusader.* Baton Rouge: Louisiana State University Press, 1985.

McCabe, James D., Jr. *A Centennial View of Our Country and Its Resources.* Philadelphia: Hubbard Brothers, 1876.

McNamara, Brooks. *Day of Jubilee: The Great Age of Public Celebration in New York, 1788–1909.* New Brunswick, N.J.: Rutgers University Press, 1997.

*The Memorial Volume of the Edwards Family Meeting at Stockbridge, Mass., September 6–7, A.D. 1870.* Boston: Congregational Publishing Society, 1871.

*Mooney & Morrison's Directory for the City of San Antonio, 1877–1878.* Galveston, Tex.: Galveston News, 1877.

Moore, Harriet Brown. *Saint Mark's Church, San Antonio, Texas: A Parish With Personality.* San Antonio, Tex.: Naylor, 1944.

Moore, John W. *Roster of North Carolina Troops in the War Between the States.* Vols. 1–3. Raleigh: State of North Carolina, 1882.

Morgan, Susan, ed. *The Romance of the Harem.* Victorian Literature and Culture Series. Charlottesville: University Press of Virginia, 1991.

Mott, Frank L. *American Journalism: A History of Newspapers in the United States through 260 Years: 1690 to 1950.* Rev. ed. New York: MacMillan, 1950.

———. *A History of American Magazines, 1865–1885.* Vol. 3. Cambridge, Mass.: Harvard University Press, 1938.

Murray, Amelia M. *Letters from the United States, Cuba and Canada.* Vol. 2. London: John W. Parker and Son, 1856.

Murray, Elizabeth Reid. *Wake, Capital County of North Carolina.* Raleigh, N.C.: Capital County Publishing, 1983.

*Newbern, N.C., City Directory, 1880–1881.* N.p.: Charles Emerson, 1881.

Olmsted, Frederick Law. *Journey through Texas: A Saddle-Trip on the Southwestern Frontier.* Austin, Tex.: Von Boeckmann-Jones Press, 1962.

Pattee, Fred Lewis. *The Feminine Fifties.* New York: D. Appleton-Century, 1940.

Patton, John S., ed. *Poems of John R. Thompson.* New York: Charles Scribner's Sons, 1920.

Pease, S. W. *They Came to San Antonio, 1794–1865.* San Antonio, Tex.: privately printed by the author, n.d.

Perry, Carmen, ed. *San Antonio: A Historical and Pictorial Guide,* by Charles Ramsdell. Rev. ed. Austin: University of Texas Press, 1976.

Polk, William M. *Leonidas Polk, Bishop and General.* Vol. 1. New York: Longmans, Green, 1915.

Post, Robert C., ed. *1876: A Centennial Exhibition.* Washington, D.C.: National Museum of History and Technology, Smithsonian Institution, 1976.

Powell, William H. *Powell's Records of Living Officers of the United States Army.* Philadelphia: L. R. Hamersly, 1890.

Powell, William S., ed. *Dictionary of North Carolina Biography.* 6 vols. Chapel Hill: University of North Carolina Press, 1979–96.

———. *The North Carolina Gazetteer: A Dictionary of Tar Heel Places.* Chapel Hill: University of North Carolina Press, 1968.

Price, Kenneth M., and Susan Belasco Smith. *Periodical Literature in Nineteenth-Century America.* Charlottesville: University Press of Virginia, 1995.

Rauch, Basil. *American Interest in Cuba, 1848–1855.* New York: Octagon Books, 1974.

Reavis, L. U. *Saint Louis: The Future Great City of the World, with Biographical Sketches of the Representative Men and Women of St. Louis and Missouri.* Centennial ed. St. Louis, Mo.: C. R. Barns, 1876.

Rister, Carl Cooke. *Robert E. Lee in Texas.* Norman: University of Oklahoma Press, 1946.

Schiller, Herbert M., ed. *A Captain's War: The Letters and Diaries of William H. S. Burgwyn, 1861–1865.* Shippensburg, Pa.: White Mane Publishing, 1994.

Scott, Anne Firor. *The Southern Lady: From Pedestal to Politics, 1830–1930.* Chicago: University of Chicago Press, 1970.

Shaw, Cornelia Rebekah. *Davidson College.* New York: Fleming H. Revell Press, 1923.

Sherman, William Tecumseh. *William Tecumseh Sherman: Memoirs of General W. T. Sherman.* New York: Literary Classics of the United States, 1990.

Sherrill, J. B., comp. *Historical Records, North Carolina Press Association 1873–1887.* N.P.: North Carolina Press Association, 1930.

Sibley, F. Ray, Jr. *The Army of Northern Virginia.* Vol. 1 of *The Confederate Order of Battle.* Shippensburg, Pa.: White Mane Publishing, 1966.

Sifakis, Stewart. *Who Was Who in the Civil War.* New York: Facts on File Publications, 1988.

Smith, John David, and William Cooper Jr., eds. *A Union Woman in Civil War Kentucky: The Diary of Frances Peter.* Lexington: University Press of Kentucky, 2000.

Spencer, Cornelia Phillips. *The Last Ninety Days of the War in North Carolina.* New York: Watchman Publishing, 1866.

Starr, S. Frederick. *Southern Comfort: The Garden District of New Orleans.* New York: Princeton Architectural Press, 1998.

Still, William N., Jr. *The Confederate Navy: The Ships, Men and Organization, 1861–65.* Annapolis, Md.: Naval Institute Press, 1997.

Tardy, Mary T. *Southland Writers. Biographical and Critical Sketches of the Living Female Writers of the South. With Extracts from Their Writings.* Philadelphia: Claxton, Remsen, and Haffelfinger, 1870.

Tyler, Ron, ed. in chief. *The New Handbook of Texas.* 6 vols. Austin: Texas State Historical Association, 1996.

U.S. Supreme Court. *United States Reports.* October Term, 1878, vol. 8 (1879); October Term, 1882 and Rules announced at October Term, 1883, vol. 108 (1884). Blake *vs* Hawkins; Hawkins & Another, Assignees, & Others *vs.* Blake & Another.

Van Doren, Charles, ed. *Webster's American Biographies.* Springfield, Mass.: G. and C. Merriam, 1974.

*War of the Rebellion, Official Records of the Union and Confederate Armies.* Washington, D.C.: G.P.O., 1880–1901. Series 1, vol. 9 (1883); vol. 19, pt. 1 (1887); vol. 42, pt. 3, Correspondence, Etc. (1893); vol. 46, pt. 2; vol. 47, pt. 3, Correspondence, Etc. (1895); series 4, vol. 2 (1900).

*War of the Rebellion, Official Records of the Union and Confederate Navies in the War of the Rebellion.* Series 2, vol. 1. Washington, D.C.: G.P.O., 1921.

Watson, Alan D. *A History of New Bern and Craven County.* New Bern, N.C.: Tryon Palace Commission, 1987.

Webb, Walter P., ed. in chief. *The Handbook of Texas.* 3 vols. Austin: Texas State Historical Association, 1952–76.

Whitfield, Emma Morehead, comp. *Bryan/Smith.* Vol. 2 of *Whitfield, Bryan, Smith and Related Families.* Westminister, Md.: privately printed, 1950.

*Who Was Who in America, Historical Volume 1607–1896.* Chicago: Marquis–Who's Who, 1963.

Williams, Kenny J. *Prairie Voices: A Literary History of Chicago from the Frontier to 1893.* Nashville, Tenn.: Townsend Press, 1980.

Woodward, C. Vann, ed. *Mary Chesnut's Civil War.* New Haven, Conn.: Yale University Press, 1981.

Young, Kevin R. *To the Tyrants Never Yield: A Texas Civil War Sampler.* Plano, Tex.: Worldware Publishing, 1991.

Zuber, Richard L. *North Carolina during Reconstruction.* Raleigh: North Carolina Department of Archives and History, 1969.

*Published Articles*

"About Several Things." *Catholic World* 9 (May 1869): 274–79.

Alexander, Roberta Sue. "Hostility and Hope: Black Education in North Carolina during Presidential Reconstruction, 1865–1867." *NCHR* 53 (Apr. 1976): 113–32.

Atchison, Ray M. "The Land We Love: A Southern Post-Bellum Magazine of Agriculture, Literature, and Military History." *NCHR* 37 (Oct. 1960): 506–15.

Bishir, Catherine W. "'A Strong Force of Ladies': Women, Politics, and Confederate Memorial Associations in Nineteenth-Century Raleigh." *NCHR* 77 (Oct. 2000): 455–91.

Bleser, Carol K. "The Marriage of Varina Howell and Jefferson Davis: 'I gave the best and all my life to a girdled tree.'" *Journal of Southern History* 65 (Feb. 1999): 3–40.

Brabham, Robin. "Defining the American University: The University of North Carolina, 1865–1875." *NCHR* 57 (Oct. 1980): 427–55.

Bridges, C. A. "The Knights of the Golden Circle: A Filibustering Fantasy." *SHQ* 44 (Jan. 1941): 287–302.

Censer, Jane Turner. "A Changing World of Work: North Carolina Elite Women, 1865–1895." *NCHR* 73 (Jan. 1996): 28–55.

———. "Southwestern Migration Among North Carolina Planter Families: 'The Disposition to Emigrate.'" *JSH* 57 (Aug. 1991): 407–26.

Clarke, Mary Bayard. "General Sherman in Raleigh." *Old Guard,* Apr. 1866, 226–32.

————. "Mrs. Leigh's Indian Waiter; and How She Came to Get Him." *Inland Monthly Magazine,* July 1877, 48–63.

————. "The South Expects Every Woman to Do Her Duty. [BY A LADY OF NORTH CAROLINA.]." *Old Guard,* Aug. 1866, 479–83.

————. "Woman North and South." *Current Thought, Literature, Fashion, Society and Home Topics* 1 (Oct. 1877): 1.

————. "Woman as a Worker," [undated and unidentified newspaper article, 1877, Barden Collection].

————. "Woman's Work." *Signal* [undated clipping, early 1880, Barden Collection].

Crow, Jeffrey J. "Thomas Settle Jr., Reconstruction, and the Memory of the Civil War." *JSH* 62 (Nov. 1996): 689–726.

Crow, Jeffrey J., and Paul D. Escott. "The Social Order and Violent Disorder: An Analysis of North Carolina in the Revolution and the Civil War." *JSH* 52 (Aug. 1986): 373–402.

Crow, Terrell Armistead, and Mary Moulton Barden. "Mary Bayard Clarke and the Yankee Occupation of Raleigh." *North Carolina Literary Review* 8 (1999): 29–38.

Cunningham, H. H. "Edmund Burke Haywood and Raleigh's Confederate Hospitals." *NCHR* 35 (Apr. 1958): 153–66.

Faust, Drew Gilpin. "Altars of Sacrifice: Confederate Women and the Narratives of War." *Journal of American History* 76 (Mar. 1990): 1200–1228.

*Fayette County Historical Society Bulletin* 1, no. 9 (Nov. 1988): 79–82.

"The Female Religious of America." *Catholic World* 19 (June 1874): 362–75.

Gibson, George H. "Opinion in North Carolina Regarding the Acquisition of Texas and Cuba, 1835–1855, Part I." *NCHR* 37 (Jan. 1960): 1–21; "Part II." *NCHR* 37 (Apr. 1960): 185–201.

Golden, Harry L. "The Jewish People of North Carolina." *NCHR* 32 (Apr. 1955): 194–216.

Hacker, Barton C. "The United States Army as a National Police Force: The Federal Policing of Labor Disputes, 1877–1898." *Military Affairs* 33 (Apr. 1969): 255–64.

Hairston, Peter W. "J. E. B. Stuart's Letters to His Hairston Kin, 1850–1855." *NCHR* 51 (July 1974): 261–333.

Hamilton, J. G. de Roulhac. "George Patterson, North Carolinian by Adoption." *NCHR* 30 (Apr. 1953): 191–99.

Harris, William C. "William Woods Holden: In Search of Vindication." *NCHR* 59 (Oct. 1982): 354–72.

Havins, T. R. "Administration of the Sequestration Act in the Confederate District Court for the Western District, 1862–1865." *SHQ* 43 (Jan. 1940): 295–322.

Hicks, Jimmie, ed. "Some Letters Concerning the Knights of the Golden Circle in Texas, 1860–1861." *SHQ* 65 (1961): 80–86.

Johnson, Guion Griffis. "Courtship and Marriage Customs in Ante-bellum North Carolina." *NCHR* 8 (Oct. 1931): 384–402.

Jones, H. G. "A Banner for the 'Yankee Celebration.'" *The State,* Jan. 1984, 24–25.

McPherson, Elizabeth Gregory, ed. "Letters from North Carolina to Andrew Johnson, continued." *NCHR* 29 (Jan. 1952): 104–19.

———. "Unpublished Letters from North Carolinians to Polk, continued." *NCHR* 16 (Oct. 1939): 428–57; 17 (Apr. 1940): 139–40.

Newsome, A. R., ed. "Letters of Lawrence O'Bryan Branch, 1856–1860." *NCHR* 10 (Jan. 1933): 44–79.

Norris, David A. "'The Yankees Have Been Here!': The Story of Brig. Gen. Edward E. Potter's Raid on Greenville, Tarboro, and Rocky Mount, July 19–23, 1863." *NCHR* 73 (Jan. 1996): 1–27.

Olsen, Otto H., and Ellen Z. McGrew. "Prelude to Reconstruction: The Correspondence of State Senator Leander Sams Gash, 1866–1867, Part I." *NCHR* 60 (Jan. 1983): 37–88.

Padgett, James A., ed. "Reconstruction Letters from North Carolina," Part I, "Letters to Thaddeus Stevens." *NCHR* 18 (Apr. 1941): 171–95; Part II, "Letters to John Sherman." *NCHR* 18 (July 1941): 278–300.

Parramore, Thomas C. "The Burning of Winton in 1862." *NCHR* 39 (Jan. 1962): 18–31.

Schauinger, Joseph Herman. "William Gaston: Southern Statesman." *NCHR* 18 (Apr. 1941): 99–132.

Schoen, Harold. "The Free Negro in the Republic of Texas," in four pts. *SHQ* 40 (1937): 85–113, 169–99, 267–89.

Stephenson, William E. "The Davises, the Southalls, and the Founding of Wesleyan Female College, 1854–1859." *NCHR* 57 (July 1980): 257–79.

Wallace, Lee A., Jr. "Raising a Volunteer Regiment for Mexico, 1846–1847." *NCHR* 35 (Jan. 1958): 20–33.

Welter, Barbara. "The Cult of True Womanhood, 1820–1860," *American Quarterly* 18 (summer 1966): 151–74.

Whitener, Daniel J. "The Republican Party and Public Education in North Carolina, 1867–1900." *NCHR* 37 (July 1960): 382–96.

Worsley, Stephen C. "Catholicism in Antebellum North Carolina." *NCHR* 60 (Oct. 1983): 399–430.

Yearns, Wilfred B., Jr. "North Carolina in the Confederate Congress." *NCHR* 29 (July 1952): 359–78.

*Online Sources*

Clarke, Mary Bayard. "Reminiscences of Cuba, Part I." *Southern Literary Messenger* 21, no. 9 (Sept. 1855); "Reminiscences of Cuba, Concluded," 21, no. 10 (Oct. 1855); "Some Farther Reminiscences of Cuba," 21, no. 11 (Nov. 1855); "Some

Farther Reminiscences of Cuba, Part II," 21, no. 12 (Dec. 1855). *Making of America,* jointly developed by the University of Michigan and Cornell University, 1996, http://moa.umdl.umich.edu

"Dashiell, Jeremiah Yellott." *Handbook of Texas Online.* Accessed 21 Sept. 1999. http://www.tsha.utexas.edu/handbook/online/articles/view/DD/fda17.html

"Dignowity, Anthony Michael," *Handbook of Texas Online.* Accessed 27 Aug. 2000. http://www.tsha.utexas.edu/handbook/online/articles/view/DD/fdi15.html

"Hertzberg, Theodor Rudolph," *Handbook of Texas Online.* Accessed 27 Aug. 2000. http://www.tsha.utexas.edu/handbook/online/articles/view/HH/fhe65.html

"Hewitt, William M." *Handbook of Texas Online.* Accessed 16 Apr. 1999. http://www.tsha.utexas.edu/handbook/online/articles/view/HH/fhe37.html

Hoertdoerfer, Pat. "A Brief History of the Ethical Culture Movement." AEU Core Curriculum, Teacher's Handbook, Brooklyn Society for Ethical Culture Web site. Accessed 9 Sept. 2000. http://www.bsec.org/info/history.html

"Howard, Henry Peyton." *Handbook of Texas Online.* Accessed 15 Mar. 1999. http://www.tsha.utexas.edu/handbook/online/articles/view/HH/fhoay.html

"Hutchings, John Henry." *Handbook of Texas Online.* Accessed 16 Apr. 1999. http://www.tsha.utexas.edu/handbook/online/articles/view/HH/fhu50.html

"Jim Wheat's Postmasters & Post Offices of Texas, 1846–1930." Accessed 22 Nov. 2000. http://www.rootsweb.com/txpost/bexar.html

"San Antonio and Mexican Gulf Railroad." *Handbook of Texas Online.* Accessed 10 Jan. 2001. http://www.tsha.utexas.edu/handbook/online/articles/view/SS/eqs8.html

"Star of the West." *Handbook of Texas Online.* Accessed 8 Mar. 1999. http://www.tsha.utexas.edu/cgi-bin/web_fetch_doc?dataset=tsha.dst&db=handbook&doc_id=4498&query=star+of+the+west

"Sweet, James." *Handbook of Texas Online.* Accessed 14 Oct. 2000. http://www.tsha.utexas.edu/handbook/online/articles/view/SS/fsw11.html

*Unpublished Works*

Alexander, Roberta Sue. "North Carolina Faces the Freedmen: Race Relations During Presidential Reconstruction, 1865–1867." 2 vols. Ph.D. diss., University of Chicago, 1974.

Beachamp, Eula Pearl, comp., and Jo Ann E. Murphy, ed. Index to "1870 Census Craven County North Carolina." New Bern, N.C.: New Bern–Craven County Regional Library, 1999.

Crawford, Victor. Unpublished typescripts of genealogical information compiled on the Clarke, Devereux, and Robateau families. Washington, D.C.: n.p., n.d.

Elliott, Robert Neal, Jr. "The Raleigh Register, 1799–1863." Ph.D. diss., University of North Carolina at Chapel Hill, 1953.

Lancaster, James L. "The Scalawags of North Carolina, 1850–1868." Ph.D. diss., Princeton University, 1974.

Whitaker, Bessie Lewis. "Mary Bayard Clarke, 1827–0886." Unpublished typescript. Frances Martin Finnerty Papers, private collection. Brevard, N.C., n.d.

# Index

Clarke, Mary Bayard Devereux (Mai)
(*continued*)
    338; Lee's letter to, 196–97; letters to
Willie, 124, 171–72; marriage to
George Moulton, 422–23, 424nn. 1,
2; marriage to Rufus Morgan, 303n. 3;
mentioned in letters of MBC, 12, 20,
23, 25, 34, 35; mentioned in letters of
WJC, 30, 33, 44; resistance to Sherman's army, 214n. 7; at St. Mary's
Academy, 264, 265, 265n. 1, 277n. 1.
*See also* Morgan, Mary Clarke; Moulton, Mary Clarke Morgan
Clarke, Thomas Pollock Devereux (Tom),
xxxiv–xxxv, xxxvi–xxxvii, xli, liii,
37n. 2, 45n. 1, 65, 74, 104–5, 157,
164, 175, 180, 337, 424–25n. 1; education of, 108–9, 278, 296; employment, 353n. 3; health, 110, 111, 112,
301, 305, 307, 325, 396; letter to
Willie, 123
Clarke, William E. (Willie), xxxiv, xli,
xlix, lii, liii, lvi(n. 30), lxii(n. 103),
45n. 2; business ventures, 179–80,
184, 185n. 1, 230n. 3, 262, 410; education of, 110, 145, 155, 166–67,
167–68, 172, 174–75; engagement to
Katie Street, 364, 365n. 3; finances,
401; health, 13, 118, 166–67; legal
career, 340; legal studies, 334–35, 337;
letters from siblings, 123–24; letters to
WJC, 143, 148; letter to Frances
Miller, 27–28; marriage to Sarah Elizabeth Howerton, 365n. 3, 424, 424n. 1;
mentioned in letters of MBC, 18, 20,
25–26, 35, 36; mentioned in letters of
WJC, 29–30, 32; New Bern Academy
and, 294, 295n. 2; Nora Cannon's letters to, 299–300, 321–23, 326–27,
333–34; as political candidate, 364,
364n. 1, 385; teaches at New York
Institute for the Deaf, 288n. 3, 296n. 1,
314n. 5. *See also* Clarke, Mary Bayard
Devereux, letters
Clarke, William J.: on African Americans,
98, 148, 297–98; alcoholism, xlvii,

233, 233n. 1, 340, 396, 397n. 2,
398–99; on battles, 117–18, 126–27,
128–29, 149–50; captures federal flag,
165; on children's education, 115,
116n. 7, 118, 133, 145, 148–49, 154,
294, 298; clerkship, 401, 401n. 1, 402;
as colonel, xl, 72, 73n. 1, 86–87,
113–16, 419–20; death of, 419–22;
defends MBC to Frances Miller,
284–85; disaffection from Conservative Party, xlvii–xlviii, 253–54; as editor of *Signal,* 396, 397n. 1, 398–99,
402; on executions, 144; financial
difficulties, xxxii, xxxvi–xxxvii, xliii,
44, 46–47, 49, 67, 76, 88, 142,
262–63, 363; health, xlvii, 114, 141,
333, 339, 418; on Jefferson Davis,
177–78; joins Republican Party, xxvii,
xxx, xlvii–l, 205, 271–72; Kirk-
Holden War and, 293, 297–98;
Knights of the Golden Circle and,
xxxvi, 58, 59, 160n. 3; on leaves of
absence, 139, 142; legal career, xxxvi,
18, 23–25, 28, 32–33, 36, 195,
264n. 3, 320, 328, 329, 333–35, 337,
364; marriage to MBC, xxxi–xxxii;
Masonic Address, 264, 264n. 6; Mexican War service, xxxi, xxxii, xxxviii,
45, 46n. 10, 67n. 1, 73, 419; New
Bern Academy and, 264n. 4, 278,
278n. 2, 293–94; obituary, 419–20;
ordered to North Carolina, 74–76,
76–77; political aspirations,
xxxii–xxxiii, 385; predictions for war,
154; as prisoner of war, xliv, 176–79,
181, 186n. 1; prospects in Cuba, 212;
railroad venture, xxxvi, 32, 34n. 2, 36,
43, 45n. 5, 47–48, 49; Raleigh Savings
Institution and, 51, 52n. 10; Ransom
and, 128, 136–38, 138–39, 146,
153–54, 162, 165; religious views of,
74, 75, 98, 107, 141–42, 144, 181,
410; sawmill venture, xlvi–xlvii, 195;
seeks commission in Confederate army,
xxxviii, xxxix, lix(n. 57), 66–67,
67n. 1, 69, 70, 71–72, 83, 100, 121,